SAMUEL WESLEY

The Man and his Music

1 Samuel Wesley aged around sixty. Portrait in oils by John Jackson, RA. By courtesy of the National Portrait Gallery, London.

SAMUEL WESLEY

The Man and his Music

Philip Olleson

THE BOYDELL PRESS

© Philip Olleson 2003

All Rights Reserved. Except as permitted under current legislation
no part of this work may be photocopied, stored in a retrieval system,
published, performed in public, adapted, broadcast,
transmitted, recorded or reproduced in any form or by any means,
without the prior permission of the copyright owner

First published 2003
The Boydell Press, Woodbridge

ISBN 1 84383 031 0

The Boydell Press is an imprint of Boydell & Brewer Ltd
PO Box 9, Woodbridge, Suffolk IP12 3DF, UK
and of Boydell & Brewer Inc.
PO Box 41026, Rochester, NY 14604–4126, USA
website: www.boydell.co.uk

A catalogue record for this book is available
from the British Library

Library of Congress Cataloging-in-Publication Data
Olleson, Philip.
  Samuel Wesley: the man and his music / Philip Olleson.
    p. cm.
  Includes bibliographical references (p.) and indexes.
  ISBN 1–84383–031–0 (hardback: alk. paper)
  1. Wesley, Samuel, 1766–1837. 2. Composers – England –
Biography. I. Title.
  ML 410.W515045 2003
  780'.92 – dc21   2003008634

Typeset by Joshua Associates Ltd, Oxford
Printed and bound in Great Britain by
The Cromwell Press, Trowbridge, Wiltshire.

Contents

	List of Plates	vii
	List of Maps and Figures	viii
	List of Music Examples	ix
	Preface	xi
	Acknowledgements	xiv
	Editorial Note	xvi
	Abbreviations	xviii
Chapter 1	Childhood and youth, 1766–1773	1
Chapter 2	Early upbringing and the family concerts, 1774–1787	12
Chapter 3	Adolescence: Roman Catholicism, rebellion, and Charlotte, 1780–1788	25
Chapter 4	Life with Charlotte, 1791–1797	40
Chapter 5	Beginning a career, 1797–1805	51
Chapter 6	Discovering Bach, 1805–1808	66
Chapter 7	Lectures and controversy, 1809	87
Chapter 8	A developing career, 1810–1811	101
Chapter 9	Vincent Novello and the Portuguese Embassy Chapel, 1811–1812	112
Chapter 10	The oratorio business, 1813	128
Chapter 11	The established career, 1814–1816	140
Chapter 12	Breakdown and recovery, 1816–1823	149
Chapter 13	The career re-established, 1823–1825	166
Chapter 14	The Fitzwilliam music, 1825	179
Chapter 15	Byrd, the *Confitebor*, and Handel's hymns, 1826–1828	187
Chapter 16	The return to Bristol, 1829–1830	203
Chapter 17	Last years, 1830–1837	210
Chapter 18	Wesley and his musical environment	217
Chapter 19	Sacred vocal music	229
Chapter 20	Large-scale choral music with orchestra	251

Chapter 21 Secular vocal music	261
Chapter 22 Instrumental music	281
Chapter 23 Keyboard music	294
Bibliography	323
Index of Wesley's works	335
General index	339

List of Plates

1	(Frontispiece) Samuel Wesley aged around sixty.	ii
2	Samuel Wesley aged ten.	18
3	Samuel Wesley as a young man.	34
4	Wesley's letter to Benjamin Jacob of 10 May 1813.	115
5	Jottings made by Wesley while at Blacklands House, March 1818.	158
6	The first page of the autograph of the Fugue from the Voluntary No. 1 in C minor.	307

List of Maps and Figures

Maps

Wesley's England	xxi
Wesley's London	xxii

Figures

Wesley's family tree	xx
The *Missa de Spiritu Sancto*, KO 3: overall plan	233
Specification of Surrey Chapel organ	295

List of Music Examples

19.01	'Ave maris stella', KO 15: 'Virgo singularis', bars 17–23	231
19.02	'Exultate Deo', KO 36, main themes	236
19.03	'Dixit Dominus' a 8, KO 26, bars 305–32	238
19.04	'In exitu Israel', KO 43, main themes	240
19.05	'Ut queant laxis', KO 70, bars 1–16	241
19.06	*Carmen funebre*, KO 54, bars 1–12	243
19.07	Morning and Evening Service in F, KO 71, Jubilate, 'Gloria Patri'	246
20.01	*Confitebor*, KO 20, 'Fidelia omnia', bars 224–32: coloratura writing	258
20.02	*Confitebor*, KO 20, 'Mandavit in aeternum', bars 279–95	259
21.01	'Harsh and untuneful are the notes', KO 218, bars 1–12	263
21.02	'What shaft of fate's relentless pow'r', KO 315, bars 1–14	277
22.01	Openings of first movements of Wesley's Symphony in D, KO 407, and J. C. Bach's Sinfonia in D, Op. 18. No. 4	283
23.01	Twelve Voluntaries, Op. 6, KO 621, fugue subjects	300
23.02	Voluntary in G minor, Op. 6 No. 9, KO 621, first movement, bars 23–7: chromatic writing	300
23.03	Grand Duet for the Organ, KO 604, Andante, bars 50–5: 'criss-cross work'	303
23.04	Variations on 'The Bay of Biscay', KO 708, Variation 5	320

To Cyril

Preface

One of the greatest musical geniuses that England has ever produced.
Vincent Novello

I knew him unfortunately, too well; pious Catholic, raving atheist, mad, reasonable, drunk and sober – the dread of all wives and regular families, a warm friend, a bitter foe, a satirical talker, a flatterer at times of those he cynically traduced at others – a blasphemer at times, a puleing Methodist at others.
Mary Sabilla Novello

This is a study of a supremely gifted musician and a maverick. Samuel Wesley (1766–1837) was the son of the hymn writer Charles Wesley and nephew of the preacher John Wesley and the finest organist and composer of his generation, who despite prodigious musical talents and a privileged family background and education never achieved lasting fame or material success and died in poverty. Born and brought up in the heart of Methodism, he repudiated most of the values of his family and religious background in his adolescence and converted to Roman Catholicism. He contracted a spectacularly unhappy marriage and in time left his wife for his teenage servant, with whom he had no fewer than nine children. Despite chronic mental health problems and many interruptions to his career, he played an important part in England's musical life for well over thirty years as a performer, composer, lecturer, journalist, teacher, entrepreneur, and champion of the music of J. S. Bach, and left a substantial legacy of compositions, in all genres except opera.

Wesley's character had many contradictions, of which three in particular will become clear in the following pages. One was the Methodist who converted to Roman Catholicism, later repudiated it, but retained a lifelong love of its rituals and music. Another was the rebel and non-joiner who was none the less a prominent Freemason and a director of the Philharmonic Society. Another was the musician who harboured a deep ambivalence about his profession, at times embracing it enthusiastically, but at others describing it as 'a trivial & a degrading Business to any Man of Spirit or of any Abilities to employ himself more usefully'.

Wesley lived through the reigns of three monarchs and into the first months of the reign of a fourth. This was a time of momentous changes in society. He saw the explosive growth in population of London, from around 750,000 in his childhood to around a million in 1800 and almost twice that number by the time of his death, and with it an enormous rash of new domestic building that engulfed many former country areas and incorporated them into the ever-increasing built-up area of the capital. There was a commensurate amount of new public building. In the area around the junction of Tottenham Court Road and the New Road (the present-day Euston Road), where he lived for most of his adult life, he saw the development of the Bedford estates in Bloomsbury, the creation of Regent's Park, and the building of St Pancras New Church. In the West End, there was the building of two new theatres at Drury Lane and one at Covent Garden, and later the building of Regent's Street and Piccadilly Circus. Elsewhere, he saw the building of Chambers's Somerset House in the Strand, and Nash's enlargement of Buckingham Palace, and in his final years, the beginning of the railway age with the opening of London's first railway terminus at Euston Square, a stone's throw from his old haunts. His life encompassed equally momentous changes in musical style, from the Baroque to the early Romantic. He grew up among and was taught by musicians who had known and played with Handel, whose music he had ample opportunities to hear along with the more modern music of J. C. Bach, C. F. Abel, and other composers of their generation. Later, he witnessed the introduction of the music of Haydn, Mozart, and Beethoven to London concert programmes, and later still, that of Rossini and Weber. In the last month of his life he met and played to Mendelssohn.

Notwithstanding many periods of compositional silence and the fact that composition was only one of ways in which he earned his living, Wesley's output was large: over 550 works are listed in *Samuel Wesley (1766–1837): A Source Book*, and this total rises to more than six hundred more if the individual components of sets of pieces such as organ voluntaries are counted separately. Much of this is in the form of individual songs, glees, and small organ pieces, but there are many substantial works, including seven violin concertos, five symphonies, three large choral works with orchestra, a large body of organ music, and a number of extended pieces of Latin and English church music. He was also a prolific and lively correspondent, and through the preservation of a large number of his own letters and those of other members of his family, more is known of his private and professional life and character than of that of any other English musician of this or of any earlier period.

Given Wesley's undoubted importance in English music and the richness and easy accessibility of the source material, it is surprising that there has been until now no extended study of his life and music. The lack of a biography is well-nigh inexplicable in the light of the colourfulness of Wesley's life, the complexity of his character, and his position as the prime rebel of early-nineteenth-century English music. The lack of a study of the music is more comprehensible, given the almost total neglect of his music for most of the last century and a concomitant lack of editions and recordings. The last twenty-five years, however, have seen a gradually accelerating interest, starting in 1978 with the publication of the *Confitebor*, Wesley's large-scale choral and orchestral setting of Psalm 111. Since then, publications of his music have included a volume of piano works in a facsimile edition, various volumes of organ music, including the *Twelve Short Pieces* and the *Organ Duet*, and some other compilations of miscellaneous pieces. As I write, a complete edition of the organ music is nearing completion. But apart from one or two isolated pieces in anthologies, there are no modern editions of any of Wesley's glees or songs, or of more than a few of his Latin and English sacred compositions. The situation is slightly more healthy with recordings. At the time of writing, there are recordings of all the symphonies, of one of the violin concertos, of the *Trio for Three Pianofortes*, of selected pieces of Latin and English church music, and of some of the organ music. There have been performances and broadcasts of the *Confitebor*, the *Ode to St Cecilia*, and the *Missa de Spiritu Sancto*, although as yet no commercial recordings. There is, however, still, no complete recording of the important Op. 6 organ voluntaries, of any of his glees or solo songs.

My aim in this book has been to provide a detailed account of Wesley's life and an introductory survey of his music, building on the infrastructure of my *Samuel Wesley: Professional and Social Correspondence, 1797–1837* (Oxford, 2001) and of *Samuel Wesley (1766–1837): A Sourcebook*, by myself and Michael Kassler (Aldershot, 2001). It will be evident that a good deal of detailed work remains to be done on the music, but I hope that the coverage here will give a basic outline, identifying which areas and works are central and which peripheral, and will provide a starting-point for further study in the future.

The particular nature of Wesley's output, with its preponderance of small pieces in some genres, has also determined my decision to discuss his music separately from his life. Many recent 'musical lives' have integrated the two elements, on the grounds that to separate them is artificial and encourages authors and readers to play down or disregard the essential links between works and the circumstances of their creation. This is a view to which I wholeheartedly subscribe. In the case, of Wesley, however, the existence of a large number of works that are either undated or have no known links with the events of the composer's life makes this approach impracticable. The approach I have therefore adopted has been to discuss details of the background of works, their composition, and performance (where known) in the biographical section, reserving more technical discussion of the music for separate chapters. One advantage of this is that the biographical chapters remain fully accessible to readers without technical knowledge; another is that it permits the discussion of Wesley's music on a category-by-category basis over his entire career in a way which would not be possible in an integrated narrative.

Philip Olleson
Nottingham, March 2003

Acknowledgements

The writing of this book, between September 2001 and March 2003, was made possible by a period of study leave from the University of Nottingham and a matching Research Leave award from the Arts and Humanities Research Board. The cost of preparation of maps, figures, and music examples was aided by generous awards from the *Music and Letters* Trust and from the University of Nottingham. I gratefully acknowledge the financial assistance of these bodies.

Some sections of this book have appeared in print in earlier versions elsewhere. I acknowledge with thanks the permission of the following institutions and journals to re-use it here: Library of Congress, Washington, DC; *Methodist History; Musical Times, Recusant History; Staffordshire Studies.*

Most of the literary and musical sources for this book are in the British Library, the Royal College of Music, and the Methodist Archives and Research Centre at the John Rylands University Library of Manchester. Over the years I have spent many hours at these three institutions. I would like to thank the staff for their unfailingly courteous and helpful service, and in particular Robert Parker at the British Library, Peter Horton at the Royal College of Music, and Peter Nockles and Gareth Lloyd at the John Rylands University Library of Manchester. I would also like to acknowledge the assistance of other institutions with holdings of Wesley family papers, music manuscripts, and pictures: the Beinecke Rare Books and Manuscript Library, Yale University; the Bodleian Library, Oxford; Cambridge University Library, Drew University, Madison, New Jersey; Duke University, Durham, N. Carolina; Edinburgh University Library; Emory University, Atlanta, Georgia; Fitzwilliam Museum, Cambridge; Gloucester Public Library; Hampshire Record Office; Houghton Library, Harvard University; John Wesley's Chapel, Bristol; Library of Congress, Washington, DC; London Metropolitan Archives; National Library of Scotland; National Trust; New York Public Library; Norfolk Record Office; Princeton University; Harry Ransom Humanities Research Center, University of Texas; Royal Academy of Music; Royal Institution of Great Britain; Royal Ontario Museum, Toronto; Southern Methodist University, Dallas, Texas; University of California at Santa Barbara; The Upper Room, Nashville, Tennessee.

Investigating Wesley's letters has involved me in correspondence with, and visits to, a large number of other libraries and record offices. I would like to thank the following: Avon Record Office; Birmingham Archives; British Library Newspaper Library; Bristol Central Library; Brotherton Library, University of Leeds; Camden Local Studies Library; Dorset Record Office; Freemasons' Hall,

London; Guildhall Library, London; Hertfordshire Record Office; Pendlebury Library, Cambridge; Reed Organ and Harmonium Museum, Saltaire; Royal College of Organists; Royal Society of Musicians; St Albans Public Library; Suffolk Record Office; Watford Public Library; and Wesley College, Bristol.

Working on Wesley has taken me into many unfamiliar areas, and I have been particularly fortunate in the helpfulness of those to whom I have turned with enquiries and requests for assistance of various kinds. I owe a particular debt of gratitude to the following: Andrew Drummond, for identifying and translating Wesley's quotations from Greek and Latin; Michael Kassler, for his continued sharing of his extensive knowledge of Wesley's life; Alyson McLamore, for making available her database of the Wesley family concerts; and Ian Wells for information on matters of Roman Catholic liturgy. My thanks are also due to Geoffrey Atkinson for preparing the music examples, to Chris Lewis of the Cartography Unit of the Department of Geography of the University of Nottingham for preparing the maps, and to Lisa Corbett for drawing up the family tree. I am also grateful to the following, who have answered queries, supplied copies of source material, read sections of the book in draft, or have provided assistance in other ways: Graham Barber, Clifford Bartlett, Ian Bartlett, Christina Bashford, Jennifer Bate, Donald Burrows, David Byers, Amanda Capern, Richard Carder, Rachel Cowgill, Oliver Davies, Phil and Pam Fluke, Jane Girdham, John Henderson, Peter Holman, Peter Horton, H. Diack Johnstone, John Keys, Leanne Langley, Peter Leech, Clare Lyon, Andrew McCrea, Simon McVeigh, John Morehen, Claire Nelson, Kenneth Newport, Peter Nockles, John Ogasapian, Guy Oldham, Edward Olleson, Fiona Palmer, Andrew Prescott, Peter Preston, Alvaro Ribeiro, SJ, Brian Robins, Francis Routh, Bradley Strauchen, Graham Treacher, Richard Turbet, John Vickers, John Wagstaff, Gillian Ward Russell, Sir George White, Bt., John Whittle, and John Worthen. As always, I owe a particular debt of gratitude to my wife Hilary, who has borne with patience and good humour the disruption of routine and domestic good order that my work on Wesley has caused over the years, and has come to expect a Wesley dimension to every family outing.

Finally, I turn to Cyril Ehrlich, doyen of social historians of English music. Cyril has shared my fascination with Wesley from its beginnings and has always been ready to discuss, question assumptions, and encourage. To me, as to so many working in this area, he has been a inspirational teacher, a generous colleague, and a staunch friend. It is with profound admiration and the deepest possible gratitude that I dedicate this book to him.

Philip Olleson
Nottingham, March 2003

Editorial Note

Citations

References in the notes to letters of Wesley and his family are given by the names of the author and recipient and the date; dates or parts of dates in square brackets are editorially supplied. Summaries of all these documents, together with full location details, are given in *Samuel Wesley (1766–1837): A Source Book*. The texts of all Wesley's letters to his professional colleagues and friends, and some to members of his family, are contained in *The Letters of Samuel Wesley: Professional and Social Correspondence, 1797–1837*; citations of these letters are identified by an asterisk in the notes. Where citations to manuscripts, books, and articles are given in incomplete form, full details will be found in the Abbreviations or the Bibliography. References to musical works by Wesley are to the worklist in *Samuel Wesley (1766–1837): A Source Book*.

Dates of birth and death

Apart from the first two paragraphs of Chapter 1, dates of birth and death of individuals are not usually given in the text. They can be found in the General Index.

Personalia

It was the practice of the Wesley family to choose Christian names for their children from a very small range. To distinguish between different members of the family with the same Christian name, the following conventions are used when necessary:
   Charles Wesley senior: Charles Wesley (1707–1788), father of Samuel Wesley
   Charles Wesley junior: Charles Wesley (1757–1834), brother of Samuel Wesley
   Charles Wesley III: Charles Wesley (1793–1859), son of Samuel Wesley
   Sarah Gwynne Wesley: Sarah Wesley (1726–1822), mother of Samuel Wesley
   Sarah Wesley: Sarah Wesley (1759–1828), sister of Samuel Wesley
Details of the relationships of other family members and their dates of birth and death are given in the Family Tree (p. xx).

Letter notation of pitch

The convention used here is that in which Tenor C is designated as c and successively higher octaves as c', c'', and c''', successively lower octaves being designated as C, CC, and so on.

Currency

In Wesley's day the pound (£) was divided into twenty shillings (s), which was in turn divided into twelve pence (d). Another unit of currency, used for professional fees, was the guinea, which was worth £1 1s. A half-guinea was thus 10s 6d, and a quarter-guinea 5s 3d.

Numbering of works

Numbers of works (in the form 'KO 000' are those of the worklist in Michael Kassler and Philip Olleson, *Samuel Wesley (1766–1837): A Source Book* (Aldershot, 2001).

Abbreviations

Institutions
BL   British Library, London
CUL   Cambridge, University Library
MARC   Methodist Archives and Research Centre, John Rylands University Library of Manchester
Rylands   John Rylands University Library of Manchester
PRO   Public Records Office, London
RCM   Royal College of Music, London

Manuscripts
Reminiscences   Samuel Wesley, *Reminiscences*, BL, Add. MS 27593

Publications
ABG   *Aris's Birmingham Gazette*
BCP   *Book of Common Prayer*, 1662
BD   Philip H. Highfill et al. (eds), *A Biographical Dictionary of Actors, Actresses, Musicians, Dancers, Managers & Other Stage Personnel in London, 1660–1800*, Carbondale and Edwardsville, Ill., 16 vols, 1973–93
DNB   *Dictionary of National Biography*
EM   *The European Magazine and London Review*, 1782–1826
GM   *The Gentleman's Magazine*, 1731–1880. References are to the year and part.
Grove   *Grove's Dictionary of Music and Musicians*, followed by edition number. References to *The New Grove Dictionary of Music and Musicians*, 2nd ed., 2001, are cited as *New Grove*: see separate entry below.
HS   *Hymns and Psalms*, London, 1983. References are to hymn numbers.
JBIOS   *Journal of the British Institute of Organ Studies*, 1977–
JCW   Thomas Jackson (ed.), *The Journal of the Rev. C. W. To which are appended Selections from his Correspondence and Poetry*, 2 vols, London, 1849
JJW   Nehemiah Curnock (ed.), *The Journals of the Rev. John Wesley, A.M.*, 8 vols, London, 1909–16
JRMA   *Journal of the Royal Musical Association*

LJW	John Telford (ed.), *The Letters of the Rev. John Wesley*, 8 vols, London, 1931
LSW	Philip Olleson (ed.), *The Letters of Samuel Wesley: Professional and Social Correspondence, 1797–1837*, Oxford, 2001
MC	*The Morning Chronicle*
MHB	*The Methodist Hymn Book*, London, 1933. References are to hymn numbers.
ML	*Music and Letters*, 1920–
MM	*The Monthly Magazine and British Register*, 1790–1826
MQ	*The Musical Quarterly*, 1915–
MR	*Music Review*, 1940–84
MT	*The Musical Times*, 1844–
MW	*The Musical World. A Weekly Record of Musical Science, Literature and Intelligence*, 1836–91
New Grove	Stanley Sadie (ed.), *The New Grove Dictionary of Music and Musicians*, 2nd ed., 29 vols, London, 2001
NMMR	*The New Musical Magazine, Review, and Register of Valuable Musical Publications, Ancient and Modern*, 1809–10
QMMR	*Quarterly Musical Magazine and Review*, 1818–29
RISM	Publications of the Répertoire International des Sources Musicales
RMARC	*Royal Musical Association Research Chronicle*
SWSB	Michael Kassler and Philip Olleson, *Samuel Wesley (1766–1837): A Source Book*, Aldershot, 2001

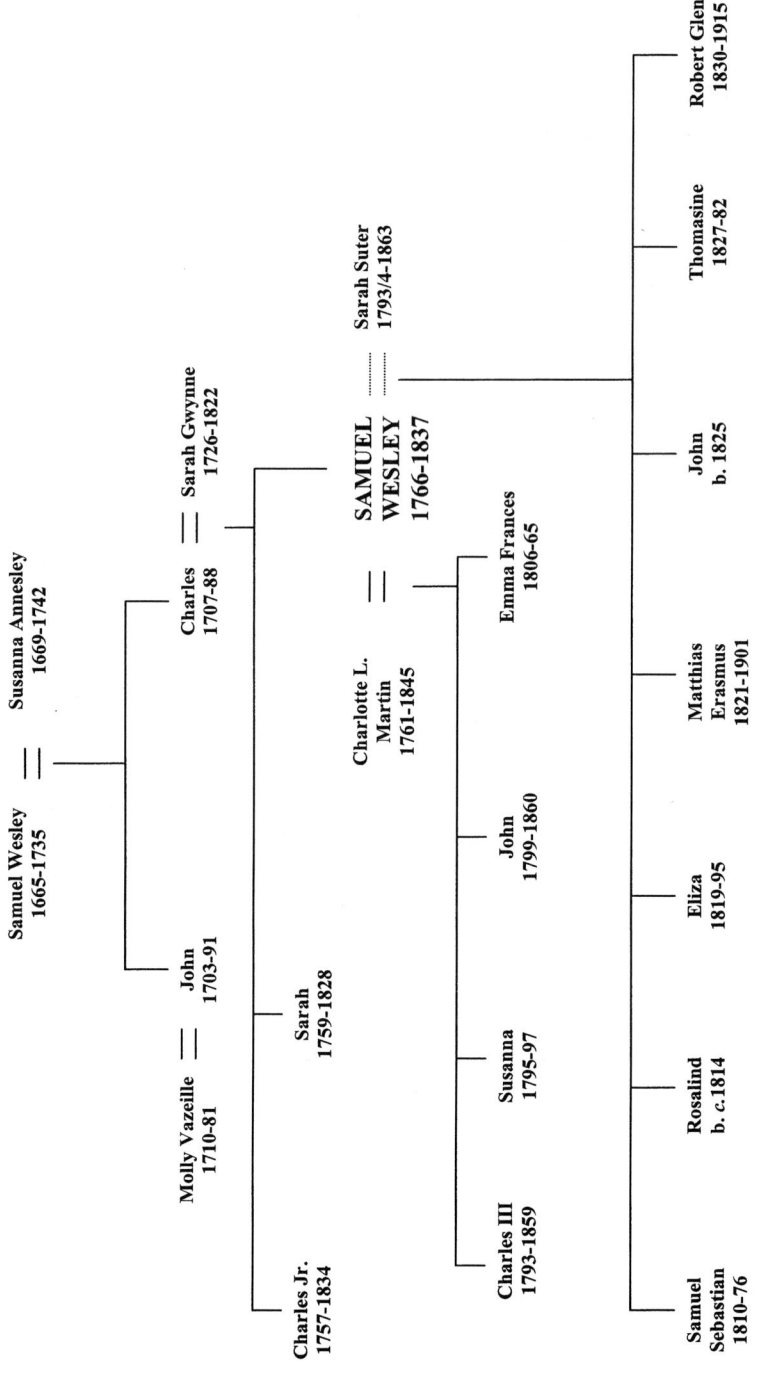

Wesley's family tree

Wesley's England

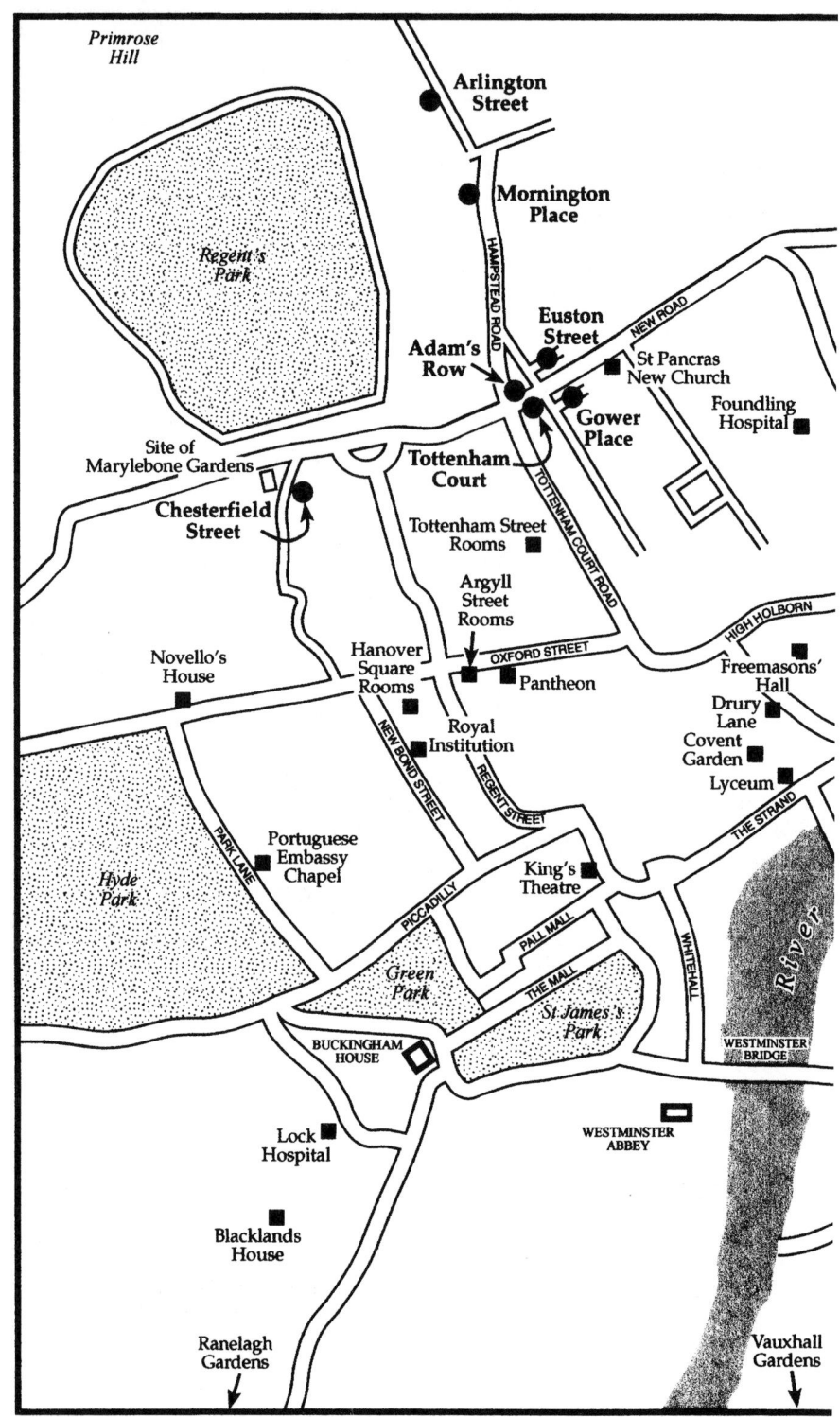

Wesley's London

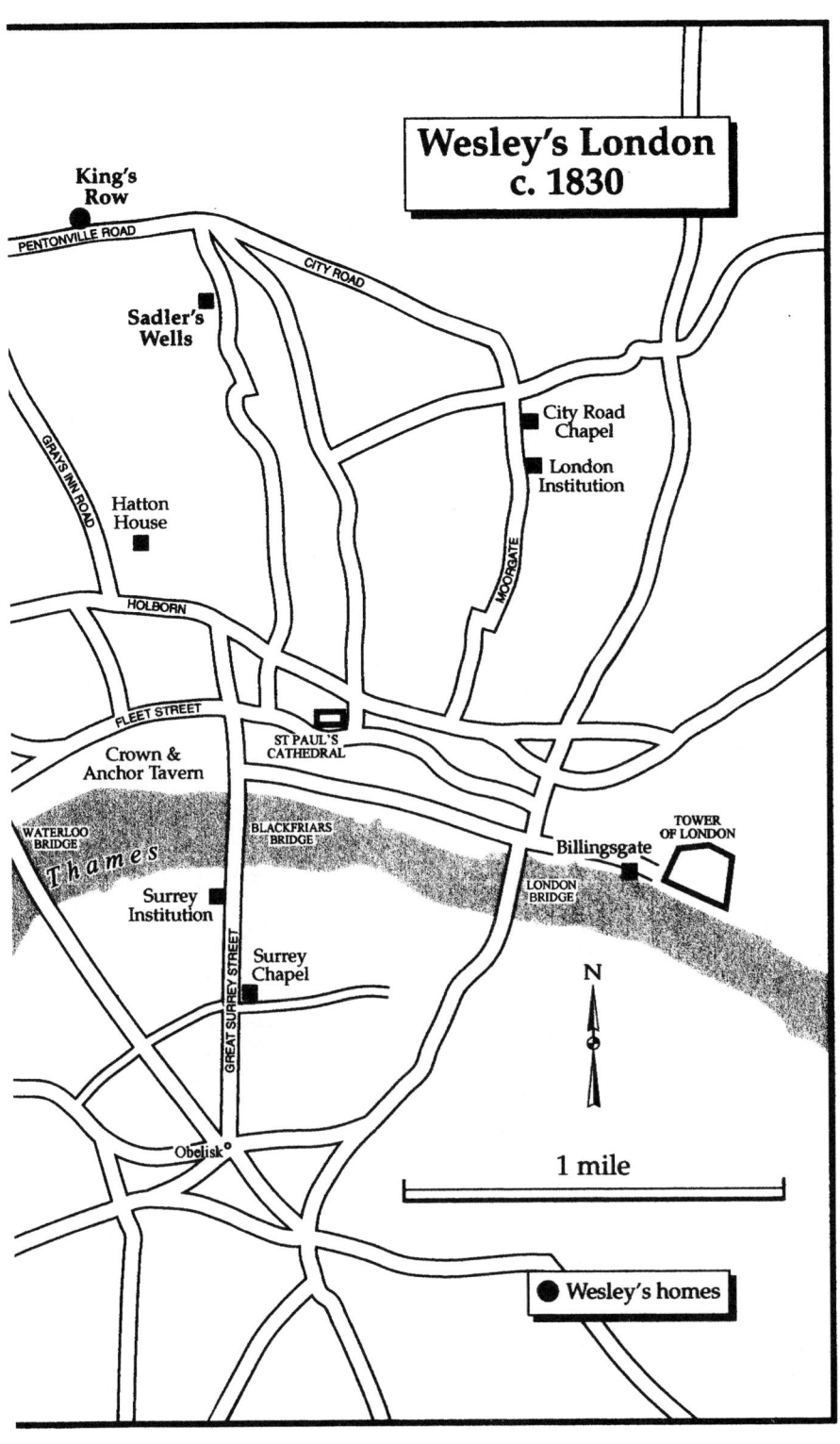

1

Childhood and youth, 1766–1773

Samuel Wesley was born in Charles Street, Bristol, on 24 February 1766. Charles Wesley (1707–88), his father, was the principal poet and hymn-writer of Methodism; John Wesley (1703–91), his uncle, was the movement's leader. Samuel was to be the youngest child, joining Charles, eight years his senior, and Sarah, almost seven years older; four other children had died in infancy or in early childhood.

Samuel's father Charles was the fifteenth or sixteenth child of Samuel Wesley (1662–1735), Rector of Epworth, Lincolnshire, and his wife Susanna (1669–1742), née Annesley. Both came from dissenting stock, their fathers being among the clergy expelled from the Church of England in 1662 for refusing to swear the oath of assent required by the Restoration Act of Uniformity. Perhaps in reaction to this background, both Samuel and Susanna had joined the Church of England in their youth and had espoused High Church principles.[1] They were markedly dissimilar in personality. Henry Rack, in his biography of John Wesley, describes Samuel Wesley senior as 'rash and hasty . . . a man of principle and courage but prone to self-dramatization', and as 'learned, zealous, pious, affectionate when his prejudices were not aroused'.[2] Vivian Green, commenting on the less positive sides of his character, describes him as 'obstinate, passionate, partisan and pedantic'.[3] His rigid adherence to principle is shown by a number of well-known incidents, of which the most striking was in 1701, when he decided to live apart from Susanna following a disagreement with her over William III's legitimacy as king of England. Noticing one day at family prayers that Susanna did not say 'Amen' to the prayer for the monarch, he raised the matter with her. On learning that she did not recognize William as king, he stated that they must henceforth live apart, and promptly left home for London. The accession of Queen Anne in March 1702 did nothing to heal the rift, and he only returned in June of the same year.[4] Susanna, on the other hand is described by Rack as 'competent, businesslike and possessed of a cool, rational mentality which contrasted strongly with Samuel's emotional and

---

[1] Newton, *Susanna Wesley and the Puritan Tradition in Methodism*.
[2] Rack, *Reasonable Enthusiast*, pp. 50, 49.
[3] Green, *The Young Mr Wesley*, p. 44.
[4] See Rack, *Reasonable Enthusiast*, pp. 48–9, which amplifies and corrects traditional accounts of this incident.

"poetic" temperament'.[5] She was a formidable figure in the home, and her authoritarian methods of child-rearing left an indelible mark, by no means always for the good, on all her children.

Of Charles Wesley's eight brothers and sisters to survive to adulthood, the only one relevant to the present study is John. Both boys went to school in London – John to the Charterhouse and Charles to Westminster. They then went on to Christ Church, Oxford, where they graduated in 1724 and 1730 respectively. In 1726 John was elected to a Fellowship at Lincoln College; he was ordained deacon in 1725 and priest in 1727. Charles later stated that his own first year at Oxford was 'lost in diversions'. In his second year, however, he settled down to study, and began to practise religion with more seriousness. It was then that he founded the 'Holy Club', a small group of like-minded fellow students who met regularly together under his leadership for Bible study and prayer. John Wesley was not in Oxford at this time, having taken a year's leave of absence from his Fellowship to assist his father in his parish at Epworth, but he joined the Holy Club on his return, and soon took over the leadership. The group, 'the spiritual birthplace of organized Methodism',[6] soon extended its activities to the practical sphere, including prison visiting.

The Holy Club continued to meet in Oxford for the next few years. In 1735, however, following the death of their father, Charles and John decided to go to America to the recently settled colony of Georgia. Part of their intention was the conversion of the Native Americans, but Charles was also engaged as secretary to General Oglethorpe, the colony's Governor. It was in preparation for this missionary work that Charles was first ordained deacon and then priest in September of that year. The visit to Georgia was not a success for either brother. Charles was the first to return, in December 1736. Back in London, his spiritual development was heavily influenced by the theologian William Law and by the Moravians, in particular Count Zinzendorf and Peter Böhler, both of whom he came to know in London in 1737 and 1738. John stayed longer in Georgia, returning in early 1738. He had been heavily influenced by the Moravians in Georgia, and continued his association on his return.

Within three days of each other in May 1738, each brother had a profound religious experience that was to change the entire tenor of their lives and lead to the beginnings of their ministry. Later in 1738, John travelled to the Moravian settlement at Herrnhut in Saxony, where he was able to observe Moravian worship and community life at first hand. The following year, the brothers started their itinerant ministry, preaching a gospel of faith leading to holiness and the personal assurance of salvation. For most of the next decade, their lives would be spent travelling across the length and breadth of England, Scotland, Wales, and Ireland to preach to mass audiences, often in the open air and in the teeth of considerable and sometimes violent opposition. In 1738 John acquired the Foundery, a former armaments factory in Moorfields, London. The

---

[5] Rack, *Reasonable Enthusiast*, p. 50.
[6] Newport, *The Sermons of Charles Wesley*, p. 13.

following year it opened as the headquarters of Methodism in London. In the same year the New Room in the Horsefair in Bristol was built to cater for the large Methodist community that had developed there; it is still in use, and is the oldest functioning Methodist chapel in the world. By now, Bristol and London were the largest centres of Methodism in England. John largely took control in London, and Charles in Bristol, although he made frequent visits to London to help John with his work at the Foundery.

In August 1747, at the age of thirty-nine, Charles met Sarah Gwynne, the twenty-year-old daughter of Marmaduke Gwynne, a wealthy landowner of Garth, Brecknockshire (now Powys). They married in April 1749. As Charles's letters to Sarah and his journal entries at the time clearly show, this was a love-match, and their marriage was long and happy; Kenneth Newport has identified the stability and responsibilities that marriage brought as a turning point equal in importance in Charles's continuing ministry as his 'conversion' experience of May 1738.[7] In September of the same year the couple moved to Bristol and settled in Charles Street, in a house that is now the Charles Wesley Heritage Centre.[8] Two years later, at the age of forty-seven, John Wesley also married, in circumstances less propitious and with altogether less happy consequences. His bride was Molly Vazeille, a well-to-do widow seven years his junior, with four children of her own. Their marriage was famously unhappy. For his part, John Wesley saw no reason to moderate his itinerant preaching so as to spend more time at home; for hers, Molly was resentful of the time that John spent away, jealous of his relationships with other women, ready to suspect him of infidelity at every turn, and on occasion physically violent. After a number of temporary separations, she left him in 1771 intending never to return, John noting in Latin in his journal that he had not deserted her, had not sent her away, and would not ask her to return. Although she did in fact come back on this occasion, a permanent separation followed in 1776, and she died in 1781.

The relationship of Charles and John Wesley, although always close, was rarely comfortable. Some of the tensions were caused by differences in temperament, some by their different views on the direction that the developing Methodist church should take. There were differences of opinion about itinerant ministry, too: after his marriage, Charles travelled less, and by 1756 had given it up entirely; John, meanwhile, travelled as much as before, and continued to do so almost up to the time of his death. As every commentator has pointed out, the differences of temperament between Charles and John Wesley repeated the differences between their parents. Charles, taking after his father, was passionate and impetuous, with a temperament that could soar to the heights of elation and plumb the depths of depression. At least one writer has suspected the presence of bipolar affective disorder or manic depression, a diagnosis that might equally be applied to his father, and – as we will see – seems inescapable for Samuel.[9] John, taking after his mother, had a far cooler

---

[7] Ibid, p. 22.
[8] Brown, *Charles Wesley, Hymnwriter*.
[9] Rack, *Reasonable Enthusiast*, pp. 51, 252.

temperament, and the obsessive eye for detail that is the mark of a great organizer. These differences were reflected in the very different roles that the two brothers took within Methodism: John as the leader and organizing genius, and Charles as the movement's principal poet and hymn-writer.

It was to be eight years before any children who survived infancy were born to Sarah and Charles. She miscarried in 1750, and one child born in 1752 died at the age of sixteen months; another was born in 1755, and died at only one month old. But on 11 December 1757 she gave birth to Charles, and eighteen months later, on 1 April 1759, to Sarah.

From his earliest years, it was apparent that Charles junior had outstanding musical abilities, the more remarkable in that his parents' own interest in music was no more than was commonplace for those of their class and background: Charles Wesley senior had played the flute a little in his youth and was generally fond of music, and Sarah played the harpsichord and sang. Charles junior was thus born into a family where music was a normal part of everyday life and where his own musical abilities were welcomed and nurtured as a matter of course. But it was not an outstandingly musical one, and nothing could have prepared his parents for the nature and extent of Charles's musical gifts and the way that accommodating them and meeting his growing needs would change the family's life for ever.

As Charles's musical gifts and early musical experiences moulded the environment into which Samuel was to be born eight years later, they are worth investigating in some detail. Fortunately, they were described in detail by Charles Wesley senior in an account that he wrote in 1776 at the request of the Hon. Daines Barrington, a wealthy lawyer and antiquarian who took a quasi-scientific interest in musical child prodigies, and also recorded his impressions of the young Mozart, whom he examined in London in December 1764, when Mozart was eight. Charles Wesley senior also provided a similar account of Samuel, and in 1781 Barrington published extracts from both accounts, together with his own impressions of Samuel, in his *Miscellanies*.[10] In this way, the early lives of both brothers were chronicled in detail, giving an unparalleled insight into their musical development.

According to Charles Wesley senior's account, from soon after the birth of Charles junior his mother found that she could quiet and amuse him with her harpsichord playing. By the time he was three he was picking out tunes, always putting a proper bass to them. Edmund Broderip, the organist of St James's, the

---

[10] For Barrington's description of Mozart, see 'Account of a Very Remarkable Musician', *Transactions of the Royal Society* 9 (1770), p. 54. The manuscript of Charles Wesley's account of the musical experiences of his two sons is at MARC, DDCW 8/2, DDCW 8/24, and DDCW 10/2. Barrington's account was reprinted as 'An Account of the very extraordinary musical talents of Messrs Charles and Samuel Wesley' in *Westminster Magazine* 9 (1781), pp. 233–6, and 289–95. A more complete, but selectively edited, version of Charles's accounts of the two children, drawing on the manuscript sources cited above, appeared in Jackson, *Life*, vol. 2, pp. 330–5, 337–45.

family parish church, heard him around this time, and said he would make a great player. When he was four, his father took him to London, where he was heard by John Beard, the celebrated tenor soloist for whom Handel had written many oratorio parts, and who was now proprietor of Covent Garden Theatre. Beard was highly impressed by him, and offered to recommend him to William Boyce, the Master of the King's Music, to have him admitted as one of the Children of the Chapel Royal at St James's. This would have placed him on the traditional training route for a church musician and ensured him a solid grounding in church music, but at this stage his father had no thoughts of bringing him up as a musician, and did not take up Beard's offer. Someone whom Charles Wesley describes only as 'a gentleman', but who was probably Barrington himself, then took him to play to the blind organist John Stanley, who expressed much pleasure and surprise at hearing him, saying that he had never met one of Charles's age with so strong a propensity to music. Charles also played to the organist, harpsichordist, and composer John Worgan, who told his father that he would become an 'eminent master', if he was not sidetracked by other studies.

Back in Bristol, there were no notable teachers for Charles to study with, and he was left to 'ramble on' until he was nearly six. He was then sent for lessons to a Mr Rooke, whom his father described as 'a man of no name but very good-natured, who let him run on *ad libitum* whilst he sat by, more to observe than to control him'.

It is worth pausing here to consider the background to this first section of Charles Wesley senior's long account of his elder son's musical experiences. The names he gives make up a roll-call of many of the most prominent musicians in London at the time, and it is apparent that Charles Wesley was able to make contact with them quickly and easily, even though he was unlikely to have known them previously. One key figure was John Beard. If Charles Wesley did not know him already, he would have had an easy introduction through the former actress Priscilla Rich, a Methodist convert. She was the widow of the playwright and theatre manager John Rich, Beard's predecessor at Covent Garden, who had died in 1761, and Beard was married to one of Rich's daughters by a previous marriage. In his capacity as proprietor of Covent Garden and as a leading tenor soloist, Beard occupied a position at the hub of London's theatre and musical life, and would have been able to introduce Charles Wesley and his son to a wide variety of musicians.

Another contact was the evangelical preacher and amateur musician Martin Madan, who was to become Samuel's godfather and would play a particularly important part in his life. Madan was the honorary chaplain of the Lock Hospital, a charity founded in 1746 by the surgeon William Bromfield for the benefit of men and women suffering from venereal diseases. He was a member of a wealthy and highly influential family – his father was an army officer, his mother Judith, née Cowper, was the daughter of a judge and the niece of Earl Cowper, the Lord Chancellor, and his cousin was the poet William Cowper – and had been an associate of both John and Charles Wesley since 1750, if not earlier.[11] He was one of John Wesley's more spectacular converts. Like Charles, he was educated at Westminster School and Christ Church, Oxford. After coming down from Oxford he had settled in London, where he was called to the Bar in 1748 and became a member of a 'very free-speaking and deep-drinking' group of young men who met in a tavern near Temple Bar and called themselves the Poetical Club. Two years later, hearing that John Wesley was due to preach in the area, the group despatched Madan to go and hear him, so that he could observe his mannerisms and later entertain the group by mimicking him. He was converted on the spot by Wesley's preaching on the text 'Prepare to meet thy God', and when asked on his return to the club if he had 'taken off the old Methodist' he replied, '*No*, gentlemen, but he has taken *me* off.' After this experience his life changed completely. He was ordained deacon in 1757 and priest the following year, and at the same time offered his services as chaplain of the Lock Hospital, where he rapidly acquired a reputation as a forceful and charismatic preacher.

Like many other philanthropic institutions, the Lock Hospital attracted many patrons from the world of the performing arts. Among its early governors were the actor David Garrick and Felice Giardini, Thomas Linley senior, and other musicians, and in its early years theatrical and musical performances were regularly held in various London theatres as part of its fund-raising activities. Handel, in addition to his better known support of the Foundling Hospital, also took an interest in the Lock Hospital. In 1754 he donated the proceeds of a performance of *Judas Maccabaeus* there, and in consequence was elected a perpetual governor. At the daily services at the hospital, Madan established a lively musical tradition, and in 1762 was responsible for the building of a fine new chapel seating eight hundred. Before long it became a fashionable place of worship, noted for the carriages that flocked to its doors every Sunday. Madan's *A Collection of Psalms and Hymns*, containing words only, was published in 1760, and subsequently ran to thirteen editions. The musical repertoire of the chapel can be seen in the companion volume, *A Collection of Psalm and Hymn Tunes* (1769), containing thirty-four tunes by such composers as Boyce, Giardini, Worgan, and Jonathan Battishill, with the largest number by Madan himself.

With the completion of the new chapel, the fund-raising concerts were able to transfer there. From 1763, there was an annual oratorio performance, in emulation of the similar tradition at the Foundling Hospital, where Handel's *Messiah* had been performed annually since 1750. The work that came particularly to be associated with the Lock Hospital was *Ruth*, to a libretto by Madan's assistant Thomas Haweis, and with music originally by Avison and Giardini; Boyce was also to have contributed, but had to withdraw because of illness. In this form it was first performed in 1763 and again in 1765, and in a

---

[11] Information in this paragraph is taken from Falconer Madan, *The Madan Family*. See also Paananen, 'Martin Madan and the Limits of Evangelical Philanthropy'; McVeigh, 'Music and Lock Hospital in the 18th Century'.

revised version with music by Giardini alone every year from 1768 to 1780. Other oratorios performed in the chapel in the early years were Arne's *Judith* in 1764 and Worgan's *Manasseh* in 1766 and 1767. It was no doubt through his friendship with Madan that Charles Wesley achieved his introductions to Arne, Boyce, Giardini, Arnold, Worgan, and many others.

It was into this environment that Samuel was born in Bristol on 24 February 1766, thus – as his father was delighted to point out – sharing his birthday with Handel. Following the death of a further child, John James, in early infancy in 1768, he was to remain the youngest in the family. The family house in Bristol was full of music, and it was not long before Samuel was showing unmistakeable signs of musical ability. According to his father, he was not quite as precocious as his elder brother, as it was not until he was nearly three that he first 'aimed at a tune', but from the start he showed a keen interest in music, and while his brother was playing, he used to stand at his side with a toy violin, scraping away and beating time.

By the late 1760s, the demands of Charles's duties in London had become such that it became essential for him to have a permanent base there. His brother John had originally hoped that Charles would be able to find a house near the Foundery, but in late 1770 he was offered the use of a large fully-furnished house in Chesterfield Street, Marylebone by Martha Gumley, a wealthy well-wisher whose late husband had been a Methodist convert. This was an inconveniently long way from the Foundery, but the offer was too good to miss, and Charles accepted it. He moved in with Charles junior in February 1771, for the time being leaving his wife and his other two children in Bristol. For the moment the family kept on the Bristol house and divided their time between Bristol and London, but in 1778 they moved permanently to London.

Although the primary reason for the move to London was the increasing demands of his ministry, Charles Wesley senior would also have been aware of the benefits for his two children of living in the capital, where they would be able to take advantage of the musical opportunities on offer. In the preceding few years the question of Charles junior's continuing musical education had continued to be a concern to his parents. One part of the problem was the lack of good teachers in Bristol. Another was the large cost, which would include substantial expenditure not only on lessons but also on music and would have been quite outside Charles Wesley's limited means. On a visit to London around 1764, however, Charles junior was heard by Lady Gertrude Hotham, a Methodist convert and friend of the family, who gave him all her music. This formed the basis of his library, together with copies of songs by Handel and Purcell and keyboard sonatas by Scarlatti that Mrs Rich and Beard gave him. There was also the promise of an organ and substantial patronage from Lady Hotham's son Charles, another Methodist convert, but this came to nothing when he went abroad and died shortly afterwards.

Charles junior's musical education continued 'with the assistance of nature only, and his two favourite authors, Handel and Corelli', until he was around ten, when it was clear that it needed to be put on a more formal basis. A Mr Rogers, described by Charles Wesley senior as the oldest organist in Bristol, advised that it was 'high time to put him in trammels'. Bernard Granville, a friend in Bath who had known Handel, had more specific advice: Charles should have nothing to do with any 'great master', who would spoil him and destroy any spark of originality in him. Instead, he should study Handel's 'Lessons' (i.e. the two sets of harpsichord suites, HWV 426–33 and 434–42) until he had mastered them. In Granville's opinion, the only person suitable to teach them to him was the eminent organist and harpsichordist Joseph Kelway, organist of St Martin's in the Fields and the music master of Queen Charlotte, but Granville was sure he would refuse to take Charles on. Charles was then taken to play to some of the other principal keyboard players in London, starting, at the recommendation of Bromfield, with John Keeble and his pupil John Burton. Both encouraged him, and Keeble advised him to keep on with his general education until the age of fourteen before applying himself in earnest to music. This advice was echoed by Arne. Samuel Arnold advised him not to restrict himself to any one composer or style, but to study and adopt what was best in all of them. Meanwhile, others had more radical plans. The opera composer Mattia Vento, whom Charles Wesley senior would have known through the Lock Hospital, thought that no-one but an Italian teacher would do, and Giardini was all for sending him to Bologna or Paris for his education – a suggestion that his father thought ludicrous.

Despite the unanimous agreement of all who heard him that Charles was destined to be musician, his father still had his doubts and misgivings. These were instantly allayed in August 1769, when Bromfield at last took father and son to see Kelway. On hearing Charles junior play, Kelway immediately invited him to come to see him whenever he was in London, and offered to teach him for nothing. He did this for two years, starting Charles off with Handel's *Lessons* before turning to his own sonatas, published five years earlier, those of his teacher Geminiani, and the sonatas of Scarlatti, whose music had had a cult following in England since the early 1740s, and which he greatly admired.[12] His father recorded some of Kelway's comments on Charles from their first meeting to late October 1770, by which time he had given him well over one hundred lessons.

At the same time, Charles's musical education was also continuing in less formal ways. In addition to harpsichord lessons from Kelway, he was having thorough-bass and composition lessons from Worgan and composition lessons

---

[12] Newton, 'The English Cult of Domenico Scarlatti'. For Kelway's interest in Scarlatti, see also Burney, *History*, vol. 2, p. 1009: 'Kelway, a scholar of Geminiani, kept Scarlatti's best lessons in constant practice, and was at the head of the Scarlatti sect. He had, in his voluntaries on the organ, a masterly wildness, and long supported the character of a great player, in a style quite his own, bold, rapid, and fanciful. With his harpsichord playing I was not acquainted, but have often been assured, that he executed the most difficult lessons of Scarlatti, in a manner peculiarly neat and delicate.'

from Boyce. Worgan, who was a great admirer of the music of Geminiani and Scarlatti and had edited a volume of Scarlatti's sonatas in 1752, often played the harpsichord to him, greatly impressing him with the boldness of his playing. Worgan and Battishill introduced him to the English oratorio repertoire, often playing and singing whole works to him, and Kelway played through *Messiah* to him, to show him how Handel himself had performed it. Samuel was no doubt also present on many of these occasions, sitting quietly but absorbing all he heard. At around this time Charles also attended oratorio rehearsals and performances at both Covent Garden and Drury Lane, comparing the performers at the two houses with each other and with his teachers. He also attended opera performances at the King's Theatre in the Haymarket.

Samuel was three when Charles started his lessons with Kelway. From the start, he took a great interest, insisting on being present and accompanying his brother 'on the chair'. At around this time he was also heard by Arnold, who said that he 'set him down as one of my family', but the family were not disposed to pay much attention to this compliment in view of the adulation that Charles had already received. But it soon became apparent that Samuel was likely to rival his brother's precocity. According to his father's account, at four years old he taught himself to read from a copy of Handel's *Samson*, and by the time he was five knew the whole of *Samson* and *Messiah* by heart. At the same time he was also able to recognize the composer of whatever music his brother played, and to say what sort it was. This was also the time of Samuel's first compositions. He frequently improvised oratorio scenes at the keyboard, and the family noticed that when he came to repeat them, the music was always the same. In this way, before he was six he had composed some of the airs of an oratorio, *Ruth*, which he then remembered until he was able to write them down, over two years later.

Samuel began his formal musical education at the age of six with lessons from David Williams, a Bristol organist, who taught him to read music. Even at this stage, his father noted, 'it was hard to say which was the master and which the scholar', and Samuel stated in his manuscript *Reminiscences*, written in 1836, that Williams had given him a free choice in what he played. He then started to teach himself the violin, going on to have a few lessons from a Mr McBean,[13] an army musician, and then around twenty lessons from William Kingsbury, with whom he studied the music of Corelli. At seven he played a psalm at a service at St James's church in Bristol,[14] and at around the same time, while staying at Bath when the rest of the family were away in Wales, performed a number of organ voluntaries at the Abbey at Sunday services and played the violin at several private concerts. It was probably at around this time that he first experienced Handel's choral music, in the form of a performance of the

---

[13] McBean's name is not given in Charles Wesley senior's account, but is supplied in *Reminiscences*, fol. 36.
[14] SW to Charles Wesley, 20 Apr. 1773.

'Dettingen' Te Deum at Bristol Cathedral, the opening of which he later remembered had left him 'thunderstruck'.[15]

In 1774 Samuel learned to write music, and was at last able to commit his compositions to paper. A volume entitled 'Pasticcio Book 1774–5', now in the British Library, contains these earliest works, in several genres: Anglican hymns and anthems, settings of the canticles, glees and catches, organ music, pieces for violin and bass, fugues, canons, and even a miniature cantata, *Derdham Downs*, to words by his father. It is an untidy manuscript, often to the point of near-illegibility, but its untidiness (as Samuel admits in an apologetic note at the beginning) is that of haste rather than uncertainty or changes of mind, and the overall impression is one of great profusion of invention, with which Samuel's as yet incompletely developed music-writing skills were sometimes unable to keep pace.

Samuel was now also at last able to write down his oratorio *Ruth*. The autograph score, also in the British Library, is as untidy as the Pasticcio Book, and the signs of inexperience in notation are as clear: Samuel notes at the beginning that the viola part is written an octave too low throughout. But these are comparatively minor details. With its full complement of recitatives, arias, ensembles, and choruses, *Ruth* is an amazing production for a child of eight, let alone one of six, which was when he conceived much of the music. Later in the year, Boyce called at Chesterfield Street, saying that he had heard that there was an 'English Mozart' in the house. After examining the score of *Ruth*, he commented that 'these Airs are some of the prettiest I have seen; this Boy writes by Nature as good a Bass as I can by Skill and Study'.[16] Samuel later presented the score of *Ruth* to him, and received in return a gracious reply in which Boyce thanked his 'very ingenious Brother Composer' for the gift and assured him that he would keep it with the greatest of care, as the 'most curious Product of his musical Library'.[17]

It must also have been at around this time that Charles Wesley wrote in verse on Samuel's behalf to Boyce to request a copy of his *Cathedral Music*, a three-volume compilation of English church music from the sixteenth to the early eighteenth century, the last volume of which was published in 1773:

> The humble Petition
> Of a rhiming Musician,
> (A Petition of Natural Right)
> Undeniably shews
> That, wherever he goes,
> Church-Music is all his delight:
>   That he never can rest,
> Till enrich'd with the best,
> His Talent aright he employs,
> And claims for his own,

[15] *SW to Jacob, 17 Sept. 1808.
[16] *Reminiscences*, fol. 33.
[17] Ibid.

> As true Harmony's Son,
> The Collection of good Doctor Boyce.
> > Three volumes of yours
> Which his Prayer procures,
> Will afford him Examples enough,
> And save Poet Sam
> (Your Petitioner's Name)
> From a Deluge of Musical Stuff.
> > So, good Doctor, if now
> His suit you allow,
> And make him as rich as a king,
> Taken into your Choir,
> To his Organ and Lyre,
> Your Petitioner ever shall – Sing![18]

The association of Boyce with the family, both as a personal friend and as the composition teacher of Charles, continued until his death in 1779.

---

[18] Kimbrough and Beckerlegge, *Unpublished Poetry of Charles Wesley*, vol. 1, p. 279.

2

Early upbringing and the family concerts, 1774–1787

Traditional Methodist attitudes to child-rearing were harshly authoritarian, taking their cue from the celebrated and often quoted statement of Susanna Wesley, Samuel's paternal grandmother, that she insisted on 'conquering the will of children betimes, because this is the only strong and rational foundation of a religious education, without which both precept and example will be ineffectual'.[1] Such attitudes were not, however, shared by Charles Wesley senior, who held more modern views that stressed the rationality of the child and the benefits of more humane treatment. He was a devoted family man, and his hymns, poems, and letters all attest to his involvement with his children: his anxiety when they were ill, the care he took over their upbringing, his delight at their successes, and his disappointment and hurt when they failed to measure up to his high standards of behaviour.

But he had come to marriage and fatherhood late: he was forty-one when he married, forty-nine at the time of the birth of Charles, the first of his children to survive to adulthood, and fifty-eight by the birth of Samuel. This large difference in age between Charles and his children inevitably revealed itself in some awkwardness in his dealings with them. Nonetheless, he appears to have made every effort to understand them, to enter into their world, and to bring them up in the way most appropriate to their personalities and talents. Some aspects of his approach – notably his seriousness and his insistence on discipline – reflected orthodox Methodist thinking. In other respects he was far more liberal, as can be seen in the following letter to the seven-year old Samuel:

> Come now, my good friend Samuel, and let us reason together. God made you for Himself, that is to be ever happy with Him. Ought you not, therefore, to serve and love Him? But you can do neither unless He gives you the power. Ask (He says Himself) and it shall be given you. That is, pray Him to make you love Him: and pray for it every night and morning in your own words, as well as in those which have been taught you. You have been used to say your prayers in the sight of others. Henceforth, go into a corner by yourself, where no eye but God's may see you. There pray to your heavenly Father who seeth in secret: and be sure He hears every word you speak, and sees everything you do, at all times, and in all places.
>
> You should now begin to live by reason and religion. There should be sense even in your play and diversions. Therefore I have furnished you with maps and

---

[1] Susanna Wesley to John Wesley, 24 July 1732, quoted by him in his journal entry for 1 Aug. 1742 (*JJW*, vol. 3, p. 36), and in his sermon *On Obedience to Parents* (1784).

books and harpsichord. Every day get something by heart: whatever your mother recommends. Every day read one or more chapters in the Bible. I suppose your mother will take you now in the place of your brother, to be her chaplain, to read the psalms and lessons, when your sister does not. . . .

Foolish people are too apt to praise you. If they see anything good in you they should praise God, not you, for it. As for music, it is neither good nor bad in itself. You have a natural inclination to it: but God gave you that: therefore God only should be thanked and praised for it. Your brother has the same love of music much more than you, yet he is not proud or vain of it. Neither, I trust, will you be. You will send me a long letter of answer, and always look on me both as your loving father, and your friend.[2]

As his verses for his children show, he was not unremittingly serious with them, and had a well-developed, if rather ponderous, sense of fun.[3] And as can be seen from the letter to Samuel above, he also (and unlike his brother) recognized the important role of play in children's lives: Samuel was allowed to keep a small menagerie of pets and to engage in kite-flying and other similar activities.[4] But the Wesley children were kept apart from others of their own age: in an undated letter to his wife Charles Wesley senior warned against the children having friends of their own age, on the grounds that children were 'corruptors of each other'.[5]

The attitude of Charles Wesley to his sons' musical talents was perhaps inevitably ambivalent. As a music-lover himself, he was delighted that his children were gifted musicians, and regarded their abilities as God-given talents, to be developed to their full potential. On the other hand, he would have been very aware of the less welcome consequences of their childhood celebrity: the boys received a degree of attention and adulation that would not always have been welcome or desirable, and they inevitably missed out on many of the features of a more normal childhood. Such problems are attendant on child prodigies and their parents in any age. In the case of the Wesleys, they were exacerbated by Charles's prominent position within Methodism, which had some deep-rooted misgivings of its own about music. John Wesley's views on music, later set out in his treatise *On the Power of Music* (1780) were decidedly uncompromising.[6] While committed to the value of hymn-singing in worship, he was distrustful of music's sensual appeal and its association with worldly entertainments, in particular with dancing and the theatre. At the root of his problem was a complete lack of comprehension about music as a source of entertainment and pleasure: he simply could not see the point of any music that was not associated with religious devotion. Charles Wesley was aware that

---

[2] Charles Wesley to SW, 6 Mar. 1773.
[3] Kimbrough and Beckerlegge, *Unpublished Poetry of Charles Wesley*, vol. 1, pp. 279–86.
[4] SW to Prudence Box, 16 July [c.1771–5] and [Aug.–Dec. 1776].
[5] Charles Wesley to Sarah Gwynne Wesley, n.d., in *JCW*, vol. 2, p. 246.
[6] Dated Inverness, 9 June 1779 and published in *Arminian Magazine* 4 (1781), pp. 104–107. For John Wesley's views on hymns, see his Preface, dated 20 Oct. 1779, to *A Collection of Hymns for the Use of the People called Methodists* (London, 1780).

there were many within the Methodist community who were disposed to criticize him for what they saw as an over-worldly style of life. In 1771 John Fletcher had written to warn him that he had enemies who complained of 'his love for musick, company, fine people, great folks' and how he had abandoned his former 'zeal and frugality'.[7] There must have been many other criticisms of a similar nature. And he had reservations of his own about music. For all his love of the art and his desire to see his children receive the best possible musical education, he nonetheless would have had misgivings about where their musical activities might lead them. To a certain extent his attitudes would have been affected and coloured by his Methodism, but in essence they would have been shared by all parents of his class. For music was, in Deborah Rohr's apt phrase, a 'profession of artisans':[8] largely working-class and family-based, and notoriously insecure. Musicians earned their livings from a 'basket of activities', which might include some or all of performing, teaching, composing, and (in the case of organists) church appointments. There was no career progression and little chance of substantial earnings, and musicians could in general look forward to an impoverished or destitute old age. The life of a professional musician was not one that a gentleman would in normal circumstances consider for his son, given the competing attractions of the three traditional 'learned' professions of the church, medicine, and the law. Of course, for Charles Wesley, circumstances were anything but normal. The two boys were the most outstanding musical child prodigies that England had ever known, and the directions their lives had taken as a result had built up a momentum that must have made progression into music as a career appear almost inevitable. This did not mean, however, that Charles Wesley was happy about the prospect.

We have already seen how important Martin Madan was in fostering Charles junior's early musical education and introducing him to many of London's leading musicians. As Charles Wesley senior's account makes clear, Madan was to play an even more crucial role in the musical development of Samuel, and as the boy's godfather, he also had a considerable influence on his spiritual development.

As a gentleman of private means, Madan had ample time to travel and to cultivate his friendships with his musician and aristocratic friends. It was probably in the early 1770s that he started to take Samuel with him on his visits. In this way Samuel soon encountered Worgan and Burton (both of whom had earlier heard his elder brother), Joah Bates (soon to become the first director of music of the Concert of Ancient Music), and the music historian Charles Burney. All who heard him were amazed at how 'just and regular' his extemporary fugues were, and could not believe that he had had no lessons in composition. They also commented on his ability to play at sight anything that was put in front of him, to improvise variations on any melody, and to imitate

---

[7] Fletcher to Charles Wesley, 13 Oct. 1771.
[8] Rohr, *The Careers of British Musicians, 1750–1850*.

the works of leading composers, whether Johann Christian Bach, Handel, Schobert, or Scarlatti.

Samuel was evidently as precocious a child in his conversation and general demeanour as in his music. When showed some of the music of Mozart – ten years his senior – and asked how he liked it, he commented gravely that it was 'very well for one of his years'. His father also commented on his great love of punctuality and order: how he could not be persuaded to attend any evening event, on one occasion insisting on leaving a performance of *Messiah* after the first part, so as to be home in time for bed. At the same time, he was also at pains to stress how natural and unaffected his behaviour was, and how his head had not been turned by the praise and attention that was lavished on him, stating that 'whenever he went into the company of his betters, he would much rather have stayed at home; yet when among them, he was free and easy, so that some remarked, he behaved as one bred up at court, yet without a courtier's servility.' But Charles Wesley was over-confident about his son's attitude to this attention. Another child might have enjoyed the experience more, but Samuel later stated that he had felt humiliated by it, and had resented his father's behaviour in allowing Madan to carry him around 'like a raree show', adding: 'this soured my temper toward him at an early age. I contracted a dislike of my father's conduct, which grew with my growth, and strengthened with my strength.'

Charles Wesley's account of Samuel's musical experiences takes the story up to late 1776. Madan had recently taken Samuel to visit yet more leading musicians. One was Carl Friedrich Abel, the celebrated composer and impresario, who with Johann Christian Bach had for many years promoted the most prestigious series of public concerts in London. He produced a subject for Samuel to improvise on, saying afterwards that 'not three masters in town could have answered it so well.' The violinist Wilhelm Cramer, the leader of the orchestra at the Bach-Abel concerts, also took a great liking to him, played some trios with him and his brother, and offered to teach him the violin, saying that he was confident that a few lessons would 'set him up for a violinist'. Samuel was also heard by James Nares, the Master of the Children of the Chapel Royal at St James's, who like everyone else could scarcely believe Samuel's ability in composition, sight-reading, and improvisation. Shortly afterwards, Boyce paid another visit to Chesterfield Street. Taking up a setting of the Jubilate that was lying on a table, he immediately assumed it was by Charles. When told that it was in fact by Samuel, he stated that he could find no fault in it, that he had never come across such a natural composer, and that it was as if Samuel had 'come among us dropt down from heaven'.

The story of Samuel's musical development is now taken up by Barrington. He recalled his meeting with Samuel in late 1775, just before his tenth birthday. Like everyone else, he had found his harpsichord-playing astonishing, and recorded much the same impressions: how Samuel was able to play the most difficult passages at sight and to improvise in the style of all the best known composers, adding that he was also able to execute difficult transpositions at sight, and if presented with one treble part of a trio sonata, could add a second treble part and a bass. He also related an anecdote involving the music publisher Robert Bremner. On hearing about Samuel's sight-reading ability, Bremner had produced a manuscript of keyboard music that had supposedly been written for Elizabeth I, and contained passages that no-one else could play. This, Bremner thought, would be certain to 'gravel' him. The manuscript was no doubt the Fitzwilliam Virginal Book, compiled at the beginning of the seventeenth century (although not in fact for Elizabeth I), which Bremner at this time owned. Its considerable notational idiosyncrasies caused Samuel some problems at first, but on a second playing he was able to execute the troublesome passages without difficulty.

Barrington also commented on Samuel's amazing memory for the music of others, and on the seemingly inexhaustible store of invention in his improvisations: how he could play upwards of fifty variations on a melody, all of them different, and all showing excellent taste and judgement. When extemporizing freely, he would often stray off into distant keys, to the extent that his brother would 'tremble' for him, but he would always manage to return safely to the home key. He had many more anecdotes of Samuel's exploits: how he had composed a march for one of the Guards regiments, and took the band to task when it was not performed correctly; how he improvised a solo for the organ which required the use of the swell pedal, which he was not able to reach from a sitting position, and so performed it standing up, with one foot on the ground and the other on the pedal; and of the great speed at which he composed and the neatness of his manuscripts, which were almost entirely without mistakes or blots. But for all these accomplishments he was not arrogant: on one occasion, he had appeared with the three-year-old William Crotch, another musical child prodigy, and went out of his way not to upset or upstage him.

Barrington repeatedly stressed the precocity of Samuel's conversation and behaviour and his readiness to speak his mind. When confronted with the Fitzwilliam Virginal Book (if this indeed is what Bremner's manuscript was) and asked if he approved of one of the compositions in it, Samuel said he did not, as attention had not been paid to the 'established rules'. Later, when told that Bremner had said that many great composers took similar liberties, he commented that 'when such excellent rules are broken, the composer should take care that these licenses produce a good effect; whereas these passages have a very bad one'. Similarly, when asked his opinion of a Bach-Abel concert that he had attended, he replied that he was happy with the music and the performances, but that the works were badly arranged in the programme, as there had been four consecutive pieces in the same key. Clearly, Samuel was entirely at home with adults, and expected to be treated as an adult himself. Barrington spoke of his 'great serenity' in telling the Guards band that they had not performed his march correctly, and the complete composure with which he pointed out their mistakes and insisted that they perform it again. And as correspondence from this period shows, the adults of his acquaintance were ready to acknowledge his particular gifts and to defer to his superior musical knowledge and experience. Barrington recorded that the Earl of Mornington, a notable amateur musician and a regular visitor to the Wesley family home, told him that he always consulted Samuel on any compositional problem, as he knew no-one who could give better advice or information.

But not all of Samuel's time was taken up with music. In the summer of 1776 the Wesley children made an extended visit to their friends the Russells in Guildford. They were a well-to-do and influential family in the area: John Russell Senior was a printer who had several times been mayor of Guildford, while his elder son, John Russell, was a noted portrait painter who during this visit painted the portrait of Samuel in court dress that he exhibited at the Royal Academy the following year and that now hangs in the Duke's Hall of the Royal Academy of Music (Plate 2). He also painted portraits of Wesley's father, mother, brother, and sister, of Boyce, and of an unidentified clergyman who may well have been Madan.[9]

The Russell portrait shows Samuel as a very self-assured child who gazes confidently at the observer in a nonchalant pose with one leg crossed carelessly over the other. He is caught in the midst of composition: in his right hand is a quill pen; in his left is the manuscript of his anthem 'I said, I will take heed to my ways', KO 90. Behind him is a chamber organ, and at his feet the full score of his oratorio *Ruth*. The portrait is of course to some extent idealized, and the pose was a popular one of the day, possibly deriving from a celebrated and widely influential marble sculpture of Mercury well known in England at the time, both from copies and from illustrations.[10] But Samuel's very adult composure and serenely confident expression are none-theless remarkable.

The visit to the Russells combined music with other less serious pursuits. In a letter to her mother at the end of June, Sarah related that Samuel set off a cannon every morning and a fire-cracker every evening, and that he would probably not agree to play 'if not rewarded by gunpowder'.[11] Later in the visit there was a public firework display organized by the family, with handbills printed by John Russell senior that were distributed all over Guildford and ensured a good attendance.[12] Three weeks later, Sarah wrote again to describe a visit of the son and daughter of Sir Fletcher Norton, the Speaker of the House of Commons, to hear Samuel play. Also present on this occasion was an acquaintance of Worgan, who gave Samuel a subject upon which to improvise and was amazed to hear how he treated it. He was even more surprised to see Samuel then rise from the harpsichord and go off to join in a game of cricket. The maker of the gunpowder, with whom Samuel had struck up a friendship, was the experimental scientist James Price, a close friend of the Russell family.

---

[9] Williamson, *John Russell*; SWSB, pp. 715–16.
[10] For an illustration of this sculpture, in the Uffizi Gallery, Florence, and a discussion of its widespread influence, see Francis Haskell, *Taste and the Antique: The Lure of Classical Sculpture, 1500–1900* (London, 1981), pp. 266–7. I am grateful to Janet Snowman for this suggestion.
[11] Sarah Wesley to Sarah Gwynne Wesley, 30 June 1776.
[12] Sarah Wesley to Sarah Gwynne Wesley, 18 July 1776.

2 Samuel Wesley aged ten. Mezzotint by William Dickinson after the portrait by John Russell, RA. By courtesy of the Royal Academy of Music, London.

Sometimes described as the last of the alchemists, he committed suicide in 1783 at the age of thirty-one after being unable to replicate in public his claims that he was able to transmute lead into gold.[13] He wrote to Samuel only a few days before his death with a long account of his latest experiments, and left him a house in Guildford and £1,000 in his will.[14]

By early 1777, further thought was being given to the future direction of Samuel's musical education. Barrington, writing to Charles Wesley in late February, mentioned one plan currently under consideration. The Bishop of Oxford had recommended Samuel to the Bishop of London as a 'singing boy extraordinary' (i.e. a chorister at St Paul's Cathedral who would be allowed to live at home rather than having to board at the choir school). Barrington understood that this proposal had the support of the Bishop of Durham, and commented that its great advantage would be that it would leave Samuel's education entirely in his father's hands. But nothing became of this plan, and Charles Wesley evidently decided against it.[15]

Barrington also talked of further concert appearances, including a suggestion that Samuel should play at the private concerts for Queen Charlotte at Buckingham House directed by J. C. Bach. Barrington, however, thought that this would 'never do', as the professional musicians who were engaged there would never tolerate a child amongst them.[16] This opposition may have been as much a matter of class as of age, and one can readily imagine the jealousy of professional musicians – many of whom would have children of their own whom they were training for the profession – at the attention and adulation that was being lavished on a child prodigy from such a privileged background. Further indications of opposition from the profession are contained in a letter of June 1778 to Charles Wesley from Philip Hayes, the recently appointed Professor of Music at Oxford University, and a friend of the Wesley family from his London days. Hayes was sorry to say that too many in the profession looked narrowly and sometimes uncharitably on 'rising merit', but thought that 'merit must in the end stand forth, by all confessed', and that his young friends had no need to be dismayed by idle remarks.[17]

As we have seen, Samuel had many opportunities to perform to visitors and at private gatherings during his boyhood, and not all were as welcome to him as his father imagined. But Charles Wesley never exhibited his two sons in public, no doubt considering that it would have been inappropriate for one in his position to do so, not to mention being damaging for the boys' development. Nor is there any record of Samuel performing at any public concerts in the 1770s, apart from on one occasion on 20 May 1777 when he played an extempore voluntary at a concert at Hickford's Rooms organized and directed

---

[13] *DNB*.
[14] Price to SW, 28 July 1783.
[15] Barrington to Charles Wesley, 24 Feb. 1777.
[16] Ibid. For the Queen's Concert, see McVeigh, *Concert Life*, pp. 51, 185.
[17] Hayes to Charles Wesley, 15 June 1778.

by J. C. Bach.[18] This was evidently intended as a showcase for talented young musicians, and also featured the thirteen-year old Elizabeth Weichsell (later to achieve international fame as the operatic soprano Elizabeth Billington) on the piano and her brother Charles on the violin. In this concert Wesley was in highly distinguished company. Among the adult musicians were Wilhelm Cramer, Johann Christian Fischer (the principal oboist of the Bach-Abel concerts), and the singer Gasparo Savoi, a long-standing member of the Italian opera company at the King's Theatre in the Haymarket. That this was an isolated event is suggested by Samuel's recollection of it in his *Reminiscences*, where he also recalled that Arne, who was present, had insisted that he played a second time, after which he had placed his hand on Samuel's head, saying 'this is a Head, indeed'.[19]

The early musical activities of Samuel and Charles were crowned by a series of private subscription concerts at the family home that ran for nine seasons from 1779 to 1787. In anticipation of the inevitable criticism from the Methodist community for allowing and encouraging his children to organise these concerts, Charles Wesley felt obliged to put on paper his 'reasons for letting my sons have a concert at home':

(1) To keep them out of harm's way: the way (I mean) of bad music and bad musicians who by a free communication with them might corrupt both their taste and their morals.
(2) That my sons may have a safe and honourable opportunity of availing themselves of their musical abilities, which have cost me several hundred pounds.
(3) That they may enjoy their full right of private judgment, and likewise their independency; both of which must be given up if they swim with the stream and follow the multitude.
(4) To improve their play and their skill in composing: as they must themselves furnish the principal music of every concert, although they do not call their musical entertainment a concert. It is too great a word. They do not presume to rival the *present great masters* who excel in the variety of their accompaniments. All they aim at in their concert music is *exactness*.[20]

This statement is full of Charles's ambivalence about the music profession and his uncertainty about the direction his two sons' future involvement with music should take. In practice, what the concerts did was to provide them with a complete introduction to the best aspects of professional music-making while shielding them from its less attractive aspects. For nine seasons, Charles and Samuel were able to perform music of their choice with professionals who would have been carefully vetted for their respectability, before a doubtless

---

[18] Advertisement in *Public Advertiser*, 20 May 1777, quoted in Lightwood, *Samuel Wesley, Musician*, p. 44.
[19] *Reminiscences*, fols. 87–8.
[20] Charles Wesley memorandum, c.14 Jan. 1779.

adoring audience of family and friends. Each series consisted of seven concerts and cost three guineas: an amount roughly comparable to what was being asked at public subscription concerts at the time. For this, audiences were entertained with music performed by the two Wesley brothers and a small professional ensemble.

The criticism from Methodists was more muted than might have been expected, perhaps reflecting some sympathy with Charles's position and the difficult choices he had to make with regard to his sons' musical education. In the eyes of some Methodists, Charles was no doubt damned from the moment he began to encourage his children's musical education, but others would have realized the dilemma he was in: whether to give them every opportunity to make the most of their gifts, even though this might lead them to adopt careers of which he – quite as much as other Methodists – heartily disapproved; or to attempt to discourage them from pursuing music, and to force them against their will into other careers. Charles had already dealt with this question as early as 1769, when he had stated, to a correspondent who objected to Charles junior playing in public, that he had intended him for the Church, but that nature had 'marked him for a musician', and that the only way he could have prevented this would have been to cut off his fingers.[21] By allowing his sons to organize concerts at home, Charles was at least keeping them out of bad company. But he could not expect his brother's whole-hearted support. In a letter to him in April 1779, Charles stated: 'I am clear without a doubt that my sons' Concert is after the will and order of Providence', continuing, 'we do not repent that we did not make a show or advantage of our swans. They will still make their fortunes if [I] would venture them into the world: but I never wish them rich.'[22] When John Wesley came to publish this letter ten years later in the *Arminian Magazine*, however, he added in a footnote that he was '"clear" of another mind'. Others were completely won over, however: Thomas Coke, in a letter to John Wesley of December 1779 in which he commented on how he had revised his opinions on Charles's character and actions, stated: 'I looked upon the Concerts which he allows his sons to have in his own house, to be highly dishonorable to God; and himself to be criminal, by reason of his situation in the Church of Christ: but on mature consideration of all the circumstances appertaining to them, I cannot now blame him.'[23]

Records of the concerts, kept from season to season by Charles Wesley, provide a remarkably full record of the music performed, the performers, and the audiences. There are also accounts of the expenditure on candles, oil, refreshments, and the like, as well as the fees paid to the musicians. The list of subscribers and their guests gives a full picture of the family's social circle, while the list of musicians is equally enlightening on the musical circles in which the

---

[21] Eleanor Laroche to Charles Wesley, 3 Feb. 1769. Charles Wesley's draft reply is written on the same sheet.
[22] Charles Wesley sen. to John Wesley, 23 Apr. 1779, in *Arminian Magazine* 12 (1789), pp. 386–8; quoted in Lightwood, *Samuel Wesley, Musician*, p. 52.
[23] Thomas Coke to John Wesley, 15 Dec. 1779, in *Arminian Magazine* 13 (1790), pp. 50–1.

two brothers moved. Finally, the concert programmes give an invaluable picture of the repertoire of the concerts, and in many cases enable us to trace the Wesley brothers' own works from composition to performance. Numbers of subscribers to the nine seasons of concerts varied between twenty-four and fifty-two, and audience numbers for individual concerts between twelve and sixty-two, with attendances typically in the forties or fifties. The subscribers and their guests came from a wide cross-section of society. A large proportion came from the aristocracy, many of them with Methodist connections, including the Earl of Exeter and Sir Watkin Williams Wynn, who were directors of the Concerts of Ancient Music, the prestigious series of subscription concerts founded in 1776. The higher echelons of the Church of England were represented by Robert Louth, the Bishop of London, and Antony Shepherd, the Dean of St George's Chapel, Windsor. There were also foreign diplomats: Count Brühl, Baron Dreyer, and Baron Nolcken, the ambassadors respectively of Saxony, Denmark, and Sweden. The world of letters was represented by Samuel Johnson, who notwithstanding his supposed aversion to music subscribed for the 1780 and 1781 seasons and attended many of the concerts. Among others who attended were Pascal Paoli, the former ruler of Corsica and a member of Johnson's social circle, and General Oglethorpe, with whom Charles and John Wesley had travelled to Georgia in 1735. There were also a number of family friends, including the antiquarian and historian James Pettit Andrews and the traveller and writer Richard Twiss. From Sarah Wesley's side of the family came members of the Waller family (Elizabeth Waller was Mrs Wesley's sister) and her cousin Thynne Gwynne. From Charles Wesley's side came his brother John, who attended a concert in January 1781 and recorded afterwards that he was 'a little out of my element among lords and ladies. I love plain music and plain company best'.[24] Nonetheless, he attended a further four concerts in the 1784 season, and according to Samuel did so to show that he considered them 'no sin'.[25] From the family's circle of friends in Guildford came John Russell Senior, the Revd James Pollen, and – for one season only, before his suicide in 1783 – the scientist James Price. From the London Methodist community came Samuel Tooth, the timber merchant and builder who had recently been responsible for the building of the City Road chapel, the banker Ebenezer Blackwell and his wife, and Martha Gumley, who had made the Chesterfield Street house available to Charles Wesley. The audiences also included many musicians who had been associated with the two boys and had become friends of the family, and many also performed from time to time. They included Arnold, Worgan, Bremner, Battishill, Wilhelm Cramer and his young son Francis, and Thomas Attwood, a trumpeter in the royal band whose son (also Thomas) would later study with Mozart and become organist of St Paul's Cathedral.

The instrumental ensemble for the concerts was small, consisting usually of one or two first violins, one or two seconds, one viola, one cello, and two horns,

---

[24] Journal entry for 25 Jan. 1781 (*JJW*, vol. 6, pp. 303–4).
[25] *Reminiscences*, fol. 3.

with Samuel usually leading and Charles playing harpsichord or organ continuo. The players were paid half a guinea per concert except for the horns, who received only 5s. Most of the players were presumably middle-ranking professionals, and nothing more is known about most of them than their names. A few, however, are known from other contexts. One of the violins in the first two seasons was William Kingsbury, who was one of Samuel's first violin teachers; he died early in 1782. Among the cellists who played from time to time was Hugh Reinagle, who is known to have had a career as a soloist before his early death in 1784; his brother Alexander played the violin at the concerts. In the 1785 season the brothers Lewis and Vincent Leander, later to become the leading English horn players of their generation, played at three of the concerts.

Like the instrumentalists, most of the singers at the concerts are unknown in wider contexts. Most were probably amateurs, although on the evidence of the music they performed, of a good standard. One, a Mr Harrison, was a professional, and his name and fee are recorded alongside those of his instrumental colleagues. He was probably Samuel Harrison, who had been an outstanding boy treble and would later have a successful career as a tenor soloist and impresario. At the concert on 30 March 1780, when Charles's *Ode on the Death of William Boyce* was performed (Boyce had died the previous year), the singers included two boy trebles who would later be close professional colleagues of Samuel: Thomas Attwood and Samuel Webbe the Younger. And at the concert on 19 February 1784, when a small choir was assembled, some or all of the four sons of the bassoonist and impresario John Ashley were imported to sing treble, along with three choristers from the Chapel Royal. All the Ashley children would later follow their father into the profession as instrumental players and impresarios, and Wesley would encounter them in these capacities later in his career.

A draft prospectus in the hand of Charles Wesley for the second series of concerts in 1780, presumably following the wording of that for the previous season, promised that the music would be of three types: that of Handel, Corelli, Scarlatti, and Geminiani, the 'most excellent of a later date', and music by Charles and Samuel themselves, and that it would consist of 'Oratorios, Concerto's, Quartetto's, Trio's, Duets (particularly for 2 Organs), Sonatas, Solo's, Extempore Lessons on the Harps^d, & Voluntaries on the Organ'.[26] Across the nine seasons, this was a more or less accurate description of what was performed. In the first category Handel predominated, both in instrumental and vocal items, and in numerous arrangements for organ duet that Samuel and Charles played together. He was closely followed by Corelli, whose Op. 6 Concerti Grossi were particular favourites: No. 8, the 'Christmas Concerto', was performed at least six times, and possibly more. Geminiani was chiefly represented by violin concertos, with Samuel as soloist, along with more recent violin

---

[26] Duke University, Frank Baker Collection. A similarly worded printed prospectus for the 1781 season is quoted in Lightwood, *Samuel Wesley, Musician*, pp. 50–1.

concertos by Borghi, Cramer, Giardini, and Giornovichi. The only other 'ancient' composer performed with any frequency was Purcell, represented by 'Mad Bess', 'From Rosy Bowers', and a duet and chorus from *Bonduca*. Notwithstanding the promise in the 1780 prospectus, Scarlatti scarcely featured at all. Among the more 'modern' composers were Arne, Cramer, Giardini, and Lord Mornington, with occasional songs by other composers. Interestingly, and possibly significantly, no music by Abel or J. C. Bach was performed, apart from one unspecified song by Bach. But it was compositions by the two Wesley brothers that accounted for most of the modern music performed. In the case of Samuel, these included four symphonies, a sinfonia obbligato (a genre that combined elements of the concerto and the symphony, after the manner of the concerted symphonies of J. C. Bach), seven violin concertos, and two overtures.

Charles and Samuel also dominated the concerts as performers. The first concert of the first season, on 14 January 1779, set the pattern. Out of twelve items, six were by Charles, three by Samuel, two by Handel, and one by Lord Mornington. Charles featured as the soloist in one of his own organ concertos and in two of his own organ voluntaries, in a harpsichord lesson by Handel, and with Samuel in an organ duet. Samuel played an extempore lesson on the harpsichord, an organ voluntary, and joined Charles in the organ duet. He was also the first violin in the instrumental group. Much the same emphasis can be seen in a sample concert from the seventh season, on 14 April 1785, where the music included the overture from Handel's *Tamerlano*, an arrangement for organ duet of the 'Dead March' from *Saul*, and Corelli's Concerto Grosso Op. 6 No. 5, along with extempore organ voluntaries by Charles and Samuel, and a symphony and a violin concerto by Samuel, the latter with Samuel as soloist.

3

Adolescence: Roman Catholicism, rebellion, and Charlotte, 1780–1788

It was in the 1780s, during the period of the family concerts, that the first signs of major problems in the Wesley family started to become apparent. By now Samuel was an adolescent. Charles and Sarah were adults, but continued to live at home, as indeed they continued to do after their father's death. Charles's worldliness and lack of spirituality was apparently a matter of concern both to his father and to his uncle at this time,[1] but the inoffensive dullness of his later life suggests that this was unlikely to have been a particularly serious problem. But the case of Samuel was another matter entirely. As early as September 1778, his father believed that 'Sam will have many more escapes. Great will be his trials; but the Lord will deliver him out of all. . . . Sam wants more pains to be taken with him. If I should not live to help him, it will lie all upon you. Make him a living Christian, and he will never wish to be a dead Papist.'[2]

Exactly what Charles's concern amounted to is not clear, but it probably involved Samuel's attendance at Roman Catholic services. This can only have been at one of the London embassy chapels, as these were at this time still the only places where Roman Catholic rites could legally be celebrated. Although the first Catholic Relief Act of earlier in the year had repealed some of the penal laws, public worship was still illegal and would remain so until the passing of the second Catholic Relief Act in 1791. Because of the politically convenient provisions of extra-territoriality, however, the chapels of foreign embassies were technically on foreign soil, and thus outside the jurisdiction of English law. Following long-standing tradition, they catered for large numbers of London Roman Catholics in addition to the embassy communities and foreign nationals for whom they were ostensibly established. The largest and most important chapels were those of the Sardinian, Bavarian, and Portuguese embassies, all of which maintained large establishments of clergy and an extensive programme of services. Here, the mass and the offices were celebrated with magnificence of ritual, in a manner that has been described as 'Baroque and triumphalist, bringing the atmosphere of the European counter-reformation to English worship'.[3]

---

[1] Jackson, *Life*, vol. 2, pp. 354–5, quoting John Wesley to Charles Wesley jun., 4 Aug. and 8 Sept. 1781.
[2] Charles Wesley to Sarah Gwynne Wesley, 7 Sept. 1778.
[3] Norman, *Roman Catholicism in England*, p. 50.

The appeal of the embassy chapels to the young Samuel must have been powerful. A large part of the attraction – perhaps initially the whole – was undoubtedly musical: they provided a wealth of music not to be found in Anglican worship, where even in cathedrals the musical standards were deplorably low, and still less within Methodism, where the only music was unaccompanied hymn-singing. There would also have been ample opportunities for Samuel to become involved, both as a performer and as a composer, thus enabling him to justify his regular attendance and involvement as a part of his musical education, and in this way partly to assuage the family's worries. He would soon have met Samuel Webbe, the organist of both the Portuguese and Sardinian chapels, and the most important and influential figure in London Catholic church music. Webbe would undoubtedly have welcomed him as a chorister and as an additional pair of hands on the organ. He also offered free instruction in Roman Catholic church music to all-comers and no doubt gave Samuel some composition lessons, and by the autumn of 1780 Samuel was composing his first works for the Roman rite. There may also have been a more personal dimension to Samuel's relationship with Webbe, as one of his sons, two years younger than Samuel, was also destined for a career in music. It is easy to imagine Samuel as a frequent visitor to Webbe's welcoming home in Red Lion Square, experiencing a form of family life and professional musical activity very different from what he was used to in Chesterfield Street.

It may be the case, as Samuel was later to assert, that what initially drew him to Roman Catholicism was its music rather than its doctrines. One needs, however, to put this statement in the context of his later violent opposition to Catholicism and his attempts to play down the extent and nature of his early involvement. But the mere fact of attendance at Roman Catholic chapels would have been a severe test for the tolerance of even the most liberal father, and it is hard to imagine that the reaction of Charles Wesley senior could have been anything other than dismay and alarm. The origins of Samuel's interest in Roman Catholicism remain unclear. As we have seen, his father expressed his concern on the matter as early as September 1778, and by later in the same year Samuel was beginning to append the initials 'SDG' ('Soli Deo gloria' – 'To God alone be glory') to his signature and the date at the end of his compositions. While this practice was not confined to Roman Catholic composers, Samuel's adoption of it at this time was probably a result of his involvement, or at the very least an indication of a growing piousness. But whatever the precise date of the beginning of Samuel's interest, it was singularly inopportune, given the strong wave of anti-Catholic feeling that had followed the passing of the first Catholic Relief Act, and later erupted in June 1780 in the appalling violence of the Gordon Riots. It is easy to imagine Charles Wesley's profound disquiet at his son's involvement with Roman Catholicism and his anxiety not only for his spiritual well-being but also for his physical safety in a society that was becoming increasingly intolerant of Roman Catholics.

Throughout all Samuel's early involvement, the main worry of his family would always have been that he would convert to Rome. In early 1784, when

Samuel was just sixteen, all their worst fears were realized. Although there is little information on the background to his conversion, and in particular, who in the Roman Catholic community was responsible for his instruction and reception into the Church, a good deal is known about one lay figure who was involved: Mary Freeman Shepherd, an intellectual who befriended Samuel and appointed herself his spiritual adviser and mentor. Educated in a convent in Rome, she was on her mother's side descended from an aristocratic Italian family, and was a cousin of Ebenezer Blackwell. In early adulthood she worked first as a translator of the foreign mails and later as a proof-corrector on the *Public Advertiser*, and was thus associated with Alexander Cruden, the compiler of the biblical concordance that bears his name. Though a strict Roman Catholic, she was strongly attracted to Methodism, and was a great admirer of John Wesley, who according to one account she would have been prepared to marry; John Wesley's thoughts on the matter are not recorded. A change in style in early 1784 from 'Miss Freeman' to 'Mrs Freeman Shepherd' suggests marriage at around that time, but nothing is known of a husband.[4] Biographical sketches and copious amounts of correspondence indicate that she was an intelligent and forceful woman with strong opinions that she had no hesitation in voicing. She also had a reputation for acquiring young protégés, whose opinions and tastes she attempted to shape. According to one account, this was 'the more singular, as her person was unwieldy and her manners were unpolished and even boisterous; notwithstanding these disqualifications for social intercourse her acquaintance was felt to be a gain and her society always profitable and frequently pleasant and delightful'.[5]

When Shepherd first met Samuel, probably late in 1783, she was in her vigorous early fifties and was quick to take him under her wing. Many years later, she confided to his sister Sarah that she had 'loved [him] as a fond mother a darling child', and had hoped that he would enter the priesthood. This, at any rate, is the implication of her statement that she had wished and hoped that 'he would be to our old Gothic structure, unencumbered with the clumsy ornaments, and top heavy additions of later ages, a Nehemiah, an Ezra, and help to build up in England a second temple, more glorious than the first, into which the Lord himself should come and reside'.[6] But she denied all accusations of being involved in 'making him a Catholic', claiming that this had taken place over two years before she met him. She had first heard that Samuel was a Catholic from Lord Traquair, who in turn had heard it from his confessor;[7] this was probably early in 1784, and it is interesting to note that the Earl and

---

[4] SW to Shepherd, 26 Dec. 1783, is addressed to 'Miss Freeman'; SW to Shepherd, 19 Mar. 1784, is addressed to 'Mrs Freeman Shepherd'.
[5] [Clarke], *An Account of the Infancy, Religious and Literary Life of Adam Clarke*, vol. 2, pp. 231–2.
[6] Shepherd to Sarah Wesley, 14 Mar. 1794.
[7] Shepherd to Sarah Wesley, 12 Mar. 1794. Later, Shepherd claimed that she had heard the news from 'Mr Payton [i.e. Stephen Paxton], a famous performer on the viol-de-gamba': see Shepherd to Adam Clarke, undated [1810–1813], in [Clarke], *An Account of the Infancy, Religious and Literary Life of Adam Clarke*, vol. 2, pp. 126–7.

Countess of Traquair attended one of the family concerts on 4 March of that year. At this point, Shepherd called on Samuel's brother Charles, who was worried that the news might come to his father's ears. By this time, stories of Samuel's conversion were being circulated by the Roman Catholics, which Shepherd did her best to stop. Some time later, Charles junior was told that Samuel had been seen at a Roman Catholic chapel, distributing the chalice at the altar. It now became imperative to break the news of his conversion to his father before he heard about it from elsewhere. Samuel, fearing for the consequences if his father heard the news directly from him, tried to persuade Shepherd to tell him herself, but she refused, on the grounds that Charles would take it as an 'insulting triumph' if it came from her as a Roman Catholic herself. They then went to consult Bishop Talbot, the Roman Catholic Vicar Apostolic of the London Region, to seek his advice. Talbot suggested sending Arthur O'Leary, an Irish Capuchin priest and an old adversary of John Wesley, but Shepherd dismissed this suggestion too, insisting that Charles Wesley should be treated with the greatest possible respect and sensitivity, as a gentleman and as a father.[8] In the end, it was decided that the news should be broken to him by the Duchess of Norfolk, in her capacity as the wife of the leading Roman Catholic layman in England, and more particularly as the mother of a son who had recently converted the other way, abandoning Roman Catholicism for the Church of England. The interview with the Duchess, which took place in April or May 1784, must have been one of excruciating embarrassment for Charles Wesley and the Duchess alike.[9] He received her in full clerical dress, and with great dignity. The Duchess for her part gave the news 'with tenderness and feeling', suggesting in a desperate attempt to offer some crumb of comfort that it might have been divine providence that brought about these strong religious convictions.

The intense pain caused to Charles by Samuel's conversion is amply shown in a collection of poems he wrote at that time, in the best known of which he expressed his grief at what he inevitably saw as an act of betrayal, and likened his 'sacrifice' to that of Abraham:

> Farewell, my all of earthly hope,
> My nature's stay, my age's prop,
>   Irrevocably gone!
> Submissive to the will divine

---

[8] On 18 January John Wesley's *A Letter to the Printer of 'The Public Advertiser' occasioned by the late Act passed in Favour of Popery* was published. In response to this attack, O'Leary published six letters in defence of Roman Catholics in *Freeman's Journal*; they were subsequently reprinted as 'Remarks on Rev. John Wesley's Letters on the Civil Principles of Roman Catholic and his Defence of the Protestant Association' in O'Leary's *Miscellaneous Tracts* (1781). For an account of this controversy, see Butler, *Methodists and Papists*, pp. 63–8.

[9] According to Shepherd (Shepherd to Sarah Wesley, 14 Mar. 1794), these events took place between Easter and Whitsuntide 1785. In fact, it is clear that they occurred in 1784. Easter Sunday in 1784 was on 11 April, so the date must have been between then and Whitsuntide, six weeks later.

> I acquiesce, and make it mine;
>   I offer up my Son!
>   But give I God a sacrifice
> That costs me nought? My gushing eyes
>   The answer sad express,
> My gushing eyes and troubled heart
> Which bleeds with its belov'd to part,
>   Which breaks thro' fond excess.[10]

John Wesley's response was more measured. In August he wrote a long letter to Samuel which in its tolerance contrasted strongly with the inflammatorily anti-Catholic pronouncements he had made after the passing of the first Catholic Relief Act. After voicing his disquiet at Samuel's general behaviour, he stated that he was unconcerned about the precise form, 'Protestant or Romish', that Samuel's religious observance took, but was more worried about his spiritual health:

> Whether of this church or that, I care not: you may be saved in either, or damned in either, but I fear you are not born again; and except you be born again you cannot see the kingdom of God. You believe the Church of Rome is right. What then: If you are not born of God, *you* are of *no church*. Whether Bellarmine [a sixteenth-century Roman Catholic theologian] or Luther be right, you are certainly wrong, if you are not *born of the Spirit*; if you are not renewed in the spirit of your mind in the likeness of Him that created you. . . .
>
> O Sammy, you are out of your way! You are out of God's way! You have not given him your heart. You have not found, nay, it is well if you have so much as sought, happiness in God! And poor zealots, while you are in this state of mind, would puzzle you about this or the other church! O fools, and blind! Such guides as these lead men by shoals to the bottomless pit. My dear Sammy, your first point is to repent and believe the Gospel. Know yourself a poor guilty helpless sinner! Then know Jesus Christ and him crucified! Let the Spirit of God bear witness with your spirit, that you are a child of God and let the love of God be shed abroad in your heart by the Holy Ghost, which is given unto you; and then, if you have no better work, I will talk with you of transubstantiation or purgatory.[11]

To mark his conversion, Samuel composed an elaborate mass, the *Missa de spiritu sancto*, which he dedicated to Pope Pius VI. If there are any doubts remaining about the sincerity of his conversion in the light of his subsequent denials that he had ever been a Roman Catholic,[12] they should be dispelled by this work. In its size and scale, it stands apart from any of the Roman Catholic

---

[10] Kimbrough and Beckerlegge, *Unpublished Poetry of Charles Wesley*, vol. 1, p. 304. The poem of which these stanzas form part is also printed in Jackson, *Life*, pp. 361–4, and Stevenson, *Memorials of the Wesley Family*, pp. 505–6.

[11] John Wesley to SW, 19 Aug. 1784 (*LJW*, vol. 7, pp. 230–1). See also the similar views expressed in his letter to Charles Wesley jun., 2 May 1784 (ibid., pp. 216–17).

[12] See SW's obituary in *The Times*, 12 October 1837, much repeated by later biographers: 'he disclaimed ever having been a convert to the Roman Catholic Church, observing, that although the Gregorian music had seduced him to their chapels, the tenets of the Romanists had never obtained any influence over his mind.'

church music he had composed in the past or would compose in the future. As befitted the circumstances of its composition and its dedication, it is extremely ambitious, written for large vocal and orchestral forces. With a duration of around ninety minutes, it is far longer than any Mass settings that Samuel would have known, and longer than any settings in the present-day repertory, with the exception of Bach's B Minor Mass and Beethoven's *Missa Solemnis*. Given its length and the forces it requires, it could not have been performed in any of the London embassy chapels, and the conclusion must be that it was composed as a presentation work, not intended for performance but to demonstrate the sincerity of Samuel's conversion and his prowess in composition. He completed it on 22 May 1784, and in early September sent a lavishly bound fair copy to Pius VI, together with a covering letter from Bishop Talbot.[13] On the first page was Wesley's dedication, in Latin: 'This Mass (the first fruits of his conversion) is with the greatest of humility dedicated to our Holy Father Pius VI by his most unworthy son and most obedient servant, Samuel Wesley.'[14] In due course Pius VI acknowledged the gift in a letter to Talbot, in which he stated that the Mass had given him great pleasure, particularly as he understood that Samuel had written it to express his gratitude to God for the gift of admission to the Catholic Church, from which his ancestors had been excluded. What pleased him even more was Samuel's skill in arguments of faith, in which Talbot had told him he excelled.[15]

Samuel's conversion to Roman Catholicism was not the only aspect of his behaviour to cause concern to his family. Perhaps more worrying was a general unruliness and rebelliousness that seems to have gone far beyond the usual excesses of adolescent behaviour. There are few contemporary family documents and letters to give much idea of life in the Wesley family in the mid-1780s, but references in later correspondence give a picture of some of the most serious incidents, which included drunkenness, staying out until the early hours of the morning, and striking and otherwise abusing servants. In what must have been an excruciatingly humiliating incident in the summer of 1785, Charles Wesley senior felt obliged to visit Talbot to ask him to take Samuel to task for his behaviour and to watch over him as his pastor, as he no longer had any control over him himself.[16] Shepherd was involved in this disagreeable incident, having been asked by Talbot to remonstrate with Samuel and to try to persuade him to mend his ways. Whether her efforts had any effect is not known, but the ensuing correspondence led to an estrangement between them, and with her

---

[13] The fair copy of the Mass is dated 1 Sept. 1784. See also SW to Shepherd, 6 Sept. 1784. Talbot's covering letter has not survived, but is referred to in Pius VI's reply.
[14] 'Beatissimo Patri nostro PIO SEXTO haec Missa humilitate maxima dicatur (primitiae Ecclesiae) suo indignissimo filio et obsequentissimo servo Samuel Wesley.'
[15] Pius VI to Talbot, 4 May 1785. The *WBRR* account of SW's life (p. 370), states that this letter, or a copy of it, was subsequently acquired by Shepherd, who suggested to SW that he should show it to his father, so that he might take pleasure in the praise that the Pope had lavished on his son.
[16] SW to Shepherd, undated [?June–July 1785].

departure from England in August 1785, the end of their relationship for the time being.

From these and other incidents it is clear that Samuel was in open revolt from his father and family and all that they stood for. It is possible to interpret his behaviour as a particularly extreme form of adolescent rebelliousness, but it is far more likely that it was a part of a hypomanic phase of the manic depressive illness that was to afflict him for the rest of his life. Although Samuel's extended periods of depression throughout his life have long been acknowledged by his biographers, the diagnosis of bipolar affective order or manic depression is a more recent one. It is, however, strongly borne out by the events of his life, the pattern of his creativity, and the testimony of his own letters and of family correspondence.[17] Manic depression has a strong hereditary component, and as we have seen above, it is possible to see indications of it in the behaviour of both Wesley's father and his paternal grandfather.

And yet Samuel's relationship with his family, and in particular with his father, was not unremittingly troubled. In August 1785, not long after the incident with Talbot, Samuel composed an ambitious and extremely long setting for six voices of an ode by Horace. In the process he had occasion to write to his father, at the time on a visit to Bristol with his sister Sarah, for advice. His letter,[18] notable for being the only one from him to his father to have survived, shows him in a deferential, highly respectful mode, and also sheds valuable light on how he regarded his future at this time. Samuel began with the news that his setting of the ode 'Qualem ministrum' was now finished. It had been praised both by musicians and classical scholars, and he had been advised to publish it by subscription. Proposals were being printed, and he would publish it only if enough subscriptions were received: he needed two hundred, but would be happy to proceed with only one hundred and fifty, as the subscription was to be half a guinea. He asked his father's advice on two points. One concerned a disputed reading in the text; the other the advisability of omitting a few 'foolish' lines which he had set, but which he could easily cut without damage either to the musical or the verbal sense. He added that Horace improved on better acquaintance, that he was reading his finest odes every day, and becoming ever more delighted with them. He then turned to the question of his classical studies. He took issue with his father's criticism that he wanted to be a scholar without putting in the necessary effort, pointing out that he was prevented from devoting more time to study by his pursuit of music. He would gladly exchange this time for study, but as he had been born 'with a trade not a fortune' in his hands, it was necessary for him to make the most of it. He estimated that with moderate effort he could understand Latin perfectly within three years, but was less sure that he would ever have time to master Greek. Only his musical commitments prevented him from studying

---

[17] On manic depression, see Goodwin and Jamison, *Manic-Depressive Illness*; on manic depression and artistic creation, see Jamison, *Touched with Fire*.
[18] SW to Charles Wesley, 22 Aug. [1785].

more, and these could not be abandoned until his purse was considerably fuller than at present.

This letter is revealing in the glimpse it gives us of an otherwise unrecorded aspect of the relationship between Samuel and his father. Equally, it shows Samuel's seriousness about studying the classics and, crucially, that he regarded music not as something to be enjoyed, but as a burden imposed on him by the need to make a living. This was a theme to which he would often return in the future. In 1830, writing to an unidentified friend, he stated:

> My Mind is not that of a *mere* Musician: I have (from a Boy) been a Lover of more of the Alphabet than the seven incipient English Letters, & had I not been an idle Dog, under the Instruction of my classical Father (whose Loss is by me daily felt, *more than 40 years since its Occurrence*) I might long ago have been well qualified to bandy Latin & Greek along with Parr & Porson [two leading classical scholars]. My *Trade* is Music, I confess; & would to Heaven it had only been destined for mine Amusement, which would certainly have been the Case, had I availed myself of the Advantages which were offered me in Juvenescence, of rendering myself eligible for any one of the learned Professions; but it was (it seems) otherwise ordained; & I was to attend only to the Cultivation of *one* Talent, which *unluckily cost me no Trouble to do*: had there been any up-Hill Work for me in Music, I should soon enough have sacrificed it altogether.[19]

One tantalising question that remains about this incident is why Samuel chose to compose a piece of the character and length of 'Qualem ministrum' at all, and why he should have chosen this particular text. What is certain is that Horace's ode, written to celebrate the victories in AD 15 of Drusus, stepson of the emperor Augustus, over the Rhaeti and other Alpine tribes, was not an obvious text for a musical setting. Nor was Samuel's setting, which lasts for almost forty minutes and is extremely taxing, a remotely saleable proposition, except perhaps to family friends and other admirers. No copies of a published edition have been traced, and it seems likely that Samuel was unable to collect enough subscriptions to proceed. One possible explanation for its composition is that he intended it as a secular analogue to the *Missa de Spiritu Sancto*: another presentation work, this time for his father, written not with performance primarily in mind, but as a conciliatory gesture after all the disturbances of the preceding few months, and one that at the same time demonstrated his devotion to the classics and his skill in composition.

Of all the sources of tension between Samuel and his family in the 1780s, the greatest was undoubtedly his relationship with Charlotte Louisa Martin, the daughter of a surgeon at St Thomas's Hospital.[20] They had first met in October 1782, when Samuel was sixteen and Charlotte twenty-one or twenty-two. From

---

[19] *SW to an unidentified recipient, 7 Mar. 1829.
[20] Deed of separation, 25 Mar. 1812. In *WBRR* 3 (1851), p. 407, he is referred to as 'Captain Martin, of Kensington'; in Stevenson, *Memorials of the Wesley Family*, p. 512, as a 'Demonstrator of Anatomy at St Thomas's Hospital'.

the start, the relationship was a passionate one and was strongly opposed by the family, largely on the grounds of what they saw as Charlotte's unsuitability of character. We can also assume that Samuel's extreme youth and the difference of age between them would also have come into the matter. Charles unwisely tried to insist that Samuel should break off the relationship; Samuel predictably refused, and it continued up to the time of Charles's death in 1788 as a potent source of conflict between father and son.

Samuel's earliest biographers were extremely tight-lipped about Charlotte. All that the author of the earliest account, in the *Wesley Banner and Revival Record* for 1851, was prepared to say about her appearance and character was that she was 'celebrated for her beauty, and for various female accomplishments'.[21] The author was probably George Stevenson, and it is interesting that when he went over the same ground more than twenty years later in the chapter on Samuel in his *Memorials of the Wesley Family* he felt it necessary to add that opinions differed on the question of her personal attractions.[22] There is a little more information about her in an important letter from Samuel to his mother of November 1792, just after he had set up house with Charlotte in Ridge, Hertfordshire. Here, he detailed some of the criticisms that had been made of Charlotte by the family and by others. She had been represented as a 'fickle and unsteady character'; as being of a 'careless, prodigal Disposition, & as closely resembling an extravagant Father & a vain Mother'. She had been called 'a Coquette, nay more; a wanton'. It had also been reported that Samuel had helped her financially, and had agreed to liquidate her debts as soon as he came of age. Wesley angrily refuted these accusations, which he described as having been 'engendered in the Heart of Envy, & vomited from the Mouth of Malice'.[23] From this and from other scraps of information scattered here and there, a picture of Charlotte emerges as a physically attractive, spirited, and possibly flirtatious young woman, from a family that had some financial irregularities in its past, had now fallen on hard times, and was clearly very different in outlook from the Wesleys.

Wesley reached his majority in February 1787. He had become a young man of below average height and of slight build and delicate features. In this he resembled his uncle and father, and he had also the prominent nose that was characteristic of all the male Wesleys (see Plate 3). As we have already seen, he was far from being committed to music as a career. He was earning some money from teaching music at Oxford House, a girls' school in Marylebone High Street run by a Mrs Barnes, but otherwise taking no part in professional music-making. It was presumably now that he came into his inheritance from James Price: a house and an adjoining property in Guildford, £1,000 in 3% Consols, £50 in money, and all Price's musical instruments, music, and books

---

[21] *WBRR* 3 (1851), p. 407.
[22] Stevenson, *Memorials of the Wesley Family*, p. 512.
[23] SW to Sarah Gwynne Wesley, 7 Nov. 1792.

3 Samuel Wesley as a young man. Watercolour copy by Frederick Gilling of a miniature by an unknown artist. By courtesy of the British Library, London.

on music.[24] This was a sizeable bequest. On their own the Consols were worth around £750, and would have yielded £30 per annum. This, and the money in the bequest, immediately gave Wesley a measure of financial independence and meant that he was not totally reliant on music to earn his living. The property remained to be let or sold. Nothing is known of its eventual fate and how much

---

[24] PRO, PROB 11/1107, proved 7 Aug. 1783.

it yielded Wesley, but it still remained unsold, amidst disputes about Wesley's right of title and accusations by Wesley of legal chicanery, as late as January 1800.[25]

Price's legacy can probably be seen as one of the main reasons, if not the main reason, why Wesley did not pursue a musical career in the late 1780s. This financial cushion removed the need for him to make his way in a profession for which he had little enthusiasm, and allowed him for the moment to pursue his enthusiasm for the classics. As he was still living at home, his outgoings would have been few, and he was no doubt able to make enough additional money from his teaching at Mrs Barnes's school to live comfortably. It was in any case not immediately clear how Wesley would make his living in music. For one of his particular gifts, the most appropriate position, and the one that would to some extent assuage his father's misgivings about the respectability of music as a profession, would have been an appointment at a cathedral or major parish church. But Wesley's Roman Catholicism told against him here, as did his Methodist background. With a little perseverance he could have made a reasonable living as an orchestral violinist, but he had by this time largely given up the violin and it is unlikely that he would have considered this as an acceptable solution. In fact, notwithstanding his superior abilities as a performer and composer and his glittering career to date, what was on offer was no more than was available to any keyboard player at this time: a 'basket of activities' consisting of teaching (adults or children, or both), playing the organ in church, a limited amount of performing, and composing. The only one of these from which a respectable living might be made was teaching, which although well paid – musicians of Wesley's calibre could demand fees of half a guinea per lesson – presented no musical challenges and could be soul-destroyingly tedious. This prospect might have looked reasonably enticing for someone less naturally talented than Wesley and without his early experiences in music, but for Wesley it can have held out few attractions. Like many musical child prodigies before and since, he was faced as he reached adulthood with the question of what he was going to do for the rest of his life, and no very clear answers.

It was around this time that Wesley is said to have sustained a serious injury that affected the course of his subsequent life. According to the account in Wesley's obituary in *The Times*, it occurred in 1787. On his way home late one night from visiting a friend, described as one of the oldest members of the Madrigal Society, he is said to have fallen into a building excavation in Snow Hill, where he seriously injured his head and lay until morning before being discovered. It was then suggested that he should undergo the operation of trepanning, which would have involved the cutting of a small hole in his skull. Not surprisingly he refused, and the wound was allowed to heal. According to the obituary account, this was a decision he regretted for the rest of his life, as the head injury was supposedly the cause of 'those periodical states of high

---

[25] *SW to unidentified lawyers, 5 Jan. 1800.

nervous irritability' that were later to afflict him.²⁶ Although this is one of the more memorable and better known anecdotes about Wesley, it deserves to be treated with caution. There are a number of features that arouse suspicions both about its total accuracy and the suggestion that it was the cause of Samuel's mental health problems. First, it is uncorroborated in any contemporary or subsequent family correspondence, and its appearance in Wesley's obituary in *The Times*, a full fifty years after it is supposed to have happened, is the first time that it surfaces. Second, and as we have seen, it is clear that the first signs of Wesley's mental health problems occurred some time before the fall. Finally, given the long interval between its occurrence and Wesley's death there must be some doubts about the year of the incident. On the other hand, the obituarist – who was evidently someone who knew Wesley well or had access to family information – appears to have drawn his account fom Wesley himself. For this reason, it would be unwise to dismiss the account out of hand, although there is room for some scepticism about the precise year in which it occurred.²⁷

By the time of the last season of family concerts in 1787, Wesley was twenty-one and his brother Charles was thirty. Charles Wesley senior was seventy-eight, and no doubt very glad to be relieved of the disruption that the concerts must have caused. His health had been declining since the beginning of the 1780s, and although he continued to preach at the City Road chapel twice every Sunday except when ill or away from London, he was evidently finding it more and more of a strain. By early 1788 he was very weak, but still able to go out occasionally.²⁸ His brother John, seeing this decline, advised him repeatedly that he should 'go out every day, or die'.²⁹

As his health continued to decline, Charles Wesley had a good deal of time to brood on the disappointments his children had brought. Neither Charles nor Sarah was showing any signs of whole-hearted commitment to God, but this was as nothing compared to the worries that Samuel's behaviour was continuing to cause. Despite a very public conversion to Roman Catholicism almost four years earlier, he was living a life that would have alarmed any parent, let alone one of Charles Wesley's cast. Rebellious, in open defiance of all the values held most dear by his family, he was by turns morose and unnaturally exuberant, wild in behaviour, and heavily involved with a woman of whom his parents thoroughly disapproved.

The spiritual health of the Wesley children was also a matter of concern to John Wesley, who in mid-March 1788 wrote to his brother with characteristic bluntness that 'never was there before so loud a call to all that are under your roof. If they have not hitherto sufficient regard either [for] you, or the God of their fathers, what is more calculated to convince them, than to see you so long hovering upon the borders of the grave.'³⁰ At the same time he wrote separately

---

[26] *The Times*, 12 Oct. 1837.
[27] Olleson, 'The Obituary of Samuel Wesley', p. 127.
[28] Jackson, *Life*, vol. 2, pp. 433–7.
[29] John Wesley to Charles Wesley, 18 Feb. 1788 (*LJW*, vol. 8, p. 36).
[30] John Wesley to Charles Wesley, 17 Mar. 1788 (*LJW*, vol. 8, pp. 45–6).

to Charles junior and to Samuel. To Charles, as the elder, he stated his determination to be a father and friend to both of them.[31] To Samuel he wrote at greater length, reiterating some of the points he had made in his long letter at the time of Samuel's conversion. At one time, he said, Samuel might have taken his advice, but now Shepherd had 'taught him another lesson'. He continued to be unconcerned about the church Samuel belonged to, as long as he was a Christian, but thought it a great loss that Samuel had turned away from Methodist preaching, which might have made him into a 'real scriptural Christian'.[32]

During Charles Wesley's final decline in March 1788, his two sons were preoccupied with other matters. For his elder son, there was the prospect of the organist's appointment at St George's Chapel, Windsor, unexpectedly vacant following the sudden death of Edward Webb on 3 March.[33] Well connected at court since his boyhood and a good friend of Dr Shepherd, the Dean of Windsor, Charles would have been a strong contender for the position, but his father was strongly opposed to his candidacy, and forbade him to canvass for it. Nothing deterred, on 25 March Charles junior wrote to Shepherd to state disingenuously that although it was his father's dying wish that he should not canvass for the post, he was nonetheless interested in it, and would be happy to serve, should this be the King's desire.[34] Meanwhile, and more mundanely, Samuel was continuing to see Charlotte, and in one of his few letters to her that have survived, wrote on 27 March to cancel an arrangement to meet, as his father's death was expected on the following day.[35]

In fact, Charles Wesley died two days later on 29 March, with all his family round him. A few days later, Sarah reported some of the events of his final days in a letter to John Wesley. On 14 March he had prayed for all his enemies, including Shepherd, imploring God that she should be spared the pangs of eternal death, and when Sarah read to him John's recent letter to Charles junior, he said that he was sure that his brother would be kind to all his children after his death. On 19 March, he took Samuel's hand and said 'I shall bless God to all eternity, that ever you were born. I am persuaded I shall!'[36] These words came too late to end the estrangement between father and son, and this lack of reconciliation was to weigh heavily on Samuel for the rest of his life. In 1824, he would compose his *Carmen Funebre*, a setting of some of the last words his father had addressed to him, describing it as a 'Testimony of my Veneration for the Dictates of a Parent whose Value was utterly unknown to me till he was translated to Society alone worthy of him!'[37]

---

[31] John Wesley to Charles Wesley jun., 16 March 1788 (*LJW*, vol. 8, p. 45).
[32] John Wesley to SW, 18 Mar. 1788 (*LJW*, vol. 8, p. 47).
[33] Shaw, *Succession of Organists*, p. 347.
[34] Charles Wesley jun. to Antony Shepherd, 25 Mar. 1788, quoted in Lightwood, *Samuel Wesley, Musician*, p. 74.
[35] SW to Charlotte Louisa Martin, 27 Mar. 1788.
[36] Sarah Wesley to John Wesley, 4 Apr. 1788, quoted in Jackson, *Life*, vol. 2, p. 443.
[37] *SW to Novello, 14 June [1824].

In December 1788 Wesley became a Freemason. The lodge he joined, Preston's Lodge of Antiquity, had strong musical affiliations: among its members when Wesley joined were the organ builder John Avery and the music publisher Robert Birchall; later musician members included Thomas Attwood, Richard Clark, James Elliott, Charles Evans, George Goss, John Jeremiah Goss, William Hawes, William Linley, and Samuel Webbe senior and junior. Wesley appears to have been an active member for a while and attained junior office in 1789, but his membership lapsed in 1791 because of non-payment of lodge dues.[38] Wesley's involvement with Freemasonry at this time has sometimes been taken to indicate that he had now turned away from Roman Catholicism. But although there was some official disapproval of Freemasonry from the Vatican at this time, there were many English Roman Catholics who were also Freemasons and who evidently had no difficulty in reconciling their membership with their religious observances. There may have been more active opposition to Freemasonry from the Methodists, however, and it may have been for this reason that Wesley did not become a Mason immediately on reaching his majority, but waited until after the death of his father.

There is strikingly little information about Wesley's day-to-day activities during the late 1780s. He continued to give piano lessons at Mrs Barnes's school, and possibly at one or more others. But he was not performing in public and seems to have been at a loss about the future direction his life should take. There are few compositions from this period, and it is likely that much of it was spent on his continuing classical studies, interspersed with further attacks of spiritual doubt and depression, and with Charlotte.

One of his problems was a deep-seated hatred of London that would surface at various stages later in his life. Whether it was the noise and foul air of the capital or other aspects of life there is difficult to tell, but in July 1789 he spent some time in Bramfield, a small village in Hertfordshire, certainly in escape from London, and possibly convalescing after a period of illness. In a letter to his mother he expressed his satisfaction at how well he was being looked after, noting that it was 'the sort of Situation which no one but he who loves Retirement as well as I would perhaps be contented in', but that it was for that purpose he had gone there, and that he was content with it. He then turned to dwell on his situation in London. He hated the life of a professional musician, and thought it was a 'cruel mistake' in his education that he had been forced into it. At the same time, one good consequence of his experience of the profession to date was that he was now very willing to leave a world that he might have valued, had he not experienced it at first hand. Meanwhile, he was expecting to return to London in the next few days, as the new school term was about to begin and he was determined to carry out his duties punctually for as

---

[38] Firebrace, *Records of the Lodge Original*. For Freemasonry and English musical life at this time, see McVeigh, 'Freemasonry and Musical Life in London in the Late Eighteenth Century'.

long as he continued with them.³⁹ Notwithstanding his discontent with his present way of life, no very obvious alternatives offered themselves. One of his plans had been to go to France, but in a letter of 29 July 1789, only two weeks after the storming of the Bastille, his sister Sarah wrote to a friend to say that he had abandoned this idea for the moment, adding that it would in any case be unwise to do so in the present 'commotions', even though as a Roman Catholic he could possibly visit places where Protestants would be unwelcome.⁴⁰

Meanwhile, John Wesley was continuing to keep a watchful eye over Samuel's spiritual welfare, in accordance with the promise he had made to his brother. In September 1789 he wrote to express his satisfaction that Samuel was going to bed at 10p.m. and rising at 4a.m. and was undertaking a systematic course of reading. He recommended a number of books for Samuel's close study, all of which he would find in his father's library at Chesterfield Street.⁴¹ They featured lives of prominent Roman Catholics, and included his biographies of Gregory Lopez and Gaston de Renty and his translation of Thomas à Kempis's *The Imitation of Christ*.⁴² The following April Wesley was still continuing his studies, and his uncle was recommending that he should follow the method of Kingswood, the school near Bristol that he had founded in 1748.⁴³ At the same time, he was still concerned about Samuel's way of life, and worried that he might feel when it was too late that he had not paid sufficient attention or given sufficient affection to his nephew. At the end of the month, in what he thought would be the last letter he wrote to Samuel, he poured out his heart, reiterating what he had written previously. If Samuel had lacked clothes or books or money, he could have supplied them. But he feared that what he lacked most of all was religion: not 'external religion' but 'the religion of the heart', as enjoyed by à Kempis, Pascal, and Fénelon. If Samuel had read even a small part of his uncle's writings or had attended his ministry, he would know a great deal more of true religion than he did at present, and he lamented that Samuel had stopped attending Methodist places of worship, where alone it was inculcated. He was unconcerned whether Samuel was to be called a Roman Catholic or a Protestant, but grieved that he was a 'heathen'. He was certain that 'the general religion both of Protestants and Catholics' was better than heathenism, but Samuel was called to better things than this. Despite his prejudices, he should go and hear the word that could save his soul.⁴⁴

---

[39] SW to Sarah Gwynne Wesley, 22 July 1789.
[40] Sarah Wesley to Penelope Maitland, 29 July 1789.
[41] John Wesley to SW, 16 Sept. 1789 (*LJW*, vol. 8, p. 171).
[42] *The Life of Gregory Lopez* (1735), *An Extract of the Life of Monsieur de Renty* (1741) and *The Christian's Pattern; or, a Treatise of the Imitation of Christ* (1735).
[43] John Wesley to Sarah Wesley, 11 Apr. 1790 (*LJW*, vol. 8, p. 213).
[44] John Wesley to SW, 29 Apr. 1790 (*LJW*, vol. 8, pp. 218–19).

4

Life with Charlotte, 1791–1797

Throughout the late 1780s Wesley and Charlotte remained as committed to each other as ever. After the death of Wesley's father, it might have been expected that they would consider marriage. By this time they had known each other for over five years, and their commitment had been tested by constant family opposition, at least on Wesley's side. In addition, as we have seen, Wesley had come into money left to him by James Price that gave him a measure of financial independence. As he and Charlotte intended to spend the rest of their lives together and were openly conducting a passionately physical relationship, there were no very good reasons, family disapproval aside, why they should not marry, and several compelling reasons why they should.

In fact, the question of marriage does not seem for the moment to have been considered, and when the subject came up in the spring of 1791, the grounds of the family's concern had shifted. By now, they recognized the strength and apparent permanence of Wesley's commitment to Charlotte, and had abandoned their former attempts to persuade him to give her up. Instead, they now attempted to persuade him to regularize the situation by marrying her.[1] Part of their concern would have stemmed from worries about Charlotte becoming pregnant and the stigma of illegitimacy that would attend any resulting children. Indeed, it appears from a remark in a letter of December 1791 from Shepherd and an allusion in a letter from Sarah in May of the same year that Charlotte may by this time have already had a child by Samuel.[2] Nothing further is known of this child and its fate, however, and it seems most likely that it was stillborn or died in early infancy, or possibly that it was given away for adoption.

It was in Wesley's response to family suggestions that he should marry Charlotte that events took a totally unexpected turn. He simply refused, on the grounds that he considered them to be married already by virtue of their sexual intimacy, and that going through a religious ceremony would do nothing to alter matters. This position, which Wesley set out in detail in a remarkable series of letters to Sarah in the spring and summer of 1791, derived from arguments which his godfather Martin Madan had elaborated, but for very different purposes, in his controversial *Thelyphthora*. In his capacity as chaplain of the

---

[1] Sarah Wesley to SW, 27 May 1791.
[2] Shepherd to SW, Dec. 1791; Sarah Wesley to SW, 27 May 1791.

Lock Hospital, Madan was constantly confronted with women who had been seduced and then abandoned, their reputations and future prospects of marriage and employment ruined. In an attempt to find a solution for the social problems that resulted, he argued that men should be obliged to take responsibility for the consequences of their sexual behaviour. This on its own was unexceptionable, although obviously difficult to enforce. Madan's next step was to argue that the essence of marriage lay not in a legal ceremony but in sexual intercourse. If this could be established and enshrined into law, a man who had sexual intercourse with a woman could be held to be married to her, and thus to be responsible for her maintenance and that of any resulting child or children. Madan claimed that this well-intentioned, if eccentric, position was supported by scriptural authority, arguing that there was nothing in the Bible to suggest that a religious ceremony was an essential component of marriage. One very obvious problem was posed by men who had sexual intercourse with more than one woman, and to cope with this, Madan was obliged to argue for polygamy, once more claiming scriptural authority. Not surprisingly, it was this aspect of his argument that was to attract the most attention and opposition. The publication of *Thelyphthora* in 1780, despite appeals from friends who saw all too clearly what reception it would have, was followed by a spate of outraged pamphlets and book-length replies. Public notoriety and disgrace inevitably followed. Madan withdrew from his active work at the Lock Hospital, retired to Epsom, and died in 1790.[3]

By the summer of 1791, when Wesley appears to have first taken up Madan's arguments, this controversy was well in the past, but would have been remembered by many. Wesley gave Madan's arguments a new and personal application. If the essence of marriage indeed consisted in sexual intercourse, then he and Charlotte were already married, and there could be no reason for them to go through a church ceremony as well. It is difficult to think of a position which could have caused more offence and hurt to his family. In his refusal to marry, Samuel was claiming to be adopting not a libertarian stance, but one of principle, backed by biblical authority. At the same time he paraded his physical intimacy with Charlotte in front of his family, expressed his contempt for the marriage ceremony, and impugned the integrity of those who celebrated it. It was an extraordinary line to take, and one which – Madan and *Thelyphthora* apart – finds little resonance in any thinking of the time, although similar views may have been held by Chancellor Cowper, Madan's great-uncle, and by Westley Hall, the ne'er-do-well husband of John and Charles Wesley's sister Martha.[4] Although Madan's arguments gave Samuel's views intellectual backing of a sort, he had more down-to-earth reasons for his refusal to marry, which on occasion he was prepared to acknowledge. One was financial; another simply a refusal to conform to expected norms of behaviour.

---

[3] Madan, *The Madan Family*, pp. 115–16. For a list of the publications occasioned by the publication of *Thelyphthora*, see pp. 289–98.

[4] *DNB*, s.v. 'Madan, Martin'.

As he candidly explained to Sarah in June 1791, he had two objections to marrying: first, that he was not rich enough; second, that one of his 'irresistible antipathies' was to being tied down in any way.[5]

In December 1791, Shepherd reappeared on the scene, as prepared as she had been during Wesley's adolescence to advise and to meddle. After her departure from England in August 1785 she had lived in Italy and France, but by late 1791 was in Paris and contemplating a return to England. She re-opened contact with Wesley in a letter of introduction presented by M. Dumont, a Roman Catholic dancing-master whom she had befriended and who had recently arrived in London: Samuel might be able to help him find some employment with suitable families and schools.[6] She had been much affected by the death of John Wesley earlier in the year, and felt he was irreplaceable unless Wesley were to take over his work. She thought that Wesley would not be hindered in doing this by any want of ability, as he possessed a 'strong sense of manly understanding' and the necessary eloquence for the task. The suggestion was laughable, and Wesley annotated the letter at one point that 'the plaister of Paris' (i.e. Shepherd's flattery) was 'too coarse to produce the intended effect'. He had been an openly professed Roman Catholic for the past seven years; in addition, as his uncle had repeatedly noted, he was not remotely religious in his conduct, and had a reputation for excessive drinking and other wild behaviour. The thought of him becoming a successor to John Wesley was ludicrous, and he did not bother to reply.

By April 1792 Shepherd had returned to England, and wrote again. She had been delighted by every report that she had heard about Wesley that set him 'high in the world's opinion' and was gaining him 'fresh additional honours from the wise and the good'. More particularly, she wanted to congratulate him on his authorship of a pamphlet that he had recently published. This was *Vindex to Verax*,[7] his response to a recent anonymous pamphlet written under the pen name of 'Verax' ('Truthful') that attacked John Wesley and blackened his character.[8] Wesley's reply, written under the name of 'Vindex' ('Vindicator') and bearing on its title page an uncompromising text from Psalm 10 ('The memory of the just is blessed, but the name of the wicked shall rot'), was a

---

[5] SW to Sarah Wesley, 5 June 1791.
[6] Shepherd to SW, 7 Dec. 1791.
[7] *Vindex to Verax. Or, Remarks upon 'A letter to the Rev. Thomas Coke, Ll.D. and Mr Henry Moore'; and an Appeal and Remonstrance to the People called Methodists'*. Addressed to 'An Old Member of the Society', London, 1792. Although the pamphlet was published anonymously, a contemporary advertisement identifies SW as the author.
[8] *A letter to the Rev. Thomas Coke, Ll.D. and Mr Henry Moore; Occasioned by the Proposal for Publishing the Life of the Revd. John Wesley A.M., in Opposition to that Advertised (under Sanction of the Executors) to be written by John Whitehead M.D. Also, a Letter from the Rev. Dr Coke to the Author on the Same Subject; Together with the whole Correspondence, and the Circular Letters written on the Occasion, and a True and Impartial Statement of Facts hitherto Suppressed. To which is added, An Appeal and Remonstrance to the People called Methodists. By an Old Member of the Society*, London, 1792.

robust defence of his uncle's reputation. In her letter, Shepherd related how she had seen the pamphlet in the window of a bookseller. On enquiring about its authorship, the bookseller told her that it was by Samuel Wesley, and produced a page of Wesley's handwriting to prove it. Shepherd recognised the hand, and subsequently bought the pamphlet and showed it to several of John Wesley's friends. She felt that Wesley's defence of his uncle must do him honour and endear him to every member of his family, concluding by sending her warmest good wishes and her hope that he might 'climb the utmost summit of genius and virtue'.[9] This time Wesley did respond, saying that his failure to reply to her earlier letter did not stem from ingratitude, and that he had the most pleasant memories of their former association. The absence of correspondence between them had been caused by some irreconcilable differences of opinion between them – doubtless those caused by the incident shortly before her departure from England in 1785. He went on to discuss his present disagreements with the Roman Catholic church. He had recently written to a Roman Catholic priest setting out in detail his views on two points of doctrine, which he considered were now so far from orthodoxy that he suspected that they would lead to his censure or condemnation by the Church. But he was not prepared to be a hypocrite or change his beliefs: he was unconcerned about the possibility of excommunication, and would not be 'drubbed or flattered' into orthodoxy. It was now up to the Church to decide whether they wished to retain him or expel him.[10]

The identity of the priest with whom Wesley was in correspondence is not known, and the letter that Wesley summarised for Shepherd does not survive. But much of its tone can be gathered from a subsequent letter in the correspondence, in which Wesley replied to points made by the priest about the necessity of baptism, the need to enter the Roman Catholic Church in order to be saved, and the requirement for Roman Catholics to submit to the Church's teaching. Wesley took issue with the argument that only marriages solemnized within the Roman Catholic Church were valid, pointing out that if this were so, all those who married within the Church of England would be 'living in fornication'. As for marriage, his own definition was that it was 'a mutual agreement of male and female to love and adhere to each other', and that it deserved to be kept 'as inviolably as that enforced by all the spiritual authority in Europe'. He was prepared to admit the necessity of having a marriage ceremony, but for civil reasons rather than religious ones. In response to his correspondent's view that he was setting his own judgement against that of the Church, he argued for his right to exercise it, stating that it was 'the true spring of all that implicit faith which is asserted by ecclesiastics to be so salutary and meritorious'. As far as attending public Roman Catholic services, he considered it to be most appropriate for him to 'remain in retirement' rather than to pretend to be submissive to the Church when he was not. The Church

---

[9] Shepherd to SW, 24 Apr. 1792.
[10] SW to Shepherd, 26 Apr. 1792.

should make up its mind what its attitude to him was: if his errors were not of a serious nature he should be honourably recalled to it; if they were, he should be 'honestly excluded'.[11]

Given the strength of Wesley's commitment to Charlotte and hers to him, it could only be a matter of ?time before they decided to live together. On 18 October 1792, the Moravian minister Christian Ignatius Latrobe noted in his diary that Wesley had gone to live with a 'companion' in Hertfordshire, and that it was a pity that he should be 'lost to the world and good society'.[12] Wesley and Charlotte had moved to Ridge, a small village near St Albans, some thirteen miles from London. Although the decision to leave London is readily understandable, the choice of Ridge is less so, to the point of appearing bizarre. Completely without amenities, the village appears to have had nothing to offer except isolation. This, coupled with presumably inexpensive housing, may have been precisely what Wesley and Charlotte were looking for. But Wesley still needed to travel to Marylebone for his teaching at Mrs Barnes's school, and the distance was too far for comfort or convenience. It is hard to believe that Wesley and Charlotte could not have found equal seclusion somewhere closer to London. It is possible that the house was made available through a personal connection, and that Wesley and Charlotte took the house despite its unpromising location, simply because it was available to them.[13]

In any case, it was not the move to Ridge itself but Wesley's decision to start living with Charlotte that was the important event, marking his decision finally to leave the family home and lead his life with someone to whom he considered himself irrevocably committed. A month later Wesley wrote to his mother to explain the reasons for his decision. This was an important letter which his mother would read and re-read, pass round the family, and then keep safe to consult at intervals. It was an occasion for Wesley to set the record straight, to correct misapprehensions about Charlotte, and express as clearly as possible his commitment to her, so that the family could understand his actions, even if they were unable to give them their blessing. In it, he stressed that he had thought long and hard about the action he had recently taken. He reaffirmed his commitment to Charlotte, whom he had now known for ten years, and defended her against the accusations made about her. Far from being a 'fickle & unsteady Character', as some had claimed, she had remained constant to Wesley ever since their first meeting in October 1782. She had received many offers of marriage from men able to support her in the style to which she was originally educated, but had none the less preferred Wesley in his 'wooden cottage' and with his 'splendid fortune' of £150 per year. She had been represented as being of a 'careless, prodigal Disposition', and having the

---

[11] SW to an unidentified priest, [?May 1792].
[12] Latrobe Journal, 18 Oct. 1792.
[13] The Churchwardens' Accounts and Land Tax records (Hertfordshire Record Office) have an entry for 21 May 1793 in the name of 'Mr Webb or tenant.' This could conceivably have been Samuel Webbe.

worst features of her extravagant father and her vain mother. But for many years she had managed to live decently and out of debt on the allowance of £30 per year which she had been granted by the Bristol merchant who looked after the financial affairs of the family. It was not true that he had ever helped her in any way financially, and utterly false to suggest that he had agreed to pay off her debts as soon as he became of age. She had been called 'a coquette – nay more, a wanton'. These accusations were also false: she was a virgin when she met him, so if she had been seduced, it was by Wesley himself. Under the circumstances, it might be expected that Wesley would want to marry Charlotte, but he already considered her his wife, and she could not be made more so by a church service.[14]

If worries about the prospect of illegitimate children were the main factor in the family's earlier attempts to persuade Wesley and Charlotte to marry, these must have increased after the move to Ridge. The issue soon became pressing, for early in 1793 Charlotte became pregnant. The impending birth of a child was evidently successful in inducing a change of attitude where repeated arguments and pleas from the family had failed: Wesley and Charlotte rapidly abandoned their principles and married on 5 April. This was no ordinary hastily arranged marriage following an unexpected pregnancy, but one which involved an embarrassing retraction of views strongly held and strenuously argued for many years. Not surprisingly, the wedding was quiet, not to say secretive. It was by special licence, thus obviating the need to call the banns, and held not at Ridge but at Hammersmith, perhaps because neither Wesley nor Charlotte was known there. None of Wesley's family was present, and they were apparently not informed about it until some time later.

After the marriage Wesley and Charlotte returned to life at Ridge. There are few indications of how they spent their time. Wesley was not composing to any extent and seems to have been pursuing no other professional musical activities apart from his school teaching in London. He was evidently devoting some of his time to intensive study: in July his mother commented to a correspondent that his recent appearance of low spirits was caused by his 'great attention to books'. She boasted that he had been learning Greek, and hoped that he might one day be ordained in the Church of England: an unlikely prospect, given Wesley's still continuing Roman Catholic associations.[15] Letters from Wesley to his mother show them in apparently amicable contact over everyday domestic matters: the delivery of a goose from Ridge to Chesterfield Street, with recommendations about how long it should be left before being dressed; the conveyance of a shower bath and some music books in the opposite direction; a proposed visit by Wesley's mother to a friend in the country, and so on. Among other items discussed was an assault on Charles by some footpads, in which he had been robbed and injured; in a similar attack, Samuel had escaped with the loss of some money and his pocket watch. On 13 July there was to be a fireworks

---

[14] SW to Sarah Gwynne Wesley, 7 Nov. 1792.
[15] Sarah Gwynne Wesley to Penelope Maitland, 23 July 1793.

party at Ridge, for which the pyrotechnist Caillot had been engaged, at presumably considerable expense.

Meanwhile, the country sweltered in a sticky and oppressive heat wave with temperatures in the eighties. Wesley commented that he and Charlotte could hardly draw breath, and were eagerly waiting for the weather to break. Wesley passed on Charlotte's best wishes, but added that her health, with her confinement only weeks away, was only 'indifferent', and that the heat and her own weight were almost too much for her.[16] In August, with Charlotte's confinement rapidly approaching, Wesley and his sister resumed their earlier arguments on marriage, continuing where they had left off two years earlier. The occasion was the news that had somehow reached Sarah that he and Charlotte were now married, and Sarah's curiosity to know how he was able to reconcile his current state with his former views. There were at least five letters in each direction, written over a period of probably just over two weeks; of these, four of Samuel's, but only one of Sarah's, have survived. All the old arguments were rehearsed at length, with remarkable frankness on both sides, right up to the time of Charlotte's confinement on 25 August, when she gave birth to a son, Charles.

Wesley and Charlotte appear to have made no immediate efforts to visit Chesterfield Street after the birth, and it was not until early in the next year that they did so. On 18 January 1794, Sarah recorded in a personal memorandum that a great anxiety had been taken from her mind 'in hearing the marriage of [her] brother confirmed', that she had seen Charlotte for the first time (presumably since the marriage), and that all family enmities had ceased.[17] In a letter to his mother of the same date Wesley recorded their safe return to Ridge and their intention to visit again the following week, when Charlotte would be able to stay for a few days. The meeting had marked the beginning of a new chapter for Wesley and Charlotte and a fresh start in his relationship with his family. Now that their marriage was out in the open and they had negotiated their awkward first meeting with the family, they could put all the unpleasantness of the last few years behind them. It was time for Wesley's mother, brother, and sister to forget all their earlier misgivings about Charlotte's character and family background and to accept her, with all her faults and shortcomings, into the family. They could then settle into their new roles as grandmother, uncle, and aunt, and Sarah and Charlotte could get to know each other properly for the first time and become friends. With the steadying influence of marriage and fatherhood and without the distractions of earlier family conflicts, Samuel would perhaps now settle down. Ridge was not an ideal place to live, but he and Charlotte appeared happy enough there. Perhaps in time they would move back to London, and Wesley would be able to find some useful employment, either in music or in some other field where his intelligence and education could be put to good use. In the meantime, he was continuing with his school teaching,

---

[16] SW to Sarah Gwynne Wesley, 25 June 1793 and 10 July 1793.
[17] Sarah Wesley, 'Mercies of the Year 1794'.

walking the thirteen miles to London in all weathers, and presumably staying overnight in Chesterfield Street on occasions when this was more convenient than travelling back to Ridge on the same day.

Notwithstanding all his disillusionment with the music profession, Wesley would have been fully aware that he was absenting himself from the London musical scene at one of its most brilliant periods.[18] This was the time of the series of orchestral concerts promoted by the violinist and impresario Johann Peter Salomon at the Hanover Square Rooms, the rival series at the Pantheon in Oxford Street, and a mass of concert activity elsewhere. The high points were in 1790–1 and in 1794–5, when Haydn was in England, appearing at Salomon's concerts and directing the first performances of the 'London' symphonies, which he had composed for the series. Wesley stated in his *Reminiscences* that this was the most glorious period of London's concert life and that he had attended many of Salomon's concerts and 'received both Pleasure and Advantage in listening to a fine Band of the best vocal and instrumental Performers so judiciously selected and so ably conducted'.[19] He is known to have heard some of Haydn's concerts, presumably most of them in the 1791 season before he had moved to Ridge.

As time went on, the disadvantages of living at Ridge became more and more apparent. By the end of September 1794, Sarah was writing to Samuel to express her concern about the effect on his health of so much travelling, and her fear that he would be exhausted by the time he reached middle age.[20] Charlotte was pregnant again, and Sarah, worried about the dampness of the house, urged Wesley to find suitable lodgings in nearby Barnet for the confinement.[21] In his reply, Wesley hoped that he and Sarah could agree to differ on his decision to continue to live at Ridge. Although he would be in better health if he were less agitated, the walking was not doing him any harm. As for Sarah's suggestion that he should keep a horse, this was not possible, as he could scarcely afford to keep a family, and there was little prospect of his fortunes improving. In response to her enquiry about Charlotte's health, in which she had expressed the hope that she was 'tolerable', he replied that he could not say she was 'tolerable' in any sense, adding that 'the poison of her mind works in proportion to the uneasiness of her body, which must be lightened by the last load I shall ever cause, I think, within this fortnight'. Meanwhile, he would be travelling to and from London as normal, as he needed to be in Ridge as much as possible to prevent the house being 'wrecked' by the servant and nurse who had been employed to attend Charlotte during the final stages of her pregnancy.

This ominous letter was Wesley's first to his family to contain any indication

---

[18] For a summary of the development of London's concert life in the later eighteenth century and the 'rage for music' of the 1780s and 1790s, see McVeigh, *Concert Life*, pp. 2–8; on orchestral concerts at this time, see McVeigh, 'The Professional Concert and Rival Subscription Series in London, 1783–1793'.

[19] *Reminiscences*, fol. 123.

[20] Sarah Wesley to Charles Wesley jun., 19 Sept. 1794.

[21] Sarah Wesley to SW, 25 Sept. 1794.

that all was not well between him and Charlotte. From now on, he would make no bones about the deterioration of their relationship and their increasing unhappiness together. In the meantime, Wesley's mother had decided to go to Ridge for the birth. She arrived some time in the middle of the month, but as the baby had not arrived by 20 October and Charlotte was not sure of the expected date of her confinement, she returned to London. As Wesley later commented to Sarah, this defeated the whole purpose of her visit, which was to comfort and look after Charlotte when she needed her most.[22] Four days later, her servant Hannah Williams travelled to Ridge to take her place to look after Charles and to assist at the birth. Meanwhile, Wesley himself was forced to remain at Chesterfield Street, where he was suffering with a bowel complaint that had troubled him for several days.[23] On 26 October, however, he was back in Ridge, and writing to Sarah that the birth was expected within hours. Once again there was an indication that all was far from well between him and Charlotte:

> May God help her and make her happy whether she live or die. I love her, as you know, but the event has proved that she was never designed for my second self. I dwell on her virtues even now, and as little on her faults as she will let me. But where can esteem be for her or him who knows not to bridle the tongue?[24]

In the event the baby, a daughter, was born almost two weeks later, probably on or around 9 November. She was named Susanna, after her redoubtable great-grandmother, the mother of John and Charles Wesley senior. Three days later, Sarah wrote with her congratulations, sending affectionate greetings to Charlotte and hoping that the child would be happier than had been the lot of other females in the family.[25]

The summer and early autumn of 1794, during the later stages of Charlotte's pregnancy with Susanna, saw Wesley returning to composition after a virtually total silence since moving to Ridge two years earlier. In October and November he composed a piano sonata, a short organ piece, and, most notably, completed the *Ode to St Cecilia*, KO 207. Although the first two of these are relatively small-scale works, the *Ode to St Cecilia*, completed on 21 October 1794, was a major project that must have occupied Wesley for some considerable time. It is a setting for soloists, chorus, and orchestra of an unpublished poem written a hundred years earlier by his grandfather and namesake. In its subject matter, length, and forces, it was suitable for one of the Lenten oratorio concerts that took place each year at Covent Garden theatre and sometimes at this time also at Drury Lane, and it seems most likely that Wesley wrote it with an eye to a performance in the following year's season. There was no performance in 1795, however, and the *Ode* had to wait over four years for its premiere.

There is little information about Wesley's activities in 1795, but his relation-

---

[22] SW to Sarah Wesley, 26 Oct. 1794.
[23] Sarah Gwynne Wesley to Sarah Wesley, 23 Oct. 1794.
[24] SW to Sarah Wesley, 26 Oct. 1794.
[25] Sarah Wesley to SW, 12 Nov. 1794.

ship with Charlotte was evidently continuing to deteriorate. At midsummer the schools broke up, and Wesley's new-found leisure at the same time obliged him to spend more time with Charlotte and gave him the opportunity to consider his position. In a letter to Sarah of 27 June he stated that he and Charlotte had spent the previous two days without any arguments, but that he was afraid that this calm would prove to be only a lucid interval, and that 'whenever the Fit of Mania returns . . . all its Consequences [would] return also'. This remark, coupled with Wesley's comment in an earlier letter on the 'poison' of Charlotte's mind, makes it clear that Wesley interpreted Charlotte's behaviour as a form of madness. Two weeks later, on 8 July, he wrote again. He thought that it was likely that by this time Charlotte had written to Sarah in an attempt to enlist her support in a fresh quarrel. If so, it was up to Sarah to decide whether or not to become involved, but she should know that Wesley had made his mind up to leave Charlotte, and that there was nothing that anyone could say or do to alter this decision. Charlotte's 'open violence' towards him would have no other effect than of 'driving [him] into comfort' sooner than he had expected. Wesley did not specify what form this might take, but stated later in the letter that he could earn his living anywhere in Europe, as could a 'similar sufferer' with him. Wesley did not say who this was, but in the light of later developments it is likely that it was Anne Deane, a close friend of Sarah's, with whom he appears to have been conducting a clandestine affair.

Precisely what happened next is unclear, but it led to a temporary separation during which Sarah and Charles took Charlotte and the two children with them to Bristol in an attempt to provide a breathing space for all concerned. Here, as Sarah reported to Wesley on 30 September, Charlotte and the children had been installed in lodgings in Clifton at a rent of 10s 6d per week. Since her arrival Charlotte had not mentioned any more 'disagreeable subjects', but appeared dejected and looked unhealthy. Little Charles was fretful, but was better behaved than when with his father, and the baby Susanna was much admired on all sides. Charlotte was doing her best to be economical, but had little skill in household management. Sarah commented that Charlotte's life at Ridge, in a cold and comfortless house and far from a market, did not encourage her to cultivate habits of good housekeeping; nonetheless, Sarah was pleased to see that she was not squandering money on herself. Although her temper was mended, her spirits were not, and Sarah thought that she would not live long. She reminded Wesley, who by now had moved back into Chesterfield Street, that in the year of his marriage his prayers were answered and he had made a vow of obedience to God. He should now 'sin no more'.[26] It is difficult to know what to make of Sarah's remarks about Charlotte's health, in particular whether she thought Charlotte's present physical condition would lead to her early death, or that she would soon commit suicide. In fact, Charlotte was once again pregnant, and her condition may have contributed to the unhealthy appearance that Sarah remarked upon. Sarah's exhortation to her brother to 'sin no more' is clearer,

[26] Sarah to SW, 30 Sept. 1795.

and suggests that the immediate cause of the separation was Wesley's continuing love-affair with Anne Deane.

Sarah, Charles, Charlotte, and her children returned home from Bristol some time in November. From an undated letter from Wesley to Sarah written probably in early December, it is evident that the temporary separation had done nothing to improve the situation. Charlotte's confinement was approaching, and Wesley would need to decide what to do with his son Charles: whether to bring him to London, where he would be spoiled and indulged, or to leave him at Ridge, where he would be likely to disturb Charlotte in childbed and for which Wesley would be sure to be blamed. No more was heard about the birth of this child, and it must be assumed that it was still-born or died soon after birth.

5

Beginning a career, 1797–1805

By the beginning of 1797, any attractions that life at Ridge may once have held had long since disappeared. The house was damp, uncomfortable, and inconveniently situated, and Wesley's incessant travelling to and from London was becoming increasingly tiring. In addition, Wesley and Charlotte were cut off from London friends and family, and had no adult company but each other. Wesley at least had his regular trips to London to ease the monotony of country life, but Charlotte had no such recourse, and for her the isolation must have been particularly burdensome. For a couple as quarrelsome and disputatious as the Wesleys, their situation made little sense: the more they were together, the more they quarrelled, and their best chance of remaining on even minimally amicable terms would be to lead more independent lives. The beginning of 1797 was particularly unhappy and led Wesley, not for the first time, to contemplate permanent separation. In a letter of January 1797 to his old friend James Kenton, he described his predicament in unprecedented detail. Charlotte's disposition was 'diabolical, ungovernable, ferocious, ungrateful', and he and Kenton had long ago agreed that she was 'incurable among Lunaticks'. Any remaining tenderness in Wesley's attitude to her had disappeared. Living with her had taken its toll on his health: since his marriage he had aged twelve years, his memory was weakened, and he was rarely calm. In the face of these difficulties, he considered it a miracle that he was still able to carry on with his engagements. If he stayed with her, he feared being so incapacitated as to be unable to continue to support his children. All in all, he felt he owed it to himself, to his children, and to his friends to leave her.[1]

Amid the unhappiness at Ridge, Wesley was beginning to involve himself in practical music-making in London. The first indication of this activity occurs in two letters of late February 1797, one to the amateur singer Joseph Payne Street,[2] the other to the violinist George Polgreen Bridgetower,[3] both concerning a music party to be held at the house of the mother of Anne Deane in Paddington on the following Friday. In his letter to Street, Wesley informed him that they were to be joined by 'our friend Vincent', and 'young Danby'.

---

[1] SW to Kenton, 18 Jan. 1797.
[2] *SW to Street, 21 Feb. 1797.
[3] *SW to Bridgetower, 23 Feb. 1797.

Wesley hoped that they could have a sing-through of a 'Miserere' (i.e. a setting of verses from Psalm 51) that he had composed some years ago, and wanted to let Street have a copy to look at beforehand. The letter to Bridgetower, whom Wesley evidently only knew slightly, was to invite him to perform at the party, and to assure him that Wesley would be glad to return the favour at a future date.

These and later letters indicate the circles in which Wesley was now moving and the nature of the music-making he was involved in. Street, who was to become a lifelong friend, was probably of around Wesley's own age, and was a businessman in the City, probably a stockbroker or a banker. He was also a keen amateur singer of near-professional standard, and the librarian of the Madrigal Society. 'Our friend Vincent' was no doubt the alto singer J. Vincent,[4] while 'young Danby' was presumably Eustace Danby, the fifteen-year-old nephew of the Roman Catholic composer and organist John Danby; from Wesley's remarks he was evidently also a singer.[5] They were comparatively minor figures. Bridgetower, on the other hand, was one of the age's leading violin virtuosos, who would in 1803 in Vienna give the first performance of Beethoven's 'Kreutzer' Sonata, Op. 47. Wesley's association with Bridgetower at this early stage in his own return to music is a telling indication of the reputation that he must have enjoyed in London, notwithstanding his long absence from the musical scene. His invitation may have been in connection with a performance of his Sonata in F for violin and piano, KO 508, which he had written for Salomon and had completed only a few days earlier. Like Bridgetower, Salomon was in the first rank of London's professional musicians, and Wesley's association with him is another indication of the distinguished company he was now keeping.

Among other musicians, amateur and professional, who appear in Wesley's letters from around this time are William Drummer, a gentleman of independent means, and his brother John, a singer who made his living as a coal merchant. Both may originally have been pupils of Wesley's, and like Street they became lifelong friends. A Mr Carter, whom Wesley hoped in a letter to Street of 18 October 1799 could be persuaded to leave his office and 'part with his Coals for a Song' at a lunchtime music party, was Thomas Carter, a professional alto singer who had by this time moved into the coal trade, perhaps as an employee of John Drummer. Carter, perhaps along with some or all of the others discussed above, was a member of the Ad Libitum Society, a more or less private club where amateurs and professionals met to eat, drink, and make music in conditions of easy familiarity. For them, Wesley in December 1799 composed 'Near Thame's fam'd banks', a celebration of the society's meetings, where 'harmony and Friendship ever reign':

---

[4] Doane, *Musical Directory*. Zelophead Vincent, also listed as a male alto in Doane, had died in 1793.
[5] Selby Whittingham, 'A Letter from John Danby Found', *ML* 76 (1995), pp. 68–71.

> Since here each pleasure gains new grace
> And jocund smiles in every face
> Our jovial rites begin,
> Come push the sparkling wine around
> While echo shall this strain resound.
> Here sadness is a sin.

On these occasions, when differences in social status counted for little and what was most important was instrumental or vocal ability, Wesley could feel at home.

It is apparent from his compositions at this time that Wesley also had some limited involvement with glee clubs: more formally constituted societies that met regularly at inns and taverns to dine and sing glees. The most prestigious and longest-established was the Madrigal Society, founded in 1741; others included the Noblemen and Gentlemen's Catch Club, and the Glee Club. All were amateur organizations, although they also had professional musicians as honorary members, who paid no membership dues and presumably also dined free in exchange for their contribution to the meetings. More recent was the Concentores Society, a small professionals-only society founded in 1798. Wesley does not appear to have been a regular attender at this time at any of these societies, and would probably have found the combination of often second-rate music and no doubt self-congratulatory all-male company tedious in any but the smallest quantities.

As Wesley's involvement in music grew, the move from Ridge to somewhere closer to London must have appeared more and more essential. Thoughts of separation were obviously abandoned, and by mid-February 1797 Wesley's sister Sarah was writing to her mother that the time was approaching when Wesley and Charlotte would leave Ridge, and hoping that their next house would have 'more comfortable necessaries' (i.e. sanitary arrangements) than they had there.[6] In fact, it was not until July 1797 that Wesley and Charlotte were able to move. It was to Finchley, another outlying village, but one a good deal more convenient for London. Unlike Ridge, it was a sizeable community. With its good transport links to London it had much of the character of a commuter village and was much favoured by those whose work was in London but who preferred to live away from the noise, smoke, and pollution of the capital. It was on the road between London and Ridge, and so somewhere that Wesley had come to know well over the last few years. With the move, evening concerts and social engagements became a good deal more feasible and it became less necessary for Wesley to stay overnight in Chesterfield Street, although he still did so on occasion.

The move to Finchley was clouded by the death in December 1797 of the Wesleys' daughter Susanna. Writing to his mother shortly after the death, Wesley was able to reassure her that Charlotte was as well as could be expected. She had had a good deal of fever – presumably the same illness that had caused

---

[6] Sarah Wesley to Sarah Gwynne Wesley, 15 Feb. 1797.

Susanna's death – but was now recovering. Wesley was sure that she was continuing to feel the loss of their child acutely. As for him, Susanna's death was a crushing blow: 'a Loss, to *me irreparable by any that can come after. I would* not love another Child as I did her, & I am certain that I never shall.'[7] He was later to commemorate her death with 'Beneath, a Sleeping Infant Lies', KO 208, a setting of an epitaph by his uncle and namesake Samuel Wesley (1691– 1739).

With the beginning of 1798 came a return to composition. Wesley had written nothing in 1795 and 1796 and little more in 1797, apart from the sonata for violin and piano mentioned above and a few other isolated pieces. From early 1798, however, the flow of compositions increased. A manuscript volume inscribed 'Harmony 1798' now at the Royal College of Music contains a large part of this output: it was obviously Wesley's fair-copy book, in which he wrote down new compositions, either as he finished them or in batches at a later stage. The inclusion of Latin sacred music in this volume indicates that Wesley had resumed his attendance at Roman Catholic worship. It is likely that by this time he was attending for solely musical reasons: his disagreements with the Church on matters of doctrine had brought him to the brink of leaving it in 1792, if not actually to that point, and there is no indication that he had subsequently changed his opinions. As with the Latin church music compositions of his adolescence, there is no evidence to tie the compositions of this period to any one location, but they were most probably written for the Portuguese Embassy chapel, where the young Vincent Novello had recently been appointed organist.

Novello was born in 1781, the son of a pastry-cook from Piedmont who had come to England in 1771 and had set up in business as a confectioner. Anxious that Vincent and his elder brother Francis should have a good education, his parents had in the early 1790s sent them to a school near Boulogne, from which they returned in 1793. Vincent then became a chorister at the Sardinian Embassy Chapel under Samuel Webbe, and when his voice broke became assistant organist there, also serving with John Danby at the Spanish Embassy Chapel in Manchester Square. He was appointed to the organist's position at the Portuguese Embassy Chapel at the age of sixteen in 1797 or 1798. Under his direction, the standard of music at the chapel reached unprecedented heights. In time, he introduced the Masses of Mozart and Haydn and much other Catholic church music by continental composers, and in 1811 he published by subscription a two-volume selection of the music sung there. This was the first of his many publications of Roman Catholic church music over the next seventeen years, after which he handed over the management of what had now become a highly successful business to his eldest son Alfred.[8]

Whichever establishment Wesley's latest church music compositions were

---

[7] SW to Sarah Gwynne Wesley, 22 Dec. 1797.
[8] For the Novello family and the firm, see Hurd, *Vincent Novello – and Company*.

written for, they show clearly how much Roman Catholic choirs had grown both in size and competence since his earlier involvement with them. Many pieces are in five, six, or even eight parts, and are conceived on a far larger and more ambitious scale than previously. Included are such pieces as the five-part 'Exultate Deo', KO 36, and the magnificent eight-part settings of 'Deus majestatis intonuit', KO 23, and 'Dixit Dominus', KO 26, that are among the most ambitious of all Wesley's Latin sacred music.

At the same time, Wesley was looking for a church position of his own, and in March 1798, the post of organist at the chapel of the Foundling Hospital became vacant. This was a prestigious appointment. Founded in 1742 by Thomas Coram for the benefit of children abandoned by their parents, the Foundling Hospital had had a long and distinguished musical history. In its early days Handel was a generous benefactor who had from 1749 given annual performances of his music in the chapel, had donated an organ in 1750, and had left the hospital the autograph score of *Messiah* in his will.[9] Although these days were long past, the chapel still maintained a choir of foundling children and had a strong musical tradition. Moreover, its organ, a 1768 instrument by Parker, was celebrated for an unusual mechanism that allowed additional pitches to be brought into operation to improve intonation in the less frequently used keys.

The committee minutes give an unusually full picture of the appointment process. There were eight candidates, who were required to play the services on successive Sundays, with the opportunity to rehearse the choir on the preceding Friday and Saturday. This took from 18 March until 6 May. There was then an election, at which John Immyns, a relative nonentity, was appointed on 9 May with fifty votes, the second candidate receiving forty-one, the third two, and everyone else, including Wesley, none. But this elaborate selection process was a sham, and the appointment of Immyns came about more through the patronage of Joah Bates, one of the Governors of the Foundling Hospital, than through any musical merits that he may have possessed.

This outcome would have come as no great surprise to Wesley or to other observers: patronage of this sort played a large part in such appointments, and as was well known, the appointment of R. J. S. Stevens, another nonentity, as organist of the Charterhouse in 1796 had come about in much the same way.[10] Nonetheless, Wesley felt sufficiently aggrieved to protest. He published a newspaper advertisement thanking those who had supported him and stating that he had no doubt 'that their kind & liberal Exertions would have been attended with good Success had the Election been fairly conducted'.[11] He also published a ballad entitled *The Organ Laid Open: Or, The True Stop Discovered*,

---

[9] Nichols and Wray, *The History of the Foundling Hospital*; McClure, *Coram's Children*.
[10] Argent, *Recollections of R. J. S. Stevens*, pp. 102–4. For an astringent assessment of Stevens, see Ehrlich, *Music Profession*, pp. 32–5.
[11] *SW to Seward, 16 June 1798.

in which he satirised the election process and the role of Bates in securing the election of Immyns. The words were by Martin Madan, the son of Wesley's godfather, and a friend and drinking-companion of his at this time:

> Come all my brave boys who want organist's places,
> I'll tell you the fun of the thing.
> Curse all your bravuras,
> Your fine 'poggiaturas,
> All the demis and semis you'll bring.
>
> You may strike up (no matter)
> Malbrook, Stoney Batter,
> Or the jig that comes into your pates.
> For let Handel or Worgan
> Go thresh at the organ,
> If you've got the right key with JO B——.
>
> The Foundling's grand organ was lately the gift,
> And all were determined to try;
> Each made his best shift
> With a finger so swift,
> And 'Cock sure of election am I.'
>
> But to give 'em their trimmings
> Up popp'd Master Immyns,
> And quickly decided their fates.
> I can't, it is true,
> Move my fingers like you,
> But I've found out the stop of JO B——.

Subsequent verses, even more scurrilous, in the personae of Immyns, a Foundling Hospital Governor, and Bates himself, were not included in the published version, but survive in one of the manuscript sources. According to the verses ascribed to Immyns:

> I've taught all the Bastards at Cripplegate Church
> The Hundred and Fourth, do ye see.
> And little suspected
> That Jo in his Search
> Would have found a Musician in me.
>
> Then who cares a Damn
> For extempore Sam
> Like Lightning his Fingers may go
> Let him play to his Grannum
> While I touch per Annum
> To the Praise and the Glory of Jo.
>
> When first this Competitor enter'd the List
> In vain all the Pretensions of mine
> Sure the Devil said I
> Has got into his Fist
> As a Legion once enter'd the Swine.

> Such Frolicks and Freaks
> His Fancy bespeaks
> As would turn Jo himself wrong outside
> His fugues then must be
> Greek and Hebrew to me
> Who don't know a chord from a Cow Turd.[12]

Although this squib may have increased Wesley's reputation as a wit and a rebel, it can have done nothing for his chances of success in any subsequent election. One person who certainly shared the joke was Immyns, who was a friend of Wesley's and was as aware as anyone of the absurdity of his appointment. As it happens, he did not last long in the post. In early 1800, as a recently discovered letter from Wesley to Latrobe shows, he was ready to resign, complaining about the low pay and sure that the authorities of the Foundling Hospital were as tired of him as he was of them.[13] In the end he lasted in post for a further year before being dismissed on 1 April 1801 for unpunctuality and slovenly dress. This was not, however, the end of his dealings with the Hospital, and he continued to act on occasion as deputy to his successor, William Russell.

Notwithstanding the move to Finchley and Wesley's budding musical and social life, the situation with Charlotte was no happier. Another crisis in late May 1798 led Wesley and Charlotte once more to contemplate separation as their only way forward. As Wesley later related to Sarah, at their last altercation Charlotte had been 'villainously abusive'. When he had insisted that she should not leave the room until she had heard what he had to say, at the same time holding the door to prevent her leaving, she struck him: 'a sharp Blow in the Face, given properly not, womanlike, with an open Palm, but with a clenched Fist, and sooth to say, it made my Teeth ache for 2 or 3 Minutes'. This, and Charlotte's subsequent unwillingness to apologize for her actions, was too much for Wesley. He was now once again 'coolly and quietly' contemplating how to arrange separate maintenance, and not a little ashamed not to have reached this point before.[14] But for all their determination, and continuing a by now familiar pattern of behaviour, Wesley and Charlotte once more failed to separate. In the late summer of 1798 they moved again, this time to Hornsey Lane, near Highgate. They were to live here for less than a year before moving to Highgate itself, where their second son, John William, was born in late June 1799.

The most significant musical event of early 1799 for Wesley was on 22 February, when his *Ode to St Cecilia* received its premiere, over four years

---

[12] BL, Add. MS 35007, fols 85–93.
[13] SW to Latrobe, 2 Jan. 1800 (Pennsylvania Historical Society), quoted in Kassler and Olleson, 'Some New Samuel Wesley Discoveries'.
[14] SW to Sarah Wesley, 23 May 1798.

after its completion. This was Wesley's first major composition to be publicly performed in London, and was a major breakthrough in his career. The performance was part of the Covent Garden Lenten oratorio season, an annual series of concerts that had begun in Handel's lifetime and exploited the official ban on theatrical performances on Wednesdays and Fridays during Lent.[15] Handel's own oratorio concerts had consisted entirely of his own works, and such was the esteem in which he was held that his music dominated the oratorio concerts that continued after his death, to the extent that few works by other composers were performed. Until the early 1780s, the concerts consisted in the main of performances of entire Handel oratorios, but the 1784 Handel Commemoration and subsequent Handel festivals in 1785, 1786, 1787, 1790, and 1791 introduced programmes of extracts that set the pattern for the repertory of all succeeding oratorio seasons and for provincial music festivals. By the 1790s, the only works to be given in full were the ever-popular *Messiah* (performed at least twice in most seasons), *Acis and Galatea*, *Alexander's Feast*, and *L'Allegro*, together with the Coronation Anthems and Handel's own *Ode to St Cecilia*. The remainder of the concerts consisted of 'Grand Selections' of favourite vocal and choral items, mostly by Handel, lumped together in no particular order and with no great regard for consistency of subject matter or mood.

The oratorio concerts were designed to cater for a different audience than that for such prestigious subscription series as the Concert of Ancient Music. Unlike the latter, which prided itself (and to a large extent sold itself) on its royal and aristocratic patronage and its social exclusiveness, the oratorio concerts were open to all, and tickets were sold for individual concerts. Tickets were far cheaper: at this time from 6s for a place in a box down to 1s for the upper gallery, compared with the half-guinea (10s 6d) that was the usual cost per concert for the Concert of Ancient Music or other subscription series. This was the point of the phrase in newspaper bills advertising oratorios 'at playhouse prices'. And the capacity of Covent Garden, at well over 2,000, dwarfed that of the Concert Room at the King's Theatre, where the Concert of Ancient Music was at this time held. In fact, the oratorio concerts offered a comparatively low-cost opportunity to hear the top performers of the day, in repertory that was in the end not very different from that of the Ancient Concerts. Although Handel dominated the programmes of the oratorio concerts, he was not the only composer to be performed there, and instrumental music by more recent composers was also included. But in choral music he reigned supreme, and the achievement of Wesley in securing a performance of his *Ode to St Cecilia* at Covent Garden in 1799 was therefore remarkable. Unfortunately, almost nothing is known about how it came to be included, the performance, or its reception. All Wesley had to say about it in his *Reminiscences* was that it was 'universally approved and applauded', that the house was

---

[15] For the background to the regulations under which oratorios were mounted, see Sachs, 'The End of the Oratorios'.

'crammed', and that in the same concert he had also played a Handel organ concerto with an extemporized fugue.[16]

Almost all of the music that Wesley composed in the late 1790s was written for very specific private or semi-private contexts or for worship. The one striking exception to this pattern is 'Confitebor tibi, Domine', KO 20, an hour-long setting of Psalm 111 for five vocal soloists, chorus, and orchestra, which he completed on 14 August 1799 and evidently intended from the start for public performance. As with the *Ode to St Cecilia*, we know nothing about the circumstances of its composition, but it seems most likely that Wesley, encouraged by the reception of the *Ode to St Cecilia* earlier in the year, composed it with an eye to performance in the following year's Covent Garden oratorio season, and with substantially the same forces. In this he may have had some agreement or understanding with John Ashley, the manager of the Covent Garden oratorios. But no performance took place, and it may have been edged out by the first performances of Haydn's *Creation*, which took place at the end of the 1800 season.

The composition of the *Confitebor* also brought Wesley into contact once more with the music historian Charles Burney. He and Burney had met at a dinner party earlier in the year, for the first time since Wesley's childhood.[17] Any initial correspondence that may have followed this meeting has been lost, but by the time he had completed the *Confitebor*, Wesley felt that he knew Burney well enough to send the score to him for his opinion. As we know from Wesley's account in his *Reminiscences*, Burney commented that it was on the whole 'an admirable composition in florid Counterpoint and in the best style of Church Music'.[18] Now, in November 1799, Wesley had occasion to write to Burney again, with an enquiry concerning a misprint that he thought he had detected in Burney's discussion of the Greek modes in his *General History of Music*, which he had recently been studying.[19] This was a passage that Burney had written in 1773, on a topic that he had probably never needed to consider since that time. Nonetheless, he gave Wesley's enquiry his full attention, replying by return to say that he would need to look further into the matter, but that it appeared at first sight that Wesley was correct.[20]

The abortive *Confitebor* project notwithstanding, it is clear that by late 1799 Wesley was rapidly, if belatedly at the age of thirty-three, establishing his position in London's professional musical life. 1800 marked a distinct further increase in activity. On 31 March he played an organ voluntary at one of a series of oratorio concerts organized by Barthélemon at Hatton House, Hatton Garden.[21] On 21 April he took part in a concert that marked out his now well-established celebrity as an organist: a performance of Haydn's *Creation*

---

[16] *Reminiscences*, fols 34, 139.
[17] Burney to Latrobe, early Feb. 1799; Latrobe to Burney, 7 Feb. 1799.
[18] *Reminiscences*, fol. 38.
[19] *SW to Burney, 28 Nov. 1799.
[20] Burney to SW, c. 29 Nov. 1799; see also *SW to Burney, 30 Nov. 1799.
[21] *Times*, 27 Mar. 1800.

organized by Salomon at the King's Theatre, hard on the heels of the first two performances in England at Covent Garden on 28 March and 2 April. On this auspicious occasion he also performed one of his own organ concertos, probably the Concerto in D, KO 414, that was to become one of his most enduringly popular and frequently performed compositions.[22]

Wesley and Charlotte remained at Highgate during the remainder of 1800 and 1801, in what appears to have been one of the less turbulent periods of their marriage. In late July 1801, however, Wesley's sister Sarah recorded in a personal memorandum that they were about to separate on account of the affair that Wesley was continuing to conduct with Deane. It is not known whether or not the separation occurred, but Wesley appears to have gone on living at Highgate, spending the occasional night or longer periods at Chesterfield Street and continuing to associate with some of the leading musicians of the day. In a letter of 16 October 1801 to his mother, at the time visiting Brighton, he gave details of a recent music party at his house attended by the singer Miss Richardson, the flautist John George Graeff, the violinist Francis Cramer, the violinist and pianist George Frederick Pinto, and the viola player Johann Wilhelm Moralt, who 'formed the sweetest Harmony consisting principally of Mozart & Haydn's Musick, which of course they performed with the most exquisite Precision & Effect.' He did not, however, record whether or not Charlotte was present on this occasion.[23]

Early in 1802 Wesley and his brother Charles promoted a subscription series of 'Miscellaneous Concerts of Vocal and Instrumental Music' at Hyde's Concert Rooms in Tottenham Street, off Tottenham Court Road, the one-time venue of the Ancient Concerts. Information on the series is sparse: as was usual for subscription series, where advertisements for individual concerts were unnecessary, there was only one press announcement, a week before the first concert, and this did little more than give the dates of concerts and the names of some of the principal performers. There were to be six concerts on alternate Thursdays, starting on 4 February, and finishing, after a break for Easter, on 6 May. Only three vocal soloists were listed: Mrs Dussek, Miss Richardson, and Mr Morelli. Names of some of the principal orchestral players were also given. Tickets, at 3 guineas for the series, were at much the same price as at other subscription series. The Wesleys had assembled a reasonably strong line-up. The best known singer was Giovanni Morelli, the principal bass for the last ten years at the King's Theatre, and thus an artist of known ability and considerable experience. The soprano Sophia Dussek was the wife of the composer and pianist Jan Ladislav Dussek, and the daughter of the singing teacher and music publisher Domenico Corri. She was twenty-six, had performed in London as a singer from 1790 or 1791, most frequently in oratorio concerts, and was closely involved

---

[22] For the first London performances of *The Creation*, see Landon, *Haydn: The Years of 'The Creation'*, pp. 572–7; Temperley, *Haydn, 'The Creation'*, pp. 19–20.

[23] SW to Sarah Gwynne Wesley, 16 Oct. 1801.

with the introduction of Mozart's music to London audiences: she included the duet 'Ah! perdona' from *La clemenza di Tito* in her benefit concert on 23 April 1800, and was one of the soloists in the first London performance of the *Requiem* in 1801. She was also an accomplished harpist and pianist. About Miss Richardson nothing very much is known, although her name appears in advertisements for other concerts around this time, and she was among those attending Wesley's music party the previous October. Also performing in at least one concert, although not included in the press advertisement, was Mrs Cimador, an otherwise unknown soprano who was presumably the wife of the singer and music publisher Giambattista Cimador, and Joseph Stageldoir Peile, a fifteen-year-old pianist. There were some well-known players in the orchestra, from the King's Theatre and elsewhere. The leader, Cesare Bossi, had led the King's Theatre orchestra between 1796 and 1800, and had also written the music for a number of ballets performed there. Also performing were Robert Lindley, the leading cellist of the time and the desk-partner of the celebrated double-bass player Dragonetti, the viola player William Shield, the double-bass player William Boyce (son of the composer), and the bassoonist James Holmes.

But the concerts had some stiff competition, notably from the Vocal Concerts and the Ancient Concerts, the two main subscription series. Directly under the brief advertisement for the Wesleys' concert in *The Times* for 29 January was the much longer preliminary announcement for the forthcoming series of Vocal Concerts, under the direction of Samuel Harrison, Charles Knyvett, and James Bartleman, due to begin on 19 February at Willis's Rooms. The Ancient Concerts were due to start on 3 March, with much the same vocal and instrumental forces, at the King's Theatre. Also in prospect were the oratorio seasons at Covent Garden and Drury Lane, due to start on 5 March and to continue on every Wednesday and Friday in Lent. Meanwhile, there was Italian Opera at the King's Theatre on every Tuesday and on some Thursdays and Saturdays. Salomon had his own series of subscription concerts on Tuesdays, starting on 6 April, and after Easter there were the annual benefit concerts of individual musicians. These rival series were all well established, under experienced management, and could already count to a large extent on their own clienteles. For two novices such as Wesley and his brother Charles to attempt to compete in this crowded market-place was brave, if not downright foolhardy. Wesley, at least, seems to have had misgivings about the series from an early stage. In a letter to Burney, written probably just before the beginning of the series, and with what sounds like a clear presentiment of the disaster that was about to befall them, he expressed his regret that he and Charles had not been able to engage the services of the soprano Elizabeth Billington, who would have 'laid us the golden Eggs; & would have been a *cheap* Bargain at any Price:– but this won't *argufy* now'.[24]

Wesley had good reason to be concerned about the absence of Mrs Billington, as she was the singer whom London audiences in early 1802 were most avid to

[24] *SW to Burney, undated [Feb.–May 1802].

hear, following her return the previous summer after seven years of steadily increasing fame on the Continent.[25] She had begun her career in London, and was still warmly remembered for her performances in English opera at Covent Garden in the late 1780s and early 1790s. Sir Joshua Reynolds had painted her portrait as Saint Cecilia, and later Haydn is said to have remarked to him, 'you have painted her listening to the angels: you should have painted the angels listening to *her* divine voice.'[26] In 1794 she went to Italy, her departure possibly influenced by the publication two years earlier of the anonymous *Memoirs of Mrs Billington*, which contained lurid and very probably false details of her private life. She went first to Naples, where she spent two highly successful years and became a personal friend of Emma Hamilton, before making a triumphant progress round the other major opera houses. She had returned to England the previous summer to a public anxious to hear how she had developed during her time away. The newspapers in July and August had been full of accounts of her signing contracts with both Covent Garden and Drury Lane, and the huge sums – variously put at between £4,000 and £5,000 – she was expected to earn from her performances in the coming season. Now in her mid-thirties,[27] she was at the height of her powers and a singer of international reputation. In the previous autumn she had taken London by storm with her performances in *Artaxerxes* and *The Duenna* at both Covent Garden and Drury Lane, but the main 1802 winter season would mark her return in earnest to the London opera scene. In addition to her continuing engagements in English opera at Covent Garden and Drury Lane, at each of which she was to sing once a week, she would appear at the Ancient Concerts, the Vocal Concerts, and the Covent Garden oratorio series, some of these engagements requiring her to perform twice on the same night. The only area in which she as yet had no engagements was Italian opera, where her reputation now chiefly lay. Engagements at the King's Theatre were for the moment out of the question in view of her obligations to Covent Garden and Drury Lane. Later in the season, however, she would be invited by Brigida Banti, the King's Theatre's reigning *prima donna*, to appear with her in her benefit, and given her own choice of opera. That performance, of Portogallo's *Merope* on 25 March, marked her King's Theatre debut, and set the seal on her success. In succeeding seasons she would appear alongside Banti and eventually supplant her, before being in turn supplanted by Angelica Catalani. Under these circumstances, it was unfortunate but not surprising that the Wesley brothers were not able to engage Billington for their concert series, and it is in any case doubtful whether they could have afforded her fee.

In his letter to Burney, Wesley gave the programme of one of the concerts:

[25] Christiansen, *Prima Donna*, pp. 46–8.
[26] [Stendhal], *Lettres . . . sur le célèbre compositeur Haydn* (Paris, 1814), quoted in Christiansen, *Prima Donna*, p. 47.
[27] There is some uncertainty about her date of birth. The date given in *Baker's Biographical Dictionary of Composers*, a reference work that usually goes to a good deal of trouble to track down elusive dates of birth, particularly for singers, is 27 Dec. 1765.

probably the first of the series. It was a varied selection of modern and older music, orchestral and vocal, intended, like the family concerts of twenty or so years earlier, to showcase the talents of the two brothers. Each half began and ended with an orchestral item: a symphony by Wesley and an organ concerto by Charles in the first part, and a symphony by Mozart and a 'full piece' from the overture to Handel's *Atalanta* in the second. The programme also included a three-part glee by Charles; a song for each of the three vocal soloists (Mrs Dussek accompanied her contribution, an aria by Sarti, on the harp); the duet 'Ah! perdona' from *La clemenza di Tito*, sung by Miss Dussek and Mrs Cimador; a trio for viola, bassoon and cello by Robert Lindley, played by Shield, Holmes, and Lindley; a piano concerto by Dussek, with Peile as soloist; and an organ duet adapted from the final chorus in Handel's *Esther*, performed by Wesley and Charles.

This was attractive programming, but could not compete with the more spectacular offerings elsewhere. Not surprisingly, the series was an expensive failure. The losses might have been smaller had the performers agreed to waive or reduce their fees, but many of them, including Mrs Dussek, who was due £70, insisted on the full amount, and Wesley and Charles were left with a shortfall of around £120 each.[28]

After the subscription concerts had ended, Wesley suffered an extended period of depression that resulted in his complete withdrawal from public performance. Although this was not his first serious attack of depression in adult life, it is the first which is extensively documented in letters, both by Wesley himself and by other family members. On 12 August, Wesley described his condition at length to his sister Sarah. He was 'heartless and hopeless', weighed down with self-reproach and guilt for all his past follies. Everyone who knew his story could not fail to be convinced that he had destroyed himself, and it was only the needs of his two children that kept him from suicide. Further letters, later in August and in September, continued in the same vein. He was now suffering 'paroxysms' which he was thankful that his mother had not witnessed, and on some days his state was so bad that he was almost on the point of cancelling his teaching engagements. He had not been obliged to do so yet, but felt that it was only a matter of time before he did so, as he felt he was often incapable of doing his pupils any good and was finding that teaching only made his condition worse. He was trying as much as possible to conceal his suffering and distress from others, but this was not always possible, particularly in the mornings when he was unable to suppress his groanings and tears.

Although Wesley's depression may have been triggered partly by the failure of the concert series and its financial consequences, it is likely that a more important contributory factor was guilt engendered by his continuing love

---

[28] SW to Sarah Gwynne Wesley and Sarah Wesley, 8 Sept. 1802. See also SW to Charles Wesley jun., 31 May 1811; Charles Wesley jun. to John Langshaw jun., 11 Jan. 1827.

affair with Deane, whom he appears to have been unwilling to give up. One important complicating factor was the effect that the affair had on his relationship with Sarah. Deane had been a particularly close friend and confidante of Sarah's, and Wesley's illicit affair with her brought to an end their long friendship. To have to endure one's closest friend having an adulterous relationship with one's brother would have been a difficult situation for any woman to bear, but for Sarah, who was always particularly possessive and jealous in her friendships, it was intolerable. Following some ill-advised remarks that Wesley made in the course of one of the many arguments that followed, Sarah broke off all contact with him and exiled herself from Chesterfield Street until he recanted. A long period of silence followed that lasted until around April 1802, when Wesley took back his hasty words and apologized. It was an action which did little to ease the situation with Charlotte and Deane, but it did at least have the effect of re-opening communications between Wesley and Sarah and gave him the opportunity once more to pour out his heart to her.

In November, Shepherd also felt impelled to become involved. At this time, Wesley and Charlotte were still living together but were once more actively contemplating separation, and it appears that Wesley had written to Shepherd to inform her of his intention of leaving Charlotte for Deane. If he was hoping for Shepherd's sympathy with his predicament and her blessing on his proposed course of action, he was to be disappointed. Her reply was in particularly forthright terms, even for her. Answering his letter point by point, she was at pains to stress the ruinous consequences of extra-marital relationships, and to remind him of his responsibilities as a husband and father. Her advice was blunt: he should immediately break off the relationship, make his peace with God, and attempt to come to some rational accommodation with Charlotte by which they could live amicably together. Should this not be possible, they should separate, at least for the moment, and a formal maintenance agreement should be drawn up. As for Wesley's dissatisfaction with the music profession and his remark that he found it ill-chosen, she felt that it should not be too irksome for him to follow it as a lawful way of earning his living.[29]

What followed next is unclear. Wesley and Charlotte appear to have separated early in 1803. The Highgate house was given up some time later, probably in May of the same year,[30] and Wesley and Charlotte went their separate ways. Charles appears to have been entrusted to the care of his uncle and aunt, much as he was during the separation in 1795. In time he was sent away to a school at Wateringbury, in Kent; a number of his letters to his grandmother, aunt, and uncle, stiffly and formally phrased and in a careful copperplate hand, survive. The three-year-old John William presumably remained with his mother. There is no record of the movements of Charlotte and Wesley after the move from Highgate. There was some talk of Charlotte moving to Yorkshire, presumably as a governess or school teacher, and an alternative plan that she should find

---

[29] Shepherd to SW, 17 Nov. 1802.
[30] Sarah Gwynne Wesley to Sarah Wesley, 30 Apr. 1803.

employment in a school in St Albans.[31] Meanwhile, Wesley appears to have moved back to Chesterfield Street for a time before going to live elsewhere. Few of his letters survive from this period, but those from other members of his family describe his condition in terms that suggest ongoing serious depression, accompanied with physical ailments and incidents of self-harming.

---

[31] SW to Sarah Wesley, 3 May 1803.

6

Discovering Bach, 1805–1808

In the spring of 1805 Wesley and Charlotte reached a limited rapprochement and started living together again. Their move to a house in Arlington Street (now Arlington Road), Camden Town at around this time probably coincided with or closely followed their reconciliation. With the move came the return home of their son Charles, now aged eleven, from his school in Wateringbury, and his admission in August to St Paul's School, probably with the aid of a personal intervention by Sarah to Dr Richard Roberts, the High Master.[1] The Wesleys were now closer to London than they had been in Finchley or Highgate, although still sufficiently far away for Wesley to be able to state his address to an out-of-town correspondent as 'Camden Town, near London'.[2] Established as recently as 1791, the settlement was less than a mile north of the New Road (now Marylebone Road, Euston Road, and Pentonville Road), the great highway built in 1756–7 as London's northern perimeter road. A later, grimly industrialized stage in its development was described by Dickens, who had lived there as a boy, in *Dombey and Son*. This, however, was after the advent of the railways and the establishment of coal wharves on the as yet unbuilt Regent's Canal. For the moment, Camden Town was still a semi-rural location which combined easy access to London with some of the pleasures of the country. Arlington Street was on its extreme western edge and had been established only very recently. At this stage, it had houses only on its east side, and the Wesleys had open views to Primrose Hill and the fields which a few years later would become Regent's Park.

By this time Wesley was thirty-nine and Charlotte forty-three. It is difficult to tell what lay behind their reconciliation, and to what extent – if at all – it was anything more than an expedient patching up of differences for the sake of the children and for reasons of financial necessity. The birth of a third child, Emma Frances, in February 1806, suggests that at least some of the original strong physical attraction between them remained, despite all the strains put on their relationship over the last few years. Shepherd perhaps accurately summed up its highly-charged and volatile nature when she remarked, just before Charlotte's confinement, that 'by and by they will be quarrelling again, like cats that fight when they cease caterwauling'.[3]

---

[1] F. Roberts (wife of Richard Roberts) to Sarah, 16 Aug. 1805; see also Sarah Wesley to Thomas Maurice, 17 Jan. 1817.
[2] *SW to John Langshaw jun., 26 Dec. 1809.
[3] Shepherd to Sarah Wesley, 15 Jan. 1806.

The years of separation had inevitably taken their toll on Wesley's finances, and the birth of Emma added further to his financial burdens. By now, much of his inheritance from James Price had disappeared, and he could no longer rely on the cushion that his modest investment income had provided in the past. He had his earnings from school teaching, but nothing of any substance from elsewhere, and few other avenues appeared to be open to him. As he had discovered in the past, his chances of an organist's appointment at an Anglican church were adversely affected by his Methodist background and his continuing links with Roman Catholicism, and although there were concert engagements to be had, they were not as regular or as frequent as they would have been if he had been an orchestral player. His financial problems came to a head at the end of March 1806, principally because of an acute shortage of money caused by the non-payment of fees and loans due to him from a number of quarters. Intriguingly, the largest amount due was caused by the death of his former lover Anne Deane in early January. Nothing is known of the outcome of Wesley's affair with her that had precipitated his separation from Charlotte in 1803, although it had presumably come to an end, one way or another, by the time of his reconciliation with Charlotte in the spring of 1805. But he had continued to teach at Deane's school in Paddington, and at her death his account for the previous half-year was still outstanding. It became one of the charges on her estate, and he was told that it was unlikely that it would be paid for at least a year.[4] He also had money owed to him from other sources, including a debt of more than twenty guineas from the parents of one of his pupils at Mrs Barnes's school, £60 from the wealthy landowner and businessman Justinian Casamajor which he had given up as 'eternally lost', and £10 from his friend William Kingston.[5]

Wesley was now faced with two main alternative ways to raise the £100 he needed, neither of them very palatable: he could either sell some of his remaining investments, or borrow on interest. He could also approach friends and acquaintances for a personal loan, but he was not optimistic about his chances of success with anyone he had dealt with in the past. He came to the conclusion that his best course of action would be to realize the money from his investments, which he considered as being 'certainly preferable either to being arrested or even *dunned*, for I had almost as soon be the one as the other'. Faced with these problems, it was clear that some drastic economies would have to be made at home. One of the first casualties would have to be the twelve-year-old Charles's education: he would need to leave St Paul's School, less than a year after going there, and be placed in some trade or profession. Wesley was not in any case satisfied with the teaching Charles had been receiving, commenting that Roberts was 'really almost disqualified for Teaching' and that the master of Charles's form was 'very far from a deep Scholar'.[6] He was relatively indifferent

---

[4] SW to Sarah Gwynne Wesley, 1 Apr. 1806.
[5] Ibid.
[6] SW to Sarah Gwynne Wesley, 21 Apr. 1806.

about the way in which Charles should make his living, but was determined that the matter should not be left to chance, which he claimed had happened in his own case and had led to his present 'total ruin'. He ruled out the three 'learned' professions of the church, medicine, and the law as being impossible without either wealth or powerful patronage, and had a jaundiced view of other professions and trades, agriculture excepted, which he held to be 'truly noble, & innocent, useful & necessary'.[7]

Wesley's financial problems inevitably exacerbated the depression that he was still suffering. He described his state as being that of one 'hating to live, & fearing to die'. He had no chance of regaining any tranquillity in life, and he regarded his mental health as damaged beyond repair. In this black mood, he was inclined to oscillate between self-hatred and blaming others for his situation. Chief among his dissatisfactions was the profession that he found himself in. As on previous occasions, he cursed the day that his father had ever allowed him to be a musician: no-one made any money from music but a few singers, and he considered it to be 'a trivial & a degrading Business to any Man of Spirit or of any Abilities to employ himself more usefully.[8] By late April, his financial situation had further deteriorated, and with it his health. On 14 April he was taken ill at Mrs Barnes's school with sickness and headache, and later in the day was affected by the most severe earache he had ever experienced, which not even a large dose of laudanum was able to alleviate. The subsequent application of an infusion of camomile flowers helped a little, but he still had to spend most of the following week in bed, and was in almost constant pain. He was sure that he would never regain real health, and his happiness and comfort had disappeared long ago.

Wesley's illness had prevented him from making progress in securing a loan and getting to the Bank of England to collect the half-year dividend on his investments. Now down to his last guinea, he was being harassed by threatening letters and daily visits from his creditors. In the end he did what he should have done a good deal earlier, and applied for a loan of £100 on interest. This would only be a temporary measure, however, and would do nothing to solve the basic problem of supporting his family on his present income. He had five people to support: Charlotte, Charles, John, the baby Emma, and a servant. Charlotte, who should be making every effort to economise, was a 'thoughtless, not to say a determined Spendthrift'. His chances of additional income were slim. Even if another school offered him work at the same rate as Oxford House – which he considered unlikely – this would be no help, as he could not bear the drudgery of more teaching. Thus, he concluded, he was left without resource. He would be glad to accept any 'quiet employment' that would pay him £200 per year, but although he had many friends who were ready to offer advice, none were prepared to help him in practical ways. Altogether, he was desperate about the future for himself and his family, and his only scant comfort was that 'all human

---

[7] SW to Sarah Gwynne Wesley, 1 Apr. 1806.
[8] Ibid.

Miseries in this World must have an End', and that the state of his health was such that he could not imagine that his life would last much longer.

The two despairing letters to his mother of April 1806 from which the preceding paragraphs are drawn show Wesley at a particularly low ebb. They are, of course, snapshots, and it should not be assumed that his mental state at the time of writing was his constant one at this time. Clearly, however severe his depression, he was able – at least, when not incapacitated by physical illness – to fulfil his teaching commitments and to carry out the normal business of everyday life. And as we will see later, he was also engaged on a task that was later to have a huge impact on the rest of his life and career: making a copy of J. S. Bach's *Well-tempered Clavier* (the '48').

Notwithstanding what he had previously written to his mother about finding employment for Charles, Wesley in time decided that he should continue with his education, and after removing him from St Paul's School proceeded to teach him at home himself. Charles was a promising classical scholar and a rewarding pupil: less than a year later he provided a translation of a Greek epigram for his father to set to music,[9] and in the following year, doubtless encouraged by him, he wrote to the *Monthly Magazine* to query the interpretation of a passage in Ovid's *Metamorphoses*. In the first weeks after Charles's removal from St Paul's, father and son spent a good deal of time together, and were probably as close emotionally as they ever became. In late May, when his financial problems had been temporarily solved and some of his depression had lifted, Wesley was sufficiently pleased with Charles's progress to propose a day out as a reward, inviting his friend Street to join them. Wesley suggested 4 June, the King's birthday, when they could visit the Tower of London to hear the guns fired (as they were, and still are, at noon on the Sovereign's birthday). They would then go on to the fish market at nearby Billingsgate, where they could have a meal of such fish as remained at that time of day, then stroll over to a tea-garden at Chalk Farm before returning home to an 'unceremonious Crust of Bread & Cheese' at Arlington Street.[10]

By the middle of the year, Wesley had resumed composition after the almost complete silence of the previous three years, and on one day in August wrote two hymn tunes ('He's blest, whose sins have pardon gain'd', KO 131, and 'O Lord my rock, to thee I cry', KO 143) for his friend Matthew Cooke, organist of St George's, Bloomsbury. His health continued to improve, and in mid-January 1807 he was able to declare to his mother that in 'corporal health' he had recovered far more than he ever expected, despite an attack of lumbago brought on by the current frosty weather. Meanwhile, the black depression and hopelessness of the previous year had lifted.[11] In a long letter of the same date to his brother Charles, he further described the improvement in his mental health, in

---

[9] 'Life is a jest', KO 225. SW's autograph and notes that the translation is by 'Charles Wesley junior' (i.e. Charles Wesley III).
[10] *SW to Street, 30 May 1806.
[11] SW to Sarah Gwynne Wesley, 15 Jan. 1807.

consequence of which he was now able 'to bear the Bustle of Society with much less Perturbation of Spirits than heretofore'. The rest of the letter bears this out. From Wesley's exhaustive account of his activities, it is clear that he had resumed the round of private music parties, glee clubs, and professional appearances of the years before his illness. On 18 December he was a visitor at a meeting of the Society of Harmonists, where his glee 'When Bacchus, Jove's Immortal Boy', KO 248, which he had composed in early September, was performed.[12] After dinner, as Stevens recorded, he entertained the company with a keyboard improvisation that contained some of the most astonishing Harmonies that Stevens had ever heard.[13] On Christmas Day, his newly composed Responses to the Litany were to have been sung at St Paul's Cathedral, but Thomas Attwood, the organist, had misread the rubrics: there was no place in the service for the Litany on this occasion, and the performance had to be postponed for the moment. Two days later, he attended a meeting of the Concentores Society at the invitation of the bass James Elliott. This was the occasion of the first performance of Wesley's new three-part setting of the Vesper Psalm 'Dixit Dominus', KO 27, which he had completed on Christmas Day. On 11 January he attended a large music party in Dulwich at the home of the Revd Edward Barry, and on 14 January a lecture by William Crotch at the Royal Institution, in which Crotch had discussed the music of Pleyel, Kozeluch, and Mozart.

The cheerful tone of this eleven-page letter was in strong contrast to the despair of the previous spring. Two months later, however, Wesley was at pains to point out to his brother that despite his activity and apparent good spirits he was still suffering a deeper malaise. He needed to keep himself continually busy as his only defence against insanity, and although he was often obliged to 'bustle about with a crazy Carcase, *as if nothing was the Matter*', often to the point of exhaustion, this was preferable to reflecting on his 'Sacrifice of Peace, Liberty, Honour, & Independence' to Charlotte.[14] Notwithstanding this description of his continuing inner despair, Wesley seemed cheerful enough in his description of his current activities, which included a 'literary business' that he was not at liberty to discuss further. In fact, this was a lengthy review for *The British Critic* of Callcott's *A Musical Grammar*.[15] He also reported wearily on the fate of his Litany Responses, which had been awaiting their first performance at St Paul's since the previous Christmas, and were now scheduled for Easter Sunday. But after so many disappointments, Wesley was by now philosophical about their chances of performance, and would not be at all surprised if it did not happen.[16]

---

[12] *A New Glee, for Three Voices, The Words translated from the 27th Ode of Anacreon . . . by Thomas Moore, Esq Composed, Presented & Performed at the Society of Harmonists, on Thursday Decr 18th, 1806, & respectfully Inscribed to the Translator.*

[13] Argent, *Recollections of R. J. S. Stevens*, p. 150.

[14] *Wesley to Charles Wesley jun., 21 Mar. 1807.

[15] *The British Critic* 29 (1807), pp. 398–407, 597–605. Wesley was later identified as the author of this review by Kollmann in *Quarterly Musical Register* 1 (1812), pp. 5, 129.

[16] *SW to Charles Wesley jun., 21 Mar. 1807.

In the midst of all these financial and emotional troubles of 1806, and maybe at the time almost completely overshadowed by them, was an event which was to change the course of his life and give him a cause on which to concentrate his considerable energies: his discovery of the music of J. S. Bach.

At the beginning of the nineteenth century, Bach's music was still very little known, either on the Continent or in England. Although he had been renowned as an organist, composer and teacher, little of his music was published in his lifetime, and his reputation was largely a local one. Because of changing styles and fashions his music had come to be considered old-fashioned by many, including his son Carl Philipp Emanuel, even in his lifetime, and after his death much of it was completely forgotten. But in some quarters his memory was revered and his music was kept alive. By the 1770s and 1780s there was a modest resurgence of interest in Bach amongst antiquarians and historically-minded musicians. In Vienna, the diplomat, amateur musician, and patron Gottfried van Swieten introduced Bach to Haydn, Mozart, and Beethoven, with discernible effects on their subsequent music. In Berlin, there was a strong group of enthusiasts, led by a number of Bach's former pupils. In Göttingen, the music historian Johann Nikolaus Forkel was working on a study that would be the first biography of him, and indeed the first comprehensive biography of any composer.

Some of this activity was paralleled in England. In 1796 the German-born composer and music theorist A. F. C. Kollmann included an analysis of the F minor fugue from Book 2 of the '48' in his *Essay on Musical Harmony*, and three years later printed the C major Prelude and Fugue from Book 2 and the organ Trio Sonata in E♭ in his *Essay on Practical Musical Composition*, also quoting from other pieces in Book 2 and from the *Chromatic Fantasy and Fugue*, the *Musical Offering*, and the *Art of Fugue*. In 1800, William Shield included the D minor Prelude from Book 1 of the '48' in his *An Introduction to Harmony*. More significantly, Kollmann was also planning to publish a complete edition of the '48'. This would have been the first anywhere, but he was forced to abandon his plans after Forkel reported them in the Leipzig *Allgemeine Musikalische Zeitung*, thus prompting three continental publishers to publish editions of their own in 1801.[17]

It seems likely that someone as well-read and intellectually curious as Wesley would have been aware to at least some extent of the publications of Kollmann and Shield and the examples of Bach's music they contained. Similarly, it is probable that he would have come across one or other of the continental editions of the '48' when copies reached England, probably some time in 1801 or 1802. But there is no evidence that Bach's music made any substantial impact on him at this time, and it was not until around 1805 or early 1806 that his interest started to be aroused. According to his *Reminiscences*, he was first introduced to the '48' by the violinist and composer George Frederick Pinto.[18]

---

[17] Yo Tomita, 'The Dawn of the Bach Movement in England'.
[18] *Reminiscences*, fol. 42.

This must have been some time before 23 March 1806, the date of Pinto's early death at the age of twenty, but there is no mention of this event in Wesley's (admittedly not extensive) correspondence of the period, and the precise date remains unknown. What is certain is that by late May 1806 Wesley had made his own manuscript copy of the '48' from a copy of the Nägeli edition lent to him by his friend Graeff. As Wesley explained to Graeff, the copying had taken a number of months, largely because his other commitments were such that he could only devote odd moments to it. In fact, as we have seen – and as Wesley was perhaps not prepared to admit to Graeff – he had had preoccupations of a personal nature during at least part of this period, and these no doubt also contributed to the delay in completing his transcription.[19]

Having gone to the considerable labour of making a full copy of the '48', Wesley seems for the moment not to have proceeded further with his detailed study of Bach. That, at any rate, is the conclusion to be drawn from the complete absence of references to Bach in Wesley's letters during the remainder of 1806 and all of 1807, including a number to Charles in which it is difficult to imagine him not mentioning a newly-discovered enthusiasm amongst all the other news of his musical activities. In fact, Wesley's interest appears not to have been fully aroused until some time early in 1808. By early April, as we know from a letter to Burney, he knew the '48' well, and considered them 'the highest Stretch of harmonic Intellect, & the noblest Combination of musical Sounds that ever immortalized Genius'.[20] Keen to share his enthusiasm with others, he played individual preludes and fugues to his fellow professionals, to most of whom Bach's music was completely unknown and who were disposed to be prejudiced against it. All, however, were surprised and delighted by what they heard, and showed interest in acquiring copies of their own. From their enthusiastic response Wesley gauged that there might be a market for a new edition of the '48', and his next move was to write to Burney to ask for his advice. As far as can be seen, he and Burney had not been in touch since early 1802, and it was only in March 1808 that he resumed contact. His initial letter, of 22 March, was not concerned with Bach at all, but in the next, of 12 April, he was able to raise the subject at length. After describing his recent study of the '48', how his enthusiasm was shared by all those to whom he had played them, and how copies of them had become scarce and almost unattainable, he turned to his plans for a new edition, to be edited by him, and asked Burney for his advice and opinion.

As Wesley immediately saw, the only way in which he could contemplate publication of the '48' was by subscription, the usual method for major projects for which large sales could not be predicted with confidence. By issuing a prospectus and inviting subscriptions, he would risk little. If sufficient subscriptions were received, he could proceed to publication, paying his engraver and printer with the money received. If insufficient subscriptions materialized,

---

[19] *SW to Graeff, 21 May [?1806].
[20] *SW to Burney, 12 Apr. [1808].

he could abandon the project with no expenses except those incurred in printing the prospectus and in any associated press advertising. This was a procedure of which Burney had extensive experience. He had published his own *General History of Music* in this way, and although he had in the past remarked to Wesley that subscriptions were 'troublesome things',[21] in this case there were no other means available.

In his letter of 12 April Wesley pointedly remarked on the prejudices of his fellow professionals that led them to find Bach's music '*dry, harsh, & unmelodious*'. This was more than a little mischievous, as Wesley knew well that much of this prejudice stemmed from the writings of Burney himself. In one place in his *General History of Music*, for example, Burney had criticized both Bach and his son Carl Philipp Emanuel for the complexity of their music, remarking that if they had written for the public or the stage in one the great capitals of Europe, their music would have been a good deal more intelligible.[22] Elsewhere in the *History*, Burney had compared Bach unfavourably to Handel as a composer of fugues, stating:

> Handel was perhaps the only great Fughist, exempt from pedantry. He seldom treated barren or crude subjects; his themes being almost always natural and pleasing. Sebastian Bach, on the contrary, like Michael Angelo in painting, disdained facility so much, that his genius never stooped to the easy and graceful. I never have seen a fugue by this learned and powerful author upon a *motivo* that is natural and *chantant*; or even an easy and obvious passage, that is not loaded with crude and difficult accompaniments.[23]

In his letter, Wesley suggested that Burney shared his high opinion of Bach, knowing full well that this was not the case. Burney was understandably reluctant to concur with Wesley's opinion, saying evasively that in order to be consistent with himself and before he could 'precisely coincide' with Wesley's view, he would need to refer to what he had written on Bach at various times. All the same, he would be very glad for Wesley to visit him and play Bach to him, especially as – and this was a surprising revelation – he had never heard any of his music. Furthermore, he owned a 'very curious & beautiful' copy of the '48' that he had been given by Bach's son Carl Philipp Emanuel when he visited him in Hamburg in 1772, and he would be delighted to show it to Wesley. This was an enticing prospect, and Wesley would have made his way to Burney's apartments at Chelsea with considerable excitement and anticipation. Once there, however, he discovered that the manuscript was full of errors, to the extent that he had great difficulty in playing from it even those fugues that he thought he knew best.[24] Nonetheless, Burney expressed his delight with what he heard and his wonder at 'how such abstruse Harmony & such perfect & enchanting Melody could have been so marvellously united.' Wesley's playing

---

[21] Ibid.
[22] Burney, *History*, vol. 4, pp. 594–5; Mercer, vol. 2, pp. 954–5.
[23] Burney, *History*, vol. 3, p. 110; Mercer, vol. 2, p. 96.
[24] *SW to Jacob, 17 Sept. 1808.

on this occasion thus resulted in Burney completely revising his former opinions of Bach and also made it clear to Wesley that they had been falsely based. Burney's comparison between Bach and Handel in the *History* had resulted from his failure to acquaint himself sufficiently with Bach's music, and the episode at Burney's apartments was proof that Burney only needed experience of the truth to make him ready to acknowledge it.[25] To have persuaded someone of Burney's great age and eminence to have retracted views so trenchantly and publicly expressed was no mean feat, and Wesley was understandably exultant. Following his 'conversion' of Burney – the term is Wesley's own, and typical of the religious imagery he used in discussing his promotion of Bach – his enthusiasm for Bach continued to grow. Now that he had Burney actively on his side, he began to consult him repeatedly for advice on how best to proceed.

Although much of Wesley's correspondence with Burney in April and May 1808 was concerned with his plans for the promotion of Bach, it was another matter that had been the occasion of his first letter: the wish of his friend William Linley to be introduced to Burney. Linley was a member of a large and highly distinguished musical family. His father Thomas Linley senior had been the principal music teacher in Bath from the mid-1750s to the mid-1770s, and had been sufficiently successful to have been able to buy one of the large and imposing houses in Royal Crescent, Bath's most fashionable address. His brother Thomas Linley junior was an exceptionally gifted and prolific composer who had drowned in a boating accident at the age of twenty-two in 1778. Another brother, Ozias, was a canon at Norwich Cathedral. But what would have raised Burney's interest most was his sister Elizabeth, who before her marriage in 1773 to the playwright and MP Richard Brinsley Sheridan had had a short but brilliant career as a singer, and had come to know Burney well. After her marriage she had given up her public career, but continued for a while to sing at private concerts, sometimes accompanied by Burney. She had died of tuberculosis at the age of thirty-seven in 1792. Burney had been exceptionally fond of her, commenting to Wesley that 'that most charming and accomplished of female beings I adored, and regarded her as an angel, in correctness and form, conversation and voice, indeed I c^d neither look at her nor listen to her divine breathings, but with extatic rapture'.[26] Burney would have remembered, too, the occasion when she had taken the principal soprano part in a performance of his Mus.D. exercise 'I will love thee, O Lord, my strength' in Oxford in 1772. He had not realized that she had a brother living, and looked forward to making his acquaintance.

Quite apart from being the brother of a singer whom Burney remembered with such affection and tenderness, Linley was a man of considerable interest in his own right. Born in 1771, he had been educated at Harrow and St Paul's School and was a pupil of Abel. In early adulthood he joined the East India

---

[25] *SW to Jacob, 17 Sept. 1808
[26] Burney to SW, 23 Mar. 1808.

Company, and lived in India from 1790 to 1795 and from 1800 to 1807. Between these two extended tours of duty he was in London, for some of the time sharing the management of Drury Lane Theatre with his brother-in-law and composing two unsuccessful operas. He returned from his second tour of duty having made sufficient money to be able to live as a gentleman amateur man of letters and composer. He wrote two novels, several sets of songs, and some elegies and glees. His most important publication was a two-volume anthology of Shakespeare settings by himself and others, published in 1816.[27] On receiving Burney's gracious reply to his initial letter, Wesley sent it to Linley, who read the remarks about his sister to his mother, who was charmed with the 'delicate & affectionate Panegyric' that Burney had bestowed on her late daughter.[28] Burney later invited Wesley to arrange a day and time for his visit with Linley, at the same time suggesting that if Wesley also wanted the opportunity to discuss Bach with him without Linley present he should arrange an additional time. Although no details have survived, there seems little doubt that the requested meeting between Linley and Burney took place, some time in the week beginning 19 April.

When Wesley first wrote to Burney about Bach, he was intending to proceed immediately with issuing proposals for his new edition of the '48', but Burney thought this premature and ill-advised. Wesley would do better to wait until he had had time to increase public awareness of the '48', and of Bach's music generally, by performances and lectures: sound advice, and a necessary brake on Wesley's impetuousness. Notwithstanding the encouraging response that Wesley had experienced from his fellow professionals, Bach's music was still known to comparatively few people. If Wesley were to announce a new edition of the '48' at this early stage he would almost certainly fail to receive enough subscriptions to proceed. Consequently, he should now concentrate on promoting Bach by any means at his disposal, and only then, having 'played and lectured the work into favour',[29] should he announce his intended edition to a receptive public.

The first, and easiest, way for Wesley to stimulate interest was to include Bach in his public performances, which indeed he had already started to do. Salomon was present at one such occasion – probably an organ recital that Wesley gave on 15 March at Surrey Chapel[30] – and was delighted by Wesley's playing, commenting that although he had heard Bach played by some of the finest organists in Germany, he had never heard anyone produce so smooth an effect. He regretted that Bach's music was not known in England, where everyone pretended to be musical, and suggested that if Wesley were to organize a morning concert in a large room with a good organ, charge 7s for tickets, and play some Bach fugues interspersed with his own voluntaries, he would make a

---

[27] *New Grove*, s.v. 'Linley (6)'; *DNB*.
[28] *Wesley to Burney, 12 Apr. [1808].
[29] Burney to SW, [c. 13 Apr. 1808], quoted in *LSW*, p. 61, n. 9.
[30] See Argent, *Recollections of R. J. S. Stevens*, p. 156.

profit.[31] Doubting the effectiveness of promoting Bach by performance alone, Wesley also consulted Burney on the timing of a lecture course: whether he should organize one now, despite the late state of the season, or wait until the following year. On this, Burney was unequivocal in his reply: Wesley should leave the lecturing to one side until the following season, when Burney was sure that he would be invited by the Royal Institution of Great Britain, and where he would follow on from Crotch and Callcott and show that he was 'not only a great Musician but a Scholar & a man of letters'.[32]

Once more, Burney's advice was sound. By now, some time in late April or May, the season was near its end, and a hastily organized lecture course would be unlikely to attract a large audience. An invitation to lecture at the Royal Institution the following season, however, would be another matter. This prestigious organization had been founded in 1799 with the aim, as one of its first prospectuses proclaimed, of 'diffusing the knowledge and facilitating the general introduction of useful mechanical inventions and improvements, and for teaching by courses of philosophical lectures and experiments the application of science to the common purposes of life'. As one of its first actions it built the handsome building in Albemarle Street that it still occupies today, complete with laboratories, workshops, reading rooms, a library, and a large lecture theatre. By 1804 the Institution's specialized lectures on science had begun to be augmented by a programme of courses covering a wider range of subjects and aimed at a fashionable lay audience, with the aim of increasing the Institution's subscriber base and generating additional income to support its primary activities. The 1804 programme included a highly successful course on moral philosophy by the Revd Sydney Smith, and courses on history, physiology, botany, painting, and engraving by other well-known speakers. The first course on music was given early the following year by Crotch, by now Professor of Music at Oxford University, followed by a further five courses by him in 1806 and two more in 1807. In 1807 Callcott was also engaged to lecture, and gave one course and part of a second before a breakdown in his health forced him to abandon it. In lecturing at the Royal Institution, Wesley would reach a large and influential audience who would be certain to spread the news about Bach far and wide. In addition, his Royal Institution lectures would probably lead to invitations from one or more of the many similar philosophical and literary institutions that had recently been founded in London in emulation of it.

If issuing proposals for publication or organizing lectures in April or May 1808 was ill-advised, there could be nothing but advantage for Wesley to take immediate steps to promote the sort of concert that Salomon had suggested, and he proceeded to book the Hanover Square Rooms for 11 June. This was very late in the season, but probably the earliest date that could be fitted in at short notice. It was the first concert that Wesley had promoted since the disastrous series at the Tottenham Street Rooms in 1802 and marked an

---

[31] *SW to Burney, [mid-Apr.–mid-May 1808] (fragment).
[32] Burney to Wesley, [mid-Apr.–mid-May 1808].

important point in his career as a performing musician, showing to the public and to his fellow professionals that he now once more considered himself a force to be reckoned with. His concert was of the type known as a benefit: a term which denoted a concert organized by one or more musicians in order to display their talents, to assert their position in the profession, and perhaps to make a modest profit on ticket sales, although that was not the primary object of the exercise. Wesley's concert differed, remarkably, from most other benefits in two important ways: first, by being a solo recital instead of involving a number of musicians, and second, by being built not around his own music and personality but that of Bach. As the finest organist in England and an inspired improviser, Wesley could expect to draw a good audience for his first solo recital in central London, but his main purpose here was to promote the Bach cause.

No details of the programme have survived. The press advertisement promised that Wesley would 'perform on the Organ . . . several admired compositions of the celebrated Sebastian Bach, together with several extemporaneous voluntaries'.[33] The Bach pieces would have been preludes and fugues from the '48', carefully chosen to demonstrate Bach at his most approachable and immediately attractive, and to counter accusations of difficulty, abstruseness, and lack of melody first made in print by Burney and endlessly repeated by Bach's detractors. Although the press advertisements promised only improvised voluntaries by Wesley, it is probable that he would also have taken the opportunity to play one or more of his published organ works: possibly one or more of the Op. 6 voluntaries, which had been appearing singly at intervals since 1802, and of which eight had been published by this time.

Although no critical reaction to the concert is recorded, it evidently had the desired effect of stimulating interest in Bach's music. On 23 June Wesley wrote to Burney to recount an anecdote told to him by the pianist and organist George Griffin, who had been approached by an aristocratic lady pupil with an urgent request for the loan of a copy of the '48', as there were none to be had in the music shops. After a great deal of heart-searching, Griffin had refused, on the grounds that his copy was so precious to him that he never let it out of his possession. Wesley was naturally delighted at the interest that his recital had engendered, writing to Burney to inform him that his prophecy that Bach's music might be 'played into fashion' had been fulfilled, and that although he had given only one concert, it had 'electrified the Town'.[34] A few days later, Wesley wrote to Burney again. In addition to informing him that Griffin's pupil was in fact Lady Chambers, the widow of the architect Sir William Chambers, he took the opportunity to let him know that on the previous night he had been raised to the rank of Master Mason, the third and highest rank of Craft Masonry, at the Somerset House lodge. His renewed involvement with Freemasonry, for the first time since his early twenties, in fact dated back to earlier

---

[33] *MC*, 7 June 1808.
[34] *SW to Burney, 23 June 1808.

in the year, when he was admitted to the lodge. Like the Lodge of Antiquity, to which he originally belonged, the Somerset House Lodge had strong musical traditions and many professional musicians among its membership. Wesley would have known many, if not most, of these musician members already. But his membership also provided him with a number of useful contacts in areas outside the musical world. An examination of the lodge records reveals the names of many men who later became Wesley's friends and acquaintances, and whom he probably first met at the lodge. Foremost among them was the wealthy architect and antiquarian Joseph Gwilt, who with his brother George was for some years a member of Wesley's social and musical circle, and involved in many of his activities.

With his benefit concert behind him and the school term ended, Wesley was free to leave London. In late June 1808 he went to Cambridge, which he had not visited for around twenty years. His friend William Carnaby was about to receive his D.Mus. degree, and Carnaby and Charles Hague, the Professor of Music, had invited him to attend and participate in the Commencement ceremonies, to be marked as usual by a music festival. Wesley had known Carnaby for a long time and thought highly of him: after a music party that they had both attended in January 1807, he commented to his brother Charles on his intelligence as a musician and described his vocal compositions performed on this occasion as 'highly finished, & extremely delightful'.[35] The Commencement opened on Thursday 30 June with a service at the University church of St Mary the Great that included contributions from Carnaby and Wesley. In the evening there was a concert in the Town Hall. The following morning there was a concert at Addenbrooke's Hall that included selections from *Messiah* and *Creation*, the choruses of which were conducted by Wesley, and in the evening another concert at the Town Hall. Carnaby's doctoral exercise, described by Wesley as 'a very pretty and correct anthem', was performed after the service at Great St Mary's on the following Sunday by a group of singers led by Thomas and Elizabeth Vaughan and Robert Leete.[36]

Wesley thoroughly enjoyed his visit to Cambridge, subsequently remarking to Burney on its beauty and the magnificence of its buildings. He had been charmed by the elder graduates and the 'venerable masters' he had met, and stated to Burney that he had 'never quitted any Sejour, even in the happy Days of Childhood, with more Regret'.[37] He had been much in demand by those who wanted to hear him play the organ. Once again, he had taken every opportunity to play Bach, both on the organ and on the piano at evening glee parties, and was particularly gratified to see how attentive his audience were. Between items, some of them would sit down and try a few bars for themselves. On becoming 'set fast', they would exclaim that if they had a copy of their own they could

---

[35] *SW to Charles Wesley jun., 15 Jan. 1807.
[36] *SW to Burney, 7 July 1808; *Cambridge Chronicle and Journal*, 25 June, 2 and 9 July 1808.
[37] Ibid.

practise them daily, and that they had been mistaken in thinking that Handel's fugues were not only the best but the hardest in the world.[38] He returned to London in early July, well satisfied with the progress he had made in promoting Bach. In the space of only a few months, he had already done much to publicize the music by playing it in concerts and private music parties. His benefit had been a success, and there were encouraging signs of growing public interest. All of this he could turn to his professional and financial advantage by the publication of an edition of the '48'. But there was still much more promotion for him to do in the forthcoming season before he could proceed further on this front: more performances, perhaps another benefit, and – if Burney's reading of the situation was correct – the prospect of a course of lectures at the Royal Institution. Eventually, the time would be ripe for him to announce his forthcoming edition.

Wesley was not the only musician in London to be promoting Bach's music at this time. In 1806, Kollmann published an edition of the *Chromatic Fantasia*,[39] and in the spring or early summer of 1807, Charles Frederick Horn an arrangement of twelve fugues, from the '48' and elsewhere, for string quartet.[40] In addition, Bach's music was being discussed and played by Crotch and Callcott at their lectures at the Royal Institution.[41] Little of this activity is reported in Wesley's letters of the spring and summer 1808, however, and it appears that he was at this time working on his own. Later in the year, however, it is clear that he made contact with other Bach enthusiasts and started to work with them. From around July or August 1808 his principal collaborator was Benjamin Jacob, the organist of Surrey Chapel.[42] From now to the end of 1809 they would be in frequent contact, their activities in promoting Bach chronicled in a series of letters from Wesley to Jacob – none in the opposite direction have survived – that give a uniquely personal and idiosyncratic view of the English Bach movement at a crucial stage in its history. Jacob was thirty, and had been since 1794 the organist of Surrey Chapel in Great Surrey Street (now Blackfriars Road), an independent chapel where the minister was the Revd. Rowland Hill. As far as can be seen, the earliest surviving letter from Wesley to Jacob, of 13 August 1808, dates from near the beginning of their correspondence, and marks Wesley's first move to join forces with Jacob and others in promoting Bach's music. Wesley stated his view

---

[38] Ibid.
[39] *J. S. Bach's celebrated Fantasia Chromatica for the Pianoforte. With some additions by A. F. C. Kollmann* (1806).
[40] *A Sett of twelve Fugues composed for the Organ by Sebastian Bach . . . arranged as Quartettos for two violins, tenor, and bass, with the addition of a Pianoforte part, or Thorough Bass* (1807). The Preface is dated 1 May 1807.
[41] Crotch included a fugue by Bach in his *Specimens*. On 14 January 1808 Callcott had played a fugue by Bach on the piano at one of his Royal Institution lectures (Argent, *Recollections of R. J. S. Stevens*, p. 155.
[42] Jacob appears to have signed himself as 'Jacobs' at the beginning of his correspondence with SW, but to have later changed his name to 'Jacob'.

that Bach's music was having the sort of effect that would soon lead to it becoming a 'party business', and proposed the formation of a society to promote it and defend it from attacks:

> I can think of nothing more expedient than the Formation of a Junto among ourselves, composed of characters who sincerely & *conscientiously* admit & adhere to the superior Excellence of the great musical High Priest; & who will bend their Minds to a zealous Promotion of advancing the Cause of Truth & Perfection.– Such a society would *at least* produce one happy Effect, that of rendering *thoroughly* public what as yet is but partially so.– I look upon the State of Music in this Country to be very similar to the State of the Roman Church when the flagrant Abuses & Enormities had arisen to such a Height as to *extort* a Reformation.– We know what Wonders were wrought by the Resolution & Perseverance of a single Friar, & that Martin Luther, having *Truth* for his firm Foundation (for this was the Reason of his Success) managed in a very short Time to shake the whole Fabric of Ignorance & Superstition, although sanctioned by the Precedence of many former Ages, & enforced by the most despotic Authority both ecclesiastical & civil.
>
> It is high Time that *some* Amendment should take place in the Republic of Musick, & I know of no Engine equally powerful with the immortal & adamantine Pillars of Sebastian's Harmony.– I really think that our constant & unremitted Question to *all* who call themselves Friends to Excellence should be 'Who is on our Side, who'?– And I have but little Doubt that by the Establishment of a *regular Society* in Defence of the Truth, we should e'er long reap some good Fruits of our laudable Endeavours.–
>
> I really think that all those who have the Courage to speak out in Defence of the greatest of all Harmonists ought to coalesce & amalgamate in a Mode which should render their cordial Sentiments & Judgement *unequivocal* in the Face of the World, & that we ought to stigmatize such Hypocrites as affect to be enchanted with Sebastian on one Day, & on the next, endeavour to depreciate & vilify him.

The excitable and hyperbolic language of this letter is characteristic of all Wesley's writing to Jacob about Bach. But when one looks behind the extravagant expression, it is clear that Wesley was proposing something very specific and down-to-earth: a pooling of interests to focus the energies and activities of all those currently involved in promoting Bach's music. The letter also tells us a great deal about how Wesley conceived the cultural politics of the situation. In his letters to Burney earlier in the year, Wesley had stressed the enthusiasm with which his performances had been received; now, he turned his attention to the resistance the Bach crusade was encountering. Earlier in the letter he had deftly identified three sources of opposition: the reactionary 'ancient music' camp, who saw any promotion of Bach as being a threat to their veneration of Handel; the lovers of modern music, who would no doubt consider Bach's music to be old-fashioned, along with that of Handel; and a third category consisting of music lovers who preferred light and popular pieces. It is evident from Wesley's remark that it was 'high Time that *some* Amendment should take place in the Republic of Musick' that he hoped that the introduction of Bach's music would challenge these entrenched positions and bring nothing less than a full-scale revolution in public taste.

One of Wesley's first ventures with Jacob was a public demonstration of a new design of organ by the builder Thomas Elliot incorporating a newly patented mechanism by William Hawkes which – it was claimed – greatly improved the intonation of keyboard instruments.[43] This was an attempt to solve a perennial problem in their tuning, inherent in the physics of sound and the construction of western musical scales. In the system of temperament in general use at this time, keyboard instruments were tuned so that the most commonly used keys (with key signatures of up to three sharps and flats) were comparatively well in tune. The less commonly used keys were correspondingly less well in tune, however, and the most remote keys so out of tune as to be almost unusable. Over the years there had been a variety of attempts to solve the problems of keyboard temperament, particularly on organs. One way was to provide additional pitches, allowing (for example) the organist to select either D♯ or E♭, or F♯ or G♭, according to the context. But such solutions tended to involve split keys or other devices and could be cumbersome and difficult to use. Another solution was equal temperament, the system which triumphed in the end and is now in general use for keyboard instruments, in which all keys are rendered equally in (or out of) tune. But it did not have widespread support at this time, and experiments with temperament tended to be concerned with systems that gave better results in some keys than were possible with equal temperament.

The basis of the Hawkes mechanism was the provision of additional pitches for each of the short or 'black' keys, controlled by a pedal which selected either one combination of pitches or another, depending on the key of the piece. It used a normal keyboard, and this and its claimed simplicity of operation were its principal selling points. There were seventeen pipes to each octave: one for each of the seven 'white' notes, and two each for the five 'black' notes, providing separate pipes for C♯ and D♭, D♯ and E♭, and so on. The selection of pipes was controlled by the pedal, by which the player engaged one or other of two alternative sets of pipes, one consisting of the white notes plus all the flats (the 'flat scale'), the other of all the white notes plus all the sharps (the 'sharp scale'). Spectacular improvements in intonation were claimed, particularly in the less frequently used keys. If the Hawkes system was as effective and as simple in operation as was claimed, there would be potentially large sales for organ builders – and also piano makers, for Hawkes had patented a similar system for use in pianos – who incorporated it in their instruments.

Given their prominence as organists and their current promotion of Bach's

---

[43] For Hawkes, see Kassler, *Science of Music*, pp. 479–83. For Wesley's relationship with Elliot and further details of the Hawkes-Elliot organ, see my 'The Organ-builder and the Organist: Thomas Elliot and Samuel Wesley' and '"The Perfection of Harmony Itself": The William Hawkes Patent Organ and its Temperament'.

music, it was not surprising that Wesley and Jacob were involved in the demonstration of the organ. Clearly, an instrument which improved intonation in the less frequently used keys would be of great value in playing the '48', which contained preludes and fugues in all keys, major and minor. According to a report of the demonstration, almost certainly written by Hawkes and Elliot themselves, in the *Monthly Magazine* for September 1808, Wesley and Jacob had played some fugues by J. S. Bach and some extempore pieces, and those present had been unanimous in thinking 'that a more valuable discovery had never been made for the improvement of musical science, as it will substitute perfection for imperfection, and pure harmony for harsh discord.'[44]

Wesley's friendship with Jacob and the work of the Bach 'junto' continued at a high pitch of intensity through the remainder of 1808 and into 1809. On 17 September, in response to a 'full & circumstantial account' of his study of Bach from Jacob, Wesley replied with an equally full account of his own experiences, and in particular, the occasion earlier in the year when Burney had shown him the copy of the '48' given to him by Carl Philipp Emanuel. This appears to have been prompted by Jacob's quotation of some of Burney's disparaging comments on Bach – perhaps an extract from his article on Bach in Rees's *Cyclopaedia*, which Wesley had evidently not seen before. Wesley was able to assure Jacob that Burney's judgement of Bach was now very different from when he had 'imprudently, incautiously, and we may add, *ignorantly* pronounced so rash & false a verdict'. The credit for the change belonged, of course, to Wesley. A month later, Wesley was able to report to Jacob on a new member of the group: Charles Frederick Horn, a German-born musician who had come to England in 1782 and had become the music teacher of Queen Charlotte and one or more of the royal princesses. Perhaps through his contacts in Germany, or through court connections, he possessed 'vast quantities' of music by Bach that had never been published, including 'centuries of pages' that he had copied himself. These included the whole of the '48', which he had written out on specially large paper ruled in such a way as to obviate the necessity of page turns, and the six Trio Sonatas for organ, BWV 525–30.[45] He already had well-developed plans for the promotion of Bach, and his ultimate goal was to publish a complete edition of all Bach's music that could be found. As Wesley explained to Jacob, he had been 'longing to find some spirited enthusiast like himself, to co-operate in bringing the musical World to Reason & Common Sense, & to extort a Confession of the true State of the Case against the Prepossession, Prejudice, Envy, & Ignorance of all *anti-Bachists*'.[46] In Wesley he had found his man, and he and Horn soon decided to collaborate. Their first plan was to publish by subscription an English translation of Forkel's *Über Johann Sebastian*

---

[44] *MM* 26 (1808), pp. 151–2. The report appeared in the 'Varieties, Literary and Philosophical' section, for which contributions from readers were actively solicited.
[45] *SW to Jacob, 17 Oct. 1808.
[46] Ibid.

Bachs Leben, Kunst, und Kunstwerke, published in Leipzig in 1802, as a preparatory measure to publishing the '48'. The translation was to be by Edward Stephenson, a banker and amateur musician who was a neighbour and long-standing friend of Horn and the godfather of Horn's son Charles Edward.[47]

One important theme running through Wesley's letters to Jacob in 1808 and 1809 is the strong opposition to Bach's music encountered from Handel enthusiasts, who were unprepared to admit that Bach could be considered as a composer of equal stature to their idol. Of the three categories of music lovers enumerated by Wesley in his letter of 13 August, it was the Handelians that he mentioned first, and it was their conversion that he saw as his greatest challenge. It was for this reason that he was so delighted with his meeting with Burney earlier in the year, and the change of heart that it had brought about. One of those he had in his sights was 'Gaffer' Stevens, whom he regarded as one of those who 'ought to know & do better, [but who] give a Decision hap-Hazard upon sundry Matters which they have never duly considered.'[48] Two others were George Ebenezer Williams, the deputy organist of Westminster Abbey, and John Stafford Smith, the Master of the Children at the Chapel Royal, whom he later described to Jacob as two 'pigmy puerile Puppies'.[49] Rather closer to home was Wesley's brother Charles, who had retained his early love of Handel and was generally extremely conservative in taste and in his own music. He remained a keyboard player of exceptional abilities, and was particularly renowned for his playing of Handel: as Wesley reported to Jacob, Kelway considered that he played it 'in a vastly superior Manner even to Handel himself'.[50] Although he did not pursue a career as a performer and generally kept a low profile, Charles's prowess as a keyboard player was well known, and his views were influential. To Wesley he represented the Handelian camp at its most conservative and inflexible, and for this and for personal reasons his conversion presented a particular challenge. On the likelihood of this happening, however, Wesley was not optimistic. Some time in early November Charles and Jacob had spent some hours playing the organ together, Jacob playing Bach and Charles playing Handel, in an attempt to compare and contrast the styles and merits of the two composers. On this occasion Charles had professed his enthusiasm for Bach, but Wesley was suspicious of the 'Sincerity of sudden Conversions', and suspected that in the company of other Handelians he would readily 'relapse into blasphemy'.[51]

Notwithstanding Wesley's frank criticisms of Charles in letters such as these, the two brothers were at this time on good terms and in regular contact. It is from a letter to Charles of 28 October, for example, that we know of Wesley's

[47] *New Grove*, s.v. 'Stephenson, Edward'.
[48] *SW to Jacob, 19 Oct. [1808].
[49] *SW to [Jacob], [?30 Sept. 1809]
[50] *SW to Jacob, [?17 Nov. 1808].
[51] Ibid.

participation on this date in a 'musical meeting' at the Portuguese Embassy Chapel.[52] This was probably to mark the re-opening of the organ after a recent major rebuild by George Pike England. The original organ was a one-manual instrument of eight stops by Abraham Jordan presumably dating from around 1747, when the Chapel opened in its current location at South Audley Street and South Street.[53] To this England had added extra stops to the Great, and completely new Swell and Choir divisions. The result was a large and substantially new three-manual instrument.[54] According to Wesley, the work had cost £400, and the enlarged organ was 'a most sublime one'.[55] That the authorities of the Portuguese Embassy should have been prepared to incur this amount of expenditure at this time is telling evidence of the importance they attached to the role of music in their services, and the support they gave to Novello as organist and choirmaster.

No records of the programme of the concert have survived, but it was no doubt intended to display the new organ, with solos by both Wesley and Novello, duets by the two of them together, and choral items. Some of Wesley's own compositions may have been performed: perhaps the large-scale settings of 'Dixit Dominus' and 'Exultate Deo' from 1799 and 1800, which would have shown off the choir to its best advantage. And it may have been for this occasion that Wesley composed his exuberant setting of 'Domine, salvam fac reginam nostram Mariam' with its virtuoso organ part. The concert would also have been another opportunity for Wesley to play Bach's music in public, thus continuing the process of public education that he had begun earlier in the year. He would have included preludes and fugues from the '48', and perhaps also some of the Trio Sonatas. If so, Wesley and Novello would have played them as organ duets on the three manuals, one player taking one treble part on one manual, the other the second treble part and the bass on the other two. This would have been a particularly effective demonstration of the capabilities of the organ and the new tonal possibilities opened up by its recent enlargement.

At the same time as informing Charles of the concert at the Portuguese Embassy chapel, Wesley invited him to St Paul's Cathedral to hear his new settings of the Te Deum and Jubilate (the canticles appointed to be sung at Matins, which together make up a morning service), which were to be sung on the following Sunday, along with his 1806 setting of the Litany Responses. Little is known about the circumstances of composition of these works. They were no doubt written at the invitation of Attwood, the organist of St Paul's, who would have been looking for a new setting of the morning canticles to supplement the existing repertoire and his own Service in F, which he had written in 1796, the year of his appointment. The invitation to compose a morning service for St Paul's might appear to have been a singular honour, notwithstanding Wesley's

---

[52] SW to Charles Wesley jun., 28 Oct. 1808.
[53] Olleson, 'The London Roman Catholic Embassy Chapels'.
[54] Boeringer, *Organa Britannica*, vol. 3, pp. 253–4.
[55] *SW to Charles Wesley jun., 28 Oct. 1808.

friendship with Attwood. But in fact the music there was not of a particularly high standard at this time, and little attention would probably have been paid to the event. Neither was the post of organist at St Paul's one of great importance or prestige, and Attwood's appointment in 1796 had not excited a great deal of attention. As far as Attwood himself was concerned, it was a second-best, as he only applied for the St Paul's post after failing to be appointed to the more lucrative position at the Charterhouse earlier in the year.[56] His duties as organist were not onerous, and he appears to have spent more time during the early years of his tenure pursuing his career as a theatre musician than at St Paul's.

In late November 1808, just as Burney had predicted, Wesley was invited by the Royal Institution to deliver a course of lectures early in the following year.[57] This was to be Wesley's first experience of lecturing, and it was natural for him to turn once more to Burney for advice. Anxious to have his lectures ready in good time, he wrote to Burney on 6 December with proposed titles for the first two: 'On the Power of musical Prejudice' and 'On the Power of Musick upon Morals'. At the same time he requested Burney's views on what would be 'the most taking style' for his first lecture, stating that his aim was 'to endeavour to dispel a few of the Clouds of Partiality & Prejudice which certainly have too long overshadowed *Apollo* in this Country'.[58] This was the beginning of a long stream of similar enquiries. Two weeks later, Wesley was beginning to express his anxieties about his lack of experience as a speaker. Should he begin with 'a little prefatory Apology' to defuse any criticism that might arise from any shortcomings in his delivery? And was it necessary to have any music examples at the first lecture – which he now decided would be 'On Music considered as an Art & as a Science' – in view of its extremely general subject?[59] To these queries, Burney replied by return: he approved of Wesley's proposal about the 'prefatory apology' and agreed that he should hold back his music examples until there was some specific point to illustrate.[60]

Among his other preparations for his lectures, Wesley needed to negotiate with the Royal Institution about the supply of a piano and an organ for his music examples. Unsurprisingly, he stipulated that the organ should be by Elliot. As was appropriate for an instrument that had to be erected in a restricted space, it was a small one, consisting only of three stops.[61] It also – crucially in the light of future events – incorporated the Hawkes patent mechanism which Wesley had demonstrated with Jacob the previous summer, and indeed may have been the same instrument. Given the amount

---

[56] Stevens was appointed instead: see above, p. 55. For Attwood's account, said to have been given to Stevens by Attwood himself, see Argent, *Recollections of R. J. S. Stevens*, pp. 102–4.
[57] Royal Institution, Minutes 4.
[58] *SW to Burney, 6 Dec. 1808. Burney's incomplete draft reply is on the address panel of this letter.
[59] *SW to Burney, 20 Dec. 1808.
[60] Burney to SW (draft), 20 Dec. 1808.
[61] *SW to C. J. Smyth, 10 Jan. 1810; see also Royal Institution, Minutes 4, cited in Kassler, 'Royal Institution Lectures', p. 16.

of Bach's music that Wesley was no doubt intending to include as examples, the choice of the Elliot organ was important: its patent mechanism would give a more pleasing intonation than that available on a conventional instrument, particularly in the less frequently used keys. In addition, and as will be seen later, it – or rather the Hawkes patent mechanism – would fully come into its own in the third lecture, which Wesley would devote entirely to a demonstration of the merits of the Hawkes system and the near-miraculous improvements in intonation that were claimed to result from its use.

Wesley approached the end of 1808 with great expectations. In the course of the preceding year his life and professional fortunes had been transformed by his discovery of Bach's music. All the strategies suggested by Burney in the spring were now bearing fruit. He had held one highly successful benefit concert and had done much to publicize Bach's music in other ways. He had made contact with Jacob and other Bach enthusiasts, and, most importantly, with Horn, and he was now about to lecture at the Royal Institution. The end of the year also brought some pleasurable diversions. In late November, Jacob had asked Wesley if he would be willing to have his portrait painted. The artist was to be John Bacon, a sculptor and a keen member of Jacob's Bach circle, and the first sitting took place on 21 December. The previous evening, Wesley had been a guest at the Madrigal Society, and on Christmas Day his Te Deum, Jubilate, and Litany Responses were again performed at St Paul's. He spent the immediately post-Christmas period as a guest of Richard Brinsley Sheridan at his farmhouse near Leatherhead, Surrey; the visit may have come about through William Linley, who knew Sheridan well, not only as his former brother-in-law, but also through having been manager of Drury Lane with him in the late 1790s.[62]

---

[62] *SW to Bacon, 28 Dec. 1808.

7

Lectures and controversy, 1809

On his return to London at the beginning of January 1809, Wesley fitted in another sitting with Bacon before setting off for an extended visit to Bath.[1] His original intention was to stay there for the remainder of January and the first half of February before returning to London in good time for his lectures at the Royal Institution. He would need to miss the first few weeks of the new term at his various schools,[2] but he made arrangements for a 'Mr Cooke' (probably Matthew Cooke, organist of St George's, Bloomsbury) to deputize during his absence. The Bath visit had been planned for some time, and was part-professional, part-social. Despite a decline since its peak of popularity in the 1790s, the town still remained the wealthiest and most important of England's resorts, and its musical culture was second only to that of London. The main concert venue was the Upper Rooms (the present Assembly Rooms) in Bennett Street, where the veteran castrato Venanzio Rauzzini presided over a series of concerts in which local musicians were joined by leading players and singers from London. There were also concerts at the Lower Assembly Rooms in Terrace Walks, and at the Pump Room adjoining the hot springs that were the original reason for Bath's emergence as a resort. Among the large numbers of wealthy visitors who rented rooms or entire houses for the season were many who took the opportunity to have music lessons, either from Bath's resident teachers or from visiting musicians. Someone of the eminence of Wesley would be in demand as a teacher and could probably charge higher rates than in London: perhaps a guinea per lesson rather than the half-guinea that was his usual rate in the capital. There would also be opportunities to play in concerts and to give a recital or two. On 19 January 1809 the *Bath Chronicle*, in a notice probably written by Wesley himself, announced his presence in the town, and expressed the hope that 'his numerous friends will prevail on him to make a public display of his wonderful abilities on the organ before his departure.' During this time Angelica Catalani, London's current leading operatic soprano, was also present in Bath, giving two concerts at the Assembly Rooms and four performances of extracts from Italian opera at the Theatre Royal during a stay of over three weeks. Her presence, the length of her stay, and the number of

---

[1] *SW to Bacon, 1 Jan. 1809.
[2] There is no record of precisely when the schools at which Wesley taught resumed after the Christmas break, but most schools in London restarted in mid- to late-January.

performances she gave are all telling indications of the town's musical importance, its wealth, and the size of the potential audience.

The rich pickings to be had from teaching and performing may have been the main reason for Wesley's visit to Bath, but there were also social reasons. Bath had its own glee club, the Bath Harmonic Society, founded some years earlier by Henry Harington, one of its most prominent citizens. Wesley's brother Charles had directed one of its concerts during his visit in the winter of 1806–7, and Wesley's three-part 'Dixit Dominus' setting may have been performed at the immediately following meeting.[3] Among others in Bath whom Wesley would have known were Benjamin Millgrove, the Precentor of the Countess of Huntingdon's Connexion chapel in Vineyards; Thomas Haweis, a senior member of the Connexion and Madan's former assistant at the Lock Hospital; the organist and music teacher James Windsor, who owned several manuscripts of Wesley's music, some of them perhaps acquired during this visit; and Dr Edward Sheppard, an old family friend and a well-known Bath eccentric of the time. Whereas his mother, brother, and sister were frequent visitors, this was Wesley's own first stay in Bath since his childhood, and his visit can be seen as another example of the upward movement of his career, and another sign of his improved health, mental and physical. Three years ago the prospect of a visit would have thrown him into panic, but he was now able to look forward with enthusiasm to the 'Bustle of Society' that he would encounter there.

Wesley had originally intended to stay in Bath until around mid-February, but such were the demands on his time that he decided to remain for a further fortnight.[4] This necessitated the hurried postponement of the beginning of his course of lectures at the Royal Institution – doubtless to the considerable annoyance of William Savage, the Secretary – and the making of arrangements for Cooke to continue to deputize for him during his extended absence. He eventually returned to London on 27 February, later remarking to Jacob that in Bath he had been 'a greater Slave *during the Holidays* than . . . when in the Mill-Horse Road of A B C Drudgery: hurried & dragged about from Pillar to Post'.[5] As a result, he had had less free time than he would have liked to prepare his first lecture. Nonetheless, by the time of his return all was reasonably well in hand: the first lecture had been ready for some days, and he had outlines for the second and third. He had decided on good subjects for the fourth and fifth lectures, and intended to devote the last to 'the miracles of Sebastian'.[6] Wesley conveyed this news to Jacob on 2 March in a cheerful letter. Only two days earlier, however, on the day following his return, he had written to Savage to announce that because of a heavy cold and accompanying hoarseness he would not be able to deliver his first lecture on 3 March as planned, and to request a further postponement until 8 March.[7] This date was not suitable to the

---

[3] *SW to Charles Wesley jun., 15 Jan. 1807.
[4] SW to Sarah Gwynne Wesley, 28 Jan. [1809]; *SW to George Smith, 23 Apr. 1809.
[5] *SW to Jacob, 2 Mar. 1809.
[6] Ibid.
[7] *SW to Savage, 28 Feb. 1809.

Governors, and the course eventually started on 10 March. Wesley may indeed have been afflicted in the way he described, but the absence of any mention of illness in his letters to Jacob of 2 and 3 March lead one to suspect that his assurance in his letter to Savage that 'nothing short of Illness should have occasioned this Procrastination' may not have been entirely truthful.

The titles of some of Wesley's lectures are known from his letters, to Savage, Burney, and others. As we have seen, the first was originally to have been 'On the Power of musical Prejudice' but he later – perhaps to avoid starting the course with a controversial subject – changed it to 'On Music as an Art and Science', the original lecture presumably being postponed to later in the course. The second was 'On the Power of Musick upon Morals'. The third, on 22 March, concerned tuning and temperament, and the final lecture was on Bach. This was a far cry from Wesley's plans the previous April to devote a whole course of lectures to Bach and his music, but Bach no doubt featured prominently in lectures that were not explicitly devoted to him. Given that Wesley had explained to Burney in his letter of 6 December 1808 that the 'grand aim' of his lecture on musical prejudice was 'to endeavour to dispel a few of the Clouds of Partiality & Prejudice which certainly have too long overshadowed *Apollo* in this Country', it seems likely that on this occasion he would have concentrated on Bach's music and the prejudices that had inhibited its acceptance in England. Similarly, in the light of Wesley's strong belief in the power of Bach's music as a general force for good, we can assume that part of his second lecture, on music and morals, would also have included some discussion of Bach's music.

When Wesley returned to his teaching at Oxford House in early March 1809, it was to find that his extended absence had been taken amiss by Mrs Barnes. Wesley's school pupils had not been neglected in his absence as they had been taught by Cooke, but no doubt Mrs Barnes considered that what was acceptable for a week or two was less acceptable for a longer period. Later in March, she gave Wesley notice that his services would not be required after the midsummer holidays, on the ostensible grounds that he had not been allowing his pupils enough time for them to make progress.[8] Wesley was outraged at his dismissal after more than twenty-five years of service. He suspected, probably correctly, that the reason given for his dismissal was not the real one, particularly as no similar complaint had been made at the other schools where he taught. Mrs Barnes lost no time in appointing a replacement: William Horsley, the organist of the Asylum for Female Orphans, where he had first been assistant to Callcott and had succeeded him in 1802. As an organist, teacher, and composer, he occupied much the same part of the music profession as Wesley, with the crucial difference that he was no performer and that his compositions were few and relatively insignificant. Although he may have been regarded by Mrs Barnes as a more reliable and suitable teacher than Wesley for her pupils, there could be no comparison between them in musical ability and accomplishments. Horsley

---

[8] *SW to Smith, 23 Apr. [1809]. Horsley's diary entry for 21 Mar. had noted: 'Wesley finally rejected by Mrs Barnes. School offered to me at Midsummer' (Horsley Papers).

was not a member of Wesley's circle of friends, but the two men would have known each other professionally and through the Concentores Society, of which he was a prominent member.

For the moment Wesley remained at Oxford House, working out his notice, and dealing with problems that had arisen from the lessons he was giving to his most promising pupil, a Miss Smith. Wesley had taught her for some time and considered her to have exceptional talents. In the previous August he had written to her father to discuss future arrangements for her lessons. Between them they had decided that she would for the moment abandon any plans to learn the organ, as she had no prospect of finding an instrument to practise on. She would continue to have piano lessons with Wesley, but as a 'private' rather than as a 'school' pupil: i.e. the arrangements for her teaching, and the payment for it, would be made direct with Wesley rather than through the school. This was an arrangement that allowed the most musically talented pupils to have more time for lessons than the meagre allocation (of probably no more than fifteen minutes per week) given to those who took their lessons through the school. The next question was whether Wesley should teach her for one or two hours per week. In his letter to her father, Wesley stated that she had 'the most illuminated musical Intellect' that he had met for many years. In the light of her progress to date, he thought that one hour per week would do great things, adding that his opinion of her musical talent was so high that he would be prepared to teach her for nothing if necessary. Smith could judge from this that 'pecuniary consideration' had little to do with Wesley's plans for her future musical education. Indeed, he was looking forward to the time when she could perform in public, which he was confident he would be able to do if she continued to make progress at her present rate.[9] This was high praise from Wesley, and his enthusiasm was a long way from his usual attitude to his school pupils. It appears from this and other comments on his best pupils that it was not music teaching *per se* that he objected to, but the mind-numbing tedium of teaching a long succession of pupils with no interest or aptitude. In Miss Smith he clearly had an outstanding pupil, and her appearance in due course as his star pupil on a public stage would be a great advertisement for his teaching.

By April 1809, however, arrangements between Wesley and Smith over the teaching of his talented daughter had run into difficulties. Some weeks earlier, probably at around the time when she had given Wesley notice, Mrs Barnes had written to Wesley to say that she thought that Smith would be extremely angry to hear how much his daughter had been neglected by him; at the same time she had apparently proposed to Smith that his daughter would make more progress with another teacher. It appears that during his extended stay in Bath Wesley had made no arrangements for the continued teaching of his private pupils, as he had for his school pupils, and that consequently Miss Smith had had no lessons during his absence. Even though Wesley had given her additional lessons on his return, Mrs Barnes still felt that she had been badly treated, and had

---

[9] *SW to Smith, 14 Aug. 1808.

suggested a change of teacher to her father. It now fell to Wesley to write to Smith to enquire whether he wished him to continue as his daughter's teacher or whether he was intending to appoint someone else.

This was on 24 April. Smith replied by return, informing Wesley that he felt that his daughter would make more progress under Johann Baptist Cramer, whom he had presumably already approached with an initial enquiry. Wesley replied with a terse note on 26 April to say that in that case Smith should engage Cramer immediately, and that he would inform Cramer of his intention. The fact that it was Cramer whom Smith approached is significant in what it tells us about Smith's knowledge of music, his ambitions for his daughter, and her musical ability, for Cramer was one of the most distinguished pianist-composers of his age, known as 'glorious John' to his admiring audiences. As a teacher he was much in demand, and was able to charge a premium rate of a guinea per lesson. Fine pianist though Wesley was, he was not (as he would have been the first to admit) in his league. In a further letter, Smith appears to have explained in greater detail his reasons for removing his daughter, at the same time accusing Wesley of acting incorrectly in the affair. By this time, Smith's mind was no doubt made up, but Wesley still wanted to put the record straight and to conclude the matter with as much dignity as he could manage. In a long reply he stated his desire to provide an 'unequivocal Explanation of [his] Conduct relative to the Misunderstanding at Oxford House', no doubt in the belief that it had been maliciously misrepresented by Mrs Barnes. He admitted that he had made arrangements for his school pupils to be taught by Cooke, although he had omitted to do so for his private pupils. On his return from Bath, Mrs Barnes had expressed her full approval of Cooke's performance. Her subsequent decision to dismiss Wesley had come out of the blue, and was apparently 'without any Kind of reasonable Pretext'. As far as Smith's daughter was concerned, Wesley conceded that he should have approached Smith to seek his approval for Cooke to teach her during his absence. Had he done this, Smith would no doubt have granted it, and these 'unpleasant Consequences' could have been avoided. It was, of course, Smith's prerogative to engage as many teachers for his daughter as he wished, and to change them as often as he pleased, but Wesley was none the less puzzled why he should now wish to move his daughter to another teacher, given his former satisfaction with Wesley. Wesley had always been committed to making Miss Smith an excellent player, and had assumed that she would be considered exclusively his pupil. He stressed that he and Cramer were good friends, and that there was no chance of Cramer suspecting Wesley of any jealousy. Notwithstanding Cramer's pre-eminence as a performer, there was no question but that Wesley understood the principles of piano teaching as well as Cramer, and that Cramer would readily acknowledge this himself. If Smith would like to reconsider his decision, Wesley would be glad to continue to teach his daughter, irrespective of what arrangements Mrs Barnes might make for the teaching of the other pupils at Oxford House. This appears to have been the end of the correspondence between Wesley and Smith, and it must be assumed that notwithstanding Wesley's rearguard action Smith decided to send his daughter for lessons with Cramer, or with some other teacher.

Wesley's third Royal Institution lecture, on 22 March, was titled 'the Improvement of the Chromatic Scale, evinced in the Construction & Effects of the Patent Organ, designed by Willm Hawkes Esqre and built by Mr Elliot'.[10] He started by acknowledging the value and usefulness of equal temperament before turning to discuss and demonstrate the merits of the Hawkes system, including its superior intonation in the less frequently used keys. Most, if not all, of his examples would have been taken from the '48', which, with its preludes and fugues in all the keys, might have been tailor-made for demonstrating the advantages of the Hawkes system.

The lecture gave rise to a lengthy and acrimonious controversy in the pages of the *New Musical Magazine, Review and Register of Valuable Musical Publications* (henceforth *NMMR*), a short-lived periodical published by Joseph Kemp.[11] In the May 1809 number an anonymous correspondent signing himself 'J. P.' launched a savage attack on Wesley, accusing him of failing to point out imperfections and shortcomings of the Hawkes system of which he could not fail to be aware, and – what was worse – of using his authority as a lecturer at the Royal Institution to promote a commercial product. A letter from Jacob defending Hawkes and Wesley against the accusations made by 'J. P.' was published in the July number, and the controversy continued for the rest of the year and into early 1810. There was a good deal of substance in these accusations. The charge that Wesley had used his platform as a lecturer at the Royal Institution to recommend the Hawkes system was undeniable, and it was also true that the claims made for the system were inflated. The improvements in intonation in the less commonly used keys, though considerable, fell short of the perfection that was claimed; in addition, as 'J. P.' was quick to point out, since the system required the player to select either all sharps or all flats it was impossible to play a sharp and a flat simultaneously, as was frequently necessary (for example) in minor keys. Nonetheless (and as Jacob remarked in his letter) there was more to the affair than might at first appear from the high-minded accusations of partiality of 'J. P', for the *NMMR* itself supported a rival patented system by one David Loeschman which claimed equally impressive results by different means.[12] Although the identity of 'J. P.' remains unknown, there are good grounds for suspecting that the pseudonym concealed Kemp himself, or someone close to him.

Amid Wesley's lectures at the Royal Institution, his arguments with Mrs Barnes and the father of his pupil Miss Smith, and the burgeoning *NMMR*

---

[10] *SW to Savage, 16 Mar. [1809].

[11] *NMMR* ran for thirteen numbers between Mar. 1809 and Mar. 1810. For Joseph Kemp and *NMMR*, see Kassler, *Science of Music*, pp. 625–32, 1235–6. For the controversy caused by SW's lecture, see Emery, 'Jack Pudding'.

[12] For Loeschman and his system, see Kassler, *Science of Music*, pp. 697–700.

controversy, his collaboration with Horn in promoting Bach's music continued. Earlier plans for the publication of a translation of Forkel's *Life of Bach* appear to have been shelved or abandoned, and the projected edition of the '48' was for the moment postponed. Instead, Wesley and Horn decided as their first venture to publish the six Trio Sonatas. The first was given to the engraver early in March 1809 and was published probably a few weeks later; the remaining five appeared at intervals over the course of the next few months.[13]

The decision to publish the Trio Sonatas at this stage instead of the '48', and in individual numbers, made good business sense. As Wesley had seen from the beginning, the only sensible way of proceeding with the publication of the '48' was by subscription. The problem, of course, lay in persuading would-be purchasers to commit themselves to expenditure on the basis of an advertising prospectus alone. This was particularly acute in the case of unfamiliar music: in such cases there was a pressing need for prospective publishers to do whatever they could to stimulate public awareness and hence demand for their wares. It was considerations of this kind that had led Wesley in April 1808 to consult Burney about the best way to proceed, and to Burney's advice that the '48' might be 'played into fashion'. By late 1808, Wesley and Horn may have felt that the right time for their edition had still not arrived, and their chances of securing an adequate number of subscribers would be improved by an extended period of promotion that would lead to a greater public awareness of Bach's music. As Wesley remarked to Jacob in March 1809, 'we must for the present confine & repress our Inclination to publish *too hastily* our Creed in the transcendant Merits of this marvellous Man: it will all go on well by slow Degrees.'[14] In the meantime, and as part of this process, they could proceed with publication of the Trios. Although it was a major undertaking, it was still considerably less ambitious than an edition of the '48'. Moreover, it was one that Wesley and Horn could afford to finance as a speculative venture. By publishing the Trios individually, they could minimize their financial outlay and their potential exposure to loss, and income from the sales of each separate number could be put towards the cost of the next. If all went according to plan, those who bought copies would have their appetite whetted, and would be more likely in time to subscribe for the edition of the '48'.

Although the title-page of the Trios proclaimed the joint editorship of Wesley and Horn, it is likely that most, if not all, of the editorial input was in fact by Wesley. His statement on 3 March to Jacob that he was 'about to put the 1st *Trio* of the Six lent me by Horn, into the Engraver's hands almost immediately', suggests that he was the active partner, and that Horn's contribution amounted to no more than providing the copy from which Wesley then prepared the edition.[15] And there can be no doubt from its

---

[13] *SW to Jacob, 3 Mar. 1809.
[14] Ibid.
[15] This implication is repeated in Wesley's statement in his *Reminiscences*, fol. 46, that 'the late C. F. Horn also brought to me in manuscript six Organ Trios, the bass part of which was originally intended to be performed on Pedals: I also published an edition of these with a preface; they met

wording that Wesley was the author of the lengthy introduction that preceded the first trio of the set.

Wesley's 1809 benefit, on 3 June, was an altogether larger and more ambitious event than its predecessor a year earlier. The 1808 benefit had involved only Wesley; this one involved Wesley, Jacob, and a group of five singers. The key work in the concert was Bach's motet 'Jesu meine Freude', BWV 527, included to demonstrate that Bach was 'no mere organist' but that he could also write effective choral music.[16] Of all the Bach motets available in print at this time, 'Jesu, meine Freude' must have seemed the most appropriate for this purpose. In five vocal parts – in contrast to the others, which are all in eight – it was at the same time cheaper to perform, easier to rehearse, and more transparent in musical texture. At around twenty-five minutes in length, it was a substantial work. Most important, its structure as a set of varied treatments of a memorable chorale melody interspersed with free movements was straightforward, and would be immediately comprehensible to the audience. But Wesley was not happy with performing it in German, a language that he found harsh and unpleasant, and translated the text into Latin.[17] There are no details in press advertisements of the other pieces performed at the concert. From a remark in a letter of late May to Jacob, however, it appears that one of the Trio Sonatas – perhaps the first, which had recently been published – was to be performed by Wesley and Jacob as an organ duet.[18] It is likely that the programme also included a selection of preludes and fugues from the '48', some further choral items by Wesley himself, and some organ music, either extemporized or from the Op. 6 voluntaries, or both.

After the concert, Wesley's engagements rapidly fell off as the end of the season approached. On 22 June, he performed an extempore organ voluntary at a concert at the King's Theatre promoted by the actor and theatrical manager Willoughby Lacy,[19] and four days later he gave another extempore performance, this time on the piano, at a concert organized by the singer Charles Smart Evans at the Green Man Inn, Blackheath.[20]

By late August 1809, Wesley's thoughts were turning to his forthcoming engagement at a music festival to be held at Tamworth, a prosperous manufacturing town on the Staffordshire-Warwickshire border, some thirteen miles from Birmingham.[21] This was his first encounter with the world of the

---

with universal approbation, and have been found eminently serviceable to all who aspire to excellence in the true Organ style.'

[16] *SW to Jacob, [?29 May 1809].
[17] *SW to Jacob, c. 15 May 1809.
[18] *SW to Jacob, [?29 May 1809].
[19] Wesley to Lacy, 20 June 1809; *The Times*, 22 June 1809.
[20] *The Times*, 23, 24 June 1809.
[21] Olleson, 'The Tamworth Music Festival of 1809'.

provincial music festival; a world which was to take him in the next few years to Birmingham, Norwich, Ipswich, and elsewhere.

The music festival was a well-established feature of cultural life in larger towns and cities. The Three Choirs Festival, the oldest in Britain, was founded around 1718 and had continued its annual rotation between Gloucester, Hereford, and Worcester ever since. The festival at Birmingham dated back to 1768, and had been mounted triennially since 1778, most recently in the previous year. Festivals were held typically in late summer or early autumn, when the weather was still good, the nights relatively light, and travel was easy. This was also the London off-season, when wealthy land-owners would tend to be in the country and when London orchestral players and singers would be only lightly employed, if at all. Many festivals, including the Three Choirs, had originated in an annual charity service with music, and continued to be organized for the benefit of a local charity. More recently, some festivals had come to be promoted solely as business ventures, by such London entrepreneurs as the Ashley family.[22] In each case, the musical aim was the same: to bring large-scale performances of vocal and choral music featuring predominantly London players and singers to local communities. Festivals conformed to a pattern which varied little from place to place and consisted of two or three days of concentrated music-making. They usually started with an extended church service in which all the performers participated, continuing with morning performances of oratorios or oratorio extracts in the local church or cathedral and evening performances in the theatre or assembly rooms. Since the Handel Commemoration of 1784 and the succeeding Handel festivals in 1785, 1786, 1787, 1790, and 1791, they had involved increasingly large numbers of performers: in 1808, Birmingham had advertised 'almost 200' in the choir and orchestra. *Messiah* was almost invariably performed, and by this time it was often joined by Haydn's *Creation*, which had gone immediately into the provincial festival repertory following its first London performances in 1800.

The Tamworth festival followed this pattern, over two days. The forces were almost as large as those at Birmingham the previous year, and the soloists almost as prestigious. Many of the same soloists were engaged: Mrs Vaughan, Miss Hawkins, and Miss Melville (sopranos), Simeon Buggins (boy treble), John Jeremiah Goss (counter-tenor), John Braham and Thomas Vaughan (tenors), and James Elliott (bass). These were all leading singers. The star attraction was Braham, at this time thirty-five years old and in his prime as the leading English tenor of the time. Unlike the festival at Birmingham, the Tamworth festival was a one-off event, organized to celebrate and at the same time to defray the costs of the recent alterations to the church and the enlargement of the organ by Thomas Elliot. Its organizers were the vicar, the Revd Francis Blick, and two of his churchwardens. All arrangements for the booking of the players and singers would have been handed over to a London 'fixer', most probably Charles Jane Ashley, who was a member of the orchestra. Wesley's role was as the director at

---

[22] Pritchard, 'The Provincial Festivals of the Ashley Family'.

the keyboard – at the organ in the church, and on the piano at the evening concert at the theatre – and thus responsible with Francis Cramer, the leader of the orchestra, for the overall control of the performances. He was also engaged to play an organ concerto in the second morning performance, to perform extempore at the final concert and doubtless to accompany the vocal soloists in the concert at the theatre. In addition, 'Father of Light and Life', his 1801 setting of lines from Thomson's *The Seasons*, was to be performed at the final concert by four of the vocal soloists.

Wesley first mentioned his visit to Tamworth in a letter of 4 September to Jacob in which he discussed the copying of orchestral parts for the organ concerto and requested Jacob to obtain him some suitable manuscript paper.[23] The concerto was the one in D that Wesley had probably first performed at Salomon's *Creation* performance in April 1800, now revised and rescored. Wesley had taken the opportunity to insert as an additional movement between the second movement and the concluding Hornpipe a transcription of the D major fugue from Book 2 of the '48', to be played first by the organ soloist, and then by the full orchestra. He was thus able at the same time to take his promotion of Bach to the provinces and to achieve his ambition – expressed to Jacob less than a year earlier – of hearing Bach played 'on a full orchestra'.[24]

Wesley set off from London for Tamworth by overnight coach on 18 September 1809: a journey of over a hundred miles. As he later related to Jacob, it was a windy, rainy, night, and any hopes he may have had of a peaceful and relatively comfortable journey were soon dashed by the presence of 'a restless Companion who was continually jerking the Windows up & down for what he called *Air*, but which was a furious Wind & pelting Rain'.[25] Once arrived in Tamworth, he had the rest of the day free to recuperate and to exchange news and gossip with his fellow performers, who would have been assembling throughout the day. Among them were many London friends and colleagues as well as musicians from nearby towns and cities. The next day was taken up with rehearsal. On the following day, 21 September, the festival began. The opening concert, at 11a.m. at the parish church, was a performance of *Messiah*, followed in the evening by a 'Grand Miscellaneous Concert' at the theatre and a ball at the Town Hall. The second day contained another morning oratorio concert: this time an abridged performance of *Creation* in the first two parts of the concert, followed by a third part containing Wesley's organ concerto and extracts from Handel oratorios. In the evening there was a concluding 'Grand Selection of Sacred Music' in the church, which was now specially illuminated for the occasion. Notwithstanding its billing, it did not consist exclusively of sacred music, although most of the items were – as befitted a concert in church – serious, or at least dignified and edifying in tone. In a prominent position at the beginning of the second part was an improvised

[23] *Wesley to Jacob, 4 Sept. 1809.
[24] *Wesley to Jacob, 19 Oct. 1808.
[25] *Wesley to Jacob, 25 Sept. 1809.

voluntary by Wesley that would have demonstrated both his powers as an organist and the additions to the organ. Despite a prohibition on applause at the church, the performances were met with great enthusiasm: Wesley remarked on the attentivess of the audiences, and how they 'seemed to long for the Privilege of clapping and rattling their Sticks'. His concerto was particularly well received: the Bach fugue produced a 'glorious effect' in its orchestral form, and he found the members of the orchestra humming its subject whenever he met them in the street.[26]

On the day after the final concert, Wesley packed his bags and headed for Birmingham. Samuel Buggins, who played the trumpet in the orchestra at Tamworth and was the father of the treble soloist, had taken the opportunity to mount a concert at the Theatre Royal with many of the Tamworth performers, repeating many of the items played in the evening performance on 21 September.[27] As at Tamworth, Wesley directed the concert from the piano, and as a solo item played a 'fantazia' (i.e. an improvised piece) which he concluded with the refrain from 'A frog he would a-wooing go'.[28]

On Wesley's return to London at the end of September 1809 he was immediately confronted with various matters that required his immediate attention. The most pressing was an urgent request from Burney to hear Bach's Sonatas for Violin and Harpsichord, BWV 1014–19, a copy of which Wesley had recently bought. Burney, informed of this by Salomon, had first written to Wesley before his departure for Tamworth to ask him if he could arrange a performance with Salomon, but this had proved impossible. Now Burney was about to leave London himself, and was anxious to hear the sonatas before his departure. By this time Salomon was unavailable, but Burney knew that Wesley had recently taken up the violin again, specifically to be able to play the sonatas, and was happy to have them played by Wesley on the violin with Jacob on the piano. His only available day before leaving London was two days later, on 2 October. Wesley was prepared to go to considerable lengths to satisfy Burney's demands, commenting to Jacob that 'the Triumph of Burney over his own Ignorance & Prejudice is such a glorious Event that surely we ought to make *some* sacrifice to enjoy it.'[29] He could rearrange the lessons of the three private pupils he was due to teach that day, and urged Jacob to make similar efforts.

Following the success of his Royal Institution lectures, Wesley was invited in late 1809 to give a course at the Surrey Institution. Like the London Institution, its counterpart in Finsbury Circus, at which Wesley would also later lecture, it had recently been founded in emulation of the Royal Institution. It occupied the Rotunda in Albion Street, an imposing building at the north end of Great Surrey Street, close to Surrey Chapel and Jacob's house. It contained a lecture

[26] Ibid.
[27] *ABG*, 18 Sept. 1809.
[28] *Wesley to Jacob, 25 Sept. 1809.
[29] SW to Jacob, [?30 September 1809?].

theatre with a capacity of five hundred, reading and conversation rooms, a chemistry laboratory, offices, committee rooms, and living accommodation for the Secretary. The reading-rooms had opened as recently as the previous year, and the programme of lectures on chemistry, mineralogy, natural philosophy, and other subjects had started only in the previous November. The first Secretary and Librarian was Adam Clarke, a distinguished Methodist minister and scholar who had been a long-standing friend of John and Charles Wesley and had been President of the Methodist Conference in 1806.[30] Wesley's course was to begin on 7 November. Invited by Jacob to call at his house after the lecture, Wesley had replied that he would probably exercise his 'blanket privilege'[31] and stay the night there rather than travelling home to Camden Town. This would be a good opportunity for them to discuss the progress of their promotion of Bach, and in particular the large-scale concert that they were organizing for later in the month. This was to be at Surrey Chapel on 29 November, with the agreement and encouragement of Rowland Hill, the minister, and was their most ambitious piece of Bach promotion to date. In addition to organ music, Wesley was to perform two of the Violin Sonatas with Jacob on the organ, and some of Handel's music was also to be included, presumably for purposes of comparison. Tickets were free, and Jacob had handbills printed giving containing details of the programme, which he then circulated in all areas where stocks of tickets were deposited. Meanwhile, Wesley was engaged in sending tickets to everyone of influence he could think of, and asking Jacob if he could borrow a copy of the *Court Guide* (an annual directory of the upper echelons of society) to aid the process. Among those they hoped would attend were a number of bankers, described by Wesley as being musical and 'sure to prate about the thing'. At the same time, Wesley took care to have advertisements for the Bach Trio Sonatas distributed at the concert, having first established with Jacob that Hill would have no objections. According to Jacob's later account in Sainsbury's *Dictionary of Musicians*, the concert lasted four hours. Wesley's and Jacob's concentrated publicity drive had attracted an audience of around 3,000, composed of 'persons of the highest respectability, also many in the first rank of professors and amateurs.'[32] Even allowing for a certain amount of exaggeration by Jacob, this was a very large number indeed, and probably a good deal more than the capacity of the chapel. It is likely that members of the audience were encouraged to arrive and leave at will, and that Jacob's figure referred to the total number attending, rather than to the number in the chapel at any one time.

After the Surrey Chapel concert, Wesley was able to turn his attention to the *NMMR* controversy, still rumbling on more than seven months after the lecture that had given rise to it. In early September, he had sent an open letter to 'J. P.'

---

[30] *DNB*, s.v. 'Clarke, Adam'.
[31] *SW to Jacob, ?21 Nov. 1808.
[32] Sainsbury, *A Dictionary of Musicians*, s.v. 'Jacob'; Jacob to Sainsbury, 15 Jan. 1824 (Glasgow University Library, Euing Collection). The article was compiled from the information supplied in Jacob's letter. See also SW's account in *Reminiscences*, fols 51–2.

for publication in the following month's *NMMR*, in reply to the attack of 'J. P.' on him in the August number, stating that he was ready to defend any position that he had advanced at his Royal Institution lecture, but that he did not propose to engage in further controversy with anonymous adversaries. If 'J. P.' wished his further attention, he should disclose his name.[33] By this time Wesley was thoroughly enjoying himself, no doubt aware that the continuing quarrel would, if nothing else, keep his name in the public eye, and that this could only favour his promotion of Bach. Before leaving for Tamworth he had referred in a letter to Jacob to his quarrel with 'Jack Pudding' including a scrap of doggerel for Jacob's amusement:

> Tho' J. P. refuses to give up his Name
> To muffle his Malice a Hood in,
> The Matter amounts to exactly the same,
> For his Nonsense proclaims 'tis J-ack P-udding.[34]

On his return from Tamworth, he had been informed – with what accuracy he did not know – that 'J. P' was the Honourable George Pomeroy, an amateur musician and music-theorist associate of Kemp whom Wesley had met and had disliked as a 'most conceited Pretender to musical Criticism.'[35] In the October number of *NMMR* there was a further attack on Wesley, this time from a new correspondent signing himself 'X.Y.Z.', whom Wesley considered in fact to be the same person as 'J. P.'. On 9 October Wesley wrote to *NMMR* to announce his Surrey Institution course of lectures, in which he would reply to his critics, adding that if 'J. P., X.Y.Z., or any other such LITERARY Gentlemen, choose to attend, they may hear their gross ignorance, and defamatory falsehoods, duly exposed.'[36]

The lecture in question was to be on 5 December, six days after the Surrey Chapel concert. From Jacob, Wesley acquired the numbers of *NMMR* that had contained the initial criticisms. These, and particularly the May number, which had included the first attack by 'J. P.', would provide sufficient material for his 'cannonade'. Wesley anticipated 'fun alive' at his lecture, particularly if 'J. P.' and 'X.Y.Z' could be persuaded to attend. The lecture, which appears to have been as robust as Wesley had promised, did not go unnoticed. Some days later, Knight Spencer, who by now had succeeded Clarke as the Secretary of the Surrey Institution, wrote to Wesley to complain about its personal tone, and to suggest that Wesley might like to give an additional lecture to make amends. This brought a long and carefully reasoned, if rather disinguous, response from Wesley. Had the controversy been a merely private matter between him and his two anonymous critics, he would have been happy to agree with Spencer that it was not a matter of sufficient importance to merit so much attention. However, he regarded the *NMMR* attack as having been directed not solely at

---

[33] *NMMR*, Oct. 1809, pp. 134–6.
[34] Enclosed with *SW to Jacob, 4 Sept. 1809.
[35] *SW to Jacob, c. 28 Sept. 1809.
[36] SW to the editor, *NMMR*, 9 Oct. 1809, published in *NMMR*, Nov. 1809, p. 154.

him but at the whole music profession, which it traduced as being 'no better than a Banditti of Pick-Pockets'. Wesley would have been 'an unworthy Deserter' of his profession if he had not taken the opportunity to reply to his critics when such an ideal opportunity as his lecture had presented itself. In any case, given that the subject of his lecture was musical deception, it would have been strange if he had not discussed so flagrant an instance of it. He could not agree with Spencer about the need for him to make amends, as he did not consider his behaviour unreasonable. If it had given offence, he was sorry, as he had assumed that the sincerity of his intentions to 'do good by exposing imposture' would have been understood and his motives would have been favourably construed. Under the circumstances, he would have to decline Spencer's suggestion that he should deliver an additional lecture.[37]

---

[37] *SW to Spencer, 9 Dec. 1809.

8

A developing career, 1810–1811

As 1809 came to an end, Wesley could look back with considerable satisfaction on his professional activities. It had been an unprecedentedly busy year, starting with an extended stay in Bath, continuing with the Royal Institution lectures in March and April, the Hanover Square Rooms concert in June, a trip to Tamworth in September, a further course of lectures at the Surrey Institution in November and December, and the important Surrey Chapel concert with Jacob in November. It had also been an eventful year on the personal front, and he was now contemplating the imminent breakdown of his marriage to Charlotte. At some time during the second half of the year he started an intimate relationship with Sarah Suter, the family's live-in servant or housekeeper. By this time, any hopes of a genuine reconciliation with Charlotte had long since disappeared. In a letter to his mother written shortly after the separation he stressed the unpleasantness of life with Charlotte, reiterating his complaints about her extravagance, insolence, and vulgarity. In addition, except for the fact that she had claim on some of his property, it was 'a joke, or rather a lye' for her to term herself his wife. In the 'true, and only original & scriptural sense' she had not been this since the birth of Emma, and he had good grounds for divorce in the ecclesiastical courts whenever he chose.[1]

Because of the reluctance of family correspondents even to mention her name, let alone discuss her, and the reticence of Wesley's first biographers, very little is known of Sarah Suter. From her death certificate it emerges that she was sixty-nine at her death on 12 September 1863. She was thus only fifteen, or at most just sixteen, at the beginning of her relationship with Wesley. Nothing is known of her background or family: no letters from her to Wesley have survived, and almost the only evidence of her existence lurks in a collection of forty-two letters to her from Wesley written between 1810 and 1830. Early accounts of Wesley's life ignored her existence, and her role as Wesley's partner for the last twenty-seven years of his life and the mother of nine children with him was first mentioned in print only in 1899 in his *Dictionary of National Biography* article.[2]

The final break with Charlotte came in early 1810, probably precipitated by

---

[1] SW to Sarah Gwynne Wesley, undated [early 1810].
[2] By F. G. Edwards. She had, however, put in a shadowy appearance in the pull-out genealogy in Stevenson's *Memorials of the Wesley Family*, but without further mention in the text.

the discovery of Sarah's pregnancy. Wesley then moved out of the marital home and set up house with Sarah at Adam's Row, near the intersection of Hampstead Road with the present Euston Road. This was far from being a fashionable address: on the very edge of London, the area had only recently been developed and was characterized by a rash of cheap speculative buildings of which Adam's Row no doubt formed part. But it met the need for inexpensive accommodation that would allow Wesley to support not only himself and Sarah but also Charlotte and their three children. The separation was inevitably acrimonious. Wesley claimed that he would 'no longer remain with an abominable creature in female shape', and that he had already endured life with Charlotte for far longer than most men would have tolerated. For her part, Charlotte would have seen herself as abandoned by a husband of forty-three for a young woman no older than their eldest child. Now forty-eight, she would have little prospect of finding another partner, and the near-certainty of poverty lay ahead. Divorce was impossible, requiring a special Act of Parliament, and was an option only for the aristocracy and the wealthy. No matter what practical arrangements were made in the future, Wesley and Charlotte would have to remain married.

The magnitude of Wesley's decision to leave Charlotte for Sarah can hardly be overstated. The unhappiness of his marriage was probably as well known to his friends and professional colleagues as it was to his family, and a separation, with appropriate arrangements for maintenance, would probably have been accepted by most as a practical solution to an intractable problem. But the real scandal lay in Wesley's abandonment of Charlotte for Sarah, who was a servant and little more than a child. This outraged his family, and must have strained to the utmost the tolerance of even his most broad-minded friends. Although it does not appear to have had an adverse effect on his playing career, it must have damaged his personal reputation and chances of employment in those areas where respectability and moral probity were of importance: in applications for church positions, for example, and also in his teaching, both at schools and with his private pupils, where many parents would understandably have been uneasy at the thought of entrusting their daughters to his care.

Following their separation, each of the Wesleys was vulnerable to the ill-will and vindictiveness of the other. Charlotte was dependent on Wesley to pay adequate maintenance to her and to the children: should he refuse or be unable to meet his responsibilities, destitution would soon follow. For his part, Wesley was vulnerable to the financial liabilities that Charlotte could place on him. Like any other married woman at this time, Charlotte had no separate legal existence. She could not enter into contracts, and any debts she incurred were Wesley's responsibility. In theory, it was open to her to ruin Wesley by incurring heavy expenditure for which he would then be liable. In practice this would be counterproductive, as a husband who was financially ruined in this way would not be able to continue to pay maintenance. Nonetheless, it was not unknown for a deserted wife to engage in extravagant spending as a way of revenging herself on her husband, and Wesley must have been apprehensive that Charlotte would act in this way. Wesley was fully aware of his responsibilities to Charlotte and their three children, and was determined to fulfil them. To his mother he stated that, so far as was possible, he had no intention of leaving Charlotte 'distressed, or even straitened', and that he would do all in his power for his children. Eventually, after two years, a formal separation arrangement was drawn up that protected the legal position of both parties. In his letter to his mother shortly after the separation Wesley discussed the urgent necessity of such a settlement, and in February he informed his brother Charles that he was 'busy in arranging a Plan which *must* deliver me from many Vexations, & which if longer delayed would eventually cause me to *look through a Grate* for life', adding that he had been 'a Dupe & a Slave too long to the most unworthy of Women'.[3] But even without a formal settlement, there were still steps that could be taken to mitigate the worst of the problems attendant on separation. One was for the husband to make an informal agreement to pay maintenance; another was for him to let it be known, either in person or by an announcement in the newspapers, that he would no longer be liable for his wife's debts. As is clear from a later letter to his mother, Wesley took both these steps.[4]

Amidst the turbulence of his personal life, Wesley's increasingly active professional life continued, seemingly without interruption. He had secured some concerto engagements at the Lenten oratorio concerts at Covent Garden, now managed by General and Charles Jane Ashley following their father's death in 1805. This was a significant development which placed Wesley as never before in the public eye. The post of regular organist for the series, however, which Wesley no doubt would have dearly liked, was held by John James, another member of the Ashley family.

The oratorio concerts followed much the same pattern as they had done in 1799, when the *Ode to St Cecilia* received its sole performance. Although more modern music was now included, notably Haydn's *Creation*, the music of Handel still predominated. Each season invariably contained at least one, and often two or more, performances of *Messiah*, and selections of favourite vocal and choral extracts from Handel's other oratorios formed a substantial part of the programmes of other concerts. At times in the past, isolated oratorio seasons had been held at Drury Lane and the King's Theatre as well as at Covent Garden, but in recent years the Covent Garden series stood alone. The previous year, following the burning down of the theatre in October 1808, the Ashleys had been obliged to move to the King's Theatre, but in 1810 they returned to the new theatre, where they continued as before. Despite inevitable season-to-season variations in box-office takings, the oratorio concerts were highly profitable. Both the old and the new Covent Garden theatres had a capacity of well over 2,000. This was more than twice that of the Hanover Square Rooms, and a full house generated considerable takings. In fact, the oratorio concerts were achieving particularly good audiences at this time. In the 1810 season, for

---
[3] *SW to Charles Wesley jun., 16 Feb. 1810.
[4] SW to Sarah Gwynne Wesley, 24 Oct. 1811.

example, all the available Wednesdays and Fridays in Lent were taken up with concerts, and many programmes were repeated in response to popular demand. Much of this success was a consequence of the engagement of Catalani: with their lower ticket prices, the oratorio concerts provided a low-cost way of hearing her rather than going to the King's Theatre or to one of the major subscription series where she was also engaged.

In 1808 Ashley for the first time organized a concert on 30 January, the anniversary of the execution of Charles I, and a day when spoken drama was prohibited. Up till then there had been some doubt whether any sort of entertainment was permissible on this date, but in 1807 Ware, the leader of the Covent Garden orchestra, used it for his benefit, and as there was no comeback from the office of the Lord Chamberlain it was incorporated into the oratorio season the following year.[5] It was on this day in 1810, between the first and second parts of *Messiah*, that Wesley performed his organ concerto in D with the interpolated Bach fugue that he had played at Tamworth the previous September. In this way he continued his policy of promoting Bach at every possible opportunity, and reached a far larger audience than ever before. He repeated the same concerto in the oratorio series proper on 12 March. He was also performing Bach in other places: as we know from a letter to his mother, on 21 January he performed the Fugue in E♭, BWV 552 (the 'St Anne') after evensong at St Paul's Cathedral, in what was probably a private performance to a few invited friends.[6] More private again would have been the party on 1 April at Edward Stephenson's house in Queen's Square, Bloomsbury, to celebrate Bach's birthday, to which all members of the Bach circle were invited.[7]

Work continued on various Bach projects throughout 1810. As we have seen, Wesley had had an edition of the '48' in mind since the beginning of his active interest in Bach in early 1808, but had shelved his plans in late 1808 or early 1809 in favour of the Trio Sonatas. By some time in the second half of 1809, however, it must have appeared to him and to Horn that the ground was now adequately prepared and that they could press forward with their plans for publication. Although they would have ensured that their intention to publish a new edition of the '48' was widely known – no doubt by publicizing it at the concert at Surrey Chapel on 29 November 1809 – it was not until the beginning of March 1810 that the first formal announcement appeared, in the form of a paragraph in the *Monthly Magazine*.[8] Titled *S. Wesley and C. F. Horn's New And Correct Edition of the Preludes and Fugues of John Sebastian Bach*, it was to be in four parts, to be published separately and at intervals. Each part was to be priced at 9s for subscribers and 12s for non-subscribers. After the appearance

[5] Parke, *Musical Memoirs*, vol. 2, p. 32. Parke mistakenly states that this happened in 1809.
[6] *SW to Sarah Gwynne Wesley, 18 Jan. 1810.
[7] *SW to Bridgetower, 29 Mar. 1810. Bach was born on 21 Mar. (OS) or 1 Apr. (NS) 1685.
[8] *MM* 29 (1810), p. 170. See also Horsley's diary entry for 26 March 1810 (Horsley Papers), where he noted that he had 'subscribed to Bach's fugues at Birchall's, for Miss Walker'.

of the proposals Wesley and Horn would have had an anxious period of waiting to see if they would receive enough subscriptions to proceed. As no copies of the proposals have survived, it is impossible to know what the terms of the subscription were, but it is likely that they would have involved subscribers in an initial payment, followed by further instalments in advance of each subsequent part. In this way, Wesley and Horn could finance each successive volume with its own subscription income, with minimum risk or financial outlay. In fact, Wesley and Horn had little to worry about: as the printed list which accompanied the first part of the edition shows, there were eventually 152 subscribers, who between them subscribed for 183 copies. Although some subscribers came in at the last minute, it must have been apparent to Wesley and Horn from an early stage that the edition was viable and that they could safely proceed with any outstanding editorial work before passing the copy over for engraving. By this stage there was probably relatively little to do. The music text was basically the manuscript copy that Wesley had made from the Nägeli edition in 1806, which would now need to be checked and re-checked, any additional editorial interventions incorporated, and an introduction added.

On 19 May, in what had become a regular part of the season and of his own annual timetable, Wesley held his benefit concert at the Hanover Square Rooms. The programme followed much the same plan as the previous year, with vocal and choral items and organ solos and duets. The star attraction was Mrs Billington, whose participation Wesley had at last been able to secure. The other vocalists included Mr and Mrs Vaughan, Goss, Elliott, and Street; Salomon played the violin, and Joseph Major joined Wesley in the organ duet items. Once more Bach dominated the programme, which included an unaccompanied sonata played by Salomon, one of the sonatas for violin and harpsichord played by Salomon and Wesley, an organ trio sonata played by Wesley and Major, and parts of 'Jesu, meine Freude', repeated from the previous year.[9] One new feature of the 1810 benefit, however, was the inclusion of two major choral compositions by Wesley himself. One was 'Father of Light and Life', the vocal quartet that the Vaughans, Goss, and Elliott had performed at Tamworth the previous September; the other was 'In exitu Israel', a motet for double SATB ensemble that Wesley had written specifically for this occasion and had completed only two weeks earlier.

As we saw earlier, in the previous September or early October Wesley had played Bach's Violin Sonatas for Burney. Another similar performance, this time of the *Goldberg Variations*, BWV 988, took place in July 1810. As with the Violin Sonatas, this was a work that was evidently completely new to Burney, and one that Wesley himself had probably only recently discovered. Plans for the performance only gradually emerged. In a letter to Wesley of

[9] John Marsh, *Journal*; Edwards, *Bach's Music in England*, p. 655.

27 June, Burney expressed his wish to make the acquaintance of Novello, whom Wesley had previously described to him in glowing terms, and suggested a day in the following week for Wesley and Novello to visit him. At this stage there was no mention of a performance of any kind, but some time later Wesley must have suggested to Burney that this would be a good opportunity for him and Novello to play the *Goldberg Variations* to him. The performance needed careful planning, as Burney did not possess the two-manual harpsichord for which the work is written. Although Wesley would have had no hesitation in performing it on the piano, he evidently did not consider it playable on a single instrument, as many variations call for the use of two manuals. In fact, as many modern pianists, including Rosalyn Tureck, Glenn Gould, and Angela Hewitt have demonstrated, the *Variations* can be performed on one piano, but Wesley and Novello came up with the idea of a performance on two pianos: one of them to be Burney's own Broadwood grand, the other a matching instrument to be moved into Burney's apartments for the occasion.

Burney initially turned down this suggestion on the grounds of lack of space in his apartments and fear of the damage that might ensue, suggesting instead that Wesley and Novello might like to find a suitable piano shop where they could play the *Variations*. The drawback to this arrangement, as Burney subsequently acknowledged in a letter to Wesley of around 17 July, was that he himself would have no part in it, as he had made up his mind never again to go out 'into the open air'. On further reflection, however, he decided that his desire to hear the *Variations* outweighed any worries about possible damage to his apartments, and that there would after all be enough room in his parlour for two grand pianos. He therefore requested Wesley to arrange the delivery of the additional piano, suggesting at the same time that he and Novello might like to 'decimate' the *Variations* and perform them over three separate visits, ten variations at a time.[10] By 19 July, when Burney wrote again, the delivery of the piano had been arranged for the following day, and all that was left was to make the final arrangements. Burney had now abandoned his previous suggestion that Wesley and Novello should visit three times and decided that he wanted to hear the *Variations* all at once, after which it would be possible to discuss them, or possibly have a repeat performance.

There are no retrospective references in the correspondence to the performance of the *Variations*. But what in the end turned out to be a single visit on 20 July appears to have been a great success. Wesley subsequently presented Novello with Burney's letter to him of 17 July, which Novello annotated as being a memento of

> the very pleasant meeting we had together at the Doctor's apartments in Chelsea Hospital, when I played the whole of the "30 Variations" by Sebastian Bach, as Duetts with Sam Wesley, to the great delight of Burney, who acknowledged to us

---

[10] Burney to SW, c. 17 July 1810. For the text of this letter and a fuller account of this incident, see my 'Dr Burney, Samuel Wesley, and Bach's *Goldberg Variations*'.

both, that he had formed a very inadequate opinion of Sebastian Bach's fertility of invention and versatility of style, till he had heard our performance of those extraordinary specimens of counterpoint, called the "30 Variations".

By the time of the *Goldberg Variations* performance, Sarah's pregnancy was well advanced. On 14 August 1810 she gave birth at Adam's Row to her first child, Samuel Sebastian, named after his father and his beloved Bach. Attending the confinement and the period immediately after it were a nurse and Sarah's sister. Wesley was able to reassure his mother, who had evidently heard news to the contrary from Charlotte's servant, that the birth had incurred little extra expense, and that the nurse and Sarah's sister were the only additional people in the house – a very different situation from the time of Charlotte, when it was 'full of Gossips & Hangers on from Morning till Night'.[11] Moreover, although the separation had taken its toll on Wesley's finances and he had been forced to realize his remaining investments in government stocks in order to provide for Charlotte, he was at present in a comfortable financial situation. A month later, on 17 September, the first part of the '48', consisting of the first twelve preludes and fugues from Book I, was published; the remaining parts would follow at intervals, the last in July 1813. The final list of subscribers included many of the expected names, both from the music profession and from Wesley's circle of friends and acquaintances. There were also many out-of-town subscribers, indicating that awareness of Bach's music had by this time reached far beyond London.[12]

Early in November, Wesley went to Birmingham to visit Joseph Moore, the organizer of the Birmingham festival, to discuss arrangements for the following year's festival, which Moore had invited him to direct. This was probably the first time that Wesley had been away from home since setting up house with Sarah, and certainly the first time since the birth of Samuel Sebastian. One of the letters that he wrote to her on this trip has survived, containing an urgent request for Sarah to send on the copy of Haydn's *La Tempesta* that Vaughan had asked him to take with him to Birmingham, and which he had forgotten. The tone is solicitous and tender, Wesley addressing Sarah as 'Pexy' (his pet name for her throughout their relationship) and referring to himself as 'Mr Pug' and 'Mr Faw':

> Pexy must not expect Mr Pug till *Sunday.*– Mrs Moore will not let me go till Saturday– I shall return in the Post Coach which sets out at 8 in the Evening & arrives at the Green Man & Still about *one* o'Clock, when Pexy may come there & wait for Mr Faw who will be very glad to see her again, though every body here is doing everything possible to make me comfortable.

This is the first surviving letter from Wesley to Sarah. Further letters followed at intervals over the next twenty years, written on every occasion that Wesley was

---

[11] SW to Sarah Gwynne Wesley, 12 Sept. [1810].
[12] See Kassler 'The Bachists of 1810'.

away from home: in turn from Margate, Norwich, Great Yarmouth, Winchester, Birmingham again, Nottingham, Leeds, and finally Bristol.

Wesley began 1811 with a visit to Tunstall, near Woodbridge, Suffolk, at the invitation of his friends Christopher Jeaffreson, the incumbent there, and his wife, to whom Wesley had given music lessons in London in late 1809.[13] He had a difficult journey. After a mild Christmas, the temperature had dropped to below freezing on New Year's Eve. It remained bitterly cold for the next ten days, dropping to as low as 18°F on the night of 3 January and rarely rising above freezing. There was snow and wind on the first three days of the year, and the prospects for Wesley's trip to Suffolk cannot have seemed promising. On 5 January, when he set out early in the morning for Tunstall via Ipswich and Woodbridge, it was cold but clear. He reached Colchester, fifty-two miles from London, between 2 and 3p.m., but was told that the coach could not go any further that day, as there were snow-drifts of up to ten feet deep ahead, blown by the strong easterly wind. Reluctantly, he decided that there was nothing for it but to spend the night in Colchester. The following morning he and two of his travelling companions decided not to wait for the coach, but to walk the eighteen miles to Ipswich, leaving their baggage in the care of the inn keeper to put on the stage coach later. They arrived in Ipswich 'without being much fatigued' at around 2p.m., and Wesley set off again in a local coach on the seven further miles to Woodbridge at around 4p.m.

Wesley conveyed this news to Sarah in a letter written at Woodbridge, where he was to spend the night before embarking on the final stage of his journey the following morning. Sarah's reply, a few days later, contained the news that 'Little Boy Blue' (the baby Samuel Sebastian) was not well, and enclosed a much-needed pound note in response to Wesley's request, presumably to make good the additional expenses he had incurred on his journey because of the delays caused by the weather. A few days later, Wesley wrote again, thanking Sarah for the money, and asking for further news of Samuel Sebastian's health. At the same time he asked Sarah to ask Novello if he had the proofs of 'the fugues' (i.e. the second part of the '48' edition) that the engraver Lomax had sent him, and to enquire what progress he was making.[14] He also sent his best wishes to friends at home, including the eccentric traveller Robert Twiss, whom Wesley had known since the time of the family concerts and had been a neighbour of Wesley and Charlotte in Camden Town. Nothing is known of Wesley's friendship with him, but John Thomas Smith in his *Nollekens and his Times* (1828) has left an intriguing vignette of the discussions of these two 'celebrated originals' as they walked

---

[13] SW to Sarah Gwynne Wesley, 9 Dec. [1809].
[14] SW to Sarah Suter, ?9 Jan. 1811. The imminent publication of the second part, containing the second half of Book I, had been announced in *MC* on 24 November 1810, where it was stated that it was 'in the hands of the engraver', and would shortly appear. See also SW to Sarah Suter, 15 Jan. 1810.

round Camden Town with Twiss's large poodle, wearing an outsize pair of pasteboard spectacles on his nose.[15]

Wesley's stay with the Jeaffresons passed very agreeably, Wesley telling Sarah that if he had not friends in London he would be happy to stay with them permanently. On 11 January the cold spell at last came to an end, and Wesley was able to go out riding. Three days later he went to the coast, afterwards setting down for Sarah his account of the sea, which he described as 'a great Body of Water to which you can see no End, & this you will not very much wonder at when I tell you also, that in the Part of the Coast where I viewed it, it is full a Hundred & twenty Miles across before you come to any Land; & when the Wind blows hard, the Waves are lifted up much higher than the highest House you ever saw, so that the Sea in a Storm is the very grandest Object in the World, & quite as astonishing as Sebastian Bach'.[16] But for all the warmth of his reception at Tunstall, Wesley was missing Sarah and Samuel Sebastian, not to mention Emma, John William, and Charles, and was anxious to have news of them. Even though the Jeaffresons lived 'like Kings and Princes', Wesley still longed for the simple pleasures of home, such as a boiled beefsteak cooked by Sarah and a glass of brandy and water. It was not luxury that he wanted, but comfort, and he had that as much at Adam's Row as at Tunstall. By 20 January, still anxious to know how his 'poor brats' were, he was preparing for his return journey. His coach fare, which Jeaffreson had already booked for him, would be 18s. This would leave him with just 11s in his pocket, of which he needed to give the servants 5s. But against this he would return home with another 18s, in payment for two copies of the first book of the '48' for Zebedee Tydemann, a music teacher who lived in Framlingham, eight miles away.

Wesley returned to London on 22 January. His next engagement was a second course of lectures at the Surrey Institution: clearly, his disagreement with Spencer at the end of his previous course had not been sufficiently serious to prevent Spencer engaging him again. The course was originally advertised to start on 14 January. At some point in late December, Wesley wrote to Spencer to request a postponement, but Spencer replied to say that this was not possible. On 3 January, just before setting off for Tunstall, Wesley wrote again, apparently agreeing to begin the course on the advertised date. At the same time, he informed Spencer that he would not after all require two pianos for his lecture, but only one, and also the organ by Elliot used for his previous course. This was for his lecture on tuning and temperament, and would need to have some alterations made which would cost an additional £5. He hoped that there would be no objection to doing this, as he felt that it was indispensable in order to 'render clear a Doctrine in the Distribution of the musical Scale which is of the utmost Importance in the Improvement of Harmony on keyed Instruments'.[17] Wesley did not give his impending trip to Suffolk to Spencer as the reason for

---

[15] Smith, *Nollekens and his Times*, p. 149 n.
[16] SW to Sarah Suter, 15 Jan. 1811.
[17] *SW to Spencer, 3 Jan. [1811].

his request for a postponement of the beginning of the course, stating instead that it was because the text of his first lecture had 'fallen among thieves', and that he would need additional time to prepare a replacement.

On 14 January, the date of his first lecture, Wesley was still in Tunstall, and did not return to London until eight days later. It is impossible to tell whether he genuinely planned to return in time for the beginning of his course, or whether he intended from the first to stay in Tunstall and to force a postponement on some manufactured pretext, as one suspects he had done at the Royal Institution two years earlier. At all events, the new course started on either 4 or 11 February with Wesley's lecture on tuning and temperament. According to Wesley, this was the replacement for the lecture that had 'fallen among thieves', although we may suspect that the original was lost rather than stolen. It is clear from Wesley's description of the lecture and from his request for the organ by Elliot that he had used during his previous course, that it was a close cousin to the Royal Institution lecture that had sparked off the controversy in *NMMR*. As it happens, the text has survived, albeit heavily altered from its original state to suit the differing circumstances of the many subsequent occasions on which Wesley delivered it.[18] Annotated 'the first lecture of the second Course', and dated 3 January 1811 (the date of Wesley's letter to Spencer), it is entitled 'The most eligible Method of acquiring a Command of Keyed Instruments – Tuning – Old & new Method – Equal Temperament'. In the first part of the lecture as preserved, Wesley recommended keyboard players to become proficient in all keys, continuing with a discussion of the respective merits of different forms of temperament, including equal temperament. At this point in 1811, Wesley would no doubt have gone on to discuss the merits of the Hawkes-Elliot instrument and its tuning, probably using the instrument to give an instant comparison between the 'old' and the 'new' methods. This part of the lecture has disappeared, however, no doubt discarded by Wesley when he no longer had the Hawkes-Elliot instrument at his disposal.

The course ended on 10 April with a lecture that dealt, as Wesley informed Spencer, with 'the Necessity of establishing a Standard Pitch for all keyed Instruments, & the Propriety of teaching Beginners on *good* Instruments, & not on Rubbish picked up at the Shops of Brokers, apparently cheap, but eventually very dear'. It may also have included, at the request of subscribers, a performance by the Italian violinist Paolo Spagnoletti.[19]

Wesley's 1811 benefit concert, on 27 April, was again at the Hanover Square Rooms. By now he was including more music by himself and less by Bach. Two compositions were given their first performances: the Trio for Three Pianofortes, played by Wesley, Novello, and Wesley's former pupil Charles Stokes, and a glee described in press advertisements as being to words by Peter Pindar. This was presumably 'O Delia, every charm is thine', KO 229, the only known

[18] BL, Add. MS 35014, fols 2–16. See also *SW to Spencer, 1 Feb. 1811.
[19] *SW to Spencer, 7 Apr. [1811].

glee by Wesley to words by Pindar, the *nom-de-plume* of the clergyman and doctor John Wolcot. Also performed were 'In exitu Israel' and 'Dixit Dominus' (presumably the eight-part setting), and there was the usual organ improvisation. Bach was represented by a solo violin sonata, played by Salomon, and one of the sonatas for violin and harpsichord, performed by Salomon with Wesley on the piano; there were probably also some preludes and fugues from the '48'.[20]

The novelty of the concert was the Trio for Three Pianofortes, one of the few works in the repertory for this unusual combination. As we know from a lecture delivered in 1826, Wesley's inspiration was Mozart's Sonata for Two Pianos, K 448, which he had first encountered on his visit to Cambridge in the summer of 1808 and had played with the daughter of his friend Hague.[21] The Trio, a substantial piece in three movements lasting for around twenty minutes, is a lively *jeux d'esprit*. Because of the difficulty and expense of assembling three pianos on the same platform, there could only be occasional public performances, and domestic performances would be equally infrequent. For this reason there was no point in Wesley attempting to publish it. But Wesley did arrange a number of subsequent performances at benefits and play-throughs in the showrooms or workshops of piano-makers for his own amusement and that of his friends. One of these was on 25 July 1814 at the premises of Clementi and Co. in Tottenham Court Road; another was on 18 May 1816 at Kirckman's premises, when Clementi and Kalkbrenner were among those present.[22]

---

[20] *MC*, 20 Apr. 1811; *The Times*, 24 Apr. 1811.
[21] BL, Add. MS 35014, fol. 36. SW recollected that he had encountered the Mozart sonata in Cambridge 'around 15 Years ago', but his only visit to Cambridge at this period was the one in 1808.
[22] *SW to Novello, [19 July 1814], [13 May 1816].

9

Vincent Novello and the Portuguese Embassy Chapel, 1811–1812

May 1811 is a watershed in our knowledge of Wesley's day-to-day activities, for it was then that Novello started to preserve the most memorable of the letters that Wesley was now writing to him in large numbers. It is clear that the first surviving letter, dated 22 May, did not mark the beginning of the correspondence, much less the beginning of their friendship and professional relationship. Wesley had probably known Novello since his boyhood, and almost certainly since the time of his appointment as organist at the Portuguese Embassy Chapel at the age of sixteen in 1796 or 1797. Their more recent association probably dated back a year or two, and there seems little doubt that Wesley's most recent pieces of Roman Catholic church music would have been written for Novello and his choir. As we have seen, the setting of 'Domine salvam fac' may have been written for the re-opening of the chapel's organ in 1808, and this piece was included in Novello's first publication, *A Collection of Sacred Music*, published in May or June 1811.

At the Portuguese Embassy Chapel, Wesley acted as Novello's unofficial assistant, helping as organist and choirmaster and deputizing as necessary. It was an arrangement that suited Wesley well. Although he had not been an observant Roman Catholic for many years and regarded the doctrines of the Church with something approaching contempt, he still retained his deep love of Gregorian chant and a fascination with the complexity and richness of the liturgy, summing up his ambivalence in his remark to Jacob that 'if the Roman Doctrines were like the Roman *Music* we should have Heaven upon Earth'.[1] Novello, it appears from a comment in one of Wesley's later letters, had similar views.[2] Together they could devote themselves to the music of the chapel without being overly concerned with matters of personal religious observance. Wesley's role at the chapel also gave him access to the organ, and a regular duet partner with whom to play Bach.

Wesley's letters to Novello about the chapel music give a lively sense of all the last-minute improvisations and changes of plan attendant on working with a volunteer choir of fluctuating numbers and composition that many present-day church musicians will recognize. In the earliest extant letter, discussing the

---

[1] *SW to Jacob, 5 Nov. [1809].
[2] *SW to Pettet, 29 July 1816.

arrangements for a service on Ascension Day 1811, on which he was to deputize for Novello, he pleaded:

> I must also desire to know exactly what is to be performed; for I am an aukward Devil when hurried, & you will acknowledge that there are very sudden Stage-Tricks played in your Choir with Regard to immediate Reversions of original Intentions, & which if not methodized a little for *me* who am not up to your very clever Harlequin Jumps from a Kyrie on the Desk to another at the Bottom of a Well, or to be fetched from Mr Fryer's in S. Audley Street, while they are singing the Gloria of the Introit, then the Mass must stand still in a very decorous & edifying Manner to the Congregation.[3]

Wesley's involvement with the chapel also gave him further opportunities to compose for the Roman rite. From this period come a number of works written for various liturgical purposes, including some revisions of earlier music, a setting of the plainsong *Missa pro Angelis*, and some smaller pieces. One, a setting of the hymn 'Ut queant laxis' for the feast of the birth of John the Baptist on 24 June 1812, caused Wesley a good deal of amusement. The Gregorian melody for this hymn is traditionally ascribed to Guido d'Arezzo, and the hymn and its melody have a special place in music theory. The opening syllables of its six lines ('ut', 're', 'mi', 'fa', 'sol', and 'la') use all five different vowel sounds and six different consonants, and are set to successively higher notes in the scale. The hymn was used as the basis of the medieval and Renaissance system of solmization, and the traditional pitch-names were in the nineteenth century used in the sol-fa systems developed by John Curwen and others. On 22 June Wesley sent his new setting, in which the melody followed the original plainsong by starting each line on a successively higher note of the scale, to Novello. In his covering letter he stated that he thought it appropriate to 'cobble up something of the sort for the Occasion', and hoped that Novello would be able to select suitable singers to enable it to be sung to best advantage at the forthcoming Feast. Two days later Wesley wrote again to thank Novello for his comments, adopting the line-by-line structure of the hymn itself:

> SW feels the **UT**most Satisfaction in **RE**turning his Acknowledgements for the **MI**nute Mention of the Circumstances attending his Tune, in which there is not discoverable any Trait of the **FA**stidious Disposition of most musical Criticks, which is as clear as **SOL** at Noon Day: the Author however fears that the Partiality of Friendship may have operated to pronounce too favourable an Opinion of a Composition which many may perhaps consider only **LA**-la after all.[4]

From 1811 until early 1826, when they quarrelled and broke off communication for over four years, Novello was Wesley's closest professional colleague and friend. At the same time, Wesley's association with Jacob appears to have diminished. If there was no cooling of relations between the two men, there certainly appears to have been a parting of their professional ways at around this

---

[3] *SW to Novello, 22 May [1811].
[4] *SW to Novello, 24 June [1812].

time. After the end of 1809, there are only two further extant letters from Wesley to Jacob. One, of May 1813, is friendly, but is couched in terms which suggest that Wesley and Jacob were no longer meeting regularly. The tone of the other, of February 1816, in response to a request from Jacob for a contribution to a publication of church music, suggests that by this time they had substantially lost touch with one another.[5] And when Jacob came to organise his next mammoth recital of Bach's music at Surrey Chapel in April 1811, Wesley was not involved, nor did he take part in the subsequent recitals there in 1812 and 1814.[6] What probably happened is that as Wesley's professional opportunities in central London increased, he had less time to travel to the Blackfriars area south of the river, and that in consequence the two men gradually lost touch.

Wesley's relationship with Novello extended far beyond the confines of the Portuguese Embassy Chapel. As we have seen, in the previous summer Novello had joined Wesley in a play-through of the *Goldberg Variations* to Burney. He now became Wesley's preferred duet partner and his principal collaborator in the promotion of Bach. This role would have arisen naturally from their sharing of the organist's duties at the Portuguese Embassy Chapel: Wesley recorded in his *Reminiscences* that they frequently played Bach's organ music together on the chapel's organ as voluntaries.[7] In time, as we shall see, Novello would join Wesley for duet performances of Bach at the Lenten oratorios and at other public concerts.

Many of Wesley's surviving letters to Novello are to make or confirm arrangements or for other equally mundane purposes. Few are simply that, however. Almost all contain some additional information, witticism, or piece of gossip that could have easily been saved until their next face-to-face meeting. Sometimes, indeed, the primary purpose of the letter appears almost as an afterthought. In one case, Wesley devotes most of a letter to discussing a word of Greek that Novello had seen painted on the wall of a building in Welbeck Street and had subsequently asked Wesley about, pointing out an error in its orthography and wondering what precisely its significance could be, before finally asking Novello if he required his services the following Thursday at the chapel.[8]

Novello's evident enthusiasm for Wesley's company does not appear to have been shared by his wife Mary Sabilla, whom he had married in August 1808. A devoted wife, home-maker, and mother (the Novellos' eldest child, Mary Victoria, was born in June 1809; the second, Joseph Alfred, in 1810) she would doubtless have been outraged at Wesley's abandonment of his wife and family and his liaison with Sarah Suter. And she would have had little time for his outspokenness, wild behaviour, and not infrequent drunkenness. She was

---

[5] *SW to Jacob, 10 May 1813, 15 Feb. 1816.

[6] Jacob did, however, continue to play Wesley's music at these recitals. He performed a voluntary in 'C natural' (i.e. Op. 6 No. 2 or 6) at the 1811 recital, a voluntary in D (Op. 6 No. 1, 5 or 8), at the 1812 recital, and Op. 6 No. 10 (described in the programme as 'new'), at the 1814 recital.

[7] *Reminiscences*, fol. 51.

[8]. *SW to Novello, 12 Aug. [1811].

> Dear Sir
>
> I have the Pleasure to inform you that I have arranged a Plan with Birchall, which will enable me to bring out the 4th Number of the Preludes & Fugues by the 1st of July next, & shall give a public Notice of it within a few Days hence. — The Subscribers in general have been exceedingly remiss in their Applications for their 3d Number, which has been one Reason (& the chief one) for the remaining Book being so long delayed. — I was however always resolved, ... at all Hazards, to perform my Engagement in this Business with the Public, which I would have much sooner done, could I have coaxed the Engravers into better Humour before. With best Wishes to Mrs Jacob & Family, I remain dear Sir
>
> very truly yours
>
> Wesley
>
> Monday
> 10th of May.
> 1813.

4 Wesley's letter to Benjamin Jacob of 10 May 1813, discussing arrangements for the publication of the fourth part of the Wesley-Horn edition of the '48'. By courtesy of the Royal College of Music, London.

also becoming well known as a hostess, and the family home at 240 Oxford Street was fast becoming the centre of a literary and artistic circle that included Charles and Mary Lamb, John and Leigh Hunt, and would later include Keats, Charles Cowden Clarke, and Edward Holmes. The Novellos are frequently mentioned in the letters of Leigh Hunt and Charles Lamb, and Vincent Novello's playing and Mary Sabilla's hospitality are affectionately described by Lamb in his essay 'A Chapter on Ears'. It is notable that there is no mention of Wesley in any of the accounts of this circle, and it is hard to escape the conclusion that he would have been far from welcome there. A few years after Wesley's death, Mary Sabilla wrote to the bass singer Henry Phillips with her recollections of him. She was characteristically forthright:

> I have great pleasure in sending you two of Wesley's letters, which are particularly interesting, as shewing the mind of a man in its opposite extremes of mad fun and excessive depression, to which alternations Wesley always was subject. I knew him unfortunately, too well; pious Catholic, raving atheist, mad, reasonable, drunk and sober – the dread of all wives and regular families, a warm friend, a bitter foe, a satirical talker, a flatterer at times of those he cynically traduced at others – a blasphemer at times, a puleing Methodist at others.[9]

Shortly after Samuel Sebastian's birth the previous August, Wesley had remarked to his mother that he was 'never so little financially embarrassed as at present'.[10] By the end of May 1811, however, there was a new set of financial problems to contend with. The immediate cause was a sudden demand made on Charlotte's account. Paying this had exhausted the money which otherwise would have lasted Wesley until the midsummer quarter-day, when he expected to receive his half-yearly fees for teaching at his two schools. He therefore asked his mother for a short-term loan until that time.[11] On the following day he wrote to his brother Charles. Pointing out that he made every effort to avoid giving his mother any trouble, he gave details of the exorbitant demands that had suddenly been made on him for the payment of Charlotte's debts, and which had obliged him to ask his mother for money. This, he stressed, was solely to allow him to keep his head above water, to avoid being 'dragged off to jail', and to ensure that his children did not fall into distress.

Here, Wesley came to the point and raised a matter that had evidently been on his mind for some time. He reminded Charles that after the disastrous series of concerts in 1802 he had lent Charles and Sarah £100, which he had been able to raise from selling some of his holdings in government stock. For this, he had received a note of hand signed by them both. He was now anxious that the debt should be repaid, in whole or part, so as to help his current situation. Charles and Sarah were evidently not able to repay the loan, and shortly afterwards Wesley began to explore other possibilities. In the will of his aunt Rebecca Gwynne, who had died in 1799, Wesley and his son Charles had been left £100

---

[9] Mary Sabilla Novello to Henry Phillips, n.d. [1841 or 1842] (BL, Add. MS 31764, fol. 34).
[10] SW to Sarah Gwynne Wesley, 12 Sept. 1810.
[11] SW to Sarah Gwynne Wesley, 30 May 1811.

that was to come to them on his mother's death, the interest on the sum to be paid to her during her lifetime. He was now anxious to know if it would be possible for him to receive his share of this legacy in advance. He appears to have discussed the matter with Charles and Sarah around the beginning of June before raising it in writing with his mother a month later. He was prepared to pay his mother the interest that she would forego by letting him have his legacy in advance, so that she would be financially no worse off by the transaction. By this time, he was anxious to have a quick decision. He was expecting several bills soon that he was at present unable to pay, and needed to lay out £50 as part of a payment for Charles's apprenticeship to an apothecary. Meanwhile, he had still not been paid for his teaching at his two schools. He suggested that his mother should consult James Pettit, a Bank of England official, for a professional opinion of his proposal.[12]

Wesley's mother acted quickly in consulting Pettit. Less than a week later she had replied with his opinion, apparently to the effect that the terms of the will could not be altered in the way that Wesley had suggested. Wesley was not convinced about the accuracy of this response. He had presumably also had an unsatisfactory reply from Charles and Sarah about the repayment of the money they owed, as he later stated to his mother that it was 'not a little mortifying' that in the two quarters that he was applying for money, and in which he was doing no more than asking for what was really his own, no-one was prepared to help him.[13] Negotiations dragged on through July, in the course of which Wesley escaped to spend a few days with the Jeaffresons in Tunstall. By the beginning of August, Wesley's mother appears to have come up with a limited amount of money – although not, it appears, the £50 that Wesley was hoping for – so that Wesley could write to thank her for her 'very welcome and opportune assistance', hoping that he would soon be in a position when he would not need to inconvenience his friends and family any further. His present situation, he reminded his mother, was all the fault of 'the vilest of women', without whose continuing demands he would have been able to manage his affairs without difficulty. In the meantime, he had heard of an excellent school for his second son John within twelve miles of London, to which he was contemplating sending him.[14]

The help of Wesley's family appears to have been enough to avert this latest crisis, but it was perhaps only to be expected that another one would be waiting in the wings. Less than three months later, Wesley was obliged to return with a request for another emergency loan. Charlotte's landlord had appeared to demand a quarter's rent, despite having been warned in the presence of witnesses that Wesley would no longer be responsible for her debts. When Wesley refused to pay, he issued a writ, which Wesley bailed and was prepared to defend in court, confident that he would win his case. He was unwilling to

---

[12] SW to Sarah Gwynne Wesley, 4 July 1811.
[13] SW to Sarah Gwynne Wesley, [10 July 1811].
[14] SW to Sarah Gwynne Wesley, 1 Aug. 1811.

allow any more money for Charlotte's maintenance beyond the £100 that he had agreed. In the meantime, he had one bill for £7 10s. outstanding, and asked his mother if she would contribute £5 towards it. If she could not, his credit would be destroyed.[15]

On 27 September, Wesley travelled to Birmingham to conduct the Birmingham festival, which followed its usual pattern of three days of concentrated music-making: a church service in St Philip's church (now Birmingham Cathedral) on the morning of Wednesday 2 October, a performance of *Messiah* and a 'Grand Selection of Sacred Music' there on the Thursday and Friday mornings, and miscellaneous secular concerts at the New Theatre in the evenings. The eleven vocal soloists were headed by Catalani and Braham. The choir numbered 119, and the orchestra, led by Francis Cramer, seventy-four, making (with Wesley at the organ and piano) a total (with the soloists) of 205 performers, which the newspaper advertisements proudly proclaimed was 'the largest Band ever assembled on the like Occasion'.[16] Among the works performed was Wesley's 'Exultate Deo' of 1800, probably now in its revised version with full orchestral accompaniment.[17]

Although Wesley had worked with many of the soloists in 1809 at Tamworth, this was the first time he had appeared professionally with Catalani, and it may also have been the first time that he had met her. He would have known her well by reputation, however, and had probably heard her sing on more than once occasion. She had arrived in London from France in 1806, making her triumphant London debut at the King's Theatre in Portogallo's *Semiramide* on 13 December. *The Times* was ecstatic, remarking that the range of her voice exceeded that of any other female singer and that its volume was such that she could fill the theatre without any sense of strain. Then came the inevitable comparisons. In the neatness and rapidity of her execution she was almost the equal of Billington, while in other aspects she combined the best features of such earlier stars as Banti, Mara, and Grassini. During the 1807 and 1808 seasons she carried all before her, appearing in a succession of operas by Portogallo and others that were little more than a vehicle for her spectacular vocal abilities. Her earnings were legendary: in the 1808 season she was paid £5,250 to appear twice a week between January and August, and was guaranteed the proceeds from two benefit performances. In the following season her demands were too great for the King's Theatre and she was not re-engaged, but she was able to find sufficient engagements at concerts, both in London and in the provinces: as we have seen, she was in Bath in early 1809 at the same time as Wesley. Unlike many of her contemporaries, including Billington and Banti, her life was free of scandal: Mount-Edgcumbe commented that there was 'not an amiable trait in her character' and that the

---

[15] SW to Sarah Gwynne Wesley, 24 Oct. 1811.
[16] *ABG*, 29 Sept. 1811.
[17] The performing material is written on paper with a 1810 watermark.

conduct of her private life was irreproachable.[18] She was also generous: in Birmingham on this occasion she is said to have given fifty guineas to the hospital charity for the benefit of which the festival was organized.

This was the only occasion on which Wesley was to direct the Birmingham festival. The 1802 and 1805 festivals had been directed by Thomas Greatorex, the director of the Concert of Ancient Music, but for some reason – perhaps out of some dissatisfaction with his performance or simply a wish to have a change – Moore did not engage him for the 1808 festival, which was directed instead by Crotch. Moore may have found Crotch unsatisfactory – an isolated letter from him to Moore concerning the arrangements for the festival suggests that he may have been overbearing and heavy-handed in his approach – and Moore may have decided to look elsewhere for the 1811 festival.[19] His choice of Wesley would have been influenced by Wesley's growing reputation and probably by good reports of his performance at Tamworth the previous September. Nothing is known about how well Wesley fulfilled his function at Birmingham, but for the 1814 festival Moore decided to revert to Greatorex, who then conducted every succeeding festival until his death in 1831.

In March 1812, more than two years after the final breakup of their marriage, Wesley and Charlotte were able to effect a formal separation agreement.[20] It is in a form more or less standard for such agreements, between Wesley, Charlotte, and George Oliver, described as a linen draper of Skinner's Street in the City of London, who acted as Charlotte's trustee. The inclusion of a trustee was necessary, for as we have seen, a married woman had no power to enter into agreements or contracts. The agreement afforded important protection to both Wesley and Charlotte. For his part, Wesley agreed to pay annual maintenance of £130 to Charlotte and Emma, renounce any claim on any Charlotte's personal possessions, and allow her to live without molestation as if she were a single woman. This last clause was important, as it prevented Wesley from entering a suit for criminal conversation against anyone with whom Charlotte should consort in the future. Charlotte for her part agreed not to take any legal action against Wesley on account of the separation or to hold him liable for any debts she incurred. All this was subject to one highly important provision: maintenance was payable in monthly instalments, and if Wesley fell in arrears by fourteen days, the agreement would be void and he would become liable for Charlotte's debts.

Perhaps the most significant detail in the document is the amount at which maintenance was set. At the time, it was typically set at around one third of the husband's income, with perhaps an additional amount for dependent children. The figure agreed by Wesley suggests an annual income of around £400, and is perhaps the most accurate indication we have of his earnings at this time. It

---

[18] Mount-Edgcumbe, *Musical Reminiscences*, pp. 109–10.
[19] See my 'Crotch, Moore, and the 1808 Birmingham Festival'.
[20] MARC, DDCW 6/88. For private separation at this time, see Stone, *Road to Divorce*, pp. 149–82.

equated to the income of a moderately successful lawyer or doctor, and suggests that the primary cause of Wesley's continuing financial problems was not, as has sometimes been supposed, his lack of income, but his personal and family circumstances.

In fact, it is difficult to see how Wesley's income was made up at this time. It certainly was not coming from his public performances. Apart from a single guest appearance at the second of Knyvett and Vaughan's Vocal Concerts on 9 March, at which he performed an extempore organ voluntary and fugue on a subject from the duet 'Ah! perdona' from Mozart's *La clemenza di Tito*,[21] he does not appear to have performed in public at all in the first three months of 1812. One can only presume that the bulk of his income was coming from his teaching.

Wesley's benefit in 1812 was late in the season, on 5 June. It was his most ambitious concert yet, involving for the first time an orchestra in addition to the vocal and keyboard performers of the previous three years' concerts. Planning had begun in good time. By the end of March, he had arranged the date and the venue, and had secured the participation of Catalani: a major achievement, as her presence on its own would virtually guarantee financial success. On 6 April the preliminary press advertisement appeared, announcing that Catalani and 'Signor Fisher' (i.e. Joseph Fischer, the son of Mozart's first Osmin in *Die Entführung aus dem Serail*), had agreed to participate. The programme would include the Trio for Three Pianofortes and a new organ concerto, written specially for the occasion. On 31 March Wesley gleefully announced the news of Catalani's agreement to participate to Novello, adding that she had invited him to dine with her the following Sunday and had recommended him to speak to her then on the 'Bertinotti Question'.[22] We can only speculate about what this was. The soprano Teresa Bertinotti was Catalani's principal rival in London, and had sung with her at the King's Theatre during the previous two seasons. In early 1812, she and a number of other singers had lost patience with William Taylor, the manager of the theatre, who had not paid their salaries for some considerable time, and defected to form a rival Italian opera company at the Pantheon. By the end of the season the company had failed, but not before it had cost Taylor and the King's Theatre £6,000 in lost receipts. One of its productions, on 2 May, was to be of the first two acts of Mozart's *The Marriage of Figaro*, in which Bertinotti was to play the Countess. This anticipated the projected English premiere of the complete opera at the King's Theatre, in which Catalani was to play the same role. Under the circumstances, direct comparisons between Bertinotti and Catalani could hardly fail to be made. Wesley's remark suggests that there was some question of her performing at the benefit as well as Catalani. If so, the 'Bertinotti question' would certainly need the most tactful and careful handling.

In early May, disaster struck. Paul Valabrègue, Catalani's husband and

---

[21] *The Times*, 7 Mar. 1812.
[22] *SW to Novello, 31 Mar. 1812.

manager, wrote to Wesley to announce her withdrawal from the concert, saying that under the terms of a new arrangement ('or rather derangement', as Wesley commented) she had come to with Taylor, she was prohibited from singing anywhere else but the King's Theatre, under threat of a penalty of £1,300. Wesley was appalled at this news, as without Catalani's participation the success and profitability of his concert was thrown into question. He was not disposed to believe a word of Valabrègue's story, pointing out to Novello that Catalani was advertised to sing at the Ashley brothers' benefit concert at Covent Garden on Whitsun eve, and that she continued to sing every Friday at the Vocal Concerts. He threatened to expose the whole matter in the newspapers, as a result of which he was sure both Catalani and Valabrègue would attract widespread censure. But perhaps all was not lost: Novello, who had played continuo in the Pantheon company and thus knew Bertinotti, said to Wesley that he might have enough influence with her to persuade her to perform without charge. If she agreed, the situation might not be a total disaster. Wesley remarked that as far as he was concerned Bertinotti was 'a Dish worth a whole *Course* of Catalanis', adding that unfortunately this opinion was not shared by the public.

By this time, with the concert still a month away, Wesley was run off his feet with the arrangements for the concert and a host of other activities. He had recently moved house to Tottenham Court, almost directly across the New Road from Adam's Row. In mid-April, he appeared at Goss's benefit concert, playing an extempore organ voluntary.[23] On 10 May, he was to give the opening recital on the new organ at Christ Church, Blackfriars; it was by Elliot, and the only one of his instruments known to have incorporated the Hawkes patent action.[24] On 16 May, he was to appear at Salomon's benefit concert at the Hanover Square Rooms, where he was to accompany no less a singer than Braham at the piano in an English version of Beethoven's *Adelaide*, adapted to words by Milton.[25] Under the circumstances, it was not surprising that he was describing himself to Novello as

> up to the A–e in all Manner of omnium Gatherum: what with signing Tickets, teaching those never meant to learn, see, hear, or understand; looking after Scrapers & Chorus-Bawlers, answering & *honouring* Bills for such as have done *me* the Honour to ruin me; laying a *musical* Siege to Badajos [i.e. composing his piano sonata *The Siege of Badajoz*, KO 706] for Mr Preston; (& for Bread & Cheese;) collecting Ammunition for the 5th of June, & snatching every Moment to write a *Bar* at a time (not more) of the Duet for the same Occasion; that by the Brains of Locke, Newton, & Mugnié! my Sconce is so bewildered & *betwattled* (as the Wenches say) that it is odds but I shall break down like a winded Post-Horse before the Day shall arrive.–[26]

---

[23] John Marsh, *Journal*.
[24] *SW to Novello, 6 May [1812].
[25] *The Times*, 12, 14 May 1812.
[26] *SW to Novello, 6 May [1812].

It was perhaps just as well that he was not also involved in the latest of Jacobs's mammoth Surrey Chapel recitals, to be held on 21 May.

There had also been important developments on the masonic front. The Grand Lodge of Modern Freemasons, under whose jurisdiction the Somerset House lodge fell, had decided to create the office of Grand Organist, and Wesley, as a Mason and the leading organist of the day, was invited to be its first incumbent. This was the highest musical position in English Freemasonry. It may have been created in anticipation of the union between the Moderns and their rivals the Ancients, about which negotiations had been proceeding for some time. A good deal of music would be required at the elaborate ceremonies to mark the union, which Wesley could help to provide. The appointment was a highly advantageous one for Wesley, as it put him in regular contact with many people of influence who were in a position, directly or indirectly, to distribute significant amounts of patronage. The Duke of Kent was the Grand Master of the Ancients and the Duke of Sussex of the Moderns, and other members of the royal family and the aristocracy were heavily represented in the upper reaches of both Grand Lodges. Many also held positions as patrons of the Ancient Concerts and the Vocal Concerts, or had influence in other areas that could be to Wesley's advantage. The contacts that Wesley could make in the lodge could be of inestimable value in the furtherance of his career, if only he could make good use of them. But Wesley was, characteristically, less than delighted at being elected to the post, and appears to have raised some objection to paying the lodge dues that went with the position. This was the occasion for a blunt letter from Lucius Coghlan, Grand Chaplain of the Moderns, who had evidently been instrumental in securing his appointment. He reminded Wesley that he had achieved his position in Grand Lodge in a short time and at little expense, whereas it took others over thirty years. Moreover, Wesley had obtained it to the 'extreme mortification and utter disappointment' of another – probably Sir George Smart – for whom it was originally intended (and who no doubt greatly coveted it). Coghlan believed that Wesley already earned more from music than he did from his own profession, and could soon expect to earn twice as much, if he would only cultivate the friends he would make as Grand Organist. His patronage had raised Wesley to a point where he might 'shine with a present lustre and future emolument'. He concluded with a postscript: if Wesley should still think his time wasted, Coghlan would have no objection to his resignation. Then, thinking better of it, he added another: he would ensure that Wesley did not have to pay for his attendance at the following day's meeting or on any future occasions.[27]

Meanwhile, amid the organizing of the benefit, concert appearances, and masonic meetings, everyday life went on. Despite all the other pressing calls on

---

[27] Part of Coghlan's reply to SW is printed in Lightwood, *Samuel Wesley, Musician*, p. 168: see also Fox, 'A Biographical Note on Samuel Wesley', p. 75.

his time, Wesley still had to fit in his teaching and cope with demands for money from Charlotte. Other financial problems continued to press, to which the organization of the benefit no doubt contributed. On 22 May Wesley confessed to his mother that he was 'rather in a hobble': he needed to honour a bill for £35 in three days' time, but at present had only £10 available. He needed to borrow £25 for the month, and wondered if she knew anyone who might be prepared to help.[28] By the day of the benefit, there were many changes to the original programme and list of performers that had appeared in *The Times* at the beginning of April. Both Catalani and Fischer had withdrawn, and the hoped-for involvement of Bertinotti had also failed to materialize. The new organ concerto had evidently not been completed, and was replaced by a concerto described as having been composed for the last Birmingham Festival.[29] Even so, the programme was an attractive one, including 'In exitu Israel', 'Exultate Deo' (no doubt in its second version with orchestral accompaniment), the Trio for Three Pianofortes, and premieres of Wesley's newly composed Grand Duet for the Organ, KO 604, and of an arrangement by Novello of Bach's Prelude in E♭, BWV 552, for organ duet and orchestra. Although it was not advertised, it is probable that Wesley would also have performed his latest piano novelty, *The Siege of Badajoz*, celebrating the recent allied victory in the Pensinsular War.

One of Wesley's major projects at this time was to compile a collection of harmonizations of Gregorian chant. Its publication was to be financed by his friend Joseph Gwilt, and it was hoped it would be widely used in the Roman Catholic church. This was an enormous task which could easily get out of hand. In early November 1811, he had written to Novello to request a meeting to discuss the matter and to try to decide on a format for the publication that would be useful and attractive while at the same time not being too unwieldy.[30] Work on the harmonizations continued through the early part of the following year. But in June 1812 Wesley wrote again to Novello to outline some serious difficulties that had only just become apparent. Wesley had recently played at a dirge (i.e. a funeral service and Requiem Mass) at the Portuguese Embassy Chapel, and had suggested to William Fryer, the chapel's principal chaplain, that he should provide an organ accompaniment for the whole of the funeral service. Fryer demurred, on two grounds: first, that there might be important variations between his own copy, from which Wesley had made his harmonizations, and the book in general use in the Chapel; and second, that it would be better not to make the innovation of performing the funeral service with the organ all at once, as the usual practice on these occasions was to use the organ only for the Mass. Wesley saw the wisdom of this, and therefore agreed that the

[28] *SW to Sarah Gwynne Wesley, 22 May 1812.
[29] The identity of this work is a mystery. The press advertisements for the 1811 Birmingham Festival offer no clarification on what concerto Wesley played on this occasion, and no very likely candidate survives in manuscript.
[30] *SW to Novello, 11 Nov. 1811.

organ should be silent until the beginning of the Mass, in which he thought there would be no problem about variant texts. But he was surprised to find that there were in fact large differences between the version he had harmonized and the one the choir was singing. These anomalies, as he put it to Novello, were a 'ten-barred Gate' against his proceeding any further. If the inconsistencies between different musical texts were as great as those he had just experienced, it would be a waste of time to attempt to produce a volume for the general use of choirs, when perhaps they would be of service to no more than three or four, whose books might by chance happen to correspond with Wesley's. Wesley could see no other way forward than to examine the books of the various different Roman Catholic chapels and to see to what extent they agreed and disagreed. This was a task that Wesley viewed with little enthusiasm, and he felt that Gwilt's offer to cover the entire cost of printing and publication was insufficient reward for such a difficult, time-consuming, and tedious job.[31]

There the matter rested for the moment. By early October Wesley had evidently still not abandoned the project, as he stated in a letter to the prominent Roman Catholic lawyer and amateur musician Charles Butler that a volume of harmonized melodies would be generally useful and that he was ready to undertake it, particularly if Butler would himself contribute an introductory essay.[32] But by early December he had become disillusioned. Despite the state of affairs he had discovered back in June, he had continued with harmonising a Mass of the Fifth Tone, and had now completed it. He was intending to try to sell it, but was not intending to undertake any further harmonizations as there was no profit in them. In any case, he added, the clergy were beginning to turn against Gregorian chant, and now was not a good time to be promoting it.[33]

In September 1812, Wesley went with Samuel Webbe, the son of his old mentor, on a concert visit to Ramsgate and Margate, leaving Sarah, by now seven months pregnant with a second child, at home at Tottenham Court with Samuel Sebastian. These seaside towns were popular holiday resorts for Londoners, and it was largely the influx of summer visitors that Wesley and Webbe hoped would flock to the concert that they intended to organize. The visit appears to have been a speculative venture, undertaken without local knowledge or contacts. Wesley and Webbe set off on 18 September by boat, sailing first down the Thames and then round the coast. Once installed in their lodgings in Ramsgate, their first task was to establish some contacts and prepare the ground for their concert. At the suggestion of Webbe's father, they approached the incumbents of the two parish churches with the offer of free recitals in their respective churches, in the hope that this would make them known, not only as artists, but also as 'lads of some liberality & obliging

---

[31] *SW to Novello, 27 June [1812].
[32] *SW to Butler, 7 Oct. 1812.
[33] *Wesley to Novello, 5 Dec. [1812].

propensity'. To Wesley's amazement, both William Baylay, the vicar of Margate, and Richard Harvey, the curate of Ramsgate, refused, Baylay stating that their suggestion was 'highly indecorous & improper'.[34]

These fruitless negotiations with the two clergymen, whom Wesley described to Novello as 'two black Crows in the Shape & Guise of *Parsons*; one of them a Blockhead & the other a Brute',[35] had wasted a good deal of time, as no arrangements could be made about the time and place of the main concert until they had given their decision. It was not until 26 September, a full week after their arrival, that Wesley and Webbe were able to arrange the concert for the evening of 3 October, the following Saturday, at the Ramsgate Assembly Rooms. The decision to hold the concert in the evening rather than in the morning had come after some considerable deliberation and conflicting advice from different quarters. There were arguments in favour of a morning concert, on the grounds that some visitors would be unoccupied at that time, and would welcome a diversion. On the other hand, as Wesley put it to Novello, all the 'fine Folk' were likely to be occupied in the day in 'prancing about on their Palfries, & bowling about in their Tumbrils for 2 or 3 Hours after scrubbing their mangey Carcases in the Sea' and were therefore unlikely to be prepared to attend a concert until the evening.[36]

Wesley and Webbe had engaged the soprano Catherine Stephens, then eighteen years old and at the beginning of her career, as their vocal soloist, Wesley remarking to Novello that she had a 'very sweet Voice' and sang in a 'pretty style'. She would sing two songs, and Wesley and Webbe would join her in two glees. There would also be a sonata by Pleyel, played by Wesley on the violin and Webbe on the piano, a piano solo ('a rattler') by Dussek, and two piano duets, played by Wesley and Webbe. Wesley would then play a 'fantazia, with some St Giles' Ditty or other' on the piano: this was presumably an improvisation incorporating a popular melody of the day, along the lines of his improvisation at his concert in Birmingham in 1809, which he had ended with the refrain of 'A frog he would a-wooing go'. Wesley and Webbe were not expecting to make a large amount of money from the concert, but they would be happy if they were able to cover their costs, and were reasonably optimistic about their chances of doing so. In the meantime, Wesley and Webbe had been amusing themselves with seaside delights. Scorning bathing machines as having 'neither prospect nor sea-room', they took to swimming every other day 'in puris naturalibus'. On one such occasion, just as they were about to undress, and much to Wesley's amusement, they met William Horsley with his fianceé, Elizabeth Callcott, the eldest daughter of John Wall Callcott, and her mother. Elizabeth Callcott remarked to Wesley that she would have recognized him by sight at any distance, on which Wesley later commented to Novello that she had narrowly escaped the chance of exercising this skill 'in his birthday suit'.[37]

[34] *SW to Novello, 1 Oct. [1812].
[35] Ibid.
[36] Ibid.
[37] Ibid.

Wesley and Webbe returned to London on 5 October, reasonably satisfied with their visit. Their concert had been attended by all the fashionable people left in Ramsgate, but many had had to return to London on account of the general election, and the audience was therefore a good deal smaller than would otherwise have been expected. Wesley and his party had received a warm reception, however, and made friends who assured them that if they returned the following year and put on an oratorio and two or more concerts in the Assembly Rooms they would have a great success. Although they had done no better than break even on this visit, they had established their reputation with the local people and had prepared the ground for future occasions.

One of Wesley's first tasks on his return was to arrange a further play-through of Bach's music to Burney. On 7 or 8 October 1812 he received a letter from Butler informing him that he had just received a note from Burney summoning them to visit him on the following Sunday.[38] This was a request that Wesley was glad to comply with, even though it meant that he would have to miss High Mass at the Portuguese Embassy Chapel to do so. A less pleasant task was to attend to his mounting financial problems. During Wesley's time in Margate and Ramsgate he had had some minor and short-term money worries which had left him temporarily short of ready cash.[39] But there were also some more serious problems on the horizon, and for these Wesley was hoping to call on his mother for assistance. They were evidently too urgent to wait until his return from Margate and Ramsgate, and in his absence he had asked his friend James Ball to raise them with her, and to report back with her decision. Ball called at Wesley's house on 4 October with the news that she was prepared to help. Wesley returned home the following day and almost immediately wrote to her. By this time, the matter was urgent, as she was about to set off with Charles and Sarah for an extended visit to Brighton, and any arrangements would need to be made before her departure. He explained that he had bills for over £40 which he was obliged to meet. He had already postponed them once, and was now sure that if he failed to pay them on the due date, 'the most serious Mischief' would follow.

Mrs Wesley was presumably able to provide the money before leaving for Brighton. Perhaps in the hope of putting a stop to any further demands while she was away, she omitted to leave Wesley her Brighton address, but he acquired it from a family friend, and soon wrote again, even more importunately, to state that he needed her immediate assistance. Aware that she had already recently helped him with money, he suggested, as he had also done earlier in the year, that he should receive part of his inheritance immediately rather than after her death.[40] By 4 November, the situation had deteriorated further, and Wesley was desperate. Unless £100 could be found immediately, he would be imprisoned.

---

[38] Butler to SW, 7 Oct. 1812.
[39] Wesley to Sarah Suter, 29 Sept. 1812.
[40] SW to Sarah Gwynne Wesley, 21 Oct. 1812.

£200, on the other hand, would see him 'compleatly free of embarrassment', and as he was in good health and spirits he was confident that his exertions in the music profession would be ultimately successful. Given this, he felt that it was hard that the advance of £100 which he was requesting, and which was in any case his own money, should have been so long delayed. Meanwhile, he thought it was very inconsiderate of her to stay so long in Brighton, where she was not available to sign the financial documents that were necessary to avert his impending crisis. Had she returned to London around 21 October, as she had originally planned, Wesley's situation would have been easier; as it was, she was intending to remain in Brighton until Christmas, and contact with her was far from easy.[41]

The precise cause or causes of this crisis are not known. Part, no doubt, was the continuing strain of paying maintenance to Charlotte. Another was a bill for £50 for John's school fees, presumably for the previous half-year, as by this time he had left school and Wesley was looking for a suitable job for him. Another may have been the expenses associated with an edition of the first three of Bach's Six Little Preludes, BWV 933–8, that Wesley had published at around this time. But whatever the cause, the incident must have done little to improve relations between Wesley and his mother, whom he had put under considerable pressure.

---

[41] SW to Sarah Gwynne Wesley, 4 Nov. 1812.

10

The oratorio business, 1813

In December 1811, to celebrate the seventieth anniversary of its foundation, the Madrigal Society offered a silver cup worth ten guineas to the composer of the best madrigal 'in not less than four or more than six parts . . . after the manner of madrigals by Bennett, Wilbye, Morley, Ward, Weelkes, Marenzio and others'[1] Wesley was among the competitors with his madrigal 'O sing unto mie roundelaie'. The Madrigal Society took their time over judging the entries, but in January 1813 awarded the prize to William Beale for his madrigal 'Awake, Sweet Muse'. Writing to Novello on 17 February, Wesley attempted to conceal his disappointment under a show of indifference, saying that he could not 'prevail upon [himself] to scrawl absolute Nonsense, even for a silver Cup.'[2] In any case, Joseph Gwilt had agreed to have the madrigal printed at his own expense, and it was already in the hands of the engraver Robert Skarratt. Wesley presented five manuscript copies to the Madrigal Society on his next visit there on 9 March. His disappointment at not winning the Madrigal Society cup would have been tempered by his appointment to a position that he had no doubt coveted for years: that of organist at the Covent Garden oratorio concerts. His appointment may well have been connected with the fact that Drury Lane was offering a rival oratorio series in 1813, and the determination of Charles Jane Ashley, the manager of the Covent Garden series, to make his own concerts as prestigious as possible.

The musical director of the Drury Lane series was Sir George Smart, one of the most successful and certainly one of the most ambitious musicians in London at this time. Born in 1776, the son of a music-seller, he had a conventional musical education as one of the Children of the Chapel Royal under Ayrton, learning the organ from Dupuis, piano from J. B. Cramer, and composition from Arnold. He made his public debut in 1790 at the King's Theatre, playing a piano concerto by Dussek. He subsequently became the deputy to Arnold at the Chapel Royal and Westminster Abbey, and also taught and played the violin. He was in the orchestra for some of Haydn's concerts in London, where he was instructed by Haydn himself in the basic principles of playing the timpani. He also sang in the chorus of the Ancient Concerts, and later at the King's Theatre. All this shows a not unusual pattern and range of

---

[1] *Grove3*, s.v. 'Madrigal Society'.
[2] *SW to Novello, 17 Feb. 1813.

activities for a young professional musician of no very outstanding abilities or talent. But what set Smart apart from his fellow musicians and made him an object lesson for others who wished to make progress in the music profession was his clear understanding of the extent to which success as a musician could be achieved by sheer energy and the assiduous development of social skills and contacts.[3] From his earliest years in the profession, his steady rise in social status can be seen in his meticulously kept account books and his journal. In June 1795 he became a Freemason. The following year found him cultivating his contacts with the aristocracy, making professional visits to Lord Charles Spencer, through whom he also met the Marquis of Blandford. In 1800 he joined the Royal Westminster Volunteers, a fashionable regiment that further widened his circle of contacts. By 1801, his teaching practice well established, he was making professional visits to Bath and other resorts. The following year he purchased the lease on a large house in Great Portland Street. In 1805 he had started an association with the Earl and Countess of Charleville. In 1806 he became a liveryman of the Grocers' Company – another move designed to increase his social standing. In 1808 he made the acquaintance of the Duke of Sussex, whom he was later to entertain to dinner.[4] His most profitable move, however, was at the beginning of 1811, when on a visit to Dublin he purchased a knighthood from the Lord Lieutenant, causing the oboist William Parke to refer to him in his *Musical Memoirs* as 'a recently dubbed knight; an Irish one, who might have said with Faulconbridge, in Shakspeare's King John, "Now can I make any Joan a lady".'[5]

Smart's relentless pursuit of social standing, of which his knighthood was the culmination, was evidently the source of much derision among other musicians. Wesley habitually referred to him in terms of amused contempt, fully aware of the wide discrepancy between his success and his limited musical accomplishments, and also in the realization that he himself was temperamentally unable to act in such a way to further his own career. Now, at the beginning of 1813, Smart evidently had his eye on diversifying into concert promotion and direction. The route he chose was by establishing his own series of oratorio concerts at the new Drury Lane theatre, which had opened the previous October to replace the earlier one that had been destroyed by fire in February 1809.

In the recent past, Drury Lane had only occasionally put on seasons of Lenten oratorio concerts, most recently in 1794 in the opening season of the previous theatre. Covent Garden, on the other hand, had a long tradition of oratorio concerts going back to Handel's lifetime. In the last three seasons, largely because of the participation of Catalani and Braham, the Covent Garden concerts had been outstandingly successful, with unprecedentedly high takings and many concerts having to be given twice in response to overwhelming public

---

[3] For a forceful exposition of this point, illustrated by reference to the careers of the 'success stories' of Smart, Crotch, and R. J. S. Stevens, see Ehrlich, *Music Profession*, pp. 30–42.
[4] Cox and Cox, *Leaves from the Journal of Sir George Smart*, pp. 5–9, 46–7; Ehrlich, *Music Profession*, pp. 37–42.
[5] Parke, *Musical Memoirs*, vol. 1, p. 83.

demand.⁶ It must have appeared to a person of Smart's ambition that there was room for two rival series in this lucrative market place. The problem was that there was a severely restricted number of dates available for oratorio concerts. By long tradition, oratorios took place on Wednesdays and Fridays in Lent, on which days plays were prohibited at the London theatres. As there was no concert on Ash Wednesday, and none in Holy Week, there were only eleven days available for concerts. If an oratorio season were to be set up at Drury Lane, it would inevitably be competing directly with the established Covent Garden series, and on the same days.

This was the background to Charles Jane Ashley's approach to Wesley in early January 1813 to become the regular organist for the Covent Garden series. Wesley had known Ashley and his brothers for many years: as we have seen, some or all of the Ashley brothers had sung at one of the Wesley concerts in 1784, and their paths would have crossed on many occasions since that time. Wesley's appointment now as the regular organist, in succession to John James Ashley, would add lustre to the series and would be a selling point in its competition with the Drury Lane series. It would also ensure that he was on hand at every concert to perform concertos and to accompany soloists at the piano or organ as required. On 12 January, Wesley reported the outcome of his negotiations with Ashley to Novello, saying that he had come to an agreement with him about terms: as we know from his *Reminiscences*, he was to be paid six guineas for a normal concert, and ten guineas when he played a concerto.⁷ He also took the opportunity to inform Ashley that Smart was intending to introduce more modern music into his programmes at Drury Lane, suggesting that Ashley should think about doing the same at Covent Garden. Ashley was less than enthusiastic about the idea, on the grounds of the cost and inconvenience that it would involve. Wesley hoped that he would not 'repent of his parsimony', commenting to Novello that these were 'the silly Means by which the Progress of Science is obstructed, & we justly become the Scorn of the musical World upon the Continent.'⁸

The competition from Drury Lane may have not given Ashley much immediate cause for concern: oratorio promotion had, after all, been in his family since the 1790s, and he himself had been promoting oratorio seasons at Covent Garden with considerable success since his father's death in 1805. He could be reasonably confident that unless they had very good reasons, his patrons would continue to come to his series rather than the upstart new series over the road at Drury Lane. Moreover, since 1810 he had been able to count on Catalani as his star soloist, and her presence alone was sufficient to ensure good houses. Nonetheless, the development should have caused him some longer-term anxieties. Even if the market for oratorio concerts was as buoyant as Smart evidently thought, the new Drury Lane series could only succeed by taking part

---

⁶ *The Times*, advertisements.
⁷ *Reminiscences*, fol. 139.
⁸ *SW to Novello, 12 Jan. [1813].

of the audience from Covent Garden, and the potential threat to Ashley's receipts was considerable.

No matter how great the potential audience, the provision of oratorio concerts in 1813 was absurd and extravagant. Starting with their pre-season performances of *Messiah* on 30 January and continuing for most of the Lenten season proper, the two companies mounted competing concerts with almost indistinguishable programes on most of the available evenings. With little to differentiate them in terms of repertoire, the two companies attempted to compete in other ways. For their *Messiah* performance on 30 January, Drury Lane advertised a 'new and splendid Gothic orchestra', a new organ by Gray, and the appearance of the bass soloist Thomas Bartleman, who was to interpolate the aria 'He was brought as a Lamb to the slaughter' from *Redemption* (a compilation by Arnold of music by Handel and by Arnold himself). At Covent Garden there was the promise of Catalani, and Wesley was to play an organ concerto. The new stage set at Drury Lane – which was presumably used for the whole season of oratorio concerts – came in for the particular scorn of a writer in the *Gentleman's Magazine*, who commented that the painting 'would have disgraced a barn' and that the performers were left in semi-darkness.[9] Smart's use of the additional accompaniments by Mozart also aroused the ire of the same writer, who mocked the presumption that Handel's music could need such 'improvements'. Not everybody was so enthusiastic about Handel. The reviewer in *The Times*, with the air of one who knew that he was uttering blasphemy, commented that 'even Handel had not the secret of giving continued interest to a stile of music, in its nature, monotonous, complicated, and heavy', and wondered if there were not something in Handel's 'peculiar genius' that increased the inherent unattractiveness of the style.[10]

Notwithstanding the opinions of the *Times* reviewer, there were no signs that Handel's music was declining in its general appeal. But the repertory had narrowed appreciably since the beginning of the century. As then, *Messiah* and *Acis and Galatea* were the only works to be performed in their entirety, and such was the perennial popularity of *Messiah* that it invariably appeared once, and frequently twice or more, in each series. Apart from *Messiah*, the other mainstay of oratorio programmes was Haydn's *Creation*, either in full or in individual parts or selections. Most of the rest of the repertory was made up of a relatively small number of favourite Handel arias and choruses. The familiarity of these was no bar to their frequent repetition, either within an individual season or from season to season, and the same pieces also formed the core repertory of the programmes of provincial music festivals. In the 1813 season, both Covent Garden and Drury Lane followed this pattern. At Covent Garden, programmes included Part I of *Creation* followed by two 'Miscellaneous Acts'

---

[9] J. Carter, 'Thoughts on the musick of Handel, and on the mode of performing it at the present day', *GM* 1813/1, pp. 220–2: p. 221.
[10] *The Times*, 1 Feb. 1813; see also a further attack in *The Times*, 6 Feb. 1813. Wesley was outraged by these sentiments: see *SW to Novello, 17 Feb. 1813.

on 12 March, *Acis and Galatea* and a 'Grand Miscellaneous Act' on 17 March, and another *Messiah* on 19 March. There were 'Grand Selections of Sacred Music' on 24 March and on 2, 7, and 9 April, some including substantial extracts from *Messiah* and *Creation*. The programme at Drury Lane was not very obviously different in character: it included *Redemption*, on 12 March, *Creation* in full on 17 March, and 'Grand Selections of Sacred Music' on the other dates.

Of course, the oratorio series were of course far from being the only concerts in London. On the very nights when Covent Garden and Drury Lane were engaged in head-to-head competition there were also the two main subscription series: the Ancient Concerts on Wednesdays and the Vocal Concerts on Fridays, both at the Hanover Square Rooms. But in fact these two series presented no great threats to the oratorios, nor the oratorios to them, as they appealed to different sectors of the concert-going public and attracted different audiences. Both the Ancient Concerts and the Vocal Concerts traded heavily on their social exclusiveness and sold tickets only for complete series, with strict rules regulating or prohibiting the transfer of tickets to others. The oratorio concerts, on the other hand, were open to all-comers, and tickets were sold on a concert-by-concert basis. With the larger capacities of their venues, their more popular programmes, and their cheaper ticket prices, the oratorio concerts appealed to a wider and more varied audience than the two subscription series, and offered a very different musical experience. Among their other attractions, they offered relatively low-cost opportunities to hear the leading opera stars to those unwilling or unable to afford the cost of a subscription to the Ancient or Vocal Concerts.

What the oratorio concerts, the Vocal Concerts, and the Ancient Concerts had in common was a heavy emphasis on vocal and choral music. Although orchestral music was to be heard, usually in the form of concertos, it did not form a large part of the programmes. It was in an attempt to redress the balance in favour of orchestral music that a group of professional musicians came together in early 1813 to form a new concert-giving organization, to be called the Philharmonic Society. An initial meeting was held on 24 January at the house of the violinist and keyboard player William Dance, followed by a second meeting on 6 February at which the constitution of the new society was established. The resulting prospectus noted the 'utter neglect' into which instrumental music had fallen, and proposed the formation of a society to 'procure the performance, in the most perfect manner possible, of the best and most approved Instrumental Music; consisting of Full Pieces, Concertantes for not less than three principal Instruments, Sestetts, Quintetts, Quartetts, and Trios, excluding Concertos, Solos, and Duets'. Vocal music, if introduced, should have full orchestral accompaniments, and should be subject to the same limitations. The society was to be governed by seven directors, and membership, which was to cost three guineas, was to be limited to thirty full members and an unlimited number of associates, from whom future full members were to be drawn. There were to be no distinctions of rank within the orchestra, and no-one was to be paid for playing. Exclusivity among the audience was to be ensured by requiring that subscribers should be introduced by members.[11] Considerable care had been taken with the wording of this prospectus. The exclusion of solo and duo concertos and the requirement that vocal music should have full orchestral accompaniment were designed to put the emphasis on the music rather than the performers and to rule out unseemly displays of empty virtuosity. At the same time, chamber music, up to now given little exposure in public concerts, was to be encouraged.

In an already overcrowded market, finding an appropriate night for the concerts was not easy. Tuesdays, Thursdays, and Saturdays were all potential opera nights, and were on the whole avoided by concert promoters so as to be able to call on the members of the opera orchestra. Wednesdays and Fridays were the usual days for the Ancient Concerts and the Vocal Concerts, and in Lent also for the oratorio concerts. That left Monday night as the only night not already occupied. There was also a problem with a shortage of appropriate venues, exacerbated by the fact that the lease of the Hanover Square Rooms was held by the Ancient Concerts, who might be expected to be unwilling to let the hall to a rival concert-giving organization. This consideration may have prevented the formation of the Philharmonic Society at an earlier date, but in March of the previous year the Argyll Rooms on the corner of Argyll Street and Oxford Street had become available as an concert venue, and became the home of the Society's concerts. The first season consisted of eight concerts on alternate Mondays from 8 March to 21 June, setting a pattern that was to continue in following years. Music by Haydn, Mozart, Beethoven, and Cherubini dominated the programmes; other composers performed were J. C. Bach, Boccherini, Clementi, Dussek, Gluck, Pleyel, Romberg, Viotti, and Wölfl.[12] For the moment, Wesley had no involvement in the Philharmonic Society, either as a member or as an associate. But the benefits of membership must have been clear to him from the foundation of the society, and by the end of 1813 he had paid his three guineas and had become an associate.

The addition of oratorio commitments to Wesley's existing workload made for an extremely busy few weeks during Lent, with eight concerts and their associated rehearsals. In this first season, he gave only two solo performances: on 17 March, when he gave the first performance of his recently-composed Organ Concerto in B♭, KO 415, and on 9 April, the final concert of the series, when he joined with Novello in a performance of the arrangement by Novello of Bach's Prelude in E♭ they had first performed at Wesley's benefit in April of the previous year.[13] For the season he would have been paid fifty-two guineas (£54

---

[11] Philharmonic Society, First Prospectus (BL, K.6.d.3). For the early history of the Philharmonic Society, see Ehrlich, *First Philharmonic*, pp. 1–14; Foster, *Philharmonic*, pp. 8–12.
[12] Foster, *Philharmonic*, pp. 8–12.
[13] *The Times*, 9 Apr. 1813.

12s). At the same time, he was having to fit in all his other activities. His teaching commitments continued, although he may have been able to engage a deputy to take some of the load from his shoulders. Early March was particularly busy, with last-minute preparations for the first performance of his new organ concerto on 17 March, including the copying of orchestral parts and probably the composition of some of the music. Later in the month there was also a personal tragedy to contend with: the death of Wesley's infant daughter, born in the previous November. Some time in late March, she had been inoculated with small-pox (at the insistence of Sarah, instead of cow-pox, as Wesley would have preferred), and had subsequently fallen gravely ill. Until 29 March there had been some hope for her recovery, but she died that evening. On the following day, Wesley wrote to Novello to apologise for his absence from a meeting they had arranged that evening at St Paul's, at which they had been intending to play through some fugues from the '48', and he had also had to forego a dinner engagement with George Gwilt at his house in the Borough.[14] One day later he wrote to his friend Robert Glenn, the music master at Christ's Hospital, to give his apologies for not being able to be present at a party the following day, saying that Sarah was very ill at present, and that he needed to be with her as much as possible.[15] On the same day he wrote to Novello, enclosing a newly composed piece for the choir of the Chapel which he described as 'put together in Sorrow of Heart, consequently not in the merriest Style', but which he thought that Novello would none the less like.[16] This was the understandably sombre 'Ecce panis angelorum', KO 33.

The death of Wesley's daughter occurred at the very busiest time of the season. Because of the period of mourning that had followed the death of the Countess of Brunswick on 23 March and closed all places of entertainment for a week, there was mercifully no oratorio concert on the Wednesday evening, but there was one on the Friday, at which Wesley would need to perform. Its programme must have seemed particularly poignant: it included the 'Dead March' from Handel's *Saul*, in which Wesley played the obbligato organ movement, and the chorus 'When the ear heard her' from Handel's *Funeral Anthem for Queen Caroline*.[17] He also had a teaching engagement on Saturday morning at his school in Turnham Green, and two further concerts in the following week, the second of which involved a performance with Novello of his arrangement of Bach's Prelude in E♭. This brought the unremitting grind of concerts to an end. The next week was Passion Week, when all the theatres were closed, and when few musical events, with the exception of certain charity concerts, were scheduled. In fact Wesley played at one of these: the Anniversary Festival of the Freemasons' Charity for Female Children, on 14 April.[18] After Easter, Wesley's engagements mostly involved playing in the benefits of others,

[14] *SW to Novello, 30 Mar. 1813.
[15] *SW to Glenn, 31 Mar. 1813.
[16] *SW to Novello, 31 Mar. [1813].
[17] *The Times*, 2 Apr. 1813.
[18] *The Times*, 6 Apr. 1813.

and in his own. On Low Sunday, 25 April, he played at a charity sermon at Spitalfields Church, where he was heard by John Marsh.[19] On the following day he accompanied Braham at Salomon's benefit concert at the Hanover Square Rooms.[20]

Wesley's own benefit this year was on 4 May at the Argyll Rooms, and was originally intended to include performances of an organ concerto, a new piano concerto (now lost), the Trio for Three Pianofortes, the Grand Duet for the Organ, and 'O sing unto mie roundelaie'. As in 1812, only one work by Bach was advertised: Novello's arrangement of the Prelude in E♭, repeated from the previous year's concert and its recent outing at Covent Garden on 9 April. An organ by Flight and Robson was erected specifically for the occasion, as the Argyll Rooms had no instrument of its own.[21] This would have been an additional expense for Wesley, unless the proprietors of the Argyll Rooms bore the cost themselves or Flight and Robson were prepared to supply it for nothing in order to advertise it.

As in the previous year, this concert was an affair of disappointments and changed plans. The performance of the Trio for Three Pianofortes had to be abandoned because of lack of room on the platform once the organ had been erected. Wesley had also hoped that the boy treble King (probably the son of the composer Matthew Peter King) would appear and sing a song by Linley. But much to Wesley's displeasure, Bartleman, King's teacher, 'in his usual obliging & Christian-like Style of Conduct', had vetoed the proposal, presumably on the grounds that King's presence would steal the thunder from his own concert, which Bartleman was currently arranging for 3 June at Willis's Rooms. On the next day it was discovered that the organ to be supplied by Flight and Robson's had only one manual, and this ruled out the performance of the Organ Duet. The problem lay in the slow movement, which, as Wesley reminded Novello, had 'some Criss-Cross Work' that involved extensive crossing of hands between the players, and could not be executed on a one-manual instrument.[22]

As if these complications were not enough, Wesley was also having difficulty in finding enough players for his orchestra. As the concert was on a Tuesday, an opera night, members of the King's Theatre orchestra were not available, and there were problems in finding suitable players elsewhere. As it happened, the situation was complicated by events at the King's Theatre, and it was by no means a foregone conclusion that the advertised opera performance there would take place. At this time Catalani was engaged in a long and acrimonious dispute with Taylor over the non-payment of her

---

[19] John Marsh, *Journal*; *The Times*, 24 Apr. 1813.
[20] *The Times*, 24 Apr. 1813.
[21] *The Times*, 1, 3 May 1813.
[22] *SW to Novello, ?1 May 1813. For the 'criss-cross work' in the slow movement, see below, p. 302, and Ex. 23.03.

salary. On the previous Tuesday she had withdrawn from a performance of Ferrari's *L'Eroina di Raab*, and after further cancellations and forced changes of programme later in the week, the advertisements for Pucitta's *La caccia d'Enrico IV*, in which she had been scheduled to sing on 1 May, announced that she had withdrawn her services. Her non-appearance was too much for her admirers, and there was a riot at the theatre, which *The Times* later described as 'one of the most extraordinary disturbances, in all its circumstances, which we ever knew in a place of public entertainment'.[23] As a result, the advertised performance on the evening of Wesley's benefit was cancelled. Wesley's dark aside to Novello in his letter of 30 April (the day before the riot) that 'there are who say that Opera on Tuesday there will be *none*. Could I know this for certain To-morrow, I might yet go on Bowling Green' suggests that the riot may not have been as unexpected or as spontaneous as it appeared. This inside knowledge was no help to Wesley, however, as he needed to book his orchestra without further delay, and could not afford to wait for the possibility that the opera players might suddenly become available after all.

The concert as eventually given had a far more conventional look to it than those of previous years. In addition to Wesley's own music, there was a varied programme of works by Mozart, Haydn, Beethoven, Handel, and Bach, thus demonstrating the excellence and catholicity of Wesley's taste. Contemporary English music was represented in the shape of Wesley's own compositions and a glee by his friend Samuel Webbe. The leader of the orchestra was Salomon and the vocal soloists were Braham, Mrs Bianchi Lacy, Thomas and Elizabeth Vaughan, Charles Evans, and Robert Leete. The soloist in Wesley's piano concerto was the seventeen-year-old Charles Wilson, Wesley's most promising pupil. Wesley was the soloist in his own organ concerto – no doubt the Concerto in B♭ that he had premiered at the oratorio concert on 17 March – and accompanied the solo items at the piano.

After his benefit, Wesley's involvement in the season was virtually at an end, apart from a few appearances in the benefits of others. On Whitsun Eve, 5 June, he took part in the Ashley brothers' benefit at Covent Garden, playing Handel's fourth organ concerto and an additional movement by Bach,[24] and on 10 June he took part at the piano in Webbe's benefit. On 21 June he attended a gala concert at Vauxhall Gardens, where a female pupil was appearing, in consequence having to miss the final Philharmonic Society concert of the season. But the concert gave him the opportunity to hear James Hook, the organist and composer at Vauxhall, who played a voluntary which Wesley, to his surprise, found to be 'exceedingly good: in thorough Organ Style, & with knowing Modulation'. After the performance he introduced himself to Hook, who told him he had just published a voluntary dedicated to him. Wesley bought three copies, later describing the style to Novello as 'none of the worst, & the Fugue

---

[23] *The Times*, 3 May 1813; Fenner, *Opera in London*, p. 78.
[24] *MC*, 4 June 1813; *The Times*, 5 June 1813.

much more in the Shape of one than any Thing I ever yet heard Crotch do upon the Organ.'²⁵

Having made arrangements with Birchall's to send the long-delayed proofs of the fourth and final part of the edition of the '48' to Novello for his attention, Wesley was able on 25 June 1813 to leave London for Ipswich, to take part in a music festival organized by his friend Hague. As the largest town in Suffolk and a prosperous port on the estuary of the River Orwell, it must have appeared to Hague as a place where a musical festival would be well attended and successful. It was Wesley's first extended visit there, although he had stopped there on his way to visit the Jeaffresons in Tunstall in January 1811. Two days after his arrival, he was taken by Thomas Green, a local man of letters, to the town's principal church, St Mary le Tower. As Green later recorded, after the service Wesley improvised 'in a most stupendous style' for an hour. He told Green that he never thought beforehand about what he was going to play, and never remembered afterwards, and could always play if he set his mind to it. He then played a voluntary which 'took away the breath'.²⁶ The following day he dined with Green, Hague, and others. Green described him on this occasion as

> full of life, and spirit, and anecdote. . . . [He] got prodigiously elated in the evening, and extemporised most stupendously: joined in singing, with good effect: mentioned that he was perfectly versed in all the minutiae of the Roman Catholic religion; could perform masses as a priest: wonderfully quick and brilliant. He drained all the bottles; and it required much management in getting rid of him at twelve.²⁷

The festival took place on 6, 7, and 8 July, and consisted of morning performances at St Mary le Tower of *Messiah* and *Judas Maccabaeus*, and evening concerts at the Assembly Rooms. Wesley played his D major organ concerto at one of the morning concerts and improvised at the piano at the evening concerts, the *Ipswich Journal* marvelling that in his extempore performances 'nothing is discoverable, that would not be eagerly claimed by the first composers of the age'.²⁸ In one performance, according to the *Suffolk Chronicle*, he had taken the Scottish tune 'Maggie Lauder' and 'wrought it nearly through the harmonic scale, and treated his subject with a display of science, and occasionally with an eccentric and unexpected change of key, which astonished and delighted his hearers'.²⁹ He returned to London on 11 July.

As we have seen, in 1798 Wesley was an unsuccessful candidate for the organist's position at the Foundling Hospital. By 1813, the organist was William

---

[25] *SW to Novello, 21 June [1813], 23 June 1813. For the advertisements for this concert, see *The Times*, 7 June 1813; *MC*, 10 June 1813.
[26] Green, *Diary of a Lover of Literature*, 27 June 1813, in *GM* 1838/1, p. 468.
[27] Ibid, 28 June 1813.
[28] *Ipswich Journal*, 10 July 1813.
[29] *Suffolk Chronicle*, 10 July 1813.

Russell, who had replaced Immyns in 1801. He was a fine player, and as a composer of organ music – his two books of voluntaries were published in 1804 and 1812 – was second only to Wesley himself. Although he does not appear to have been an active member of Wesley's Bach circle, he is known to have played Bach with Wesley and Novello on the organ at St Stephen's, Coleman Street, on 6 November 1811,[30] and in the following year had the distinction of giving the first performance of Bach's music in East Anglia at the opening recitals for the new organ at St Nicholas, Great Yarmouth, on 8 and 10 September 1812.[31] Now, little more than a year later, he was dying from a lingering illness, and it was apparent that his post at the Foundling Hospital would soon be vacant. With his now greater reputation, Wesley decided to apply for it, no doubt hoping that the events of the 1798 election had been forgotten. On 8 November he wrote to the governors of the Foundling Hospital to say that he understood that the post of organist was vacant by the death of Russell, and to offer his services.[32] At the same time, he had a letter printed containing much the same sentiments, which he distributed to his friends for them to endorse with their recommendations and to send to various governors of the Foundling Hospital. One of these has survived: addressed to Christopher Idle, it bears a recommendation from William Kitchiner, a wealthy man of science, inventor, musician, and epicure whose celebrity dinner parties were the talk of London, recommending Wesley as 'a worthy man, and an incomparable Organist.'[33] It was presumably another of these canvas letters that Wesley was referring to in a deliberately circumlocutory letter to Novello of around the same time:

> You will give me Credit (I think) for not intentionally bothering *any* Body, & hardly suspect me of intentionally teazing *you*; but being pretty well aware of your hostile Disposition to Doctor Samuel Weasel-Eye, therefore I presumes like, upon your Remembrance of your Word given to the said outlandish unaccountable excommunicable omnium-gatherum Son of the Whore of Babylon's great Grandson, that you will not be *over slack* upon the Business relative to the *Bottom* of a certain printed Paper, very generally circulated in Times like the Present.– I have no other particular Reason for pressing the *Motion*, than that the Point gained would prove a knock-down Blow to a few malicious Opponents who (by the way) are likely to be worsted either with or *without* Privilege.[34]

Unfortunately, Wesley had been misinformed about Russell's death: he was still alive, and did not die until 21 November. But despite this embarrassing mistake, Wesley proceeded with his application. On 24 November, he wrote to Samuel Cox, the Treasurer of the Hospital, to offer his services at the organ on the following Tuesday, St Andrew's Day, either at Matins or Evensong, stating that he was prepared to attend for a rehearsal with the choir at any convenient time on the preceding Saturday.

---

[30] Argent, *Recollections of R. J. S. Stevens*, p. 184.
[31] Norfolk Record Office, A. H. Manns, notebooks on music in East Anglia.
[32] *SW to the Governors of the Foundling Hospital, 8 Nov. 1813.
[33] *Kitchener to Idle, c. 10 Nov. 1813.
[34] *Wesley to Novello, c. 10 Nov. 1813.

By the day after his letter to Cox, Wesley had already seen him in person, and had come to the conclusion that he was backing another candidate. Cox declined Wesley's offer to play for services on the coming Sunday, on the grounds that John Nightingale, Russell's former deputy, had already been engaged. Wesley did not believe this, having been told from another quarter that Nightingale would be playing at his church at Deptford then. He had also done some lobbying with his masonic contacts: on the previous evening he was at a meeting of the Grand Lodge and spoke to the Duke of Sussex, who said he would do what he could for him. Wesley was not building up his hopes, however, and was determined not to worry, however the matter went.

The process of the election did not follow the lengthy procedures of 1798. Instead, the General Committee proceeded on 22 December to draw up a shortlist. Four candidates went forward: Nightingale with ten votes, Wesley with six, and a Mr Firth and a Mr Linton with four each. The ballot was held on 29 December, Nightingale receiving twenty-one votes, Linton fifteen, and Firth and Wesley eleven each. Nightingale was duly elected.[35] Although Wesley was no doubt disappointed at this result, he was not downhearted. A few days later, he was writing to Novello to say that he was 'cruelly in the Dumps at having missed the *Certainty* of being kicked & cuffed about by the worthy Governors of the Sunday Bawdy House'. He had met Immyns that day, who had congratulated him on his escape, saying that he would 'not have been a Fortnight in the Situation without spitting in Mr Treasurer Cox's Face.'[36]

Wesley's year came to an end in a flurry of masonic activity with his involvement in the elaborate ceremonies to enact the union of the two Grand Lodges of England to form the United Grand Lodge of Ancient Freemasons of England. Wesley's role included playing the organ and the composition of a new three-part anthem, 'Behold how good a thing it is', for the occasion.[37]

---

[35] London Metropolitan Archives, Foundling Hospital, General Committee Fair Minutes, May 1812–Mar. 1814 (A/FH/K02/032); General Committee Rough Minute Book, July 1812–June 1814 (A/FH/A03/002/027); General Court Minutes 1802–1818 (A/FH/K01/005).

[36] *SW to Novello, 4 Jan. 1814.

[37] The anthem is lost. For an extended account of the ceremonies, and the texts of the poetry recited and music sung, see *EM* 65 (1814), pp. 6–12, 49–52.

11

The established career, 1814–1816

Wesley began 1814 with a further addition to the number of his activities as a musician: in February he was invited by James Asperne, the publisher of the *European Magazine*, to contribute a monthly column of reviews of new musical publications. It was the first time that the *European Magazine* had ventured into this area, but similar columns were from time to time a feature of such other monthly journals as the *Monthly Magazine*, the *Gentleman's Magazine*, and more recently of Rudolph Ackermann's *Repository of Arts*. This was not Wesley's first encounter with musical journalism: as we have seen, in 1807 he had contributed a lengthy review of Callcott's *A Grammar of Music* to *The British Critic*, and he may also have written other anonymous reviews or articles.

Given Wesley's knowledge of the repertory and his facility with words, he was well suited to reviewing. Notwithstanding his obvious suitability, his actual appointment may well have come about through masonic connections. Stephen Jones, the editor of the *European Magazine*, was a prominent Freemason who had been Master of the Lodge of Antiquity, Wesley's former lodge, in 1801 and 1802, and was later to occupy other offices in the lodge. Since his appointment as editor in 1807, the *European Magazine* had included extensive coverage of masonic events, most recently the previous month, when it had given a particularly full account of the Union, including full lists of those taking part and the texts of the poetry and vocal music performed. Payment was evidently not discussed at the time of Wesley's appointment. Six months later, he wrote to Novello to ask him what he had received for his own reviewing, as Asperne was refusing to pay him until he had found out what the usual rate was. Wesley would have preferred to have been paid an annual sum rather than 'to go higgling about *Sheets* &c', and thought that around twenty-five guineas for the year was reasonable.[1] In the end, however, as subsequent letters to Jones show, he was paid in the usual way, by the sheet.[2] For three years, he contributed a monthly column of reviews, mostly of popular piano music or songs, amounting to one or at most two pages. As was usual practice at the time, his column was unsigned, and his authorship would remain unknown today were it not for some passing remarks in his letters. On 17 March 1814, for example, he mentioned to Novello in a letter that there was a 'funny blunder' in

---

[1] *SW to Novello, 9 July [1814].
[2] *SW to Jones, 15 Feb., 26 Dec. 1816.

the current number that he had asked the editor to correct. This was in his review of John Cramer's piano piece *Rousseau's Dream*, where his description in the fourth variation of 'the sound of a side drum' had been printed as 'the sound of a sick dream'.[3]

Easter was fairly late in 1814, and as a result the Lenten oratorios did not begin until 25 February. By this time, competition between the Covent Garden and Drury Lane series had intensified, and there were oratorio concerts at both houses on every available Wednesday and Friday. At Drury Lane, Smart put into action the plans he had announced the previous year of introducing modern repertoire alongside the more traditional oratorio fare. He gave the English premiere of Beethoven's oratorio *Christus am Ölberge*, in a translated and adapted version entitled *The Mount of Olives*, on the first night of the series, and repeated it at almost every subsequent concert. Never one to let an opportunity slip, in the same year he also published a vocal score of the English version. Other novelties included two performances of Mozart's Requiem, two programmes of selections from *The Magic Flute*, two performances of an orchestral arrangement by Charles Weichsell of the final movement of Beethoven's String Quartet in C, Op. 59 No. 3, and on 16 March the belated British premiere of Haydn's *Te Deum* in C of 1802, to celebrate Marshall Blücher's victory at the battle of Laon a week earlier, news of which had only recently reached London. There were also appearances at two of the concerts by the virtuoso horn-players Andreas and Gottfried Schunke, on a visit from Berlin.

This was work-led programming with a vengeance. It was a good deal more enterprising than anything Ashley had to offer at Covent Garden, where the repertoire contained few surprises and catered for more conservative tastes. But Ashley could still offer Catalani and Braham among his vocal soloists and Wesley at the organ. Wesley's contribution to the series included another new organ concerto. Described as 'composed expressly for these performances', its premiere was advertised for the concert on 4 March, and again in identical terms for the following concert on 9 March. This was the Organ Concerto in C, KO 417, and the dated autograph score and a letter of 8 March to Glenn together clarify what happened. The concerto was not ready in time for the 4 March concert, and had to be postponed. In fact, it was not completed until 5 March, and Wesley and Novello then sat up copying the orchestral parts until the early hours of the following morning so that it could have its delayed first performance at the next concert.[4] It was repeated 'by popular demand' on 11 March, and Wesley also performed a concerto – whether the same one or a different one is not clear – on 30 March. Plans to include a performance of Novello's arrangement of Bach's Prelude in E♭ at one of the later concerts appear to have come to nothing.[5]

---

[3] *EM* 65 (1814), p. 138. For the correction, see ibid., p. 233.
[4] *SW to Glenn, 8 Mar. 1814.
[5] See *SW to Novello, 17 Mar. 1814: 'I told Ashley I should like to perform Bach's Prelude with

The increased number of concerts in the season was good news financially for Wesley. There had been no oratorio performance on 30 January as it had fallen on a Sunday, but with concerts on every possible Wednesday and Friday in Lent, he had appeared eleven times in the season. On three of these occasions he played a concerto, thus boosting his earnings on those evenings from six to ten guineas, and bringing his total fees for the season up to 74 guineas (£77 14s).

After the oratorio season, Wesley was involved in two other major events. One was a concert of music by Thomas Linley the Elder on 25 April for the benefit of Queen's Lying-In Hospital that Wesley had agreed to organize. In addition to the music by Linley that made up most of the programme, Wesley performed an organ concerto and a voluntary.[6] The other was a benefit concert for the widow and two young children of William Russell, for which a committee consisting of Wesley, Attwood, Horsley, John and Francis Cramer, and others had been set up to make the necessary arrangements.[7] It was agreed that the concert should be at the Foundling Hospital chapel, and should consist of Russell's oratorio *Job*, which he had left unfinished at his death. It then became the task of the committee to put the oratorio into a performable condition. It met first on 24 March, and again on 19 April, to play through the work. Wesley was not impressed with its quality, referring to it in a letter to Novello after the second meeting as 'poor Russell's (I am sorry to say) poor Oratorio', and reporting that everyone had agreed that it could only bear a single public performance.[8] This was on 15 June, when Wesley and Novello also performed an arrangement for organ duet of Bach's 'St Anne' Fugue by Novello, preceded by an introduction that Wesley had composed for the occasion.

In 1814, for the first time since 1808, Wesley did not have his own benefit concert to arrange. He did, however, perform at the benefits of others, notably Charles Ashley's at Covent Garden on Whitsun Eve, 28 May. As the manager of the Covent Garden oratorios, Ashley had taken to arranging his own benefits on this day, another when spoken drama was forbidden and theatres traditionally remained closed. From the audience's perspective, the concert was indistinguishable from the Lenten oratorio concerts, with the same singers and instrumentalists and the same repertory. There was an important difference for Ashley, of course, in that the performers would have appeared without fee and that his profits would have been the greater as a result. Wesley also appeared on 6 June at Salomon's benefit at the Hanover Square Rooms, where he accompanied him in a Bach violin sonata,[9] and on 22 June at a concert organized by James Elliott and the alto Charles Smart Evans at the Green Man, Blackheath, where he played a piano concerto and an improvised

---

your Arrangement, which he readily agreed to, but it *must* be rehearsed.' The work did not appear in press advertisements for the remaining concerts in the series.
[6] *MC*, 18, 22 Apr. 1814.
[7] *The Times*, 9 May 1814.
[8] *SW to Novello, 20 Apr. [1814].
[9] *The Times*, 4 June 1814.

piano piece.[10] More informally, there was a play-through of the Trio for Three Pianofortes at Clementi's piano factory in Tottenham Court Road on 25 July, at which Wesley's pupil Charles Wilson also played a piano concerto by J. B. Cramer.[11]

In early October 1814 Wesley visited Norwich, leaving London on 5 October and staying with William Linley's brother Ozias at his house in Dean's Square. Here, in a city with a thriving musical culture, he was well entertained. Linley introduced him to all the principal people in the city, and at the request of the clergy in the choir he played for at least three choral services at the Cathedral. He found the Norwich people 'uncommonly hospitable and hearty', and before he left they organized a special dinner in his honour at the Assembly Room.[12] The principal reason for his visit was a concert at St Peter Mancroft, the parish church. Advertised as including 'the most celebrated Organ Compositions of the first Masters, as well as Extempore Voluntaries and Organ Duetts', it had originally been arranged for 12 October, but had to be postponed to the following week: partly because Edward Taylor, a local bass singer who was also taking part, had suffered a recent family bereavement and could not appear in public so soon afterwards, but also because the following week was Assize Week, when there would be more people in Norwich and therefore the prospect of better audiences.[13]

On 16 October, Wesley wrote enthusiastically to Sarah Suter about his experiences. The outlook was looking promising for a profit on the concert, and he had been assured that he would be sure of success with a concert on a subsequent visit. He was on the lookout for some choice items of food to bring back with him, anxious about the state of Samuel Sebastian's health, chiding about the items of clothing that Sarah had omitted to pack for him, and impatient to get back to the simple pleasures of home.[14]

With the beginning of 1815 came round another season of oratorio concerts. As in the previous two years, Covent Garden and Drury Lane were in direct competition, every available evening being taken up with performances in both houses. As usual, both mounted *Messiah* on 30 January: in the case of Drury Lane a programme of selections coupled with *The Mount of Olives* and a 'Grand Miscellaneous Act' consisting mostly of Handel selections. But the relative positions of the two series were now beginning to change. Catalani had left England for France, and her absence from the Covent Garden series removed much of the competitive edge it had formerly enjoyed over Drury Lane.[15]

---

[10] *The Times*, 22 June 1814.
[11] *SW to Glenn, 22 July [1814].
[12] SW to Sarah Gwynne Wesley, 12 Oct. 1814.
[13] *Norwich Mercury*, 1, 8, 15 Oct. 1814; *Wesley to Novello, 5 Oct. 1814.
[14] SW to Sarah Suter, 16 Oct. [1814].
[15] See the review of the previous season in *The Times*, 2 Apr. 1814, stating that the Covent Garden oratorio season had been more popular than the Drury Lane one, and attributing this to the presence of Catalani and Braham at Covent Garden.

Meanwhile, Drury Lane had secured the services of Mrs Dickons, the leading English soprano since the virtual retirement of Mrs Billington. From the programmes for the coming season it appeared that the competition between the two houses would once more be on the basis of repertory. At Drury Lane, Smart had further novelties to introduce. Chief among them was Beethoven's *Battle Symphony*, Op. 91, written to celebrate Wellington's decisive victory over the French at the Battle of Victoria on 21 June 1813, and dedicated to the Prince Regent. Although it had been performed in Vienna in December 1813, it had not yet been played in London, and received its British premiere on 10 February 1815 at the first concert of the season. It was then repeated at every subsequent concert in the series, much as *The Mount of Olives* had been in 1814. With its appeal to patriotic sentiments, special effects, and broad, not to say vulgar, popular appeal, it was the perfect piece to draw the crowds. As the programme for the New Musical Fund concert on 6 April described it:

> The Sinfonia commences with a March of the English Army to the Air of *Rule Britannia*; next follows a march of the French Army to the Air of *Marlbrook* ['Marlbrook s'en va en guerre']. The Music then expresses the Battle between the two Armies, and Imitation of the Firing of Cannon and Musquetry, and the Retiring and Defeat of the French Army: a GRAND MARCH and INTRADA OF DRUMS and TRUMPETS announce the VICTORY: and concludes with *GOD SAVE THE KING*; the Solos of which will be sung by the Principal Vocal Performers and Full Chorus.[16]

Although the victory specifically celebrated in the *Battle Symphony* was now well in the past, its general patriotic theme was still timely. The French wars had effectively come to an end with the defeat of Napoleon's forces at the Battle of the Nations in October 1813, Napoleon's abdication in April 1814, and the restoration of the monarchy later in the same month. During the 1815 season Napoleon would return from Elba and temporarily regain power in France, but this too would come to an end with his defeat at the Battle of Waterloo in June 1815. Rather more serious fare was provided by Beethoven's Mass in C, adapted to English words that disguised its original religious function; part received its English premiere on 22 February, and the remainder on 24 February. *The Mount of Olives* was revived from the previous season and received three further performances, and there were two performances of Mozart's Requiem. There were also five performances of *Elijah raising the Widow's Son*, an apparently new oratorio that was in fact a compilation from the music of Peter Winter, adapted to a new libretto by William Thomas Moncrieff.

At Covent Garden, Ashley's response to this barrage of new works was to fall back on tried and tested favourites. In response to Drury Lane's constantly repeated performances of the *Battle Symphony*, all he could do was to programme Haydn's 'Military Movement' (i.e. the slow movement of the Symphony No. 100, with its military effects); later in the season, he would

---

[16] Quoted in Young, *Beethoven: A Victorian Tribute*, p. 9.

put on the whole symphony. Wesley's one concerto appearance was on 8 March, when he played his D major concerto with the Bach fugue, and *In exitu Israel* was performed on 1 March. He was still doing well financially out of the oratorios: he had appeared in all twelve concerts, and had earned seventy-six guineas (£79 16s).

After the season had ended, Wesley took the opportunity to make another visit to Norfolk. This time, he was visiting the seaside town of Great Yarmouth, twenty-three miles from Norwich, at the invitation of its organist, John Eager. Despite its small population, the town had a lively musical culture. As we have seen, the re-opening of the organ at the parish church after a substantial enlargement by George Pike England three years earlier had been marked by two recitals by Russell, and there was also a recently founded music society which gave weekly concerts.[17] Eager was the main musician in the town: according to Wesley, in addition to being the organist of the church he played and taught most other string and wind instruments, and also dancing. Wesley's concert, which he gave at the church with the singer and organist Charles Smith, was on 12 July. This was not part of a music festival, but the concluding item of a week of entertainments that had started with a 'water frolic' on nearby Breydon Water on 7 July and a cricket match on the following day. The concert included the 'St Anne' fugue, played by Wesley and Smith as a duet, which according to Wesley was received 'with the same kind of Wonder that people express when they see an Air Balloon ascend for the first Time'.[18] On the following day, they performed the *Goldberg Variations* on the organ at St Nicholas. On 27 July, Wesley travelled to Norwich, where later in the day he was to play at the Cathedral at an anniversary sermon for the benefit of the local hospital and on the following day at St Peter Mancroft in his own concert.[19] His visit and concert coincided with Assize Week, when a number of entertainments, including a balloon ascent by the aeronaut James Sadler, were on offer for the numerous visitors flocking to the city for the occasion.

When Wesley returned to London on 30 or 31 July, it was to find a large number of letters requiring his attention, including one from Novello asking him 'to do his Popish drudgery' at the Portuguese Embassy Chapel for the next two Sundays. But he was able to find time to write to his friend Alfred Pettet, the assistant organist of St Peter Mancroft, to express his regret at not having had more time to spend with him on his brief visit to Norwich, and to raise a number of matters in connection with his visit there.[20] Seven weeks later, on 22 September, he wrote to Pettet again. By now he had further points to raise, of which the most important concerned an edition of the 'Credo' of Bach's B

[17] Norfolk Record Office, A. H. Mann, Notebooks on Music in East Anglia, *Norwich Mercury* advertisements.
[18] *SW to Novello, 18 July 1815.
[19] Advertisement, *Norwich Mercury*, 22 July 1815; report, *Norwich Mercury*, 29 July 1815.
[20] *SW to Pettet, 31 July 1815.

Minor Mass that he was hoping to publish by subscription, and for which Taylor, the singer who had appeared with him at his concert in Norwich the previous year, had been helping to raise subscriptions.[21] As Wesley had explained in a letter to Shield a week earlier, he would need seventy subscribers to cover his costs, which he estimated at £60 to £70. This would have been the first edition of the Credo anywhere, and a notable contribution to the Bach cause. Unfortunately, the edition does not appear to have materialized, probably because of a lack of sufficient subscriptions.[22]

By the time of Wesley's next letter to Pettet a week later, it was to thank him for his efforts on behalf of the Bach edition, and to say that he had received a further four subscriptions from the Hall Concert, a local concert-giving organization. He regretted not having earlier offered his services to the forthcoming music meeting in Norwich, and stated that he would be very glad to play on future occasions. Finally, he asked Pettet to pass on his thanks to their friend Thomas Pymar, the organist of the parish church at Beccles in Suffolk, for his gift of some game.[23]

Having joined the Philharmonic Society as an associate member in the year of its foundation in 1813, Wesley applied for full membership in May 1815, and was elected on 1 June. Thereafter he appears to have thrown himself with a will into the business of the Society. He chaired committee meetings on 27 September and 16 October, and on 22 November was elected one of the seven directors. This development was highly significant, showing that he had now become fully accepted into the inner circles of London's concert life. Although he was a director for a relatively short time, his involvement in the society's affairs was considerable, and discussions in his letters at this time shed light on various aspects of its activities. As a director, Wesley could also expect to be more involved in the planning of concerts and the choice of repertoire, and from time to time to direct concerts from the piano. There might also be opportunities for his own music to be performed: perhaps the Symphony in B♭, or other works that he would compose specially. But these exciting possibilities were for the future, when he had further consolidated his reputation and his position in the Society. At the time of his election, the programmes for the forthcoming season were no doubt largely already decided. Nonetheless, he did have one piece performed in the 1816 season: 'Father of Light and Life', which was sung at the concert on 29 April 1816.

Before this, however, was the current season of Lenten oratorio concerts, for which Wesley had once more been engaged. By this time, common sense had begun to prevail in the scheduling of concerts and the two theatres were dividing the available dates between them, Drury Lane taking Wednesdays and Covent Garden Fridays. The competition between Covent Garden and Drury

---

[21] *SW to Pettet, 22 Sept. 1816.
[22] *SW to Shield, [13] Sept. 1815.
[23] *SW to Pettet, 29 Sept. [1815].

Lane of the previous three seasons may have been financially damaging to both series, but in the end Smart and his Drury Lane company must have been pleased with the outcome: in three seasons they had broken the Covent Garden monopoly and by the 1816 season had gained control of more than half the oratorio business. By this time some retrenchment was probably in any case necessary. With the end of the Napoleonic Wars, the large number of foreign players who had flocked to London from the Continent were free to return and many did so, thus depleting the pool of available musicians. At Drury Lane, Smart was continuing his policy of repeated performances of new works and crowd-pleasing old ones: the *Battle Symphony* was performed at four of the six concerts, and probably would have been performed at the other two were it not for the inclusion in the programme on these occasions of Peter Winter's *The Liberation of Germany*, a work which was presumably cast in a similarly patriotic vein and fulfilled much the same function in Smart's programming.[24] There were also two further performances of *The Mount of Olives*, two of selections from *Israel in Egypt*, one each of *Messiah* and *Creation*, and selections from Mozart's *Requiem*. At Covent Garden, Ashley's programmes continued the conservative course of the last few seasons, with many 'Grand Selections' and 'Grand Miscellaneous Acts'. Specific details of what these contained are only infrequently available: now that directly clashing oratorio concerts were a thing of the past, neither house felt the necessity to provide full details of their programmes in their newspaper advertising, and programmes are only to be found in surviving individual concert bills. One such was for the Covent Garden concert on 29 March 1816,[25] where the principal attraction was Josephine Fodor-Mainvielle, the current sensation at the King's Theatre, where she had made her London debut on 13 January. With her were Madame Marconi, also from the King's Theatre, Braham, Catherine Stephens, and the bass Charles Tinney. The principal instrumental soloist was the French virtuoso flautist Louis Drouet, on his first visit to England and making a repeat appearance at this concert, by the particular request of many patrons. The first part of the concert consisted of favourite solo and choral items from *Messiah* followed by a concerto by Drouet; the second part contained 'select parts' of *Acis and Galatea*, including 'Love in her eyes sits playing' from Braham, 'O ruddier than the cherry' from Tinney, and the trio 'The flocks shall leave the mountains'. The third part opened with the overture to Cherubini's *Anacreon*, a frequently performed orchestral work in London at this time. Elsewhere, Mme Fodor sang an unidentified 'grand bravura' and, with Braham, the duet 'Ah! perdona' from Mozart's *La clemenza di Tito*. The mixture of the sacred and the secular at oratorio concerts was nothing new, of course, but this programme, typical of many in the season, shows how far that the balance had now tilted towards the secular, to the extent that it was now difficult to reconcile the oratorio concerts

---

[24] Lost, but presumably a translation of his *Germania* of 1815.
[25] Concert bill at BL, Add. MS 56411, fol. 33.

with their original aim of providing spiritual entertainment on those evenings in Lent when spoken drama was prohibited.

The reduction in the number of oratorio concerts meant that Wesley's earnings from this source were reduced in 1816 to roughly half of the level of the previous year. On the other hand, he was more at leisure. In particular, he was now able to attend occasional oratorio performances at Drury Lane and see for himself what Smart and his company were doing there: something that in the previous three seasons would have been impossible. Even so, other commitments tended to get in the way, so that Wesley could complain ironically to Novello in March that 'there seems to be Fatality against my ever hearing the grand Battle Symphony, & my learning how to conduct Choruses from the noble Knight-man.'[26]

Wesley did not hold a benefit of his own in 1816, preferring to repeat the arrangement he had come to with Ashley the previous year, and sharing his benefit on Whitsun Eve, 1 June.[27] As in previous years, this was in effect an additional oratorio concert, with many of the same performers and much the same repertory as in the main Lenten series. The vocal soloists once more included Fodor, Marconi, Stephens, Braham, and Tinney, performing their favourite concert pieces, and Drouet performed a concerto at the end of the first part, just as he had at the oratorio concert discussed above. The programme began with *The Intercession*, a new sacred oratorio by King, based on words from *Paradise Lost*, followed by two miscellaneous acts 'from the compositions of the most favourite Authors – ancient and modern'. Also included was one new choral piece: 'Hail then, all hail! Illustrious pair', by William Hawes, to words by J. Taylor, in honour of the marriage on 2 May of Princess Charlotte and Leopold Saxe-Coburg-Saalfeld. At the end of the second part, Wesley played what was described in advertising as a new concerto on the organ, in which, 'in allusion to the glorious 1st of June', he was to introduce the National Air of 'Rule Britannia'. In fact the concerto was not new at all, but a revised version of the Concerto in C of March 1814, with a newly composed set of variations on 'Rule Britannia' replacing the original finale. This was yet another gesture towards the prevailing mood of patriotism, and alluded to the famous naval victory on 1 June 1794, at which the British fleet under Lord Howe conclusively defeated the French fleet in the Atlantic some four hundred miles off the Breton peninsula.

---

[26] *SW to Novello, 4 Mar. 1816.
[27] Concert bill at Duke University, Frank Baker collection.

12

Breakdown and recovery, 1816–1823

Wesley reached the end of the 1816 season in exuberant good spirits and ready for another visit to Norwich, where he was to perform at the anniversary sermon for the Norfolk and Norwich Hospital in the Cathedral on 15 August. In addition, he had just completed his *Twelve Short Pieces with a Full Voluntary Added*, KO 617, to be published the following year by Clementi. On 29 July he wrote to Pettet to state that he was looking forward to his visit, and proposing that as both Pettet and Beckwith, the organist of the Cathedral, had invited him to stay with them, he should make himself a 'joint concern' and spend part of his time with each. On 1 August he wrote to Novello to make arrangements for deputizing, stating that he would also be contacting Wilson, on whom he had a claim for a favour, and that he was intending to leave London on 10 August at the latest.[1]

These arrangements were plunged into disarray the following week with the serious illness of one of Wesley's children. On 7 August he wrote to Novello to say that his infant son was in a 'so precarious a state' that it was unlikely that he would be able to attend the meeting at the Surrey Chapel with Jacob that they had arranged for the following day. There were two private pupils in the Cheapside area whom he was obliged to teach, come what may, but if his child should die he would probably feel 'totally disqualified for any musical Exertion of Energy'. This child, about whom nothing else – not even his name or approximate date of birth – is known, did in fact die, and his death precipitated Wesley into his most serious and extended bout of depression for many years. Despite the events of the past few days, he managed to set off for Norwich, but collapsed on the road and never reached his destination. After spending some time at a nearby inn, he limped back to London, considerably out of pocket. Here, he appears to have been able to continue working, and on 15 August composed a song, 'In radiant splendor', to words by John Davies, in celebration of the recent royal wedding.

Wesley had been expecting to make £100 from the Norwich visit, and the loss of this income coupled with the additional expenditure caused by his collapse plunged him into immediate financial crisis. As a result, he was obliged once more to try to borrow money against the £100 that was to come to him on his mother's death, and for which he had now persuaded Charles and Sarah to give

---

[1] *SW to Novello, 1 Aug. [1816].

security, should he predecease her. By 28 August, however, his applications had been largely fruitless. One person to whom he applied was prepared to give £50 on the £100, which Wesley felt would have been useless, and an absurd sacrifice. Without immediate assistance, he was facing the prospect of surrendering himself to the hands of 'officers', whose visit he daily feared. If he could not pay certain debts by the coming Saturday he would be arrested in his current weak and near-delirious state. He was thus obliged to approach Charles and Sarah direct for a loan, proposing that they should let him have £90. This would ease his present difficulties, and the remaining £10 would be two years' interest to his mother in advance.[2]

Despite his financial difficulties and deteriorating health, Wesley continued to carry out his engagements through the autumn. On 25 September, for example, he played an organ concerto at an ambitious concert at All Saints', High Wycombe organized by the organist, R. H. Pontyfix.[3] But by early October his health had evidently deteriorated further and he moved temporarily to lodgings in Hampstead, probably in an attempt to recover his health in the purer air of what was still a country area, and in the awareness that it was better for all concerned for him to spend some time on his own. In a letter to Novello he described himself as being 'very low and ill', and on two occasions had to ask him to stand in for him in his teaching engagements. In late December, he asked Novello to help him with his column for the *European Magazine*. Although he did not realize it at the time, this column was his last, as Asperne subsequently discontinued it.[4]

Despite the continuing decline in his mental and physical health as 1816 moved into 1817, Wesley was still continuing to work. Apart from those occasions when he had to ask Novello to deputize, he appears to have continued with his teaching commitments, and was at his usual place at the organ at the Covent Garden Lenten oratorio series in February and March 1817. He also appears to have taken on a church appointment at Kentish Town Chapel, a chapel-of-ease to St Pancras Parish Church, although nothing is known of the details.[5] Nonetheless, matters were clearly going from bad to worse. In February he had another attack similar to the one of the previous August, and Alexander Sutherland, the physician at St Luke's, London's main hospital for mental illnesses, was consulted. He prescribed complete rest and a change of scene, neither of which was possible for one in Wesley's position. At the same time, or later, Wesley's sister Sarah consulted Sir Thomas Bagshawe, another eminent medical man, whom she may have known socially. By the end of April, Wesley's

---

[2] SW to Sarah Wesley and Charles jun., 28 Aug. 1816.
[3] Lightwood, *Samuel Wesley, Musician*, pp. 181–2; R. S. Downs, *The Parish Church, High Wycombe: A Descriptive Guide* (1904).
[4] *SW to Jones, 13 Jan. [1817].
[5] A receipt for £45 dated May 1818 from Mr Hornby, treasurer of the organ committee, for eighteen months salary paid to Sarah Gwynne Wesley, is at MARC, DDWF 27/4A. Wesley's duties were presumably entrusted to deputies during his illness. The church is now known as St John the Baptist, Highgate Road.

condition had deteriorated further and was giving serious cause for concern. On 3 May he went to stay with his mother, in such a state of agitation that his sister Sarah had to engage a keeper to look after him. A day or so later, lodgings for him were arranged in the neighbourhood. On 6 May, while still at his mother's, and with her sitting at his side, he threw himself out of an upper-storey window, imagining himself set upon by creditors sent to him by Charlotte. He sustained serious injuries, and for a time it was thought that he was unlikely to survive.[6]

Although the earliest published account of Wesley's life, in the *Wesley Banner and Revival Record* for December 1851, described Wesley's illness at some length, it completely omitted details of this incident, leaving its statement that 'on May the 8th, it was pronounced that he had but a few days to live' curiously unexplained. But it did report at length the immediately following scene, when Wesley's death was thought to be imminent. The source was his sister's diary:

> He was then perfectly in his senses, aware of his danger, and able to receive a visit from Mrs Mortimer, who, as an old friend of the Wesley family, hastened to the scene of sorrow, to comfort the aged mother in this hour of maternal anguish. . . . She remarked, that she was sorry to see him in this situation, and wished to read a hymn of his father's which was a prayer of mercy, asking, 'if he did not wish for mercy?' He answered, 'Yes! mercy!' Mrs Mortimer remarked that he had resisted the mercy of the Redeemer, and provoked His wrath. He added, – 'Reviled, blasphemed Him, and he feared it was too late to repent.' She, upon this, directed him to some of the promises made to the penitent sinner. He expressed a fear that 'his repentance was not of the right sort, arising more from the fear of punishment than from hatred to sin.' Upon which she said, 'If you are spared, would you live as you have done?' He replied, 'I hope not.' He wished to see several persons with whom he was connected.– particularly his wife and children; and said 'he was a great sinner – had been an undutiful son, – and had sadly abused the talents God had given him.' On being urged to ask for repentance, he still appeared to feel it was too late, but often lifted up his hands in prayer. Some encouraging Scriptures having been repeated, he was asked 'if he had any hope?' He paused some time, and replied, '*A little.*' He expressed himself as having felt, some days previously, 'as though surrounded with evil spirits, and feared it was a foretaste of hell and of his companions there.' Mrs Mortimer again dwelt upon the nature of repentance, and inquired 'if he did not hate his former courses, and wish to live another kind of life?' To which, without hesitation, he replied, 'Yes!'[7]

Prominent among the friends of Wesley who were involved in the crisis was Linley, who visited him on the day after the fall and subsequently went to break the news of his condition to Charlotte and her children. On 8 May he reported in a letter to Sarah that he had not been able to see Charlotte, but had left a note with Emma. He had then visited Mrs King (presumably a friend or neighbour), who had assured him that she would bring Charlotte and her children to see Wesley as soon as possible. He continued:

---

[6] Sarah Wesley to Wilberforce, c.12 May 1817.
[7] *WBRR* 3 (1851), p. 440.

> In doing my duty today, my nerves have been much shaken; this would not have been the case if I had been more accustomed to scenes of distress. It is, however, a painful satisfaction to know that I have seen my dear friend once more, agreeably to his wishes. If your poor brother departs easily, it will afford me great consolation to hear it, and that the last stages of his life were, through the mercy of Providence, without any bitter pain, either of mind or body. The sight of his wife and children, and the reconciliation which I hope may take place, will prepare his mind more than anything for the last and most sacred consolation of religion, and which I fervently recommend may be administered to him before it is too late.[8]

A few days later Wesley was pronounced out of danger. Thoughts now turned to the question of his treatment: how it was to be managed and financed, and – most important – where he should live while it took place. Wesley's medical care appears to have been entrusted to Bagshawe and a Mr Heaviside, while his financial affairs were put into the hands of Linley, Glenn, and Kingston. On 19 May, Wesley's son Charles wrote to one of these, probably Linley, to thank him for his assistance so far, and to give his view of the issues:

> I understand that my father clamours exceedingly after his spurious children. This circumstance greatly distresses my aunt; especially as the two surgeons are solicitous to comply with his demands. 'If moved to lodgings of his own', they observe, 'he may see whom he pleases without let or hindrance. This is very true; and lamentable would be the result of such license: all hope of reconciliation with his lawful family would thus be cut off, and his insanity (I doubt not) become permanent and incurable.
>
> That he must be moved from his present abode is agreed on all hands. The question is, where? We could not concur in any proposal unsanctioned by your authority. The manner in which himself, his wife, and daughter are to be supported till it may please God to restore his reason is next to be considered, since the limited incomes of myself and my brother place it out of our power to take this duty upon ourselves. I anxiously await the counsel which your kindness and experience will suggest on these points.[9]

On 23 May, on the orders of his two doctors, Wesley was removed to temporary lodgings, or perhaps a private asylum, in Chapel Street. In the meantime, discussions were continuing about the management of his condition in the longer term. A week later, as Stevens recorded in his diary, a meeting was held on whether to place him in St Luke's or in a private asylum.[10] The outcome is not recorded. It may have been decided that Wesley's condition did not after all require his immediate confinement, or perhaps there was no suitable accommodation available at the time, either at St Luke's or in a private asylum. At all events, Wesley was not committed at this stage, but was sent off to Southend to convalesce. Not surprisingly, there is little information about

---

[8] Linley to Sarah Wesley, 8 May 1817.
[9] Charles Wesley III to ?Linley, 19 May 1817.
[10] R. J. S. Stevens, diary entry for 29 May 1817 (Cambridge, University Library, Add. MS 9110).

Wesley's state of mind in these crucial few weeks. He did, however, write one heart-rending letter to Novello on 31 May:

> Here I am in the greatest Agonies of Mind and Body too, tho' the latter are the less– *All forsake me*: why is this?– If you think you *ought* not to come and comfort me I must submit, but I trust this is not so.– O come my dear Novello, and leave me not utterly in my deep Distress.– My Prayer is unavailing, else how do I long for a Release from my offended Maker!– It is *hardest* that even my little ones are with-holden from seeing me. Alas, alas, Despair is for ever in Prospect.
> *Will* you come this Evening. Do, for Pity's sake.[11]

On 7 July Wesley's sister Sarah wrote to Glenn to ask him to make arrangements for Sutherland to take over her brother's treatment. This was to be under the superintendence of Glenn and Kingston only, as Linley – for reasons that may have had to do with a quarrel with Wesley's son Charles – had by now given up his share of responsibility for Wesley's affairs. This marked the beginning of the process that would lead to Wesley's committal to Blacklands House, a private lunatic asylum in Chelsea owned by Sutherland. Sarah also requested Glenn to arrange for Sutherland to consult Dr Tuthill, another specialist in mental illnesses and the physician to Bethlem Hospital and other institutions. This was presumably to obtain the obligatory second signature on the certificate attesting Wesley's insanity that would be necessary for his committal to Blacklands House.

The deliberations about Wesley's treatment were not guided solely by medical considerations and a disinterested concern for his best interests. In the background, and no doubt contributing to the problem, was a tangle of family squabbles. Three separate groups can be identified, each with its own interests and views on how Wesley's illness should be treated and the situation managed. One consisted of Wesley's sister Sarah, his brother Charles, and his mother. A second comprised Charlotte and her three children: Charles, now twenty-three and effectively head of the family, John William, aged seventeen, and Emma, aged ten. Finally, there was Sarah Suter, with her two young children Samuel Sebastian and Rosalind, and whatever support she may have been able to call upon from her own relatives.

Little love was lost between any of these groups, although there was some common ground between the first and the second in the hatred that each bore Sarah Suter. The relationship between Wesley's family and Charlotte, never easy since the time in the early 1780s when she had first appeared on the scene, continued to be as prickly as ever. Sarah and Charles evidently found Charlotte and her son Charles difficult allies, and this feeling was no doubt reciprocated. The views of Charlotte and Sarah Suter on the situation are not recorded, but can easily be imagined. It seems unlikely that Charlotte, after six years of separation, would still have wanted or expected a reconciliation with her husband, and probably hoped for nothing more than that he would be restored

---

[11] *SW to Novello, 31 May 1817.

to health as soon as possible and resume the regular payment of her maintenance. Sarah Suter's desires would have been even more straightforward: to see her partner recovered and returned to her, and in a position once more to maintain her and their two young children.

For Wesley's sister Sarah, however, nothing less than the ending of Wesley's relationship with Sarah Suter and his return to his lawful family would do. This, as she saw it, was the essential first step to his return to sanity and a more godly and respectable life. In her eyes it was her brother's liaison with Sarah Suter that was at the root of all his mental problems. It was this belief, which seems to have been shared by Kingston and Glenn, that lay behind her determination first to place Wesley at Blacklands House or some other similar establishment, and then to keep him there for as long as possible. The longer he was separated from Sarah Suter, the greater the likelihood that she would find another partner or remove herself from the scene. As another part of this strategy, Sarah was keen to separate the six-year-old Samuel Sebastian from his mother, and a plan was devised to send him away to Heywood Hall school, twelve miles from Manchester, at the family's expense.

Wesley was admitted to Blacklands House and the care of Mrs Bastable, its superintendent, some time in July or August. The asylum was a large house in its own grounds in Blacklands Terrace, Chelsea. For most of the eighteenth century it had been used as a girls' boarding school, and by a bizarre coincidence Burney had taught music there in the 1770s and 1780s.[12] Its date of conversion to an asylum is not known, but it continued in this form until the 1930s. It was a very much more suitable place for Wesley's treatment than the public wards of St Luke's, where conditions were overcrowded and insanitary. Blacklands was a relatively small institution, with probably no more than thirty patients at any time. Here, Wesley would probably have received reasonably liberal and humane treatment by the standards of the day, with his own room, the freedom to pursue his own interests, and little or no use of restraint except when considered absolutely necessary.[13]

Wesley's condition at the time of his admission to Blacklands is not known. On 23 August, however, Kingston spent five hours with him, following a letter in which he appears to have explained to Wesley the reasoning behind the decision to place him there. On arrival he was courteously received by Mrs Bastable, who took him round the extensive enclosed gardens and discussed Wesley's case with him. She then made tea for him and Wesley, and left them alone together. Kingston subsequently reported to Sarah on his visit, in the process giving the only account we have of Wesley's condition while at Blacklands. He had found Wesley calm and self-possessed and full of questions on the content of Kingston's letter. He did not deny the soundness of Kingston's arguments, or condemn the reasons for the actions of those entrusted with his

---

[12] Burney to Wesley, 17 Oct. 1808.
[13] On private madhouses in the early nineteenth century, see Parry-Jones, *The Trade in Lunacy*; Porter, *Mind-Forg'd Manacles*.

treatment, but could not be convinced of its appropriateness. His hopes, fears, and wishes were all 'extravagant':

> They encumber the efforts of his reason, & he knows it, but he will not part from them – they drag him about over all the thorns & briars of a wilderness of misery, out of which he can see no path; & yet he clings to them, like a child to a vicious horse that is about to leap with him down a precipice.

Wesley did not consider that what his friends were doing for him was for his good, and held that his conduct did not justify his being treated as a madman. His dissatisfaction with himself, with his friends, and with everything, was total. Kingston concluded that there was no improvement in Wesley's mood, and there was nothing he could do to persuade him to act rationally.

At the request of Wesley's mother, Kingston also took the opportunity to tell him about the plans to send Samuel Sebastian away to school in Yorkshire. Although able to see some of the advantages, Wesley was violently opposed to the plan, saying that it was intended to send Samuel Sebastian out of his reach and that he would never see him again. Growing more and more agitated, he asked Kingston to intervene and prevent Samuel Sebastian's departure, or at least to delay it. By now, the time allotted for their meeting was over, and Mrs Bastable came in with a keeper to bring it to a close. Kingston promised Wesley to let the family know of his opposition to the plan, at which Wesley retired, 'dissatisfied, irritated'. The visit had not been a success. Kingston thought that Sutherland had been over-hasty in allowing him to visit, and that visits from Wesley's other friends at this stage were highly improper and unhelpful to his recovery.[14]

In her reply to Kingston two days later, Sarah was able to make her position about Samuel Sebastian clear. Had she been at home when he called before his visit to Blacklands, she would have opposed her mother's wish to inform Wesley about the plans to send Samuel Sebastian to Heywood Hall, and would presumably have carried them out without consulting him. In her opinion, Wesley's insanity stemmed from his 'vile connection' with Sarah Suter, and his continuing association with her and their children did nothing but perpetuate his illness. Sutherland had been too sanguine in his assessment of Wesley's condition, and had thought him better than he was. She agreed with Kingston's opinion that Wesley's insanity was mostly self-will: if he were now to be discharged from Blacklands, he would show clear signs of this by returning to Sarah Suter, where 'on the first contradiction' from her, he would kill himself.[15]

Kingston's meeting with Wesley had at least one positive effect, in that Sarah immediately cancelled the arrangements for Samuel Sebastian to go to Heywood Hall. In future, if he were to be sent away to school, it would have to be at someone else's expense. Sarah had done what she could to help, but her efforts to take over Samuel Sebastian's education had been rebuffed both by Wesley

---

[14] Kingston to Sarah Wesley, 24 Aug. 1817.
[15] Sarah Wesley to Kingston, [26 Aug. 1817].

and by Sarah Suter, whom Sarah had tried to persuade by way of an intermediary.[16] In fact, arrangements were made later in the year to have him placed at the Chapel Royal at St James's.[17] Here he came under the care of William Hawes, who had recently been appointed Master of the Children. His treatment there would have been rough-and-ready at best: Hawes had a reputation for being a harsh disciplinarian, but in practice was too busy with his many other occupations to pay much attention to the boys in his charge.[18] But he was better off at the Chapel Royal than he would have been at Heywood Hall: he was still in London, within reach of his family, and would have the opportunity to gain a solid musical education.

By early 1818, Wesley's condition showed signs of improvement, and he was beginning to look forward to his discharge from Blacklands. In a letter of 3 January he asked Glenn to bring him a copy of the current *Ordo Recitandi Divini Officii* (the annual publication containing the local rubrics for the services of the Roman Catholic church) and his 'great music book'. On 23 March, in apparent good spirits, he was asking Glenn to visit, and commenting on a current dispute between the piano teacher Johann Bernard Logier and the Philharmonic Society over Logier's controversial system of group music teaching.[19] Meanwhile, those responsible for his care had themselves been assessing his condition and wondering when he could be released. In early March, Sarah reported to her nephew Charles that a Mr Cook had offered to take Wesley as a boarder for two guineas per week. She had agreed to convey this proposal to Glenn and Kingston, but without any great expectation that it would be agreed by Sutherland, who had earlier counselled against her brother's early release. Sarah had earlier asked Glenn about the reasons for this: the reply was that in Sutherland's experience patients rarely recovered in less than twelve months, and that doctors were unwilling to risk their reputations by discharging them before this time had elapsed. As Sarah stated to Glenn, there were further reasons for Wesley to be kept at Blacklands. The longer he was out of circulation, the greater the chance of Sarah Suter 'disposing of herself' (by which Sarah presumably did not mean committing suicide, but removing herself from the scene). It would be a disaster if Wesley were to return to her, and a sure proof that he was not cured. What was worse, the return to 'the same scene of disorder & misery' would be sure to make his condition worse and lead to him doing away with himself.[20]

Amidst all the discussions about Wesley's treatment, the London concert season was proceeding without him. Jacob had taken his place at the organ at the Covent Garden oratorios, where he played concertos or solos at four of the six concerts; he also played at Ashley's Whitsun Eve benefit on 9 May. But

---

[16] Sarah Wesley to Kingston, [26 Aug. 1817].
[17] *SW to Hawes, 28 Nov. 1817.
[18] For Hawes's exploitation of the boys under his charge, see *MW*, 17 May 1838, pp. 45–6.
[19] *SW to Glenn, 3 Jan. 1818; *SW to Glenn, 23 Mar. 1818.
[20] Sarah Wesley to Charles Wesley III, 4 Mar. 1818.

Wesley's fellow musicians were taking steps to help him financially: a committee was set up to organize a benefit concert for him, to be conducted by Smart. It was arranged for 17 June, but had to be postponed at the last moment because of the lateness of the season.[21]

Only three letters by Wesley survive from his time at Blacklands. One is a letter he wrote to Hawes in November 1817 thanking him for agreeing to take Samuel Sebastian at the Chapel Royal; the other two are those to Glenn mentioned above. None shows any evident signs of insanity. As we have seen, on his visit the previous August Kingston had found Wesley sane and rational, although understandably angry about being detained against his will and at the prospect of Samuel Sebastian being taken from him. But there is no doubt that Wesley also had violent attacks, similar to the one that had led him to throw himself out of the window in May 1817. It seems likely that his condition was volatile and unpredictable from day to day and even from hour to hour, and that periods of relative calm alternated with episodes of agitation and acute distress, during the most severe of which he may have had to be placed under restraint. The only other evidence of Wesley's state of mind while at Blacklands is a single sheet of music manuscript containing musical sketches and other jottings written while Wesley was there (Plate 5). Two of the sketches bear dates during March and April 1818, and the other jottings were presumably made around the same time.[22] All graphically convey Wesley's state of mind at this time: his acute misery and sense of hopelessness, coupled with dissatisfaction at his confinement against his will, a sense of grievance at those who had put them there, and a strong belief that he was not insane. Among the statements contained are the following: 'How the foolish & and the malicious confound *pure Distress of Mind* with *Insanity, or Madness*'; 'Agitation proves no more than strong & irritable Feelings. What is he worth who never had these?'; 'There was never more unprovoked Cruelty than that which I am doom'd to undergo ab indignissimis & villissimis [from the most unworthy and vile people] continual unceasing and increasing'; and 'O God help the helpless!'

By late June 1818, Wesley was at last considered sufficiently recovered to be discharged from Blacklands.[23] What happened next is unclear in detail, but at some stage he and Sarah Suter were reunited and started living at a house in Euston Street, Euston Square (the present Melton Street), close to their previous house in Gower Place. They were to stay there until 1830.

Wesley now needed to pick up the threads of his ruined career. As he must have realized all too well, this would not be easy, particularly in his still debilitated and only half-recovered state. Arrangements painstakingly built up over a period of years had been disrupted, some never to return. During his

---

[21] *The Times, MC*, 16 June 1818.
[22] RCM, MS 4025, fol. 30.
[23] Sarah Wesley to an unidentified recipient (possibly Miss Ogle), 26 June 1818.

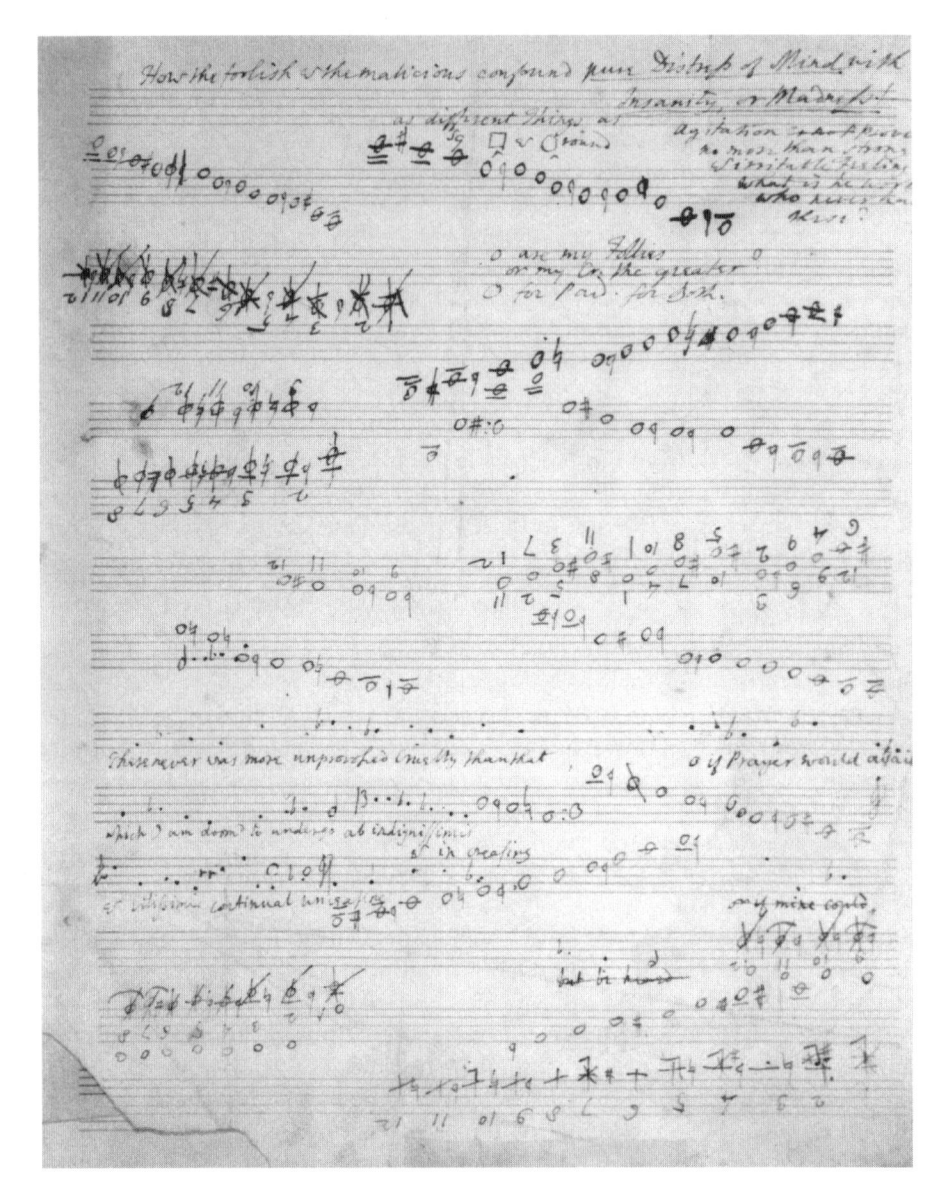

5 Jottings made by Wesley while at Blacklands House, March 1818. By courtesy of the Royal College of Music, London.

absence from the concert platform, other musicians would have gladly stepped into his shoes, and much of his teaching practice would have disappeared as his pupils found other teachers. For the next few years, Wesley would need to take whatever work he could find, rebuilding his contacts and once more establishing his role in London's musical life. Nonetheless, there were offers of help. In

November 1818 the Philharmonic Society proposed that he should be employed for the scoring of a symphony; the suggestion appears to have been made at the instigation of Smart. This was a thoughtful gesture, but any gratitude that Wesley might have felt was nullified by the exceptionally low rate of 1s 6d per sheet that the Society offered. Wesley pointed out to Novello that this was no more than the going rate for copying many years ago, and commented that if he were younger, he could make 'a dozen Fold more by running Errands than arranging Scores on such Terms'. As a result, Novello raised the matter with the Society, and the rate was doubled.[24] Wesley also found that he was able to return to the Covent Garden oratorios after his year of absence. At the first concert of the 1819 season he announced his return by performing the organ concerto in D with its Bach fugue, and at the last an unspecified Bach fugue (perhaps the 'St Anne') as a duet with Novello. As in the past, his friend Glenn was on hand to turn pages, pull stops, and generally to assist during performances.[25]

In February 1819 Wesley was contacted by Edward Hodges, a Bristol organist who would later play a significant role in helping to arrange his visits to Bristol in 1829 and 1830. Hodges was twenty-two and largely self-taught as a musician. He was already organist at St Nicholas's church, and later in the year would be appointed to St James's, where Wesley had been baptized and had his first organ lessons.[26] From his boyhood he had taken a keen interest in mechanical improvements to organ design, and it was about his latest invention that he now wrote to Wesley. This was a 'typhus pedal', a device that enabled any number of keys to be held down for an indefinite length of time.[27] Hodges appears to have been alone in his enthusiasm for it, and Wesley's response was guarded. Thanking Hodges for letting him know about his invention, he commented that it was 'exceedingly ingenious', and that a 'great increase of grand effect will be produced in the hands of a complete master of Modulation and of the Organ'. But it was only in such hands that it would achieve this end, and he had his doubts about its general usefulness among organists at large.[28]

On 6 May 1819 Eliza, Wesley's second daughter with Sarah Suter, was born, joining the eight-year-old Samuel Sebastian, now away at the Chapel Royal, and Rosalind, aged four or five. She would become the most musically talented and successful of Wesley's daughters, following in his footsteps as an organist and holding a number of church appointments. She was also a crucial figure in keeping alive her father's memory and promoting his music, and eventually bequeathing a large quantity of family papers to the British Museum.

---

[24] *SW to Novello, 17 Nov. 1818; Philharmonic Society Directors' Minutes, 15 Dec. 1818 (BL, Loan 48.2/1).
[25] *SW to Glenn, 17 Mar. [1819].
[26] Ogasapian, *Edward Hodges*.
[27] Faustina Hasse Hodges, *Edward Hodges*, pp. 199–200.
[28] *SW to Hodges, Feb. 1819.

A further instance of Wesley attempting to pick up the threads of his professional life is shown by a letter of early June to Richard Mackenzie Bacon, the owner of the *Norwich Mercury* and the publisher of the recently founded *Quarterly Musical Magazine and Review*, England's first long-run music journal. Horsley, who had been heavily involved with Bacon in setting it up, had told Wesley that Bacon needed someone to help in his 'musical publication' and that he had recommended him, whereupon Wesley wrote to Bacon to ask for further details.[29] As it happens, the 'musical publication' was probably not the *Quarterly* itself, but a projected dictionary of music that Bacon was planning at this time. A prospectus, naming Horsley and Wesley as contributors, appeared in the *Quarterly* for 1822, but the project appears not to have been completed, and the dictionary was never published.

Wesley would have been very glad of any work that Bacon could put his way on the *Quarterly* or on any associated publication. It would take the place of his discontinued column of reviews for the *European Magazine* and would help him to regain a foothold in the world of musical journalism. Moreover, the *Quarterly* must have appeared to offer the prospect of a continuing association. Its format was ambitious, each number running to over a hundred pages and containing lengthy articles on historical aspects of music, features on composers and prominent musicians, reports on concerts in London, the provinces, and abroad, and copious reviews of music, which were lengthy and considered, in contrast to the rather perfunctory round-ups of recent publications in general monthly journals such as the *European Magazine*. And although it was edited by Bacon from Norwich with the assistance of two of his daughters, it relied heavily on a team of London contributors for its London coverage. With his depth of knowledge of music of all periods, his strong opinions, trenchant prose style, and experience in musical journalism, Wesley might have considered himself well qualified to be part of this team. But in fact he never wrote for the *Quarterly*. The timing of his illness may have been partly to blame: he had fallen ill precisely at the time of the run-up to the launch of the *Quarterly* and the launch itself. By the time he had sufficiently recovered to be thinking again about musical journalism, the organization of the *Quarterly* was well established, and there may have been no room for any contributions from him.

The years following Wesley's illness are particularly sparsely documented. Although such a lack of documentation need not necessarily indicate a corresponding lack of activity, in this case it seems to do so. From the almost complete absence of letters to Novello of the period it is apparent that Wesley had ceased for the moment to be involved with the music at the Portuguese Embassy Chapel and now saw Novello only infrequently: on one occasion he remarked to him that he found the music at the chapel 'too overwhelming' for

---

[29] *SW to Bacon, 5 June 1819.

him to bear.³⁰ He had, however, made some new friends: the organist Stephen Francis Rimbault, the artist William Behnes and his two brothers Henry and Charles, and Henry Delafite, an Anglican clergyman who lived in Somers Town, a short distance from Wesley's home in Euston Street.

But Wesley had still to re-establish his place as a public performer. After the 1819 season Ashley had given up the management of the Covent Garden oratorios, and it passed into other hands: first to Sir Henry Bishop, and later to the French emigré Nicholas Bochsa and to Smart. At the same time, the shift in the repertory continued, to the extent that extracts from Handel were now almost completely replaced by extracts from more modern works, predominantly operas. In April 1820 a writer in the *Quarterly* complained that the oratorio concerts had now departed almost entirely from their original conception, and it was a mockery to prohibit the theatres from staging plays in Lent, only to allow them to put on concerts like these. He continued:

> Our remark can scarcely need a more ample justification than is to be found in Covent Garden bill of March 3. The first part consisted of selections from *Il Don Giovanni*, the most licentious of all Italian operas. In the second part, '*Non piu andrai farfallone amoroso*' from *Figaro*, stood between 'Waft her Angels' [from Handel's *Theodora*] and 'O magnify the Lord' [from Handel's eighth Chandos Anthem]. The third commenced with the first part of *Acis and Galatea*, and concluded with the *Battle Sinfonia* [by Beethoven]; and this is called an oratorio during Lent.³¹

In fact, this development merely marked an acceleration in a process that had been going on for some time. While Ashley was in charge at Covent Garden, the core of the old programming remained, but once he left, the oratorios dropped all pretence at being religious entertainments, and were given over almost entirely to secular music, with the heavy emphasis on opera that the *Quarterly* contributor noted. In this there was little or no place for an organist, let alone one of such conservative tastes and views as Wesley. Nor was Wesley able to regain his old position in the Philharmonic Society. At the time of his illness his membership had lapsed, presumably because of the non-payment of his subscription, and he never rejoined. It is possible that he had no desire at this stage to renew his contacts with the Society; it is also possible that the Society, with its habitual anxiety about respectability and social status, made no moves to welcome him back or even that it actively cold-shouldered him.

1820 was a year of depression and considerable financial difficulty. A rare letter from Wesley to Novello, written in late August on the occasion of the death of Novello's son Sidney at the age of four, gives a good indication of his mental state and his finances. After offering his condolences, he continued:

> My Views of any Peace of Comfort on Earth have long since terminated, and could I only secure a Probability that my poor Children would not exist in

---

³⁰ *SW to Novello, 29 Aug. [1820].
³¹ 'Sketch of Music in London', *QMMR* 2 (1820), pp. 373–391: p. 388.

> Wretchedness, I could perhaps drag out the sad Remainder of my melancholy Journey in less Horror and Agitation.– To be starved one's self is dismal enough, but to become the Cause of similar Destruction to others, and worst of all to those we do and ought to love, is insupportable by any but a Heart of Adamant.[32]

In November, he wrote again to Novello to beg for some copying, either literary or musical, leaving the terms for Novello to decide. For Wesley to be reduced to this was a sign of how low his fortunes had sunk. Novello later angrily annotated the letter:

> I wish to place this affecting Note on record, as an eternal disgrace to the pretended Patrons of good music in England, who could have the contemptible bad taste to undervalue & neglect the masterly productions of such an extraordinary Musician as Sam Wesley, and who had the paltry meanness of spirit, to allow such a real Genius (who, like Purcell, was an honor to the Country where he was born) to sink into such poverty, decay and undeserved neglect, as to be under the necessity of seeking employment as a mere drudging *Copyist* to prevent himself from starvation![33]

This was understandably a time of low creativity. But Wesley was able to publish some of his earlier compositions, and thus to earn a little from the sale of their copyrights. Perhaps in response to the accession of George IV on 29 January, he published sets of variations for organ on 'God Save the King' and on 'Rule, Britannia'. At around the end of the year he published 'Father of Light and Life' and *The Hornpipe and Variations from a favorite Organ Concerto*, an arrangement for piano of the last movement of his Organ Concerto in D.

There appears to have been little family correspondence during the year. One letter from Wesley's sister Sarah in December shows that old family arguments were still continuing. She took Wesley to task for turning down an advantageous offer of employment, apparently on the grounds that it would mean that he would have to leave London and would lose the financial assistance of his friends. In her opinion, his duty was to pay his bills and to avoid contracting further debts, and had he accepted the offer he would have been able to do this. She thought that it was a miracle that he had not died as the result of his fall, but while he continued to live with Sarah Suter there could be no hope for him. He should now repent and end his relationship with her, paying her an allowance to live elsewhere with the children. One thing Sarah evidently did not realize was that Sarah Suter was again pregnant; another son, Matthias Erasmus, was born in May of the following year.

1821 was scarcely more eventful than 1820. In August Wesley canvassed for the organist's appointment at the new St Pancras Parish Church that was nearing completion on the New Road, within sight of his house. In late September, Novello asked him to compose a Latin setting of the Magnificat for a collection of church music that he was compiling. Despite protestations

---

[32] *SW to Novello, 29 Aug. [1820].
[33] Annotation by Novello on *SW to Novello, 20 Nov. [1820].

that all his 'inventive spirit' had long since evaporated, Wesley completed the piece promptly. It was his first new composition of any size since his illness. But his financial situation was still desperate. In late November he was again writing to Novello to beg for copying, stating that although as a composer he was a 'cripple', as a copyist he remained as accurate, although perhaps not as quick, as before. At the same time, his thoughts had been turning to his *Confitebor*, the score of which he had temporarily mislaid, and wondering whether he might be able to publish it.

Wesley entered 1822 in no better spirits. Samuel Sebastian was still boarding as a chorister at the Chapel Royal, where his outstanding treble voice was giving him a measure of celebrity in his own right, and on at least one occasion he was invited to sing before George IV at the Royal Pavilion at Brighton. In February Wesley was unsuccessful in the election for the organist's position at the new St Pancras Church. In May, he submitted a glee, 'While ev'ry short-liv'd flower of sense' for a Glee Club competition, but without success. But later in the year he was invited by the newly-founded Royal Academy of Music to become an honorary member: an appointment which involved no teaching duties but granted him admission to the concerts, rehearsals, and examinations of the institution, and placed him on a list of fifty-seven leading musicians who were similarly honoured.[34]

The end of the year was more active, however. In the early autumn Wesley was commissioned to arrange some music for the barrels of a finger- and barrel-organ that Walter McGeough, a wealthy Irish landowner, was having built for The Argory, his new house in Co. Armagh; at around the same time his friend Behnes received a commission for a portrait bust of McGeough. It is not known whether the request came directly from McGeough, or through James Bishop, the organ builder who had taken over the contract from James Davis, who had originally been engaged. Wesley had had close relationships with various organ builders over the years, but this was the first time he had undertaken this particular task. As well as actually arranging the music for the barrels, it involved liaising with McGeough over the choice of music and the number of barrels required, and presumably also with Bishop over technical matters. In November 1822 he wrote to McGeough to give him details of the fourteen pieces that he had already arranged: they included pieces by Handel, Mozart, and Wesley himself as well as such popular pieces as 'Scots wha' hae wi' Wallace bled' and 'Grammachree Molly'.[35] By timing these, Wesley had established that there were already too many to fit onto the six barrels that McGeough had specified. As there were other pieces that McGeough had also requested, Wesley now needed to know how he wished to proceed: whether to order further barrels, or to substitute some pieces for others. It took until March 1824 to agree all the details of the project, and it is evident that there were many more

---

[34] *SW to Burghersh, 2 Sept. 1822. For honorary membership of the Royal Academy of Music, see 'The Royal Academy of Music', *QMMR* 4 (1822), 370–400, 516–26: pp. 378, 518–19.

[35] *SW to McGeough, 11 Nov. 1822.

letters between McGeough and Wesley than the three from Wesley that have survived. Bishop's final specification and estimate provided for only six barrels, with any additional ones to be charged at £15 each. The organ, an outstanding example of its type, still survives in working order at The Argory (now a National Trust property), together with three of its original barrels. They contain five pieces arranged by Wesley: Mozart's variations on Fischer's Minuet; the Overture and March of the Priests from Mozart's *Die Zauberflöte*; the Overture to Arne's *Artaxerxes*; and 'See the Conqu'ring Hero Comes' from Handel's *Judas Maccabaeus*. The remaining three barrels, which presumably contained some or all of the other pieces listed by Wesley, plus any extra pieces that McGeough ordered, are missing, and were probably destroyed in a fire at The Argory in 1898.[36]

In addition to Wesley's fee for arranging the music and liaising with McGeough, he was due payment of commission from Bishop. As he later explained to him, McGeough's original order to Davis had been placed at his recommendation, and Davis had agreed to pay him fifty guineas, probably representing ten per cent of the cost of the organ, in return. Now that the contract had been transferred to Bishop, the responsibility for paying the commission also passed to him, and Wesley looked forward to receiving his fee as soon as the organ was completed.[37] In this he was to be disappointed: as a remark in a subsequent letter to Novello shows, Bishop declined to pay, and Davis – not surprisingly under the circumstances – was not himself disposed to admit any responsibility for the commission.[38]

The completion of the work on the organ for The Argory and Wesley's difficulties over his commission lay in the future, however. Wesley's main task in late 1822 was the composition of settings of the Magnificat and Nunc Dimittis, the two canticles sung at Evensong in the Church of England. Their composition brought to completion the full morning and evening service that he had begun with his settings of the Te Deum and Jubilate fourteen years earlier in 1808, and marked his return to serious composition. For this was not a matter of a competition entry, like his glee of earlier in the year, nor a response to a request, like his Latin Magnificat for Novello the previous year, nor yet an opportunistic recycling of old material for publication and a quick profit such as the Variations on 'Rule, Britannia' and 'God Save the King' of 1820. With the Magnificat and Nunc Dimittis he was now back in action in one of the main arenas of composition. Nonetheless, and possibly indicating his continuing lack of confidence, he had chosen to complete something already half-made rather than to undertake a completely new project.

On 28 December Wesley's mother died, aged ninety-six. Although she had

---

[36] For the innovative registrations, presumably by SW himself, see Bicknell, *The History of the English Organ*, p. 221.
[37] *SW to Bishop, 28 Feb. [1824].
[38] *SW to Novello, 8 Mar. 1824.

gone blind and had been in failing health for some time, she still retained full command of her mental faculties. In an undated memorandum, Wesley's sister Sarah recorded his last meeting with her, probably on 10 December. It seems characteristic of all Wesley's dealings with his family, and recalls the equally unsatisfactory interview he had with his dying father over thirty years earlier. Wesley knelt at her mother's bedside and begged her forgiveness. She blessed him and his children, and expressed her satisfaction that they were all well and prospering. When Wesley mentioned Samuel Sebastian, his mother said, 'God bless all your children'. Then, suddenly remembering who Samuel Sebastian's mother was, she commented that Sarah Suter was an 'impudent baggage' to take her name (i.e. to call herself Mrs Wesley) and hoped that Wesley would be led in the right way. At this Wesley rose and soon left the room.[39]

---

[39] Sarah Wesley memorandum, Dec. 1822.

13

The career re-established, 1823–1825

The early part of 1823 was a barren time. Wesley was still making applications for church appointments, although by this time with few hopes of success. In January he failed to be elected at St Lawrence, Jewry, polling a humiliatingly small number of votes; George Frederick Harris, a total nonentity, was appointed.[1] By now he had become resigned to the unlikelihood of ever gaining a major church appointment, and when a year later he applied for the organist's position at St George's, Hanover Square he remarked to Novello that his past experience made him reasonably philosophical about the outcome, but that he wanted to disprove the impression that many had that he was 'averse from all musical Employment', even though he hated it as a 'source of great misery'.[2]

Most of the remainder of 1823 was also uneventful, but Wesley's fortunes started to change with a performance of his new Magnificat and Nunc Dimittis at Evensong at St Paul's Cathedral on Christmas Day.[3] Whether or not this was the first time they had been heard there is unknown, but it was no doubt as a result of favourable comments following this performance that Wesley decided early in 1824 to publish the full Service by subscription. By late February he had issued proposals,[4] and shortly afterwards started to make arrangements with Attwood to have the complete Service performed at Matins and Evensong at St Paul's on a date when potential subscribers could come to hear it. Wesley's decision to publish the Service was a highly significant step, signalling his return to active participation in the London musical scene. Before his illness he had been a highly respected figure in the world of church music, renowned both for his learning and the robustness of his opinions. Most of his own church music up to now had been for the Roman rite, however, and of this, very little had been published. By publishing the Service, he was making a large statement in one of the most important forms available to a church musician, and could expect that it would attract widespread attention and detailed comment.

In late February or early March 1824, Wesley's Norwich friend Pettet wrote to request a composition from Wesley for a collection of church music he was compiling, taking the opportunity to enclose a gift of Norfolk sausages. In his

---

[1] Dawe, *Organists of the City of London*, p. 48.
[2] *SW to Novello, 17 Feb. [1824].
[3] *SW to Novello, 19 Dec. 1823.
[4] Charles Wesley jun., pocket-book entry for 24 Feb. 1824, quoted in Stevenson, *Memorials of the Wesley Family*, p. 464.

reply, Wesley stated that he had a suitable piece, a Latin setting of the first two lines of Psalm 65, which he proposed to adapt to English words. This was 'Te decet hymnus', KO 66, written in 1798, which in English would become 'Thou, O God, art praised in Zion', KO 114. As the piece was little known, Wesley was confident that it would appear as a novelty and would suit Pettet's purposes just as well as the Collect that he had originally requested. At the same time he informed Pettet about the proposed publication of the Service, stating that proposals for this 'dose of egotism' were printed and that the whole Service was due to be performed in May.[5] On the same day he also wrote to Novello with copies of the proposals and an update on plans for performance: Attwood favoured a Sunday, when there would be the largest congregation, and therefore the largest number of potential subscribers.[6] Ten days later, when Wesley wrote again to Pettet, it was with more definite news: the performance was to be soon, and Wesley commented with his tongue firmly in his cheek on his 'dread Anxiety for the Verdict of the learned Canons, Vicars-Choral, Vergers, Bellows Blower &c.'[7]

The performance of the complete Service took place on 3 April – a Saturday – instead of the previous Sunday, as previously arranged. The change of date was Attwood's suggestion, so as to coincide with a Philharmonic Society rehearsal, when many of those who would be in London for the occasion could be expected to take the opportunity to come to St Paul's for Matins, and perhaps also for Evensong. On the following Tuesday, Wesley was finally able to send his anthem to Pettet, commenting that the Service had been performed 'very respectably', and that there were already plans for a further performance on a Sunday.[8] This second performance was originally arranged for 25 April. On 23 April, however, Wesley commented to Novello that there had been 'a little *friendly* manoeuvring among the vocal Operators at St Paul's to cause a Disappointment on Sunday next'. Wesley suspected the involvement of Hawes, who was Master of the Children at St Paul's in addition to all his other positions, and was not optimistic that the performance would take place. To Novello, he was able to express his candid opinion of the standard of the previous performance and the quality of the choir. Unless the Service was sung with more feeling and precision than before, Wesley would rather it were not performed at all. Given that the choir was made up of 'half-schooled Musicians and dignified Parsons', he was not confident that this would happen, and as one of the choir was apparently intent on mischief, it would a miracle if a 'butchery' of his Service did not ensue.[9]

Despite Wesley's forebodings, the Service received its second full performance on 25 April as arranged. Wesley did not comment directly on how it was performed or received, but it appears that some remarks were made on a

[5] *SW to Pettet, 8 Mar. [1824].
[6] *SW to Novello, 8 Mar. 1824.
[7] *SW to Pettet, 18 Mar. 1824.
[8] *SW to Pettet, 6 Apr. 1824.
[9] *SW to Novello, 23 Apr. 1824.

progression in the Jubilate that could not be explained in terms of orthodox harmonic theory.[10] Wesley enclosed a copy of the relevant passage in a letter to Novello, asking for Novello's opinion.[11] Novello's reply, containing some blunt references to the 'plodding Pedants' and 'tasteless Drones' who had criticized the progression, delighted Wesley, who was now able to reveal that among his critics was none other than Attwood. As for his 'inoffensive appoggiatura', Novello had convinced him of its legitimacy, and he proposed to do nothing to change it.[12]

In May 1824 Wesley was at last successful in his search for a church appointment. It was at Camden Chapel, Camden Street, a chapel-of-ease in the St Pancras parish, newly built to cater for the increase in population that had followed the large amount of building in the parish over the last few years. Wesley's appointment may have benefited from his connections at the parish church: as we have seen, he had briefly been organist at Kentish Town chapel before his illness, a candidate for the organist's position at the new church in 1822, and was doubtless also well known to the church authorities by virtue of living close by. In addition, the first incumbent of Camden Chapel was Alexander d'Arblay, son of Mme d'Arblay (née Frances Burney) and grandson of Charles Burney. It is from Mme d'Arblay that we have a description of Wesley playing at the consecration service on 15 July, when his skills in improvisation were put to good use during an extended wait for the arrival of the Bishop of London, who conducted the service.[13] The Camden Chapel appointment was by no means a prestigious appointment for one of Wesley's abilities, and his acceptance of it may have marked a realization that he would now never gain a major church position. As it was a new church, there was no music tradition, and Wesley would have the job of forming and training a choir from scratch. In addition, the organ at the church was not large or in any way distinguished. At £63 per annum, the salary was only modest, but it would have been a welcome addition to the family finances at a time when Wesley was still struggling to make ends meet.

Wesley's next substantial composition, in June 1824, was the *Carmen Funebre*, a setting of words taken in part from Ecclesiastes: 'Omnia vanitas et vexatio spiritus, praeter amare Deum et illi soli servire' ('All is vanity and vexation of spirit, except to love God and to serve Him alone'). The words had a particular significance to Wesley as almost the last spoken to him by his father before his death. As Wesley explained to Novello, he thus regarded the piece as a belated memorial to his father, whose true worth he had not appreciated in his lifetime. He also intended that it should be sung at his own

---

[10] See below, Example 19.07, bar 17.
[11] *SW to Novello, 26 Apr. [1824].
[12] *SW to Novello, 12 May 1824.
[13] Mme d'Arblay to Mrs Barrett, c.16 Aug.–2 Sept. 1824, in Joyce Hemlow et al., *The Journals and Letters of Frances Burney (Madame d'Arblay)* (Oxford, 1984), vol. 9, pp. 543–9.

funeral, and asked Novello to ensure that his wishes were carried out.[14] For the present, however, the plan was that the *Carmen Funebre* would receive its first performance by Novello's 'well-drilled corps' at a vocal party that Novello was organizing. This was no doubt the July meeting of the Classical Harmonists Society, a private concert-giving organization that Novello had founded in 1821 and that met on the first Thursday of the month at the Crown and Anchor Tavern in the Strand.

It was also at around this time that Wesley resumed his practice of attending music parties with members of a circle of amateur musician friends. One was John Harding, a doctor from Kentish Town, whom Wesley described to Novello as 'an extreme & unpretending Lover of the Organ'.[15] Harding had known Wesley for some time: he had given Wesley his support in his application for the St Pancras appointment in 1822,[16] and was the dedicatee of six organ voluntaries published around 1824. Another was the Revd Allatson Burgh, vicar of St Lawrence, Jewry, and author of *Anecdotes of Music, Historical and Biographical; in a Series of Letters from a Gentleman to his Daughter* (1814). Caroline, the daughter in question, may have been a pupil of Novello's at this time. Yet another was a keyboard player, also from Kentish Town, known to us only by his nickname of 'Pug'. It was in the company of these men and of Novello that Wesley went out to play some of the notable organs of London, particularly those with pedal boards and pedal pipes. A projected visit to Westminster Abbey came to nothing because the guides were not prepared to have organ music disrupting their activities, but Wesley was able instead to arrange a visit to St Sepulchre-without-Newgate, Holborn, where his friend George Cooper was organist, and where the Thomas Harris organ of around 1676 had recently been the subject of major work by Gray which included the addition of an octave of pedals and pedal pipes.[17] Another visit was to St Lawrence, Jewry, Burgh's own church, where the 1686 Renatus Harris organ had had a set of pedals added by Hugh Russell earlier in the year.[18] Yet another visit, described many years later by the writer and journalist Edward Holmes, was to the German Chapel at the Savoy in the Strand. Here, the chief attraction was the historic Snetzler organ, one of the few instruments in London at this time to have a full pedal-board, and for this reason a favourite of Wesley's. Holmes recalled that the music consisted entirely of Bach fugues, performed as duets, Wesley playing with each of the others in turn and allowing each his own choice. Afterwards Wesley started to improvise:

---

[14] *SW to Novello, 14 June [1824].

[15] *SW to Novello, 18 Sept. [1824].

[16] Ibid. For Harding's assistance to SW in 1822, see Harding to Sarah Wesley, 16 Jan. 1822.

[17] *SW to Novello, 25 Sept. [1824]; *SW to [Harding], 27 Sept. 1824; *SW to Novello, 28 Sept. [1824]. For the alterations, which took place in 1817, see Plumley, *The Organs of the City of London*, 123–6; Boeringer, *Organica Britannica*, vol. 2, pp. 206–7.

[18] *SW to Novello, 12 Nov. 1824, 23 Nov. 1824. For the organ, see Plumley, *The Organs of the City of London*, pp. 82–5; Boeringer, *Organica Britannica*, vol. 2, pp. 181–3.

He treated the organ in a manner which, to a young man who had never heard any of Bach's trios, appeared extraordinarily new and difficult. He began with a soft air, and then with his right hand on the Swell, his left on the Diapasons of the Great Organ, and his feet sliding over the pedals, he made it the subject of a trio, of which the parts for the two hands continually crossing or involved together, produced a very beautiful effect. A more difficult mode of improvisation cannot be imagined; it discovered the most profound head and the most refined taste.[19]

Holmes went on to comment that a good idea of the style of these improvisations could be gained from the theme and variations movement of the *Trio for the Piano forte and two Flutes*, KO 514, composed two years later.

It was probably in the late summer of 1824 that Wesley started making piano accompaniments for vocal music published by the Royal Harmonic Institution, a firm of music publishers run by Thomas Welsh and the ubiquitous Hawes.[20] Wesley's task was to supply realizations of the figured bass parts of Handel songs and duets for a generation of keyboard players without this skill. The first publication he worked on was Handel's *Thirteen Celebrated Italian Duets*, first published in 1777, which he started in September and which occupied him until around mid-November.[21] At around the same time, he was also providing similar realizations for songs from the oratorios, which were published, like the Italian duets, as individual numbers. Meanwhile, the publication of the Service was approaching. On 13 September Wesley wrote to Novello to ask him to forward the names of those who had subscribed for copies through him, so he could add them to the printed subscription list. On 18 October he was able to inform Novello that the Service was about to be published in the coming week,[22] and on 6 November, perhaps after a last-minute delay, he was at last able to send copies to his brother Charles.[23]

The publication of the Service was the clearest indication yet of Wesley's return to health and full activity. It attracted widespread attention and achieved good sales, with 205 subscribers purchasing a total of 230 copies, and an unknown number of further copies sold at non-subscription prices. The subscription list contained many familiar names. From among Wesley's closest professional associates were Novello, Attwood, Glenn, Major, Cooper, and the blind organist and Bach enthusiast John George Emett. Among other London professional musicians who subscribed but were not members of this inner circle were Busby, Horsley, Shield, Smart, and Stevens. Wesley's amateur musician friends were represented by Street, Drummer, Miss Burgh (the eldest daughter of Allatson Burgh), Harding, Holmes, Ozias and William

---

[19] Holmes, 'Cathedral Music and Composers', p. 234. For the arrangements for this day, on 22 Sept. 1824, see *SW to Novello, 18 Sept. [1824]; *SW to Novello, 20 Sept. [18]24.

[20] Krummel and Sadie (eds.), *Music Printing and Publishing*, s.v. 'Regent's Harmonic Institution'.

[21] *SW to Novello, 13 Sept. 1824, 18 Sept. 1824. See also *SW to Charles Wesley jun., 6 Nov. 1824.

[22] *SW to Novello, 18 Oct. 1824: 'That Eye Sore to our royal Composer (my Church Service) means to be troublesome to him (& perhaps to others) in the course of next Week.'

[23] *SW to Charles Wesley jun., 6 Nov. 1824.

Linley, and Henry Robertson, the treasurer of Covent Garden Theatre. There were also many subscribers from outside London. Pettet had evidently worked hard to find subscribers from among his friends in East Anglia, recruiting Eager from Great Yarmouth, Pymar from Beccles, and Tydemann from Framlingham. Other subscriptions came from church musicians both in London and the provinces who would have wanted to assess the suitability of his new Service for their own use before perhaps going on to buy further copies. The largest order of all came from the Dean and Chapter of Exeter Cathedral, who subscribed for ten copies, with other dignitaries from the Cathedral taking a further four.

The publication of the Service was narrowly preceded by an incident that at the same time caused a good deal of innocent amusement and ensured that Wesley's name was on everybody's lips: an exchange of correspondence in *The Times* between Wesley and the publishers John Sainsbury and Co. following the statement in the article on Wesley in their recently published *Dictionary of Musicians* that he had died around 1815. The error presented Wesley with an opportunity for self-promotion that was too good to miss. In a letter to *The Times* on 12 October, he humorously pointed out the error, at the same time taking the opportunity to state that he had recently composed a church service that was now in the press and was shortly to be published. At this point, the wisest course of action for the publishers of the *Dictionary* would have been either silence or an unreserved apology for their error. Instead, they chose to try to explain and justify themselves, claiming that they had approached Wesley by letter some time previously with a request for some biographical details about him, but had received no reply. Consequently, they had to compile his entry from the best previously published authorities. One of these was the article on Wesley's brother Charles in the recently published *Public Characters of All Nations* which had referred to him as 'the late Mr S. Wesley'.[24] In addition, a compiler working on the *Dictionary* had later been told of a confusion of Charles with Samuel, and that Samuel had died 'about the year 1815'. They commented that this isolated error did not detract from the accuracy of the *Dictionary* as a whole, and complained that Wesley had been less than grateful towards them, given that their article on him contained a 'very warm' and 'very just' eulogy of his merits.

It was not to be expected that as adept a self-publicist as Wesley would let this absurdity pass. In a second letter to *The Times*, he pointed out when people made public blunders, it was more creditable for them to admit their errors and apologize than to try to bolster up their cause by 'sophistical evasion'. He had indeed received a request from Sainsbury's for information about his career some twelve months ago but had declined to answer, on the grounds that he felt no obligation to give strangers information about himself for their own publications. He further pointed out that he held egotism to be 'generally nauseous and disgusting', and that it was 'both indelicate and in bad taste to

---

[24] *Public Characters of All Nations*, vol. 3, p. 599.

publish the history of any living artist'. He had no desire to injure the reputation of the *Dictionary*, but did want to correct the error it had made about him. In addition, Sainsbury's account of the misunderstanding was inconsistent. If they really believed that he had died around 1815, it was strange that they had written to him eight years later, and if they did not, it was even more strange that they had stated that he had died then. This goaded Sainsbury's into yet another ill-advised reply. They now claimed that they had known personally that Wesley was alive in 1814, but were out of England for the whole of 1815, and thus would not have seen any announcement of his death, had he in fact died then. When later told that he had died, they concluded that it must have been in 1815, but qualified their statement in the *Dictionary* by the word 'about'.

All this made good copy, and the affair was picked up in the 16 October number of the *News of Literature and Fashion* in a humorous article, possibly by the humorist Edward Dubois, entitled 'The Ghost Extraordinary'. Wesley took the opportunity to reply in similar vein, and his article, entitled 'A Voice from Charon's Boat', was printed in the following week's number, along with the entire *Times* correspondence for the benefit of those who had missed it on its first appearance. In time, the whole correspondence and the two *News of Literature and Fashion* articles were reprinted in the *Harmonicon*, a monthly musical journal that had been launched the previous year under the editorship of William Ayrton.[25]

The past year had been an eventful one. It came to an end with an excursion by Wesley and Samuel Sebastian to visit his old friend Sir Robert Peat, the vicar of St Lawrence, Brentford, and a chaplain to George IV, whom Wesley had probably first got to know through Masonic circles. Wesley thought highly of him, describing him to Novello as 'a good Scholar, a very *feeling* Lover of Music, a Man of superior Manners, & what *we* think better than all these, his Heart is warm and sincere.'[26] In late November he had invited Wesley to bring a party down to Brentford to perform the Service to him, offering them beds for the night if necessary. He was particularly keen to meet Novello, whose services he had attended at the Portuguese Embassy Chapel and whom he knew well by reputation. Samuel Sebastian was to sing treble, if Hawes could be persuaded to allow him leave of absence from the Chapel Royal. Wesley would sing bass, and Novello would direct from the piano. Various other singers were suggested for the other parts, including Robertson and Novello's brother Francis, who sang bass in the Portuguese Embassy choir and whose assistance Wesley thought would be worth 'an Octave of Pedal Pipes'. But there were difficulties in finding a suitable date, and then Novello fell ill with a recurrence of a digestive disorder that had been troubling him for some time. Wesley was unwilling to leave Novello out of the party, and on 13 December wrote to him to suggest a

---

[25] *Harmonicon* 2 (1824), pp. 210–12. See also Ritchey, 'The Untimely Death of Samuel Wesley; or, The Perils of Plagiarism'.
[26] *SW to Novello, 29 Nov. 1824.

postponement until his health was improved, at the same time urging him to consult John Abernethy, the eminent specialist in digestive disorders (and inventor of the biscuit that bears his name), about his continuing ill-health. The visit had to be further postponed when Peat fell and injured his back, and in the end it was only Wesley and Samuel Sebastian who made the journey to Brentford, on 29 December.[27]

Wesley's Service received its first review in the January 1825 number of the *Harmonicon*.[28] The anonymous reviewer began by commenting on and explaining the relative paucity of new church music publications, pointing out that in the past there had been a tendency to value only what was old, and that there was therefore no stimulus for composers to publish new works. In addition, the church authorities were conservative, and tended to be resistant to new works on account of their 'alleged gaiety'. No such criticisms could be levelled against Wesley's service on this score, however: it was written according to the practice of church music, and its composer had evidently studied Gibbons and Child as well as more recent composers of church music.

In fact, it was Wesley's familiarity with earlier English church music that the reviewer was to use against him. Remarking that Wesley's adoption of a long-established style had precluded any 'bold attempt at novelty', he drew attention to some errors in emphasis that he had discovered in the setting of the words. With this, he moved to more detailed criticism, first regretting that Wesley did not make the Service truly complete by supplying a setting of the Nicene Creed, which was sung in all cathedrals, and commenting that the settings of the Sanctus and the Kyrie Eleison were not so likely to please as the other parts of the service. But it was in his comments on individual passages that the reviewer was most critical. Of the chord in the Jubilate to which Attwood had taken such exception the previous April, he remarked that it was a chord of the 7th and 2nd 'in an extremely bare, crude, state, and to our ears very cacophonous, though Dr Blow might have enjoyed it much'– a reference to some famously discordant passages in the church music of Purcell's most celebrated English contemporary. He also criticized the final cadence of the same movement, and took objection to a passage in the Gloria Patri section of the Magnificat. Having thus achieved the 'impartial discharge of [his] critical duty', he rounded off his notice with a return to the tone of Olympian praise with which he had begun it, commenting on the work's many beauties, including the aptness of the word setting and the skill of the imitative writing.

The review could be read in two ways: either as an extremely favourable notice with a few comments on minor shortcomings, or as a hostile one that cloaked its destructive criticisms beneath a thin veneer of courtesy and praise. Wesley was in no doubt about its intention, commenting to Novello that 'the

---

[27] *SW to Novello, 29 Nov. 1824, 3 Dec. 1824; Peat to Wesley, 19 Dec. 1824; *SW to Novello, 20 Dec. 1824, 21 Dec. [1824], 22 Dec. 1824.
[28] *Harmonicon* 3 (1825), 10–11.

Rats have been nibbling at my poor Service', and adding that he felt 'obliged to accommodate them with a Kick, not merely out of Respect, but because it is a Pity that the *innocent* part of the musical World should be humbugged and insulted by Lies, hypocritically forwarded to it as Truth & Candour.'[29] At first, perhaps surprisingly, he had no idea who had written the review. He approached Linley to see if he knew, but Linley denied all knowledge, and attempted to dissuade Wesley from the immediate response that he was considering. To Wesley's scorn, Linley also had the temerity to suggest that the review had been written with friendly intent. Ten days later, Wesley wrote to tell Novello that he had been reliably informed that William Ayrton was 'one of the head-Pigs at the Trough' at the *Harmonicon*, and that he had no doubt that Attwood was similarly involved. Crotch was another possibility, although Wesley was inclined to think that he 'could hardly write such nonsense as the others'.[30] In fact, to anyone who was at all conversant with the organization of the *Harmonicon*, William Ayrton, as the editor, was from the first the leading contender for the authorship of the review.

By 27 January, Wesley had completed his 'Apology for all my mortal Sins committed against holy Counterpoint' and was ready to show it to Novello for his comments. He had no confidence that the *Harmonicon* would print it, and had in any case decided to have no more to do with them as a 'Junto of mere book-making Blunderers, interspersed with a few half-in-half Musicians with just knowledge enough to betray their Ignorance'.[31] When in time the *Harmonicon* predictably declined to publish his reply, Wesley turned his attention elsewhere. The *Examiner* was the first and most obvious next journal to approach. It was a weekly, and was edited by Novello's old friends John and Leigh Hunt. It was certainly no stranger to controversy: in 1813, an attack on the Prince Regent had landed the two brothers in prison for two years for criminal libel. Moreover, Leigh Hunt was a member of the Novello salon, and so might well be amenable to persuasion from Novello. By 25 March, however, it was apparent that the *Examiner* was not going to co-operate. It was now almost three months since the appearance of the *Harmonicon* had been published, and Wesley, aware that the topicality of his response was fast disappearing, felt that it was high time that his 'Animadversions on Mr Ayrton's Nonsense' appeared, if they were to appear at all. He now turned his attention to the monthly journals, which he had been told were often avid for controversy. He had been told that the venerable *Gentleman's Magazine* now refused nothing, and in consequence had lost much of its former reputation.[32] Part of Wesley's information was correct, but the *Gentleman's Magazine* did not make a practice of publishing controversial material, and in the unlikely event of it accepting Wesley's article, the soonest it could appear would be in the May number. His

---

[29] *SW to Novello, 8 Jan. 1825.
[30] *SW to Novello, 27 Jan. [1825].
[31] Ibid.
[32] *SW to Novello, 25 Mar. [1825].

next approach, a few days later, was to Edward Dixon Pouchée, the publisher of the weekly *News of Literature and Fashion*, which had printed 'The Ghost Extraordinary' and 'A Voice from Charon's Boat' the previous year. Pouchée at this point claimed to be unconcerned by the inclusion in Wesley's article of musical quotations requiring specialist engraving or typesetting, and agreed to give it his full consideration.[33] Two weeks later, however, he turned down the article on the grounds that it was too long for a newspaper. At this point Wesley enlisted the aid of Joseph Street junior, the son of his old friend, to make further attempts to find a monthly journal that would be prepared to accept it.[34]

For all his obsession with the *Harmonicon* review of the Service, Wesley was occupied in the early part of 1825 with other activities and projects. Perhaps most important, he was again playing the organ at the Covent Garden oratorio concerts, the management of which Hawes included with all his other activities. This was the first time Wesley had been engaged for the oratorio concerts since 1819, and by now they were looking very different, with programmes consisting in the main of modern music. In 1824 and 1825 the most favoured composer was Weber, whose *Der Freischütz* had received its first London performances in July 1824. The 1825 oratorio concerts were dominated by his music, the most frequently performed item being the Hunting Chorus from *Der Freischütz*, which was to be heard at almost every concert.

At the same time, he was continuing to arrange Handel oratorio songs for the Royal Harmonic Institution. It was presumably these arrangements that he was referring to when he wrote at the end of April to Mary Russell, the widow of William Russell, in response to a request for his advice on how to proceed with commissioning a piano reduction of her late husband's oratorio *Job* for its projected publication.[35] Wesley advised that rather than attempting to find a single person to make the entire reduction, she should aim to appoint three, each of them to undertake one act. He regretted that he was too busy with a similar task to be able to help himself, but offered to suggest the names of two or three suitable people. In due course, he would also be willing to help with the revision of the arrangements, the reading of proofs, and any other necessary tasks connected with seeing the publication through the press, as a token of his friendship.

On 2 May 1825 Wesley acted as 'umpire' or consultant in the appointment of the organist at the new church of St Matthew's, Brixton. The preliminary stages of the appointment process had been handled with due seriousness and correctness. Candidates had been asked to put their names forward, and by the time of the Select Vestry meeting of 25 April a short-list had been drawn up consisting of William Ling, Henry Boys, Emett, and Robert Williams. Williams, the organist of St Andrew by the Wardrobe, Victoria Street, was one of Wesley's

---

[33] *SW to Novello, 29 Mar. [1825].
[34] *SW to Novello, 12 [Apr. 1825].
[35] *SW to Mary Ann Russell, 16 Apr. 1825.

pupils, and was also known to Novello, who in 1818 had written in support of his application for membership of the Royal Society of Musicians. Wesley thought highly of him, and when Williams wrote to him earlier in the month to ask Novello if would be prepared to write him a reference, he described him to Novello as clever and worthy, and stated that Novello could 'safely give him a favourable Word without Dread of a Charge of Falsehood from the Editors of the Harmonicon or musical quarterly Review.'[36]

The short-listed candidates were required to appear before the select vestry on 2 May and to perform three pieces: an own-choice voluntary lasting not more than ten minutes, the 104th Psalm, and the Pastoral Symphony from *Messiah*. Having heard the candidates, Wesley recommended that Williams should be appointed, on the grounds that he had exhibited 'real organ style'.[37] Despite this recommendation, Williams received only one vote in the ballot. Emett received two, Boys five, and the winner was Ling with twelve votes. Both Wesley and Williams were understandably upset by this decision, suspected some underhand dealings, and published letters expressing their concern at the conduct of the election.

This affair, subsequently referred to by Wesley as the 'Brixton squabble',[38] was soon overtaken by more urgent matters. Later on the same day Wesley returned home to be served notice that Charlotte was having him arrested for debt, and was ordered to give himself up two days later for imprisonment in a 'spunging house' or debtors' prison. Wesley had no great expectation of being able to find the money to clear the debt and secure his early release, and thought it unlikely that he would be able to attend the meeting of Novello's Classical Harmonists Society on the coming Thursday. He also had his doubts about being able to fulfil his commitments at Camden Chapel on the following Sunday.[39] In fact, Wesley remained in the spunging house, in Cursitor Street, off Chancery Lane, for only three days. He was released on the Saturday, and was thus able to appear the following day at Camden Chapel, presumably saying nothing to the authorities there of his recent ordeal. The debt, which cost £25 to clear once legal expenses had been met, was no doubt a consequence of non-payment of maintenance to Charlotte. By now, this had been reduced from £130 per year, the amount set in 1812, to £25, probably in recognition of Wesley's reduced means and the fact that Emma, a dependent child at the time of the original settlement, was now grown up.

Charlotte's action in having Wesley arrested was prompted by their son Charles. Following the upheavals which had precluded his going to university at the normal age, he had gone up to Christ's College, Cambridge in 1819 and had been ordained in 1821. He was now thirty-one, and on the first steps of a successful career in the Church. For the moment he was the curate of St Mary's,

---

[36] *SW to Novello, 19 Apr. [1825].
[37] *Courier*, 9 May 1825.
[38] *SW to an unidentified recipient, [14 June 1825].
[39] *SW to Novello, 3 May [1825].

Pimlico, but would go on later to a number of appointments at court, ending his career as Sub-Dean of the Chapel Royal at St James's and Chaplain-in-Ordinary to Queen Victoria. There was little love lost between him and his father. He would have remembered clearly the family quarrels of his childhood and the circumstances of his father's desertion in 1810. At that time he was sixteen, and in other circumstances might have been looking forward to going to university. Instead, he was forced to abandon these ambitions and was two years later apprenticed to an apothecary – a procedure that cost his father £200, but could only have been an unsatisfactory alternative to what had originally been envisaged. In his father's absence, he had also been forced to become the head of the household, and had observed and experienced for himself the financial privations and emotional turmoil that characterized his mother's life following the separation. Of the many crises that he had lived through, the greatest had been the one surrounding his father's breakdown of May 1817, in which destitution had stared the entire family in the face. Under the circumstances, it was not surprising that he harboured a deep antipathy to his father. By nature rather stiff and formal, he found it hard to understand, much less to countenance or condone, any aspect of his father's behaviour. For his part, Wesley was not disposed to think well of his eldest son, feeling that Charles's position as a clergyman sat badly with his uncharitable behaviour towards him in the present crisis, as in others before it.[40]

Wesley was considerably shaken by his experiences in the spunging house. Three days after his release, as he explained to Novello, he had still not recovered from 'the Effects of close Air, & what is still worse, the witnessing Scenes of Misery impossible for me to relieve'.[41] He now needed to pick up the threads of everyday life. There were letters to write: principally to his brother and sister, to let them know the true circumstances of the case and to correct any false accounts put about by Charlotte and her allies. He also needed to write to Evans, to turn down a request to participate in his forthcoming benefit, and to Novello. There was also the continuing saga of the Brixton organ squabble to deal with. Following the publication of the letters by Wesley and Williams, the story had been picked up in the *Courier* in a brief paragraph published on 9 May. The purpose of this was not, however, to investigate any alleged irregularities in the appointment, but a lame and tedious attempt at humour. Noting that Wesley had declared that 'the superiority of *real* organ style was evinced by Mr. Williams', it continued: 'it is, however, admitted, that Mr. Ling was *really* elected. This, perhaps, was the origin of the statement said to be erroneous, as it was not supposed that the select vestry gentlemen had declined attending to the umpire, to give the preference to superiority of *un*"real organ style", after "the very respectable exertions of the other gentlemen".' Having read the *Courier* paragraph, Wesley wrote to Williams to say that he wished to discuss it with him, going on to declare that 'the Trustees, Vestry or whatever they call

---

[40] SW to Charles Wesley jun., 10 [May 1825].
[41] *SW to Novello, 10 May 1825.

themselves are no better than a Bundle of Swindlers, & were I you I would expose them to the uttermost.– There ought in fact to be an entirely new Election.' The affair evidently rumbled on: in a further letter to Williams two days later, Wesley enclosed another paper – whether a personal letter to Wesley or another newspaper column is not clear – on the matter. Wesley did not know whether or not the writer had produced an accurate account of the case, but was inclined to doubt it, remarking that bitter experience had forced him to distrust the professions of every man. He concluded by signing himself 'Your hoaxed & belied Umpire'.[42]

---

[42] *SW to [Williams], 12 May 1825.

14

The Fitzwilliam music, 1825

By far the most exciting and potentially profitable item of business confronting Wesley in the spring of 1825 concerned the important collection of music manuscripts bequeathed to the University of Cambridge in 1816 by Lord Fitzwilliam. For eight years the University had done nothing about it, but in December of the previous year set up a committee to consider how parts of the collection might be published. Novello, hearing of this, approached the University and offered his advice.[1] He visited Cambridge for a few days in the Christmas vacation to inspect the collection, and later submitted a catalogue and report, outlining three ways in which selections might be published: by the University itself, by a third party, or by the University in partnership with a third party.[2] Novello's preferred option was that the University should act as publisher and employ him as editor, but he was also prepared if necessary to edit and publish selections himself. The Senate considered the report at its meeting on 18 March, and immediately granted him permission to publish any parts of the collection that he should think fit, but at his own expense and at his own risk.

It must have been apparent to Novello as he examined and catalogued the Fitzwilliam collection that it contained material for far more than the selection that he was contemplating. He evidently discussed the matter with Wesley, and appears to have suggested that Wesley should make his own approach to the University and negotiate permission on his own account to publish a further volume or volumes of selections. Wesley appears to have made his initial enquiries in late April or early May 1825. His contact in Cambridge was the Anglican clergyman and Hebrew scholar Daniel Guilford Wait, at this time in Cambridge cataloguing the oriental manuscripts in the University Library. In the week following his release from the spunging house, a letter from Wait was among those that demanded his attention. Wait informed him that he had visited Thomas Le Blanc, the current Vice-Chancellor, who considered that the Senate would in time be prepared to grant Wesley permission to publish a

---

[1] His main contact in Cambridge was John Lucius Dampier, a Fellow of King's College and a member of the committee: see Dampier to Novello, 18 Jan. 1825 (Leeds University Library, Brotherton Collection, Novello–Cowden Clarke Collection).

[2] Novello to Le Blanc, 27 Jan. 1825 (Cambridge University Library, University Archives, CUR 30.1 (60)).

selection, but not before Novello had published his own.³ In Wait's opinion, the collection contained a great deal that would reflect credit on Wesley if he were to publish it, and the undertaking would be 'of the most lucrative nature'. He was about to come to London, and suggested that Wesley should accompany him back to Cambridge, where he could then make a preliminary inspection of the collection before proceeding any further. There, for the moment, the matter rested. Novello would continue work on the collection at various stages in 1825, making at least one further visit to Cambridge in the course of the year, and the first part of his five-volume selection, consisting entirely of sacred choral music by Italian composers of the sixteenth to eighteenth centuries, was published as *The Fitzwilliam Music* in December 1825 or January 1826.⁴

Even as Wesley was still attempting to secure a reply to the *Harmonicon* notice, the Service received its second review, in the April 1825 number of the *Quarterly Musical Magazine and Review*.⁵ This was three times the length of its counterpart in the *Harmonicon*, and far more detailed in its comments. It was also, after its initial courtesies, decidedly more hostile, containing many detailed criticisms of specific points of harmony, in a manner very close to that formerly practised by Wesley himself in the *European Magazine*. The writer began by regretting the current decline in church music, and saluted Wesley for his courage and initiative in writing in such a neglected and unfashionable field. After praising Wesley's profound learning and refined taste, he remarked that he seemed to compose little and that the Service was the largest composition by him that he had encountered. This he put down to Wesley's prowess as an improviser, which saved him from 'the drudgery of the desk and the waste of midnight oil'. He praised the Service for its melody, its pure harmony, the 'truly ecclesiastical' character of its modulations, and the total lack of anything vulgar or theatrical: there were no 'lack-a-daisical chromatics nor stage effects', and the Service was imbued by the 'simplicity that should be the chief characteristic of church music'. At this point, however, he shifted from praise to censure, commenting on a lack in the Service of the elevation of expression achieved by previous composers, the harshness of some of the modulations, and the carelessness of much of the writing. Finally there were four pages of detailed criticisms of Wesley's word-setting, harmonies, and the negative tenor of the whole was only partly saved by a conciliatory conclusion.

Although Wesley appears initially not to have known who had written the review, his enquiries soon revealed that it was generally thought to be by Horsley, and Wesley accordingly wrote an 'inquisitorial line' to him on the

---

³ Wait to SW, 11 May 1825.
⁴ The preface is dated Dec. 1825, and the volume was reviewed in *Harmonicon* 3 (Feb. 1826), 32–4. Subsequent parts appeared and were reviewed at intervals through 1826 and early 1827.
⁵ *QMMR* 7 (1826), pp. 95–101.

subject in late April.⁶ Wesley and Horsley, of course, had known each other for a long time. There are no indications in Wesley's letters up to this time of any great friendship between the two men, but no signs of any great antipathy either, beyond a predictably snide remark by Wesley in a letter to Novello of 1814 about Horsley's Oxford Mus.B. degree.⁷ More recently, as we have seen, Horsley had been heavily involved in the *Quarterly*, and had become Bacon's chief assistant. His recommendation of Wesley to Bacon in 1819 suggests that he was at this time well disposed to Wesley. On the other hand, Wesley had reviewed two works by Horsley in his columns for the *European Magazine*, one of them not entirely favourably, and although the reviews were anonymous, Horsley may have discovered or suspected that Wesley was the author, and may have long contemplated revenge.⁸

Whatever the reason or reasons, by early 1825 there appears to have been little love lost between Wesley and Horsley. In a letter to Novello of 27 April, Wesley described him as 'a Musician of abundant Merit, which however I have long known to be lamentably counterbalanced by an Exuberance of Envy', before going on to quote Pope's couplet about critics who 'Damn with faint praise, assent with civil leer, / And without sneering, teach the rest to sneer'.⁹ When challenged about the review, Horsley not surprisingly denied any involvement with it, but Wesley by now had little doubt that he was the author, and Horsley's reply¹⁰ did nothing to persuade him otherwise. In fact, given Horsley's position as Bacon's leading associate on the *Quarterly* and its chief reviewer of church music, his authorship cannot ever have been seriously in doubt to anyone familiar with the journal's organization.

In mid-June 1825, Wesley was finally successful in finding in the *Literary Chronicle* a home for his response to the *Harmonicon* review.¹¹ A long-standing family connection with Samuel Benson, one of the editorial staff, probably helped to secure its insertion: Benson was the son of the Methodist minister Joseph Benson, who had been a close friend of both Wesley's father and his uncle John, and the next generation of Wesleys and Bensons had continued their association.¹² Wesley's article is a heavyweight rejoinder in which he is at

---

[6] *SW to Novello, [27 Apr. 1825]; SW's letter to Horsley is not preserved. SW was correct in his supposition: Horsley's authorship of this review is indicated in Horsley's own copy of QMMR, now at the Sibley Library, Eastman School of Music, Rochester, NY, USA.

[7] *SW to Novello, 13 [Apr. 1814].

[8] SW had reviewed Horsley's *Elegiac Ode for Five Voices, composed in Memory of Samuel Harrison* in *EM* 67 (1815), pp. 151–2, and his glee 'Hail, sweet patroness of song' in *EM* 69 (1816), p. 535. His review of the former was generally complimentary, but in the latter he took Horsley to task on some points of harmony and word setting.

[9] *SW to Novello, [27 Apr. 1825]. The quotation is from Pope's *Epistle to Dr Arbuthnot* (1735), 1. 201–2.

[10] Not preserved, but mentioned in *SW to Novello, 2 May 1825.

[11] *Literary Chronicle*, 11 June 1825, pp. 377–80. For the *Literary Chronicle*, see Sullivan, *The Romantic Age*, pp. 230–9.

[12] See also Benson to Sarah Wesley, 12 Apr. 1827, in which Benson approached Sarah with a request for material for publication in the *Literary Chronicle*.

pains to take issue with his critic on every possible point, from his knowledge of musical repertoire and grasp of the rules of harmony to his knowledge of Greek and his use of English. It is larded with quotations from and references to the works of Shakespeare, Pope, Swift, Johnson, Horace, and Cicero, at one point even invoking the authority of Scapula's Greek Lexicon to point out an incorrect usage. On the musical side, Wesley countered the accusations of harmonic incorrectness by reference to the practice of Tallis, Farrant, and Purcell and with quotations from their works from Boyce's *Cathedral Music*.

Wesley was finally able to go to Cambridge in the second half of June 1825; it was his first visit since 1808, when he had attended the Commencement ceremonies at the invitation of Hague and Carnaby. This was not the best of times, as Sarah was heavily pregnant and needed help in the house, or at least a watchful eye to ensure that she did not over-exert herself. But it fitted in with Wait's timetable: in early June he was in London attending to business matters but was soon due to return to Cambridge, when Wesley would be able to join him and stay at his house. Wait would then be able to make the necessary introductions, and Wesley would be able for the first time to inspect the Fitzwilliam collection for himself.

The original plan was that Wesley and Wait would travel on 14 June, a Tuesday, but Wait was delayed by various urgent business commitments, and the journey was postponed, first to the next day and then to the Friday. Apart from the inconvenience of having to kick his heels in London for two days, Wesley was particularly disappointed at this second postponement, as it meant that he would not have Wait's company for the journey. When he finally got to Cambridge, it was ahead of Wait, who was further delayed, and followed the next day. In Wait's absence Wesley was entertained by his wife Eliza, who like Sarah was heavily pregnant, with her confinement expected within the next month or six weeks. On the day of his arrival Wesley spent the evening with a scholar whom Mrs Wait had invited to meet him in her husband's absence. Wesley later described him to Sarah as 'so glorious a Companion that even were Wait not to come back, I could pass all the Days here without feeling much loss.'[13] But he was missing Sarah and his children, and anxious that she should not over-exert herself in his absence.

The real work of the visit began after the weekend, when Wesley was able to gain access to the Fitzwilliam collection. Although he had not yet received official permission to publish, he evidently considered it a mere formality, and was already beginning to select and transcribe material. On 21 June he wrote to Novello to ask him which composers he was intending to include in his own selection, so that he could avoid duplicating his work.

Wesley's stay in Cambridge was not entirely taken up with the Fitzwilliam collection, and he also found time to play some of the more notable organs, Wait having presumably made the necessary arrangements for access. He

---

[13] SW to Sarah Suter, 19 June 1825.

commented to Novello on the mischief that had been done to the Trinity College organ by 'that Brace of Quacks' Flight and Robson: a reference to the botched alterations that they had made in 1819–20 to the 'Father' Smith organ, over which they had been taken to court by the Master and Fellows.[14] Of the small Snetzler organ at Peterhouse, he remarked that it was 'a sweet little instrument', and of the 'Father' Smith organ at St Mary's, the University Church, that it uttered 'the true ecclesiastical Sounds'.[15] But he was unable to try the Avery organ at King's as the Provost had refused to make the key available. On 25 June he returned to London, immediately writing to Novello to inform him of his return and that he had a letter from Wait for him.[16] Sarah had still not given birth, but she did so in the course of the following week, to another son, John.

In late July Wesley returned to Cambridge for a further two weeks. In view of Eliza Wait's still impending confinement he stayed in lodgings, taking breakfast and tea with the Waits but making his own arrangements for other meals. For some of the time Novello was also in Cambridge, and some of Wesley's transcriptions on this visit may have been for him. But Wesley was certainly also transcribing manuscripts on his own account, and was able to report back to Samuel Sebastian that they were likely to 'turn to excellent account'. Among them, and a source of particular interest, was a manuscript dating from around 1740 containing motets by William Byrd.[17]

Wesley and Novello took the opportunity of their joint stay in Cambridge to forward the cause of the *Confitebor*, which Wesley had by now decided to attempt to publish by subscription. The work had never been performed, and if it were to be published at this stage it would be vital to bring it to public attention by giving a public performance in London. As an experiment, and in an attempt to gauge public reaction, Wesley and Novello gave an informal performance of the work in the chapel of Trinity College as an organ duet, before an invited audience. The response was encouraging, and several members of the audience indicated their enthusiasm to subscribe to a published edition in due course. Foremost among these was Mary Frere, the wife of William Frere, Master of Downing College, and a force to be reckoned with in the social life of the Cambridge at this time. Wesley described her as a 'great Patroness of all musical Schemes', and was confident that she would on her own bring him a good number of subscriptions. Wait evidently had a hand in these arrangements, and Wesley commented to Samuel Sebastian – inaccurately, as it

---

[14] *SW to Novello, 21 June 1825.
[15] Ibid.
[16] *SW to Novello, 25 June 1825.
[17] Cambridge, Fitzwilliam Museum, MS 114: see Fuller Maitland and Mann, *Catalogue of the Manuscript Music in the Fitzwilliam Museum, Cambridge*, pp. 58–9. There are twenty-one items in the manuscript, of which only seventeen are listed in the catalogue, and only twenty are in fact by Byrd: the remaining one ('Quia illic interrogaverunt nos') is by Victoria. See my '"Byrde's excellent Antiphones": Samuel Wesley's Projected Edition of Selections from *Gradualia*'.

happened, in the light of Wait's later disastrous business dealings – that he 'would not encourage me in any Risk, nor suffer me to venture on proceeding until I should be sure of a very liberal Subscription before beginning to print'.[18]

Wesley returned to London some time before 9 August, much buoyed up by the good reception that the *Confitebor* had had in Cambridge, and anxious to proceed with publicizing the work in preparation for a full-scale performance. His next step was to write a paragraph for the *Examiner* in which he described the Cambridge performance and its reception, and expressed the hope that the work would be performed in the following year's Lenten oratorio season, at the same time including a puff for Novello's forthcoming edition of selections from the Fitzwilliam collection. He then sent the paragraph to Novello, who was able to call on his long-standing friendship with Leigh Hunt to secure its appearance in the *Examiner* on the following Sunday.[19] At the same time, Wesley was continuing in his efforts to secure a London performance of the *Confitebor*. In late August he approached the bass singer Henry Phillips with a proposal that he might like to sing the bravura aria 'Confessio et Magnificentia' at a forthcoming concert, and later reported to Novello that he was delighted with it, and would 'drain the Marrow of his Bones to give it Effect'.[20] Wesley had in mind Mary Anne Paton as his principal soprano soloist, and felt she would do justice to the florid aria 'Fidelia omnia mandata eius'. With these two outstanding young singers as his preferred soloists, Wesley was certainly aiming high. Phillips was twenty-four, and already well established as the outstanding bass of his time. In the previous year he had made his stage debut in the taxing role of Artabanes in Arne's *Artaxerxes* and had gone on to take the part of Caspar in the first English production of Weber's *Der Freischütz*.[21] Paton was a year younger. After appearing as a child performer between 1810 and 1813, she had made her adult stage debut as Susanna in *The Marriage of Figaro* in October 1822. Since then she had sung Polly in *The Beggar's Opera*, Mandane in Arne's *Artaxerxes*, and Agathe in *Der Freischütz*. In the following year, both singers would create major roles in Weber's *Oberon*.

Persuading the managers of the Covent Garden oratorios to pay the high fees for these two soloists might be difficult, however. Robertson told Wesley that Phillips had asked more at the previous year's Covent Garden oratorio series than they were prepared to pay, to which Wesley commented that they had made good profits, and that they should be prepared to 'squeeze out an extra 10 or 20 Guineas for the Credit of a national Concern'.

Now that Wesley had returned to London, he was ready once more to take up the cudgels against Horsley and the *Quarterly*. Before leaving for Cambridge in June he had written to Horsley, and it was during his absence that Horsley's reply arrived. Neither letter has survived, but it can be imagined that by this

---

[18] *SW to Samuel Sebastian Wesley, 1 Aug. 1825.
[19] *Examiner*, 14 Aug. 1825.
[20] *SW to Novello, c. 26 Aug. 1825.
[21] For a contemporary account of his early career, see *QMMR* 7 (1825), pp. 463–7.

stage the correspondence was becoming steadily more bad-tempered on both sides. By 17 August a further letter from Horsley arrived which Wesley sent on to Novello with the comment that it put him in mind of a favourite remark of his godfather Martin Madan, that it was 'a lamentable affair that so many people could not be quietly contented to remain fools, but felt obliged to let all the world know it'.[22] By 31 August, Wesley had received yet another letter from Horsley, which he again forwarded to Novello, this time enclosing some satirical verses on him that he had written for Novello's amusement. It was at much the same time that Wesley wrote to Bacon to ask if he would include his reply to the review in a forthcoming number of the *Quarterly*.[23] He had no great hopes of Bacon's agreement, as he suspected that Horsley had 'put him up either to Evasion or Refusal'.[24] After the anticipated refusal, he then turned to Novello's friend (and future son-in-law) Charles Cowden Clarke, hoping that his contacts in the world of periodical journalism would help to find it a home.[25] Clarke, who at this time had connections with the *London Magazine*, appears to have used his good offices on Wesley's behalf with Henry Southern, the editor, and for a while Wesley was confident that his article would appear in the November number.[26] All, however, came to nothing, and it was at this point, almost eleven months after the appearance of the *Harmonicon* review, that Wesley tacitly admitted defeat and allowed the matter to drop.[27]

On 12 August 1825 Wesley received an invitation from his friend Sir James Gardiner to spend a week at his home at Roche Court at Fareham, Hampshire. Wesley was glad to accept, particularly as Sir James offered to pay his coach fare and other travelling expenses,[28] and set off on 1 September. His visit was a time for relaxation and good company: he found Gardiner and his family delightful, and Gardiner introduced him to several 'prime sensible Folk' of his acquaintance, among them William Carnegie, seventh Earl of Northesk, the Rear Admiral of the Navy, with whom Wesley and Gardiner spent two pleasant days at his seat at Longwood House, Owslebury, just outside Winchester. Wesley's visit coincided with the Three Choirs Festival meeting at Hereford and in consequence the absence from Winchester of George Chard, the organist of the Cathedral, who was one of the vocal soloists at the festival and was having one of his own compositions performed there. A native of Winchester, he was a near-contemporary of Wesley, whom he may have met in London when he was a chorister at St Paul's. He had returned to Winchester in 1791, first as a lay vicar and since 1802 as organist, and would serve another twenty-four years until his death in 1849, when he would be succeeded by Wesley's son Samuel

[22] *SW to Novello, 17 Aug. [1825].
[23] Letter not preserved, but written between 12 and 19 Aug. 1825.
[24] *SW to Novello, 19 Aug. 1825.
[25] *SW to Novello, 31 Aug. [1825].
[26] For Clarke's connections with the *London Magazine*, see Altick, *The Cowden Clarkes*, pp. 51–2.
[27] *SW to Novello, 23 Nov. [1825].
[28] *SW to Novello, [12 Aug. 1825].

Sebastian. Wesley found him to be 'much less disagreeable than Musicians in general' – high praise indeed – and although he did not meet him in Winchester he was able to play for the service at the Cathedral on two occasions.

Wesley returned to London around 10 September. Nine days later, he received a letter from Wait in Cambridge reporting that difficulties had arisen in the negotiations with the University which threatened the whole Fitzwilliam enterprise.[29] At root was the unease which some members of the Senate felt over the fact that if Wesley was granted his permission, two different sets of selections from the Fitzwilliam collection would be published in quick succession and in apparent rivalry. For a while, it seemed likely that permission from the University would not be forthcoming and that all Wesley's work during the summer had been for nothing.

The absence of key parts of the correspondence makes it impossible to chart all the stages of the crisis, but it is clear that a number of letters were exchanged between Wesley, Wait, Novello, Novello's friend Dampier, and the University authorities to try to clarify the situation and to ensure that Wesley would gain his permission. On more than one occasion Wesley complained to Novello about the lack of straightforwardness of some of those involved. The affair dragged on through October and November and into December, until eventually Wesley wrote to Novello to say that permission would be granted if Novello were to state in writing that he was intending to restrict himself to Italian repertoire, and that he was happy for any other parts of the collection to be published by anyone who was granted permission from the University. Novello made this declaration in the Preface to the first volume of his collection, which was published later in the month or early in the following year. This brought the negotiations to a close, and on 1 March of the following year Wesley was granted permission to publish. But this seemingly satisfactory outcome had been achieved at the cost of the friendship between Wesley and Novello. There was a serious quarrel between the two men some time early in 1826, almost certainly concerning the Fitzwilliam collection, that resulted in a complete cessation of communication between them for over four years.

---

[29] Not preserved, but see *SW to Novello, 19 Sept. [1825].

15

Byrd, the *Confitebor*, and Handel's hymns, 1826–1828

Now that the all-important permission had been granted by the University, Wesley was anxious to get to work on the Fitzwilliam project. Commitments in London detained him throughout March 1826, but he was able to leave London on Easter Monday, 27 March, returning on 4 April.[1] This visit was probably taken up with transcribing the Byrd motets discovered on a previous visit. He soon decided – if he had not done so earlier – that these would form his first volume of selections. An edition of some or all of these would be a reasonably sized and self-contained project that would tap into existing antiquarian interests in English music of the Elizabethan and Jacobean periods. Wesley appears to have transcribed the whole manuscript, and most of his transcriptions are now at the British Library.[2] It was presumably shortly after his return from Cambridge that Wesley issued proposals for his edition, and it was certainly before the end of the month, when he wrote to his sister Sarah to correct a rumour that she had heard that he was expecting to receive £300 from the publication. In fact, he would be happy to receive a third as much, but hoped that his edition would lead to other volumes in the future.[3] The Byrd edition did not materialize, for reasons that Wesley was to explain over four years later in a letter to Street. He had received over two hundred subscriptions, which was sufficient to ensure a profit on the venture, and had had nine plates engraved, but then ran out of money and was unable to proceed.[4]

The visit to Cambridge was squeezed in before the beginning of an exceptionally busy period culminating in his benefit on 4 May. On 14 April he began a course of six weekly lectures at the Royal Institution: his first engagement there since 1811, and the first of three courses to be delivered there over the next two seasons. The *Harmonicon* for May 1826 printed the titles of the lectures: 'On Music, considered in the two-fold Sense of a Science, and as an Art'; 'On Musical Taste'; 'On Musical Prejudice'; 'On the Distinction between Sublime, Beautiful, and Ornamental Style'; 'On the General Management of

---

[1] Samuel Sebastian Wesley to Emett, 25 Mar. 1826; *SW to Glenn, 4 Apr. 1826.
[2] BL, Add. MS 35001, fols 86–144, erroneously described in the printed catalogue as being by SW himself.
[3] *SW to Sarah Wesley, 27 Apr. [1826].
[4] *SW to Street, 25 May 1830.

Musical Performances in England'; and 'On the Advancement and Improvement of Musical Knowledge and Taste'.[5] The texts of some of these lectures, sometimes in revised and altered form from delivery on subsequent occasions, are identifiable among the papers bequeathed by Wesley's daughter Eliza to the British Museum. Wesley appears to have taken a good deal of care in their preparation. From the existence of several versions of some passages, differing only slightly in wording, it appears that he probably read out the lectures directly from the written texts. If so, they show him in a stiffly formal and self-consciously learned vein. As might be expected from their titles, their subject matter was very general, and Wesley treated them as opportunities to ride hobby-horses and to retail anecdotes in an overall structure that can only be described as rambling. Each lecture had a number of music examples which were only loosely connected, if at all, with the subject. And Wesley was not above puffing the work of his friends: in the last lecture of the course, on 19 May, he devoted a good deal of time to discussing the merits of Linley's *Shakspeare's Dramatic Songs*, and included two of them among his musical examples. The lecture theatre at the Royal Institution must have been exceptionally crowded on this occasion, as the lecture concluded with a performance of the Trio for Three Piano fortes.

Wesley's main preoccupation in early 1826, however, was his benefit. It was his first for many years, and would include as its principal item the first performance of the *Confitebor*. Plans for a performance at the Covent Garden oratorios, which Wesley had been anticipating the previous year, had fallen through, probably because of a change of management. Hawes, who managed the 1825 season and had employed Wesley as organist for the series, had now been replaced by Smart. Whatever Smart's attitude to Wesley, he clearly did not consider his continued presence at the organ indispensable, and he was not employed for the 1826 season. Indeed, there appears to have been no organist at all for the series, perhaps in recognition of the radically changed nature of the programmes and the diminished proportion of 'old' music. Under the circumstances, it was not surprizing to find that Smart had no room in his programme either for Wesley's *Confitebor*, a work now twenty-six years old and still awaiting its first performance; instead, there was a heavy emphasis on the music of Weber. In early March Weber himself arrived in London for the rehearsals and first performances of *Oberon*, commissioned in 1824 by Charles Kemble for Covent Garden. His first appearance, three days after his arrival, was at the oratorio concert on 8 March, when the audience rose to its feet to greet him. He conducted the first part of this concert, consisting of a selection from *Der Freischütz*, and repeated the process for the three remaining concerts in the series.

Given this turn of events, Wesley had no option but to promote his own performance of the *Confitebor*, with all the hard work and financial risk that this

---

[5] *Harmonicon* 4 (1826), p. 94.

involved. Preparations for the concert, which was to be at the Argyll Rooms on 4 May, began in earnest in late March or early April with the copying of chorus and instrumental parts and the assembling of a chorus made up of Wesley's amateur and professional singer friends.[6] By 13 April, Wesley was anxious to place press advertisements without further delay, and wrote to Smart to ask for confirmation that some of his pupils could be included.[7] These were presumably boy trebles, who would have formed some or all of the soprano line of the chorus in the *Confitebor*. A complicating factor was that they were already due to appear in a performance of *Oberon* at Covent Garden on the same evening – probably as extras or members of the chorus – but Wesley was confident that their duties there would finish in good time for them to come on to the Argyll Rooms and sing in the *Confitebor*, which formed the second half of his own concert.

The first part of the concert consisted of an extempore organ voluntary by Wesley and a piano concerto by Moscheles, with the composer as soloist. The *Confitebor* followed. The principal soprano and bass soloists were Paton and Phillips, as Wesley had planned; also taking part were the sopranos Harriet Cawse and Miss Hammersley, the tenors Braham and Vaughan, and the basses Knyvett and Sale.[8] This was a generous complement of soloists, as the *Confitebor* contained separate parts for only five soloists, but presumably the arias and ensembles were shared out between the soloists, in the usual oratorio fashion. Wesley later remembered that the performance had been 'universally approved',[9] but in fact it appears to have made little or no impact. The concert as a whole was briefly reported in the May number of the *Harmonicon* in its round-up of benefits, Wesley's improvisation receiving more coverage than the *Confitebor*, which was described merely as 'a work which contains some very fine composition, and many beautiful passages'.[10] There was no other press comment, and Wesley seems for the moment to have abandoned or postponed his plans for publication.

Notwithstanding some tart comments about the popularity of Weber's music and no doubt a strong feeling that it had played a large part in crowding out his own, Wesley had nothing against Weber personally. On 26 May he attended Weber's benefit concert at the Argyll Street Rooms. This was Weber's last public appearance: he died at Smart's house in Great Portland Street, where he had been staying, ten days later. Wesley offered to play the organ at the performance of Mozart's Requiem at his funeral on 21 June, but his offer was declined and Attwood played instead.

Wesley's quarrel with Novello earlier in 1826 brought to an end their correspondence, and with it a fruitful source of information about his activities. Some additional light on their disagreement is provided by a letter from an

[6] *SW to Glenn, 4 Apr. 1826.
[7] *SW to Smart, 13 Apr. 1826.
[8] *Harmonicon* 4 (1826), p. 31.
[9] *Reminiscences*, fol. 38.
[10] *Harmonicon* 4 (1826), p. 131.

anonymous correspondent signing himself 'Jubal' that appeared in the June number of the *Harmonicon*.[11] 'Jubal', who described himself as a subscriber to Novello's *Fitzwilliam Music*, remarked that the 'peculiar nature' of the work could hardly be expected to repay Novello financially for the time, labour, and expense of preparing it for publication. He and others were therefore surprised to read the announcement of another publication with the same title, and compiled from the same source, by Wesley. His surprise was increased by the knowledge that Novello had long been 'the intimate, the active, the tried friend' of Wesley. As he could not believe that any 'mercantile rivalry' had arisen between Novello and Wesley he professed to be at a loss to understand how two such specialised publications could be produced advantageously to their editors at the same time. He subsequently made it his business to enquire further into the situation, and found that Novello had no connection with Wesley's publication. He pointed out that Novello, in addition to his other acts of friendship to Wesley, had introduced him to the University and had 'acquiesced' in the Grace by which Wesley was given permission to transcribe and publish from the Fitzwilliam collection. It was scarcely worth pointing out that Novello's friendly actions had been undertaken in ignorance of the steps that Wesley was intending to take to produce a rival publication. He forbore to comment whether Wesley's actions were worthy of a 'respectable member of an enlightened profession', but trusted that the editor would submit the facts of the case to his readership.

The identity of 'Jubal' is unknown, but his letter sheds light on some aspects of the quarrel between Novello and Wesley. As we have seen, the whole of Wesley's negotiations with the University had been carried out openly and frankly, and Wesley had taken care to keep Novello in touch with all developments. The evidence of Wesley's letters to Novello clearly shows that the accusation that he had behaved in an underhand way was unfounded, and that it was absurd and malicious of 'Jubal' to suggest that Wesley had kept Novello in the dark about his intentions to publish selections from the Fitzwilliam collection. Wesley could not let the accusations of 'Jubal' go unanswered. He prepared a response, which he sent to the *Harmonicon* for insertion in the July number. It was evidently both lengthy and intemperate in tone, and the editors declined to print it, merely noting on the contents page of the July number that it had been held over until the following month and that in the meantime Wesley would be hearing from them. Wesley's response has not survived, but the revision of his response appears to have been the subject of an undated letter to his sister Sarah of around this time, in which he mentioned having 'thrown out one "silly", and trimmed a Word or two elsewhere', and stated that his 'Squib' should 'now explode'.[12] This revision was evidently not sufficiently thorough-going for the editors of the *Harmonicon*, however, who

---

[11] 'Jubal' to the editors of the *Harmonicon*, 20 May 1826, *Harmonicon* 6 (1826), p. 113.
[12] SW to Sarah Wesley, [?8 July 1826]. The letter, which is dated only 'Saturday noon', was probably written on 8 July, but could also have been written on 15 or 22 July. I am grateful to Michael Kassler for establishing its date and pointing out its relevance to the 'Jubal' affair.

noted on the contents page of the next month's number that although they had desired Wesley to shorten and to moderate his expression, he had declined to do so, 'in terms that do not show much discretion'.[13]

Wesley had planned another visit to Cambridge at the end of July to undertake further work on the Fitzwilliam collection, but a short-term financial crisis obliged him to postpone it for the moment. As he explained to his sister Sarah, he was owed nearly £40 from a variety of sources, including £10 from the organ builder John Gray, £15 due to Samuel Sebastian – presumably for appearances as a boy treble arranged by Hawes – and four guineas from Robert Elliston, the licensee of Drury Lane, in respect of some lessons that Wesley had given one of his employees. The situation was grave: Wesley himself was 'in utter distress, even for quotidian expenses', and Sarah Suter was so anxious and perturbed that Wesley feared for her brain. Wesley considered the cancellation of his visit to be particularly unfortunate, as he thought Novello's friends would conclude that it had been brought about by cowardice, following the attack by 'Jubal' in the 'rascally Harmonicon'.[14]

Wesley was eventually able to get away to Cambridge in early September. Writing to Sarah Suter from the Castle Inn on the evening of 13 September, he was in good humour and able to report that all was going well, despite Sarah's failure to pack up tea and sugar in his luggage so as to save money. He had spent eight hours copying that day, entirely without tiredness. A week later, nearing the end of his visit, he was able to look forward to his return on the following Saturday. By now he was full of anxiety about money. Cambridge inns were expensive, and it was only the previous day that his friend Ridgeway had discovered an eating house where he had dined for half the price he had paid elsewhere. He had only £1 6s to last until his return, out of which he had to find the cost of his lodgings and of breakfast and tea for the whole of his visit. There was also the cost of a shirt, to replace the one that Sarah had omitted to pack, and he needed to give his landlady 2s 6d for her attendance. He also reported that he had dined once with Mr Key, the Procurator of the Fitzwilliam Museum and had breakfasted with Edward Henslowe, whose wife Cecilia was the daughter of Barthélemon, who had died in 1808. The following year she published a commemorative volume of selections from her father's 1776 oratorio *Jefte in Masfe*.[15] Some of the keyboard reductions in this were by Wesley – others were by Crotch and Attwood – and it is possible that it was on this occasion that the arrangements for the edition were made.

On this visit, Wesley turned his attention to the extensive collection of Handel autographs in the Fitzwilliam collection. Although he had not located the score of *Gideon* – a compilation by Handel's copyist and amanuensis John

---

[13] *Harmonicon*, Aug. 1826 (collection of Jamie and Michael Kassler). The covers of most extant copies of the *Harmonicon* have not survived, having been discarded when the volumes were bound.
[14] SW to Sarah Wesley, 29 July 1826.
[15] For a review, see *QMMR* 9 (1827), p. 238.

Christopher Smith of music by Handel and by Smith himself – that he had hoped to find, he was well pleased with what he had discovered, and was confident that everything he was transcribing was unpublished and would therefore 'prove an entire novelty'.[16] He was also hoping to transcribe a mass by Scarlatti', and requested Sarah to send half a quire of fourteen-stave manuscript paper for the purpose.[17] Wesley's most important discovery on this visit was entirely unexpected: a single sheet of manuscript in Handel's autograph containing three hitherto unknown tunes by him to hymns by Wesley's father: 'Sinners obey the Gospel Word', 'O love divine, how sweet thou art', and 'Rejoice! the Lord is King'. This was a major find that would be of interest to music-lovers and Methodists alike. No direct connection between Handel and Charles Wesley had previously been known, and the discovery appeared to Wesley to indicate that the two men had known each other.[18] Wesley was quick to see the commercial possibilities of his discovery. Publication of the hymns could be done cheaply, quickly, and easily, and there would then be the near-certainty of large sales to Methodist congregations, who could immediately begin to use the new tunes in their services. He was confident of success, and accordingly had the hymns engraved even before sounding out his contacts in the Methodist community.

His first approach, on 31 October 1826, was to Eliza Tooth, a close friend of his brother and a member of a prominent Methodist family whose links with the Wesley family went back over fifty years.[19] A week later, probably at Tooth's suggestion, he wrote to Thomas Jackson, the Methodist Connexional Editor and editor of the *Wesleyan Methodist Magazine*, repeating the information that he had given Tooth and pointing out that the words of the hymns were well known to Methodists and were to be found in all hymn books. Moreover, the tunes could be sung to any other hymns in the same metre, and the style of the tunes was 'simple, solemn, and easy of Execution to all who can sing or play a plain Psalm Tune'.[20] Although he did not intend this letter for publication,[21] it nonetheless conveniently set out both the background to the hymns and Wesley's plans for their publication, and Jackson included it, with a few minor alterations, in the December number of the *Wesleyan Methodist Magazine*.[22]

That Wesley should have had the plates engraved even before writing to Jackson to enlist his support was a measure of his confidence in the success of

---

[16] SW to Sarah Suter, 13 Sept. 1826.

[17] This was presumably the five-part *Missa tutta in canone di diverse specie* by Alessandro Scarlatti, MS 30 F 7, the only example of a Mass setting in the Fitzwilliam collection by either Alessandro or Domenico Scarlatti.

[18] SW to Sarah Suter, 13 Sept. 1826. In this letter Wesley talks of having discovered six hymn tunes by Handel, but this must have been an error.

[19] *SW to Tooth, 31 Oct. 1826.

[20] *SW to Jackson, [8] Nov. 1826.

[21] See *SW to Roberts, 6 Jan. 1827, where SW refers to 'my Letter which was published (totally without any Intention of mine)'.

[22] *WMM* 4 (1826), pp. 817–18.

the publication. In fact, as we know from a further letter to Tooth, by this time all that needed to be done was the engraving of the title page, on the design of which Wesley wished to consult John Jackson, the Methodist artist who at around this time painted the portrait of him that now hangs in the National Portrait Gallery (see Frontispiece).[23] The publication appeared by the end of November. Titled *The Fitzwilliam Music, never published. Three Hymns, the Words by the late Revd Charles Wesley, A.M . . . and set to Music by George Frederick Handel*, it contained the voice part and a harmonized accompaniment of the three hymns, together with the words of the first verse of each, amounting to no more than three pages of music and the title page. The price was 1s 6d, a considerable amount for such a slim publication. If 1,800 copies were sold, as Wesley stated in a later letter to Jackson, the profits must have been substantial.[24]

Wesley was right to realize the importance of the hymns, but may have been over-hasty in his conclusions about the relationship between Handel and his father. Wesley's sister Sarah set out the connection as she understood it in a letter in October to the Methodist minister John Gaulter, and later in a memorandum that Jackson published in the *Wesleyan Methodist Magazine* for December, along with her brother's letter to him.[25] According to Sarah, the connection had come about through Priscilla Rich, the wife of John Rich. Impressed by Charles Wesley's preaching, Mrs Rich had converted to Methodism and had then promptly retired from the stage. Both John and Priscilla Rich were friends of Handel, who taught their daughters, and Charles Wesley and his wife had heard Handel's 'fine performances' when visiting the Richs' home. Sarah claimed to have this information from Mrs Rich herself, whom she remembered visiting in her youth.[26]

This was plausible enough in essentials, although Sarah's acquaintance with Mrs Rich must have been in the 1770s or early 1780s, long after the events she described, and a certain amount of dimming of the memory and embroidery of the details may have occurred in the intervening period.[27] But in fact it is highly unlikely that Charles Wesley and Handel knew each other at this time, and in any case unnecessary to assert that they did to explain how Handel came to compose the tunes. As Donald Burrows has shown, it is virtually certain that Handel used as the literary text for the hymns the collection *Hymns on the Great Festivals and Other Occasions* by John Frederick Lampe, first published in 1746, which contains them all.[28]

Following the publication of the hymns at the end of November 1826, Wesley wrote again to Jackson on 19 December. There had been a good deal of interest

---

[23] *SW to Tooth, 8 Nov. 1826.
[24] *SW to Jackson, 17 May 1828.
[25] *WMM* 4 (1826), p. 818.
[26] Sarah to Gaulter, 25 Oct. 1826.
[27] Sarah was born in 1759 and did not move to London until the early 1770s. Mrs Rich died in 1783.
[28] See Burrows, *Handel: The Complete Hymns and Chorales*, pp. 2–3.

in the hymns from members of various non-Methodist congregations, but he had gathered from John Kershaw, the steward of the Methodist Book-Room and manager of the Methodist Printing House, that there had as yet been little from Methodists, who on the whole seemed unaware of them. Wesley requested that there should be an advertisement for them in the following month's *Wesleyan Methodist Magazine*. At the same time he enclosed a copy of the proposals for the Byrd edition, requesting that an advertising slip for the edition should also be included in the same number.[29] By early 1827, sales of the *Hymns* were going so well that Wesley was contemplating a second edition. On 19 February he reported to Jackson that several people had suggested that the hymns would be more useful if they could be published in four-part harmonizations and with the words of all the verses, instead of in their present form, containing the treble and bass parts and the first verses only. Wesley had been glad to take up this suggestion, and expected that the new edition, incorporating these changes, would be published on 1 March. He also informed Jackson that the words of 'Rejoice, the Lord is King' had inadvertently been omitted from the latest (1825) edition of John Wesley's *A Collection of Hymns for the Use of the People Called Methodists*, which still remained, forty-five years after its first publication and after many subsequent editions, the standard hymn-book of the Methodist Connexion.[30] The new edition of the hymns, 'ramified into a Score for 4 Voices', was published on schedule, and a week later Wesley was able to send a copy to the Methodist minister Thomas Roberts, who was one of those who had suggested the revisions.[31]

Wesley's correspondence in late 1826 with Jackson about the Handel hymns also had the effect of opening up communications with the headquarters of London Methodism at the City Road chapel. Since the death of his father, his mother, sister, and brother had kept in regular contact with City Road, although they usually worshipped elsewhere, either at Marylebone Parish Church, where Charles Wesley senior was buried, or at the Methodist chapel in West Street, off Charing Cross Road. Wesley's own contacts with Methodism and Methodists since his adolescence had been few. He had rejected the whole Methodist ethos at the time of his conversion to Roman Catholicism, and since then, his dealings with individual Methodists had often been far from happy. For Methodism, Wesley was of course a considerable embarrassment: a son of one of the founders of Methodism who had converted to Roman Catholicism, had professed scandalous views about marriage, and had later abandoned wife and children for a servant young enough to be his daughter. Worse still, he was still unashamedly living with her, and they had five children together. Nor did he hold an anonymous or insignificant place in society, where he could be quietly forgotten, but had a high public profile. What was more, his son Samuel

---

[29] The advertisement appeared on the wrapper of the Jan. 1827 number of *WMM*, and is quoted in Lightwood, *Samuel Wesley: Musician*, p. 198.
[30] *SW to Jackson, 12 Feb. 1827.
[31] *SW to Roberts, 8 Mar. 1827.

Sebastian was at the age of sixteen showing signs of following his father into the music profession and was already beginning to appear at concerts with him. Wesley's story, or at least part of it, must have been known to all Methodists, and to everyone with an interest in music. Nonetheless, and notwithstanding the awkwardness and uneasiness of the relationship, bridges were beginning to be built. The relationship with Jackson had so far been characterized by courtesy on both sides, and Jackson had welcomed Wesley's discovery of the Handel hymns and had shown himself helpful in promoting his edition of them. After these promising beginnings, it was time to proceed further.

The next step was an invitation to Wesley to attend the Breakfast for the Children of the Methodist Preachers at the City Road Chapel on 3 May 1827. This was an annual event which Wesley had never before attended, although his brother and sister had done so in previous years. Wesley was delighted with his invitation, enclosing it in a letter to his sister Sarah with the comment that it proved that the Methodists were well disposed to him.[32] The breakfast began at 7a.m., requiring Wesley to set off an hour earlier in order to walk the distance of over three miles between his home in Euston Street and the City Road chapel. He was warmly welcomed, and thoroughly enjoyed the occasion. The preacher prayed 'lustily' for all three of Charles Wesley's children, and was delighted when Wesley's own presence was announced.[33]

The early part of 1827 was also a time for family reconciliations. For Wesley, faced with his own advancing age and that of his brother and sister, it was a time for drawing a line under old quarrels. His relationships with Charlotte and his children with her were probably beyond repair, but he could at least make peace with his brother and sister. By now, Sarah was increasingly frail, and in addition to deafness was struggling with a progressive degeneration of sight that made reading difficult and sometimes impossible, and required her on occasion to use Charles as her amanuensis.[34] For his part, Charles cut an increasingly pathetic figure. Completely unworldly and wrapped up in his music, he was able to do little for himself and was heavily dependent on Sarah for almost everything.[35]

Nonetheless, old patterns of plain speaking between Wesley and his sister continued. In mid-April, Sarah wrote to take him to task for promoting Samuel Sebastian as a musician, warning him that his illegitimacy would prove a major barrier to his success, and suggesting that it would be better if Samuel were to do his best not to advertise the fact that Samuel Sebastian was his son.[36] Her letter may have been occasioned by learning that Wesley and Samuel Sebastian were to appear together later in the month at a concert at Christ Church, Newgate Street. Weary of criticism of this kind from her,

---

[32] SW to Sarah Wesley, 29 Apr. 1827.
[33] SW to Charles Wesley jun., 4 May 1827.
[34] SW to Sarah Wesley, 8 Jan. and 22 Jan. 1827; Charles Wesley jun. to Marianne Francis, 5 May 1827.
[35] See Stevenson, *Memorials of the Wesley Family*, pp. 447–70, *passim*.
[36] Letter not preserved. This summary of its contents is inferred from SW's reply.

Wesley replied with a plea for peace: he was now doing his best to avoid controversies, and found disputes concerning his own flesh and blood particularly painful. If there were topics on which he and Sarah could not agree, they should avoid them. In any case, Sarah was mistaken about Samuel Sebastian suffering any discrimination because of his illegitimacy. Wesley reminded her that when he was presented to George IV it was as 'the son of Sam. Wesley of musical Celebrity'.[37] After this and all the other occasions on which Samuel Sebastian's name had appeared in concert bills, it was impossible, even if Wesley wanted to, to conceal the fact that Samuel Sebastian was his son. He similarly dismissed Sarah's view that his relationship to Samuel Sebastian would adversely affect the sale of the hymns.

Although the tone of Wesley's letter was as robust as ever, it does not seem to have given undue offence, and succeeding letters between Wesley and Sarah show a relationship more relaxed than for some time. Part of the reason may have been Wesley's improved financial situation, presumably brought about by receipts from the Handel hymns. He still had financial problems, some of them of a temporary and short-term nature, but with money coming in from the Handel hymns he was less likely to be seeking loans or gifts from Sarah and Charles. In addition, there seems to have been a marked change of attitude on the part of Charlotte's trustee Oliver, who was now 'inclined to be civil' and was thought unlikely to harass Sarah again over her brother's debts, as he had so often done in the past.[38]

With no engagements at Covent Garden oratorio concerts or at any other of London's principal venues, Wesley's concert activities had by now significantly reduced, and consisted for the most part of organ recitals and occasional appearances at concerts in churches. He was still in considerable demand as a recitalist, and his improvisations could still be relied on to astonish and delight. On 1 March he directed a 'Grand Selection of Sacred Music' at St Saviour's, Southwark and played an extempore voluntary;[39] his involvement no doubt came about through Benson, who was chaplain there. Four days later he was at Flight and Robson's with Jacob for the trial of a new organ, playing Bach's 'St Anne' fugue and part of a Mozart Mass as duets.[40] On 27 April he appeared with Samuel Sebastian in a concert of 'Ancient Music' at Christ Church, Newgate Street, the church associated with Christ's Hospital School, where his friend Glenn was music master.[41] Other performances during the year included a recital on 8 June at Beresford Chapel, Walworth,[42] and on 24 June the opening recital of the new organ by John Gray at the recently built Somers Town Chapel

---

[37] SW to Sarah Wesley, 20 Apr. 1827.
[38] SW to Charles Wesley jun., 4 May 1827. For Oliver, see also SW to Sarah Wesley, 8 Jan. and 29 Apr. 1827.
[39] Handbill in private collection.
[40] Unidentified press report, 6 Mar. 1827, cited in an undated cutting from *Musical Standard* (BL, Music Library Deposit 1995/19, item 7).
[41] *Atlas*, 27 Apr. 1827, quoted in Lightwood, *Samuel Wesley, Musician*, p. 202.
[42] *The Times*, 8 June 1827.

(now St Mary the Virgin, Eversholt Street), another chapel-of-ease in the St Pancras parish.[43]

On 9 October Wesley set off for Brighton, leaving the heavily pregnant Sarah Suter at home with the children. Although his primary purpose was to give music lessons, he also took with him a letter from Flight and Robson's to Henry Michell Wagner, the Vicar of Brighton, concerning the bid that the firm was making for the supply of an organ for the church of St Peter, York Place, which was currently under construction. Wagner was a highly significant figure in the nineteenth-century history of Brighton. He was an Old Etonian and had been a Fellow of King's College, Cambridge, subsequently going on to be tutor to the two sons of the Duke of Wellington. He was rich and powerful, and moved easily in the highest circles, including those of the royal family and the court. On his appointment as Vicar of Brighton at the age of thirty-one in 1824 he immediately began an energetic programme of church building, of which St Peter's was the latest project.[44] Flight and Robson's already had experience of Brighton and of Wagner, having installed the organ at St Margaret's, another of Wagner's new churches, in 1824, and were clearly hoping for the commission for St Peter's.[45]

Wesley visited Wagner on the day after his arrival with the letter from Flight and Robson's. As he reported to Sarah Suter, Wagner received him well, inviting him to play the organ at the parish church on the following Sunday and to dine with him the day after. Wesley added that Wagner had behaved 'in the kindest Manner respecting *dutiful* Master Sam' on a point that Robson had suggested to him.[46] This may have been a request for a reference or testimonial for Samuel Sebastian, in connection with his application for the organist's position at St Stephen's, Coleman Street: Wagner may have heard him sing at the Royal Pavilion and would thus be in a position to comment on his abilities.[47] Otherwise, Wesley's main contact in Brighton was a Mr Wellings, of whom Wesley thought extremely highly. As he wrote to Sarah Suter on 14 October, he was to give daily lessons to two female pupils, whom he described as 'two of the most delightful Women in the Creation'. One was Wellings's sister, the widow of an army officer, who was to pay a guinea per lesson; the other was to pay 15s, perhaps for a shorter lesson. Altogether, Wesley was hoping to earn £15 5s from his visit. He was particularly impressed by the accomplishments of Wellings's sister, and asked Sarah to tell Samuel Sebastian that she had shown him one of her compositions in which he had found no more than three notes that he could change for the better. Everyone in Brighton had been very welcoming and hospitable, and he was being '*muched* & *cuddled*' from morning till night. In the churches, the parsons

---

[43] *SW to Glenn, 15 June 1827.
[44] Wagner and Dale, *The Wagners of Brighton*, pp. 28–42.
[45] Boeringer, *Organa Britannica*, vol. 3, p. 147.
[46] SW to Sarah Suter, 10 Oct. 1827.
[47] The election was on 1 Nov.; Samuel Sebastian was not elected (Dawe, p. 66). I am grateful to Peter Horton for this suggestion.

were more interested in hearing his voluntaries than preaching their sermons, and Wesley had found it quite impossible that morning to 'play the people *out* of the church', to the extent that Wellings had told him that he was robbing half the congregation of their dinner. He went on to give his engagements for the coming week: he was invited to dinner with Wagner on the following day, with Price, a local doctor, on the Wednesday, and with Wagner again on the Friday, before returning to London on the Saturday.

By the time of Wesley's next letter to Sarah two days later, he was becoming increasingly concerned about her condition as her confinement approached, and was impatient to return home. He reported that the letter to Wagner from Flight and Robson's had been in vain, as it was now apparent that the order was to be placed through Attwood, who in addition to his position at St Paul's was also organist at the Royal Pavilion. Wesley had heard that the church authorities wanted the organ erected by December, but thought that it would not be possible to install anything more than 'a mere box of whistles' in the time. He had also heard that Attwood was recommending an existing organ, and did not know how that could be unless it was to be the instrument that had formerly been at St Katherine's-by-the-Tower, and had been dismantled when the church was demolished in 1824 to make way for St Katherine's Dock.[48] In this he was mistaken: the organ from St Katherine's had been moved, along with the collegiate foundation of which the church had formed part, to St Katherine's Hospital, Regent's Park.[49]

In early 1828, as in the previous two years, Wesley was heavily engaged in lecturing, with courses at the Russell Institution in Bloomsbury, at the London Institution in Finsbury Circus, and at the Royal Institution, where he gave six lectures starting in April. On 21 May he set out for Birmingham to take part in a series of concerts to mark the opening of the Elliot and Hill organ at the newly built church of St Peter, Dale End, for which he had been engaged at a fee of twenty-five guineas. His journey took thirteen and a half hours, prompting a grumble to Sarah Suter that 'the Pretence of driving the Coaches down in 12 Hours is all my Eye & my Elbow & my A – .'[50] He stayed with a Mr Tolly, who informed him that Joseph Moore, the organizer of the Birmingham festival that Wesley had directed in 1811, was no longer the influential figure that he once was, and now had only £100 per year to live on; Wesley doubted the truth of this. On the following day was the rehearsal, before which Wesley dined with Mr Freer, one of the churchwardens. There were two concerts on the next day: 'grand selections of sacred music', at which Wesley played extempore voluntaries, and a Miss Symonds, a Miss Heaton, and a Miss J. Fletcher, presumably

[48] SW to Sarah Suter, 16 Oct. 1827.
[49] For St Katherine's-by-the-Tower, see Williamson and Pevsner, *London Docklands: an Architectural Guide*, p. 212; for its organ, see Plumley, *The Organs of the City of London*, pp. 173–4. The organ eventually erected at Brighton was a three-manual instrument by W. A. A. Nicholls: see Boeringer, *Organa Britannica*, vol. 3, pp. 146–7.
[50] SW to Sarah Suter, 22 May 1828.

all local singers, performed vocal solos. Between the two concerts, Wesley dined with Mr Greave, the organist.[51] He returned to London on 25 May.

The healthy sales of the Handel hymns prompted Wesley to consider other ways in which he could exploit his Methodist connections. One obvious way was to write tunes of his own for the hymns currently in use in Methodist chapels. In April 1828 he wrote to Jackson to suggest the idea, and after an encouraging response moved quickly, composing thirty tunes in a variety of metres.[52] Before setting off for Birmingham he had written again to Jackson to offer the copyright to the Book Room committee, suggesting £150 as a 'fair and moderate' price, and pointing out that his edition of the Handel hymns had sold 1,800 copies and that he had afterwards been able to dispose of the plates for a considerable sum.[53] The committee turned down this proposal, and Wesley was obliged to publish at his own expense: a more risky, but at the same time a potentially more profitable course of action. The result was the *Original Hymn Tunes, adapted to every Metre in the collection by the Rev. John Wesley*, which were published by late August and reviewed in glowing terms in the *Wesleyan Methodist Magazine* for October.[54]

In early September 1828, Wesley travelled to Leeds to open the organ at the Methodist Brunswick Chapel. As he would have been aware, the installation of the organ had provoked a major controversy within Methodism between those who thought that hymns should be accompanied by the organ, as in the Church of England, and those who rejected any use of instrumental music in Methodist worship. The dispute, which at bottom was really about where decision-making lay within the movement, led in time to the formation of the Protestant Methodist Connexion, a breakaway group that set up its own assembly, separate from the main Methodist Conference. Wesley was not implicated or involved in the controversy, but it ensured that the opening of the organ had maximum publicity in the local press.

At the end of August, a preliminary notice in the *Leeds Mercury* announced that the trustees of the chapel had written to invite Charles Wesley to play for the opening of the organ on 12 September, but he was away from home and they had so far received no reply.[55] In fact, since mid-August Charles had been in Bristol with Sarah, where her health had been giving increasing cause for concern. When he eventually received the invitation, he turned it down,

---

[51] SW to Sarah Suter, 22 May 1828; St Peter's, Dale End, Birmingham, Vestry Minutes (Birmingham Archives EP 27/5/2/1); *ABG*, 19 May 1828. For St Peter's, Dale End, which was demolished in 1899, see *VCH, A History of the County of Warwick*, vol. 7, *The City of Birmingham*, p. 394.

[52] *SW to Jackson, 21 Apr. 1828.

[53] *SW to Jackson, 17 May 1828.

[54] *WMM*, October 1828, quoted in Lightwood, *Samuel Wesley, Musician*, p. 211. The review has not been traced in surviving copies of this number, and may have been on the wrapper.

[55] *Leeds Mercury*, 30 Aug. 1828. The same announcement appeared in the *Leeds Intelligencer*, 4 Sept. 1828.

suggesting that Samuel should play instead.[56] The following week the *Mercury* announced that 'Samuel Wesley, the celebrated performer' would perform, and that the services of the day promised to be of a very interesting and attractive kind.[57] Notwithstanding this clear statement, there was apparently still some uncertainty about which of the two brothers was 'the celebrated Wesley'.[58]

Wesley set off from London on 10 September with a Master Bennet, breaking his journey at Nottingham and continuing to Leeds on the following day. His performances at Leeds took the form of half-hour voluntaries preceding three special services on Friday 12 September, at which the sermons were preached by Robert Newton, William Bunting, and Theophilus Lessey. There were further services on the following Sunday, at which Wesley also appears to have played.[59] The *Leeds Intelligencer* reported that the organ had been universally admired.[60] Still under the impression that it was Charles rather than Samuel who was the celebrated player, the *Intelligencer* went on to state that Wesley's performances had nonetheless delighted all who had heard them, and that he was 'worthy of any celebrity'. After the weekend, there was a recital at which Wesley was joined by Latrobe (the Moravian Church had a large settlement at Fulneck, near Leeds) and some local organists, and at which his performances of a fugue on a subject by Boyce and a set of variations on 'Rule Britannia' attracted particular attention.[61]

In Leeds, Wesley and Bennet stayed with William Smith and his family, who entertained them generously. He was also made much of by the Leeds congregation, and remarked to Sarah Suter that if he had a guinea for each time he had shaken hands since his arrival, he would have enough money to enable them to go on holiday to Gravesend every week for the next year and still have money to spare. There was a proposal that he should go to York, twenty-four miles away, to see the cathedral, but he was unwilling to incur the additional expense and undergo the additional travelling that the journey would involve. He returned to London on 16 September, well pleased with his visit, and with the prospect of further lucrative visits to Leeds in the future.[62]

While Wesley was in Leeds, his sister Sarah's health had declined further. On 18 September 1828 Charles wrote to tell him that she was 'near a crown of glory', revealing at the same time that she had fallen ill five weeks earlier at the house of Lady Herschel in Slough while on their journey to Bristol, and had been unable to eat ever since. She died on the following day, and was buried in St James's churchyard, in the family plot that already contained her brothers

---

[56] Charles Wesley jun. to SW, 18 Sept. 1828.
[57] *Leeds Mercury*, 6 Sept. 1828.
[58] *Leeds Intelligencer*, 11 Sept. 1828.
[59] Ibid; handbill at Leeds Public Library, Local Studies Dept., L 287.I B 838.
[60] *Leeds Intelligencer*, 18 Sept. 1828.
[61] *Leeds Intelligencer*, 18 Sept. 1828. For the organ, by Booth of Wakefield, see Boeringer, *Organa Britannica*, vol. 3, pp. 333–4.
[62] SW to Sarah Suter, 10 Sept., 13 Sept. 1828.

and sisters who had died in infancy. Disapproving to the last of her brother's liaison with Sarah Suter, she left her entire estate to Charles, except for £50 to John William, in recognition of the part he had played in securing Samuel's release from the spunging house in May 1825.[63]

With Sarah's death, another link to the past was severed. Since the death of her father, and increasingly as her mother grew older and more frail, she had effectively come to occupy the position of head of the family. Hers had been a life of minor humiliations and disappointments. Although intelligent and talented herself, she had from her childhood been obliged to take a back seat to her two musician brothers, and even more of a subsidiary role than would have otherwise been expected for one of her sex. Always bookish and reclusive by nature, she had become increasingly averse to going into company after smallpox disfigured her appearance in her teens. But her early adulthood had been active enough: she had travelled abroad to France and Italy, and had known Samuel Johnson through her aunt Martha Hall. In her middle years she hovered on the fringes of London's literary world, longing for an acceptance that never materialized. Henry Crabb Robinson, who met her at a party at the novelist Elizabeth Benger's in May 1812, left a devastating vignette of her as 'a very lively little body, with a round short person, in a constant fidget of good-nature and harmless vanity: the author of novels that did not sell, who was reputed to have said on being introduced to Maria Edgeworth that "we sisters of the quill ought to know one another"'.[64] There had also been a succession of extended visits to different families as a house-guest or governess. Latterly, her time had been more and more occupied with caring for her mother and brother.

From early adulthood, her relationship with Samuel had been characterized above all by an understandable disapproval of his way of life and behaviour. From her vantage point of seven years' seniority, she witnessed both the adulation he had received in his childhood and the events of his stormy adolescence. In the early 1780s she saw his growing fascination with Roman Catholicism, culminating in his conversion in 1784 and observed at first hand the pain it caused her parents. At the same time she saw his involvement with Charlotte and the pain that this too had caused. After their father's death, she did battle with him over his views on marriage, and saw the complete volte-face that had followed Charlotte's pregnancy. After the marriage she had put all past disagreements behind her, welcomed Charlotte into the family as her sister-in-law, and did her best to become her friend. She had received countless letters from Samuel describing his misery with Charlotte and the depths of his depression. She had seen the many quarrels and separations between Samuel and Charlotte, had been obliged to look after her nephew Charles at times of crisis, and for a time was responsible for his education. Later, she had seen her brother's final separation from Charlotte and his subsequent relationship with Sarah Suter. In 1817 she was closely involved with the events surrounding his

---

[63] Sarah Wesley, will, 16 Nov. 1827.
[64] Sadler, *Diaries, Reminiscences, and Correspondence of Henry Crabb Robinson*, vol. 1, pp. 201–2.

breakdown in health and his subsequent period at Blacklands House. Most recently, she saw his temporary imprisonment for debt, and the unseemly squabbles that eventually resulted in his release. During all this time, Samuel had made repeated financial demands on her and her mother, which progressively drained their already limited resources.

Wesley heard about his sister's death on 22 September, just before setting off for a few days holiday in Gravesend advised by his doctor in the hope that sea air would help to settle his troubled digestion.[65] He interrupted his holiday at the weekend to come back to London to carry out his duties at Camden Chapel, but then returned to Gravesend early in the following week. In a letter of 1 October to Sarah Suter he was in good spirits and reporting that his health was much improved, although he grumbled at Sarah for not packing his razor strop, complained that he had had to pay 2s 6d for a hot bath at his lodgings, and was disappointed that Sarah had not been able to join him. The previous day he and a party of friends had been shown round Cobham Hall, the seat of the Fourth Earl of Darnley, which Wesley had found magnificent. As usual in his letters of this period, he ended with a small sketch and message for his children: on this occasion a picture of a cow for the three-year-old John with the caption 'O Johnny! Look! There's one of your Cows, All flown up in the Air, With her ragged Bum Fiddle bare'.

The remainder of 1828 appears to have been uneventful. There was, however, a dispute over Sarah's decision in her will to leave her entire residual estate to Charles, instead of to Charles and Samuel equally. The evidence in the correspondence is too patchy to fill in any of the details, but it is clear that solicitors were involved, among them Wesley's former organ pupil Henry Gauntlett, at this time earning his living as an articled clerk.[66]

---

[65] *SW to Emett, [?21 Sept. 1828].
[66] Gauntlett to Glenn, 27 Nov. 1828.

16

The return to Bristol, 1829–1830

The early part of 1829 was also uneventful, with no concert appearances or lecture engagements. Wesley had approached Hawes to offer his services at the Covent Garden oratorio concerts, but Hawes appointed Thomas Adams instead and did not even bother to reply to Wesley's letter, earning himself a rebuke from Wesley for this discourtesy.[1] But in mid-September Wesley travelled to Bristol with the prospect of giving a number of organ recitals in the city of his birth. Unlike his brother and late sister, Wesley had no great affection for Bristol, and this was the first time, apart from a brief visit while in Bath in 1809, that he had returned there since leaving it as a boy over fifty years earlier. The visit no doubt came at the suggestion of Wait, who in addition to his scholarly activities had the living at Blagdon, a village nine miles away. Hodges was also involved at an early stage. By this time he was organist of both St Nicholas's and St James's, and was well known in Bristol as an organist and an organ designer, with recent contributions to the building or renovation of the instruments at St Nicholas's, St James's, and the new Clifton Parish Church.

Wesley stayed initially with Wait at Blagdon. From here, he and Wait despatched a series of letters to Sarah detailing the progress of their negotiations about the recitals. The first few days were taken up with negotiations with the authorities at St Mary Redcliffe, Bristol's parish church, about the recital that he wished to give to mark the reopening of the organ after its extensive renovations and enlargements by John Smith, a local builder. On 18 September Wesley was able to announce to Sarah that the recital had been agreed and that there were prospects of at least three further recitals elsewhere, including one at Wells Cathedral, twenty miles away. At St Mary Redcliffe, Wesley thought an advantageous outcome was virtually assured, and he was similarly optimistic about other projected recitals. On 23 September he went with Wait to the church to try the organ, as yet still not quite completed, and to meet the churchwardens. He pronounced his 'decided approbation' of the recent work on the organ, at the same time recommending an extension of its compass.[2] At this meeting it was agreed that Wesley was to have the use of the church for a recital, giving part of his profit to the church's organ fund. Two days later, Wesley and Wait dined with a number of church dignitaries, whom Wesley

---

[1] *SW to Hawes, 24 Jan. 1829.
[2] *Bristol Gazette*, 24 Sept. 1829.

described as being 'in hoity-toity Spirits upon the Occasion and . . . eager to do me all the Service they can'.[3] They included Cornelius Bryan, the organist of the church, Smith, the churchwardens, and several members of the vestry. It seems to have been on this occasion that it was decided that Wesley should give not one recital as originally agreed, but three. The first, on 1 October, would mark the formal opening of the organ, and would be followed by further recitals on 5 and 7 October. It was also agreed that the church would bear all the costs of the advertisements and meet the fees of the singers who would also participate. The charge for admission was to be 3s for the body of the church and 4s for the chancel for single concerts, or 7s 6d for the church and 10s for the chancel for all three concerts.[4]

Wait was cock-a-hoop at how matters had turned out. In his part of a joint letter to Sarah Suter the following day, he urged her not to 'hurry Mr Wesley back, for the harvest will be rich beyond his expectations: he will have three days at Redcliffe church, & some at Clifton church, besides some in other places', adding in a triumphant postscript the news about the advertisements and singers.[5] He was also able to announce that the Redcliffe authorities had promised Wesley three further recitals the following summer, and he scented the possibility of yet more recitals in years to come. For this reason, he urged Sarah not to mention Wesley's Bristol recitals to anyone, in case others should feel inclined to 'try the experiment in this rich ground themselves'. In his own portion of their letter, Wesley was equally insistent on this point. Part of the original plan for the recitals was that Wesley would share the playing with George Cooper, who would come down from London for the purpose. Subsequent discussions of the finances of the recitals led to a rethink and the proposal from Wait that Samuel Sebastian should play instead. Wait urged this particularly strongly, arguing that if Cooper were involved he would take from Wesley's receipts and might be tempted at a later stage to organize recitals on his own account. For his part, Wesley still wanted to keep his options open, and asked Sarah once more to sound out Cooper about his terms.[6] Two days later, he wrote again to say that Bryan had been 'so very civil & attentive' that there was no need of Cooper's assistance.[7] There was no mention of Samuel Sebastian in this letter, however, suggesting that Wesley had not yet come to any decision on whether he should come or not. Eventually it was decided that he should come, and he arrived in Bristol towards the end of the month.

One complication in these arrangements was the presence in Bristol of Wesley's brother Charles, who was also giving organ recitals and being mistaken for his more famous brother – a confusion he was apparently actively fostering and had probably exploited in Bristol for a number of years. As a result, as Wait

[3] SW to Sarah Suter, 23 Sept. 1829.
[4] Wait to Sarah Suter, 25 Sept. 1829; *Bristol Mercury*, 29 Sept. 1829; *Bristol Gazette*, 1 Oct. 1829.
[5] Wait to Sarah Suter, 25 Sept. 1829.
[6] SW to Sarah Suter, 23 Sept. 1829.
[7] SW to Sarah Suter, 25 Sept. 1829.

informed Sarah, they had been obliged to place an advertisement in the newspapers to clarify matters.[8] On 24 September Charles had given a recital at St James's: largely, Wait thought, in an attempt to steal the thunder from Wesley's own forthcoming recitals. Wait suspected that Hodges was involved in this spoiling operation, adding his opinion that it showed that Hodges was 'close to Charles Wesley's Backside, & now shows his *cloven* Foot'.[9]

The concerts at St Mary Redcliffe were a great success. The principal attraction, as always, was Wesley's extempore playing, but there were also solo contributions from Samuel Sebastian, organ duets, and solo vocal and choral items. Hodges attended all the concerts and noted his reactions both in reports for the *Bristol Mirror* and in his diary, in the process leaving the most detailed and perceptive first-hand accounts of Wesley's playing that we have. Writing in his diary about the first recital, he commented that it was

> the most wonderful I ever heard, more even than I had before been capable of conceiving; the flow of melody, the stream of harmony, was so complete, so unbroken, so easy, and yet so highly wrought and so superbly scientific, that I was altogether knocked off my stilts. Before such a man and organist I am less than nothing and vanity. A Duett was performed by him and his son, Samuel Sebastian Wesley. The Concluding Fugue was sublime. A few Choruses and Songs were interspersed but I wished them away. . . . I exchanged a few words with the old man and his son on the performance being over. I walked home afterwards, but my head was full of naught but Samuel Wesley and his seraphic genius. . . . He is the Prince of Musicians and Emperor of organists.[10]

Hodges's accounts in his diary of Wesley's playing in the two subsequent concerts were less ecstatic. After the second concert, he commented that he had not enjoyed Wesley's playing as much as before, but was not sure whether this was from 'a sense of satiety' in himself or from some falling off in Wesley's performance. After the third recital, however, he stated that he had begun to work out how Wesley worked his magic. On repeated hearing, his harmonies and modulations became less amazing than at first, and Hodges noticed that certain melodic passages occurred over and over again. He still found Wesley's extempore fugues to be as effective as before, but on further acquaintance he found that the subjects were 'the illegitimate offsprings of Sebastian Bach', and that Wesley had carefully prepared their openings.[11]

With the St Mary Redcliffe concerts behind him, Wesley could turn his attention to arranging recitals at other churches in Bristol. At the same time, he needed to do battle over the payment of his share of the takings, about which he was in dispute with the church authorities. In a letter to Sarah on the morning of his final concert he had stated that he had not yet received any money, and

---

[8] Wait to Sarah Suter, 23 Sept. 1829. The 'advertisement' was presumably the note stating that both Samuel and Charles Wesley were in Bristol that appeared in the account of SW's visit to St Mary Redcliffe in the *Bristol Gazette* on 24 Sept.
[9] Wait to Sarah Suter, 25 Sept. 1829.
[10] Hodges, diary entry for 1 Oct. 1829, quoted in Hodges, *Edward Hodges*, pp. 48–9.
[11] Hodges, diary entry for 7 Oct. 1829, quoted in Hodges, *Edward Hodges*, pp. 51–3.

was intending to press the church for immediate settlement.[12] On 11 October, four days later, he had still received nothing, and was complaining to Sarah that the Redcliffe churchwardens were attempting to cheat him as much as they could, but that he was prepared to fight them with their own weapons and if necessary to expose their behaviour.[13] On the following day, a meeting with the churchwardens failed to resolve matters, although Wesley appears to have been paid some of what he was owed. Samuel Sebastian then returned to London with part of the takings and a host of alarmist stories – which Wesley subsequently denied – about how badly his father had been treated and how inattentive Wait had been to his interests.[14]

By the end of the week, Wesley had made progress with his negotiations for other recitals. On 18 October he reported to Sarah that he was sure of making money, notwithstanding all the lies and misrepresentations that had been put about by his brother and his friends and that had up to now been an obstacle to his success. He still retained his low opinion of the Bristolians, however, commenting that they were 'not to be managed at all by *Kindness*, for they are unfeeling Brutes, but principally by *Fear* – Money is their God, & in the Proportion any one can produce it for them just in that Degree, & no further can you work upon their safe Spirits'.[15] On 22 October, he went to stay with Hodges at his house in the Cathedral cloisters while Wait went to London on business. Wait returned on 24 October, only to go back to London the next day, and Wesley lodged with Hodges for the remainder of his visit. For all the time that Wesley had known him, Wait had been involved in questionable business ventures. By now, one of them had evidently failed, and his financial situation appeared desperate. Gauntlett and his brother Edward (described by Wesley as 'a brace of hell-hounds') appear to have been acting for his creditors: Wesley had to explain to Sarah that the only reason that Wait had not visited her when in London was that he was afraid that they would be lying in wait for him in the vicinity, knowing his friendship with the family.[16]

From his new base at Hodges' house Wesley gave a number of recitals at other Bristol churches: at the Moravian Chapel on 26 October (the organ of which he later described as 'a capital and delicately toned instrument'),[17] at St Nicholas's on 28 October and at St James's on 29 October.[18] At the same time, he was managing to send money home. On 27 October he instructed Sarah to go to a bank in the Poultry, where she would receive £30 that he had sent, and on 30 October wrote again to let her know that there was a further £50 waiting. He was also able to fix the date of his return, which would be on the following Monday or Tuesday. By now, he had a clearer view of the outcome of his visit.

---

[12] SW to Sarah Suter, 7 Oct. 1829.
[13] SW to Sarah Suter, 11 Oct. 1829.
[14] SW to Sarah Suter, 18 Oct. 1829.
[15] Ibid.
[16] SW to Sarah Suter, 25 Oct., 29 Oct. 1829.
[17] *Reminiscences*, fol. 54.
[18] SW to Sarah Suter, 21 Oct., 29 Oct. 1829.

He had done far better than expected out of the churches, and was delighted at how things had turned out, despite being disappointed by how he had been treated by the 'shabby, scabby' churchwardens of St Mary Redcliffe. Many people had contributed to a subscription for him, which Wesley was expecting to amount to at least £50. He had made several friends who were intent on promoting his interests whenever he should decide to pay a return visit.[19] In fact, shortly before his departure he was approached by Edward Bowles Fripp, a local amateur musician, on behalf of the Bristol Philosophical and Literary Institution with an invitation to give a course of lectures on music there in the following January. When he left, on 2 or 3 November, the dates and his terms had been agreed.[20]

Wesley returned to London to a writ for £22 issued by a tradesman. On 16 November, as he informed Eliza Tooth, his house was besieged by several law officers and he was obliged to hide at the house of a friend to escape them; he now wondered if his brother Charles could come up with a loan of £25 to cover the writ and the associated legal expenses. The following day, still anxious to avoid his creditors, he went to Watford, Hertfordshire, where he was preparing a concert with William Bird, the organist of the parish church. But despite these current problems, he was at pains to assure Tooth that his financial prospects were at present looking more healthy than they had done for years.

Before Wesley left Bristol, it had been agreed that his course of lectures would consist of eight lectures on the Science and Practice of Music, for which he would be paid £50 plus a half share of any profits. On his return visit in early January 1830, he wished to stay in Bristol no longer than was necessary. His usual practice in London was to lecture weekly, but in order to minimize the time spent away from home he would now lecture three times a week, on Mondays, Wednesdays, and Fridays at 1p.m., and to repeat each lecture on the same day at 7.30p.m. In this way he would be able to compress the course into seventeen days, starting on 11 January and finishing on 27 January. It was later agreed that he would bring Mr Collyer, a singer, with him, at a cost not exceeding 20 guineas, and that an organ would be erected for the course at a cost not exceeding £20. The admission charge was to be £1 for the whole series, or 3s 6d for individual lectures.[21]

On this visit, Wesley stayed in lodgings at 62 Park Street, just across the road from the Bristol Institution. His landlady was Deborah Sherriff, a confectioner, who had long ago been a great friend of his uncle John. Staying with Wait in Blagdon would have been impracticable, given the winter weather and Wesley's heavy lecture commitments. In any case, Wesley had had a disagreement with Wait occasioned by some alleged sharp practice by Wait over the financial

---

[19] SW to Sarah Suter, 29 Oct. 1829.
[20] Bristol Philosophical and Literary Institution, minutes of the sub-committee for lectures and philosophical apparatus 1824–36, 29 Oct., 2 Nov. 1829 (Bristol Record Office, 32079/33).
[21] Bristol Institution Minutes, 11 Nov., 28 Nov., 16 Dec. 1829; *Bristol Mirror*, 2 Jan., 9 Jan. 1830.

arrangements for Wesley's Mary Redcliffe recitals the previous October. In a letter of 14 January Wesley commented to Sarah Suter on how Wait and his family had 'robbed' him, adding that it was 'a grievous Thing that a Man so fitted to make his fellow Creatures happy should exert the Powers of such a Head only to deceive & plunder them.'[22]

Wesley's lectures were popular and well attended, and by the end of the course he was confidently predicting to Sarah that he would come away with twenty guineas in addition to his fee. In fact, as the minutes of the Bristol Institution show, the final sum after expenses was £36 7s 6d, of which Wesley gave half to Hodges in recognition of his help.[23] At the same time, he was able to make additional money by selling copies of the *Original Hymns* that he had with him. He also gave copies to Hodges, to Fripp (who had earlier given Wesley a copy of his own compilation of hymn tunes)[24] and to a Mr Badham, who had helped to arrange his recital at the Moravian chapel during his previous visit to Bristol. Plans for an organ recital at the parish church at Frome, twenty-one miles away, to take place after the lecture course had finished, had to be abandoned because of the bitterly cold weather and the consequent likelihood of poor attendance.[25]

The Bristol lectures were the last Wesley gave. Although no syllabus for the course has survived, many of the lectures are identifiable among the papers bequeathed to the British Museum by Eliza. Some were adaptations of existing lectures (including those given at the Royal Institution in 1826); others appear to have been specially written (or written out afresh) for this course. They included the following: 'On Musical Prejudice' (13 January); 'The sublime, the beautiful & and the ornamental in Music' (15 January); 'The most eligible method of acquiring an easy command of keyed instruments. Transposition. Tuning, old and new method. Equal Temperament' (18 January); 'On the distinction between good and faulty musical composition' (22 January); 'Progress of Music in General among us' (25 January) and 'On the most eligible mode of advancing the cause of music theoretically and practically' (27 January). The texts also give a good idea of what music was performed. At the lecture on musical prejudice, Wesley performed the Benedictus from the Mozart Requiem on the organ. Collyer, despite a heavy cold, sang two Vauxhall ballads ('How sweet is the Love' and *The Death of Old Robin Gray*) and a song by Hook. He was unable to sing at the next lecture, on temperament and tuning, but Wesley played an arrangement of Handel's coronation anthem 'The King shall Rejoice' on the organ. At the following lecture Collyer was back in action, and sang a recitative and aria from Méhul's *Joseph* that had been performed at the previous year's Birmingham Festival. Like the examples at the Royal

---

[22] Wesley to Sarah Suter, 14 Jan. 1830.
[23] Bristol Institution Minutes, 28 Jan. 1830.
[24] *Church Psalmody: A Collection of Tunes, Harmonized for Four Voices with an Organ Accompaniment; expressly adapted for A Selection of "Psalms and Hymns". By a Layman.* SW's copy, annotated by him as a gift from Fripp, and dated Oct. 1829, is at the BL.
[25] Wesley to Sarah Suter, 14 Jan., 17 Jan., 22 Jan., 26 Jan. 1830.

Institution course in 1826, these were introduced solely as musical interludes, and appear to have had no discernible connection with the subjects of the lectures.

In his final lecture, Wesley expressed the hope that he had covered all the points in his syllabus and that his audience had enjoyed the 'vocal and instrumental effusions' that he and Collyer had introduced. He concluded with a long leavetaking:

> I cannot quit the Spot which gave me Birth without adverting to some affecting Remembrances which I confess have awakened melancholy Thoughts. Everyone in this City whom I well remember during my Childhood is now no more upon earth, and their Descendents [sic] recognize me only by consanguineous Alliance to mine illustrious & revered Father & Uncle. I feel, therefore, at present, not as a Stranger at Home, but alas! rather at Home as a Stranger.
>
> Let me not be hence understood to insinuate that I consider myself to have been here inhospitably received. No – on the contrary, I feel (as I ought) that I have experienced a warm & hearty Welcome: should my Services be hereafter required in this Place, and should my precarious Existence be providentially prolonged to render them, I hope and trust that Power of exerting such Services may not be wanting – the *Will*, I am sure shall not.
>
> It has been elegantly affirmed that the last Word, the last Look – the last any Thing is a gloomy Idea. Yet, the flattering Reception I have experienced in this Place encourages, & even compels me to bid you all cheerfully Farewell.[26]

---

[26] BL, Add. MS 35014, fol. 165. Wesley's underlinings, inserted to aid his delivery, have been omitted.

17

Last years, 1830–1837

Wesley returned to London on 28 January 1830. Two months later, the family moved house to Mornington Place, at the north end of Hampstead Road, close to Mornington Crescent and not far from the former house in Arlington Street. For the occasion, he wrote a prayer:

> Almighty God the Father, we humbly implore thee for this House, & for all its Inhabitants & Contents, that thou mayest vouchsafe to bless sanctify & increase it with all good Things: give O Lord Abundance from the Dew of Heaven & the Substance of Life from the Fat of the Land to them who dwell therein, & lead their Desires to the Experience of thy Mercy. Therefore at our Entrance do thou vouchsafe to bless and sanctify this House, as thou didst vouchsafe to bless the House of Abraham & Isaac, & Jacob: and may the Angels of thy Brightness inhabit it, & preserve both it & all who reside in the same, through Christ our Lord. Amen.[1]

In June, he resumed contact with Novello after the silence of over four years that had followed their disagreement over the Fitzwilliam music. On 11 May, Novello had written to Wesley in connection with his researches into Purcell, to ask if he had any relevant information.[2] This was one of a number of similar letters to other musicians, but Novello no doubt also intended it as a way of reopening communication with Wesley and ending their long estrangement. It took almost a month for the letter to reach Wesley, possibly because Novello had sent it to Euston Street. Wesley's reply of 10 June was markedly generous in tone and brought about the desired reconciliation.[3] But there was no resumption of their correspondence. By this time, their paths had diverged: neither was now actively involved in Roman Catholic church music, and without this shared activity there was little reason for them to be in regular contact.

In his letter Wesley sounded his usual self, commenting on the neglect of Purcell's church music in favour of the easier, but duller, services of more modern composers. But as we know from a letter from his brother Charles to Eliza Tooth of the same date, he was seriously ill; Charles thought, rightly or

---

[1] BL, Add. MS 35013, fol. 108. Eliza's recollection, noted in the index to this collection, that this prayer related to the move to King's Row, Pentonville, was mistaken: the move to King's Row took place over two years later.
[2] Letter not preserved.
[3] *SW to Novello, 10 June 1830.

wrongly, that drink was the cause.[4] He evidently recovered from this attack, but early in August he fell ill again; this time Charles reported to Eliza Tooth that he was 'deranged and strapped down', and later in the month, that he was having repeated convulsions.[5] The family now once more faced destitution. In March 1831 Stevens recorded in his diary that bailiffs had seized Wesley's property, and that he had given £6 to a subscription set up by Wesley's friends.[6] A copy of the printed appeal has survived: addressed to the members of the Glee Club, the Madrigal Society, and the Somerset House Lodge, and bearing the names of Novello, Linley, and John Capel, MP (the President of the Glee Club), it noted that Wesley faced total ruin, and that without financial assistance he would be 'unable to settle himself on an establishment, which, there is every reason to hope, would prevent a recurrence of his present annoyances.'[7]

The illness of 1830 marked the end of Wesley's public career, although he continued to compose, to publish, and no doubt to teach a few private pupils. In the late summer or early autumn of 1832 the family moved yet again, to 8 King's Row, Pentonville Road. Rosalind, his eldest daughter, was now grown-up, and in May 1834, at the age of around twenty-one, she married Wesley's old friend Robert Glenn, who at fifty-eight was only ten years Wesley's junior. In virtual retirement, Wesley had more time to spend with his large family. Samuel Sebastian had long left home, and was rapidly establishing his career as an organist and composer. After a number of church appointments in London, he had in July 1832 been appointed organist of Hereford Cathedral at the age of only twenty-one. Eliza, aged fifteen at the time of Rosalind's marriage, was now the eldest child remaining at home. She was a promising organist, and evidently Wesley's favourite, and much of his organ and piano music from this time, including some duets, was written for her to play. The other children were much younger: Matthias Erasmus, born in 1821, followed by John (1825), Thomasine (1827), and Robert Glenn (November 1830).

Some of Wesley's final years were undoubtedly clouded by depression and general ill health. But 1834 seems to have marked an upturn in his spirits, sufficient for him to hope that he might be able to come out of retirement to take part in the Handel Commemoration festival, to be held at Westminster Abbey in June. In March he wrote to Lord Burghersh, the Chairman of the committee, to propose himself as organist for one of the concerts, but his offer was not taken up.[8] On 23 May his brother Charles died. For the funeral service, Wesley composed an anthem, 'All go unto one place', KO 77, that was to be his last major church music composition, and on 7 August he accompanied a

---

[4] Charles Wesley jun. to Tooth, 10 June 1830.
[5] Charles Wesley jun. to Tooth, 5 Aug., 27 Aug. 1830.
[6] R. J. S. Stevens memorandum, Mar. 1831 (Cambridge, University Library, Add. MS 9111, vol. 2, p. 21).
[7] Printed appeal at BL, Add. MS 56411, fol. 34, quoted in Lightwood, *Samuel Wesley, Musician*, p. 219.
[8] *Wesley to Burghersh, 6 Mar. 1834.

performance of it at a concert of the Sacred Harmonic Society at Exeter Hall. This was his last public performance.

Charles left his brother £300 in his will, which must have done much to ease the family's financial situation in difficult times. In addition, with Charles's death the annuity of £50 per annum initially granted to his mother by the Methodist Book Room in respect of the copyright of his father's hymns, and after her death paid in turn to Sarah and to Charles, passed to him.[9] Wesley now became the last surviving member of his generation. His relationship with Charles had never been close and had often been strained. He had looked with scorn on Charles's musical conservatism, and no doubt pitied him for his failure to break away from his mother and sister and make his own way in the world. For his part, Charles viewed his brother's irregular private life and frequent excesses and financial crises with considerable distaste. As can be seen in his behaviour in Bristol in 1829 at the time of Samuel's recitals, he was also jealous of his brother's greater success.

After Charles's death, Wesley renewed his contacts with Thomas Jackson, who as Secretary of the Book Room, was responsible for making the weekly annuity payments that were now due to him. In his *Recollections*, Jackson spoke warmly of the care Wesley took at this time to uphold the honour of the family despite his poverty, and remembered the exquisite manners of Matthias Erasmus, who would sometimes come to collect his father's pension in his place.[10] In private, however, Jackson was far from impressed by Wesley's reduced state, adding the comment 'beggarly ending of a great line' on one of Wesley's many begging letters.[11]

Most of Wesley's compositions in his final years were on a small scale. In 1834 he started to compose hymn tunes for Novello's compilation *The Psalmist*. He was also continuing to publish, in some cases through the Novello & Co, the firm established in 1829 by Novello's son Alfred, sometimes adapting earlier works or making up collections from pieces that he had composed many years earlier. Meanwhile, Vincent Novello was including pieces by Wesley in his multi-volume compilation *Select Organ Pieces*, which began to appear around 1830. Some were reprints or arrangements of music that had already been published, while others were appearing for the first time. Wesley was also making money from the sale of some of his church music. Two letters to Gauntlett from the summer of 1836 show him negotiating about an unspecified piece that was probably his 1827 setting of 'Tu es sacerdos', KO 69, which Gauntlett was intending to publish in an arrangement to English words.[12]

Early in 1836, Wesley wrote his manuscript *Reminiscences*, in which he recorded on scraps of paper all he could remember of his life in music. The project was evidently undertaken at the suggestion or insistence of Wesley's

---

[9] Jackson, *Recollections*, p. 231.
[10] Jackson, *Recollections*, pp. 231–2.
[11] Annotation on *SW to Jackson, 28 Jan. 1837.
[12] *SW to Gauntlett, 16 June, 30 Sept. 1836. The arrangement by Gauntlett with English words ('He is our God and strong salvation') is at the RCM, MS 5253.

family, who were no doubt anxious to have a permanent record of Wesley's memories and anecdotes and may also have wanted to find something to occupy his time. Wesley was apparently an unwilling participant in this exercise, remarking at one point that it was now time to end 'what perhaps will be considered a tedious farrago of Egotism, but I was required and pledged to write it, and therefore have been wholly unable to help myself.'[13] Although containing much of interest, the *Reminiscences* completely lack the fire and uncompromising judgements that make Wesley's letters so entertaining and so valuable a source. There are few adverse comments on other musicians, suggesting that Wesley may have been writing with at least half an eye on publication, and wanted to avoid giving offence. It is also apparent from the laborious handwriting of some sections and the frequent repetitions how much his physical and mental powers had declined.

At around the same time as writing the *Reminiscences*, Wesley contributed an article to the first number of the *Musical World*, a new periodical published by Novello's and edited by Charles Cowden Clarke, who in 1828 had married Novello's eldest daughter Mary Victoria. Entitled 'A Sketch of the State of Music in England from the Year 1778 up to the Present', it concluded with an account of the first performances in England of Haydn's *Creation* in 1800, and was intended to be followed by one or more further instalments.[14] But no continuation appeared, possibly because Wesley was incapable of supplying one. A long section of historical material evidently intended as part of the second instalment appears in the middle of the manuscript volume that contains the *Reminiscences*, but it would have been too long for its intended purpose, and is in any case about Haydn rather than about music in England. Cowden Clarke's invitation to Wesley to write for the *Musical World* should probably be seen as an act of kindliness to an old friend who had fallen on hard times, who Cowden Clarke mistakenly thought could resume his writing career to their mutual advantage.[15]

Later in 1836, Wesley amused himself by helping Eliza to compile an autograph album – incidentally, the beginning of a collecting habit which was to last for the rest of her life. The first item, dated 1 July, was by Wesley himself: a setting for soprano and piano of some lines from Dryden's *A Song for St Cecilia's Day*. Further contributions, many of them solicited by Wesley himself, came from Dragonetti, Crotch, Gauntlett, Attwood, Benedict, Ole Bull, Mori, and – in September 1837 – Mendelssohn. Some time in the late spring or summer of 1837, Wesley's health improved dramatically. In late May he was visited by the distinguished Norwegian violinist Ole Bull, on his first visit to London, and they played over some music together; he and Eliza may also have attended Bull's farewell concert on 19 May. In July 1837 he wrote out from

---

[13] *Reminiscences*, fol. 131.
[14] 'A Sketch of the State of Music in England from the Year 1778 up to the Present', *MW*, 22 March 1836, pp. 1–3.
[15] See my 'Samuel Wesley and the *European Magazine*', p. 1111.

memory the full score of his *Ode to St Cecilia* of 1794, which he believed was lost; comparison with the original score, which subsequently re-appeared, shows how accurate his memory was. On the same day that he completed the *Ode* he composed 'O give thanks unto the Lord', an anthem for the coronation of Queen Victoria, who had acceded to the throne the previous month. Her coronation would not take place until the following year, after Wesley's death. It was no doubt at much the same time that he arranged the March from the Overture to the *Ode to St Cecilia* for piano as the *Grand Coronation March*, in a further attempt to profit from the new queen's accession.[16] At some time in the late summer he also composed five short pieces for the seraphine, a type of reed organ invented around 1830 by the music publisher John Green.

Wesley's last appearance in public was in the morning of 12 September, when he was taken by Eliza and Rosalind to hear a recital given by Mendelssohn, at the time on his fifth visit to England following his marriage earlier in the year, at Christ Church, Newgate Street. This appears to have been the first time the two men had met, plans for a meeting during Mendelssohn's visit to England in 1833 having fallen through.[17] Mendelssohn had probably already met Eliza, however: on 7 September he made a contribution to Eliza's autograph book, and it seems likely that Eliza had visited him in person on this date with her request. Mendelssohn's contribution was nine bars of two-part counterpoint, and two days later Wesley used the upper part as the subject of a short fugue in B minor, which he inscribed 'Fugue composed expressly for Dr Mendelssohn'.

The Christ Church recital had been hurriedly arranged by Henry Gauntlett, who was organist of the church. It was intended to make amends both to Mendelssohn and his audience for their unhappy experiences at St Paul's Cathedral the previous Sunday. On this occasion, Mendelssohn played after Evensong, but his performance was brought to an undignified halt in the middle of Bach's Fugue in A Minor, BWV 543, when the vergers, who wished to close the cathedral, ordered the organ-blower to stop blowing. The *Musical World* correspondent, while deploring the vergers' conduct, was ecstatic about Mendelssohn's playing, stating that he 'had never previously heard Bach executed with such fire and energy – never witnessed a composition listened to with greater interest and gratification'.[18] It was on the 1690 Renatus Harris organ that had recently been substantially enlarged by Elliot and Hill, but still at this stage lacked the full pedalboard and pedal pipes that would be added in a comprehensive rebuild by Hill the following year.[19] Mendelssohn had already played it, and declared it to be the finest organ he had yet played in England.[20]

---

[16] SW used an earlier arrangement of this piece for organ as the last movement of his Voluntary in D dedicated to William Drummer, KO 623, published in 1830. It was also one of the pieces he arranged for McGeough's barrel organ.

[17] Mendelssohn to Glenn, 26 July 1833.

[18] *MW*, 15 Sept. 1837.

[19] Boeringer, *Organa Britannica*, vol. 2, pp. 199–200; Plumley, *Organs of the City of London*, p. 159.

[20] *MW*, 15 Sept. 1837.

Wesley, despite his growing frailty, was particularly anxious to attend. According to Charles William Pearce, whose account came from Eliza, on the way to the church Wesley asked her if Mendelssohn was better than Adams, saying that he thought that Adams had 'the finest finger in Europe'. Eliza replied that Mendelssohn was considered to play more in Wesley's style than in that of any other organist, and that she hoped that he would play too, to which Wesley's response was, 'I will do as well as I can. I have thought of my subject'.[21]

Mendelssohn's recital consisted of six improvised fantasias and the Bach fugue that he had not been allowed to finish at St Paul's. After the first piece, Wesley turned to Eliza, saying 'this is transcendent playing! Do you think I dare venture after this'. The *Musical World* correspondent was equally entranced, commenting on Mendelssohn's improvisations in terms which inevitably bring to mind the many reports of Wesley's own improvisations:

> The enthusiasm, the fire and energy, with which the whole was carried on, was perfectly marvellous; he sat at the keys as one inspired, casting forth one gorgeous jewel after the other, sparkling in all the radiance of light throwing out a succession of bright passages, any one of which would have made the reputation of an ordinary performer. His invention never failed him for a moment; there was no return to any phrases or expressions used at an earlier part of his performance, and his genius appeared less unwearied and more boundless than during the first half hour.

After Mendelssohn had finished playing, he asked Wesley to come forward and play himself. Wesley's extemporization, according to the *Musical World* correspondent, was characterized by 'a purity and originality of thought for which he has rendered his name ever illustrious'. After he had finished playing, Mendelssohn, who had been standing by his side, complimented him on his performance, to which Wesley could only shake his head and say with a smile: 'Ah, Sir! You have not heard me play; you should have heard me forty years ago!' This incident was also described by Mendelssohn in his diary:

> Old Wesley, trembling and bent, shook hands with me and at my request sat down at the organ bench to play, a thing he had not done for many years. The frail old man improvised with great artistry and splendid facility, so that I could not but admire. His daughter [Eliza] was so moved by the sight of it all that she fainted and could not stop crying and sobbing. She believed she would certainly never hear him play like that again; and alas, shortly after my return to Germany I learned of his death.[22]

On his return home, Wesley hung up his hat in the hall, saying that he would never go out again alive. Thereafter, although clearly in rapidly declining health, he continued to work. In early October he wrote eight hymn-tunes for the third volume of *The Psalmist*, the last of them (*Cesarea*) on 7 October. Two days later, he tried to write a testimonial for a friend, but was by now so weak that he could

---

[21] Pearce, *Notes on Old London City Churches*, pp. 28–9.
[22] Diary entry for 11–12 Sept. 1837: see Jones, *The Mendelssohns on Honeymoon*, p. 103.

only add his signature. In the morning of 10 October, he called Eliza to him, and said, 'My child, the Almighty will take care of you'. On the same day, he was visited by his friend and former pupil the organ builder Frederick Davison, whom he thanked for his many kindnesses. By the evening, it was clear that his death was not far away.

Wesley died at around 4.20p.m. on 11 October and was buried on 17 October in the burial ground adjoining St Marylebone Old Church, joining his father, mother, and brother. Among family members attending the funeral service at St Marylebone New Church were Charles and John William, Wesley's two sons with Charlotte, Samuel Sebastian and Matthias Erasmus, his two eldest sons with Sarah, and Robert Glenn, his brother-in-law; according to the usual custom of the time, no female members of the family appear to have been present. Among his friends and professional colleagues were Thomas Jackson, Henry and Edward Gauntlett, Adams, and Harding. Moscheles, Crotch, and Attwood were out of town and unable to attend.[23]

The service was conducted by Wesley's sons Charles and Samuel Sebastian with full clerical and musical honours. A choir of choristers from Westminster Abbey had been assembled; they were conducted by James Turle, the organist there and a former chorister at the Portuguese Embassy Chapel under Novello and Wesley; they were joined by a large number of other singers, many of whom were listed in the *Times* report of the funeral. According to a hastily inserted announcement in the *Musical World* two days after Wesley's death, the original proposal was to include Wesley's *Carmen Funebre*, the anthem that he had himself requested to be sung at his funeral, and 'All go unto one place', which he had composed three years earlier on the death of Charles, along with Boyce's 'If we believe that Jesus died', with the proviso that if it proved too difficult to rehearse the Wesley pieces the funeral service of Purcell and Croft would be substituted, together with an anthem by Greene or Battishill.[24] There was no mention of these pieces in the *Times* report, however, which recorded only that the burial service in the church was sung to music by Purcell and Croft, and that afterwards the choir and congregation moved to the burial ground, where the choir formed a large circle around the grave and sang the chorus 'His body is buried in peace, but his name liveth for evermore' from Handel's *Funeral Anthem for Queen Caroline*.

---

[23] *The Times*, 18 Oct. 1837; Jackson, *Recollections*, p. 232.
[24] *MW*, 13 Oct. 1837.

18

Wesley and his musical environment

Earliest musical experiences

There can be few composers whose early musical lives are as fully documented as are those of Wesley and his brother Charles. First through the accounts of their father and then through those of Daines Barrington, their earliest musical experiences and the music and musicians they encountered are recorded in great detail.

Samuel's early musical development was greatly aided by the fortunate accident of having a child prodigy for a brother. Although his father was well-disposed to music and his mother sang and played the harpsichord, the family was not a particularly musical one before the extraordinary musical talents of their elder son started to become apparent. From then on, they were projected into a world of professional music and music-making of which they had previously known little. Through the singer John Beard, Charles Wesley senior gained access to one wide circle of London's leading musicians; through Martin Madan and the Lock Hospital, to another. By the time he was ten, Charles Wesley junior had met almost everyone of consequence in the London musical world, with the exception of the large German expatriate community: to name only those who appear in his father's account, Arne, Arnold, Battishill, Beard, Boyce, Burton, Giardini, Keeble, Kelway, Savage, John Christopher Smith, Stanley, Vento, and Worgan. Had Handel still been alive (he had died in 1759), Charles would doubtless have met him too.

Charles Wesley senior's account is equally informative about his elder son's musical tastes and the music he played and owned. From the start it was apparent that his favourite composer was Handel, closely followed by Corelli – a preference that he would retain for the rest of his life. With Kelway, who taught him from the age of eleven, he studied Handel, then Kelway's own sonatas, Scarlatti, and Geminiani. Worgan and Battishill played over whole oratorios to him – presumably mostly by Handel, but no doubt also the Lock Hospital oratorios, and Kelway himself played *Messiah*, in order to demonstrate Handel's tempos and performance style. Beard and Mrs Rich gave him songs by Handel and Purcell and sonatas by Scarlatti, and Gertrude Hotham gave him her entire music library, its contents unspecified by Charles Wesley senior. In or around 1773 John Wesley gave him the three volumes of Boyce's *Cathedral Music*, after which

Charles declared his enthusiasm for church music and made a special study of Handel's oratorios.

This was the environment in which Samuel grew up, and it was an ideal one for the development of his own musical talents. From his earliest years he was able to soak up the music that he heard in the house, and as soon as he showed any signs of musical ability, there was help and advice on hand. As he grew older, he would discover a house full of printed and manuscript music, and adults who would help him to discover it.

Charles Wesley senior stated that Samuel was playing his first tunes at just before three, taught himself to read from a copy of Handel's *Samson* at four, and by five knew the whole of *Samson* and *Messiah* by heart; this was presumably through hearing Battishill, Worgan, and Kelway play these works to his brother. It was presumably the same experiences which led him to improvise music in a similar style himself, and in time to the composition of parts of his oratorio *Ruth* at the age of six and his subsequent committal of the completed work to paper two years later. This incident points to a phenomenal receptiveness and a particularly well-developed aural memory from a very early age. More generally, Samuel would have heard the keyboard music that Charles was studying with Kelway: the suites of Handel, the sonatas of Kelway himself, and those of Scarlatti and Geminiani. To this can no doubt be added keyboard music by the other composers mentioned in Charles Wesley senior's account: Burton's *Ten sonatas for the harpsichord, organ or pianoforte,* Worgan's *Six Sonatas,* and the earlier volumes of Keeble's *Select Pieces for the Organ.* And Charles would also have been playing music by other composers of the day: notably piano sonatas and other works by such composers as Schobert, Vento, and J. C. Bach.

As Samuel grew older, he became able to discover this music for himself. He could also explore the contents of Boyce's *Cathedral Music.* From this he would have got to know the historical repertoire of Anglican church music from the sixteenth century onwards, and have laid the foundations of his knowledge of English music of previous ages. From the Elizabethan and Jacobean periods there were works by Byrd, Farrant, Gibbons, Morley, Parsons, Tallis, and Tomkins. From the seventeenth century, there were Aldrich, Blow, Child, Clarke, Humfrey, Lawes, Locke, Purcell, and Wise, and from the eighteenth century, a few works by Croft and Weldon.

Concerts, theatre performances, and music in church, 1774–1787

There is little information in Charles Wesley's account about the public performances Samuel attended during his childhood and boyhood, but it is clear (*pace* Charles Wesley's biographer Thomas Jackson) that he and his brother were encouraged to attend concerts, oratorio performances, and even operas in London.¹ His first concert experience, however, may have been in Bristol, when he heard Handel's 'Dettingen' Te Deum at Bristol Cathedral in a performance involving over a hundred musicians.² In London, he would have had repeated opportunities to hear Handel oratorios, for the most part in their entirety. The repertoire of the annual Lenten oratorio series at Drury Lane and at Covent Garden at this time included *Acis and Galatea*, *Alexander's Feast*, *L'Allegro*, the Coronation Anthems, *The Ode to St Cecilia*, *Judas Maccabaeus*, *Messiah*, and *Samson*, with occasional outings for *The Choice of Hercules*, *Deborah*, *Esther*, *Jephtha*, *Joseph and his Brethren*, *Joshua*, and *Solomon*. There were also a few oratorios by other composers, such as Arnold's *The Prodigal Son* (1773), Thomas Linley the Younger's *Omnipotence* (1774), *Shakespeare Ode* (1776) and *The Song of Moses* (1777). Wesley would also have attended at least some of the annual charity performances of *Messiah* at the Foundling Hospital and of *Ruth* at the Lock Hospital, until these came to an end in 1777 and 1780 respectively.

Wesley is also known to have attended the public rehearsal for the annual Festival of the Sons of the Clergy at St Paul's Cathedral on at least one occasion.³ Here, he would have encountered Anglican church music on its grandest scale, much as he had in Bristol Cathedral. Among the works associated with the Festival were Purcell's Te Deum in D, Handel's 'Dettingen' and 'Utrecht' Te Deums, and the four anthems written for the coronation of George II in 1727. Wesley would also have heard 'Lord, thou hast been our Refuge', and 'Blessed is he that considereth the Poor', the two anthems that Boyce had composed in 1755 especially for the festival.

As far as public concerts were concerned, Wesley had a good deal of choice, as the period of his boyhood and youth was one of great abundance of provision in London. By 1774 the Bach-Abel concerts, which presented a predominantly German repertoire dominated by the works of Bach and Abel themselves, were being challenged by a rival series headed by Arnold and Vento offering Italian and English music at the newly opened Pantheon in Oxford Street. In the following year the Bach-Abel concerts moved into the newly-built Hanover Square Rooms. Their popularity was on the wane, however, and after the death of Bach in early 1782 the series was substantially reorganized in 1783 as the Hanover Square Grand Concert and in 1785 as the Professional Concert, headed by Wilhelm Cramer and the flautist Friedrich Hartmann Graf. In these new guises, the music of Bach and Abel continued to be performed, but the repertoire expanded to include a greater range of composers, including Graf, Stamitz, and most notably Haydn, whose symphonies began to be performed in almost every concert from the 1783 season onwards. Symphonies and piano concertos by Mozart also began to be performed, but with nothing like the same

---

¹ References in Charles Wesley's account to Wesley and his brother attending such events are suppressed by Jackson in his quotations in *The Life of the Rev. Charles Wesley*.
² *SW to Jacob, 17 Sept. 1808.
³ For the history of the Festivals of the Sons of the Clergy, see Weber, *Rise of Musical Classics*, pp. 104–13.

frequency. At the rival Pantheon series in 1784 and 1785 Wesley would have heard a broadly similar repertory. Both series included a good deal of vocal music, mostly taken from the Italian opera repertory, but not generally including arias from operas currently in performance.

In 1776 the Ancient Concerts had been founded, with an aggressively conservative policy of playing only music over twenty-five years old, and in consequence a repertory that was dominated by Handel and Corelli. Two of the original directors (Sir William Watkins Wynn and the Earl of Exeter) would later be among the subscribers to the Wesley family concerts.

If Samuel attended opera performances, he would have been able to see both Italian opera at the King's Theatre in the Haymarket and English opera at Covent Garden. At the King's Theatre, he would have had the opportunity to see operas by composers such as Anfossi, J. C. Bach, Sacchini, Giordani, Paisiello, Piccini (whose *La buona figliuola*, based on Samuel Richardson's *Pamela*, was a staple of the repertory), and Traetta, as well as many pasticcios, stitched together from the works of a number of composers. Here, the outstanding singers were the castratos Rauzzini and Pacchierotti, and later the German soprano Elisabeth Mara. At Covent Garden he could have seen Arne's *Love in a Village* and *Artaxerxes*, both popular works of the early 1760s that were still regularly performed, and *The Beggar's Opera*. At the same theatre he may also have seen Sheridan's *The Duenna*, the runaway hit of the 1775–6 season, with music by Thomas Linley senior and junior and others. Among the singers he may have heard there was Elizabeth Billington, who made her stage debut in Arne's *Love in a Village* in 1786. If he attended spoken drama at Drury Lane, he may have seen David Garrick at the very end of his career, and Sarah Siddons and her brother John Philip Kemble at the beginning of theirs.

Wesley would also have been able to hear music in the London pleasure gardens. It is not known if he ever visited Ranelagh or Vauxhall – he later stated to Thomas Jackson that his father was implacably opposed to such places[4] – but it is very likely that he visited Marylebone Gardens in his childhood, as they were only a short distance from the family home in Chesterfield Street. By the early 1770s, Arnold was in charge of the music, the orchestra was led by Barthélemon, and James Hook played organ concertos. Concerts were given out of doors, and there was a hall in which small-scale operas were performed. In the five summers from 1770 to 1774, no fewer than fourteen of these were staged, including Pergolesi's *La Serva padrona*, which received fifty-five performances in an English version.[5]

Between 1779 and 1787, information both on the music favoured by the Wesley brothers and on the musicians they associated with is contained in the records of the family concerts. The concerts, with their explicit policy of including both 'ancient' and modern music, included a great deal of Handel and Corelli, the more modern repertory consisting largely of the compositions

---

[4] *SW to Jackson, 12 Nov. 1835.
[5] For Marylebone Gardens see Fiske, *English Theatre Music in the Eighteenth Century*, pp. 384–9.

of Samuel and Charles themselves. Many of the works by other composers – Borghi, Cramer, Geminiani, Giardini and Giornovichi – were violin concertos, the solo parts of which were taken by Samuel, and supplemented the seven violin concertos that he composed for his own performance during this period. Little instrumental music by other contemporary composers was played, apart from a symphony by Boyce and some items by Lord Mornington, who was a close family friend and (according to some accounts) a distant relative. The vocal items consisted in the main of Handel oratorio songs, but there were also some items by other composers, including Purcell's 'Mad Bess' and the celebrated soprano bravura aria 'The soldier, tir'd of war's alarms' from Arne's *Artaxerxes*, both of which, bizarrely, were sung by Jonathan Battishill, who in addition to being a composer and keyboard player had a fine tenor voice. The absence of any instrumental music by J. C. Bach and Abel is probably explained by the presence of so much by Samuel and Charles rather than by any deliberate exclusion of their works.

Roughly contemporary with the family concerts was the period of Wesley's first involvement with Roman Catholic worship, at the embassy chapels. Here, the repertoire included masses by Samuel Webbe senior, Arne, Stephen Paxton, and the Italian Francesco Pasquale Ricci. Some of this repertory has been lost, but much survives in various publications of Roman Catholic church music that appeared in the 1780s and early 1790s.[6]

One large-scale musical event in which neither Wesley nor his brother took part was the Handel Commemoration. This massive celebration, in May and June 1784, consisted of three performances of Handel's music at Westminster Abbey and one at the Pantheon, with unprecedented numbers of singers and players. The performances were on such a scale as to include almost all musicians of note, both amateurs and professionals, adults and children, from London and the provinces, and the names of all those participating are given in Charles Burney's printed account.[7] Some light on the absence of Samuel, at any rate, is shed by his statement to Thomas Green, almost thirty years later, that at around this time he had been 'seized, from particular circumstances, with a nervous horror against music' that had caused him 'torment and pain'.[8]

The withdrawal from music, 1787–1797

It is not known how long this 'nervous horror' lasted: not long, presumably, as Wesley was able to compose for and participate in three further seasons of family concerts, and to continue to compose Roman Catholic church music. But it may have been a recurrence of this problem, or one similar, that led to his

---

[6] Olleson, 'The London Roman Catholic Embassy Chapels', pp. 108–10.
[7] Charles Burney, *An Account of the Musical Performances in Westminster Abbey*, London, 1785.
[8] Green, *Diary of a Lover of Literature*, entry for 28 June 1813, *GM*, 1838/2, p. 468.

virtual disappearance from the musical scene for ten years from around 1787, when the family concerts came to an end, to around 1797. In this period, for four years of which he was living well out of London at Ridge, there is no record of public performances, no family or other correspondence which bears on music in any way, and – with the exception of the *Ode to St Cecilia* and some works for piano – very few compositions. Apart from his school-teaching, which he continued for purely financial reasons, Wesley appears to have turned almost entirely away from music during these years, and he may well have been suffering for some of the time from depression.

We do know, however, that he attended London concerts during this period. In one place in his *Reminiscences*, he states that the Salomon-Haydn concerts had formed 'a grand Epoch of new musical Excellence by the Introduction of Haydn and his inimitable Symphonies into this Country', while the rival Professional Concert of 1792, featuring Ignace Pleyel as a counter-attraction, was 'by no means comparable in Merit and Dignity', In another he records that he attended Salomon's concerts 'very frequently, and received both Pleasure and Advantage in listening to a fine Band of the best vocal and instrumental Performers so judiciously selected and so ably and skilfully conducted'.[9] And we know from another comment that one of the concerts that he attended was that on 2 March 1792, when Haydn played a brief obbligato part on the piano in the first performance of his Symphony No. 98 in B♭.[10]

Personal influences: Boyce, Webbe, Burney, Latrobe, and Battishill

Given the wide range of musical influences on Wesley, it is difficult to pick out any one composer, type of music, or teacher likely to have been more important to Samuel than another, in the way that Handel, keyboard music, and Kelway were to his brother Charles. It is in any case clear that Wesley soaked up music like a sponge wherever he encountered it, and that – unlike his brother – his tastes were wide and eclectic. But in the light of Wesley's future development the most important influence was probably 'ancient' music, and in this William Boyce played a crucial role. As we have seen, as his brother's composition teacher Boyce was a frequent visitor to the family home, and took a particular interest in Samuel from the time in 1774 that he arrived announcing that he had heard there was an 'English Mozart' in the house. Later, he had introduced the young Samuel to the assembled musicians at a rehearsal of the Festival of the Sons of the Clergy and told them that he would surpass them all. And as we have seen, there was a copy of Boyce's *Cathedral Music* in the family home from around 1773. As a noted collector with a large library of books and music, part of which he had inherited from Maurice Greene, Boyce may have been the first,

[9] *Reminiscences*, fols 40, 123.
[10] *Reminiscences*, fol. 70.

or one of the first, to arouse in Samuel an interest in the music of the past. Samuel was not quite thirteen when Boyce died in early 1779, but he may well have had occasion to use Boyce's extensive library before this time, and thus to study much music that would otherwise not have been available to him.

Another particularly important influence, a little later, was Samuel Webbe senior. As organist of the Sardinian and Portuguese Embassy chapels from around 1776 he was the most important figure in Roman Catholic church music in London at this time. When Wesley started to take an interest in Roman Catholicism it could have not been very long before he encountered Webbe, who would have encouraged him to sing in his choir, and in time to compose for it. The result was a considerable body of Latin church music dating from the period 1780 to 1787, utterly distinct from the instrumental music composed for the family concerts of the same period. Like Boyce, Webbe was a collector of books and music and a man of wide general culture, and he too may have made his collection available to Wesley. It was no doubt also at this time, and largely through Webbe, that Wesley began his lifelong fascination with Gregorian chant.

Two other important musical influences later in Wesley's life should also be mentioned. The first was the historian of music Charles Burney. Burney had first encountered Wesley in Wesley's childhood, but after that their paths did not cross again until early in 1799, when they met again at a dinner party. Thereafter they corresponded from time to time until early 1808, when Wesley began to consult Burney extensively over his plans to promote the music of J. S. Bach. The result was a warm friendship that continued until Burney's death in 1814, and involved Wesley in several visits to Burney's apartments at Chelsea College and doubtless many opportunities to consult his extensive library. The second was the Moravian minister and musician Christian Ignatius Latrobe, a key figure in introducing the music of Haydn into England in the 1780s, and who between 1806 and 1825 published *A Selection of Sacred Music from the Work of some of the Most Eminent Composers of Germany and Italy*, a six-volume compilation that first anticipated and later overlapped with the similar publications of Novello. In the summer of 1784 Latrobe had returned to England after studying in Germany, and it is likely that Wesley had first got to know him at this time: Latrobe and Charles Wesley senior were certainly in constant touch by 1786, and Latrobe attended one of the family concerts in 1787. It is apparent from his journal of 1788–9 that Latrobe was at this time a regular visitor at the Wesley family home, and from a letter of early 1799 from Wesley to him that the two men were still in contact then.[11] Lack of evidence makes it impossible further to document the nature and extent of their relationship, but it is possible that Latrobe introduced Wesley to printed and manuscript music in his large collection, which included many items acquired direct from continental publishers and not generally available in England at this time. In this way Wesley may have got to know a good deal of music by Graun,

---

[11] For Latrobe, see Cowgill, 'The Papers of C. I. Latrobe'.

Hasse, Pergolesi, Haydn, and Mozart, some of which Latrobe was later to include in his *Selection of Sacred Music*.[12]

Pursuing further musicians who Wesley may or may not have come into contact with and have been influenced by is inevitably speculative, but one other may be mentioned: Jonathan Battishill, whose brilliant career as a keyboard player and composer was latterly marred by his over-indulgence in drink. As we have seen, he was an early associate of Wesley's brother Charles, and appeared as a tenor soloist in some of the family concerts. In a letter of 1800 to Thomas Busby, one of Battishill's pupils, Wesley referred to him as his friend, stating that it would give him great pleasure to meet him at Busby's house.[13] Battishill possessed an extensive library of theology and works by classical authors, and it is easy to see how Wesley, with his scholarly tendencies and interests in these two subjects as well as in music, might have cultivated Battishill's acquaintance.

Starting a career, 1797–1802

When Wesley returned to an active interest in music around 1797, he was thirty-one. This was decidely late to be making an adult professional debut, and he appears to have been content for a while to stay on the fringes of professional music making, taking part in informal music gatherings, while at the same time becoming involved once more in the music of the Roman Catholic church, this time most probably with Novello at the Portuguese Embassy chapel. But the performance of his *Ode to St Cecilia* in February 1799 and the composition of the *Confitebor* later in the same year are both, notwithstanding our lack of knowledge about their respective backgrounds, clear indications of his desire to become fully involved in London's professional musical life, and his performance of an organ concerto at a performance of Haydn's *Creation* in April 1800 indicates his full acceptance into this world. Further evidence of his range of activities at around this time is to be found in the publication of his Sonatinas, Op. 4 and his Four Sonatas and two Duets, Op. 5, and the promotion with his brother Charles of what turned out to be a disastrous concert series in early 1802. Among his professional associates at this time were the Ashleys, Barthélemon, Bridgetower, and Salomon, and it was also at this time that he got to know Charles Burney.

At the turn of the century, Wesley's reputation was chiefly as an organist. In 1798 William Seward, in an article in the *European Magazine*, praised his powers of improvisation and bracketed him with Mozart as one of the few child prodigies whose later achievement was commensurate with their early talent.[14] Up to this time he had not published any organ music, but in 1802 published the first of the Op. 6 voluntaries. Six more appeared over the next four years,

---

[12] For a list of their contents, see *Grove 1–3*.
[13] *SW to Busby, 21 Mar. 1800.
[14] *EM* 34 (1798), p. 161. For a quotation from this article, see below, pp. 297–8.

and a further five at irregular intervals thereafter, consolidating his reputation as the most important composer of organ music of the period.

The discovery of Bach

After the failure of the 1802 concert series Wesley again dropped out from the musical world, emerging from another debilitating attack of depression only around three years later. It was not until his discovery of the music of J. S. Bach early in 1808, however, that his career started the rapid ascent that would place him at the centre of London's musical life until the breakdown of his health in 1817. His first West End concert, a solo recital at the Hanover Square Rooms in June 1808, was largely devoted to Bach's music, but later concerts included increasing amounts of his own compositions and involved increasing numbers of other musicians. His appearances at the Tamworth Festival in September 1809 and at the Birmingham Festival in October 1811 further consolidated his reputation.

Among the works of Bach that Wesley performed either in public or in private at this time were the '48', the *Goldberg Variations*, the Sonatas for Violin and Harpsichord, the Trio Sonatas for organ, the 'St Anne' Fugue, and various other organ chorale preludes. But it is difficult to say how much direct influence any of Bach's music had upon his own style. Wesley does not quote or allude to material by Bach, nor are there any obvious signs of him adopting Bach's formal procedures, except perhaps in the conclusion of the fugue of the Voluntary in C minor dedicated to Thomas Adams, KO 606. It is possible, however, to detect in some of Wesley's more involved two-part writing, particularly in the shorter pieces for organ, some echoes of Bach's style in (say) the slower and more ruminative of the *Goldberg Variations*. But Wesley's organ style was well established long before he made his first acquaintance with Bach's music, and any perception of the influence of Bach is just as likely to be of a more generalized Baroque style. Some contemporary observers, however, blamed the influence of Bach for much of the conservatism of Wesley's later style: Holmes commented that 'he carried his idolatry [for Bach] to an almost injurious extent – for his own original powers were in a manner absorbed in the object of his admiration; and many think that the change wrought in his subsequent way of thinking and composing infused a stiffness into his original compositions from which at first they were entirely free.'[15]

The oratorio concerts

In 1810 Wesley appeared twice at Covent Garden oratorio concerts in performances of his own organ concertos, and in 1813 was appointed the

---

[15] Holmes, 'Our Musical Spring', p. 590.

regular organist of the series. This marked the beginning of the highest point in his career, and his greatest public exposure. It was also in this year that he joined the Philharmonic Society as an associate member, although it was to be another two years before he applied for and was elected to full membership. During these peak years, Wesley was exposed to most of the new music performed in London. Because of direct clashes with his Covent Garden oratorio engagements he would not, however, have been able to hear the innovative programmes that Smart was introducing at the rival Drury Lane series and that included the first English performances of Beethoven's *The Mount of Olives*, the Mass in C, and the 'Battle Symphony', as well as many other new works. But he would have attended the concerts of the Philharmonic Society, where he would have heard further performances of Beethoven, in addition to Mozart, Haydn, and Cherubini, and a good deal of music by other contemporary composers.

Wesley's appointment as a director of the Philharmonic Society in late 1815 and his active involvement in its affairs indicates his acceptance into the innermost circles of London's concert life, and – equally important, for one of his constitutionally rebellious character – his own acceptance of the benefits this association could bring. But his assimilation into this world was not total. It is worth noting that he was never one of the small number of musicians who were office-holders or committee members of such organizations as the New Musical Fund. Nor (one performance apart) did he ever appear at the two most prestigious subscription series, the Ancient Concerts and the Vocal Concerts, or, as far as is known, at any of the many private concerts that took place in the houses of the aristocracy. It was in these circles that real advancement in the music profession lay, and for whatever reason – his outspokenness, his unconventional private life, or his own unwillingness to become involved – he never became part of it.

Breakdown and recovery

Wesley's collapse in April 1817, following a progressive deterioration in health since the previous August, brought this career to an abrupt halt. After his release from Blacklands House in June 1818, his return to full health and full involvement in London's music was slow. He was engaged for the 1819 Covent Garden oratorio series, but after that was not engaged again until 1825. The intervening period was one of depression, inactivity, and low productivity. By this time, most observers had probably written Wesley off as a sadly anachronistic figure. In addition, the oratorio concerts, in which he had played so prominent a role before his illness, had changed in character and were now largely occasions for performances of operatic extracts. London's musical public were now increasingly following new enthusiasms, largely operatic. The first was for Rossini, whose music had been performed in London since 1818, and who visited in 1823–4, conducting no fewer than nine of his operas at the

King's Theatre.[16] The second was for Weber, whose music was all the rage in the 1824–5 season, following the first English performance of *Der Freischütz* on 22 July 1824. His one visit to England was in early 1826, to rehearse and conduct the first performances of *Oberon* at Covent Garden, which he managed to do before his death in London in June of that year.[17]

And yet Wesley proved that he was not yet a spent force. In 1824, in a return to full activity that appears to be inexplicable except in terms of spontaneous recovery, he sprang back to action. This year saw his appointment as organist of Camden Chapel, and the publication of the Service in F and two important sets of organ voluntaries. Early in 1825 he appeared for the last time at the organ at the Covent Garden oratorio concerts, but much of the rest of this year was taken up with negotiations with the University of Cambridge about permission to publish extracts from the Fitzwilliam collection and in dealing with the reviews of his Service in the *Harmonicon* and the *Quarterly*. He was also making plans for a performance and the subsequent publication of the *Confitebor*.

What these activities all indicate is a withdrawal from the concert platform, on which he doubtless felt he could no longer compete with younger men, to areas where he could still make an effective contribution and a living. Conservatism of style was no problem in the composition of church music or organ voluntaries, and was irrelevant to any editing he might undertake. By the same token, he was able to put his age and experience to good use in lecturing on music, which he resumed in a course at the Royal Institution in 1826 after an absence of fifteen years.

Amongst all the activity of the mid-1820s, there was a distinct narrowing of horizons. With his abandonment of the concert scene – or it of him – Wesley lost contact with many of his former colleagues and with new developments in London's musical life. His letters of the period, for all their liveliness, contain little that is not concerned with a few circumscribed topics: music parties with his friends, his obsessive pursuit of the critics of the Service, and the protracted negotiations over the Fitzwilliam collection. One looks in vain for any extended commentary on the main musical events of the day: the visits of Liszt, Rossini, and Weber, for example, or the first performance of Beethoven's Ninth Symphony at a Philharmonic Society concert in March 1825.

Final years

Wesley's next bout of illness, after two highly successful visits to Bristol in late 1829 and early 1830, brought his public career to an end. By the time he died seven years later, he was largely forgotten, except by a few old friends such as Vincent Novello, and by organists, who still regarded his music highly and retained fond memories of his extraordinary extempore performances. During

---

[16] For Rossini in England, see Weinstock: *Rossini*, pp. 135–42, 436–7; Kendall, *Rossini*, pp. 121–5.
[17] Kirby, 'Weber's Operas in England, 1824–6'; Warrack, *Weber*, pp. 345–64.

much of this final period he appears to have been in declining health, but he was far from inactive, and a host of publications, largely of small collections of organ pieces, show him still doing what he could to earn some money from his profession. Finally, in the last month of his life came the famous meeting with Mendelssohn when Wesley played for the last time, after Mendelssohn's recital at Christ Church, Newgate Street.

19

Sacred vocal music

Latin sacred music

Wesley wrote around seventy pieces of Latin church music, from simple harmonizations of hymns to large-scale settings in up to eight parts, some with instrumental accompaniment. His output falls into main three periods, coinciding with those times when he was most actively involved in Roman Catholic worship. The first, covering 1780 to 1787, was the period of Wesley's first involvement with Roman Catholicism, including his conversion in 1784. The second, covering 1797 to around 1802, was the exceptionally productive time that followed Wesley's return to music after a long silence and also resulted in a large number of compositions in other genres. Nothing is known about the background to Wesley's involvement with Roman Catholicism at this period, but it seems likely that it was at the Portuguese Embassy Chapel, where Vincent Novello had recently been appointed organist. The third was his time as assistant to Novello at the Portuguese Embassy Chapel, possibly from as early as 1808 until his illness of 1816–17. Wesley's activities for much of this period are well documented in his letters to Novello and in other sources.

The music of the 1780s

Most of Wesley's earliest pieces for the Latin rite are contained in a volume of fair copies of sacred and secular vocal compositions that he compiled in the early 1780s.[1] Included here are three settings of the Gloria Patri, two of the Domine salvum fac (the prayer for the monarch that concluded Sunday Mass), a Kyrie, and seven antiphons for two, three, and four voices, with and without accompaniment. All appear to have been written in 1780 or 1781, and can have only been written for use at one or other of the embassy chapels, as these were the only places where Roman Catholic worship could legally be conducted at this time. It is not known for certain which chapel or chapels Wesley attended, but it was most probably the Sardinian or the Portuguese, where Samuel Webbe senior was in charge of the music.

These early pieces already show familiarity with the style of late Renaissance

---

[1] BL, Add. MS 31222.

polyphony and of more recent Italian church music. Some are for unaccompanied SATB choir and others for ATB, often with extremely low alto parts, typically from d to a'. It is evident that these, like those in much other English sacred and secular vocal music going back at least to the time of Purcell, were written for singers who were able to switch easily between the baritone and falsetto registers. Wesley also favours a texture of two (or less frequently, three) upper voices and continuo. Here he was probably taking his cue from the many publications of sacred and secular vocal music for this combination by such contemporary Italian composers as Mattia Vento and Giuseppe Aprile that were currently popular in England. The texture is essentially that of the Italian trio sonata transferred into vocal terms, and with its use of homophonic passages in thirds and sixths, telling use of dissonance, and occasional passages of simple counterpoint, is particularly mellifluous. Among other works of this type that Wesley would have known well were Handel's *Thirteen Celebrated Italian Duets*, first published in 1777, and Pergolesi's *Stabat Mater*, first published in 1749.

The first composition in the volume may in fact be the earliest in date: the SATB **Kyrie Eleison**, KO 10, designated by Wesley as for Holy Cross Day (14 September), and possibly written for this feast in 1780. The first dated composition is **Ecce Maria genuit nobis**, KO 32, completed on 9 November 1780. As Wesley noted, this is an antiphon for the Feast of the Circumcision (1 January). On the following day he composed **Hodie beata Virgo Maria**, KO 42, an exuberant Magnificat antiphon for the Feast of the Purification of the Virgin Mary (2 February), suggesting that he was looking well ahead in the liturgical calendar. The latter two are for two sopranos, alto, and continuo. The next dated composition is an extended SATB **Gloria Patri**, KO 40, written in the following month for the Feast of St Peter in Chains (1 August). Other pieces are either not precisely dated or not dated at all. They include particularly attractive short settings of the Marian antiphon **Ave regina caelorum**, KO 16a, and the eucharistic motet **Ave verum corpus**, KO 17a, for two sopranos and continuo. Both are notable in that Wesley returned to them many years later to recast them for larger forces, leaving them otherwise substantially unchanged. There are many other examples of the same process in Wesley's output, indicating that once he had completed a composition, he rarely saw the need to change it in essentials, and that he was sufficiently satisfied with the compositions of his early years to re-use them many years afterwards.

Most of the works considered so far are on a fairly small scale, but there are three that are more extended. One, written in October 1782, is a four-part unaccompanied setting of the Vesper Psalm **Dixit Dominus**, KO 25, a text that Wesley was to return to on several subsequent occasions. In this setting, unlike in the others, where he set only the first verse or one from the middle of the psalm, Wesley sets the entire text, producing in the process an extended multi-sectional composition of around eight minutes. Of comparable length is an ambitious **Magnificat**, KO 49, for three sopranos and continuo, composed for the feast of the Purification (6 February). The four sections into which Wesley divides the text are well differentiated and contrasted, with an effective change of key and tempo and a reduction to duet texture at 'Suscepit Israel' ('He remembering his mercy, hath holpen his servant Israel'). Fifteen years later Wesley was to reuse this section for the 'Redemptionem misit populi' movement in the *Confitebor*.

Wesley's largest and most impressive piece of Latin sacred music of this period, and the only one (the *Missa de Spiritu Sancto* apart) involving instruments, is **Ave maris stella**, KO 15, of 1786, for two sopranos, strings, and continuo, which inevitably prompts comparisons with Pergolesi's *Stabat Mater*, written for the same forces. Wesley divides the seven verses of the hymn into four movements: a leisurely opening Andante, an Allegretto in the dominant, a Poco Largo, for one of the sopranos only, in the tonic minor, and an exuberant closing Animoso movement featuring the repeated use of a plainsong psalm tone as a cantus firmus. The emotional centre of the piece is 'Virgo singularis', the minor key movement, which sets the fifth verse of the hymn ('Virgin unequalled, gentle among all others, released from our sins, make us gentle and pure') in a most effective manner, with some restrained use of coloratura (Ex. 19.01). Here, as elsewhere, it is clear that Wesley is strongest as a melodist in minor keys.

Example 19.01, 'Ave maris stella', KO 15, 'Virgo singularis', bars 17–23

The Missa de Spiritu Sancto

Standing completely apart from the rest of Wesley's Latin church music of this time is the *Missa de Spiritu Sancto*, the work that he completed in May 1784 to mark his conversion to Roman Catholicism. Because of its enormous length (around 90 minutes) and the vocal and orchestral forces it requires, it could not have been performed in any of the London embassy chapels, and there is no evidence to suggest that Wesley expected that it would be performed in Rome either. It is best regarded as a presentation work, intended by Wesley as a mark of the sincerity of his conversion and an example of his prowess as a composer. The purpose for which the Mass was written goes a long way to explaining its enormous dimensions. As an actual performance was not in prospect, Wesley could give free expression to his conception of what a large-scale setting of the Mass should be like. His basic model was the Neapolitan cantata mass, in which the individual sections of the Mass are divided into separate sections and set as choruses, solos, and ensembles: a genre familiar to present-day listeners from the Masses of Haydn and Mozart. Wesley's own models were presumably Masses by such composers as Pergolesi and Hasse which he had got to know through published editions or manuscripts owned by Samuel Webbe or other musicians in his circle. But there was nothing in this repertoire remotely approaching the dimensions of the *Missa de Spiritu Sancto*, and the overall conception of the Mass can only have been Wesley's own. From outside Roman Catholic church music, Wesley would also have been able to draw on his knowledge of large-scale Anglican church music by Purcell, Handel, Boyce, and others, and of Handel's oratorios.

The Mass is scored for SSAATB soloists, choir, and an orchestra of flutes, oboes, horns, trumpets, timpani, and strings. The layout of the work (Fig. 2) shows the customary division into choral and solo movements, with the choir used for the outer sections of the Kyrie, at the opening and conclusion of the Gloria, for the opening, the 'Et resurrexit' and 'Et in unam sanctam apostolicam ecclesiam' sections of the Credo, for the Sanctus, the Osanna, and the concluding 'Dona nobis pacem'. Similarly, sections such as the 'Christe eleison', the 'Laudamus te', and the Benedictus are allocated either as solos or ensembles. Wesley's use of the soloists favours the upper voices: neither the tenor nor the bass soloist has a solo number, and they appear only in ensembles. This disposition of voices may reflect either his personal preference for soprano and alto voices, or the conditions he was familiar with in the embassy chapels.

Dominating the Mass are the extended choral fugues that conclude each main section: the 'Cum sancto spiritu' at the end of the Gloria, the 'Et vitam venturi saeculi' at the end of the Credo, the 'Hosanna in excelsis' at the end of the Sanctus, and the 'Dona nobis pacem' at the end of the Agnus Dei. Here, in accordance with the usual practice for these sections, Wesley draws upon elements of the 'ancient' style that he knew so well. The result is particularly successful, showing Wesley's mastery of contrapuntal techniques and a striking

Kyrie
Kyrie I	Chorus
Christe	Soprano, tenor, bass solo
Kyrie II	Chorus

Gloria
Gloria in excelsis	Chorus
Et in terra pax	Chorus
Laudamus te	Soprano, alto solo
Domine Deus	Chorus, soprano solo
Quoniam tu solus sanctus	Chorus

Credo
Credo in unum Deum	Chorus
Et in unum Dominum	Soprano 1 and 2 solo
Deum de Deo	Chorus
Qui propter nos homines	Soprano 1 and 2 solo
Crucifixus etiam pro nobis	Soprano solo
Et resurrexit	Chorus
Et in Spiritum Sanctum	Alto
Et in unam sanctam	Chorus

Sanctus
Sanctus	Chorus
Benedictus	Soprano 1 and 2, bass solo
Hosanna	Chorus

Agnus Dei
Agnus Dei	Soprano 1 and 2, alto 1 and 2 solo
Dona nobis pacem	Chorus

Figure 2: The plan of the *Missa de Spiritu Sancto*

command of structure in very long fugal movements. There are some examples of thematic integration, too. The short fugue in Kyrie I is extended to form Kyrie II, and then returns at the end of the Mass as the main material of the 'Dona nobis pacem' movement. Rather more surprising in this movement is the way in which Wesley introduces, in the order in which they first appear, the subjects from all the other main fugal movements in the work: the 'Cum sancto spirito' from the Gloria, the 'Et vitam venturi saeculi' from the Credo, and finally the 'Hosanna' from the Sanctus. The result is a contrapuntal tour-de-force, and a highly satisfying conclusion to the work.

Apart from the big set-piece fugues, where the use of Baroque idioms was the norm, the style of the Mass is thoroughly modern. The solo and ensemble movements are operatic in style, perhaps reflecting Wesley's familiarity with Italian operas by such composers as Sacchini, Giordani, and Paisiello that he may have seen at the King's Theatre. There are extended movements, sometimes extremely florid, for the soprano and alto soloists: the soprano 'Domine Deus, Agnus Dei', pastoral in character with prominent flute parts, the alto 'Et in spiritum sanctum', the two-soprano duet 'Et in unum Dominum', and the soprano-alto duet 'Laudamus te'. There are also ensembles for various combinations of soloists, of which the quartet for two sopranos and two altos at the beginning of the Agnus Dei is perhaps the most effective. In some places, the tessitura of some of the solo soprano and alto writing is uncomfortably low for present-day voices, and it is possible that Wesley had the range and vocal characteristics of the castrato voice in mind.

Perhaps inevitably, given the ambitiousness of its overall conception and Wesley's lack of experience in writing large-scale church music, the *Missa de Spiritu Sancto* is not a consistently successful work. At the beginning of the Gloria, for example, Wesley takes care to write a orchestral introduction of appropriate length for the substantial movement that follows, but its musical material consists of little more than repeated tonic and dominant harmony and stock scale and arpeggio figurations. The necessary massiveness is achieved, but without a great deal of thematic interest. Generally, and as might be expected in a work of this length, the treatment of the text is leisurely, with a good deal of repetition both of words and of musical material and much highly melismatic writing.

Latin sacred music, 1797–1802

Wesley's next period of composition of Latin church music was in the productive period between 1797 and around 1802, when he returned to music, re-established his contacts in London, and evidently resumed his attendance at Roman Catholic chapels. Much of it is contained in two fair-copy music books labelled 'Harmony 1798' and 'Harmony 1800', both of which also contain other compositions.[2] As before, Wesley writes for a variety of combinations, from single voice and continuo up to elaborate settings for double SATB chorus, and for a variety of liturgical contexts. If, as seems likely, these pieces were written for the Portuguese Embassy chapel, they attest to the elaborateness of the music there at this time and to the high degree of competence of the choir. But we know from Wesley's letters of the period that some of them were also sung at informal parties with such amateur musician friends as Kingston, the Drummer brothers, and Street.[3]

Much of Wesley's output from this time consists of three-part and four-part unaccompanied settings for male voices. The simplest and most straightforward pieces are settings of hymns for ATB, all featuring the very low alto parts that we have noted earlier. **Ecce iam noctis tenuatur umbra**, KO 31a, is a strophic setting in simple note-against-note style of an office hymn for Lauds, dating from August 1801. In its original three-part form it exists in two versions, one of

---

[2] RCM, MS 4020; BL, Add. MS 71107.
[3] See *SW to Street, 9 November [1799], in which Wesley proposed to bring along a 'new Chorus for a double Choir' (probably 'Deus majestatis intonuit', KO 23') to a music party at the Kingstons' on the following Tuesday.

which includes short organ interludes between the verses. In 1808 Wesley recast it for SSATB and organ. **Nocte surgentes**, KO 52, also dating from 1801, is very similar in style, as is the 1799 setting of the Marian hymn **Salve regina**, KO 59, one of three settings by Wesley of this text. As a consequence of their scoring, all these pieces are dark-textured and exploit a relatively narrow overall compass.

Many of the more elaborate contrapuntal settings of this period are also for three or more men's voices. One such is the undated ATB **De profundis clamavi**, KO 22, for ATB. As befits the text, from Psalm 130 ('Out of the deep have I called to thee, O Lord'), it is intensely expressive. The first verse, 'De profundis clamavi ad te Domine: Domine exaudi vocem meam' ('Out of the deep have I called unto thee, O Lord; Lord, hear my voice') is in C minor and exploits the harmonic implications of two simple motifs, repeated again and again. With the second verse, 'Fiant aures tuae intendentes in vocem deprecationes meae' ('O let thy ears consider well: the voice of my complaint') Wesley moves to the relative major and a duet texture for the tenor and bass only, the writing for both parts being cast particularly low. The third verse, 'Si iniquitates observaveris Domine: Domine, quis sustinebit' ('If thou, Lord, wilt be extreme to mark what is done amiss: O Lord, who may abide it?') moves to G major and returns to a three-part texture. There is then a reprise of the entire first section. This is an extraordinary piece, which in its brooding chromaticism and dark colouring looks forward to Wesley's better known *Carmen funebre* of over twenty years later.

One or two of the pieces from this period have organ accompaniment. **In te, Domine speravi**, KO 45, is a joyous setting for soprano and continuo of a non-liturgical text compiled mostly from the psalms, in which the first line ('In thee, Lord, have I trusted; let me never be confounded', taken from the Te Deum) is repeated as a rondo-like refrain after each succeeding interlude. **Beati omnes qui timent Domini**, KO 18, ('Blessed are all they who fear the Lord'), is for alto and tenor and continuo, and looks back to the church music of the 1780s.

The main distinction within the pieces of this period is between those pieces for men's voices only and those with parts for sopranos or boy trebles, which are inevitably more brilliant and fuller in texture, and allow Wesley to exploit larger voice-groupings and a greater range of sonorities. The four-part **Te decet hymnus**, KO 66, from September 1799 is on a text from Psalm 65 that also appears in the Office for the Dead. Wesley bases the whole on a striding cantus firmus that appears both in its original form and in inversion, and contrasts vocal registers and combines passages in block chords with imitative writing in a way that is wholly assured and effective. In 1824 Wesley adapted this piece to an English translation of the text ('Thou, O God, art praised in Zion', KO 114) at the request of his Norwich friend Alfred Pettet for a volume of church music that Pettet was compiling.

The SSATB **Anima nostra erepta est**, KO 14, of 1798, a setting of the last two verses of Psalm 123, is utterly different in character. Whereas 'Te decet hymnus' uses bright sonorities, this is sombrely magnificent. Wesley keeps the overall tessitura low for the first, imitative, section ('Our soul is escaped even as a bird out of the snare of the fowler: the snare is broken, and we are delivered'), only using the full soprano range in the massive chordal writing of the second ('Our help standeth in the Name of the Lord: who hath made heaven and earth'). As elsewhere, the range of the voice parts (especially the sopranos and alto) can make performance of this piece problematic, but many of the difficulties disappear if it is sung by SATTB.

Exultate Deo, KO 36 is a setting for SSATB of two verses from Psalm 81 dating from June 1800: 'Sing we merrily unto God our strength: make a cheerful noise unto the God of Jacob. Take the psalm, bring hither the tabret: the merry harp with the lute.' Unlike 'Te decet hymnus', and 'Anima nostra erepta est', both of which are specifically designated as being for voices without organ, it has a written-out organ part, which for the most part doubles the voices, but goes on to conclude the work with a ten-bar postlude. With a length of around seven minutes, it is one of Wesley's largest pieces of Latin church music. Like 'Te decet hymnus', it opens with a striding figure in the bass, although in this case not one that is used as a cantus firmus. This, with its continuation, and a third theme at 'Sumite psalmum' ('Take the psalm, bring hither the tabret') make up the whole of the thematic material (Ex. 19.02). The work is notable for its exuberant rhythmic flexibility, arising naturally out of the first theme, and for Wesley's masterly handling of contrasting textures and dynamics. Later, probably for a performance of the work at the 1811 Birmingham festival, Wesley scored the accompaniment for orchestra. In this guise, the parts for high trumpets and drums, held in reserve until the middle of the work, are then further used for the massive concluding peroration, greatly adding to the effect.

Example 19.02, 'Exultate Deo', KO 36, main themes

Dixit Dominus, KO 26, written in January 1800, is on a similar scale. It is for two SATB choirs, used sometimes antiphonally, sometimes as one eight-voice ensemble. The structure and technique follow that of 'Te decet hymnus' and 'Exultate Deo'. A strong opening theme in long notes is announced in the basses, and this and a small number of other themes constitute the material for the whole of the work. The use of thematic material is simultaneous, rather than sequential, as in classical Renaissance practice. As in 'Exultate Deo', there is some highly effective use of contrasting textures, sonorities, and dynamics, and a well developed sense of the dramatic. All of these are perhaps best displayed in the work's conclusion (Ex. 19.03). Note again the characteristic quiet ending, marked 'dulce'.

Only one of the large-scale works from this period was originally conceived with orchestral accompaniment: **Deus majestatis intonuit**, KO 23, a setting for two SATB choirs and strings of a single verse from Psalm 29. As in the eight-part 'Dixit Dominus' setting, the two choirs are sometimes deployed as one eight-part ensemble, sometimes antiphonally. The text is extremely short: 'Deus majestatis intonuit, Dominus super multas aquas ('The Lord of Majesty sounds forth, the Lord is present upon the waters'). Wesley sets it with great economy of thematic material, using only two motifs that are announced simultaneously at the opening and then used throughout the work. Whereas the strings sometimes double the voices, they more often have separate parts of their own, accompanying antiphonal block-chord passages for the two choirs.

Latin sacred music, 1806–1814

After the compositional silence that accompanied his extended bout of depression of 1802–5, Wesley started writing Latin church music again in 1806 and continued up to his breakdown of 1817. Compared with the outpouring of a few years earlier, this was not a time of great productivity: Wesley was now increasingly busy in other directions, first with the promotion of Bach, and then with the expansion of his own performing career. Although some of the pieces are on a large scale, most are short and straightforward, and evidently designed for the day-to-day requirements of the Portuguese Embassy Chapel.

The ATB setting of **Dixit Dominus**, KO 27, was written on Christmas Day 1806, and first performed two days later at a meeting of the Concentores Society that Wesley attended as a visitor and later described in a letter to his brother.[4] By the side of the massive eight-part setting of six years earlier, this is a small-scale and unremarkable piece. Notwithstanding its secular première, it was doubtless later used at the Portuguese Embassy chapel. **Deus noster refugium**, KO 24, a setting of verses from Psalm 46, dates from the following September. In 1808, Wesley recast his earlier three-part setting of 'Ecce iam noctis', KO 31a. The resulting work, **Ecce iam noctis**, KO 31b, is for five-part choir, but leaves the musical substance unchanged.

The date of composition of **Domine salvam fac reginam nostram Mariam**, KO 28a, for SATB with obbligato organ part, is unknown, but Wesley may have written it to mark the re-opening of the organ of the Portuguese Embassy

---

[4] See above, p. 70.

Example 19.03, 'Dixit Dominus' a 8, KO 26, bars 305–32

Chapel after its rebuild and substantial enlargement by George Pike England in 1808. At all events, it was published in *A Collection of Sacred Music*, Novello's first publication, which appeared in or around May 1811. Wesley had earlier composed other settings of this text, the short prayer for the monarch that concludes the celebration of the Mass on Sundays, but this one is different in two important respects. The first concerns its addressee: not 'Georgium' (i.e. George III of England), but 'Mariam' (i.e. Mary, Queen of Portugal). The second concerns its scale and character. The text was often sung to a chant, and it was certainly not usual to subject it to elaborate musical treatment. Wesley's setting, however, is highly extended, culminating in an enormous fugal setting of the 'Gloria Patri'. The sheer size of the piece and the virtuoso nature of the organ writing suggest a special Sunday High Mass, with the prayer for the monarch serving as its spectacular conclusion.

In exitu Israel, KO 43, a setting for double SATB choir of verses from Psalm 114, is Wesley's best known and most celebrated choral work, and also dates from this period. Although it may subsequently have been performed at the Portuguese Embassy chapel, it was originally written for, and was first performed at, his benefit concert at the Hanover Square Rooms on 19 May 1810, when Bach's *Jesu, meine Freude* was also performed. Wesley's setting contains many features already familiar from his eight-part setting of 'Dixit Dominus' of ten years earlier and other pieces of the same period: the large scale (around seven minutes); the use of double choir; the announcement of a strongly defined first theme (in this case a Gregorian psalm tone) by the basses alone, and its subsequent use as a cantus firmus (Ex. 19.04); the thematic economy; the masterly use of contrasting textures and sonorities, including passages in unisons and octaves; and the by now utterly characteristic quiet ending. Along with 'Exultate Deo' and the eight-part 'Dixit Dominus' setting it was one of the few pieces of Wesley's Latin church music known by Victorian and Edwardian musicians; Ernest Walker in 1907 found it 'gorgeously powerful and impressive', and 'a masterpiece that places its composer on a very lofty pedestal'.[5]

For part of the time during his collaboration with Novello at the Portuguese Embassy chapel, Wesley was involved in harmonizing Gregorian chant for liturgical use. As his letters to Novello show, some of this was evidently done on an *ad hoc* basis, but around 1812 and 1813 he was also involved in an ambitious project to publish harmonizations of all the Gregorian melodies in common use in the London chapels, the cost of publication to be borne by his friend Joseph Gwilt. As we have seen earlier, the project eventually had to be abandoned because of extensive discrepancies between the chants in the books used at the various chapels.[6] Few of Wesley's harmonizations have survived, but there is an example of a complete Mass setting based on a Gregorian chant: the **Missa pro Angelis**, KO 5, based on a chant still widely used in Roman Catholic worship.

---

[5] Walker, *A History of English Music*, p. 241.
[6] See above, pp. 123–4.

[Musical example: four staves labeled (i), (ii), (iii), (iv) with text underlay:
(i) Allegro, ff: In ex-i-tu Is-ra-el de Æ-gyp-to, do-mus Ja-cob de po-pu-lo bar-ba-ro:
(ii) f: Fac-ta est Ju-dæ-a sanc-ti-fi-ca-ti-o e - - - jus.
(iii) f: Ma-re vi-dit, et fu-git,
(iv) Jor-da-nis con-ver-sus est re-tror - - - sum,]

Example 19.04, 'In exitu Israel', KO 43, main themes

Novello included the Kyrie in his *A Selection of Sacred Music*, and Wesley completed the rest of the Mass in December 1812. To judge by the number of autographs and manuscript copies extant, it was a popular work. Wesley subjects the chant to a variety of treatments for full choir and a variety of solo groupings. A recent performance has shown it to be an attractive work, although inevitably constrained by the sectional nature imposed by the many repetitions of the chant.

For the feast of John the Baptist on 24 June 1812, Wesley composed **Ut queant laxis**, KO 70, a setting of the hymn proper to the occasion. Here he followed the principle of the original Gregorian melody by making each line of the hymn start on a successively higher degree of the scale, from C (ut) to A (la) (Ex. 19.05). This may have been a *jeu d'esprit* that gave Wesley, Novello, and the choir of the Portuguese Embassy chapel (not to mention any musical members of the clergy and congregation) a good deal of innocent amusement, but the setting is also entirely successful in its own right.[7]

---

[7] For Wesley's letter to Novello on the setting, see above, p. 113.

Example 19.05, 'Ut queant laxis', KO 70, bars 1–16

The demands of the chapel also impelled Wesley to revise some earlier compositions. Two weeks after writing his setting of 'Ut queant laxis', he completed a new version of **Ave verum corpus**, KO 17b, in which he recast his 1781 setting for two sopranos and continuo for ATTB by transposing it down a fifth, putting text to the previously untexted bass part, and adding a second tenor part at the end. At the end of March 1813 he composed **Ecce panis angelorum**, KO 33, which he entitled a 'transubstantiatorial hymn'. The text is from Lauda Sion, the Sequence for the Feast of Corpus Christi, but Wesley no doubt intended it for more general use as a communion motet. This sombre piece is probably Wesley's finest hymn setting. As we have seen earlier, it was written in tragic circumstances, immediately following the death of an infant daughter.[8]

Wesley composed two more ambitious pieces during the period, both in 1814. The first is **Tu es sacerdos**, KO 69, written in January: a highly effective setting for SATB of a verse from 'Dixit Dominus' that contains some of Wesley's most daring harmonic writing. The other is **Constitues eos principes**, KO 21, for SSATB, written in November for the Feast of Apostles. These are among Wesley's finest pieces of Latin church music. Although lacking the large

---

[8] See above, p. 134.

scale of 'In exitu Israel', 'Exultate Deo' and the eight-part 'Dixit Dominus' setting, they are equally assured in their handling of counterpoint and tonal contrast and in the richness of their harmonic language. Although there is a modern edition of both works, they remain little known and are unrecorded at the time of writing.

Latin sacred music of the 1820s

Wesley's involvement with the Portuguese Embassy chapel appears to have come to an end with his illness of 1816–17. During his convalescence, he kept away from the Chapel, remarking on one occasion to Novello that he found the music 'too overwhelming' for him to bear, and even after his health began to improve he still appears to have stayed away.[9] In 1821, however, Novello asked him to compose a setting of the Latin text of the Magnificat. Novello no doubt told Wesley that this was for a projected publication, but one suspects that this might have been a polite fiction, and his real aim was to persuade Wesley to start composing again after his long silence. Wesley was glad to comply with Novello's request, but was at this stage woefully lacking in confidence about his abilities as a composer, and feared that his setting would be 'a very poor Job'. When he had finished it, he stated to Novello that it was well if the Magnificat pleased him, as he would never again write anything that pleased himself.[10]

In a letter to Novello, Wesley enquired whether it would be acceptable to compose the Magnificat 'like one of Webbe's, in little Duets & Solos with an occasional Chorus'. He was no doubt thinking here of the setting by Samuel Webbe senior in *A Collection of Music as used in the Chapel of the King of Sardinia* of around 1785 which exactly answers this description. It was also the form that Wesley's own setting takes. The result is a work divided into no fewer than ten sections, for varied solo and full choir groupings. The result is rather short-winded and not entirely successful.

Although Novello resigned his position at the Portuguese Embassy Chapel in April 1824, he appears to have continued his association for some time longer, perhaps until a suitable successor could be found. His departure marked the end of around twenty-eight years of service, during which the music of the chapel had reached a high point that saw the introduction of Masses by Haydn and Mozart to its services, and latterly attracted large numbers of visitors who attended as much for the music as the worship.[11] For much of the time Wesley had also been actively involved, and his music had formed a substantial part of the repertoire. With Novello's resignation, his contact with the chapel ceased. He now had little occasion to write Latin church music, and of the small number of pieces that he did compose, most appear to have been in response

---

[9] *SW to Novello, 29 Aug. [1820].
[10] *SW to Novello, 2 Oct. [1821], 9 Oct. 1821.
[11] See Clarke, *My Long Life*, 11.

to specific requests, from Novello and others, for music for projected publications.

One exception, however, was his **Carmen Funebre (Omnia vanitas)**, KO 54, which Wesley composed in June 1824 in memory of his father, taking for its text some of the last words his father had spoken to him, and expressing to Novello the wish that it should be performed at his own funeral.[12] Given this heavy weight of personal significance, it is not surprising that Wesley's setting is out of the ordinary. It is for SSATTB, in the (for the time) extraordinary key of C♯ minor, and with the economy of thematic material and the mastery of sonorities and vocal textures that we have already noticed in Wesley's large-scale settings. But what marks it out from these earlier works is its extraordinary plangency and intensity of expression and the richness of its harmonic language, apparent from its opening bars (Ex. 19.06).

Example 19.06, *Carmen funebre*, KO 54, bars 1–12

By the time of composition of the *Carmen funebre*, Wesley was fully back in action. Later in the year, Novello asked him to supply a number of compositions for a projected church music publication. Wesley made a revision of his 1781 setting of **Ave regina caelorum**, rescoring it for SSATB but leaving the musical substance unchanged. At the same time he also gave Novello copies of 'Ecce panis angelorum' and some other unidentified pieces.[13]

In June 1827 Wesley composed **Tu es sacerdos II**, KO 69, his second setting of a verse from 'Dixit Dominus' that he had previously used in 1814. The aim, as in the earlier setting, is massive effect, and notwithstanding its extreme brevity (it lasts just over a minute) it shows that Wesley had lost none of his touch in writing effectively for large vocal ensembles. This was probably the piece that Wesley enclosed in a letter to Crotch on the day after its composition,

---

[12] See above, p. 168.
[13] *SW to Novello, 20 Dec. [1824].

describing it as 'a few old-fashioned bars, framed expressly in the Style of those whom you term the "Minority," and with whom I am likely to continue to vote, maugre the fashionable Mania for operatical Adulteration of Church Descant.'[14] He later sold the copyright to Henry Gauntlett, and it was probably this transaction that was the subject of a letter from him to Gauntlett in September 1836, in which he requested 'the other Pound for the Motett'. Gauntlett subsequently arranged the piece to English words as 'He is our God and strong salvation'. Together with the *Carmen funebre*, it was included by Wesley's son Samuel Sebastian in his tract *A Few Words on Cathedral Music* (1849) as an outstanding example of his father's style, and as a proof that 'talent in the highest order of Ecclesiastical Music can exist in modern times'.[15]

English sacred music

Early anthems

Although Wesley did not hold an Anglican church appointment until late in his career, he composed a good deal of Anglican church music over the years. As one might expect, there are some early anthems, chants, and hymn-tunes included among the other pieces in his Pasticcio Book of 1774–5. One of the solo anthems is **Behold, I was shapen in wickedness**, KO 83, a minor-key solo anthem of remarkable intensity on this bleak text from Psalm 51. Among other pieces from this period that are lost is the Jubilate setting that Boyce mistook for one by his brother on a visit to the family home.[16] Another is **O Lord God of hosts**, KO 101, which Barrington stated had sections for solo tenor, treble duet, and full choir, and was performed at St Paul's Cathedral and at the Chapel Royal.[17] And it is the manuscript of another anthem, **I said, I will take heed to my ways**, KO 90, that Wesley is pictured holding in the Russell portrait of 1776.[18] Wesley revised it in 1797, and in this form it was published in John Page's collection *Harmonia Sacra* in 1800.

Various other Anglican anthems, hymns, and other music for services appeared over the years. Some at least may have been written for his brother Charles and for other fellow organists with appointments in Anglican churches. **O Lord God, most Holy**, KO 100, was written in 1800; it is a setting for SATB of verses from the Burial Service that shows Wesley fully aware of the famous setting by Purcell of over a hundred years earlier. From the same year is **This shall be my rest forever**, KO 113, a setting for SATB of verses from Psalm 132. From the following year are **In the multitude of the sorrows**, KO 89, for ATB, and the large-scale SATB **All the earth doth worship thee**, KO 78, a setting of a

---

[14] *SW to Crotch, 7 July 1827.
[15] S. S. Wesley, *A Few Words on Cathedral Music*, p. 77.
[16] See above, p. 15.
[17] Barrington, *Miscellanies*, p. 307.
[18] See Pl. 2 and above, p. 17.

single verse from the Te Deum based on two thematic motifs which Wesley presents at the opening and then works out intensively over 112 bars, in a manner similar to that of his Latin church music of the period.

The Service in F

Rather more is known about Wesley's settings of the canticles for Matins and Evensong, which together make up his **Morning and Evening Service in F**, KO 71. As we have seen earlier, he composed the settings of the Te Deum and Jubilate, the canticles for Matins, in 1808, and they were first performed at St Paul's Cathedral on 30 October and repeated on Christmas Day of the same year.[19] After an interval of fourteen years, and as his first major compositions since his illness, in late 1822 Wesley composed settings of the Magnificat and Nunc Dimittis, the corresponding canticles for Evensong. The complete service was sung at St Paul's in April 1824 and was published by subscription in October of the same year, together with settings of the Responses to the Litany and the Sanctus from the Communion Service, as *A Morning and Evening Church Service for four Voices, with an Accompaniment for the Organ or Piano Forte*.[20]

The Service should be seen in the context of the generally poor state of Anglican church music in the late eighteenth and early nineteenth centuries. For generations, deans and chapters had reduced funds intended for music and choirs were cut down to the minimum. Lay clerks, who were usually appointed for life and could only be dismissed for gross misconduct, were often incompetent and neglectful of their duties; absenteeism was rife, threatening the traditional practice of antiphonal singing and even on occasion the maintenance of four-part harmony. The repertoire consisted largely of undistinguished service settings and anthems of the early eighteenth century that made few demands on the singers. Apart from a few isolated pieces, music from the Tudor and Jacobean repertoire was absent, as were the services and anthems of Purcell. This situation was to continue until well into the nineteenth century, when reforms to cathedral finances and a radical change in attitudes to the place of music in worship led to major improvements.[21]

Compared with most of the cathedral repertory of the time, Wesley's Service is a breath of fresh air. Conceived on a far larger scale than other services of the period, it incorporates repetition of words, frequent passages of imitation, some imaginative use of harmony, and some backward glances to the sixteenth and seventeenth centuries. The 'Gloria Patri' section of the Jubilate (Ex. 19.07) shows its style at its most elaborate.

---

[19] See above, pp. 84, 86.
[20] See above, pp. 167–8, 170–1.
[21] For a survey of Anglican church music during the period, see Nicholas Temperley, 'Music in Church' in Johnstone and Fiske, *The Eighteenth Century*, pp. 358–64, from which much of this paragraph is summarized.

Example 19.07, Morning and Evening Service in F, KO 71, Jubilate, 'Gloria Patri'

As we have seen earlier, Wesley's decision to publish the *Service in F* was a significant step in asserting his full return to health, and its performances at St Paul's and subsequent publication predictably attracted a great deal of attention. After the first performances of the complete Service at St Paul's in April 1824, adverse comments had been made by Attwood and others about the supposed incorrectness of the harmony on the first beat of bar 17 of the 'Gloria Patri' section of the Jubilate quoted above. When the first review of the Service appeared in the *Harmonicon* in January 1825, the same harmony was again singled out for adverse comment, along with the final cadence of the same section, and a passage in the Magnificat.

Wesley's enraged reactions to this and the later review in the *Quarterly Musical Magazine and Review*, and his repeated attempts throughout much of the rest of 1825 to find a newspaper or journal prepared to publish his reply to his critics, have already been discussed. What the incident demonstrates clearly is first, the seriousness with which Wesley regarded his Service, and second, the large amount of controversy that the publication of such a piece could engender.

From the perspective of nearly 180 years later, it is clear that the Service in F was the most important piece of Anglican church music to be published for many years. Its failure to become widely accepted into the repertoire of cathedral choirs probably had more to do with its length, its difficulty for most choirs of the time, and the reluctance of cathedral authorities to lay out money on new music, than on its musical quality. Wesley's son Samuel Sebastian certainly thought highly of it, commenting in the Preface to his own Service in E that he regarded it as 'the most perfect work of a similar nature' to his own. But he revealed elsewhere that only one cathedral had bought copies, and that Ball, the publisher, had subsequently re-used the plates for a set of quadrilles.[22]

Mention should also be made here of a short **Evening Service in G**, KO 72, published in 1897 in a series edited by Charles Vincent and C. W. Pearce, who were organists, professors at Trinity College of Music, and joint editors (with E. J. Hopkins) of *The Organist and Choirmaster*. These settings of the two evening canticles are considerably shorter than those in the Service in F and – unlike in the Service in F – there is a fully independent organ part. A note on the first page stated that the service had been published 'by permission of R. Glenn Wesley, from manuscripts in the possession of Dr Vincent and Dr Pearce'. There is now no trace of these manuscripts, and no references in any of Wesley's letters to the composition of these pieces. A paragraph published in *The Organist and Choirmaster* at around the time of publication sheds some light on the subject. The Magnificat had been originally to Latin words. Its autograph had been for some time in the possession of Vincent, and it had apparently taken little work to adapt it to English words. The Nunc Dimittis, on the other

---

[22] S. S. Wesley, *A few Words on Cathedral Music*, p. 53.

hand, was originally set to English words, and had been discovered by Pearce in one of Wesley's sketch-books.[23]

'All go unto one place', and other late anthems

Wesley composed one notable piece of Anglican church music towards the end of his life: the funeral anthem **All go unto one place**, KO 77, for SATB soloists, choir, and organ, written following the death of his brother Charles in May 1834. This was his last extended composition, and the concert of the Sacred Harmonic Society at Exeter Hall on 7 August 1834 when he accompanied it was the last time he appeared in public. The compilation of the text, from Ecclesiastes, Thessalonians, Wisdom, and I Corinthians, may have been by Wesley himself; the passages from I Corinthians are among those set in *Messiah*, and they may have been chosen partly for this reason, in recognition of Charles's lifelong veneration of Handel. Wesley lays out the anthem for a variety of choral and solo forces. 'All go unto one place, all are of the dust and all turn to dust again', the opening number, is a slow choral movement in D minor for the full choir, on a text from Ecclesiastes, in which Wesley's familiarity with the funeral music of Purcell can clearly be seen. It is followed by a duet for alto and tenor, a duet for two trebles, and a short bass recitative followed by a trio for alto, tenor, and bass. Most of this is in minor keys, but Wesley at last turns to the major in the final choral section at the words 'Death is swallowed up in victory. Thanks be to God, who giveth us the victory through our Lord Jesus Christ.'

'All go unto one place' was not quite Wesley's last piece of Anglican church music, however. In 1834 and 1835 he composed a number of other short anthems which survive only in manuscript. They include **Lord of the earth and heavens sublime**, KO 92, **The Lord is my shepherd**, KO 112, **Mansions of Heav'n, your doors expand**, KO 93, and **O give thanks unto the Lord**, KO 97. All are for one or two treble parts with organ accompaniment and a unison or two-part chorus at the end, suggesting that even at this late stage in his life Wesley had some involvement with a church choir. Some time in 1837 he inscribed a solo anthem, **I will arise and go to my Father**, KO 91, in his daughter Eliza's music book, and in July of the same year, less than three months before his death, composed a second setting of **O give thanks unto the Lord**, KO 98, which he intended – an opportunist to the last – as a coronation anthem for Queen Victoria, who had acceded to the throne a few weeks earlier.

Hymn tunes and chants

Wesley composed a large number of single hymns and chants throughout his career, some of which were published in contemporary hymn books. Probably

---

[23] *The Organist and Choirmaster* 5 (1897–98), p. 19. I am grateful to Peter Horton for drawing this article to my attention.

his best known hymn in his lifetime was **He's blest, whose sins have pardon gained** (BRISTOL or WESLEY), KO 131, one of two hymns he wrote on one day in August 1806 for his friend Matthew Cooke. Cooke included it in his *A Collection of Psalm and Hymn Tunes for the Use of the Lock Hospital* in 1808, and it subsequently appeared in three other collections.[24] Other published tunes were CHELMSFORD, KO 122, in Cooke's *Select Portions of the Psalms of David* (c.1795), ASCENSION, KO 120, in J. S. Holmyard's *The Psalms, Hymns and Miscellaneous Pieces, as sung at the Episcopal Chapel of the London Society for Promoting Christianity amongst the Jews* (before 1823), and HOOKER (**We sing the wise, the gracious plan**) KO 162, in Joseph Major's *A Collection of Sacred Music for Churches & Chapels* (1824 or after). In 1872 Wesley's son Samuel Sebastian included some of these tunes and others in his own compilation *The European Psalmist*.

In addition to conventional hymn tunes such as those listed above, Wesley also composed a number of sacred songs for solo voice and accompaniment and probably intended for private devotional use rather than in church. One fine example is **Might I in thy sight appear**, a setting of 1807 of two verses from his father's hymn 'Saviour, Prince of Israel's Race'.[25] Another is **Gentle Jesus, meek and mild**, KO 128, written in the following year, again to words by his father.[26] Both are intimate and intensely expressive. The words of 'Might I in thy sight appear' had particular personal significance for Wesley, and he later quoted them in a letter to the writer William Hone to express his own feelings of unworthiness before God.[27] Novello was particularly impressed by 'Gentle Jesus', commenting on his own copy that 'this exquisite specimen of Sam Wesley's musical genius is quite a gem of composition. The melody is full of the most energetic Pathos, & passionate expression; the harmonies are of the most refined & masterly description; & the piece, in its entire construction, is worthy of Purcell himself.'

In September 1826 Wesley discovered in the Fitzwilliam Museum, Cambridge, a manuscript containing three tunes by Handel to hymns by his father: 'Sinners, obey the Gospel Word', 'O love divine, how sweet thou art', and 'Rejoice! the Lord is King'. As we have seen earlier, he subsequently published them, first in an edition for melody and bass giving the first verse only of each hymn, and subsequently in an edition for four-part choir and with all the verses included.[28] The first two tunes are not now in general use, but 'Rejoice! The Lord is King' is sung by congregations of every denomination, and its discovery

---

[24] Benjamin Jacob, *National Psalmody* [1817]; Thomas Cahusac, *A Collection of Psalms, Hymns, Chants and Other Pieces, as sung at the Bentinck Chapel, Paddington* (c.1820); and J. S. Holmyard, *The Psalms, Hymns and Miscellaneous Pieces, as sung at the Episcopal Chapel of the London Society for Promoting Christianity amongst the Jews* (before 1823): for further details, see Temperley, *Hymn Tune Index*.
[25] *A Collection of Hymns & Sacred Poems* (1749); *MHB*, p. 348.
[26] *A Collection of Hymns & Sacred Poems* (1742); *MHB*, p. 842; *HS*, p. 738 (with altered words).
[27] *SW to Hone, 18 Aug. 1825.
[28] See above, pp. 192–4.

by Wesley must be considered his single most important contribution to hymnody.

In May 1828 Wesley composed thirty untitled tunes intended for use in Methodist congregations. The collection, entitled **Original Hymn Tunes, Adapted to Every Metre in the Collection by the Rev. John Wesley**, KO 117, was published in July of the same year. One of them, 'Come ye that love the Lord', was later known as RIDGE and under this title was included in *The Methodist Hymn Book* (1933).[29]

Between 1834 and his death in October 1837 Wesley supplied fifty-four original hymns and a further twenty-five arrangements of Gregorian melodies and tunes by other composers for Novello's four-volume compilation *The Psalmist*. Many are individually dated, and eight were written in the last two weeks of Wesley's life, including CESAREA, his last composition, written four days before his death. BETHLEHEM was later known as DONCASTER, and under this title was included in *The Methodist Hymn Book* (1933).[30]

Few of Wesley's hymns achieved any lasting popularity and fewer still have survived in present-day hymnals. RIDGE and DONCASTER, mentioned above, were his only hymns to be included in the *Methodist Hymn Book* (1933),[31] and they are also included in *Hymns and Psalms* (1983), its successor.[32] There are no tunes by Wesley in the *United Methodist Hymnal*, the most generally used Methodist hymnal in the USA, or in *The New English Hymnal* and *Hymns Ancient and Modern Revised*, the two hymnals in widest use in the Church of England.

---

[29] *MHB* 410.
[30] *MHB* 685, 807.
[31] *MHB* 410 (RIDGE) and 685, 807 (DONCASTER).
[32] *HS* 4 (RIDGE) and 306 (ii), 513 (ii) (DONCASTER).

20

Large-scale choral music with orchestra

This chapter discusses Wesley's two boyhood oratorios *Ruth* and *The Death of Abel*, the *Ode to St Cecilia*, and the *Confitebor*. Although the text of the latter is sacred, it is appropriate to discuss it here, together with the two early oratorios and the *Ode to St Cecilia* rather than with Wesley's sacred music, as – like the *Ode to St Cecilia* – it was intended from the first for performance at the Lenten oratorio concerts. The *Missa de Spiritu Sancto*, Wesley's one piece of large-scale church music with orchestra, has been discussed above.

Ruth and *The Death of Abel*

Wesley's first oratorio was *Ruth*, to the text by Haweis that had been set by Giardini and Avison for the Lock Hospital in 1763, and which in its revised version by Giardini alone would be performed annually there from 1768 to 1780. According to Charles Wesley senior's account, Wesley had composed some of the airs at six years old, but was not able to write the music down until he was eight. The dates on the autograph score, from 8 September to 30 November 1774, bear out the second part of this claim, and there is no reason to disbelieve the first, particularly as it is supported (although not in precise terms) by Wesley's own statement in his *Reminiscences*.

The composition of *Ruth* doubtless arose from the occasions during Wesley's childhood when Worgan, Battishill, and Kelway played through oratorios by Handel and others to his elder brother Charles. Wesley would have been present at many of these sessions, quietly paying attention and absorbing everything he heard. In his *Reminiscences*, Wesley remembered how he would frequently improvise oratorio scenes from oratorio word-books, and it would have been a natural step from this to the composition of parts of a complete oratorio. What is remarkable, of course, is his extreme youth at the time and the fact that he was not able to write down what he had composed.

Ruth is an amazing achievement for a child of eight, let alone for one of six. The autograph score, together with other associated fragments, contains all the necessary components of an oratorio, competently put together and showing at the very least an extraordinary skill in pastiche and imitation. The handwriting is untidy, often almost to the point of illegibility, but there is no doubting that

Wesley knew exactly what he wanted to say, even if he sometimes had difficulty in knowing how to write it down.

Wesley's other childhood oratorio was *The Death of Abel*, of which only Acts 2 and 3 are extant. As with *Ruth*, neither the text nor the music of a contemporary English oratorio on this subject has survived, but Wesley presumably took his text from the wordbook either of Arne's lost oratorio *The Sacrifice, or the Death of Abel* (1744) or of an English version of Piccinni's *La morte d'Abel* (also lost) that was performed in London in the seasons of 1768 to 1771. The date of Wesley's setting is uncertain: the overture to Act II is signed and dated 1779, but Wesley's daughter Eliza in her annotation on the autograph of the oratorio proper claimed that the work was written when he was eleven years old (i.e. in 1777 or in the first two months of 1778). Eliza may have been told this by Wesley himself, and for this reason her dating cannot wholly be disregarded, even when allowance is made for Wesley's imprecise memory at the end of his life for dates of events in the distant past. It is possible that the oratorio was written earlier and the overture added later.

Whatever the date of composition, the surviving portions of *The Death of Abel* show a great step forward. Wesley has now mastered musical orthography, and the manuscript is as a result far more legible, although not always very tidy. There is a considerable sense of drama in the interchanges between Abel and his brother Cain, in particular a duet in which Abel repeatedly tries to speak to Cain, and is repeatedly rebuffed by him. There is also an effective coloratura aria, 'Tis the same herb we see', for Abel. The overture, which is a three-movement symphony in all but name, was probably performed separately in the 1780 season of the family concerts, and is separately considered below as a piece of orchestral music.

In addition to *Ruth* and *The Death of Abel*, fragments of an oratorio apparently on the subject of Gideon have survived. There is also the concluding section of an aria and an SATB chorus from a setting of Milton's *Comus*. The words are identical to those used in Arne's setting of 1736, and presumably came, like the words of the other oratorios, from a wordbook that Wesley had found in the house.

The *Ode to St Cecilia*

During the particularly fertile period of the early 1780s, most of Wesley's creative activities were devoted to composing for the family concerts and for the Roman Catholic chapels he attended, both of which provided opportunities for performances of each new composition. As we have seen, the later 1780s and the early 1790s were by contrast almost completely barren of compositions of any kind, but in the second half of 1794, the year after his marriage, Wesley briefly returned to composition. The major work of this period was a setting of the *Ode to St Cecilia* by his grandfather and namesake, written one hundred years earlier.

Although not formally titled an oratorio, the *Ode to St Cecilia* would undoubtedly have been regarded as such by contemporary audiences, who used the term loosely to refer to any large-scale secular work for soloists, choir, and orchestra, particularly those that were performed at the annual Lenten oratorio concerts at Covent Garden and Drury Lane theatres, and at provincial music festivals. They would certainly have referred in this way to Handel's *Ode for St Cecilia's Day*, the work to which own Wesley's *Ode* is most closely related.

The *Ode to St Cecilia* was Wesley's largest secular choral work to date, involving three vocal soloists, chorus, and orchestra. With a playing length of just over an hour, it was of an appropriate length for one act or part of an oratorio concert. Nothing is known of the circumstances of its composition, but the most plausible assumption is that it was written with performance at an oratorio concert in mind, probably in the 1795 Covent Garden season. If this was the case, Wesley was for the moment disappointed, as it was not performed then, and had to wait until 1799 for its première.

As a setting of an ode to the patron saint of music, the *Ode to St Cecilia* continues a tradition that began in the lifetime of Purcell, when such pieces were performed annually on 22 November, the feast day of St Cecilia.[1] One hundred years later, however, these performances had long fallen into abeyance. On the other hand, Wesley would have known Handel's settings of two odes to St Cecilia by Dryden that had originally been set by other composers in the 1680s and 1690s: *Alexander's Feast* (1736) and the *Ode for St Cecilia's Day* (1739).[2] Of the two, the *Ode for St Cecilia's Day*, generally known at this time simply as 'Dryden's Ode', was the more frequently performed, and appeared in most oratorio seasons, either paired with *Alexander's Feast* (and thus making up a whole programme of works on St Cecilia) or with *L'Allegro*.

Wesley's *Ode to St Cecilia* has marked similarities to Handel's 1739 *Ode* in its verbal text, its character, and its overall playing length. Samuel Wesley senior appears to have known Dryden's poem, as he echoes it at several points, most strikingly at 'What passions can'st thou calm / What courage canst thou raise', which is almost a quotation from Dryden's 'What passion cannot music raise or quell?'. Mercifully, the quality is higher than in some of his other verse – he was pilloried by Pope in the 1728 edition of *The Dunciad* for his ineptitude as a poet[3] – but it is nonetheless far inferior to that of Dryden. The layout of the work is broadly similar to that of Handel's *Ode*. After the overture there are eleven movements (as against twelve in Handel), disposed for chorus and for the three soloists as solos, duets, and trios.

The *Ode to St Cecilia* was Wesley's first large-scale work for public performance, and so it is not surprising to find a marked change from the style of the music written for the family concerts. Wesley is now writing for the full orchestral forces of the Covent Garden oratorio concerts rather than for the

---

[1] For the historical background, see Husk, *An Account of the Musical Celebrations on St Cecilia's Day*.
[2] The original setting of Dryden's *Alexander's Feast* was by Jeremiah Clarke (1697: lost). That of the *Song for St Cecilia's Day* was by Giovanni Battista Draghi (1687).
[3] Pope, *The Dunciad*, line 115.

tiny instrumental ensemble that was all the music room at Chesterfield Street and the concert budget could accommodate: oboes, bassoons, horns, trumpets, drums and strings. Wesley writes effectively and idiomatically for these, with particularly full parts and many solos for the woodwind. After an attractive two-movement overture (discussed with Wesley's orchestral music below), the *Ode* proper begins with a short accompanied recitative, immediately followed by 'Numbers, Cecilia' a lengthy movement for soprano solo and chorus. The following movement, 'Music and thou, fair saint', is a duet for soprano and alto soloists. As in the preceding movement, the tempo is leisurely and the mood relaxed, with a long opening ritornello and a good deal of writing in parallel thirds and sixths for the soloists. This is followed by 'Hark, hark, Arion sweeps the sounding string', an accompanied recitative for alto with violin solo that celebrates the exploits of Arion, who rode on dolphins, charmed the sirens, and disarmed the rage of Neptune. The next movement, 'How various, Music, is thy praise', is a rather austere trio for soprano, alto, and bass soloists that celebrates music's power to inspire courage and to calm the passions. Another accompanied recitative, 'With what a natural art', this time for alto, continues the same theme, before leading into a reprise of the trio. The power of music in time of war is celebrated by an accompanied recitative and the bravura aria 'See all the hills' for the bass soloist, the aria making full use of trumpets and drums and inevitably recalling 'The trumpet's loud clangour' from Handel's setting of Dryden's ode. The mood becomes calm once more with the lengthy soprano aria 'When, heav'nly peace, wilt thou descend and tune the world again?', set as a gentle Siciliano. Two choruses, 'Tis here a sacred vestal' and 'Io, triumph! sing and play', celebrate Cecilia's ascent to heaven, and bring the work to a close.

The *Ode to St Cecilia* is an attractive work and an important precursor to the *Confitebor*, Wesley's *magnum opus* of five years later. As his first large-scale exercise in secular choral music and his first work involving an orchestra since the mid-1780s, it is inevitably of great importance in charting his development as a composer. In addition, it shows him writing for the first time for a full orchestra, instead of the very limited instrumental forces available to him at the time of the family concerts. And it is the felicity of the scoring, particularly for the wind instruments, that is one of the most striking features of the work. In overall structure the *Ode to St Cecilia* is not entirely successful, however. Despite Wesley's attempts at contrasts of mood, too many of the movements jog along at much the same slow or slowish tempo, and in much the same relaxed and leisurely way. In addition, many of the individual movements are vastly over-extended for their material, and with large amounts of repetition of both words and music. Whatever the merits of this work, conciseness is not one of them.

The *Confitebor*

According to Wesley, the *Ode to St Cecilia* was well received at its one performance at Covent Garden in February 1799, and its success appears to have spurred him on to further activity on the oratorio front. The result was a setting of the Vesper Psalm 'Confitebor tibi, Domine, toto corde meo' ('I Will give thanks unto the Lord with my whole heart'). The choice of a biblical text in Latin was unprecedented for a work intended for the Lenten oratorio concerts, but there can be little doubt that Wesley intended it for them, and it is therefore most appropriately discussed here, rather than among Wesley's Latin sacred music written for liturgical use in the embassy chapels.

No more is known about the circumstances of composition of the *Confitebor* than for those of the *Ode to St Cecilia*, but its date of completion (14 August 1799) suggests that Wesley was hoping for a performance in the 1800 season of Lenten oratorios, to follow the successful performance there of the *Ode to St Cecilia* the previous year. As we have seen earlier, it is possible that arrangements were made for a first performance then, but that these were then superceded to make way for the first English performances of Haydn's *Creation* at the end of the 1800 oratorio season.

The *Confitebor* lasts around an hour, is scored for a full complement of vocal soloists, chorus, and orchestra, and is divided into ten individual movements. In broad general outline, it is thus not markedly dissimilar from the *Ode to St Cecilia*. In a paragraph for the *Examiner* written over twenty-five years later, Wesley described it as 'a judicious mixture of the ancient and more modern church music', except for one soprano aria introduced for the sake of variety, which was a 'completely Italian bravura'.[4] In structuring the work in this way, he was playing to the tastes of his intended audience, for whom the oratorios of Handel formed the core of their listening experience, but for whom the music of J. C. Bach, Abel, and latterly Clementi, Dussek, and Haydn would also have been familiar.

Well-chosen variation is an essential part of the *Confitebor*: not just between the older and more modern styles, but also in the scoring. Wesley writes for a classical orchestra of double woodwind without clarinets, but is careful to vary his scoring throughout the work, and to give each movement its own characteristic tone colour and character. As part of this strategy, some instruments are not used at the beginning but are held in reserve until later in the work, thus maximizing their effect when they do eventually appear. The horns are silent until the soprano solo 'Fidelia omnia', more than half-way through the work, while the trumpets make a brief but telling appearance at the climax of the chorus 'Virtutem operum suorum annuntiabit populo suo', and then remain silent until the jubilant final chorus.

There is no overture, its function being taken instead by the extended opening ritornello of the first movement, a setting in G major of the first verse of the psalm. Perhaps surprisingly, given the conventions of the oratorio genre and the mood of the text ('I will give thanks unto the Lord with my whole heart') this is not a rousing chorus but a gentle solo quartet with attractive pastoral writing for flutes and bassoons in thirds, recalling similar passages in

---

[4] *Examiner*, 14 Aug. 1825.

the *Ode to St Cecilia*. The second movement, 'Magna opera Domini' ('The works of the Lord are great') introduces the chorus. With its striding main theme and the massiveness of some of the choral writing, this is a movement which looks back to Handelian traditions through the eyes of a later age, much as Mozart does in parts of the Mass in C Minor, K 427/417a and the Requiem, and Haydn in parts of the *Creation, The Seasons,* and his late Masses. The next number, 'Confessio et magnificentia' ('His work is worthy to be praised') is a bravura bass aria in G minor of the most taxing sort. The principal bass soloist in the 1799 Covent Garden season was James Bartleman, and Wesley may well have written this aria, with its many extended runs and its exceptionally wide range of almost two octaves from G to f′, with his voice specifically in mind. The following movement, 'Memoriam fecit mirabilium suorum' ('The merciful and gracious Lord hath so done his marvellous works') is a complete contrast. With its flutes and bassoons in thirds and sixths, the mood and key return to the quiet pastoralism of the opening. Against this background Wesley sets a harmonization of a Gregorian psalm-tone.

After a short tenor recitative and aria in D major for the tenor soloist, the chorus 'Virtutem operum suorum annuntiabit populo suo' ('He has shewed his people the power of his works') follows. This is a starkly powerful movement in D minor, using a texture of almost continuous unison semiquavers in the strings, against which the chorus sings in predominantly block chords in crotchets and quavers, starting quietly and building to an impressive climax with the introduction for the first time in the work of the trumpets and drums. In the boldness of its gestures and its arresting texture it is very Handelian, recalling moments in *Israel in Egypt* and *Dixit Dominus*, but it is completely original in its detailed conception, and its unexpected quiet ending is utterly characteristic of Wesley. A short recitative now leads into the soprano aria 'Fidelia omnia mandata ejus' ('He has shewed his people the power of his works'), the movement that Wesley later described as 'a completely Italian bravura'. It is an immensely long and taxing piece in B♭, using an exceptionally wide range of over two octaves from b♭ to c‴. The principal soprano soloist in Wesley's *Ode to St Cecilia* performance in early 1799 had been Gertrud Elisabeth Mara, who was famed for her vocal range of almost three octaves, and Wesley no doubt wrote the aria with her voice in mind. Some years later, probably in the summer of 1809, he gave it to Elizabeth Billington to try. She sang it at sight virtually without any mistakes, and was so delighted with it that she proposed to perform it at a forthcoming meeting of the Three Choirs Festival at Worcester. Orchestral parts were prepared but it was never performed, for reasons that Wesley darkly alleged had to do with musical politics.[5] 'Fidelia omnia' is nothing less than a show-stopper. Wesley no doubt hoped that it would be taken up as a free-standing concert item by those few sopranos who could negotiate its considerable difficulties, to join such well-established showpieces as 'The soldier, tir'd of war's alarms' from Arne's *Artaxerxes* and 'Let the bright

[5] Ibid..

seraphim' from Handel's *Samson*. With its leisurely opening and closing ritornellos, its extended passages of coloratura and its exceptionally wide leaps, it is likely to remind the modern listener most closely of some of Mozart's most florid operatic arias, notably 'Martern aller Arten' from *Die Entführung* and 'Come scoglio' from *Così fan tutte*, or (to take an example from his church music), the 'Laudamus te' from the Gloria of the C Minor Mass (Ex. 20.01). In its tonal colouring, it is differentiated from the movements that precede it by the introduction for the first time in the work of prominent parts for the two horns.

The following duet for soprano and alto, 'Redemptionem misit populo suo', is short and gentle, featuring many passages in thirds and sixths for the two soloists, bringing to mind the opening of the work. If it seems reminiscent of Wesley's Latin church music compositions of the 1780s, it is perhaps because it is adapted and expanded from the 'Suscepit Israel' section of his Magnificat setting of 1783. In the following chorus, 'Mandavit in aeternum testamentum suum' ('He hath sent redemption unto his people') Wesley returns to G minor. The writing of the first section is marked 'a cappella', indicating that the orchestra doubles the voice parts rather than having independent lines of its own. It is an imposing and austere movement based with characteristic economy on two short motifs. It is extended to enormous length, with wide-ranging modulations to keys as distant as E minor and F♯ minor, culminating in a highly dramatic ending in which the a cappella texture is abandoned: a general pause is followed by a two-bar unaccompanied timpani crescendo that leads into a fortissimo block-chord statement of 'Sanctum et terribile nomen eius ('Holy and terrible is his name'), the final line of text. (Ex. 20.02)

In the tenor aria 'Initium sapientiae timor Domini' ('The fear of the Lord is the beginning of wisdom') Wesley uses oboes as solo instruments for the first time: they previously appeared unobtrusively doubling the voices in the previous number. This is another bravura piece, the tenor soloist's counterpart to 'Confessio et magnificentia' and 'Fidelia omnia', taking him up to B♭' at one point, and with a cruelly high overall tessitura. The principal tenor in the 1799 Covent Garden company was Charles Incledon, and the part was probably written with his voice in mind. Other points to note are the attractive solo writing for the flutes, oboes, and bassoons, and another of Wesley's trademark quiet endings.

In the trio 'Laudatio eius manet in saeculum saeculi' ('The praise of it endureth for ever') for the alto, tenor, and bass soloists, Wesley introduces the full wind chorus of flutes oboes, bassoons, and horns. With the final two movements he returns to the chorus and to his original tonic, first minor, then major. In the first, 'Gloria patri, et filio, et spiritui sancto' ('Glory be to the Father, and to the Son, and to the Holy Ghost'), Wesley sets a Gregorian psalm-tone in massive block chords against an accompaniment of detached string quavers. The final movement, 'Sicut erat in principio, et nunc, et semper, Amen' ('As it was in the beginning, is now, and ever shall be, Amen'), returns to the major of the opening to bring the work to a triumphant conclusion.

Example 20.01 *Confitebor*, KO 20, 'Fidelia omnia', bars 224–32: coloratura writing

Example 20.02 *Confitebor*, KO 20, 'Mandavit in aeternum', bars 279–95

Wesley regarded the *Confitebor* as his finest work. In October 1821, in the midst of the debilitating period of depression that followed his breakdown of four years earlier, he commented to Novello that he considered that it was 'the least incorrect of my musical Scrolls, and *might* have had a Chance of becoming profitable (if published) to some of my unfortunate Progeny, when my Carcase shall be in the Churchyard'.[6] In 1825 and 1826 he attempted to publish the work by subscription, and on 4 May 1826 it received its first and only performance in Wesley's lifetime, with Mary Anne Paton, John Braham, and Henry Phillips as principal soloists. Samuel Sebastian made plans – in vain, as it turned out – to perform it at the 1834 Hereford meeting of the Three Choirs Festival, possibly with Novello's daughter Clara, then at the very beginning of her career, singing 'Fidelia omnia'. At around the same time, Wesley attempted to sell the copyright, but was unable to find anyone prepared to give him what he considered a fair price. In the year after his death there was another attempt to publish it by subscription, but this too came to nothing. Samuel Sebastian was finally able to mount a performance of parts of the work at the 1868

---

[6] *SW to Novello, 9 Oct. 1821.

Gloucester meeting of the Three Choirs Festival with Therese Tietjens singing 'Fidelia omnia' and Charles Santley 'Confessio et magnificentia'. After that, the work languished unperformed until June 1972, when it received its second complete performance, in York Minster, followed in January 1973 by a performance at the Queen Elizabeth Hall in London. The availability of performance materials now made subsequent performances a good deal easier, and in 1978 the full score was published as a volume in the *Musica Britannica* series. Although there have been a number of subsequent performances, some of them broadcast, the work still remains comparatively little known at the time of writing, and there is no commercial recording.

Few would dissent from Wesley's own judgement of the worth of the *Confitebor*, and it must be considered his finest work. Its combination of styles is finely judged, and the command of overall structure, both in individual movements and overall, is highly assured. The *Confitebor* stands as a worthy companion to Haydn's *Creation* and *The Seasons* as an outstanding oratorio of the period.

21

Secular vocal music

Glees and part songs

Wesley wrote over a hundred pieces of secular vocal music, ranging from unaccompanied glees and part songs to solo songs and duets with keyboard, and occasionally instrumental, accompaniment. They date from every part of his career, from his childhood to the last months of his life. Very few were published in his lifetime, or have appeared since. Roughly half are glees and part songs, the remainder being solo songs and duets.

Despite their large number, the glees and part songs form only a comparatively small part of Wesley's output, and composing such pieces was never one of his main preoccupations. Neither was his output large when compared with that of specialist glee composers such as Callcott, Stevens, Horsley, and Samuel Webbe the Elder, each of whom wrote well over a hundred examples, of which a large proportion were published. His choice of texts reflected the eclecticism and catholicity of his literary tastes, being drawn from members of his family, from classical Greek and Latin (either in the original or in translation), from English literature of all periods, including Akenside, Beaumont and Fletcher, Chatterton, Dryden, Gray, Hawkesworth, Peter Pindar (i.e. John Wolcot), Pope, Southey, Thomson, and Young, and from his own circle of friends.

During Wesley's lifetime, the glee was a particularly popular form in England and enormous numbers were written, a large proportion by composers who specialized in the genre and often wrote little else. David Baptie, the principal nineteenth-century historian and cataloguer of the genre, estimated around 1885 that nearly 23,000 glees and part-songs had been published since 1750, and that an equal number remained unpublished.[1] The glee was particularly associated with the all-male glee and catch clubs that flourished in London and other urban centres, in which members came together to dine and to sing glees afterwards in conditions of relaxed conviviality. But glees were also performed in the home, in the masonic lodge, and at public concerts. The subject-matter, like that of the English madrigal of the sixteenth and early seventeenth centuries, of which the glee was a descendant, varied from the religious, philosophical, and moralistic to the satirical and topical, the humorous, the risqué, the mildly indecent, and on occasion the downright obscene.

---

[1] Baptie, *Sketches of the English Glee Composers*; *New Grove*, s.v. 'Glee'.

Although most glees, reflecting the circumstances in which they were typically performed, were for male voices, there were many that called on female voices for their upper parts and were evidently designed for domestic performance. Predictably, the texts of such glees are more genteel than those written for all-male performance.

A range of vocal idioms was also used. At its most straightforward, a glee might be no more than a simple strophic setting of its text as a melody and accompaniment in note-against-note style; more ambitious examples involved greater or lesser amounts of imitative writing. Such glees tended to be through-composed and divided into a number of sections, to reflect the mood and meaning of different sections of the text. The same principle operated at a more detailed level, the meanings of individual words or phrases being represented in the music by harmony or vocal line, in ways that are familiar from the use of similar techniques in the English madrigal.

Glees and part songs of the early 1780s

Short pieces of secular vocal music were among Wesley's earliest compositions. Included in Wesley's Pasticcio Book of 1774–5 are two catches, **Three bulls and a bear**, KO 243, and **Whoes there? A granidier** [sic], KO 256. From the early 1780s there are nine glees, all contained in a group of four related autograph manuscripts, together with vocal solos and duets and Latin sacred vocal music of the period. From Wesley's choice of clefs for the upper parts (the treble clef throughout, rather than the mezzo-soprano, alto, or tenor clefs) it is clear that he intended them to be sung by female voices: a sonority that is close to some of his Latin sacred music of the period. Most of the texts, not surprisingly, are genteel and suitable to be sung in mixed company. A notable feature is the generally high tessitura of the soprano writing, no doubt reflecting the character of the voices of the individual singers for whom he was writing.

There is only one four-part glee in this group. **Circle the bowl with freshest roses**, KO 213, an accomplished setting for SSAB of an unidentified text in Anacreontic vein.[2] With its three well-contrasted sections, its lightness of touch, and its sure-footed combination of homophony and undemanding imitative writing, it is a glee in the classic mould. The rest of the glees are for three voices. Two are described by Wesley as 'serious' glees, a designation that applies primarily to the character of the texts. **Adieu, ye sweet scenes of delight**, KO 206, is a straightforward and unpretentious strophic setting in note-against-note style of an unidentified poem on lost love. **Thou happy wretch**, KO 242, is another matter, however, exploiting some poignant chromaticism to express the stark message of its text, from Young's *Night Thoughts*:

---

[2] 'While Prussia's warlike monarch blusters', erroneously listed in *SWSB* as a separate work, is in fact a later part of this glee.

Thou happy wretch! By blindness art thou blest
By dotage dandled to perpetual smiles.
Know, smiler! at thy peril art thou pleas'd;
Thy pleasure is the promise of thy pain.
Misfortune, like a creditor severe,
But rises in demand for her delay;
She makes a scourge of past prosperity,
To sting thee more, and double thy distress.

Harsh and untuneful are the notes, KO 218, is a setting of Mrs Slawkenberg's ballad in Sterne's *Tristram Shandy*. The opening is characteristically Wesleyan in its boldness, but also very much in accordance with the genre's preoccupation with word-painting. It is a particularly attractive and elegant setting in its combination of homophony with more imitative writing.

Example 21.01, 'Harsh and untuneful are the notes', KO 218, bars 1–12

Other pieces are more light-hearted. **Nella casa troverete**, KO 227, is a macaronic piece, said to have been written at an inn, which mixes Italian, French, Latin, and English words to humorous effect: 'Nella casa troverete tout ce que pouvez souhaiter[:] vinum, panem, pisces, carnes, coaches, chaises, horses, harness' ('In the inn you will find all that you can wish: wine, bread, fish, meat, coaches, chaises, horses, harness'). **There are by fond mama supplied**, KO 241, to words by Wesley's father, is a humorous piece discussing the various reasons why the young Samuel should not go out riding, the text adapted from Henry Aldrich's well-known 'Reasons for Drinking'. The *Vocal Magazine*, a compilation of the words of over 1,200 pieces of vocal music that appeared in 1781, supplied the text for **When Orpheus went down to the region below**, KO 252, a facetious version of the story of Orpheus and Euridice that Wesley sets in several sections to bring out its humour.

The most surprising piece is **When first thy soft lips**, KO 250. The anonymous text, although mild enough to modern eyes, is a very long way from the generalized expressions of love and loss that are typical of many of

Wesley's other glees and songs of this period, and must have appeared shockingly direct to delicate sensibilities at the time:

> When first thy soft lips I but civilly prest
> Oh Anna, how great was my bliss
> The fatal contagion ran quick to my breast
> I lost my poor heart with a kiss
> And when I'm supremely thus blest with your sight
> I scarce can my transport restrain
> I wish and I pant to repeat the delight
> And kiss you again and again.
>
> In raptures I wish to enjoy
> All those charms still stealing from favor to favor
> And now O ye gods let me fly to your arms
> And kiss you for ever and ever.

Wesley's treatment of the text, with its many repetitions of 'I pant to repeat the delight and kiss you again and again', and 'let me fly to your arms and kiss you for ever and ever', does nothing to lessen its impact.

The straightforward setting of the nursery rhyme **Goosy goosy gander**, KO 216, is the only item from this collection to have been published at the time, Wesley stating on the autograph that it was composed around 1778 and that he had been obliged to publish it as so many unauthorized and inaccurate manuscript copies had been circulated.

'Qualem ministrum'

As far from these predominantly short and unpretentious works as the *Missa de spiritu sancto* is from Wesley's Latin church music of the period is his six-part setting of Horace's ode **Qualem ministrum**, KO 234. By no stretch of the imagination could this immense piece be called a glee. For six voices (designated SSAABB, although the two alto parts would be more effectively taken in modern performance by tenors), and lasting for almost forty minutes, 'Qualem ministrum' is unique in the repertory of English vocal music of this period in its scale and seriousness. The background to the composition of this ode and its general features have been discussed earlier.[3] Wesley's setting matches the epic quality of the text in its grandeur and boldness of conception. He makes full use of the range of possibilities of his six-part texture: there are massive full passages in block harmony, a good deal of dense imitation, contrasts between groupings of high and low voices, and striking passages in octaves. Wesley takes care to vary the tempos, textures, and moods of the many sections into which the long text divides.

'Qualem ministrum' is one of Wesley's grandest conceptions, and is almost completely unknown. There is no record of it ever having been performed in

---

[3] See above, pp. 31–2.

public in Wesley's lifetime, and apart from a sole broadcast performance by John Lubbock and the BBC Singers in 1985 (fortunately preserved in the National Sound Archive), it does not appear to have been performed since. It awaits rediscovery by an ambitious solo vocal group or chamber choir, for whom it would present a worthwhile challenge and an exciting addition to their repertory.

Glees and part songs of 1797–1802

When Wesley returned to composition in 1797, it was as an adult, and not as the home-based adolescent of the early 1780s. He was now of an age to participate in London glee clubs, where he would have no doubt found a ready welcome. But as we have seen earlier, his involvement in the formally constituted glee clubs appears to have been limited and he seems to have composed most of his glees and part-songs of this period for more informal occasions. Nonetheless, as we have seen earlier, on occasion he attended meetings of the Society of Harmonists, the Concentores Society, and the Madrigal Society as a visitor. At a meeting of the Concentores that he attended in November 1800 two of his glees ('The Macedon youth', KO 240, and 'While others, Delia, use their pen', KO 254), were performed, and on a subsequent visit six years later his recently composed three-part setting of 'Dixit Dominus', KO 27, was sung. Wesley was evidently highly amused by this second visit, afterwards describing it to his brother Charles:

> My Invitation thither was as a Visitor only, from [James] *Elliott* (Master Elliott in Days of yore) who is a very amiable sensible Man, & I need not say much to you of his Skill and Taste in singing.– What will I think amuse you in the present Instance is, that at the *broaching* of this Dixit Dns were aiding and assisting Messrs *Harrison* & Greatorex, together with Stevens, Callcott, *little Master Tommy* [Attwood], cum *septem* aliis quæ nunc præscribere longum est ['with seven others it would take too long to enumerate']. In fine, the Verse made a great *Splash*, or as the English *French* Phrase is, a great Sensation. Old Horsefall was Bawler Maximus, as usual, & he was so transported that I feared he would be seized with some mortal Spasm or other, which (as I want no more Deaths laid at my Door) I was glad to find averted.[4]

At a later stage, Wesley was a 'perpetual visitor' of the Glee Club and acted as its regular pianist. In an article in the *Musical World* published shortly after Wesley's death, John Parry remembered that Wesley 'used to delight the company with his matchless execution of Sebastian Bach's Fugues on the pianoforte, or an extemporaneous effusion on a given subject, frequently some conspicuous passage in a glee recently sung.'[5] Wesley resigned from the club in December 1823, explaining to Richard Clark, the secretary, that he could no longer make an effective contribution as a singer, and that in his old age he

---

[4] *SW to Charles Wesley jun., 15 Jan. 1807.
[5] John Parry, 'The Glee Club', *MW*, 1 March 1838.

had grown 'a little weary of musical Chords in the shape of Glees'.[6] To Novello, however, he was more forthright:

> I forbear with the Glee Club in future to dine
> Tho' the Members are all so respectable
> Bad singing, bad Viands, false Friends, & bad Wine
> Are to me (I confess) not delectable.[7]

The glees of 1797–1802 are a very mixed bag, ranging from the serious to the lighthearted and the mildly indecent. Wesley now usually writes almost exclusively for male voices: a typical combination is ATB or AAB, the alto parts covering much the same range that we have noted in connection with the sacred music, and evidently intended for the same voice type. **Roses, their sharp spines being gone**, KO 235, written in 1798, apparently for a Glee Club competition, is a short setting for SSB of a verse from the song that opens Beaumont and Fletcher's *The two Noble Kinsmen*. Perhaps in fulfilment of the rules of the competition (about which nothing more is known), it is deliberately archaic in style, with an almost unvarying metrical pattern and a complete lack of the other usual features of the glee.

Beneath these shrubs, KO 209, is a heartfelt and dark-textured epitaph for ATB on a favourite dog, dating from 1800. **The Macedon youth**, KO 240, is one of the two pieces that were sung at the meeting of the Concentores that Wesley attended in November 1800, and was quite possibly written specifically for the occasion. Described as a 'brisk part song', it is a cheerful exhortation to abstain from deep contemplation and to devote the time to drinking instead. The other piece sung on this occasion, **While others, Delia, use their pen**, KO 254, was composed earlier in the year; it is a setting of a poem in *An Asylum for Fugitive Pieces*, a collection of humorous poetry and prose by a variety of predominantly undistinguished amateur hands. Titled 'The Rights of Man: An Address to a Lady', it alludes to Thomas Paine's famous work of 1791 and 1792, but for very different purposes.

> While others, Delia, use their pen
> To vindicate the rights which they defend:
> Those eyes, that glow with Love's own Fire
> And what they speak, so well inspire
> That melting Hand, that heaving Breast
> That rises only to be prest;
> That Ivory Neck, those Lips of Bliss,
> Which half invite the willing kiss.
> These! these and Love approves the Plan
> I deem the dearest Rights of Man.

More serious, but no more elaborate, is **The glories of our birth and state**, KO 239, a simple strophic setting for SATB of 1799 of Shirley's well-known poem.

---

[6] *SW to Clark, [c. 4 December 1823] (draft).
[7] Enclosed with *SW to Novello, [?4 Dec. 1823].

The style is note-against-note throughout, but it is highly effective in its use of chromatic harmony. **Happy the man, and happy he alone**, KO 217 is a short and straightforward setting for three male voices of four lines from one of Dryden's translations of Horace, starting off chordally and going on to some small amounts of imitation.

> Happy the Man, and happy he alone,
> He, who can call to day his own:
> He, who secure within, can say
> To morrow do thy worst, for I have liv'd to day.

Wesley appears to have been fond of setting such moralizing or 'improving' poems. In August 1799 he set Southey's recently published 'You are old, Father William', subtitled 'The old man's comforts, and how he procured them', in which Father William is repeatedly questioned by a young man about the reasons for his continuing good health, explaining that it is the result of living a pious life. The poem is now, of course, known principally through its parody in *Alice's Adventures in Wonderland* and in consequence is difficult to take seriously on its own terms. Wesley sets it in complete seriousness for ATB as **You are old, father Dennis**, KO 258; the name of the old man is the only element of the poem that is changed. Another setting of a moralizing poem is **Tobacco's but an Indian weed**, KO 245, also from 1800 and for ATB. The text had first appeared in D'Urfey's *Wit and Mirth; or, Pills to purge Melancholy* (1699–1700), but Wesley had probably obtained it from the *Vocal Magazine*, where it had later appeared:

> Tobacco's but an Indian weed,
> Grows green at morn, cut down at eve,
> It shews our decay, we are but clay
> Think of this when you smoke tobacco

There are four more verses in the same vein, which Wesley sets strophically and with grim humour. When this piece was published, it was not in conventional form, but as a single-page facsimile of Wesley's autograph manuscript, complete with signature and date.

Among Wesley's glees of this period, pride of place must go to **Father of Light and Life (Invocation to the Deity)**, KO 214, an extended setting for SATB of lines from Thomson's *The Seasons*, composed in 1801. Wesley thought sufficiently highly of it to include it in a number of his own concerts, and its generalized religious words made it suitable for inclusion in selections of sacred music. It was the only piece by Wesley to be performed at a Philharmonic Society concert, and was published in 1820. Its greater length and its scoring for SATB rather than for an all-male combination suggests that Wesley may have intended it from the start as a concert piece. The opening section immediately proclaims its serious tone; it is followed by an imitative Andante con moto section in C minor ('Save me from folly, from vanity and vice, from every low pursuit / And feed my soul with knowledge'), leading to a largely chordal final section ('Conscious peace and virtue pure, Sacred substantial never-fading bliss').

Other glees from this period continue a long tradition of celebrating the joys of drinking. One is **Mihi est propositum**, KO 226, a setting of a well known drinking song in Latin by the twelfth-century Welsh cleric Walter Map. **Hilaroi piomen oinon**, KO 220, is more extended: a setting in Greek of an ode by Anacreon in which the first two lines ('Whilst our joys with wine we raise, / Youthful Bacchus we will praise') form a rondo-like refrain.

Some of the glees of this period are parodies, often with a topical slant. **Blushete ne Carolos**, KO 211, a parody of Horace, is aimed at the politician Charles James Fox. In Horace's ode,[8] the poet's friend Xanthias is assured that he need not be ashamed of his love for his servant girl. In this version, by Wesley's friend Martin Madan (the son and namesake of Wesley's godfather), Fox is assured that he need not blush for his association with 'Parson' John Horne Tooke:

> Nay hang it, Charles, don't dread the Scorn
> Of shaking Hands with Parson Horne,
> For tho' at Parsons you may scoff,
> He long has had his Gown stript off,
> And Mobs on Hustings has harang'd
> (Arrraign'd & try'd but not yet hang'd)
> Then let Rebellion hail the Morn
> When you shook Hands with Parson Horne.

It is not this verse but an 'anglo-graecized' version of it that Wesley sets, in deliberately long-winded and pedantic vein, causing Novello to comment that it was 'one of the most exquisite burlesques ever composed, independently of its rare merit as a piece of admirable, masterly counterpoint.'[9]

Horace is again parodied in **Integer Penis**, KO 224, a parody in Latin of 'Integer vitae, sceleri purus', one of Horace's most venerated odes, often read as a declaration of high moral principles. Once again, Martin Madan was responsible for the text. The opening of Horace's ode asserts that the man who is of faultless life and is innocent of crime has no need of 'the Moorish javelins or the bow and quiver, with its clutch of poisoned darts'. In Madan's parody, it is the man who is 'integer penis, veneris purus' (i.e. free of venereal disease) who is the subject of the poem: he has no need of 'Velno's Vegetable Syrup or Brodumus's Cordial' – presumably two proprietary medicines of the time – or of any preparations of mercury. The text goes on to refer to the musical skills of Cramer (presumably the pianist John Baptist, although possibly his violinist brother Francis), who is described as 'skilful with strings and experienced with the lyre, with his flying fingers and muddled demisemidemi-semiquavers'. This is set to a melody and accompaniment of impeccable classical elegance that might have come straight from Haydn or Mozart.

---

[8] Book 2, Ode 4.
[9] BL, Add. MS 14343, fol. 35.

Indeed, one of its phrases is virtually identical to a cadential phrase in Haydn's *Creation*, but whether this is a coincidence or a deliberate quotation is impossible to tell.

'Integer penis' is a miniature of less than twenty bars. Like the previous piece, its humour operates on several levels: as a parody of Horace, as a piece of topical satire, and in the incongruity of the combination of the text and the music. It is difficult to imagine it being composed for a meeting of a glee club, or being well received there. Its true context, and that of other comparable pieces, must have been one of the many musical evenings described in several of Wesley's letters of around this time, which lasted well into the night and involved the consumption of large amounts of wine.

Later glees and part songs

Wesley composed some further glees and part-songs on his return to creativity around 1806, but fewer during his busiest period between around 1813 and 1816 – probably because he was too busy with other activities – and very few from the 1820s, after his recovery from illness. Of the glees composed from 1806 on, most appear to have been coterie pieces, one-offs probably written for performance at private gatherings and not intended for performance elsewhere, let alone for publication. An exception, however, and perhaps the finest work from this period, is **What bliss to life can autumn yield?**, KO 247, composed in 1807. The text, thought at this time to be by Samuel Johnson, is in fact by John Hawkesworth. This is a glee in the classic manner, with the music carefully matched to the meaning of the words, and three separate sections in contrasting speeds and moods to reflect the structure of the poem:

> What bliss to life can Autumn yield,
> If glooms and show'rs and storms prevail
> And Ceres flies the naked field
> And flow'rs and fruits and Phoebus fail?
> Oh what remains, what lingers yet
> To cheer me in the darkening hour?

> The grape remains, the friend of wit
> In love and mirth of mighty pow'r.
> Haste, press the clusters, fill the bowl
> Apollo shoot thy parting ray
> This gives the sunshine of the soul
> This god of health and verse and day.

The first stanza is marked 'moderately slow'. The first four lines are set as a repeated section, with a touch of localized word-painting and minor harmony for 'glooms' in the second line, and a minor-key conclusion to the section. For the last two lines of the stanza, Wesley turns to the tonic minor, closing mock-portentously in the dominant. There is a marked change of mood and tempo for the second stanza, now back in the major, for extended imitative treatment of the lines in praise of wine.

Life is a Jest, KO 225, written in January 1807, is a setting of an accomplished translation by Wesley's thirteen-year-old son Charles of a Greek epigram, evidently a product of his classical studies at this time with his father.[10] Wesley later quoted Charles's translation in a letter of 1828, stating that he thought it superior to the original:

> Life is a Jest – mere children's play:
> Go, learn to model thine by theirs:
> Go, learn to trifle life away,
> Or learn to bear a life of cares.[11]

Wesley's setting is an exquisite and dark-textured miniature for ATTB, restrained and effective in its simple and straightforward harmonies.

Undated, but probably also from much the same time, is **Here shall the morn her earliest tears bestow**, KO 219, a short but poignant setting of four lines adapted (or misremembered) from Pope's *Elegy to the Memory of an Unfortunate Lady*:

> Here shall the morn her earliest tears bestow;
> Here the first voilets of the year shall blow;
> While angels with their silver wings o'ershade
> The place, now sacred by thy relics made.

It is possible that this piece was written in memory of Wesley's lover Anne Deane, who died in early 1806. Wesley subsequently alluded to her loss in affecting terms, and as late as 1823 was requesting Novello to ensure that he was buried as close as possible to his 'transcendent and inestimable Friend'.[12]

Many of the glees of this period, as of the previous one, are humorous. One is **I walked to Camden Town**, KO 223, described by Wesley as a 'burlesca'. It is undated, but was evidently written while Wesley was living in Camden Town, where he moved some time in 1805, and probably before 23 March 1806, the date of the death of Wesley's friend Pinto, who is mentioned in the text. It appears to have been written for Wesley, Salomon, and the flautist Charles Saust to sing at a music party, as their names are indicated on the three vocal parts of the manuscript. It is in the form of a conversation, or rather an argument, between the three men, each having his own line of text. Wesley begins, describing his late-night return home, presumably to his house in Arlington Street:

> I walked to Camden Town without a single incident deserving observation. Your time and mine is much employ'd, I therefore will not trespass any longer than to say that I remain sincerely yours, Samuel Wesley.

He is then joined by Saust and Salomon, each of whom adds his own comments:

---

[10] See above, p. 69.
[11] *SW to Britiffe Smith, 4 Sept. 1828.
[12] *SW to Novello, 4 July 1823.

Saust: 'You'll get your brains knock'd out some night, you will as sure as Fate. What the devil! Are you mad? Pray be rul'd by men of sense. Where's the idea of being murder'd? I do assure you I'm in earnest and wish you not to die like a fool.' *Salomon:* 'Aye, Aye, so he will but he's as obstinate as Pinto who no advice would take, but always did what e're he lik'd, right or wrong, so Mister Saust it is in vain to preach to one as stubborn as a mule.'

The identity of the author of **If in fighting foolish systems**, KO 222, composed in May 1807, is unknown, but may once again have been Wesley's friend Madan, or indeed Wesley himself. It is another facetious piece, this time on the comparative merits of the philosophers Locke and Chillingworth:

> If in fighting foolish systems
> You would be a hearty cock
> I can give no better counsel
> Than to study Johnny Locke
>
> And if of subtle reason you would
> Buy a noble shillingsworth
> Spare your first twelve pennies
> To get hold of Billy Chillingworth

Musically, it is the occasion for a display of imitative writing, drawn out to ridiculous lengths for humorous effect.

Hurly burly, blood and thunder, KO 221, is a setting of 1810 of part of a 'burlesque ode' for the birthday of George III by the lawyer and politician Edward Thurlow, Lord Chancellor of England from 1778 to 1792.[13] Although Thurlow was a keen amateur musician and the patron of R. J. S. Stevens, Wesley probably had no personal connection with him: the ode had been published in 1785 in the first volume of *An Asylum for Fugitive Pieces*. Thurlow's ode is most charitably described as doggerel, with a chorus concluding: 'This is a day for fun and drinking / This is a day for damning, sinking; / For on this day big George was born / At twenty-three minutes past two in the morn'. Wesley's setting, for three voices, is appropriately boisterous.

Unde nil maius, KO 246, merits a small footnote in the history of the English Bach movement, as it is a eulogy in Latin on J. S. Bach, adapted from part of an ode by Horace. It dates from 1810, the time of Wesley's greatest enthusiasm for Bach, and was probably written for a gathering of his fellow Bach enthusiasts. Horace's ode is in praise of his patron the Emperor Augustus, whom he asserts to be the greatest of men, while allowing that the warrior Pallas comes closest to him in honour. The adapted text, undoubtedly by Wesley himself, simply substitutes the name of Bach for Augustus and that of Handel for Pallas. Wesley sets it in two parts: a slow opening section in praise of Bach, then an extended section parodying Handel's style. From the existence of a copy in the hand of Novello, marked up for the engraver, it is clear that it was intended to be published, but no copies have been found.

---

[13] *DNB*; Argent, *Recollections of R. J. S. Stevens*, pp. 301–2.

O Delia, every charm is thine, KO 229, is a straightforward and unremarkable four-part arrangement from around 1811 of a melody by an unknown composer on words by Peter Pindar (the pen name of John Wolcot). It was probably the glee performed at Wesley's benefit on 27 April 1811, when an unnamed glee by him to words by Pindar was advertised. The undated **Sol, do, re, mi**, KO 237, is a little solmization exercise of only sixteen bars, in which the notes are sung to their appropriate names.

At least two glees by Wesley were evidently written for use in masonic circles. One is **When friendship, love and truth abound**, KO 251, for TTB; the other is **Behold, how good and joyful**, KO 80, for ATB, to a text from Psalm 133, and composed as an anthem for the installation of the Duke of Sussex as the Grand Master of the Grand Lodge of All England on 12 May 1813.

Wesley probably regarded the composition of glees as outside his usual range of activities, and most of those that he did write as no more than trifles. With the exception of 'Tobacco's but an Indian weed' and the madrigal 'O sing unto mie roundelaie' (to be discussed below), only two of his later glees are known to have been published at or around the time of composition. In both cases the title page refers to the occasion on which the glee was performed, suggesting that copies were printed as souvenirs. No copy has been traced, nor is the first line known, of the **Glee, perform'd at the anniversary meeting of the Literary Society, May 2nd, 1799**, KO 215.[14] Copies are, however, extant of **When Bacchus, Jove's immortal boy**, KO 248, sung at a meeting of the Society of Harmonists on 18 December 1806. Like the earlier 'Hilaroi, piomen oinon', it is a setting of Anacreon in praise of wine, but this time in a translation by Thomas Moore, and dedicated to him. This, like 'What bliss to life can Autumn yield', from around the same time, is a glee in the classic mould, in several short sections, each reflecting the mood and meaning of its own portion of text.

In 1822, just as he was beinning to emerge from the extended period of depression that followed his breakdown in 1817, Wesley composed another entry for a Glee Club competition. This was **While ev'ry short-liv'd flower of sense**, KO 253, a setting for ATTB of some trite verses on the consolations of friendship. Unlike his other glees, it has a piano accompaniment, thus reflecting recent developments in the genre. This, together with the predominantly homophonic setting and a more extended use of chromatic harmony, brings us close to the world of the part-songs of Mendelssohn and his contemporaries.

O sing unto mie roundelaie

Standing apart from Wesley's glees is **O sing unto mie roundelaie**, KO 233, his unsuccessful entry for a competition organized by the Madrigal Society in 1811 for a madrigal in sixteenth- or early seventeenth-century madrigalian style.[15] As

---

[14] See RISM-A W 914, which locates a copy at McGill University, Montreal, Canada. This copy can no longer be found.

[15] See above, p. 128.

we have seen, on learning that he had not won the prize, Wesley commented to Novello that he had been able to 'prevail upon [himself] to scrawl absolute Nonsense, even for a silver Cup'.[16] By this he may have meant that he had not been prepared to write out-and-out pastiche, and this indeed may have cost him the prize, for while the surface manner is that of the earlier period, there are several instances where he departs from it in his harmonies and treatment of dissonance. This is of no particular concern to present-day listeners and singers, of course, for whom 'O sing unto mie roundelaie' stands as a early, and conspicuously successful, example of the interest of nineteenth-century English composers in re-interpreting the idioms of the English madrigal for their own purposes.

For his text, Wesley chose not a genuine piece of madrigal verse, but a mock-archaic lyric by the boy-poet Thomas Chatterton – a highly suitable choice, given the nature of the exercise.

> O sing unto mie roundelaie,
> Drop the briny tear with me
> Dance no more on holiday,
> Like a running river ever be.
> My love is dead,
> Gone to his deathbed
> All under the willow tree.

Wesley chose to set this for five voices, following the practice of the English madrigalists in some of their finest works. He thus had opportunities for contrasting textures and sonorities not available in the average glee. From his extensive experience in writing Latin sacred music, he was well used to handling groupings of this size and larger, and to working with the language and idioms of sixteenth-century polyphony. To these he added some effective word-painting (at 'dance no more' and 'like a running river'), while his shift from the minor of the opening to the tonic major for the final section recalls Wilbye's celebrated use of the same procedure in 'Adieu, sweet Amaryllis'.

Solo songs and duets

Juvenilia

Amongst its varied contents, Wesley's Pasticcio Book of 1774–5 contains two examples of his early writing for solo voice. One, to words by his father, is **Alack and alack, the clouds are so black (Derdham Downs)**, KO 260, a miniature dramatic cantata for soprano or boy treble (possibly Wesley himself) and orchestra of strings, timpani and organ, on young Samuel's adventures when out riding in uncertain weather on Bristol's most famous open space. At one stage there was clearly a concluding section that was subsequently lost or

---

[16] *SW to Novello, 17 Feb. 1813.

discarded: the last surviving section is a setting of the penultimate stanza of Charles Wesley's poem, followed by the instruction 'segue subito'.[17] **What are the falling rills**, KO 314, is another early cantata, this time for solo voice, flute, and strings. In another manuscript is the ambitious **In gentle slumbers**, KO 280, an undated setting from around this time of a poem by his godfather Martin Madan, for soprano, 'violetti' (violas?), and bass. From a little later, and of interest as being reportedly a transcription of a melody composed on the spot, is **Autumnus comes**, KO 265, composed in 1777 or 1778 and published by Barrington alongside his report on Wesley's musical accomplishments in his *Miscellanies* (1781): it is thus Wesley's first published piece of vocal music.

Solo songs and duets of the 1780s

The group of manuscripts which contains most of Wesley's glees of his teenage years also contains fourteen solo vocal items and two duets, all written at around the same time in the early 1780s. Of the solo items, nine are for voice and bass only, while four have sketched or fully written out accompaniments, in whole or part. The remaining item is a dramatic recitative that will be discussed separately below. Nine items are designated as ariettas, but they do not appear any different in form or length from the others, two of which are designated as arias, the remaining two being untitled. The two duets in the collection are for two sopranos and instrumental bass, and are similar in style and approach to the solo songs.

These songs are far from conventional. With few exceptions, they are syllabic settings of anonymous texts, many of them from the *Vocal Magazine*, and most are on the subjects of unrequited or disappointed love, or the partings of lovers. Given the date of their composition, one suspects some autobiographical significance in Wesley's choice of these particular subjects. Some, such as **When we see a lover languish**, KO 318, **Louisa, view the melting tears**, KO 285, and **One kind kiss before we part**, KO 293, are extremely short, amounting to no more than a single statement of a four-line lyric, and extending to no more than fifteen or twenty bars. Others are more extended and elaborate. In some, including the extraordinary **Love's but a frailty of the mind**, KO 288, some turns of phrase and the bold use (not always entirely successfully) of chromatic harmony for expressive purposes suggest that Wesley had the songs of Purcell in mind. Probably the most successful is **Too late for redress**, KO 311, of September 1783, a minor-key setting of a lyric of unrequited love.

Alone on the sea-beat rock (Armin's Lamentation for the Loss of his Daughter), KO 261, is a setting in recitative for soprano, two violins, and continuo of verses from the *Sorrows of Winter* by Ossian (i.e. James Macpherson). It is a miniature drama, showing Wesley trying his hand in the (to him) new medium of operatic recitative.

---

[17] For the complete poem, see Kimbrough and Beckerlegge, *Unpublished Poetry of Charles Wesley*, vol. 1, p. 283.

Wesley wrote two songs with instrumental accompaniment at around this time. One is the undated **Gentle breath of melting sorrow**, KO 275, a gently elegiac minor-key da capo aria for soprano and strings. The other is **Tergi il pianto idolo mio**, KO 302, an Italian opera aria in rondo form for soprano, oboes, horns, and strings, and similar in style and conception to many pieces by other composers published individually in score in the 1780s.

In a different category from the items discussed above, and in a separate manuscript, is **And is he then set free?**, KO 262, a setting of May 1782 for soprano, alto, two violins, and bass of an ode by Charles Wesley senior on the death of the violinist William Kingsbury.[18] As we have seen, Kingsbury had been one of Wesley's first violin teachers, had played in some of the early family concerts, and had died in penury in a poorhouse near Bristol in early February 1782. Only a few days previously, he had written to Wesley to thank him for the care Wesley had taken with his violin – presumably by selling it on his behalf – and to say that he would be even more grateful to receive the money and the watch that Wesley had offered.[19] In an annotation to the letter, Wesley's father noted that it was Kingsbury's last, and that he was 'carried soon after by the angels into Abraham's Bosom'.

Wesley set his father's poem, consisting of six six-line stanzas, as an extended funeral ode in seven movements. An opening duet is followed by a soprano solo ('Born to distress and woe') describing the poverty and isolation of Kingsbury's final days, and an alto solo ('By his own flesh forsook') describing his reliance on the charity of the workhouse and his death. The next movement ('For lo, he lives again') is an a cappella duet that dwells on Kingsbury's reward in heaven, while the soprano solo 'Happy at last might I, as meek and lamblike die', draws an instructive lesson from Kingsbury's uncomplaining death. The final movement sets the last stanza of the poem as another duet, turning to the major key and a fast tempo for the first time in the work:

> With those redeem'd of old,
> In life's fair book enroll'd
> Saviour, tune and take my soul
> With that double choir to meet.
> Then the harmony is full,
> Then the triumph is complete.

The ode is a highly effective work that shows Wesley handling the idioms of the 'ancient' style with skill and an impressive degree of command of overall structure and sensitivity to words. It would be pleasing to record that it was performed in Kingsbury's memory at one of the family concerts, but there is no record of any performance in Charles Wesley's listings. If it was so performed, and somehow was omitted by Charles Wesley, it would have probably have been in the 1783 season, as Wesley did not complete it until 30 May 1782, after the end of that year's season.

---

[18] Text in *JCW*, vol. 2, pp. 410–11.
[19] Kingsbury to SW, 24 Jan. 1782.

Songs and duets of 1797–1802

Although the few months on either side of Wesley's marriage in April 1793 were generally an unproductive time for composition, he did write a few pieces, including one song. This was the aria **Hope away! Enjoyment's come**, KO 279, written a month after the marriage; it is a bravura piece for soprano and instrumental bass, with an obbligato violin part bristling with multiple stops and rapid passage work. Further songs date from the productive time between 1797 and 1802: they were doubtless intended, like the glees of the period, for the many music parties that Wesley attended at this time, and none was published. As before, some have only a bass while others have fully written out accompaniments. Although the latter tend to be more elaborate than the former, there is no great stylistic divide between the two types, as it would have been easy for Wesley or any other competent pianist to improvise a simple arpeggio or chordal accompaniment from the voice part and the bass.

One of the most successful of the songs for voice and bass is **Little tube of mighty pow'r**, (*Address to a Pipe*), KO 283, an elegant minor-key setting dating from July 1798 of a poem that Wesley gleaned from the *Vocal Magazine*; with its extravagant praise of the joys of tobacco and pipe-smoking it would make an interesting contrast in a concert programme with the very different sentiments of 'Tobacco's but an Indian weed', KO 245, discussed above. **Come Stella, queen of all my heart**, KO 268, composed in 1801, is (like the glee 'What bliss to life can autumn yield', KO 247), a setting of lines from a poem thought at the time to be by Samuel Johnson, but in fact by Hawkesworth.[20] **Not heav'n itself**, KO 290, is a setting of two lines from a translation by Dryden of an ode by Horace, and dates from December 1804. Three years earlier, Wesley had set the whole of the stanza containing this couplet in his glee 'Happy the man', KO 217. **O that I had wings like a dove**, KO 295, is a charming miniature for soprano on a verse from Psalm 55, later memorably set by Mendelssohn. Notwithstanding its biblical text, it seems to be a secular piece.

Among the songs with written-out accompaniments from this period are some of Wesley's best works in the genre. All are for soprano and piano and are written with much the same high tessiture and wide vocal range, suggesting that they may have been written with a particular singer in mind: perhaps the Miss Richardson whom Wesley mentions in his account of a music party he gave in October 1801, and who also sang in his concert series in early 1802.[21] Three are particularly notable. One is the undated **Hark! his hands the lyre explore**, KO 278, a setting of lines from Gray's *The Progress of Poetry*, which after an initial statement of the first line as recitative, launches into a treatment with a piano accompaniment of slow-moving bass with broken chords in the right hand that continues almost until the end, ceasing abruptly at the words 'tis heard no more'. Another is **Gentle warblings in the night**, KO 276, composed in February

---

[20] *The Midsummer Wish* ('O Phoebus! Down the western sky'), first printed in *GM*, 1748/1, 232.
[21] See above, p. 60.

1799 for soprano and piano, with ad lib parts for two flutes. It also exists as **Fairy minstrels in the night**, KO 272, to completely different words by Wesley's friend William Kingston, who may have also been responsible for the words of the other version. **What shaft of fate's relentless pow'r**, KO 315, is the only song from this period (and indeed the only secular song in Wesley's entire output) to have been published in a modern edition.[22] It is a fine setting dating from around 1800 of a sonnet by Martin Madan (whether the father or the son is not known). The poignant minor-key opening section, marked 'slowly and pathetically' (Ex 21.02) gives way to a faster second section in the major, marked 'joyous', at the words 'But for the change of fortune's frown what happier stars remain / When time shall break the barrier down', leading to a triumphant conclusion and rushing piano postlude. Although clearly for

Example 21.02, 'What shaft of fate's relentless pow'r', KO 315, bars 1–14

---

[22] In Nicholas Temperley and Geoffrey Bush (eds), *English Songs 1800–1860*.

soprano, it was – as we know from a note by Novello on one of the manuscript sources – a favourite of the tenor Thomas Vaughan, and would make a highly effective recital piece today. The same manuscript is marked up for the engraver, so the song was probably published at some stage, but no copies have been traced.

Apart from two topical pieces, to be discussed below, only one song from this period was published at the time: **Love and folly were at play**, KO 286, which appeared around 1802, described as a 'favorite song'. Single song publications at this time tended to be popular and straightforward, and this one is no exception. The critic of the *Monthly Magazine* was nonetheless impressed by it, commenting, 'we are much delighted with this pretty sportful effort of the imagination. The character is strong and attractive, and an unaffected novelty prevails throughout the melody. We hope the sale of so pleasing a specimen of Mr. Wesley's taste in this province of composition will encourage him to bring forward many similar productions.'[23]

From this period also comes one piece for voice and instrumental ensemble: **Near Thame's fam'd banks**, KO 289, written in late December 1799 for performance by the singer and coal merchant Thomas Carter and the Ad Libitum Society, to the members of which Wesley dedicated it.[24] It is a charming recitative and aria for alto soloist and strings in praise of the society and the friendship and companionship it offered.

Wesley also wrote a number of songs on topical subjects at this time, at least two of which were published. **The rising sun of freedom**, KO 305, a rousing solo song with chorus, was written for the birthday of Charles James Fox in 1798 or 1799, and may have been performed at one of the elaborate birthday parties that Fox held at this time; nothing is known about what relationship, if any, Wesley had with him. **Come all my brave boys who want organists' places (The Organ Laid Open. Or, The true Stop discovered)**, KO 267, composed and published in 1798, relates to Wesley's unsuccessful application for the organist's position at the Foundling Hospital in May of that year, and satirizes Joah Bates, a Governor of the Hospital through whose patronage John Immyns was appointed.[25] The song is of no particular musical merit, but it is of considerable interest for its commentary on the affair. The background to the composition of the song has been discussed and parts of its text have been quoted earlier.[26]

From rather later, but again with topical significance, was **This is the house that Jack built**, KO 310, a satirical version of the well-known cumulative song. Wesley composed it on the occasion of the Old Price riots at Covent Garden in the autumn of 1809, when widespread disturbances followed the management's attempts to raise prices for a series of recitals by Catalani shortly after the opening of the new theatre.

---

[23] *MM* 14 (1803), p. 543
[24] See above, pp. 52–3.
[25] See above, p. 55.
[26] See above, pp. 55–7.

There are also a few duets from this period. Pride of place must go to **Beneath, a sleeping infant lies**, KO 208, a restrained setting for soprano, alto and bass of an epitaph on the death of a child, by Wesley's uncle and namesake Samuel Wesley (1690–1739). The poem was well known at the time, as it had been included by Johnson in the introduction to his *Dictionary* as an example of simple but effective versification. As a note on one of the manuscripts makes clear, Wesley's setting commemorated the death in late 1797 at the age of three of his first daughter, Susanna. **See, the young, the rosy spring**, KO 299, is a setting for two sopranos and piano of an ode of Anacreon, in the translation by Thomas Moore. Although undated, its inclusion in Wesley's 1800 music book and the fact that Moore's popular translations of Anacreon were first published in this year suggest a date of composition around this time. **There was a little boy**, KO 304, published around 1800, is a popular pot-boiler of no musical significance.

Later songs

As Wesley's public career grew more established and he became busier, he understandably had less time to devote to writing songs, and his later works in the genre were comparatively few. Some appear to have been written opportunistically for publication to commemorate a public event or to meet the mood of the moment. Such was the lost **As on fam'd Waterloo the lab'ring swain**, KO 264, in celebration of the British victory at Waterloo on 18 June 1815. It was a setting of verses brought to Wesley in June 1816 by the Revd John Davies, and was originally intended to be sung by the tenor Charles Edward Horn at a concert at the Lyceum Theatre on 23 July of the same year. At the last moment Horn decided not to perform it, much to the annoyance of Wesley and Davies.[27] It was later performed at a New Musical Fund concert in May 1817. **In radiant splendor**, KO 281, again to words by Davies, was written in August 1816 to celebrate the marriage three months earlier of Princess Charlotte, daughter of George III, to Prince Leopold of Saxe-Coburg-Saalfeld. If Wesley had plans to publish these two songs, as seems likely, these were no doubt disrupted by the onset of his illness in early August 1816 and his eventual collapse in May of the following year.

The standard of England still floats on the waves (**True blue, and old England for Ever**), KO 306, published in 1830 and reviewed in the *Harmonicon* for November of that year, was probably also written opportunistically. No copy of the print has been traced, but from the single sheet that is all of the autograph that is extant, it was a patriotic song in popular vein with an SATB refrain.

Other songs appear to have been composed as gifts or mementoes for friends. One such was the duet **Why should we shrink from life's decline**, KO 257, described on the autograph as a harvest cantata. It is a substantial and attractive

---

[27] *SW to unidentified recipient, 23 July 1816.

work for soprano and tenor with elaborate full orchestral accompaniment that Wesley composed for his friends Thomas and Elizabeth Vaughan. He completed it on 24 May 1813, possibly for the Vaughans to sing at their benefit concert at the Hanover Square Rooms four days later. It was not included in the advertising for this concert, however, and it is not known whether or not they performed it on this occasion, or indeed on any other. Another, much less elaborate, was the short Purcellian **'Twas not the spawn of such as these**, KO 312, a setting for high voice and piano of a translation of part of an ode by Horace. Wesley probably wrote it for Novello, who certainly later owned the autograph, and commented on it that it was 'a most admirable imitation of Henry Purcell's style', adding that he had always thought that Wesley's musical genius 'strongly resembled that of Purcell, with a mixture of Mozart, Handel, and Sebastian Bach in it'.

Farewell! If ever fondest prayer, KO 273, a setting of a lyric from Byron's *The Corsair*, is undated, but appears from the very shaky hand in which it is written to have been composed at some stage in the 1830s. No copies of **Looking o'er the moonlight billow**, KO 284, advertised in the *Harmonicon* for November 1831, have been traced. The undated **Go, minstrel, go**, KO 277, described by Wesley as 'A song composed on J. B. Cramer's leaving England', was presumably written to mark Cramer's permanent departure in 1835 to live abroad. It may have been written for publication, but no printed copies have been traced. Nothing is known about the circumstances of composition of **When thro' life unblest we rove**, (On Music), KO 317, written apparently at the same time, and on the same page of manuscript. The short **What folly it is**, KO 313, was composed in the following year to mark the departure from England of Mark Howell, unidentified but evidently a friend or acquaintance of Wesley's.

Also from 1836 is **Orpheus could lead the savage race**, KO 294, a short setting of lines from Dryden's *Song for St Cecilia's Day* that he wrote as the first item in his daughter Eliza's album, begun in July of that year. **Eyes long unmoisten'd wept**, KO 271, is slightly later, and is a short recitative and air from an elegy on the death of the operatic soprano Maria Malibran in September 1836; as Wesley noted, he took the words from the 2 October number of the *John Bull* newspaper. It was later published by J. Alfred Novello. His last song was probably the short **When all around grew drear and dark**, KO 316, completed on 1 August 1837 for his daughter Eliza to give to her friend Sarah Emett, the daughter of his friend the organist John George Emett, as a birthday present.

22

Instrumental music

Orchestral music

Most of Wesley's orchestral music, including all his violin concertos and all but one of his overtures and symphonies, dates from the time of the family concerts. The remaining works are later and were written for public performance at the Lenten oratorio concerts and elsewhere; they consist of a number of organ concertos, some of them lost or incomplete, and a lost piano concerto. The Overture to *The Dilosk Gatherer* of 1832 and an Overture in E of around 1834, at one time thought to be by Wesley, are in fact by his son Samuel Sebastian.[1]

Overtures and Symphonies

Apart from orchestral writing in his oratorio *Ruth*, Wesley's first attempt at orchestral music was probably the **Overture in G**, KO 401, dated 9 January 1775, contained in his Pasticcio Book of 1774–5. Although notated on two staves, some indications for scoring show that it was conceived orchestrally. But it was not until the late 1770s and early 1780s that he started to write substantial quantities of orchestral music, almost all for performance at the family concerts. The records kept by Charles Wesley senior do not usually specify precisely which overture, concerto, or symphony was performed on each occasion, but it is often possible to match works to dates and to establish probable datings for undated or only partly dated works.

Wesley's first composition for the family concerts appears to have been the **Overture in D**, KO 402. Its designation of 'Overture for 11 December 1778' points to its having been written originally for a separate concert, as yet untraced, on that date. It was no doubt the overture performed at the second concert of the first series on 28 January 1779, in a programme devoted almost entirely to music by the Wesley brothers. Like all the music for the family concerts, it is for oboes, horns, and strings. It is in three movements: a sonata-form Con Brio, an Andante in the subdominant in 2/4 time with some graceful triplet quaver figuration, and a fast and furious Presto in 6/8. In its length, proportions, and overall form, it is a symphony in all but name. Much the same

---

[1] See Horton, 'The Unknown Wesley', pp. 135–6, 141–4; Horton, *Samuel Sebastian Wesley*, pp. 25–6, 69.

can be said of the Overture to Act Two of *The Death of Abel*, dated merely 1779, consisting of an Allegro con brio, an Andante in the relative minor, and a rushing Presto finale. This could well have been the work played on various occasions in the 1780 season, when an unspecified overture appears in the concert lists.

Wesley can be assumed to have composed the **Overture in C**, KO 403, dated 26 October 1780, for the 1781 series, when it was no doubt the work performed at the first concert on 25 January. It consists of only two movements: a truncated sonata-form Allegro con brio that comes to a halt on the dominant shortly after the recapitulation, to lead directly to the second movement, headed 'La Marche, Pomposo', featuring prominent parts for horns that must have sounded particularly striking in the confined space of the music room at Chesterfield Street. It was doubtless these three works that continued to appear, identified only as overtures, from time to time in the programmes of the six remaining seasons.

The **Sinfonia Obbligato in D**, KO 404, composed in April 1781, was finished too late to be performed in that season, but was played at the first concert of the following season, on 31 January 1782. It contains extended solo parts in the outer movements for violin, cello, and organ, a combination that combines elements of Charles's organ concertos with those of Samuel's violin concertos, while at the same time also involving their friend Hugh Reinagle, who would have played the taxing cello part. Its starting point is clearly the many sinfonia concertantes of J. C. Bach and Abel that were performed in their subscription concerts, but Wesley was evidently also familiar with Bach's *Six Grand Overtures*, Op. 18: the opening of the *Sinfonia Obbligato* starts with the unison dotted note figure that Bach uses to begin four out of six of these works.

It was not until the 1784 season that works by Wesley described specifically as symphonies began to appear in the programmes; works thus described were also performed in the following year, but then were dropped for the final two series in 1786 and 1787. Of the extant symphonies from this period, two (the Symphony in A, KO 406, and the Symphony in E♭, KO 408) bear dates in early 1784, and were probably first performed at the concerts on 15 April and 29 April respectively. It is worth pointing out that this was the period in which Wesley converted to Roman Catholicism, and that at this time he was also composing the *Missa de Spiritu Sancto*, which he completed in late May. Another symphony, the Symphony in A, KO 406, is undated, and was probably written either in 1784 or 1785 for the 1785 season. A further work, the Symphony in A, KO 405, again undated, survives only in the form of parts for first and second violins; it too may have been written for the 1785 season.

The two dated orchestral works from 1784 are very dissimilar in character. The **Symphony in D**, K 407, like the *Sinfonia Obbligato*, is a work particularly close to the style of J. C. Bach. Wesley once again begins with the dotted-note figure that he had used at the beginning of the *Sinfonia Obbligato*, and continues in a manner extremely close to that used by Bach in his Op 18 No. 4 (Ex. 22.01). Although there is some further treatment of this theme's second element in the development, Wesley does not bring it back at the return of the tonic key, preferring to delay its recapitulation to the very end of the movement, where it functions as a closing theme. The second movement is a gently lyrical Andantino in 3/8 in ternary form, and the finale is a rushing sonata-form Allegro Molto in 6/8.

Example 22.01, Openings of first movements of Wesley's Symphony in D, KO 407, and J. C. Bach's Sinfonia in D, Op 18. No. 4

The **Symphony in E♭**, KO 408, completed only two months later, is a far more complex and satisfying work. The first movement, in 3/4, is notable for the richness of its thematic material, the large amount of imitative writing in the development, and the highly truncated recapitulation. The slow movement is a short and graceful Andante in the dominant that holds few surprises. The finale, however, is decidedly quirky. Unlike most of Wesley's last movements, which are rondos or sets of variations, this starts as if it is a Minuet and Trio. The second section of the Minuet is considerably extended, however, suggesting to the audience that what is about to follow will not be the expected trio section. Eventually, this section comes to a close in the dominant, and is immediately followed by what sounds like the opening of a finale in the same key. Not content with wrong-footing his audience's expectations at this stage, Wesley now does so again, by abruptly interrupting this section when it has run a good deal of its course and bringing back the Minuet to bring the movement to a close.

The **Symphony in A**, KO 406, is considerably less adventurous. In its recapitulation of the first theme right at the end as a closing theme, the first movement recalls the formal procedures of the D major symphony; the texture of the orchestral writing is thin, however, and it is not as successful as the corresponding movement of the earlier work. The slow movement is a leisurely Italianate movement in binary form,[2] while the rondo finale is based on a theme with two elements: one, marked *piano*, is in the tonic minor; the other, marked *forte*, is in the major. Of the two episodes, one is in the tonic and features a short burst of solo violin writing; the other, far longer, is in the tonic minor. Too little remains of the fragmentary and undated **Symphony in A**, KO 405, to allow

---

[2] Opening quoted in Caldwell, *Oxford History of English Music*, vol. 2, pp. 129–30.

further comment beyond that it was a substantial three-movement work consisting of an Allegro con Spirito, an Andante in the subdominant, and a concluding Allegro.

Wesley's next exercise in orchestral writing was the **Overture to the** *Ode to St Cecilia*, KO 207, completed in October 1794. Here Wesley was no longer restricted to the small forces that were available for the family concerts, but was writing for the larger resources of the orchestra of the Covent Garden oratorio concerts. By this time he would also have heard at least some of the concerts that Haydn had given on his visit of 1791–2: we know from his *Reminiscences* that he was present at the concert on 2 March 1792, when Haydn directed the first performance of his Symphony No. 98 in B♭. The results are evident in the orchestral writing, which now features prominent parts for woodwind soloists, and a particular fondness for the bassoon in its tenor register. In form, the overture shows some of the features of the Overture in C, KO 403, of 1780, albeit on a far larger and more ambitious scale. It opens with an ambitious sonata movement incorporating a good deal of imitative counterpoint in its development that breaks off half-way through the recapitulation to lead into the second movement, a rather Handelian march that achieved sufficient independent popularity for Wesley later to arrange it both for piano and organ solo, and to include it among the music he arranged for Walter McGeough's barrel organ at the Argory.[3]

The only symphony of Wesley's maturity is the magnificent **Symphony in B♭**, KO 409, composed for the ill-fated series of concerts that he promoted with his brother Charles in early 1802. The autograph of the symphony is dated 27 April 1802, just in time for performance at the last concert on 6 May. There is no record of any subsequent performance in Wesley's lifetime.

The Symphony is utterly different in scale and conception from the symphonies of the 1780s and the Overture to the *Ode to St Cecilia* of 1794. By this time, Wesley is writing for a far larger orchestra of flutes, oboes, bassoons, horns, timpani, and strings. Two features are immediately apparent: the large amount of counterpoint, and the richness of the woodwind writing. We have already noted the first of these in the earlier overtures and symphonies, and the second is apparent in some of the earlier symphonies, and to a far greater extent in the Overture to the *Ode to St Cecilia* and in the *Confitebor*. Both are also, of course, features of Haydn's symphonies, and particularly the 'London' symphonies.

But for all that the Symphony in B♭ shows the influence of the 'London' symphonies on every page, Wesley is no slavish imitator. At the outset of the work he dispenses with Haydn's customary slow introduction, preferring instead to launch immediately into a densely conceived Allegro. And Wesley is far more thorough-going in his maintenance of contrapuntal textures. Whereas Haydn's typical manner in the 'London' symphonies, as elsewhere, is to combine passages of artless simplicity with passages of imitative writing,

---

[3] See above, p. 164.

Wesley introduces counterpoint from the start and maintains it throughout the movement. The slow movement is a ruminative treatment of a single theme that subjects it to a variety of treatments in a number of keys, rather in the manner of the slow movement of Haydn's Symphony No. 102 in B♭ of 1794. The Minuet and Trio is marked 'Vivace' and is very much after the manner of the fast minuets of Haydn's 'London' symphonies, with a trio section in G minor that exploits some very Haydnesque metrical irregularities. The finale is a headlong rondo, with further examples of dense contrapuntal writing.

It is a telling comment on the state of London music in the early nineteenth century that the symphony appears to have had only one performance. At the time of its composition, there was no native tradition of composing symphonies. As we have seen earlier, most concerts in the first decade of the nineteenth century concentrated heavily on vocal music, and although instrumental music was performed, it was usually in the form of solo concertos. The formation of the Philharmonic Society in 1813 did much to restore orchestral music to programmes by banning most vocal music from its concerts, and had Wesley's membership not been first interrupted and then terminated by his illness in 1817, it is entirely possible that the symphony would have been performed there at some stage.

The violin concertos

In his *Reminiscences*, Wesley stated that as in his youth he was 'an adept on the violin', he 'found no great difficulty in mastering the compositions of the fashionable Violinists of the Day, such as Giardini, Cramer, Borghi, Giornovich, &c', and that his own solos and concertos contained 'many passages of as showy and brilliant Execution as any of those popular Authors'.[4] His performances of violin concertos, both by the composers he mentions and by himself, were a frequent feature of the family concerts.

Of his own seven concertos, five are dated between November 1779 and March 1785; of the remaining two, one is completely undated, and the other is dated merely '24 February'. Taking the evidence of the dates of composition on the autographs and the performance details in the concert register, it seems likely that Wesley wrote one concerto for each of the seven seasons between 1779 and 1785, with the two undated concertos fitting into the seasons for which there is no dated work. The following discussion is based on this hypothesis; it further assumes that the less technically demanding of the undated concertos is likely to be the earlier one, on the grounds that Wesley's writing for violin would have increased in difficulty as his own technique developed.

In 1779, in the first season, he performed no concertos by other composers, but on 25 February, at the third concert, he performed a concerto of his own. This may well have been the **Violin Concerto in A**, KO 419, which is the one dated '24th February'. In the following season he performed concertos by

[4] *Reminiscences*, fol. 100.

Borghi and Giardini and also his new **Violin Concerto in C**, KO 418, composed the previous December. In the 1781 season he performed a concerto by Cramer: presumably the Concerto in E, a complete set of parts of which in Wesley's hand is at the British Library.[5] On 10 April he completed the **Violin Concerto in D**, KO 420, and this was presumably the work performed at the final concert of the season on 26 April. There is no dated concerto for the 1782 season, but Wesley may well have written the undated **Violin Concerto in E♭**, KO 421, for it. As we have seen above, the **Sinfonia Obbligato**, KO 404, containing substantial amounts of solo writing for the violin, was also written for and performed in this season, and Wesley also performed concertos by Cramer and Giardini. Wesley also played his reworking of a concerto by Giornovichi, consisting of new accompaniments to the solo part of Giornovichi's Concerto No. 5 in E, first published by LeDuc in Paris in 1777.[6] The concerto for the 1783 season was presumably the **Violin Concerto in B♭**, KO 422, completed in September 1782. In this season Wesley also performed a concerto by Geminiani and again performed his reworking of the Giornovichi concerto.

Wesley's enthusiasm for the violin diminished after early December 1783, when – as we know from a contemporary letter to Shepherd and a later one to Burney – he lost his favourite violin after leaving it in a hackney cab. Wesley stated to Burney many years later that he had been unable subsequently to find another instrument that suited him as well, and that in consequence he had 'turned sulky at the whole *Genus*'.[7] Nonetheless, he continued for the moment to play the violin in the family concerts, and composed concertos for the following two seasons. For the 1784 season he composed the **Violin Concerto in G**, KO 423, which he completed in mid-December 1783. His last concerto, the **Violin Concerto in B♭**, KO 424, was completed on 4 April 1785 and was presumably the concerto performed by him at the concert ten days later. During these two seasons he also played one or more concertos by Geminiani. This season marked the end of his solo violin playing, however, and in the 1786 and 1787 seasons he played no concertos, either by himself or by other composers.

Wesley's violin concertos are all in a thoroughly modern style. Their model, as Chappell White points out, was the cosmopolitan Parisian concerto of the 1760s and 1770s, a fusion of stylistic elements from Italy, Germany, and France and represented by the works of Gaviniès, Leduc, Paisible, and Barthélemon, examples of which Wesley would have heard in London;[8] this is also the format of Mozart's five unquestionably authentic violin concertos, written in Salzburg between 1773 and 1775, which of course Wesley would *not* have heard. His chief personal influences in London would have been Giardini, Barthélemon, and Cramer, the three leading violinists in London at the time, all of whom Wesley must have heard on many occasions.

---

[5] BL, Add. MS 35023, fol. 32.
[6] White, 'The Violin Concertos of Giornovichi'.
[7] SW to Shepherd, 26 Dec. 1783; *SW to Burney, 4 September 1809.
[8] White, *From Vivaldi to Viotti*, p. 313.

The first movements of Wesley's violin concertos are in the hybrid ritornello-sonata form characteristic of the period and best known from Mozart's concerto first movements. Of the slow movements, only one is a romance, the form particularly associated with the concertos of Giornovichi, who is often thought to have been the first to use it. Another, the slow movement of the Concerto in C, KO 418, is – most unusually for the slow movement of a violin concerto of this period – a set of variations, on Thomas Linley the Elder's air 'When wars alarmed'. Three slow movements are in the dominant, two in the relative minor, one in the subdominant, and one in the tonic minor. The last movements are all rondos, the standard form for violin concerto finales, and in four cases, Wesley uses the French term 'rondeau' or 'rondeaux'. Throughout the concertos, Wesley's writing shows many features of contemporary Parisian practice, such as the use of two violins and bass or two violins only as accompaniment for solo passages.

Even without considering the one undated concerto and the one that is only incompletely dated, there is evidence of growing technical difficulty in the solo violin writing over the course of time. The first dated concerto, the Concerto in C, KO 418, of 1780, makes little use of double-stopping or passages in broken octaves. These features, however, are extensively used in the next dated work, the Concerto in D, K 420, completed on 10 April 1781, and they continue to be used in the remaining concertos.

The **Concerto in D**, KO 420, is the only concerto to have been recorded at the time of writing, and it is therefore appropriate to single it out for further discussion here. It is a substantial and highly accomplished work lasting around eighteen minutes. The solo part makes considerable technical demands, with frequent use of the violin's high register combined with rapid passage-work and double stops in thirds, sixths, octaves, and tenths. The first movement is an assured ritornello-sonata movement remarkable chiefly for its great length (over ten minutes) and its many passages of double-stopping in thirds and broken octaves. The slow movement, a highly Italianate Largo in triple time, langorously alternates tutti sections and solo sections, the solo sections accompanied only by the two violin parts. The last movement is a witty rondo based on a theme that incorporates a quotation from an air in Gluck's *La rencontre imprevue* (1764), known in German as *Die Pilgrimme von Mecca*.[9] As Peter Holman has pointed out, there had been no stage performance of this work in London by the time of composition of the symphony, but Wesley may have seen a copy of the score, published in Paris in 1776.[10] This movement also features some virtuoso passages for cello that were doubtless written with Hugh Reinagle in mind.

---

[9] From the Act 1 Air, 'Les hommes pieusement pour Caton nous tiennent'. This air, known in German as 'Unser dummer Pöbel meint', was later used by Mozart as the theme of a set of piano variations, K 455.

[10] Peter Holman, notes to *English Classical Violin Concertos* (Hyperion CDA 66865), 1996.

The keyboard concertos

As with almost every other form, Wesley made his first attempts at writing keyboard concertos at a very early age. The **Harpsichord Concerto in G**, KO 410, and the **Harpsichord Concerto in F**, KO 411, are contained in his Pasticcio Book of 1774–5. They have every appearance of being solo pieces, or at least having started off that way – indeed, one of them is called a 'Lesson' – but it is clear from some scattered indications for the scoring that they were conceived as concertos.

Although Wesley frequently played the organ and harpsichord at the family concerts, he did not usually play the solo in keyboard concertos, which were the province of Charles. But as we have already seen, the *Sinfonia Obbligato*, KO 404, of 1781 contains substantial amounts of solo writing for organ, and thus deserves a mention here. Wesley's next instrumental work involving organ solo was the three-movement **Quintetto in A**, KO 529, for organ, two violins, viola, and bass, with horn parts in the last movement only, completed in April 1787 for performance at the last series of family concerts, and performed on 24 April and 8 May of that year. This is a concerto in all but name, and given the extremely small forces that performed at the family concerts, the distinction between chamber music and orchestral music is only a nominal one.

Wesley's later organ concertos were all written for his own performance at public concerts, chiefly at the Lenten Oratorios at Covent Garden. Apart from the lost Organ Concerto in B♭, KO 413, discussed below, the first was the **Organ Concerto in D**, KO 414, completed on 22 March 1800. This was probably the concerto that Wesley played at Salomon's performance of Haydn's *Creation* at the King's Theatre on 21 April of that year, and it is likely that he had previously performed it on 31 March at an oratorio concert promoted by Barthélemon at Hatton House, Hatton Garden.

In its 1800 form the concerto was in three movements, and scored for two flutes, two horns, timpani, and strings. In the summer of 1809, however, when his enthusiasm for Bach was at its peak, Wesley revised it for performance at the Tamworth Festival, inserting an arrangement of Bach's D major fugue from Book I of the '48' before the final movement.[11] At the same time, he took the opportunity to add parts for oboes, trumpets, bassoons, and a single trombone, doubtless so as to use all the orchestral forces available to him on this occasion. This new version also fulfilled his long-standing desire to hear Bach played orchestrally. In October of the previous year he had enthused to Jacob about the 'glorious effect' that Bach's fugues made in Horn's arrangements for string quartet, going on to wonder 'what must they do in a full Orchestra!'[12] He now had his answer.

In its revised version, the D major concerto was the most popular and most frequently performed of Wesley's organ concertos in his lifetime. The *violino*

---

[11] *SW to Jacob, 4 Sept. 1809.
[12] *SW to Jacob, 19 Oct. [1808].

principale part bears the dates of some of the subsequent performances of the revised version and the names of the leaders on those occasions: they include General Ashley at Covent Garden on 30 January 1810, Francis Cramer at Covent Garden on 12 March 1810, Charles Hague at the Ipswich Festival on 6 July 1813, Nicolas Mori at a Covent Garden oratorio concert on 4 March 1825, and Francis Cramer at his own benefit on 5 May 1826. Press advertisements give evidence of many other performances.

The concerto is a substantial work of around twenty-four minutes in the version with the added Bach fugue, and around five minutes less in its original version. The opening Allegro spiritoso is one of Wesley's finest concerto movements, with its strong thematic materials, fully integrated counterpoint, amd its occasional glances back to Handel, whose organ concertos Wesley frequently played. Characteristically, it ends quietly. The slow movement is a leisurely Larghetto cantabile in ternary form, with a first section alternating tutti and solo sections, a short middle section consisting of a minor version of the theme for organ alone, and a shortened repeat of the first section. The Bach fugue then follows, played twice: first by the organ alone, and then by the orchestra, the strings alone until six bars before the end, where they are joined by the full wind and brass in a massive final cadence. The jaunty concluding Hornpipe and variations undoubtedly contributed greatly to the concerto's enduring popularity. Wesley was later to arrange it both as a piano solo (the *Hornpipe and Variations from a favourite Organ Concerto*, KO 711), and for Walter McGeough's barrel organ, along with the March from the Overture to the *Ode to St Cecilia*.

The only other complete organ concerto is the **Organ Concerto in C**, KO 417. This was the 'new concerto' first performed at a Covent Garden oratorio concert on 9 March 1814, and finished only four days earlier.[13] Even without Wesley's remark in a letter that he and Novello had sat up until the early hours of 6 March copying the parts, it would be clear that this was a rushed job, as the final movement is an arrangement of the last movement of the Voluntary in C, Op. 6. No. 2, written over ten years earlier. As we have seen earlier, two years later Wesley composed a new finale, a set of variations on 'Rule, Britannia'. The concerto is a substantial work with many of the features that have been noted in discussions of the Concerto in D and the Symphony in B♭: imaginative scoring and frequent use of contrapuntal textures, coupled with bravura writing for the organ. The slow movement is particularly successful, with its long opening statement by the organ followed by *concertante* writing featuring solos in turn for the bassoon, the oboe, the clarinet, the violin, and the cello. The work's most surprising feature is the totally unexpected unaccompanied timpani blow that concludes the first movement.

Wesley's other organ concertos are to varying extents and in different ways

---

[13] See above, p. 141. A later note by Henry Gauntlett on the autograph score that the concerto was written for the Birmingham Festival is erroneous, and may stem from his mistaken belief that SW directed the festival in 1814 and not in 1811.

incomplete. The most complete is the **Organ Concerto in B♭**, KO 415, which survives in the form of a complete set of orchestral parts, but with no score or solo part. It was first performed on 17 March 1813, and may have been the work that was announced in an early advertisement for Wesley's 1812 benefit, but which in the end was not performed on that occasion. It was almost certainly the concerto that Wesley played at his benefit in the following year, when he is said to have included an extempore movement. Another substantially lost work is the **Organ Concerto in B♭**, KO 413, of 1800, surviving only in an arrangement of the last movement 'with a few additions' published by Novello in his *Select Organ Pieces*. Novello describes the movement as a 'Purcellian Air with Variations' and gives the date of composition as 21 February 1800. Nothing further is known either about the composition or any performances of this concerto. Given its date, it is conceivable that it was this work, and not the Concerto in D, that Wesley performed at Barthélemon's concert little more than a month afterwards, and/or at the *Creation* performance the following month. Even more fragmentary is the **Concerto in G**, KO 416, of which only the last page of the score, dated 31 October 1813, and the orchestral parts for the lively fugue which forms its last movement, survive. Wesley later arranged this movement for organ solo, in which guise it appears in the second of the two voluntaries dedicated to Thomas Adams, KO 607.

Of all Wesley's works that have been lost, or that exist only in a fragmentary and unperformable state, the greatest loss is probably that of the **Piano Concerto**, KO 412, written for Wesley's benefit on 4 May 1813 and performed on that occasion by his star pupil Charles Wilson. Although apparently enthusiastically received, it does not appear to have been performed again: possibly because Wilson later gave up performing in public, and Wesley had no other suitable pupils to whom to entrust it. A first violin part to an otherwise unidentified concerto by Wesley may be its sole surviving remnant; if so, it was a work in E♭, consisting of a Moderato, a 6/8 Andante in C minor, and a lively Vivace Moderato in rondo form.

Chamber music

Wesley wrote a fairly small amount of chamber music, of which only one piece (the *Trio for Two Flutes and Piano*, KO 514) was published in his lifetime. Most dates from early in his career, from the time of the family concerts or during the later 1780s and 1790s, and was probably written for his own use and that of his friends.

Sonatas for violin and continuo

Wesley wrote a number of sonatas for violin and piano during his boyhood and adolescence, starting with a two movement **Sonata in F**, KO 501, in his

Pasticcio Book of 1774–5. From a little later are the **Sonata in A**, KO 502, and the **Sonata in E♭**, KO 503, both from 1778 and in a thoroughly modern style. The Sonata in A, designated as 'Solo – per Violino – con Accompagnato per Basso' is in two movements: a binary Allegro and a Rondeau with two episodes, the second in the minor, and very much longer than the first. There are no very great technical difficulties in the violin part. The Sonata in E♭ from four months later is designated 'Sonata a Violino Solo'. It too is in two movements: this time an opening sonata-form Allegro and another Rondeau similar in structure to that of the earlier sonata. The writing for violin here is more difficult – perhaps reflecting the development of Wesley's technique over the intervening period – with many semiquaver arpeggio passages across the strings and a good deal of double-stopping. In both sonatas, the compass of the bass part only extends below C for one note, and some features of the writing suggest that Wesley may have been writing for a cello – possibly to be played by his friend Hugh Reinagle – or at least keeping open this option for performance.

Three sonatas from the early 1780s follow much the same pattern, but in three movements, and on a generally larger scale. The **Sonata in B♭**, KO 504, the only one to be dated, was completed in November 1781. The **Sonata in D**, KO 505, and the **Sonata in A**, KO 506, are contained in the same manuscript collection, and undoubtedly date from around the same time. This was the period of Wesley's violin concertos, and there is much in the violin writing of these works that is reminiscent of the concertos. As in the case of their predecessors of 1778, the emphasis is firmly on the violin. They may have been performed at the family concerts, although they are not to be found in any of the concert listings. The sonatas in B♭ and in D are in three movements, each with an opening sonata-form Allegro followed by a florid Adagio and a rondo finale. The Sonata in A consists only of a single sonata movement, unsigned and undated, and it is apparent that it too was in three movements, and that the second and third movements are lost. In all three sonatas the compass of the bass part again suggests that it was conceived for cello and not for piano.

The **Duetto a due violini in D**, KO 509, dates from January 1785. Like the sonatas of 1778 and 1781, it is attractively and idiomatically written, and was evidently written for Wesley's own use. It is an attractive contribution to a rather unusual genre.

The **Two Sonatas for the Piano Forte or Harpsichord, with an Accompanyment for a Violin**, KO 507, published in 1786 as Wesley's Opus 2, are, as their title suggests, really piano music, and are discussed below with Wesley's other piano works.

Wesley's only mature work for violin and piano is the large-scale **Sonata in F**, KO 508, composed for Salomon and completed in February 1797. As we have seen earlier, only five days after its completion Wesley participated in a music party to which he also invited the virtuoso violinist Bridgetower. It seems very likely that Wesley's invitation was for the purpose of securing Bridgetower's services for the first performance of this work, doubtless with Wesley himself at the piano.[14]

Unusually for its period, when it was more usual for the violin parts of sonatas for piano and violin to be optional and entirely dispensable, this sonata is a genuine duo, in which violin and piano have parts of equal importance. The writing for violin is of considerable difficulty, exploiting the full range of the instrument, and the piano part is equally taxing. It is in three movements: an extended sonata-form Allegro; a lyrical slow movement, and a concluding rondo in 6/8 time on what sounds like a Scottish popular melody.

Works for string quartet

Wesley composed comparatively little for string quartet. His first work in the genre was the substantial three-movement **String Quartet in G**, KO 523, completed on 1 January 1780 and almost certainly the 'quartetto' performed at the family concert on 30 March of the same year. It is a particularly fresh and attractive work, with gratefully written *concertante* parts for all the instruments except the second violin, the range of the viola part extending to a″ and that of the cello, doubtless written for Hugh Reinagle, to d″. The remaining pieces are single movements dating from the first decade of the nineteenth century, and are likely to have been written for private music parties: the **Minuet in F in Haydn's Manner**, KO 528, of 1800, the **Minuet in C minor in the German Style**, KO 607, of 1807, and the immense **Fugue in B♭ on a Subject from Haydn's Creation**, KO 526, of 1800, on the opening theme of the chorus 'Achieved is the glorious work'. The latter bristles with fugal devices, all of them carefully labelled by Wesley. The impetus for its composition seems to have been Wesley's intense interest in fugue at this time, also to be seen in other free-standing fugues for piano and organ.

There is no doubt about the authenticity of these works, but there must be a considerable question-mark over that of the large-scale **Quartet in E♭**, KO 524. This exists in only one source: a set of mid-nineteenth-century parts in an unidentified hand contained in the collection of Wesley's manuscripts and papers bequeathed by Wesley's daughter Eliza to the British Museum. The quartet bears no attribution, and it is only its inclusion in this collection that links it to Wesley. It was on this decidedly flimsy evidence that it was attributed to Wesley in the British Museum catalogue and that has led to two recent commercial recordings having been made and released as being unquestionably by him. But there is no documentary evidence of Wesley having composed it, or indeed of him being involved with the composition or playing of string quartets after the first decade of the nineteenth century, when he composed the works discussed above. The style of this piece, with its elaborate concertante writing for all four instruments, suggests a far later date of composition, and is in any case quite different from anything else Wesley wrote. As Peter Holman has

---

[14] *SW to Bridgetower, 23 Feb. 1797.

pointed out, it is closest in style to the *quartets brillants* composed by such composers as Spohr, Rode, and Romberg in the 1820s and 1830s.[15] Unless firm evidence linking it to Wesley appears, it must be excluded from his output.

The Trio for Two Flutes and Piano, KO 514

The **Trio for Two Flutes and Piano**, KO 514, was completed in January 1826 and was published by J. Alfred Novello around 1830. It was dedicated to the flute maker George Rudall, whose name still survives in the company of Rudall, Carte. There is no information in Wesley's letters or elsewhere on what relationship, if any, Wesley had with him, or the circumstances of the composition of the work. As Wesley's only published piece of chamber music, and as his only composition of this period which is not vocal or keyboard music, it is of particular interest. It is a substantial and attractive two-movement work of around eighteen minutes, idiomatically and imaginatively written for all three instruments. The first movement consists of a slow introduction leading to an extended sonata-form Allegro. The second movement is an Andantino consisting of a leisurely theme and four variations, in which each successive variation except the third uses progressively shorter notes and more elaborate figuration, the third variation breaking this pattern by being in the minor and reverting to the character of the theme.

---

[15] Peter Holman, notes to *The String Quartet in Eighteenth-Century England* (Hyperion, CDA 66780), 1995.

23

Keyboard music

Organ music

Wesley's organ music is at the centre of his output. It was as an organist that he was best known in his lifetime, and it was largely through his pre-eminence as a performer that he was able to find a ready market for his compositions. His output for organ is by far the largest of any English composer of his period. Between 1802 and the year of his death, he published around fifty voluntaries, variously titled, individually and in sets. He also published an important collection of short pieces concluding with a further voluntary and a collection of twenty-four interludes for young organists. Yet more pieces, some previously published, some not, were included in Vincent Novello's *Select Organ Pieces*, published in the early 1830s, and in his *Short Melodies for the Organ*, published after Wesley's death. Wesley also composed a large number of pieces that remained unpublished in his lifetime, including juvenilia contained in his Pasticcio Book of 1774–5, two large-scale pieces from the 1780s, four or five voluntaries from his time at Blacklands House in 1817–18, and a large number of individual short pieces composed over the years, many of them probably for teaching purposes.

The organ of Wesley's time

All but Wesley's earliest organ music was written for a typical English organ of the day: of two or three manuals, with a compass from GG to f''' on the Great and Choir, a short-compass Swell from c, and either no pedals at all or a rudimentary pedal-board of an octave, or at most, an octave and a half, of 'pull-downs' that did no more than duplicate or 'pull down' the lowest notes on the Great, enabling the organist's feet to act as a third hand. In the early part of Wesley's career very few organs had separate pedal pipes, and these had only started to come in by its end. The lack of fully independent parts for pedals in most of Wesley's organ music does not mean, however, that pedals were never used: there are many passages with large and awkward stretches in the left hand where the execution is greatly eased by the judicious use of the pedals, and in the later works their use is often specifically called for.

Then, as now, organs varied greatly in size and specification. A typical

Great

Open Diapason I	8
Open Diapason II	8
Stopped Diapason	8
Principal	4
Flute	4
Twelfth	$2\frac{2}{3}$
Cornet (treble)	III ranks
Sesquialtera (bass)	II ranks
Mixture	II ranks
Trumpet I	8
Trumpet II (=Swell)	8

Swell

Open Diapason	8
Stopped Diapason	8
Principal	4
Cornet	III ranks
Trumpet	8

Pedals
One-and-a-half octaves of pull-downs.

Figure 3: Specification of Surrey Chapel Organ (Thomas Elliot, 1794)

example of a fairly large organ of the day, well known to Wesley, was the 1794 Thomas Elliot instrument at Surrey Chapel (Fig. 3). Of two manuals, it had diapason and other flue stops at 8-foot and 4-foot pitch on Great and Swell, some mutation stops, and a cornet and a trumpet on both manuals. It also had an octave and a half of pull-downs.

Wesley was one of the last English organ composers to write predominently for manuals only. By late in his career, full pedal boards had begun to be installed on English organs, and with them, separate pedal pipes and eventually whole pedal divisions. From now on, English organ music would be written on three staves and with independent pedal parts, thus bringing it into line with continental Europe. English organists would learn the art of pedal-playing, and would at last be able to play Bach's organ music in the manner in which he had intended it, instead of as duets for three hands. The introduction of pedals was a development that Wesley welcomed: as we have seen earlier, in the 1820s he made special expeditions with his friends to play organs with pedals, one of which was memorably recorded by Edward Holmes.[1]

Unfortunately, the manuals-only writing of most of Wesley's voluntaries has worked against their continued place in the repertory. Large-scale and ambitiously conceived works for manuals only are a rarity, and organists have understandably tended to pass them over for works which use the full resources

---

[1] See above, pp. 169–70.

of the modern instrument. In addition, and to compound the problem, the long manual compass of the organ for which Wesley wrote makes some of Wesley's lowest manual notes unplayable as they stand on modern instruments. In an attempt to overcome these problems, some pieces appeared during the nineteenth century in arrangements for organs with pedals, and more recently there have been further well-meaning but misguided arrangements along the same lines. It is only within the last few years that a facsimile edition and a complete modern edition of the Op. 6 voluntaries have appeared, followed by editions of Wesley's other voluntaries and shorter pieces. Despite all these efforts, comparatively little of Wesley's organ music has been recorded: at the time of writing there is, for example, still no complete recording of the Op. 6 voluntaries, and only a few isolated recordings of the other organ music.

Early works

As with every other sort of music, Wesley started composing for the organ at a very early age. Among the contents of his Pasticcio Book of 1774–5 are a five-movement **Voluntary in C**, KO 637, three **Movements for the Cornet Stop**, KO 675, and **Four Fugues**, KO 628. Another piece from the same period is an attractive short **Voluntary in D**, KO 639, dated 18 November 1775 and consisting of an Adagio for Diapasons, an Andante for Echo or Swell, and a Fugue on a distinctly Handelian subject for full organ. There were probably many other similar pieces that have not survived.

Wesley's first surviving extended piece for organ is the three-movement **Sonata per il organo**, KO 643, composed in May 1784 for John Langshaw, a young organist from Lancaster who in 1778 had been sent by his father to London to study music, and became a pupil of Wesley's brother Charles. He stayed in London until the winter of 1780–1 before returning home, but spent another three months in London in the first half of 1784.[2] The sonata dates from this second visit. On the title page, Langshaw noted that it was written for him and that the first two pages were composed while he was having his lesson from Charles, and so quickly that a good copyist could not have written the first page. The sonata is in three movements: an Allegro, a ternary Andante in the tonic minor, and another Allegro movement, designated 'fugato'. Its style is quite unlike anything else in Wesley's output for the organ. The style is thoroughly pianistic – although unlike Wesley's own writing for the piano at this time – and were it not for the title, there would be nothing to indicate that it was for the organ rather than the harpsichord or the piano. The first movement is in sonata form and features a good deal of passage work and many loud-soft contrasts. The central Andante is in ternary form, the outer sections consisting of a simple air, and the central section of semiquaver scales and figuration in the right-hand over sustained left-hand chords. The last movement, although designated

---

[2] Wainwright and Saliers, *Wesley/Langshaw Correspondence*, pp. 1–3; *LSW*, p. 133, n. 1.

'fugato', is in sonata form, and soon abandons the imitative texture of its opening for a predominantly two-part texture.

From four years later comes the **Andante Maestoso and Presto in D**, KO 627. From the 'Full' indication at the beginning of the first movement, there can be no doubt that this part of the work, at least, is for organ. But as Robin Langley has pointed out, the second movement, an extended Presto, appears from its style to be for piano, and the presence of pianistic dynamics in the first movement, perhaps added later, suggests that Wesley may have changed his mind during its composition about the instrument for which he intended it.[3] Of one point there can be no doubt: the piece is not an organ concerto, as was inexplicably suggested by one writer in the 1920s.[4]

The Preludes in all the Keys throughout the Octave, KO 636

From 1797 come the unpublished **Preludes in all the Keys throughout the Octave,** KO 636, thirty-four tiny pieces for organ or piano that Wesley probably composed for teaching purposes.[5] 'All the keys' is here not to be interpreted literally, but in the sense of 'all the keys in common use': there are two each in C, D, E, F, G, A, B♭, B, E♭, A♭, C minor, D minor, E minor, F minor, G minor, A minor, and B minor, omitting the seven most distant major and minor keys. They are thus not a collection on the same lines as the '48', although they do exemplify Wesley's firmly held belief, later expressed in one of his Surrey Institution lectures, that keyboard players should as a matter of course become proficient in all the keys. The collection is also of particular interest in that all three of the autograph sources are heavily marked with fingerings.

The Op. 6 Voluntaries, KO 621

All the pieces discussed above remained unpublished, and Wesley's debut in print as a composer of organ music was not until 1802, when he published the first of what would eventually become a set of twelve large-scale voluntaries, the rest appearing at intervals over the next twenty years or so. By this time, Wesley had an impressive reputation as an organist, and particularly as an extempore player. William Seward, in an unsigned piece in the *European Magazine* in 1798, commented:

> Mr. Wesley's power of improvisation on the organ is wonderful; his composition keeps pace with his execution; his melodies, though struck out on the instant, are sweet and varied, never common places; and his harmony is appropriate, and follows them with all the exactness and discrimination of the most elaborate and

---

[3] Langley, 'Samuel Wesley's Contribution to the Development of English Organ Literature', pp. 105–6.
[4] C. W. Pearce, 'A notable eighteenth-century Organ Concerto', *Organ* 7 (1927), pp. 38–41.
[5] Pelkey, '*Preludes in All the Keys throughout the Octave*'. This article includes copious quotations from the preludes and a complete set of their incipits.

studious master; and his execution (however impossible it may be at times to follow his flying fingers with the eye) keeps its proper place, and is never sacrificed to the superior charms of expression.[6]

More recently, Wesley had appeared as the soloist in a Handel organ concerto at the premiere of his *Ode to St Cecilia* in February 1799 and in one of his own concertos at Salomon's performance of Haydn's *Creation* in April 1800. He was by this time widely hailed as the finest organist in England, if not in Europe, and could therefore be confident that any organ music he published would attract widespread attention.

The decision of Wesley and Hodsoll, his publisher, to publish the voluntaries individually rather than as a set, as was more usual, was a shrewd one with obvious benefits for composer, publisher, and purchaser alike. For the composer, it allowed him to publish works as he composed them, and not to wait until he had completed enough for a full set, whether of three, six, or twelve pieces. Publishing in individual numbers at intervals also made sense if he had composed all (or at least some) of the works already, as it kept up interest and demand, and allowed each work to be reviewed as a separate entity. For the publisher, publication in individual numbers was equally advantageous. It spread financial outlay and minimized risk, and sets or series that failed to achieve satisfactory sales could be quietly discontinued. A *passe-partout* (i.e. universal) title page could be produced for the whole set: this would leave a blank space for the number of the individual voluntary to be filled in by hand. The advantages for the purchaser were also clear. Publishing in individual numbers allowed music to be acquired in easy instalments and the cost to be spread over a period – in the case of the Op. 6 voluntaries, a very long period indeed.

Few autographs of the Op. 6 voluntaries have survived – for the most part, they were probably given to the engraver as copy and subsequently discarded – and most of the information on their dates of composition and publication must be derived from reviews and other sources. The appearance of a review of No. 1 in the July 1802 number of the *Monthly Magazine*[7] suggests a publication date some time during that spring or early summer and a composition date perhaps in late 1801 or early 1802. The next seven voluntaries appeared at intervals over the next four years, and were all reviewed in the *Monthly Magazine*. This period was one of profound depression and almost total compositional inactivity for Wesley, and it therefore seems likely that he had composed at least some of these voluntaries earlier and that their publication was deliberately held back so as to release them onto the market at intervals.[8] After the publication of Op. 6 No. 8, some time before October 1806, there was

---

[6] *EM* 34 (1798), p. 161.
[7] *MM* 13 (July 1802), p. 601.
[8] Nos 2–8 were reviewed as follows: No. 2, *MM* 15 (Oct. 1802), 265; No. 3, *MM* 16 (June 1803), p. 439; No. 4, *MM* 16 (Oct. 1803), p. 268; No. 5, *MM* 18 (Sept. 1804), p. 153; No. 6, *MM* 19 (May 1805), p. 369; No. 7, *MM* 21 (Mar. 1806), p. 154; No. 8, *MM* 22 (Oct. 1806), p. 278.

a long break, probably best explained by Wesley's increased commitments in other directions. Nothing is known of the date of publication of No. 9, but the autograph of No. 10 is dated January 1814, and it was performed, published, and reviewed in that year.[9] Nothing is known about the dates of composition and publication of Nos 11 and 12. However, Wesley composed a separate work entitled *Voluntary '12th'*, KO 644, in November 1817 while confined at Blacklands House, and he may have originally intended this as the concluding voluntary of the set. If this conjecture is correct, it is likely that he had already composed No. 11 by this time, although whether it had been published must remain an open question. The date of composition of the true No. 12 may have been some time later, perhaps as late as 1822 or 1823, when Wesley started again to compose after the extended fallow period that followed his breakdown. It is perhaps significant that its style of engraving is markedly different from that of the remainder of the set. Even more significant is the fact that when W. F. Horncastle discussed the Op. 6 voluntaries in his extended essay on Wesley's music in the *Quarterly Musical Magazine and Review* in 1823, he commented only on the first eleven voluntaries, possibly because the twelfth had not at this time been published.[10]

It was to be expected that the first voluntaries published by an organist with Wesley's reputation would be serious works, conceived on a large scale. And in fact the Op. 6 voluntaries are unprecedented in English organ music in the grandeur of their conception and their exploitation of every aspect of organ technique. Although there is a good deal of variety in the number and order of their movements, they are of a piece in their general conception and approach. The first movements are invariably slow: sometimes reflective and sombre (No. 1), sometime lyrical (Nos 2 and 7), sometimes imposing, with the dotted rhythms and swagger of the French Overture (Nos 3 and 5). The second movements, which follow either with or without a break, are invariably Allegros, and often fugues. The last movement of No. 5 is a set of variations based on a theme by the Roman Catholic organist and composer Stephen Paxton, whom Wesley would have known in his youth. For his use of this non-original material Wesley came in for some adverse criticism from the *Monthly Magazine* reviewer, who had nonetheless earlier praised Wesley's use of the canon 'Non nobis, Domine' as the basis for the extended movement that concludes No. 4.

The fugues in Op. 6 are on widely differing types of subject: some diatonic, some chromatic, some terse, some lengthy (Ex. 23.01). Wesley's treatment of fugue, both in the Op. 6 voluntaries and elsewhere, is varied. Some examples are rigorously conceived, maintaining strict fugal texture throughout; others are more informal, largely dispensing with fugal textures and techniques after the first few bars. Some, even those that maintain fugal textures throughout, are discursive, alternating entries of the subject with leisurely interludes and making

---

[9] *New Monthly Magazine* 3 (Mar. 1815), p. 153; *GM*, 1815/1, p. 445.
[10] Horncastle, 'Remarks on Instrumental Composers', pp. 297–8.

Example 23.01, Twelve Voluntaries, Op. 6, KO 621, fugue subjects

little or no use of the devices of stretto, augmentation, diminution, and inversion. Others, such as the fugue in the first of the two voluntaries dedicated to Thomas Adams, use these devices extensively. But fugues and other large-scale movements account for only some of the writing in Op. 6. There are also shorter and more intimate movements, often slow and with a highly characteristic use of chromatic appoggiaturas (Ex. 23.02). Also to be seen is Wesley's fondness for slow movements in compound times, often with the lilting rhythms of the Siciliano, as in the first movement of No. 2: a type that he was repeatedly to return to in his later organ music.

Example 23.02, Voluntary in G minor, Op. 6 No. 9, KO 621, first movement, bars 23–7: chromatic writing

Wesley and J. S. Bach

The question of the influence of J. S. Bach on Wesley's Op. 6 voluntaries and his later organ music has often been raised, but the discussion has usually been vitiated by errors and misconceptions about the chronology of Wesley's discovery of Bach's music and the dates of composition of the individual voluntaries. As we have seen, Wesley's discovery of Bach had two distinct stages. The first was marked by the loan to him by Pinto of a copy of the '48', some time before Pinto's death in March 1806 and Wesley's subsequent making of his own manuscript copy from a copy of the Nägeli edition lent to him by Graeff, which he had completed by late May 1806. The second and more important stage was the explosive awakening of his enthusiasm for Bach's music and the beginning of his Bach crusade early in 1808. It is therefore clear that there can be no question of Bach's influence on the first eight voluntaries of Op. 6. That leaves open the question of the possibility of Bach's influence on the remaining four voluntaries of the set, and on his later organ music. There is in fact strikingly little evidence of Bach's influence, either in overall style or in the use of thematic materials or contrapuntal techniques. There is no general stylistic divide between the first eight voluntaries of Op. 6, composed before Wesley's discovery of Bach, and the remaining four, composed after it. Nor does Wesley's use of fugue change in any way that can be specifically attributed to Bach's influence. In only one case, to be discussed below, can any reference or allusion be found to Bach's own fugal procedures.

The published voluntaries and Wesley's improvisations

For contemporary organists, the relationship between Wesley's published voluntaries and his extemporizations would have been a matter of particular interest, and this was frequently commented on in reviews. The reviewer of Op. 6 No. 1, after describing it as an 'ingenious and truly scientific composition', commented that 'from the first extempore performer on the organ in this country, and perhaps in Europe, we naturally expected a production replete with ingenious evolutions of harmony, and new tracts of modulations, and were in no respect disappointed.'[11] The reviewer of No. 4 – no doubt the same person – applauded Wesley's design 'to furnish the organists of this country with a *suite* of Voluntaries in the style of his own unrivalled extemporary performances'.[12] But it is clear from a number of comments in other reviews that the published voluntaries were only pale reflections of Wesley's improvisations. Horncastle, perhaps the most thoughtful and knowledgeable contemporary musician to write on Wesley's music, stated in his 1823 article that 'the published works of this master can give not the faintest idea of his powers when he sits down unpremeditatedly to his instrument, and of the effective original combinations

[11] *MM* 13 (1802), p. 601.
[12] *MM* 16 (1803), p. 268.

of harmony in which he delights so much to indulge', before going on to express his intention of describing 'in some faint degree' some of the 'splendid evolutions of harmony, the wonderful precision of finger, the astonishing fertility of invention, and the profound learning' displayed in Wesley's performances.[13]

The Grand Duet for the Organ, KO 604

Wesley's **Grand Duet for the Organ**, KO 604, is his largest work for the instrument, and was written for him to perform with Novello at his benefit concert at the Hanover Square Rooms on 5 June 1812. Its composition flowed naturally from his regular practice at this time of playing Bach's organ music with Novello as duets on the organ of the Portuguese Embassy chapel, and earlier with Jacob on the organ of Surrey Chapel.[14] It is an enormous three-movement sonata lasting for around fifteen minutes, and can probably lay claim to being his greatest work for the organ.

There is an inevitable tendency for organ duets, like piano duets, to suffer from thick, heavy, textures. Wesley takes care to avoid this by judicious variation of textures and by antiphonal writing between the two players, while at other times exploiting the opportunities for full sound that the medium makes possible. In the expansive slow movement, he has a few tricks up his sleeve that are not available to composers of piano duets, where by and large the first player must take the treble and the second the bass. Here, Wesley writes interlocking parts for the two performers, to be played on two separate manuals. With contrasting registrations this gives at times the effect of two instruments in dialogue (Ex 23.03). The result is delightful to the listener, although at times highly uncomfortable for the performers. The last movement is an enormous fugue for full organ that brings the work to an exhilarating conclusion.

Two other organ duets should be mentioned here. One is lost: the **Organ Duet**, KO 632, described in the worklist that appeared with Wesley's obituary in the *Musical World* as 'a second grand organ duet, unpublished; the composer preferred this to the other [i.e. the *Grand Duet for the Organ*, KO 604] and considered it his best composition for the organ'. This was presumably the duet that Wesley was referring to in a letter to Burney of early 1802 in connection with his Tottenham Street concerts, when he remarked that he had recently written a duet which he thought 'too complicated for any Chance of *general* Approbation', and which he therefore did not propose to perform at his forthcoming concert.[15] The other is the **Introduction to J. S. Bach's Fugue in E♭**, KO 669, composed in 1814 to go with Novello's arrangement for organ duet of the 'St Anne' Fugue, BWV 552; the first performance was at the benefit

---

[13] Horncastle, 'Remarks on Instrumental Composers', p. 292.
[14] See *Reminiscences*, fol. 51.
[15] *SW to Burney, [Feb.–May 1802].

Example 23.03, Grand Duet for the Organ, KO 604, Andante, bars 50–5: 'criss-cross work'

concert for the widow and children of William Russell at the Foundling Hospital on 15 June of that year. It is very short (51 bars), swiftly moving from its opening key of C minor to E♭, and cadencing on the dominant to lead directly into the fugue. The thematic material is unrelated to what follows, apart from outlining the main subject of the fugue near its end.[16]

Twelve Short Pieces for the Organ with a Full Voluntary Added, KO 617

A different side of Wesley's character as a composer of organ music is seen in the many shorter pieces that he wrote throughout his career. Of these, the most accessible collection is the **Twelve Short Pieces for the Organ with a Full Voluntary Added**, KO 617, completed in July 1816, and described by Wesley in a letter to Novello of the time as 'little tiney nimminy Pippiny Voluntaries'.[17] They were published the following year by Clementi, and around 1820 in a

[16] Bars 25–39 quoted in McCrea, 'British Organ Music after 1800', p. 284.
[17] *SW to Novello, 28 June [1816].

separate edition by Hofmeister of Leipzig, thus becoming Wesley's only work to be published on the Continent in his lifetime. Two of the collection, the 'Air' and 'Gavotte' (neither title is Wesley's own) have long been his best known pieces of organ music and have been repeatedly published and recorded.

There are in fact thirteen short pieces in the set, showing Wesley's skill as a miniaturist and continuing in the vein of some of the shorter movements in Op. 6. They divide by key into four groups: Nos 1–3 are in G, Nos 4–7 are in A minor, Nos 8–10 are in F, and Nos 11–13 are in D. In each group there is a build-up to the last piece, which is for full organ, making each group a miniature voluntary of three or four short pieces, united by key. Various attempts have been made to explain the fact that there are thirteen pieces in the collection. It has been claimed that the last two pieces in fact constitute a single voluntary and thus should be counted together as No. 12. This, however, ignores the fact that in both the autograph and the Clementi edition the pieces are numbered consecutively from 1 to 13.

The **Full Voluntary** that concludes the 'Twelve Short Pieces' is a complete contrast to what has gone before. Whereas the preceding pieces are short, intimate, and above all accessible, the *Full Voluntary* shows Wesley writing on the grand scale and with few concessions to popularity or accessibility. In the first movement, Wesley evokes the style of the French Overture, in writing that is uncompromisingly and harshly dissonant. The fugue, with its angular and distinctive subject, is one of Wesley's most elaborate, and is similarly harsh in its use of dissonance. One contrapuntal tour-de-force should be pointed out: towards the end, Wesley introduces the subject in the bass in irregular augmentation, against three statements of it in the treble in its original form.

The 'Blacklands' Voluntaries

While at Blacklands House in 1817 and 1818 following his breakdown in health, Wesley not surprisingly wrote little. But in the space of just over four weeks in October and November 1817 he did compose a number of organ voluntaries. Although not among Wesley's best works for organ – it is perhaps significant that he appears to have made no subsequent attempts to publish them – they show no very evident signs of diminished competence, let alone of insanity. Similarly, the one extant manuscript of most of these pieces, which was evidently Wesley's working manuscript and not a fair copy made later, bears few indications apart from a few marginal comments of the circumstances in which it was written. This should not come as any surprise, since the chief effect of Wesley's successive attacks of depressive illness on his composing seems to have been to remove the desire to compose and the belief that anything he composed would be of any value rather than significantly to affect the quality of those works that he did manage to produce during these periods.

One of these pieces is the **Voluntary '12th'**, KO 644, already mentioned in the discussion of the Op. 6 voluntaries. Its opening movement, marked 'slow', makes effective use of octave passages on the full Great, contrasting with more flowing sections on the Swell. The following Alla Breve on full organ, like the last movement of Op. 6 No. 1, has some passages where the performer is evidently expected to provide appropriate figuration to amplify the block chords that are all that Wesley provides. The third movement, marked 'moderately slow', does not provide a very satisfactory conclusion to the work, and one suspects that Wesley did not so much conclude as abandon it, notwithstanding the fact that he appended his usual signature and the date (6 November 1817) at its end. Another is the **Voluntary and Fuga in D**, KO 640, dated 8 October, to which the immediately following **Voluntary in D**, KO 641, dated 18 and 20–21 October, probably forms a concluding movement. The fugue is based on a comparatively unmemorable subject and is unremarkable, some instances of inversion of the subject apart. The undated two-movement **Voluntary in C**, KO 638, also in the same manuscript, was no doubt also written at around the same time. It is a very lacklustre affair, consisting of little more than the sequential phrases and melodic formulae that are the stock-in-trade of the Baroque idiom.

The organ music of the early 1820s

After his release from Blacklands House in June 1818 and during the long period of convalescence that followed, Wesley composed as little organ music as he did in other genres. He did, however, publish the **Variations on 'God Save the King'**, KO 619, and the **Variations on 'Rule, Britannia'**, KO 620, both of which appeared in or around 1820 in a series entitled *Beauties for the Organ*. They are unashamed potboilers, probably undertaken for no other reason than the need to generate a little additional income at a difficult time.

Probably in the following year, his **A Book of Interludes for Young Organists**, KO 618, was published by Preston. The work was described in the *Musical World* work-list as published by Coventry and Hollier, the firm who succeeded Preston's around 1834; this was presumably a later reprint. No copies of either edition have been traced, but there was a still later edition of around 1851 by Cocks and Co, from which it can be seen that there were two interludes each in the keys of C, G, D, A, E, F, B♭, E♭, E minor, A minor, D minor, and G minor.

The Voluntaries dedicated to John Harding, KO 615 and 616

On his recovery around 1824, Wesley started once more to compose with something like his old enthusiasm. From this time come two sets of three voluntaries composed for and dedicated to his friend John Harding. It is evident from the titles of the two volumes (*A First Set of Three Voluntaries, A Second Set*), the uniform title page, the continuous pagination, and the numbering of the voluntaries from 1 to 6, that they were conceived as a whole, and that the second volume was probably published shortly after the first, if not simultaneously with it. The two sets show important structural similarities. Each voluntary is in two or three separate movements, and fugues are used only in the concluding movements of the final voluntary of each set. The voluntaries are on a far smaller scale and make fewer technical demands than the Op. 6 set, reflecting either Harding's own abilities as an organist, or perhaps Wesley's desire to reach a wider audience.

Since the time of publication of the earlier Op. 6 voluntaries around twenty years earlier, a good deal had happened in the design of organs. Now, far more English organs were equipped with pedal boards, even though most were still rudimentary and incomplete. This changed situation is reflected in Wesley's writing in the Harding voluntaries, where pedal notes are frequently indicated. Sometimes these can be played on the manuals if no pedals are available, but in other cases they cannot, and the use of pedals is necessary to play the passages in question as written.

Later individual voluntaries

This section considers seven individually published voluntaries, all but one bearing a dedication to one of Wesley's friends and colleagues. Those that are datable were published between 1826 to 1830, and it seems likely that the others are also from around this time.

Probably the earliest of this group are the two **Voluntaries dedicated to Thomas Adams**, KO 606 and 607 (*Preludes and Fugues for the Organ, intended as Exercises for the Improvement of the Hands, and suitable as Voluntaries, for the Service of the Church. Composed & Inscribed to his Friend Thomas Adams Esq. . . . No. 1 [No. 2]*). Adams, nineteen years Wesley's junior, was the leading virtuoso of his generation, best known at this time for his involvement in the ensemble recitals on the Apollonicon, the massive finger- and barrel-organ built and exhibited by Flight and Robson at their premises at 101 St Martin's Lane. With its five consoles, forty-five stops, and independent pedal department, it was the largest organ in England.[18] Here, Adams presided over recitals by up to five organists playing simultaneously, in programmes that showed the instrument to its best advantage and were dominated with arrangements of orchestral music, an area in which Adams himself was renowned. His skill as a pedal player, which Wesley would later comment on in his *Reminiscences*, would doubtless also have been in evidence on these occasions. He also composed a good deal of organ music, characterized by its extensive use of fugue and of intricate contrapuntal textures.

Wesley's two voluntaries have all the appearance of being written with Adams's particular strengths as a composer and player in mind. Both make considerable technical demands and are dominated by enormous fugues. The first voluntary, in C minor, consists of a Preludium, Arietta, and Fugue. The autograph of the Fugue is dated 24 July 1826, and that of a very much shorter

---

[18] Cowgill, 'The London Apollicon Recitals', pp. 190–202.

6 The first page of the autograph of the Fugue from the Voluntary No. 1 in C minor dedicated to Thomas Adams, KO 606. By courtesy of the Royal College of Music, London.

(and presumably earlier) version of the Arietta, in C♯ minor, 1 August of the same year.[19] No copy of the original edition, by Goulding and d'Almaine, has been traced. The sole printed source is a later edition of around 1840 published by d'Almaine and Co. (the successors to Goulding and d'Almaine), probably from the original plates. The Preludium looks back to Op. 6 No. 3, also in C minor, in its use of the French Overture style. The Arietta is more modern, almost Romantic, in its harmonic language and mood. The rather austere three-part fugue extends to 148 bars and explores all the possibilities of its subject, with entries in inversion, stretto, stretto by inversion, and augmentation. Although technically extremely difficult, it is not a showy piece, and impresses rather by the rigour and comprehensiveness of its use of fugal procedures and by the effectiveness of its overall structure. To conclude, Wesley brings in the pedals for the first time in the movement with a statement of the subject in augmentation, which he immediately follows with the final treble entry in double augmentation over a massive dominant pedal-point. In the introduction of the pedal in this manner one is reminded of Bach's use of the same procedure in the Prelude and Fugue in C, BWV 547. Anxious to ensure that his use of these fugal devices does not go unnoticed, Wesley takes care to use the analytical symbols that he first devised for his edition of the '48' to label each entry of the subject and the various contrapuntal devices used. The independent pedal writing of the final page is Wesley's most extensive to date.

The second voluntary, in G, is a complete contrast. A 35-bar Allegro Brillante is followed by an arrangement of the fugue that concluded the almost completely lost Organ Concerto in G, KO 416, of 1813 that survives only in the form of instrumental parts and the final page of the full score. It is even longer than its counterpart in the first voluntary and is of a completely different type: a bravura piece that dispenses completely with complex contrapuntal argument for the sake of sheer barnstorming excitement, rather in the manner of the concluding fugue of Beethoven's String Quartet in C, Op. 59 No. 3 – a piece that Wesley may well have known, either in its original form or in the arrangement for orchestra by Charles Weichsell.[20] As in the earlier voluntary, the writing is of great technical difficulty. Many passages for the manuals are awkward in the extreme, and some are unplayable as they stand. The pedal part, at times requiring the simultaneous use of both feet, ranges over two octaves and is even more extensive than that of its predecessor. This is a piece that could have been played by only a very few organists of the day, and on very few organs.

The only one of Wesley's voluntaries of the 1820s not to bear a dedication is the **Short and Familiar Voluntary**, KO 608, published in early 1827 and as short and straightforward as its title suggests. It is in two movements: the first is a

---

[19] Melody in C♯ minor, KO 672.
[20] See above, p. 141. Wesley would not have heard the two performances in the 1814 Drury Lane oratorio series as he was engaged at the rival Covent Garden series that year, but he may have had heard it on other occasions.

gentle Siciliano with the lilting rhythms of which Wesley was so fond in his shorter movements, and the second a rather wayward March.

The dates of composition and publication of the **Voluntary in G minor dedicated to William Linley**, KO 624, and the **Voluntary in G dedicated to H. J. Gauntlett**, KO 625, are unknown. Both were included in the *Musical World* worklist, which stated that they were published by Monro and May, a firm that started in business around 1823. No copies of the Monro and May editions survive, however, and the two voluntaries are known only from later editions by Robert Cocks and Co. that must date from 1873 or later, as they carry a reference on their uniform title pages to 'the late Emperor Napoleon III', who died in that year. The music appears to have been printed from the original plates, and it is possible that the title page is also original, with the substitution of the name and address of Cocks and Co. for those of the original publishers. If so, it is likely that the two voluntaries were published within a short time of each other, if not simultaneously. They are certainly similar in length and conception, being on a relatively small scale and of no great technical difficulty. The Linley voluntary opens with the customary Largo movement, notable only for calling for the use of pedals throughout to double the bass. The second movement is a sprightly Gavotte, easily the equal in attractiveness to its better-known counterpart in the *Twelve Short Pieces*. In this case, however, the movement has a trio section in the major, followed by a varied reprise of the Gavotte, a variation on it, and a short coda. The Gauntlett voluntary is in three movements: a slow movement, a ternary movement featuring solo stops with a middle section in the tonic minor, and a short concluding movement marked 'With spirit'. As with the Linley voluntary, there is some limited use of the pedals.

The **Voluntary in D dedicated to William Drummer**, KO 623, was published in 1828. It is conceived on a large scale and is in three movements: a ruminative Largo, a lively Fugue (Allegro Moderato), and a March, arranged from the second movement of the overture to the *Ode to St Cecilia*. The fugue is one of Wesley's best. Wesley makes no use of stretto, inversion, or any other of the technical devices of fugue, but fully exploits the rhythmic ambiguity of his subject and concludes with a magnificent peroration. Another feature of this voluntary, like the two voluntaries dedicated to Thomas Adams, is the independent pedal writing that forms a genuine additional voice, albeit one that is used sparingly and requires no great agility from the performer.

The **Voluntary in B♭ dedicated to Thomas Attwood**, KO 622, was composed in 1829 and published early in 1830. It is of similar dimensions to the Drummer voluntary, is also in three movements, and includes an extended fugue. The nature and the extent of the pedal writing is also similar. But there the similarities end. Although no more difficult than the Drummer voluntary, it is a far more showy work, with a good deal of semiquaver figuration in the second movement that is more characteristic of the piano than the organ. Whereas the fugue in the Drummer voluntary was rigorous in its maintenance of fugal texture almost to the end, the fugue in the Attwood voluntary is far more informal, with fugal texture largely abandoned after the opening, and subsequent appearances of the subject and its inversion interspersed with passages in block chords, some of them involving extraordinary harmonic progressions. This movement, one feels, may well stand in a closer relationship to Wesley's improvisations than most of his published fugues.

Other smaller sets of voluntaries

In his final years, and in retirement from public performance, Wesley composed a number of sets of short voluntaries and other pieces. One was the **Six Introductory Movements**, KO 610 (*Six introductory Movements for the Organ, Intended for the Use of Organists as Soft Voluntaries, to be Performed at the Commencement of Services of the Established Church, to which is added a Loud Voluntary with Introduction and Fugue*), published in 1831. The autographs of three of the pieces (which are all that have survived) are designated as 'desk voluntaries' – perhaps implying that they were to be kept on the organ desk to be used for any points in the service when a little filling-in was required – and the other three pieces may also have had this title.

With the *Six Introductory Movements*, Wesley repeated, although on a smaller scale, the formula of the *Twelve Short Pieces* of 1816. But the careful grouping of voluntaries by key of the former set is not present here: the individual voluntaries are in D, E, F, A, C, and E minor, and the concluding Loud Voluntary is in D. In other respects, the pieces are of much the same character as their predecessors. In one important respect, however, the set shows the developments of the intervening years. Like Wesley's longer voluntaries of the period, it demonstrates clearly the greater incidence of pedal boards, if not of independent pedal pipes to go with them, by this time. The number of occasions on which the use of pedals is indicated is far greater than ever before, often in passages that are either impossible or awkward to play on manuals only.

Much of Wesley's organ music of the 1830s was probably written in the first place for his daughter Eliza, who by this time was making good progress as an organist, and would gain her first appointment, at St Katherine Coleman, two months after his death.[21] This was probably the origin of the **Six Organ Voluntaries, composed for the use of Young Organists, Op. 36**, KO 613, a collection of straightforward and attractive short voluntaries in two or three movements, with no use of fugue except in the last movement of the sixth voluntary. Their companion pieces are the **Six Fugues with Introductions for Young Organists**, KO 612, which survive only in the autograph manuscript at the Royal College of Music. No copies of a printed edition have been traced, and it is not known if the set was ever published.[22] The slow introductions are very brief, consisting of only a few bars of chords, and are followed by long and

---

[21] Dawe, *Organists of the City of London*, p. 153.
[22] *Pace SWSB*, these voluntaries are unlikely to have been the *Six Short Voluntaries for the Organ* that were advertised as being in the press in *MW*, 13 Oct. 1837; this publication was probably a reprint of the *Six Voluntaries for Young Organists*, KO 613.

rather rambling movements that can only loosely be described as fugues, in that after the first few bars they abandon all pretence at fugal textures and procedures, apart from occasional entries of the subject. Although fluent and quite attractive, they contain few surprises and little that is particularly distinctive. Much of the writing leans heavily on routine sequential passages of a type that Wesley could probably improvise by the hour. Wesley also published **Six Short Toccatas, Intended as Short Voluntaries for the Use of Organists**, KO 611, at around this time: it was advertised in the *Harmonicon* for March 1832, but no copies have been located.

A number of miscellaneous short pieces for organ or piano also date from this period. Among them are the eight **Duets for Eliza**, KO 667 (the last is incomplete), which we know from Eliza's annotation to have been written for her to play with her father 'when a little girl'. Other pieces, including the **Introduction and Fugue in D minor**, KO 634, and the **Introduction and Fugue in G**, KO 635, are contained in Eliza's music book, a present from her father on her eighteenth birthday on 6 May 1837.

It was around 1830 that Novello began to publish his *Select Organ Pieces*, a multi-volume compilation that consisted in the main of arrangements of sacred music by Haydn, Mozart, Beethoven, and others, but also included eight pieces by Wesley. Two were reprints or arrangements of vocal and organ works that had already been published elsewhere: the fugue from the Voluntary in C minor, Op. 6 No. 3, KO 621, and the 'Sicut erat in principio' fugue from 'Domine salvam fac reginam nostram Mariam', KO 28a, originally printed in Novello's *A Collection of Sacred Music* of 1811. The remaining six pieces were appearing in print for the first time, some of them over thirty years after their composition: they comprised a **Slow Air in D**, KO 614, from 1794, a vigorous **Fugue in D**, KO 603, from 1800, the **Purcellian Air** from the otherwise lost Organ Concerto in B♭, KO 413, also from 1800, the **Largo in F**, KO 605, from 1800 or 1808, the **Fantasy in F**, KO 602, from 1809, and the undated two-movement **Voluntary in B♭**, KO 626. After Wesley's death, Novello would continue this process in another collection, his *Short Melodies for the Organ*.

Further organ music publications continued to appear until and beyond Wesley's death. In the number of the *Musical World* that announced his death, an advertisement by J. Alfred Novello announced that *Six Short Voluntaries for Young Organists* was in the press. Once again, no copies have been traced. In the same advertisement, Novello also announced the forthcoming publication of *Six Desk Voluntaries for the Organ*, presumably a collection of short pieces similar in character to the *Six Introductory Movements*, KO 610. Wesley's final compositions for organ were probably the five little pieces, KO 601, that he wrote for inclusion in *Characteristic Airs for the Royal Seraphine*, a collection compiled by the music publisher John Green for a type of reed organ that he had invented around 1830.

Piano music

Piano music (including some early compositions for piano or harpsichord) makes up the largest category of Wesley's music published in his lifetime. His first published work, in 1777 or early 1778, was a set of sonatas for piano or harpsichord, and he continued to compose and publish for the piano until the last year of his life. His known piano music publications (including those in the press at the time of his death and published posthumously) number over forty, of which copies of some thirty have been located. He also composed a number of works that survive only in manuscript. Some of these, notably four large-scale piano sonatas, an ambitious sonata for piano duet, and the Trio for Three Piano fortes, can be asserted with confidence not to have been published in Wesley's lifetime. Others, principally rondos and variation sets, were probably written with publication in mind, and some may in fact have been published; if so, no copies have been traced.

Wesley and the piano business in London

Wesley's output of keyboard music took place against a background of the replacement of the harpsichord by the piano in the 1760s and the establishment at around the same time of a large number of piano makers who within a few years made London the most important centre in the world for the manufacture and sale of pianos. With the buoyancy of piano sales grew up a host of related trades and professions, giving employment to music publishers and sellers, piano tuners, and teachers. Large amounts could be made by leading performers and from the more entrepreneurial sides of the business such as piano making and music publishing.

Many of the most important figures in the piano business combined playing, composing, and teaching with piano manufacturing and selling, and sometimes also with music publishing and selling. At the head of the profession for much of Wesley's career, and combining all these activities, stood Muzio Clementi, although from 1810 he largely ceased performing in public.[23] Lower down the hierarchy, very respectable incomes could be made from teaching the piano to children and adults. Playing the piano was a desirable accomplishment for young ladies, and piano lessons were offered as a matter of course at girls' schools, many pupils continuing their studies into adulthood. For much of the later eighteenth century and the early years of the nineteenth, the rate for lessons ranged from 5s 3d to 10s 6d (a quarter to half a guinea) per hour, depending on the prestige and reputation of the teacher. Charles Burney was charging his 'masters and misses' 10s 6d an hour in the late 1770s and early 1780s,[24] as was Stevens twenty years later. In 1806, by dint of extremely long hours and very

---

[23] See de Val, 'Gradus ad Parnassum' and 'The Ascent of Parnassus'.
[24] Lonsdale, *Burney*, pp. 234, 272.

large numbers of pupils, Stevens was able to make almost £600 from three days' teaching per week: a considerable income, comparable to the full-time earnings of a moderately successful doctor or lawyer.[25] Such teaching, particularly in girls' schools, was largely invisible, utterly lacking in prestige, and contributed nothing to a musician's public profile and reputation. As most pupils were lacking in both talent and commitment, it was tedious work, and as we have seen earlier, Wesley hated it and often complained about it.[26] But it continued through much of the year and provided a welcome amount of dependable income in a profession that was otherwise notoriously seasonal and insecure. For many musicians, including Wesley for much of his career, it provided a core income that made their other musical activities possible.

For the amateur domestic market, music was composed and published to suit all tastes and levels of competence. At the most serious and exalted level, and beyond the technical reach of all but the most accomplished amateur pianists, were sonatas and other works by such pianist-composers as Clementi, Dussek, and John Baptist Cramer, who with others made up the group now generally known as the London Pianoforte School. The same composers also wrote collections of studies for aspiring pianists, of which Cramer's *Studio per il pianoforte* (1804–10) and Clementi's *Gradus ad Parnassum* (1817–26) were the most celebrated examples. For pianists of lesser abilities, a host of minor composers wrote easier pieces in a variety of genres, of which rondos and variation sets were the most common. These, as can be seen from surviving copies and the review columns in such publications as the *Monthly Magazine* and the *Gentleman's Magazine*, appeared in great numbers, in response to apparently insatiable demand. Many were based on stage songs or popular tunes of the day, and as such were essentially ephemeral novelties whose attractiveness could be expected to be as short-lived as the materials on which they were based.

Wesley was involved with most aspects of the piano business at different stages of his career, mostly as a teacher and as a composer of piano music, but also on occasion as a performer – although he would have been the first to admit that he was not in the same league as a Cramer or a Clementi. With few exceptions, he eschewed in his published works the type of virtuoso works composed by Clementi, Dussek, Cramer, and others, and for the most part confined himself to the less technically demanding – and therefore more saleable – areas of rondos and variation sets and other short pieces. For a composer of his facility, such works were easily composed, and provided a ready source of income.

---

[25] Stevens's account book (CUL, Add. MS 9112). See also Argent (ed.), *Recollections of R. J. S. Stevens*. For a discussion of incomes from teaching, see Ehrlich, *Music Profession*, pp. 32–5; Olleson, 'Samuel Wesley and the Music Profession', pp. 29–31. For the comparison with the earnings of other professions, see Patrick Colquoun, *A Treatise on Indigence*, London, 1806, 23–4, cited in McVeigh, *Concert Life*, pp. 197–9.
[26] See above, p. 88.

Sonatas and Sonatinas

Wesley's first published compositions for piano were the **Eight Sonatas for the Harpsichord or Pianoforte**, KO 701, dedicated to Daines Barrington and published in 1777 or early 1778.[27] They are remarkably confident and assured productions, given that Wesley was only eleven or twelve when he wrote them. All except two (which are in two movements) are in three movements, with one sonata in each major key up to three flats and four sharps. There is considerable variation in length: the two-movement first sonata is the shortest at only four pages, whereas the second is twice as long, and the others fall somewhere in between. Most are in a fast-slow-fast pattern, but the sixth sonata looks back to older models with its slow first movement and concluding Giga. The finales of four sonatas are rondos, all with two episodes, the first short, and the second much longer and in the tonic minor: the same formal arrangement has already been noted in similar movements in the violin concertos and violin sonatas. The writing is straightforward and in a 'neutral' style, designed to be equally suitable for harpsichord and piano: largely in two or three parts, and with a sparing use of dynamic markings. The best sonata of the set is probably No. 7 in G, available in a facsimile edition.[28]

Also from around this period, and possibly by Wesley, are three sonatas ascribed to him in a manuscript volume bequeathed to the British Library in 2000 by the English musicologist Alan Tyson.[29] The identity of the copyist of the manuscript, which also contains a number of sonatas by Scarlatti, is unknown, but the sonatas ascribed to Wesley are of comparable length and in a comparable style to the sonatas of 1777 or 1778 discussed above, and may well be by Wesley, as the inscription on the cover asserts.

Wesley's next two piano publications are lost. One was **An Italian Rondeau**, KO 740, mentioned in a letter of June 1783 to Wesley from the castrato singer Gasparo Pacchierotti, and also publicized on an advertisement for the 1785 season of family concerts. The other was **Lunardi's March**, KO 741, included on the same advertisement, and evidently written to celebrate the exploits of the aeronaut Vincenzo Lunardi, who made the first balloon ascent in England on 15 September 1784. These were followed by the **Two Sonatas for the Piano Forte or Harpsichord, with an Accompaniment for a Violin, Op. 2**, KO 507, published no later than 1786: the British Library copy has this date inscribed on the title page, presumably by its first owner. These works are appropriately discussed here, as it was the norm at this time for piano sonatas to have

---

[27] Pace Caldwell (*English Keyboard Music before the Nineteenth Century*, p. 227), who conjectures a date of publication of 1790 on stylistic grounds, a date of publication in either 1777 or 1778 is well documented. Barrington (*Miscellanies*, 306–7) states that they were published in 1777, and they are mentioned in a letter from Tryphena Bathurst to SW of 26 Jan. 1777 or 1778: see *SWSB*, p. 107.

[28] Nicholas Temperley, *Works for Pianoforte Solo by late Georgian Composers: Samuel Wesley and Contemporaries* (*The London Pianoforte School, 1766–1860*, vol. 7).

[29] BL, Tyson MS 4.

'accompaniments' for violin or flute, and for these to be entirely optional. This appears to be the case with these sonatas, in which the piano part is completely self-sufficient. It is difficult, however, to assess what the contribution of the violin was, as it is not indicated in the piano part, and the violin part is missing from the British Library copy. Each sonata is in two movements: a binary quick movement followed by the standard rondo with two episodes.

The date of publication of the **Three Sonatas for the Piano Forte, Op. 3**, KO 702, is not known, but must have been in or before May 1789, when the partnership of Birchall and Andrews, the publishers, was dissolved. These are more ambitious works than the sonatas in the previous two sets: longer, and making greater technical demands on the performer. The first and the third are of roughly equal size and are in three movements; the second is only half as long, and in two. The predominating form is the two-episode rondo. Predictably, it is the form of the last movements of the first and third sonatas, but it is also that of the first movement of No. 3, which begins as if it is a set of variations before turning into a rondo later. The last movement of the same sonata is of a more brilliant type that contains the greatest technical challenges of the set. The second sonata starts with yet another rondo, but on a smaller scale, and concludes with a short minuet.

From around the same time is **The Favorite Duett in the Opera of La Cosa Rara, varied & adapted for the Piano Forte**, KO 709, published no later than January 1789. Notwithstanding the implication of its title, this is again a simple rondo with two episodes, and a highly attractive and gratefully written piece. It differs from Wesley's other rondos of the period and later by having both episodes of roughly the same length, by the second not being in the minor, and by the final statement of the theme being adapted to form a coda. Characteristically, it ends quietly. Its relationship with Vincente y Soler's opera *Una cosa rara* is worth mentioning. *Una cosa rara* was not performed in London until January 1789, but the duet on which the rondo is based – similar in character to the number from the same opera played by the on-stage wind ensemble in the supper scene of Mozart's *Don Giovanni* – had been included in performances of a revival of Arne's *Comus* from October of the previous year. It had become immediately popular, and Wesley evidently wrote the rondo to exploit this popularity. It was reviewed in favourable terms in the *Analytical Review* in February 1789, where the anonymous reviewer commented that it showed 'considerable taste, and a perfect knowledge of the instrument for which the duet is altered.'[30]

Two years later, in 1791, Wesley composed his only major work for piano duet, a genre that had initially been popularized in England by J. C. Bach and the young Mozart in the 1760s. Later, Burney published two sets of four sonatas in 1777 and 1778, Clementi included duets as part of his Op. 3 (1779), and Theodore Smith composed many simple works in the form from 1779

[30] *Analytical Review* 3 (1789), p. 237.

on.[31] Many of the pieces in this agreeable domestic form are understandably slight and technically undemanding, but the **Sonata in G**, KO 825, is a large and ambitious three-movement work from June 1791 of around twenty minutes that exploits the full range of the piano. In its overall conception it invites comparison with Mozart's mature duet sonatas in F, K 497, and C, K 521, of 1786 and 1787, both of which Wesley could have known, as they had been published in Vienna in 1787. Wesley's sonata was not published, and survives only in the form of the last four pages of the autograph and a complete copy in the hand of Novello. The opening movement is a sonata-form Allegro preceded by a short slow introduction in the tonic minor. It is followed by a Largo in the dominant with some elaborate and grateful figuration for both players. The third movement is a set of four variations on a leisurely theme marked 'Commodo', each successive variation using shorter note-values, and ending with a thematically related Presto coda. Once again, there is a quiet ending.

Wesley also wrote three unpublished sonatas during the late 1780s and early 1790s that show him coming closest to the manner of such better-known piano composers of the London Piano School as Clementi, Dussek, and Cramer. The first, the **Sonata in E♭**, KO 750, dates from November 1788. Its sole source is a manuscript that was evidently Wesley's composition draft. It bears all the signs of having been written extremely fast, with numerous corrections and abbreviations. The first movement, in sonata form, is wild and rhapsodic, full of abrupt switches from cantabile passages to virtuoso figuration and back again, and with a good deal of chromaticism and minor-inflected harmonies. The slow movement, a pathetic Andante, is in G minor, with further extensive use of chromaticism. The finale is a headlong Presto assai, with sonata-form elements, and ending unexpectedly quietly.

The other two sonatas, which evidently belong together, date from Wesley's first year at Ridge. The **Sonata in B♭**, KO 751, of January 1793 (marked 'No. 1' on the autograph) opens with a broadly conceived sonata-form movement based on a theme in which an initial *forte* arpeggio figure is followed by a quieter, more lyrical consequent, in a manner that looks back to the characteristic openings of works by members of the Mannheim School. Unusually, both the second and third movements are rondos, with the usual two episodes, the second in the tonic minor. The slow movement, an Andante, is based on a florid and richly decorated melody with an equally elaborate accompaniment; the final movement is a lively 6/8 Allegro. The **Sonata in A**, KO 752 (marked 'No. 2' on the autograph), dates from October 1794, and thus belongs to the period of intense activity that also saw the composition of the *Ode to St Cecilia*, which was completed a little over two weeks later. The first movement, in sonata form, is decidedly eccentric in its proportions, with a long development section culminating in an extended dominant preparation that leads to a perfunctory recapitulation consisting of no more than a statement of both main themes

---

[31] Johnstone and Fiske, *The Eighteenth Century*, pp. 8, 423.

followed by four semibreve cadential chords (marked 'perdendosi') to bring the movement to an abrupt close, almost as if Wesley had run out of interest in pursuing his musical argument any further. The ternary slow movement, in B minor, is extremely brief. The finale is an attractive set of variations.

The numbering of the sonatas suggests that Wesley at one time may have intended to publish them together, either as a pair or as the first two items of a larger set. But some of the formal features of the second sonata, identified above, and the markedly more untidy appearance of its autograph, suggests that Wesley may have been rushed in its composition, and in the end have decided not to proceed with publication. At all events, these two sonatas and their predecessor of 1788 deserve a modern edition and a recording.

Wesley probably composed the **Twelve Sonatinas for the Piano Forte or Harpsichord... Op. 4**, KO 703, in late 1798: we know from a letter of Wesley to Latrobe of early 1799 that they had then just been published.[32] They are simple one-movement pieces for beginners, complete with fingerings. The **Four Sonatas and two Duets, Op. 5**, KO 704 were published around 1801 (the dating comes from the watermark on the British Library's copy). The sonatas are in two movements, and the duets are in three, and are scarcely more technically demanding than the Sonatinas.

The **Sonata for the Piano Forte, in which is introduced a Fugue from a Subject of Mr. Salomon**, KO 705, is in an entirely different category from the earlier published sets of sonatas and was evidently aimed at a different audience. It is an ambitious and challenging two-movement work in D minor, dominated by the fugue on Salomon's theme. The first movement, in D minor, consists of a short but imposing introduction followed by the Fugue; the second is a relaxed and easy-going Rondo in the tonic major. The overall scheme, of a challenging and hard-driven movement in the minor followed by a more relaxed one in the major, may put the present-day listener in mind of Beethoven's Sonata in E minor, Op. 90: a work, however, that was not composed until six years later.

One particular point of interest about the sonata is its date of composition. As with much of Wesley's keyboard music, there is no extant autograph, but it was reviewed in the May 1808 number of the *Monthly Magazine*, and thus published probably a month or two earlier.[33] Wesley thus may have composed it in early 1808, at just the time of his explosive discovery of the music of J. S. Bach. If this were the case, it might be expected that there would be some hint of Bach's style, particularly in the Fugue. But in fact, the writing is not even remotely tinged by Bach, and the Fugue is in the austere, gritty manner that characterizes so many fugues by composers of the late Classical period, and of which other examples are to be found in the works of Mozart, Haydn, Beethoven, and Schubert. It can also be seen as a continuation of Wesley's own interest in fugue, to be seen in many other works, published and

---

[32] *SW to Latrobe, after 6 Feb. 1799.
[33] *MM* 25 (1808), p. 341.

unpublished, of the period. Fugues featured prominently in his Op. 6 organ voluntaries to date, and he had also composed three free-standing fugues for keyboard around the turn of the century. And as we have seen, at the same time he also composed a particularly involved fugue for string quartet on a theme from Haydn's *Creation* that explores all the technical devices of inversion, augmentation and diminution.

Wesley published nothing later comparable in scale to this Sonata. There is, however, a large-scale work that he appears to have started in 1813, abandoned, and then completed at a far later stage: the **Sonata in C**, KO 753. There is only the smallest amount of documentary evidence about this composition. The autograph, which is the only manuscript source, is all of a piece and bears a date of 1813–14 at the beginning and of March 1831 at the end. And in a letter to Novello of February 1814, Wesley commented that he had finished the slow movement of a sonata.[34] This suggests that Wesley had composed the first two movements of the sonata in 1813 and 1814, failed to complete it, and then recopied it in 1831, at the same time adding the final movement. He may at this time have revised the first two movements, but in the absence of any other manuscript sources, it is impossible to tell. It was eventually published around 1880 in an edition by Wesley's daughter Eliza. Like the three sonatas of the late 1780s and the early 1790s, it is a big, expansive work, very different from the published sonatas. The opening Moderato Allegro is a sprawling sonata-form movement of 220 bars, bringing to mind the first movement of the Sonata in E♭ of 1789 in its rhapsodic character and frequent shifts of mood and texture. The slow movement, a rondo with two episodes on a leisurely song-like theme, also has elements of the set of variations, in that the second and third statements of the rondo theme are successively more elaborate. The third movement is another rondo, this time again on a jerky 6/8 theme of only eight bars, its statements completely dwarfed by the two episodes, which include a good deal of rapid passage-work in arpeggios and double thirds. Like the three unpublished sonatas of the late 1780s and early 1790s, the sonata is a work well worth exploring and performing. Pianists who wish to do so would be well advised not to rely on Eliza's highly inaccurate edition, however, but to acquire a copy of the autograph from the British Library.[35]

The Trio for Three Pianofortes, KO 826

Standing apart from Wesley's other piano music is the **Trio for Three Pianofortes**, KO 826, completed on 20 April 1811 and first performed a week later at Wesley's benefit at the Hanover Square Rooms by Wesley himself, Novello, and Charles Stokes. As we have seen earlier, it was inspired by Mozart's Sonata in D for two pianos, K 448/375a, which Wesley had first encountered on

---

[34] *SW to Novello, [4 Feb. 1814].
[35] BL, Add. MS 35008, fol. 8.

his visit to Cambridge in the summer of 1808.[36] Like the Mozart sonata, it is in D major, and is a substantial work of around fifteen minutes. It is in two movements: a sonata-form movement with a short slow introduction in the tonic minor (thus recalling the Sonata in G for piano duet), and a leisurely set of variations with coda. As in the *Grand Duet for the Organ*, Wesley takes care to vary his sonorities and to include a good deal of dialogue between the players so as to avoid the heaviness of texture that would result from over-much reliance on full passages. The result is a highly attractive work, serious yet at the same time full of playfulness. It will never become a frequently performed work, but a recent broadcast and recording have perhaps made it better known and will perhaps encourage further performances.

Variation sets and rondos

Wesley is known to have published nine variation sets and seventeen rondos. There may have been more, as some works that now survive only in manuscript may also have been published, and yet more sets may have disappeared completely without trace. All those extant or known from advertising or reviews to have been published were based on well-known melodies. The variation sets include **The Bay of Biscay**, KO 708; **Jessy of Dunblane**, KO 712; **Patty Kavanagh**, KO 713; **Scots wha' hae wi' Wallace bled**, KO 715; and **The Hornpipe and Variations from a favorite Organ Concerto**, KO 711, an arrangement of the last movement of Wesley's own Organ Concerto in D, KO 414. The rondos include **I Attempt from Love's Sickness to Fly**, KO 723, based on Purcell's song; **The Christmas Carol**, KO 718, on 'God rest ye merry, Gentlemen'; **Bellissima Signora**, KO 717, on a 'favorite song' by M. P. King; **The Deserter's Meditations**, KO 719, on a 'favorite Irish Air'; **Jacky Horner**, KO 724, on the popular nursery rhyme; and **Off she goes**, KO 727, on 'a popular air'. **A Favorite Air Composed by Carl Maria von Weber**, KO 720, is on 'Wenn die Maien grün sich kleidern', Op. 71 No. 5 (the *Lied der Hirtin*), a song by Weber that was inserted into London performances of *Der Freischütz* in 1824. **The Widow Waddle**, KO 732, and **Will Putty**, KO 733, are on songs sung by the clown Joseph Grimaldi in pantomimes in 1807 and 1808, and presumably composed and published shortly afterwards.

Of the two forms, the variations set is the more straightforward: at its simplest, a series of varied treatments of the theme, using different forms of decoration and figuration. Variation sets were easy to write, even for those of limited compositional ability and talent, and not surprisingly many were tedious in the extreme in their repetitiveness and poverty of invention. What marked out a good set of variations from a bad one was the inventiveness of the composer and his skill in varying the mood and character of variations so as to construct an interesting and pleasing whole, and one with some overall sense of structure. A typical and markedly successful example is **A favorite popular**

---

[36] See above, pp. 78–9.

Polish Air, with New Variations, KO 714, published probably in late 1805 or early 1806. There are six variations of steadily increasing difficulty. Variation 1 presents the minor key theme unadorned, with an accompaniment of continuous semiquavers. Variation 2 is similar, but in the major, while Variation 3 returns to the minor and introduces triplet semiquaver movement. Variation 4 is in the major, with octaves in both hands, and right-hand passages extending to c'''', exploiting the extreme treble range of the newest pianos by Clementi; alternatives are provided for those with instruments with the more usual compass only to f'''. Variation 5, a mock-serious Lento, returns to the minor, and the final variation, an Allegro, rounds the piece off with more passage work and a further exploration of the piano's topmost register.

Rather more ambitious is the set of variations on **The favorite Air of the Bay of Biscay**, KO 708, dedicated to Clementi and published by his firm in early 1813. The melody, a sea shanty, had been popular since its inclusion in John Davy's opera *Spanish Dollars*, first produced at Covent Garden in 1805. The early variations either present the theme virtually unchanged, but with increasingly elaborate accompaniment figuration, or subject it to gentle decoration. Variation 5, marked 'Poco Largo', takes a fragment of the melody and repeats it in the accompaniment in a sequence from the top of the piano to the bottom, its last appearance coinciding with its appearance in the melody (Ex 23.04).

Example 23.04, Variations on 'The Bay of Biscay', KO 708, Variation 5

Variation 6, marked 'brillante' uses a good deal of hand-crossing. Variation 7 is an Alla Polacca, while Variation 8, marked 'Alla Fughetta', uses canon at the fourth and the sixth, in a manner that inevitably brings to mind Bach's *Goldberg Variations*, a work that Wesley knew well by this time. The Allegro final variation makes as if to bring the work to a brilliant conclusion, but in fact ends quietly.

Wesley's variation sets stand out from other contemporary English works in the genre by virtue of the superiority of their inventiveness and craftsmanship.

Much the same can be said about his rondos. In its most basic form, the piano rondo of this period consists simply of a number of statements of the rondo theme alternating with thematically unrelated episodes. In Wesley's hands, however, the treatment is less straightforward and more subtle: he blurs the distinction between statements of the rondo theme and episodes by constructing the episodes in part out of material from the theme; in addition, he varies the treatments of the rondo theme on their successive appearances, thus bringing in some of the characteristics of variation. Two good examples are the rondos on **The Widow Waddle**, KO 732, and **Will Putty**, KO 733, both of which are carefully written to appeal to pianists of only moderate technique, while at the same time presenting them with the occasional challenge. Each is fairly short, extending to only five pages of music and with only three appearances of the rondo theme and two interludes, and features felicitous points of detail that raise the standard of the whole to well above that of most other contemporary pieces in the genre.

There are similar features in the slightly more extended rondo on **The Deserter's Meditations**, KO 719, which was particularly well received by the critic of *The Repository of Arts*, whose comments could be applied to many of Wesley's rondos and variation sets:

> In this small publication we meet with ample traces of the mastery of its author. It is not a rondo patched up out of a few common-place turns and chords, just to be played once and then to be consigned to the heap of modern musical rubbish. Mr Wesley has taken up a common subject, and treated it in a manner which becomes an adept in the science of harmonies. The theme makes its appearance in a variety of protean shapes and keys, constantly diversified by the hand of sterling art. We are at one time entertained with neatly fuged contrivances, at another some masterly counterpoint claims our attention. Every bar partakes of the spirit of the subject, while it displays the skill of the composer. To the true connoisseur this rondo will afford a high treat, and to such only we wish to recommend it, as it would be thrown away upon an ear vitiated by the ephemeral sing-song products of the day.[37]

The Deserter's Meditations appears to have enjoyed continuing popularity. Ten years after its publication it was singled out by Horncastle with the comment that it was 'full of points and answers, for which the theme is well adapted, and you discern it ever and anon appearing through the rich harmony in which it is clothed, a welcome intruder'.[38] Another rondo, better known today by virtue of having been commercially recorded, is **The Christmas Carol**, KO 718, where Wesley produces a work of considerable subtlety and elegance from the well-known melody.

As is apparent from the *Repository of Arts* review of *The Deserter's*

---

[37] *The Repository of Arts, Literature, Commerce, Manufactures, Fashion and Politics*, 8 (July 1812), p. 43. Wesley was highly amused by the effusiveness of this review: see *SW to Novello, [?2 July 1812]. Its author was probably Lewis Engelbach: see Ford, *Ackermann 1783–1983: The Business of Art*, pp. 77–83.

[38] Horncastle, 'Remarks on Instrumental Composers', p. 294.

Meditations, reviewers of Wesley's music recognized and acknowledged his talent for producing works of interest and high quality in a field dominated by the workaday and the trivial. Perhaps for this reason, they were also quick to take him to task when he fell short of his usual high standards and produced out-and-out potboilers. One of these was **The Siege of Badajoz**, KO 706, written and published in 1812 to celebrate the siege and capture of the Spanish town that was one of the main British successes in the Peninsular War in April of that year. With its musical depictions of the various stages of the siege, this 'characteristic sonata' exploited the topicality of the recent campaign and the current popularity of battle pieces. The reviewer in the *Gentleman's Magazine* was far from impressed, reporting disdainfully that he had attended a performance together with some 'musical criticks', and that at the end 'it was amusing to observe their astonishment that Mr Wesley, one of the first Organists of the present age, was the author of a piece so every way unworthy of his name.'[39] Another piece in the same vein was **The Sky Rocket**, KO 743, a 'Grand Jubilee Waltz' published in 1814 and dedicated to William Congreve, the inventor of the military rocket that bears his name, in which Wesley depicted the ascent of the rocket by glissandi. About this the *Gentleman's Magazine* reviewer was equally scathing, commenting that it was 'lamentable that this very learned musician should not find it more advantageous to employ his distinguished talents on their proper objects than on unmeaning trifles, like the present', and wishing for the sake of young organists that he would continue with his voluntaries instead of wasting his time on such rubbish.[40]

Wesley continued to compose and publish piano music on an occasional basis up to the end of his life. As with the organ music of the 1830, much of the simple piano music of the period, including some duets, was written for Eliza. Some, like the **Grand Coronation March**, KO 737, published following the accession of Queen Victoria in June 1837, was opportunistic recycling: like the last movement of the *Voluntary dedicated to William Drummer*, KO 623, it was an arrangement of the March from the Overture to the *Ode to St Cecilia*. Other pieces were unpublished, and were probably written entirely for domestic use: they include a number of short movements that could equally well be for the organ.

---

[39] *GM* 1813/1 (Jan. 1813), p. 60.
[40] *GM* 1814/2 (Sept. 1814), p. 260.

Bibliography

Details of the works most frequently cited are given in the list of Abbreviations (pp. xviii–xix)

Manuscript sources

Horsley papers, Oxford, Bodleian Library, MS Eng. e. 2134
Latrobe, Christian Ignatius, Journal, John Rylands Library of Manchester, Eng. MS 1244
John Marsh Journals, San Marino, CA, Henry E. Huntington Library and Art Gallery
Royal Philharmonic Society Archive, London, BL, RPS MSS 272–417
Sir George Smart papers, London, BL, Add. MSS 41771–9, 4225
R. J. S. Stevens papers, CUL, Add. MSS 9109–12
Wesley, Samuel, *Reminiscences*, London, BL, Add. MS 27593

Printed sources

Ackroyd, Peter, *London: The Biography*, London, 2000
Almon, J. (compiler), *An Asylum for Fugitive Pieces, in Prose and Verse, not in any other Collection: with Several Pieces never before Published*, 4 vols, London, 1785–93
Altick, Richard, *The Cowden Clarkes*, London, 1948
Anon., *The Picture of London*, published annually
—— 'Mr Samuel Wesley', *The Times*, 12 October 1837
—— 'Professional Memoranda of the Late Mr. Samuel Wesley's Life', *MW* 7 (1837), pp. 81–93, 113–18
Anstruther, Godfrey, *The Seminary Priests: A Dictionary of the Secular Clergy of England and Wales, 1558–1830*, 4 vols, Great Wakering, 1969–77
Argent, Mark (ed.), *Recollections of R. J. S. Stevens: An Organist in Georgian London*, London, 1992
Arminian Magazine, 1778–97
Baker, Frank, *Charles Wesley as Revealed by his Letters*, London, 1948; rev. edn 1995
—— *Charles Wesley's Verse: An Introduction*, London, 1964; rev. edn 1988
Banks, Chris, 'From Purcell to Wardour Street: A Brief Account of Music Manuscripts from the Library of Vincent Novello now in the British Library', *British Library Journal* 21/2 (Autumn 1995), pp. 240–58
Baptie, David, *Sketches of the English Glee Composers*, London, 1895
Barrett, William Alexander, *English Glees and Part-Songs: An Enquiry into their Historical Development*, London, 1886
Barrington, Daines, *Miscellanies*, London, 1781
Bashford, Christina, and Leanne Langley (eds), *Music and British Culture, 1785–194: Essays in Honour of Cyril Ehrlich*, Oxford, 2000

Beedell, Ann, *The Decline of the English Musician, 1788–1888*, Oxford, 1992
Bennett, Joseph, 'A Novello Centenary', *MT* 22 (1881), pp. 495–7
Bicknell, Stephen, *The History of the English Organ*, Cambridge, 1996
Black, Clementina, *The Linleys of Bath*, rev. edn, London, 1971
Boeringer, James, *Organa Britannica: Organs in Great Britain 1660–1860*, 3 vols, London and Toronto, 1989
Bor, Margaret, and L. Clelland, *Still the Lark: A Biography of Elizabeth Linley*, London, 1962
Bossy, John, *The English Catholic Community 1570–1850*, London, 1975
Boyle's New Fashionable Court and County Guide and Town Visiting Directory, published annually
Brewer, John, *The Pleasures of the Imagination: English Culture in the Eighteenth Century*, London, 1997
Bridge, Tom, and Colin Coope English, *Dr William Kitchiner: Regency Eccentric*, Lewes, 1992
Broughton, Augusta Delves (ed.), *Court and Private Life in the Time of Queen Charlotte: Being the Journals of Mrs Papendiek, Assistant Keeper of the Wardrobe and Reader to Her Majesty*, 2 vols, London, 1887
Brown, James D., and Stephen S. Stratton, *British Musical Biography*, London, 1897, repr. New York, 1971
Brown, Robert W., *Charles Wesley Hymnwriter: Notes on Research carried out to establish the Location of his Residence During the Period 1749–1771*, Bristol, 1993 (privately printed: available from the Charles Wesley Heritage Centre, Bristol)
Bunce, John Thackray, *A History of the Birmingham General Hospital and the Music Festivals*, Birmingham, 1858
Burchell, Jennifer, *Polite or Commercial Concerts? Concert Management and Orchestral Repertoire in Edinburgh, Bath, Oxford, Manchester, and Newcastle, 1730–1799*, New York, 1996
Burgh, Allatson, *Anecdotes of Music, Historical and Biographical; in a Series of Letters from a Gentleman to his Daughter*, London, 1814
Burney, Charles, *A General History of Music, from the Earliest Ages to the Present Period*, 4 vols, London, 1776–89
—— *An Account of the Musical Performances in Westminster Abbey*, London, 1785
—— ed. Alvaro Ribeiro, SJ, *The Letters of Dr Charles Burney, Vol. I: 1751–1784*, Oxford, 1991
Burney, Frances, *Evelina, or, A Young Lady's Entrance into the World*, London, 1778
—— *Cecilia, or, Memoirs of an Heiress*, London, 1782
Burrows, Donald (ed.), *George Frideric Handel: The Complete Hymns and Chorales*, London, 1987
—— *Handel*, London, 1994
Burrows, Donald, and Rosemary Dunhill (eds), *Music and Theatre in Handel's World: James Harris and his Family, 1732–1780*, Oxford, 2002
Butler, David, *Methodists and Papists: John Wesley and the Catholic Church in the Eighteenth Century*, London, 1995
Caldwell, John, *English Keyboard Music before the Nineteenth Century*, Oxford, 1973
—— *The Oxford History of English Music*, 2 vols, Oxford, 1991, 1999
The Catalogue of Printed Music in the British Museum until 1980, 62 vols, London, 1987
Chappell, Paul, *Dr S. S. Wesley*, Great Wakering, 1977
Chedzoy, Alan, *Sheridan's Nightingale: The Story of Elizabeth Linley*, London, 1997

Christiansen, Rupert, *Prima Donna: A History*, London, 1984; 2nd edn, 1995

Clark, Richard, *The First Volume of Poetry, Revised, Improved, and considerably Enlarged, containing the most favorite Pieces, as performed at the Noblemen and Gentlemen's Catch Club, the Glee Club . . . and all public Societies*, London, 1824

[Clarke, Mary Ann], *An Account of the Infancy, Religious and Literary Life of Adam Clarke . . . by a Member of his Family*, 3 vols, London, 1833

Clarke, Mary Cowden, *Life and Labours of Vincent Novello*, London, 1864

—— *My Long Life: an Autobiographic Sketch*, London, 1896

Clarke's New Law List, published annually

Colvin, Howard, *A Biographical Dictionary of British Architects 1600–1840*, London, 1978

Cowgill, Rachel, 'The London Apollonicon Recitals, 1817–32: A Case Study in Bach, Mozart, and Haydn Reception', *JRMA* 123 (1998), 190–228

—— 'Mozart's Music in London, 1764–1829: Aspects of Reception and Canonicity', Ph.D. diss., King's College, University of London, 2000

—— 'The Papers of C. I. Latrobe: New Light on Musicians, Music and the Christian Family in Late Eighteenth-Century England', in Jones, *Music in Eighteenth-Century Britain*, pp. 234–58

—— '"Wise Men from the East": Mozart's Operas and their Advocates in Early Nineteenth-Century London', in Bashford and Langley (eds), *Music and British Culture*, pp. 39–64

Cox, H. B. and C. L. E. (eds), *Leaves from the Journal of Sir George Smart*, London, 1907

Crosby, Brian, 'Stephen and Other Paxtons', *ML* 81 (2000), pp. 41–64

Crotch, William, *Specimens of Various Styles of Music Referred to in a Course of Lectures read at Oxford & London*, 3 vols, London, 1808–10

—— *Substance of Several Courses of Lectures on Music, Read in Oxford and in the Metropolis*, London, 1831

David, Hans T., and Arthur Mendel, revised and enlarged by Christoph Wolff, *The New Bach Reader: A Life of Johann Sebastian Bach in Letters and Documents*, New York and London, 1998

Davies, Rupert E., *Methodism*, Harmondsworth, 1963

Dawe, Donovan, *Organists of the City of London 1666–1850*, Padstowe, 1983

Doane, John, *A Musical Directory for the Year 1794*, London, 1794

Drabble, Margaret, *The Oxford Companion to English Literature*, 6th edn, Oxford, 2000

Drummond, Pippa, 'The Royal Society of Musicians in the Eighteenth Century', *ML* 59 (1978), pp. 268–89

E[dwards], F. G., 'Bach's Music in England', *MT* 37 (1896), pp. 585–7, 652–7, 722–6, 797–800

—— 'Samuel Sebastian Wesley', *MT* 41 (1900), pp. 297–302, 369–74, 452–6

—— 'Samuel Wesley', *MT* 43 (1902), pp. 523–8, 798–802

—— 'Vincent Novello 1781–1861', *MT* 44 (1903), pp. 577–81, 650–3, 787–90

Ehrlich, Cyril, *The Piano: A History*, Oxford, 1976

—— *The Music Profession in Britain since the Eighteenth Century: A Social History*, Oxford, 1985

—— *First Philharmonic: A History of the Royal Philharmonic Society*, Oxford, 1995

Elkin, Robert, *Royal Philharmonic: The Annals of the Royal Philharmonic Society*, London, 1946

—— *The Old Concert Rooms of London*, London, 1955

Elvin, Laurence, *Bishop and Son, Organ Builders: The Story of J. C. Bishop and his Successors*, Lincoln, 1984

Emery, Walter, 'The English Translator of Forkel', *ML* 28 (1947), pp. 301–2
—— 'The London Autograph of "The Forty-Eight"', *ML* 34 (1953), pp. 106–23
—— 'Jack Pudding', *MT* 107 (1966), pp. 301–6
Farmer, D. H., *The Oxford Dictionary of Saints*, Oxford, 1978; 3rd edn, 1992
Fenner, Theodore, *Opera in London: Views of the Press, 1785–1830*, Carbondale and Edwardsville, 1994
Firebrace, C. W., *Records of the Lodge Original, No. 1, now the Lodge of Antiquity, No. 2 of the Free and Accepted Masons of England*, 2 vols, London, 1926
Fiske, Roger, *English Theatre Music in the Eighteenth Century*, Oxford, 1973
Ford, John, *Ackermann 1783–1983: The Business of Art*, London, 1983
Foster, Joseph, *Alumni Oxonienses*, 1st ser., *1500–1714*, 4 vols, Oxford, 1891–2; 2nd ser., *1715–1886*, 4 vols, Oxford, 1887–8
Foster, Myles Birkett, *The History of the Philharmonic Society of London, 1813–1912*, London, 1912
Fox, Peter, 'A Biographical Note on Samuel Wesley (1766–1837), the First Grand Organist', *Ars Quatuor Coronati* 92 (1979), pp. 64–81
Fuller Maitland, J. A., and A. H. Mann, *Catalogue of the Manuscript Music in the Fitzwilliam Museum, Cambridge*, London, 1893
Gardiner, William, *Music and Friends*, 3 vols, London, 1838–53
Gill, Frederick C., *Charles Wesley: The First Methodist*, London, 1964
Girdham, Jane, *English Opera in Late Eighteenth-Century London: Stephen Storace at Drury Lane*, Oxford, 1997
Girouard, Mark, *Life in the English Country House: A Social and Architectural History*, New Haven and London, 1978
Goodwin, Frederick K., and Kay Redfield Jamison, *Manic-Depressive Illness*, New York and Oxford, 1990
Green, Thomas, *Diary of a Lover of Literature*, in *GM* 1834/1, pp. 5–16, 246–53, 470–8; 1834/2, pp. 14–23, 227–33; 1835/1, 15–18, 127–33, 350–6, 570–4; 1835/2, 235–8, 458–62; 1836/1, pp. 459–463; 1836/2, pp. 572–8; 1837/1, pp. 353–8; 1837/2, pp. 11–14, 231–5, 455–8; 1838/1, pp. 129–3, 249–53, 464–9; 1839/1, pp. 575–9; 1839/2, pp. 455–9
Green, Vivian, *The Young Mr Wesley: A Study of John Wesley and Oxford*, London, 1961
The Harmonicon: A Journal of Music, 1823–33
Hawkins, John, *A General History of the Science and Practice of Music*, London, 1776
Heitzenrater, R. P., *Wesley and the People Called Methodists*, Nashville, 1995
Hemlow, Joyce, et al., *A Catalogue of the Burney Family Correspondence 1749–1878*, New York, Montreal, and London, 1971
Hibbert, Christopher, *King Mob: The Story of Lord George Gordon and the Riots of 1780*, London, 1958
—— *London: The Biography of a City*, London, 1969
Higgs, James, 'Samuel Wesley: His Life, Times, and Influence on Music', *Proceedings of the Musical Association* 20 (1893–4), pp. 125–47
Highfill, Philip H., et al. (eds), *A Biographical Dictionary of Actors, Actresses, Musicians, Dancers, Managers & Other Stage Personnel in London, 1660–1800*, Carbondale and Edwardsville, Ill., 16 vols, 1973–93
Hodges, Faustina Hasse, *Edward Hodges*, New York, 1896
Holmes, Edward, 'Cathedral Music and Composers', *MT* 4 (1851), pp. 207–8, 225, 233–4, 239–40
[Holmes, Edward], 'Our Musical Spring', *Fraser's Magazine* 43 (1851), pp. 586–95.

H[orncastle], W. F., 'Remarks on Instrumental Composers', *QMMR* 5 (1823), pp. 292–9
Horton, Peter, 'The Unknown Wesley: The Early Instrumental and Secular Vocal Music of Samuel Sebastian Wesley', in Zon (ed.), *Nineteenth-Century British Music Studies* vol. 1, pp. 134–78.
—— *Samuel Sebastian Wesley*, Oxford, 2003
Hughson, David (i.e. Pugh, David), *London: Being an Accurate History and Description of the British Metropolis and its Neighbourhood to Thirty Miles Extent from an Actual Perambulation*, 6 vols, London 1805–9
Humphries, Charles, and William C. Smith, *Music Publishing in the British Isles from the Beginning until the Middle of the Nineteenth Century*, Oxford, 1954; 2nd edn, 1970
Hurd, Michael, *Vincent Novello – and Company*, London, 1981
Husk, W. H., *An Account of the Musical Celebrations on St Cecilia's Day in the 16th, 17th, and 18th Centuries*, London, 1857
Illiano, Roberto, et al., *Muzio Clementi: Studies and Prospects*, Bologna, 2002
Irving, Howard, *Ancients and Moderns: William Crotch and the Development of Classical Music*, Aldershot, 1999
Jackson, Thomas, *The Life of the Rev. Charles Wesley, MA*, 2 vols, London, 1841
—— *Recollections of My Own Life and Times*, London, 1874
James, Kenneth Edward, 'Concert Life in Eighteenth-Century Bath', Ph.D. diss., Royal Holloway College, University of London, 1987
Jamison, Kay Redfield, *Touched with Fire: Manic-Depressive Illness and the Artistic Temperament*, New York, 1993
Jerdan, William, *Men I have known*, London, 1866
Johnstone, H. Diack, 'The Genesis of Boyce's *Cathedral Music*', *ML* 56 (1975), pp. 26–39
Johnstone, H. Diack, and Roger Fiske (eds), *The Eighteenth Century (The Blackwell History of Music in Britain*, vol. 4), Oxford, 1990
Jones, David Wyn, 'Haydn's Music in London in the Period 1760–1790: Part One', *Haydn Yearbook* 14 (1983), pp. 144–72
Jones, David Wyn (ed.), *Music in Eighteenth-Century Britain*, Aldershot, 2000
Jones, H. Bence, *The Royal Institution: Its Founder and its First Professors*, London, 1871
Kassler, Jamie Croy, *The Science of Music in Britain, 1714–1830: A Catalogue of Writings, Lectures and Inventions*, 2 vols, New York, 1979
—— 'The Royal Institution Lectures 1800–1831: A Preliminary Study', *RMARC* 19 (1983–5), pp. 1–30
Kassler, Michael (ed.), *Charles Edward Horn's Memoirs of his Father and Himself*, Aldershot, 2003
—— 'Samuel Wesley's "Madness" of 1817–18', *History of Psychiatry*, 14 (2003), forthcoming
—— *Music Entries at Stationers' Hall, 1710–1818*, Aldershot, forthcoming 2004
—— 'The Bachists of 1810: Subscribers to the Wesley/Horn edition of the "48"', in Kassler (ed.), *The English Bach Awakening*
—— *The English Bach Awakening: Knowledge of J. S. Bach and his Music in England, 1750–1830*, Aldershot, forthcoming 2004
Kassler, Michael, and Philip Olleson, 'New Samuel Wesleyana', *MT* 144 (Summer 2003), pp. 49–53
Kelly, Linda, *Richard Brinsley Sheridan: A Life*, London, 1997
Kelly, Michael, *Reminiscences*, London, 1826
Kendall, Alan, *Gioacchino Rossini: The Reluctant Hero*, London, 1992
Kent, William (ed.), *An Encyclopaedia of London*, London, 1937

Kimbrough, S T Jr., and Oliver A. Beckerlegge, *The Unpublished Poetry of Charles Wesley*, 3 vols, Nashville, 1988–92
King, Alec Hyatt, *Some British Collectors of Music*, Cambridge, 1963
—— 'Don Giovanni in London before 1817', *MT* 127 (1986), pp. 487–93
Kirby, Percival R., 'Weber's Operas in England, 1824–6', *MQ* 32 (1946), pp. 333–53
Kiste, John van der, *George III's Children*, Stroud, 1992
Krummel, D. W., and Stanley Sadie (edd.), *Music Printing and Publishing*, London, 1990
Landon, H. C. Robbins, *Haydn in England 1791–1795*, London, 1976
—— *Haydn: The Years of 'The Creation' 1796–1800*, London, 1977
Langford, Paul, *A Polite and Commercial People: England 1727–1783*, Oxford, 1989
Langley, Leanne, 'The English Musical Journal in the Early Nineteenth Century', Ph.D. diss., University of North Carolina at Chapel Hill, 1983
—— 'Sainsbury's *Dictionary*, the Royal Academy of Music, and the Rhetoric of Patriotism', in Bashford and Langley (eds), *Music and British Culture*, pp. 65–98
Langley, Robin, 'Samuel Wesley's Contribution to the Development of English Organ Literature', *JBIOS* 17 (1993), pp. 102–16
Lennep, William, et al. (eds), *The London Stage 1660–1800*, 5 pts in 11 vols, Carbondale, Ill., 1960–8
Lewis, Donald M. (ed.), *The Blackwell Dictionary of Evangelical Biography*, 2 vols, Oxford, 1995
Lightwood, James T., *Samuel Wesley, Musician: The Story of his Life*, London, 1937
—— *The Music of the Methodist Hymn-Book*, London, 1935
Lloyd, Gareth, 'Charles Wesley junior: Prodigal Child, Unfulfilled Adult', *Proceedings of the Charles Wesley Society* 5 (1998), pp. 23–35
Lloyd, J. E., and R. T. Jenkinson (eds), *The Dictionary of Welsh Biography: Down to 1940*, London, 1959
Lonsdale, Roger, *Dr Charles Burney: A Literary Biography*, Oxford, 1965
—— 'Doctor Burney's "Dictionary of Music"', *Musicology* 5 (1977), pp. 159–71
McClure, Ruth K., *Coram's Children: The London Foundling Hospital in the Eighteenth Century*, New Haven and London, 1981
McCrea, Andrew, 'British Organ Music after 1800', in Thistlethwaite and Webber, *The Cambridge Companion to the Organ*, pp. 279–98
McKenzie-Grieve, Averil, *Clara Novello 1818–1908*, London, 1955
McVeigh, Simon, 'The Violinist in London's Concert Life, 1750–84: Felice Giardini and his Contemporaries', D.Phil. diss., University of Oxford, 1980
—— 'Music and Lock Hospital in the 18th Century', *MT* 129 (1988), pp. 235–40
—— 'The Professional Concert and Rival Subscription Series in London, 1783–1793', *RMARC* 22 (1989), pp. 1–135
—— *Concert Life in London from Mozart to Haydn*, Cambridge, 1993
—— 'The Benefit Concert in Nineteenth-Century London: from "tax on the nobility" to "monstrous nuisance"', in Zon (ed.), *Nineteenth-Century British Music Studies* vol. 1, pp. 242–66
—— 'Freemasonry and Musical Life in London in the Late Eighteenth Century', in Jones, *Music in Eighteenth-Century Britain*, pp. 72–100
Madan, Falconer, *The Madan Family*, Oxford, 1933
Madan, Martin, *Thelyphthora; or, a Treatise on Female Ruin . . . Considered on the Basis of the Divine Law*, London, 1780
Marsh, John, 'The Latin Church Music of Samuel Wesley', Ph.D. diss., University of York, 1975

Matthews, Betty, 'Charles Wesley on Organs', *MT* 112 (1971), pp. 1007–10, 1111–12
—— 'Wesley's Finances and Handel's Hymns', *MT* 114 (1973), pp. 137–9
—— *The Royal Society of Musicians of Great Britain: List of Members 1738–1984*, London, 1985
—— 'Joah Bates: A Remarkable Amateur', *MT* 127 (1986), pp. 611–15
Mercer, Frank (ed.), Burney, Charles, *A General History of Music*, 2 vols, London, 1935, repr. New York, 1957
Milhous, Judith, Gabriella Dideriksen, and Robert D. Hume, *Italian Opera in Late Eighteenth-Century London – Volume 2: The Pantheon Opera and its Aftermath, 1789–1795*, Oxford, 2001
Milligan, Thomas B, *The Concerto and London's Musical Culture in the Late Eighteenth Century*, Ann Arbor, 1983
Money, John, *Experience and Identity: Birmingham and the West Midlands, 1760–1800*, Manchester, 1977
Mount-Edgcumbe, Richard, *Musical Reminiscences, Containing an Account of the Italian Opera in England from 1773*, London, 1824; 2nd edn 1827
Munby, A. N. L., *The Cult of the Autograph Letter in England*, London, 1962
Myers, Robert Manson, *Handel's 'Messiah': A Touchstone of Taste*, New York, 1948
Nalbach, Daniel, *The King's Theatre, 1704–1867: London's first Italian Opera House*, London, 1972
Neighbour, Oliver, and Alan Tyson, *English Music Publishers' Plate Numbers in the First Half of the Nineteenth Century*, London, 1965
Nelson, Claire M., 'The Masonic Connections of Haydn's Impresario Johann Peter Salomon', *Ars Quatuor Coronati* 110 (1998), pp. 177–91
Newman, William S., *The Sonata in the Classic Era*, New York and London, 1963; 3rd edn 1983
Newport, Kenneth G. C., *The Sermons of Charles Wesley: A Critical Edition with Introduction and Notes*, Oxford, 2001
Newton, John, *Susanna Wesley and the Puritan Tradition in Methodism*, London, 1968
Newton, Richard, 'The English Cult of Domenico Scarlatti', *ML* 20 (1939), pp. 138–56
Nichols, R. H., and F. A. Wray, *The History of the Foundling Hospital*, London, 1935
Norman, Edward, *Roman Catholicism in England: From the Elizabethan Settlement to the Second Vatican Council*, Oxford, 1986
Ogasapian, John, *English Cathedral Music in New York: Edward Hodges of Trinity Church*, Richmond, Va., 1994
Olleson, Philip, 'Family History Sources for British Music Research', in Michael Burden and Irena Cholij (eds), *A Handbook of Studies in 18th-Century Music III*, Edinburgh, 1993, pp. 1–36
—— 'The Tamworth Festival of 1809', *Staffordshire Studies* 5 (1993), pp. 81–106
—— 'Samuel Wesley and the *European Magazine*', *Notes* 52 (1996), pp. 1097–111
—— 'The Organ-builder and the Organist: Thomas Elliot and Samuel Wesley', *JBIOS* 20 (1996), pp. 116–25
—— 'Crotch, Moore, and the 1808 Birmingham Festival', *RMARC* 29 (1996), pp. 143–60
—— '"The Perfection of Harmony Itself": The William Hawkes Patent Organ and its Temperament', *JBIOS* 21 (1997), pp. 108–28
—— 'Samuel Wesley and the *Missa de Spiritu Sancto*, *Recusant History* 24 (1999), pp. 309–19

Olleson, Philip, 'The Obituary of Samuel Wesley', in Zon (ed.), *Nineteenth-Century British Music Studies* vol. 1, pp. 121–33
—— 'The London Roman Catholic Embassy Chapels and their Music in the Eighteenth and Early Nineteenth Centuries', in Jones (ed.), *Music in Eighteenth-Century Britain*, pp. 101–20
—— 'Dr Burney, Samuel Wesley, and Bach's *Goldberg Variations*', in Jon Newsom and Alfred Mann (eds), *The Rosaleen Moldenhauer Memorials: Music from Primary Sources. A Guide to the Moldenhauer Archives*, Washington, DC, 2000, pp. 169–75
—— 'Samuel Wesley and the Music Profession', in Bashford and Langley, *Music and British Culture*, pp. 23–38
—— 'Samuel Wesley and the English Bach Awakening', in Michael Kassler (ed.), *The English Bach Awakening*
—— '"Byrde's excellent Antiphones": Samuel Wesley's Projected Edition of Selections from *Gradualia*', *Annual Byrd Newsletter* 9 (2003), supplement to *Early Music Review* No. 81 (June 2003), pp. 7–9
Olsen, Donald J., *Town Planning in London: The Eighteenth and Nineteenth Centuries*, New Haven and London, 1964; 2nd rev. edn 1984
—— *The Growth of Victorian London*, London, 1976
O'Toole, Fintan, *A Traitor's Kiss: The Life of Richard Brinsley Sheridan*, London, 1977
Oxford, Arnold Whitaker, *No 4: An Introduction to the History of the Royal Somerset House and Inverness Lodge*, London, 1928
Paananen, Victor N., 'Martin Madan and the Limits of Evangelical Philanthropy', *Proceedings of the Wesley Historical Society* 40 (1975), pp. 57–68
Palmer, Fiona M., *Domenico Dragonetti in England (1794–1846): The Career of a Double Bass Virtuoso*, Oxford, 1997
Parke, William, *Musical Memoirs: Comprising an Account of the General State of Music in England, from the first Commemoration of Handel, in 1784, to the Year 1830, interspersed with numerous Anecdotes, Musical, Histrionic, &c.*, 2 vols, London, 1830, repr. New York, 1970
Parry-Jones, William Llewellyn, *The Trade in Lunacy: A Study of Private Madhouses in England in the Eighteenth and Nineteenth Centuries*, London, 1971
Pascall, Robert, 'Ein Überblick der Frühen Bach-Rezeption in England bis zirka 1860', in Ingrid Fuchs (ed.), *Johann Sebastian Bach: Beiträge zur Wirkungsgeschichte*, Vienna, 1992, pp. 147–65
Pearce, Charles William, *Notes on Old London City Churches, their Organs, Organists, and Musical Associations*, London, 1909
Pelkey, Stanley, '*Preludes in All the Keys throughout the Octave* by Samuel Wesley: An Introduction to a Forgotten Keyboard Repertory', *Early Keyboard Journal* 15 (1997), pp. 67–92
Picken, Laurence, 'Bach Quotations from the Eighteenth Century', *MR* 5 (1944), pp. 83–95
Pickering, Jennifer M., *Music in the British Isles, 1700 to 1800: A Bibliography of Literature*, Edinburgh, 1990
Plantinga, Leon, *Muzio Clementi: His Life and Music*, London, 1977
Plumb, J. H., 'The Commercialization of Leisure' in Neil McKendrick, John Brewer and J. H. Plumb (eds), *The Birth of a Consumer Society: The Commercialization of Eighteenth-Century England*, London, 1982, pp. 265–85
Plumley, Nicholas M., *The Organs of the City of London*, Oxford, 1996

Porter, Roy, *Mind-Forg'd Manacles: A History of Madness in England from the Restoration to the Regency*, London, 1987
—— *English Society in the Eighteenth Century*, rev. edn, Harmondsworth, 1990
—— *London: A Social History*, London, 1994
Price, Curtis, Judith Milhous, and Robert D. Hume, *Italian Opera in Late Eighteenth-Century London – Volume 1: The King's Theatre, Haymarket, 1778–91*, Oxford, 1995
Pritchard, Brian, 'The Music Festival and the Choral Society in England in the Eighteenth and Nineteenth Centuries: A Social History', Ph.D. diss., University of Birmingham, 3 vols, 1968
—— 'The Provincial Festivals of the Ashley Family', *Galpin Society Journal* 22 (1969), pp. 58–77
[Pyne, W. H., and W. Combe], *The Microcosm of London*, 3 vols, 1808–11
Rack, Henry D, *Reasonable Enthusiast: John Wesley and the Rise of Methodism*, London, 1989; 3rd edn 2002
Rees, Abraham (ed.), *The Cyclopaedia; or, Universal Dictionary of Arts, Sciences and Literature*, 45 vols, 1802–20
Reid, Douglas J., and Pritchard, Brian, 'Some Festival Programmes of the Eighteenth and Nineteenth centuries', *RMARC* 5 (1965), pp. 51–79; 6 (1966), pp. 3–23; 7 (1969), pp. 1–27; 8 (1970), pp. 1–33; 9 (1973), p. 138
Rennert, Jonathan, *William Crotch*, Lavenham, 1975
Ritchie, Lawrence I., 'The Untimely Death of Samuel Wesley; or, The Perils of Plagiarism', *ML* 60 (1979), pp. 45–59
Robins, Brian (ed.), *The John Marsh Journals: The Life and Times of a Gentleman Composer (1752–1828)*, Stuyvesant, NY, 1998
Robinson, Howard, *The British Post Office: A History*, Princeton, 1948
Rohr, Deborah, *The Careers of British Musicians, 1750–1850: A Profession of Artisans*, Cambridge, 2001
Rosen, Charles, *The Classical Style: Haydn, Mozart, Beethoven*, London, 1971; enlarged 3rd edn 1997
—— *Sonata Forms*, New York, 1980; 2nd edn 1988
Routh, Francis, *English Organ Music from the Middle Ages to 1837*, London, 1973
Rudé, George, *Hanoverian London, 1714–1808*, London, 1971
Rule, John, *Albion's People: English Society, 1714–1815*, London, 1992
Rushton, Julian, *Classical Music: A Concise History from Gluck to Beethoven*, London, 1986
Russell, Gillian Ward, 'William Russell and the Foundling Hospital, 1801–1813, M.Mus diss., Colchester Institute, 1985
—— 'William Russell 1777–1813: An Enquiry into his Musical Style', 4 vols, Ph.D. diss., University of Leicester, 1994
Sachs, Joel, 'The End of the Oratorios', in E. Strainchamps and M. R. Maniates, *Music and Civilization: Essays in Honour of Paul Henry Lang*, New York, 1984, pp. 168–82
Sadie, Stanley (ed.), *The New Grove Dictionary of Musical Instruments*, 3 vols, London, 1984
—— *The New Grove Dictionary of Opera*, 4 vols, London, 1992
Sadler, Thomas (ed.), *Diaries, Reminiscences, and Correspondence of Henry Crabb Robinson, Barrister-at-Law, FSA*, 2 vols, London, 1872
Sainsbury, John H. (publisher), *A Dictionary of Musicians*, London, 1824; 2nd. edn 1827

Samson, Jim (ed.), *The Cambridge History of Nineteenth-Century Music*, Cambridge, 2001
Sands, Mollie, *The Eighteenth-Century Pleasure Gardens of Marylebone*, London, 1987
Scholes, Percy A., *The Great Dr Burney*, 2 vols, London, 1948
—— *Dr Burney's Musical Tours in Europe*, 2 vols, London, 1959
Schwarz, John, 'The Orchestral Music of Samuel Wesley', Ph.D. diss, University of Maryland, 1969
Searle, Arthur, 'Julian Marshall and the British Museum: Music Collecting in the later Nineteenth Century', *British Library Journal* 9 (1985), pp. 67–87
Shaw, Watkins, *The Three Choirs Festival, c.1713–1953*, London, 1954
—— *The Succession of Organists of the Chapel Royal and the Cathedrals of England and Wales from c.1538*, Oxford, 1991
Sheppard, Francis, *London, 1808–1870: The Infernal Wen*, London, 1971
Slonimsky, Nicolas (ed.), *Baker's Biographical Dictionary of Musicians*, 8th edn, New York, 1992
Smith, J. Sutcliffe, *The Story of Music in Birmingham*, Birmingham, 1945
Smith, John Thomas, *Nollekens and his Times*, London, 1828
Smith, William C., *The Italian Opera and Contemporary Ballet in London, 1789–1820: A Record of Performances and Players with Reports from the Journals of the Time*, London, 1955
Smith, William C., and Charles Humphries, *A Bibliography of the Musical Works published by the firm of John Walsh during the Years 1721–1766*, London, 1968
Smither, Howard, *The History of the Oratorio*, 4 vols, Chapel Hill, 1977–2000
Squire, W. Barclay, 'Some Novello Correspondence', *MQ* 3 (1917), pp. 206–42
Stevenson, George J., *City Road Chapel London and its Associations, Historical, Biographical, and Memorial*, London, 1872
—— *Memorials of the Wesley Family*, London, 1876
Stone, Lawrence, *Road to Divorce: England 1530–1987*, Oxford, 1990
Sullivan, Alvin, *British Literary Magazines: The Augustine Age and the Age of Johnson, 1698–1788*, Westport, Conn. and London, 1983
—— *British Literary Magazines: The Romantic Age, 1789–1896*, Westport, Conn. and London, 1983
Summerson, John, *Georgian London*, London, 1962; rev. edn 1988
Telford, John, *The New Methodist Hymn Book Illustrated in History and Experience*, London, 1934
Temperley, Nicholas, 'George Frederick Pinto', *MT* 106 (1965), pp. 265–70
—— 'Beethoven in London Concert Life, 1800–1850', *MR* 21 (1960), pp. 207–14
—— *Haydn, 'The Creation'*, Cambridge, 1991
—— *The Hymn Tune Index: A Census of English-Language Hymn Tunes in Printed Sources from 1535 to 1820*, 4 vols, Oxford, 1998
—— (ed.), *The Romantic Age, 1800–1914* (*The Blackwell History of Music in Britain*, vol. 5), Oxford, 1981
—— (ed.), *Works for Pianoforte Solo by late Georgian Composers: Samuel Wesley and Contemporaries* (*The London Pianoforte School 1766–1860*, vol. 7, New York and London, 1985
—— and Geoffrey Bush (eds), *English Songs 1800–1860* (*Musica Britannica*, vol. 43), London, 1979
Terry, Charles Sandford, *John Christian Bach*, London, 1929; rev. 2nd edn by H. C. Robbins Landon, 1967

Thistlethwaite, Nicholas, *The Organs of Cambridge: An Introduction to the Organs of the University and City of Cambridge*, Oxford, 1983
—— *The Making of the Victorian Organ*, Cambridge, 1990
Thistlethwaite, Nicholas, and Geoffrey Webber, *The Cambridge Companion to the Organ*, Cambridge, 2000
Tomita, Yo, 'The Dawn of the Bach Movement in England, as manifested in the Manuscript Sources of the *Well-tempered Clavier* in the Second Half of the Eighteenth Century', in Kassler (ed.), *The English Bach Awakening*
Trend, J. B., 'Jonathan Battishill from the unpublished Recollections of R. J. S. Stevens', *ML* 13 (1932), pp. 264–71
—— 'R. J. S. Stevens and his Contemporaries', *ML* 14 (1933), pp. 128–37
Twyman, Michael, *Early Lithographed Music: A Study based on the H. Baron Collection*, London, 1996
Tyson, John R., *Charles Wesley: A Reader*, New York, 1989
Val, Dorothy de, 'Gradus ad Parnassum: The Pianoforte in London, 1770–1820', Ph.D. diss., King's College, University of London, 1991
—— 'The Ascent of Parnassus: Piano Music for the home by Clementi and his Contemporaries', in Illiano, *Muzio Clementi: Studies and Prospects*, pp. 51–66
Venn, J. and J. A., *Alumni Cantabrigienses*. Part I: to 1751, ed. John and J. A. Venn, 4 vols, Cambridge, 1922–7; part II: 1752–1900, 6 vols, Cambridge, 1940–54
Vickers, John A., *A Dictionary of Methodism in Britain and Ireland*, Peterborough, 2000
The Vocal Magazine, or Compleat British Songster, consisting of such English, Scotch and Irish Songs, Catches, Glees, Cantatas, Airs, Ballads & c. as are deemed most worthy of being transmitted to posterity, London, 1781
Wagner, Anthony, and Antony Dale, *The Wagners of Brighton*, Chichester and London, 1983
Wainwright, Arthur and Don E. Saliers (eds), *Wesley/Langshaw Correspondence: Charles Wesley, his Sons, and the Lancaster Organists*, Atlanta, Georgia, 1993
Wakefield, Priscilla, *Perambulations in London and its Environs*, London, 1809
Walker, Ernest, *A History of Music in England*, London, 1907
Wallace, Charles (ed.), *Susanna Wesley: The Complete Writings*, Oxford, 1997
Ward Jones, Peter (ed. and trans.), *The Mendelssohns on Honeymoon: The 1837 Diary of Felix and Cécile Mendelssohn Bartholdy together with Letters to their Families*, Oxford, 1997
Wardroper, John, *The World of William Hone*, London, 1997
Warrack, John, *Carl Maria von Weber*, Cambridge, 1968; 2nd edn 1976
Weber, William, *The Rise of Musical Classics in Eighteenth Century England: A Study in Canon, Ritual, and Ideology*, Oxford, 1992
Weinreb, Ben, and Christopher Hibbert (eds), *The London Encyclopaedia*, London, 1983
Weinstock, Herbert, *Rossini: A Biography*, London, 1968
Wellesz, Egon, and Frederick Sternfeld, *The Age of Enlightenment, 1745–1790* (*The New Oxford History of Music*, vol. 7), Oxford, 1973
Wesley, Samuel, *Letters of Samuel Wesley to Mr Jacobs, Organist of Surrey Chapel, Relating to the Introduction into this Country of the Works of John Sebastian Bach*, London, 1875. Facsimile edn with Introduction by Peter Williams as *The Wesley Bach Letters*, London, 1988
Wesley, Samuel Sebastian, *A Few Words on Cathedral Music and the Musical System of the Church, with a Plan of Reform*, London and Leeds, 1849
White, Chappell, 'The Violin Concertos of Giornovichi', *MQ* 58 (1972), pp. 24–45

White, Chappell, *From Vivaldi to Viotti: A History of the Early Classical Violin Concerto*, New York, 1992
Williams, Peter, 'J. S. Bach and English Organ Music', *ML* 44 (April 1963), pp. 140–51
Williamson, Elizabeth and Nikolaus Pevsner, *London Docklands: an Architectural Guide*, London, 1998
Wood, Arthur Skevington, *Thomas Haweis, 1734–1820*, London, 1957
Wright, Josephine, 'George Polgreen Bridgetower: An African Prodigy in England, 1780–99', *MQ* 66 (1980), pp. 65–82
Wroth, Warwick, *The London Pleasure Gardens in the Eighteenth Century*, London, 1896
Young, Percy M., *Beethoven: A Victorian Tribute based on the Papers of Sir George Smart*, London, 1976
Zon, Bennett, 'Plainchant in the Eighteenth-century English Catholic Church', *Recusant History* 21 (1993), pp. 361–80
—— *The English Plainsong Revival*, Oxford, 1999
Zon, Bennett (ed.), *Nineteenth-Century British Music Studies* vol. 1, Aldershot, 1999

Index of Wesley's Works

Numbers of works are those in the work list of Michael Kassler and Philip Olleson, *Samuel Wesley (1766–1837): A Source Book* (Aldershot, 2001).

SACRED VOCAL MUSIC
  Latin sacred music
    Masses and Mass movements
  2   Missa de sanctissima Trinitate Quinti Toni 124
  3   *Missa de Spiritu Sancto* 29, 231, 232–4, 282
  5   Missa pro Angelis 113, 239–40
    Other Latin sacred music
  14 'Anima nostra erepta est' 235–6
  15 'Ave maris stella' 231 (Ex 19.01)
  16a 'Ave Regina caelorum' I (*c.* 1781) 230
  16b 'Ave Regina caelorum' II (1824) 243
  17a 'Ave verum corpus' I (1781) 230
  17b 'Ave verum corpus' II (1812) 241
  18 'Beati omnes qui timent Dominum' 235
    Carmen funebre see 'Omnia vanitas'
  20 'Confitebor tibi, Domine' *see under* Large-scale choral works with orchestra
  21 'Constitues eos principes' 241–2
  22 'De profundis clamavi' 235
  23 'Deus noster refugium' 237
  25 'Dixit Dominus' I a 4 (1782) 230
  26 'Dixit Dominus' II a 8 (1800) 55, 84, 230, 236–7, 238 (Ex.19.03), 242
  27 'Dixit Dominus' III a 3 (1806) 70, 88, 237–8, 265
  28a 'Domine salvam fac reginam nostram Mariam' I 84, 112, 237–9, 311
  31a 'Ecce iam noctis' I (1801) 234–5, 237
  31b 'Ecce iam noctis' II (1808) 237
  32 'Ecce Maria genuit nobis' 230
  33 'Ecce panis angelorum' 134, 241
  36 'Exultate Deo' 55, 84, 118, 123, 236 (Ex. 19.02), 242
  40 'Gloria Patri' III in B♭ (1780) 230
  42 'Hodie beata Virgo Maria' 230
  43 'In exitu Israel' 105, 145, 204 (Ex. 19.04), 239, 242
  45 'In te, Domine, speravi' 235
  49 'Magnificat anima mea' I (1783) 230–1, 257
  50 'Magnificat anima mea' II (1821) 162–3, 242
  51 'Miserere mei, Deus' 52
  52 'Nocte surgentes' 235
  54 'Omnia vanitas' (*Carmen funebre*) 37, 168–9, 216, 235, 243 (Ex. 19.06)
  59 'Salve Regina, mater misericordiae' I (1799) 235
  66 'Te decet hymnus' 167, 235 *see also* 'Thou, O God, art praised in Zion', KO 114
  68 'Tu es sacerdos' I (1814) 241–2
  69 'Tu es sacerdos' II (1827) 212, 243–4
  70 'Ut queant laxis' 113, 240, 241 (Ex. 19.05)
  English sacred music
    Service music
    Jubilate (*c.* 1776: lost) 15, 244
  71 Morning and Evening Service in F 84, 164, 166, 170–1, 173–4, 180–1, 227, 245, 246 (Ex. 19.07), 247
    Jubilate 167–8, 246 (Ex. 19.07)
    Te Deum and Jubilate (Morning Service) 84, 164
    Magnificat and Nunc Dimittis (Evening Service) 84–5, 164
  72 Evening Service in G 247–8
  76 Responses to the Litany 70, 74
    Anthems
  77 'All go unto one place' 211–12, 216, 248
  78 'All the earth doth worship thee' 244–5
  80 'Behold, how good and joyful' II (1813) 272
  82 'Behold, how good a thing it is' (1813: lost) 139
  83 'Behold, I was shapen in wickedness' 244
    'He is our God and strong salvation' *see* 'Tu es sacerdos' II, KO 69
  89 'In the multitude of the sorrows' 244
  90 'I said, I will take heed to my ways' 244
  91 'I will arise and go to my Father' 248
  92 'Lord of the earth and heavens sublime' 248
  93 'Mansions of Heav'n, your doors expand' 248
  97 'O give thanks unto the Lord' I 248
  98 'O give thanks unto the Lord' II 214, 248
  100 'O Lord God, most Holy' 244

101 'O Lord God of Hosts' 244
'Sing aloud with gladness' see 'Exultate Deo', KO 36
112 'The Lord is my shepherd' II (1834) 248
113 'This shall be my rest forever' 244
114 'Thou, O God, art praised in Zion' 167, 235 see also 'Te decet hymnus', KO 66)
Hymns and sacred songs
117 *Original Hymn Tunes, Adapted to Every Metre in the Collection by the Rev John Wesley* 199, 208, 250
118 Hymns in Vincent Novello's *The Psalmist* 215, 250
120 ASCENSION 249
118 BETHLEHEM/DONCASTER 250
118 CESAREA
122 CHELMSFORD 249
'Come ye that love the Lord' (RIDGE) 250
128 'Gentle Jesus, meek and mild' 249
131 'He's blest whose sins have pardon gain'd' (BRISTOL or WESLEY) 69, 249
139 'Might I in thy sight appear' 249
143 'O Lord my rock, to thee I cry' (HERTFORD) 69
162 'We sing the wise, the gracious plan' (HOOKER) 249

LARGE-SCALE CHORAL WORKS WITH ORCHESTRA
20 'Confitebor tibi, Domine' 59, 163, 183, 184, 188–9, 224, 227, 231, 251, 254–60, 258 (Ex. 20.01), 259 (Ex. 20.02), 259
201 *The Death of Abel* 252
Overture to Act Two 281–2
202 *Ruth* 9, 10, 218, 251–2
207 *Ode to St. Cecilia* 48, 57–9, 103, 214, 222, 224, 252–4, 256, 284, 298, 309, 316, 322
Overture 254, 284, 289, 309

SECULAR VOCAL MUSIC
Choruses, glees, and partsongs
206 'Adieu ye soft scenes of delight' 262
207 'Begin the noble song' see Ode to St Cecilia under Large-scale choral works with orchestra
208 'Beneath, a sleeping infant lies' 54, 279
209 'Beneath these shrubs' 266
211 'Blushete ne Carolos' 268
213 'Circle the bowl with freshest roses' 262
214 'Father of Light and Life' 96, 105, 146, 162, 267–8
215 *Glee, perform'd at the Anniversary Meeting of the Literary Society* 272
216 'Goosy goosy gander' 264
217 'Happy the man and happy he alone' 267, 276
218 'Harsh and untuneful are the notes' 263 (Ex. 21.01)
219 'Here shall the morn her earliest tears bestow' 270
220 'Hilaroi piomen oinon' 268, 272
221 'Hurly burly, blood and thunder' 271
222 'If in fighting foolish systems' 271
223 'I walked to Camden Town' 270–1
224 'Integer penis' 268–9
225 'Life is a jest' 69, 270
226 'Mihi est propositum' 268
227 'Nella casa troverete' 263
229 'O Delia, ev'ry charm is thine' 110, 272
Ode to St Cecilia see under Large-scale choral works with orchestra
233 'O sing unto mie roundelaie' 128, 135, 272–3
234 'Qualem ministrum' (*Drusi laudes*) 31, 32, 264–5
235 'Roses, their sharp spines being gone' 266
237 'Sol, do, re, mi' 272
239 'The glories of our birth and state' 266–7
240 'The Macedon youth' 265, 266
241 'There are by fond mama supplied' 263
242 'Thou happy wretch' 262–3
243 'Three bulls and a bear' 262
245 'Tobacco's but an Indian weed' 267, 276
246 'Unde nil maius (*Eulogium de Johanne Sebastiano Bach*) 271
247 'What bliss to life can Autumn yield' 269, 276
248 'When Bacchus, Jove's immortal boy' 163, 272
250 'When first thy soft lips' 263
251 'When friendship, love and truth abound' 272
252 'When Orpheus went down to the region below' 263
253 'While ev'ry short liv'd flower of sense' 163, 272
254 'While others, Delia, use their pen' 265, 266
256 'Whoes there? a granidier' 262
257 'Why should we shrink from life's decline?' 279–80
258 'You are old, Father Dennis' 267
Songs and duets
260 'Alack and alack, the clouds are so black' (*Derdham Downs*) 273
261 'Alone on the seabeat rock' (*Armin's Lamentation for the Loss of his Daughter*) 274
262 'And is he then set free?' (Ode on the death of William Kingsbury) 275
264 'As on fam'd Waterloo the lab'ring swain' 279
265 'Autumnus comes' 274
267 'Come all my brave boys who want organists' places' (*The Organ laid Open*) 55, 278
268 'Come Stella, queen of all my heart' 276

271 'Eyes long unmoisten'd wept' 280
272 'Fairy minstrels in the night' 277
273 'Farewell! If ever fondest prayer' 280
275 'Gentle breath of melting sorrow' 275
276 'Gentle warblings in the night' 276–7
277 'Go, minstrel, go' 280
278 'Hark! his hands the lyre explore' 276
279 'Hope away! Enjoyment's come' 276
280 'In gentle slumbers' 274
281 'In radiant splendor' 149, 279
283 'Little tube of mighty pow'r' 276
284 'Looking o'er the moonlight billow' 280
285 'Louisa view the melting tears' 274
286 'Love and folly were at play' 278
288 'Near Thame's fam'd banks' 52, 278
290 'Not heav'n itself' 276
293 'One kind kiss before we part' 274
294 'Orpheus could lead the savage race' 213, 280
295 'O that I had wings like a dove' 276
299 'See the young, the rosy spring' 279
302 'Tergi il pianto idolo mio' 275
304 'There was a little boy' 279
305 'The rising sun of freedom' 278
306 'The standard of England still floats on the waves' 279
310 'This is the house that Jack built' 278
311 'Too late for redress' 274
312 ''Twas not the spawn of such as these' 280
313 'What folly it is' 280
314 'What are the falling rills' 274
315 'What shaft of fate's relentless pow'r' 277 (Ex. 21.02), 278
316 'When all around grew drear and dark' 280
317 'When thro' life unblest we rove' 280
318 'When we see a lover languish' 274

INSTRUMENTAL MUSIC
Orchestral music
401 Overture in G 281
402 Overture in D 281
403 Overture in C 282
404 Sinfonia Obbligato in D 282 286 288
405 Symphony in A (fragment) 282, 283–4
406 Symphony in A 282, 283
407 Symphony in D 282–3, Ex. 22.01
408 Symphony in E♭ 282, 283
409 Symphony in B♭ 63, 146, 284–5, 289
410 Harpsichord concerto in G 288
411 Harpsichord concerto in F 288
412 Piano Concerto 142, 290
413 Organ Concerto in B♭ 136, 288, 290, 311
414 Organ Concerto in D 60, 96, 104, 137, 145, 159, 162, 288–9, 319
415 Organ Concerto in B♭ 133, 290
416 Organ Concerto in G 290, 308
417 Organ Concerto in C 141, 148, 289
418 Violin Concerto in C 286, 287
419 Violin Concerto in A 285
420 Violin Concerto in D 286, 287
421 Violin Concerto in E♭ 286
422 Violin Concerto in B♭ 286
423 Violin Concerto in G 286
424 Violin Concerto in B♭ 286

Chamber music
501 Violin Sonata in F (1774–5) 290–1
502 Violin Sonata in A 291
503 Violin Sonata in E♭ 291
504 Violin Sonata in B♭ 291
505 Violin Sonata in D 291
506 Violin Sonata in A 291
507 *Two Sonatas for the Piano Forte or Harpsichord, with an Accompanyment for a Violin*, Op 2: 291, 314–15
508 Violin Sonata in F (1797) 54, 291–2
509 Duetto a due violini in D 291
514 Trio for Pianoforte and two Flutes 170, 290, 293
523 String Quartet in G 292
524 String Quartet in E♭ 292–3
526 Fugue in B♭ on a subject from Haydn's *Creation* 292
527 Minuet in C minor in the German Style 290
528 Minuet in F in Haydn's Manner 292
529 Quintet in A 288

KEYBOARD MUSIC
Organ music
601 Five pieces in John Green's *Characteristic Airs for the Royal Seraphine* 311
602 Fantasy in F 311
603 Fugue in D 311
604 Grand Duet for the Organ 123, 135, 302, 303 (Ex. 23.03), 319
605 Largo in F 311
606 Voluntary in C minor dedicated to Thomas Adams 225, 306–8, 309 (Pl. 6)
607 Voluntary in G dedicated to Thomas Adams 306, 308
608 A Short and Familiar Voluntary 308–9
610 Six Introductory Movements 310, 311
611 *Six Short Toccatas, Intended as Short Voluntaries for the Use of Organists* 311
612 *Six Fugues with Introductions for Young Organists* 310–11
613 *Six Voluntaries, composed for the use of Young Organists* 310
614 Slow Air in D (1794) 8, 311
615 *A First Set of Voluntaries*, ded. John Harding 169, 305
616 *A Second Set of Voluntaries*, ded. John Harding 169, 305
617 *Twelve Short Pieces for the Organ with a Full Voluntary Added* 149, 303–4, 309, 310
618 *A Book of Interludes for Young Organists* 305

619 Variations on 'God save the King' 162, 164, 305
620 Variations on 'Rule, Britannia' 162, 164, 305
621 Twelve Voluntaries, Op. 6: 77, 224, 289, 297–9, 300 (Exx. 23.01, 23.02), 305, 308, 311
622 Voluntary in B♭ dedicated to Thomas Attwood 309–10
623 Voluntary in D dedicated to William Drummer 214 n., 309, 322
624 Voluntary in G minor dedicated to William Linley 309
625 Voluntary in G dedicated to H. J. Gauntlett 309
626 Voluntary in B♭ 311
627 Andante Maestoso and Presto in D 297
628 Four Fugues 296
631 Fugue in B minor on a theme by Mendelssohn 14
632 Grand Duet 302
634 Introduction and Fugue in D minor 311
635 Introduction and Fugue in G 311
636 Preludes in All the Keys throughout the Octave 297
637 Voluntary in C (1774–5) 296
638 Voluntary in C (1817) 305
639 Voluntary in D (1774–5) 296
640 Voluntary and Fuga in D (1817) 305
641 Larghetto and Coda in D (1817) 305
643 Sonata per il Organo 296–7
644 Voluntary '12th' 299, 304–5
667 Duets for Eliza 311
669 Introduction to J. S. Bach's Fugue in E♭ 142
672 Melody in C♯ minor 306–8
675 Movements for the Cornet Stop 296
676 Movements in D (1774–5)

Piano music

Sonatas and Sonatinas
701 Eight Sonatas for the Harpsichord or Pianoforte 314
702 Three Sonatas for the Piano Forte, Op. 3: 315
703 Four Sonatas and two Duets, Op. 5: 224, 317
705 *Sonata for the Piano Forte, in which is introduced a Fugue from a Subject of Mr. Salomon* 317
706 *The Siege of Badajoz* 121, 123, 322
Variation sets
708 'The Bay of Biscay' 319, 320 (Ex. 23.04)
709 *The Favorite Duett in the Opera of La Cosa Rara, varied & adapted for the Piano Forte* 315
711 *The Hornpipe and Variations from a favorite Organ Concerto* 162, 289, 319
712 'Jessy of Dunblane' 319
713 'Patty Kavanagh' 319
714 *A favorite popular Polish Air with New Variations* 320
715 'Scots wha' hae wi' Wallace bled' 319
Rondos
717 'Bellissima Signora' 319
718 'The Christmas Carol' 319, 321
719 'The Deserter's Meditations' 319, 321–2
720 *A Favorite Air Composed by Carl Maria von Weber* 319
723 'I Attempt from Love's Sickness to Fly' 319
724 'Jacky Horner' 319
727 'Off She Goes' 319
732 'The Widow Waddle' 319, 321
733 'Will Putty' 319, 321
Miscellaneous
737 *Grand Coronation March* 214, 322
740 *An Italian Rondeau* 314
741 *Lunardi's March* 314
743 *The Sky Rocket* 322
Unpublished works
750 Piano Sonata in E♭ 316, 318
751 Piano Sonata in B♭ 316
752 Piano Sonata in A 48, 316–17
753 PIano Sonata in C 318
825 Piano Duet Sonata in G 312, 316
826 Trio for three Pianofortes 120, 123, 135, 143, 188, 312, 318–19

General Index

Abel, Carl Friedrich (1723–87), German composer 15, 24, 74, 219, 221, 255, 282
  see also Bach-Abel concerts
Abernethy, John (1764–1831), surgeon 173
Ackermann, Rudolph (1764–1834), publisher: *Repository of Arts* 140
Adams, Thomas (1785–1858), organist 203, 215, 216, 300
  organ voluntaries by SW dedicated to 306, 307 (Pl. 6), 308
Ad Libitum Society 278
Akenside, Mark (1721–70), poet 261
Aldrich, Henry (1648–1710), English divine and collector of music 218, 263
  'Reasons for drinking' 263
d'Almaine and Co, music publishers 308
Anacreon (6th century BC), Greek poet 272, 279
  'Hilaroi piomen oinon' set by SW 268
  English translations of by Thomas Moore set by SW 272, 279
Ancient Concerts (Concert of Ancient Music) *see* concert series
Andrews, James Pettit (*c*. 1737–97), antiquarian 22
Annesley, Samuel (*c*. 1620–96), SW's great-grandfather 1
Aprile, Giuseppe (1732–1813), Italian singer, composer 230
d'Arblay, Revd Alexander (1794–1837), son of Mme d'Arblay 168
d'Arblay, Frances, née Burney (1752–1840), author, daughter of Charles Burney 168
Arezzo, Guido d' *see* Guido of Arezzo
Argory, The, McGeough's house 163
  arrangements by SW of music for barrel organ at 163–4, 284, 289
Argyll Rooms *see* concert venues
Arminian Magazine 21
Arne, Thomas Augustine (1710–78), composer 7, 8, 20, 217, 219
  Artaxerxes (1762) 62, 164, 184, 220
    Overture, arr. SW for barrel organ 164
    'The soldier, tir'd of war's alarms' 221, 256
  Comus (1736) 252, 315
  Judith (1761) 7
  Love in a Village (1762) 220
  The Sacrifice, or The Death of Abel (1744) 252
  Masses 221
  music perf. at family concerts 24
Arnold, Samuel (1740–1802), composer, editor 7, 8, 9, 22, 128, 217, 220
  The Prodigal Son 219
  Redemption 131, 132
Ashley family 95, 224
Ashley, Charles Jane (1772–1843), cellist, impresario 23, 95, 103, 121, 128, 130, 136, 141, 144, 147, 156, 161
Ashley, General Christopher (1767–1818), violinist, impresario 23, 103, 121, 136, 289
Ashley, John (1734–1805), bassoonist, impresario 23, 95, 103, 130
Ashley, John James (1772–1815), organist 23, 103, 130
Asperne, James (d. 1821), publisher of *European Magazine* 140, 150
Assize Weeks 143, 145
Asylum for Fugitive Pieces 266, 271
Attwood, Francis (1775–1807), musician 22
Attwood, Thomas (1765–1838), composer, organist 22, 23, 38, 142, 174, 191, 198, 216, 265
  as organist of St Paul's Cathedral 70, 84–5, 166–8
  and SW's Service in F 166–8, 170, 173
  contributes to Eliza's album (1836) 213
  organ voluntary dedicated to by SW 309–10
Avery, John (1738–1808), organ builder 38, 183, 251
Avison, Charles (1709–70), composer 6
Ayrton, Edmund (1734–1808), organist 128
Ayrton, William (1777–1858), editor of *Harmonicon* 172, 174

Bach, Carl Philipp Emanuel (1714–1788), composer, son of J. S. Bach 71, 73, 82
Bach, Johann Christian (1735–82), composer, son of J. S. Bach 15, 19, 20, 24, 221, 282, 283 (Ex. 22.01) *see also* Bach-Abel concerts
  Six Grand Overtures 282
Bach, Johann Sebastian (1685–1750), composer, organist 126, 136, 138, 205, 271, 280, 288, 317
  discovery and promotion of by SW 69, 71–86 *passim see also* performances of by SW
  performances of by SW 75, 76–7, 78–9, 94, 96,

Bach, Johann Sebastian (1685–1750) (*cont.*): 97, 98, 104, 105–7, 110–11, 123, 133, 135, 137, 142, 145, 159, 225
works:
  instrumental music:
    Sonatas for violin and harpsichord, BWV 1014–19: 97, 98, 105, 225
  keyboard music:
    Forty-eight Preludes and Fugues (the '48') 69, 71, 79, 301
      Fugue in D major, Book I, arr. by SW for orchestra 96–7, 104, 288–9
    Goldberg Variations 105–7, 145, 225
    Six Little Preludes, BWV 933–8: 127
  organ music:
    Fugue in A Minor, BWV 543: 214, 215
    Fugue in E♭, BWV 552 ('St Anne') 104, 225
      arr. Novello for organ duet 142, 145, 302
    Prelude in E♭, BWV 552, arr. Novello for organ duet and orchestra 123, 133, 135, 141
    Prelude and Fugue in C, BWV 547: 308
    Trio Sonatas, BWV 525–30: 71, 82, 93, 225
  sacred music:
    B Minor Mass 30
    Credo 30, 145
  'Jesu, meine Freude', BWV 527: 94, 105, 239
Bach-Abel concerts 15, 16, 219
Bacon, John (1777–1859), sculptor and artist 86, 87
Bacon, Richard Mackenzie (1776–1844), editor and proprietor of *QMMR* 160, 181, 185
Badham, Mr, of Bristol 208
Bagshawe, Sir Thomas, doctor 150, 152
Ball, James (*fl. c.* 1780–1832), piano maker, music seller publisher, printer 126
balloons, air 145, 314
Bank of England 68
Banti, Brigida (*c.* 1756–1806), soprano 62, 118
Baptie, David: *Sketches of the English Glee Composers* (1895) 261
Barnes, Mrs, owner of Oxford House school 33, 35, 38, 44, 67, 68, 89–92
Barrington, Daines (1727–1800), antiquarian, writer 4, 5, 15, 17, 19, 217, 244, 274, 314
  Miscellanies 4, 274
Barry, Revd Edward (1759–1822), of Dulwich 70
Barthélemon, François-Hippolyte (1741–1808), composer 59, 191, 220, 224, 286, 288
  oratorio concert in 1800: 288, 290
  Jefte in Masfa (1776), oratorio 191
Bartleman, James (1769–1821), bass 61, 131, 135
Bastable, Mrs, keeper of Blacklands House 154, 155
Bates, Joah (1740–99), civil servant, musician 14, 55–6, 278
Bath, Somerset 9, 74, 87–8, 129, 203
Bath Harmonic Society 88

Battishill, Jonathan (1738–1801), composer, organist 6, 22, 216, 217, 218, 221, 251
  influence on SW 224
Bavarian Embassy Chapel 25
Baylay, William (1778/9–1845), vicar of Margate (1812) 125
Beale, William (1784–1854), organist, composer: 'Awake, sweet Muse' 128
Beard, John (*c.* 1717–91), tenor, proprietor of Covent Garden theatre 5, 7, 217
Beaumont, Francis (1584–1616) and Fletcher, John (1579–1625), playwrights 261
  'Roses, their sharp spines being gone' (*The Two Noble Kinsmen*) set by SW 266
Beccles, Suffolk 146, 171
Beckwith, John Charles (1788–1819), organist of Norwich Cathedral 149
Beethoven, Ludwig van (1770–1827), Austrian composer 71, 133, 136, 317
  Adelaide, Op. 46: 121
  Battle Symphony, Op. 91 (*The Battle of Vittoria*) 144, 147, 148, 161, 226
  Mass in C 144, 226
  Missa solemnis 30
  The Mount of Olives (*Christus am Ölberge*, Op. 85) 141, 143, 147, 226
  Piano Sonata in E minor, Op. 90: 317
  Sonata in A for Violin and Piano, Op. 47 ('Kreutzer') 52
  String Quartet in C, Op. 59 No 3: last movement arr. by Weichsell 141, 308
  Symphony No. 9 in D minor ('Choral') 227
Behnes, William (?1795–1864), artist 161
  bust of McGeough by 163
Benedict, Julius (1804–85), composer, contributor to Eliza Wesley's album (1836) 213
benefit concerts *see* concerts
Benger, Elizabeth (1778–1827) writer, friend of Sarah Wesley 201
Bennet, John (*fl.* 1599–1614) madrigal composer 128
Bennet, Master, companion of SW in Leeds 200
Benson, Joseph (1748–1821), Methodist minister 181
Benson, Samuel (1779–1881), Methodist minister 181, 196
Bertinotti, Teresa (1776–1854), soprano 120–1, 123
Billingsgate (fish market) 69
Billington, Elizabeth, (?1765–1818), soprano 20, 61–2, 105, 144, 220, 256
  portrait by Reynolds 62
  date of birth 64n
bipolar affective disorder 3, 31
Birchall, Robert (*c.* 1760–1819), music publisher 38, 137
Birchall and Andrews, music publishers 315

Bird, William (*fl. c.* 1811–*c.* 1840), organist of Watford 207
Birmingham 94, 107, 108
  St Peter, Dale End 198–9
  St Philip 118
  Music Festival (1808) 95
  SW's concert at Theatre Royal (1809) 125
  Music Festival (1811) 107, 118–19, 123, 198, 225, 236
  Music Festival (1829) 208
Bishop, Henry (1786–1855), composer 161
Bishop, James (1783–1854), organ builder 163–4
Blacklands House, Chelsea 153, 154–7, 202, 294, 299, 304–5
Blackwell, Ebenezer (d. 1782), banker 22, 27
Blagdon, near Bristol 203, 207
Blick, Francis, Vicar of Tamworth 95
Blow, John (1649–1708), composer 173, 218
Boccherini, Luigi (1743–1805), Italian composer 133
Bochsa, Nicholas (1789–1856), French harpist, impresario 161
Böhler, Peter (1712–75), Moravian minister 2
Borghi, Luigi (?1745–*c.* 1806), Italian violinist, composer 221, 285, 286
  violin concertos perf. at family concerts 24
Bossi, Cesare (1774/5–1802), Italian violinist, composer 61
Boyce, William (1711–79), composer 5, 6, 7, 8, 9, 10–11, 15, 17, 23, 200, 217
  visits Wesley family home (1774) 10, 222, 244
  comments on SW's abilities 10, 222
  symphony of perf. at family concert 221
  ode on death of by Charles Wesley jun. perf. at family concert 23
  influence on SW 222–3
  Cathedral Music 10–11, 182, 217, 218, 222
  'Blessed is he that considereth the poor' 216, 219
  'If we believe that Jesus died' 216
  'Lord, thou hast been our Refuge' 219
Boyce, William, double-bass player 61
Boys, Henry, organist 175, 176
Braham, John (1774–1856), tenor 95, 118, 121, 129, 135, 136, 141, 147, 148, 189, 259
Bramfield, Herts. 38
Bremner, Robert (1713–89), music publisher 16, 22
Brentford, Essex 172–3
Bridgetower, George Polgreen (?1779–1860), violinist 51–2, 224, 291–2
Brighton, Sussex 60, 126, 127, 163, 197, 198
Bristol 1, 3, 7, 9, 10, 49, 108, 200–1, 219, 227
  Clifton 49
  Clifton Church 203, 204
  Derdham Downs 273
  Kingswood School 39
  Moravian Chapel 206
  St James's church 9, 159, 203, 206
  St Mary, Redcliffe 203–6
  St Nicholas's church 159, 203, 206
  SW's recitals at (1829) 203–7
  SW's lectures at (1830) 207–9
Bristol Philosophical and Literary Institution 207–9
British Critic 70, 140
British Library 10, 187, 286, 314, 317, 318
British Museum 159, 208, 292
'Brixton squabble' (1825) 175–6, 177–8
Broderip, Edmund (1727–79), Bristol organist 4–5
Bromfield, William (1712–92), surgeon, founder of the Lock Hospital 5, 8
Brühl, Count, Saxon ambassador 22
Brunswick, Countess of (d. 1813), sister of George III 134
Bryan, Cornelius (*c.* 1775–1840), organist of St Mary, Redcliffe 204
Buggins, Samuel, Birmingham trumpeter, impresario 97
Buggins, Simeon, boy treble 95
Bull, Ole (1810–80), Norwegian violinist 213
  contributes to Eliza's album (1836) 213
Bunting, William (1805–66), Methodist preacher 200
Burgh, Revd. Allatson (b. 1769/70), clergyman, author 169, 170
  Anecdotes of Music (1814) 169
Burgh, Caroline, daughter of Allatson Burgh 169, 170
Burghersh, Lord (John Fane) (1784–1859), amateur musician 211
Burney, Charles (1726–1814), music historian 13, 61, 62, 72–7, 78, 93, 97, 126, 154, 168, 222, 224, 286, 302, 312
  renews acquaintance with SW (1799) 59
  comments on SW's *Confitebor* (1799) 59
  converted to Bach cause by SW (1808) 73–4
  performance of Bach's violin sonatas to by SW and Jacob (1809) 97
  performance of Bach's *Goldberg Variations* to by SW and Novello (1810) 105–7
  influence on SW 223
  comments on Elizabeth Linley 74
  piano teaching 312
  Four Sonatas or Duets for two Performers (1777), *A Second Set of Four Sonatas or Duets* (1778) 315
  'I will love thee, O Lord' (Oxford D.Mus exercise) 74
  A General History of Music 59, 73
    comments on Kelway in 8n
    comparison between Bach and Handel in 73
  An Account of the Musical Performances in Westminster Abbey (1785) 221
Burton, John (1730–82), English harpsichordist, organist and composer 8, 14, 217

Burton, John (1730–82) (*cont.*):
  Ten sonatas for the harpsichord, organ or pianoforte (?1766) 218
Busby, Thomas (1755–1838), composer, writer 170, 224
Butler, Charles (1750–1832), Roman Catholic lawyer 124, 126
Byrd, William (*c.* 1540–1623), composer 183, 218
  proposed edition by SW of motets by 187, 194
Byron, Lord (1788–1824): 'Farewell! If ever fondest prayer', set by SW 280

Cahusac, Thomas, *A Collection of Psalms, Hymns, Chants and Other Pieces, as sung at the Bentinck Chapel, Paddington* (*c.* 1820) 249n
Caillot, M., pyrotechnist 46
Callcott, Elizabeth Hutchins, later Horsley (1793–1875), daughter of John Wall Callcott 125
Callcott, Elizabeth Mary, wife of John Wall Callcott 125
Callcott, John Wall (1766–1821), composer, music theorist 70, 76, 79, 89, 125, 265
  A Musical Grammar (1806) 70
Cambridge 111, 179, 180
  SW's visit to (1808) 78–9
  SW's visits to (1825, 1826) 182–4, 187, 191–2
Camden Town 66, 108–9; *see also* Arlington Street, Camden Town, under Wesley, Samuel
cantata mass 232
Capel, John, MP (1767–1846) 211
Carnaby, William (1772–1839), composer, organist 78, 182
Carnegie, William (Lord Northesk (1758–1831)), Rear-Admiral 185
Carter, Thomas (1769–1800), alto and coal merchant 52, 278
Casamajor, Justinian (1746–1820), landowner 67
Catalani, Angelica (1780–1849), soprano 62, 104, 123, 129, 130, 131, 141, 143
  career and reputation 118–19
  in Bath (1808) 87–8
  in Birmingham (1811) 118–19
  and Old Price riot at King's Theatre (1809) 278
  and SW's Hanover Square concert (1812) 120–1
  and riot at Covent Garden (1813) 135–6
Catch Club (Noblemen and Gentlemen's Catch Club) 53
catch clubs *see* glee clubs
Catholic Relief Acts 25, 26, 29
Cawse, Harriet, singer 189
Chambers, Lady, widow of Sir William Chambers (1726–96) 77
Chapel Royal at St James's 5, 23, 83, 128, 156, 159, 163, 172, 177, 244

Chard, George William (1765–1849), organist of Winchester Cathedral 185–6
Charlotte, Queen (1744–1818), consort of George III 8, 19, 82
Charlotte, Princess (1796–1817), daughter of George IV 148, 279
Charterhouse 2, 55
Chatterton, Thomas (1752–70), poet: 'O sing unto mie roundelaie' set by SW 128, 273
Chelsea College (address of Charles Burney) 73, 106
Cherubini, Luigi (1760–1842), composer 133
  Overture to *Anacréon* 147, 226
Chesterfield Street, Marylebone (Wesley family home) 7, 10, 15, 22, 26, 39, 45, 46, 47, 48, 60, 65, 220, 254, 282
Child, William (1606/7–97), composer 173, 218
Chillingworth, William (1602–44), theologian, philosopher 271
Christ's Hospital 134, 196
churches, chapels, and other places of worship (in London unless otherwise stated):
  Beresford Chapel, Walworth 196
  Camden Chapel, Camden Street 168, 176, 202, 227
  Chapel Royal, St James's *see separate entry*
  Christ Church, Blackfriars 121
  Christ Church, Newgate Street 214, 228
  City Road Chapel *see* Methodism
  Foundling Hospital Chapel *see separate entry*
  German church *see* Savoy Chapel
  Kentish Town Chapel (St John the Baptist, Highgate Road) 150, 168
  Portuguese Embassy Chapel *see separate entry*
  St Andrew by the Wardrobe, Victoria Street 125
  St George, Bloomsbury 69
  St George, Hanover Square 166
  St Katherine-by-the-Tower 198
  St Katherine Coleman 310
  St Lawrence, Jewry 166
  St Martin's in the Fields 8
  St Mary, Pimlico 176–7
  St Mary the Virgin, Eversholt Street *see* Somers Town Chapel
  St Marylebone 194, 216
  St Matthew, Brixton 175
  St Pancras Old Church 150
  St Pancras New Church, Euston Road 162, 163, 168, 169, 197
  St Paul's Cathedral *see separate entry*
  St Sepulchre-without-Newgate 169
  St Stephen, Coleman Street 138, 197
  Savoy Chapel, Strand 169
  Somers Town Chapel (St Mary the Virgin, Eversholt Street) 196–7
  Spitalfields Church 135
  Surrey Chapel *see separate entry*
  Westminster Abbey *see separate entry*

Cimador, Mrs, wife of Giambattista Cimador (1761–1805), singer 61, 63
Clark, Richard (1780–1856), Secretary of Glee Club 38, 265–6
Clarke, Adam (?1762–1832), Methodist minister 98, 99
Clarke, Charles Cowden (1787–1877), musician, writer 116, 185, 213
Clarke, Jeremiah (c. 1674–1707), composer 218
 Alexander's Feast (1697) 253
Clarke, Mary Cowden, née Novello (1809–98), writer 114, 213
Classical Harmonists Society 169, 176
Clementi, Muzio (1752–1832), pianist, composer, music publisher 111, 133, 255, 312, 313, 316, 320
 piano duets by 315
 Gradus ad Parnassum (1817–26) 313
Clementi & Co., music publishers, piano makers and sellers 111, 143, 149, 303, 320
Clifton *see* Bristol
Cobham Hall, near Gravesend, Kent 202
Cocks and Co., music publishers 305, 309
Coghlan, Lucius (c. 1750–1833), chaplain to the Grand Lodge of England 122
Coke, Thomas (1747–1814), Methodist minister 21
Colchester, Essex 108
Collyer, Joseph, singer with Wesley in Bristol (1830) 207, 208–9
Concentores Society 53, 70, 90, 265
Concert of Ancient Music *see* Ancient Concerts under concert series
concert series
 Ancient Concerts 22, 58, 60, 61, 62, 122, 128, 131, 132, 220, 226
 Vocal Concerts 61, 62, 120, 122, 132, 133, 226
 Wesley family concerts (1779–87) 20–4, 25, 220–1, 281–2, 285–6, 288, 291
 Charles and SW's Tottenham Street Rooms series (1802) 60–4, 302
concert venues
 Argyll Rooms 133, 135, 189
 Crown and Anchor Tavern, Fleet Street 169
 Green Man Inn, Blackheath 94, 142
 Hanover Square Rooms 47, 76, 101, 103, 105, 110, 121, 132, 133, 135, 142, 219, 225, 239, 280, 302, 318
 Hatton House, Hatton Garden 59, 288, 232
 Hickford's Rooms 19–20
 Hyde's Concert Rooms *see* Tottenham Street Rooms
 Pantheon, Oxford Street 47, 219, 220, 221
 Tottenham Street Rooms (Hyde's Concert Rooms) 60, 302
 Willis's Rooms 61 135
concerts
 benefit concerts 77 78, 86, 94, 105, 110–11, 120–3, 133 135–6, 142, 148, 156–7, 188–9
 see also individual entries under Wesley, Samuel
 oratorio concerts 6, 9, 48, 58, 61, 103–4, 114, 161, 175, 225–6 *see also* Covent Garden Theatre, Drury Lane Theatre, King's Theatre
 subscription concerts 58, 60–1, 62–3, 224 *see also* Ancient Concerts, Vocal Concerts, Wesley family concerts
 Vocal Concerts
Cook, Mr, potential landlord for SW (1818) 156
Cooke, Matthew (?1761–1829), organist of St George's, Bloomsbury 69, 87, 88, 89, 91
 Select Portions of the Psalms of David (c. 1795) 249
 A Collection of Psalm and Hymn Tunes for the Use of the Lock Hospital (1808)
Cooper, George (c. 1783–1843), organist 169, 170, 204
Coram, Thomas (c. 1668–1751) founder of Foundling Hospital 55
Corelli, Arcangelo (1653–1713), Italian composer 8, 9, 23, 220
 music perf. at family concerts 24
Corri, Domenico (1746–1825), composer, publisher, teacher 60
Corri, Sophia, singer, harpist, pianist 60–1
Courier (newspaper) 177
Court Guide 98
Covent Garden Theatre 5, 9, 60, 62, 136, 171, 220, 278, 320
 capacity of 58
 'Old Price' riots at (1809) 278
 oratorio concerts at 9, 48, 58, 59, 61, 103–4, 114, 128, 129–32, 141–2, 144–5, 146–8, 150, 156, 159, 161, 184, 188, 225–6, 227, 253–4, 257
Coventry and Hollier, music publishers 305
Cowper, Judith *see* Madan, Judith
Cowper, William, first Earl Cowper (c. 1664–1723), Lord Chancellor 5, 41
Cowper, William (1731–1800), poet 5
Cox, Samuel Compton (*fl.* 1798–1839), Treasurer of Foundling Hospital 138, 139
Cramer, Francis (1772–1848), violinist 22, 60, 96, 118, 142, 268, 289
Cramer, Johann Baptist (1771–1858), pianist, composer 91–2, 128, 142, 143, 268, 280, 313, 316
 as teacher 91–2
 Studio per il Pianoforte (1804–10) 313
 Variations on 'Rousseau's Dream' 141
Cramer, Wilhelm (1746–99), violinist 15, 20, 22, 219, 221, 285, 286
 violin concertos perf. at family concerts 24
Croft, William (1678–1727), composer 216, 218

Crotch, William (1775–1847), composer, lecturer, writer on music 16, 79n, 119, 174, 191, 216, 243–4
  lectures at Royal Institution 70, 76
  contributes to Eliza's album (1836) 213
Crown and Anchor Tavern, Fleet Street *see* concert venues
Cruden, Alexander (1701–70), compiler of biblical concordance 27
Curwen, John (1816–80), music educator 113

Dampier, John Lucius (1793–1853), Fellow of King's College, Cambridge 179n, 186
Danby, Eustace (1781–1824), organist, composer 51–2
Danby, John (c. 1757–1798) organist, composer 52, 54
Dance, William, violinist, keyboard player 132
Davies, Revd John:
  'As on fam'd Waterloo' set by SW 149
  'In radiant splendor' set by SW 279
Davis, James (1762–1827), organ builder 163–4
Davison, Frederick (1814/15–89), organ builder 216
Davy, John (1763–1824), composer, theatre musician: 'The Bay of Biscay 320
Deane, Mrs, mother of Anne Deane 51
Deane, Anne (d. 1806), lover of SW 49, 51, 64, 67, 270
Delafite, Henry Francis Alexander (1772/3–1831), friend of SW 161
Dickens, Charles (1812–70), novelist: *Dombey and Son* 66
Dickons, Maria (1774–1833), soprano 144
Draghi, Giovanni Battista (c. 1640–1708): *A Song for St Cecilia's Day* (1687) 253n
Dragonetti, Domenico (1763–1846), double-bass player 61, 213
  contributes to Eliza's album (1836) 213
Dreyer, Baron, Danish ambassador 22
Drouet, Louis (1792–1873), French flautist 147, 148
Drummer, John, friend of SW 52, 170, 234
Drummer, William, friend of SW 52, 234
  organ voluntary by SW dedicated to 309
Drury Lane Theatre 62, 75, 86, 129, 220
  oratorio concerts at 9, 48, 61, 103, 128–30, 141, 143–4, 146–7, 226
Dryden, John (1631–1700), poet, dramatist 261
  A Song for St Cecilia's Day 213, 253
  'Orpheus could lead the savage race' (*A Song for St Cecilia's Day*) set by SW 280
  translations of Horace set by SW 267
Dubois, Edward (1774–1850), humorist 172
Dumont, M., French dancing master 42
Dupuis, Thomas Sanders (1733–96), organist, composer 128
Durham, Bishop of (1777) 19
Dussek, Jan Ladislav (1760–1812), Bohemian composer 60, 63, 125, 128, 133, 255, 313, 316
Dussek, Sophia, née Corri (1775–1847), singer, harpist 60–1, 63

Eager, John (1782–1853), organist of Great Yarmouth 145, 171
Edgeworth, Maria (1767–1849), novelist 201
Elliot, Thomas (c. 1759–1832), organ builder 81–2, 92, 95, 121, 295
  organs by used by SW in lectures 85–6, 110
Elliott, James (1783–1856), bass 38, 70, 95, 105, 142, 265
Elliston, Robert William (1774–1831), licensee of Drury Lane theatre 191
embassy chapels 25–6, 232 *see also* Bavarian Embassy Chapel, Portuguese Embassy Chapel, Sardinian Embassy Chapel, Spanish Embassy Chapel
Emett, John George (1787–1847), organist 170, 175, 176, 280
Emett, Sarah, daughter of John George Emett 280
Engelbach, Lewis, music reviewer for *Repository of Arts* 321n
England, George Pike (c. 1768–1815), organ builder 84, 145, 239
equal temperament *see* tuning and temperament
European Magazine 140, 160, 224, 297–8
  SW's reviews of music in 141, 150, 180, 181
Evans, Charles Smart (1780–1849), alto 38, 94, 136, 142
Examiner, The 174, 184, 255
Exeter, Earl of, subscriber to family concerts 220
Exeter Hall, London 212, 248

Farrant, Richard (c. 1525–30–80), composer 182, 218
Ferrari, Giacomo (1763–1842), Italian composer: *L'eroina di Raab* 136
Festival of the Sons of the Clergy 219, 222
Firth, Mr, organist 139
Fischer, Johann Christian (1733–1800), oboist 20
Fischer, Joseph, singer 120, 123
Fitzwilliam, Lord (Richard Fitzwilliam, 7th Viscount Fitzwilliam of Meryon) (1745–1816), collector 179
  music collection of 179–80, 182–3, 184, 186, 190, 191–2, 210, 227, 249
Fitzwilliam Virginal Book 16
Fletcher, John (1729–85), Methodist minister 14
Flight and Robson, organ builders 135, 183, 197, 198, 306
  Apollonicon 306
  organ at SW's 1813 Argyll Rooms concert 135
Fodor-Mainvielle, Joséphine (1789–1870), soprano 147, 148
Forkel, Johann Nikolaus (1749–1818), writer on music 71

General Index

Über Johann Sebastian Bachs Leben, Kunst, und Kunstwerke, (1802) (Life of Bach) 82–3
Foundery, The see Methodism
Foundling Hospital 6, 55
  chapel 55, 142
  oratorio performances at 6, 219
  organ 55
  appointment of organist (1798) 55–7, 278
  appointment of organist (1814) 137
  benefit concert for family of Russell at (1814) 142
Fox, Charles James (1749–1806), politician 268, 277
Framlingham, Suffolk 109, 171
Freer, Mr, of Birmingham 198
Freemasonry 77–8, 129, 139, 172, 272
  Grand Lodge 139
  Preston's Lodge of Antiquity 38, 78, 140
  Somerset House Lodge 77–8, 122, 211
  Union of two Grand Lodges of England (1813) 140
  Freemasons' Charity for Female Children 134
Frere, Mary, of Cambridge 183
Fripp, Edward Bowles (1787–1870), Bristol organist and composer 207, 208
  Church Psalmody (c. 1829) 208
'A Frog he would a-wooing go' 125
Frome, Somerset 208
Fryer, William (1768–1844), principal chaplain of Portuguese Embassy Chapel 113, 123
Fulneck, near Leeds 200

Gardiner, Sir James (1785–1851), friend of SW 185
Garrick, David (1717–79), actor 6, 220
Garth, Brecknockshire (estate of Gwynne family) 3
Gauntlett, Edward Ebenezer (b. 1808), solicitor 206, 216
Gauntlett, Henry John (1805–76), organist, composer 202, 206, 213, 214, 216, 244, 289n
  arrangement of SW's 'Tu es sacerdos' as 'He is our God and strong salvation 212 244
  contributes to Eliza's album (1836) 213
  organ voluntary by SW dedicated to 309
Gaviniès, Pierre (1728–1800), French composer 286
Gay, John (1685–1732), playwright: The Beggar's Opera 184, 220
Geminiani, Francesco (1687–1762), Italian violinist, composer 8, 9, 23, 217, 221, 286
  keyboard sonatas 8
  violin concertos by perf. at family concerts 23, 221
Gentleman's Magazine 131, 140, 174, 313
  review of rival oratorio concerts in (1813) 131
  reviews of SW's music in 322

George III (1738–1820), King of England: birthday 239, 279
George IV (1762–1830), King of England, previously Prince of Wales and Prince Regent 162, 172, 174, 196
Giardini, Felice (1716–96), Italian violinist, composer 6, 7, 8, 217, 221, 285, 286
  violin concertos by perf. at family concerts 24, 221
  Ruth 6, 219, 251
Gibbons, Orlando (1615–76), composer 173, 218
Giordani, Tommaso (c.1733–1806), Italian violinist, composer 220, 233
Giornovichi, Giovanni Mane (1735–1745–1804), Italian violinist, composer 221, 285
  violin concertos perf. at family concerts 24
  Violin Concerto No. 5 arr. by SW 286
Glee Club 53, 163, 211, 265, 272
glee clubs 53, 261
glees 261–2
Glenn, Robert (1776–1844), organist, friend of SW 134, 152, 153, 159, 170, 196, 216
  marries SW's daughter Rosalind (1834) 211
'Glorious First of June', sea battle (1794) 148
Gloucester 95
  Three Choirs Festival meeting at (1868) 259–60
Gluck, Christoph Willibald (1714–87), German composer 133
  La rencontre imprevue (1764) (Die Pilgrimme von Mecca) quoted by SW 287
Gordon riots (1780) 26
Goss, John Jeremiah (1770–1817), counter-tenor 38, 95, 105
Graf, Friedrich Hartmann (1727–95), flautist, composer, impresario 219
Graeff, John George (c. 1762-post 1824), flautist, composer 60, 72, 301
'Grammachree Molly', arr. SW for barrel organ 63
Granville, Bernard (1689–1775), of Bath 8
Grassini, Josephina (1773–1850), contralto 118
Graun, Heinrich (1703/4–59), German composer 118
Gravesend, Kent 200, 202
Gray, John (d. 1847), organ builder 169, 196
Gray, Thomas (1716–71), poet 261
  'Hark, his hands the lyre explore', from The Progress of Poesy set by SW 276
Gray, William (c. 1757–1820), organ builder 191
Greatorex, Thomas (1758–1831), organist and conductor 119
Great Yarmouth, Norfolk 108, 138, 145, 171
Greave, Mr, organist, of Birmingham 199
Green, John (fl. 1794–1848), music publisher, inventor of the seraphine 214, 311
Green, Thomas (1769–1825): Diary of a Lover of Literature 137, 221
Green Man Inn, Blackheath see concert venues

Greene, Maurice (1696–1755), composer 216, 222
Gregorian chant 223, 240
  SW's harmonizations of 123–4, 239
  SW's use of 231, 239, 257
Griffin, George Eugene (1781–1863), pianist, organist 77
Grimaldi, Joseph (1779–1837), clown 319
Guido of Arezzo, music theorist (c. 991–2-post 1033) 133
Guildford, Surrey 19, 22
Gumley, Martha, benefactor of Charles Wesley sen. 7
Gwilt, George (1775–1856), architect, friend of SW 78, 134
Gwilt, Joseph (1784–1863), architect, friend of SW 78, 123, 124, 128, 239
Gwynne, Marmaduke (?1694–1769) father of Sarah Gwynne Wesley 3
Gwynne, Rebecca (1724–99), aunt of SW 116–17
Gwynne, Thynne (d. 1826), cousin of Sarah Gwynne Wesley 22

Hague, Charles (1769–1821), English violinist, composer 111, 137, 182, 289
Hall, Martha (1706/7–91), sister of Sarah Gwynne Wesley, wife of Westley Hall 41, 201.
Hall, Westley (1711–76), Methodist minister 41
Handel, Georg Frideric (1685–1759), composer 5, 7, 8, 9, 56, 73, 80, 129, 217–18, 271, 280, 289
  alleged friendship with Charles Wesley sen. 192–3
  and Foundling Hospital 6, 55
  music by arr. SW for barrel organ 163–4
  music by perf. at Wesley family concerts 23, 24
  music by perf. at public concerts (see also individual works below) 58, 98, 103, 131, 136, 143, 161, 220
  works:
    church music:
      Coronation Anthems (1727) 58, 219,
      'Dettingen' Te Deum 10, 219
      'Dixit Dominus' 256
      Funeral Anthem for Queen Caroline 134, 216
      hymn tunes to words by Charles Wesley 192–5, 249–50
      'Rejoice! The Lord is King' 194
      'Utrecht' Te Deum 219
    harpsichord music: Harpsichord Suites, HWV 426–33 and 434–42: 8
    oratorios:
      Acis and Galatea 58, 131, 132, 147, 219
      Alexander's Feast 58, 219, 253,
      L'Allegro 58, 219, 253
      The Choice of Hercules 219
      Deborah 219
      Esther 63, 219
      Israel in Egypt 256
      Jephtha 219
      Joseph and his Brethren 219
      Joshua 219
      Judas Maccabaeus 6, 137, 164, 219
      Messiah 6, 9, 15, 55, 78, 95, 96, 103, 104, 118, 131, 132, 137, 143, 147, 217, 218, 219, 248
        'Pastoral Symphony' 176
      Ode for St Cecilia's Day 58, 219, 253
      Samson 9, 218, 219
      Saul: 'Dead March' 134
      Solomon 219
    oratorio songs arr. by SW (1824, 1825)
    organ concertos 59, 136, 298
    operas: Atalanta, Overture to 53
    Thirteen Celebrated Italian Chamber Duets 170
Handel Commemoration (1784) 58, 95, 221
Handel Commemoration (1834) 211
Handel festivals (1785, 1786, 1787, 1790, 1791) 58, 95
Handelians 80, 83
Hanover Square Grand Concert 219
Hanover Square Rooms see concert venues
Harding, John, doctor, friend of SW 169, 170, 216
  organ voluntaries by SW dedicated to 305–6
Harington, Henry (1727–1816), of Bath 88
Harmonicon, music journal 172, 187–8,
  review of SW's Service 173–5, 180, 185
  'Jubal' letter in 189–91
  pieces by SW advertised in 279, 280, 311
Harris, George Frederick, organist 166
Harris, Renatus (c. 1652–1724), organ builder 169, 214
Harris, Thomas (d. c. 1684), organ builder 169
Harrison, Samuel (1760–1812), tenor 23, 61
Harvey, Richard (1768/9–1836), vicar of Ramsgate (1812) 125
Hasse, Johann Adolf (1699–1783), German composer 224, 232
Hatton House, Hatton Garden see concert venues
Haweis, Revd Thomas (1734–1820) 88
Hawes, William (1785–1846), singer, conductor, impresario 38, 157, 167, 170, 188, 191, 203
  'Hail then! Illustrious pair' 148
Hawkes, William (fl. 1798–1810), inventor 81–2
  patent organ mechanism 85–6, 92, 110, 121
Hawkesworth, John (1715–73), poet 261
  'What bliss to life' set by SW 269
  'Come Stella, Queen of all my heart' set by SW 276
Hawkins, Miss, soprano 95
Haydn, Joseph (1732–1809), composer 47, 60, 62, 71, 128, 222, 223, 224, 268, 317

music by (see also individual works below) 133, 136, 219, 226
works:
   The Creation 59–60, 78, 95, 96, 103, 131, 132, 147, 224, 255, 256, 260, 269, 288, 298, 318
   'Blessed be his name for ever': fugue by SW 292
   Masses 232, 242, 256
   Symphonies 47, 284, 284–5
   Symphony 98 in B♭ 222, 284
   Symphony 100 in G ('Military') 144–5
   Symphony 102 in E♭ 285
   The Seasons 256, 260
   Te Deum in C 141
   La Tempesta 107
Hayes, Philip (c. 1738–1797), Professor of Music, Oxford University 19
Haymarket Theatre see King's Theatre, Haymarket
Heaton, Miss, singer, of Birmingham 198
Heaviside, Mr, doctor 152
Henslowe, Cecilia Maria, née Barthélemon 191
Henslowe, Edward Prentice 191
Hereford 95, 211
   Three Choirs Festival (1825) 185
   Three Choirs Festival (1834) 259
Herrnhut, Saxony (Moravian settlement) 2
Heywood Hall School, nr. Manchester 154, 155, 156
Hickford's Rooms see concert venues
High Wycombe, Bucks. 150
Hill, Rowland (1744–1833), Minister of Surrey Chapel 79, 98
Hill, William (1789–1870), organ builder 214
Hodges, Edward (1796–1867), organist, inventor 159, 203, 206, 208
   'typhus pedal' 159
   acount of SW's playing (1829) 205
Hodsoll, William, music publisher 298
Holmes, Edward (1799–1859), journalist, writer on music 116, 170, 225, 295
   account of SW's playing (1824) 169–70
Holmes, James (1755/6–1820), bassoonist 61, 63
Holmyard, J. S., The Psalms, Hymns and Miscellaneous Pieces, as sung at the Episcopal Chapel of the London Society for Promoting Christianity amongst the Jews (ante 1823) 249
Hone, William (1780–1842), author, publisher 249
Hook, James (1746–1827), organist, composer 136, 220
Horace (Quintus Horatius Flaccus) (65–8 BC), Latin poet 31, 182, 271
   'Qualem ministrum' set by SW 264–5
   parody of 'Integer vitae' by Martin Madan jun. set by SW 268

Horn, Charles Edward (1786–49), tenor, composer 279
Horn, Charles Frederick (1762–1830), organist, editor of music 79, 82–3, 93–4, 104–5
   arrangement of Bach fugues for string quartet 79, 288
Horncastle, W. F., writer on music 299, 301–2, 321
Horsley, William (1774–1858), composer, writer 89–90, 125, 142, 160, 170, 184–5
   involvement with QMMR 180–1
   review of SW's Service in QMMR 180–1
Hotham, Sir Charles (1730–67) 7
Hotham, Lady Gertrude (1697–1775) 7, 217
Humfrey, Pelham (1647–74), composer 218
Hunt, John (1775–1848), writer 116, 174
Hunt, Leigh (1784–1859), writer 116, 174, 184
Hyde's Concert Rooms, Tottenham Street see concert venues
Hymns Ancient and Modern Revised 250
Hymns and Psalms 250

Idle, Christopher, governor of Foundling Hospital 138
Immyns, John (1764-post 1818), organist 55–7, 138, 139, 278
Incledon, Charles (1763–1826), tenor 257
Ipswich, Suffolk 95, 108
   music festival at (1813) 137
Italian opera 62 see also King's Theatre

'J. P.', correspondent to NMMR 98–9
'Jack Pudding', see 'J. P.'
Jackson, John (1778–1831), artist 193
Jackson, Thomas (1783–1873), Methodist Connexional Editor 192–5, 199, 216, 218, 220
   Recollections (1874) 212
Jacob, Benjamin (1778–1829), organist 79–85 passim, 88–9, 92, 112, 149, 156, 196, 302
   SW's friendship with 113–14
   SW's letters to 79–80
   concert with SW at Surrey Chapel (1809) 98
   concert at Surrey Chapel (1812) 122
   National Psalmody (1817) 114, 249n
Jeaffreson, Christopher (1769/70–post 1847), vicar of Tunstall, friend of SW 108–9, 117, 137
John Bull (newspaper) 280
Johnson, Samuel (1709–1784), author, lexicographer 22, 182, 201, 279
   poems ascribed to set by SW see Hawkesworth, John
'John the Baptist's Hymn' see 'Ut queant laxis'
Jones, Stephen (1763–1827), editor of European Magazine 140
Jordan, Abraham (fl. 1712–56), organ builder 84
'Jubal', anonymous correspondent to Harmonicon 190–1

Kalkbrenner, Frédéric (1785–1849), pianist 111
Keats, John (1795–1821), poet 116
Keeble, John (1711–86) organist, composer 8, 217
  Select Pieces for the Organ (*c.* 1775–85) 218
Kelway, Joseph (*c.* 1702–82), harpsichordist, composer 8, 9, 83, 251
  Six Sonatas (*c.* 1764) 8, 217, 218
Kemble, John Philip (1757–1823), actor 220
Kemble, Charles (1775–1854), actor 188
Kemp, Joseph (?1702–82), editor of *NMMR* 92, 99
Kent, Duke of 122
Kershaw, John (1766–1855), manager of Methodist Printing House 194
Key, Mr, Procurator of Fitzwilliam Museum, Cambridge 191
King, Matthew Peter (*c.* 1773–1823), composer 135
  The Intercession 148
King, Master, boy treble 135
King, Mrs, Wesley family friend 151
Kingsbury, William (d. 1782) violinist 9, 23, 275
  'And is he then set free', ode by SW on death of 275
King's Theatre, Haymarket ('Haymarket Theatre', 'Opera House') 9, 20, 60, 61, 62, 104, 118, 120–1, 128, 147, 220, 227, 233
  concert room at 58
  oratorio concerts at 103
  Lacy's concert at (1809) 94
  riot at (1813) 135
Kingston, William B., friend of SW 67, 152, 153, 234
  'Fairy Minstrels in the Night' set by SW 277
Kingswood School, *see* Bristol
Kitchiner, William (1775–1827), inventor, epicure 138
Knyvett, Charles (1752–1822), alto 51, 120
Knyvett, William (1779–1856), bass 189
Kollmann, Augustus Frederic Christopher (1756–1829), organist, music theorist 70n, 71
  An Essay on Musical Harmony (1796) 71
  An Essay on Practical Musical Composition (1799) 71
  edition of Bach's *Chromatic Fantasia* (1806) 79
Kozeluch, Leopold (1747–1818), composer 70

Lacy, Mrs Bianchi, singer 136
Lacy, Willoughby (1749–1831), actor, theatre manager 94
Lamb, Charles (1775–1834), essayist 116
  'A Chapter on Ears' (*Essays of Elia*) 116
Lampe, John Frederick (*c.* 1703–51): *Hymns on the Great Festivals* (1746) 193
Langshaw, John (1763–1832), organist of Lancaster 296

Latrobe, Christian Ignatius (1758–1836), Moravian minister, musician 44, 57, 200, 317
  influence on SW 223–4
  A Selection of Sacred Music (1806–25) 223
Lawes, Henry (1602–45), composer 218
Leander, Lewis Henry (1769–1830) and Vincent Thomas (b. 1770), horn players 23
Le Blanc, Thomas (1773/4–1843), Vice Chancellor of University of Cambridge (1824–5) 179–80
lectures on music 76 *see also* Royal Institution; Crotch, William; Wesley, Samuel
Leduc, Simon (*ante* 1748–1777), French violinist and composer 286
Leeds, Yorkshire 108, 199–200
  Brunswick Chapel 199
Leete, Robert (*ante* 1772–*post* 1836), bass 78, 136
Lenten oratorio concerts *see* concerts
Lessey, Theophilus (1787–1841), Methodist Minister 200
Lindley, Robert (1776–1855), cellist 61, 63
Ling, William Thomas, organist 175, 176, 177
Linley, Elizabeth, *see* Sheridan, Elizabeth
Linley, Ozias (1765–1831), Canon of Norwich Cathedral 74, 143, 170
Linley, Thomas, the Elder (1733–95), composer 6, 74
  'When wars alarmed' used by SW in organ voluntary 287
  concert of music by (1814) 142
Linley, Thomas, the Younger (1756–78), composer 74
  Omnipotence (1774) 219
  The Duenna (1775) 220
  Shakespeare Ode (1776) 219
  Song of Moses (1777) 219
Linley, William (1771–1835), writer, amateur musician 38, 74–5, 86, 135, 143, 151, 152, 153, 170–1, 174
  arranges concert of his father's music (1814) 142
  Shakspeare's Dramatic Songs (1816) 75, 188
  organ voluntary by SW dedicated to 309
Linton, Mr, organist 139
Liszt, Franz (1811–86), pianist, composer 227
Literary Chronicle: article by SW in (1825) 181
Lock Hospital 5, 6–7, 41, 217, 219
Locke, John (1632–1704), philosopher 121, 271
Locke, Matthew (1621/2–77), composer 218
Loeschman, David (*fl.* 1802–29), inventor 92
Logier, Johann Bernhard (1777–1846), pianist, teacher, inventor 156
Lomax, Mr, music engraver 108
London, Bishop of (1777) *see* Louth, Robert
London Institution 97, 198
London Magazine 185
London Pianoforte School 313, 316

Longwood House, Owslebury 185
Lord Chamberlain, Office of 104
Louth, Robert (1710–87), Bishop of London in 1777: 19, 22
Lunardi, Vincenzo (1759–1806), balloonist 314
Lyceum Theatre (English Opera House) 279

McBean, Mr, early teacher of SW 9
McGeough, Walter (1790–1866), Irish landowner 163–4, 284, 289
Madan, Judith, mother of Revd Martin Madan 5
Madan, Revd Martin (1725–90), SW's godfather 5–6, 14–15, 17, 88, 217
  quoted by SW 185
  A Collection of Hymns and Psalms (1760) 6
  A Collection of Psalm and Hymn Tunes (1769) 6
  Thelyphthora 40–1
  'In gentle slumbers' set by SW 274
  'What shaft of fate's relentless pow'r' (possibly by) set by SW 277–8
Madan, Martin (1756–1809), son of Revd Martin Madan:
  'Come all my brave boys' set by SW 56
  'Blushete ne Carolos' set by SW 268
  'If in fighting foolish systems (possibly by) set by SW 271
  'Integer penis' set by SW 268
  'What shaft of fate's relentless pow'r' (possibly by) set by SW 277–8
Madrigal Society 35, 52, 53, 211, 265
  competition for composition of madrigal (1811) 128, 272–3
'Maggie Lauder' 137
Major, Joseph (1771–1828), organist, friend of SW 105, 170
  A Collection of Sacred Music for Churches & Chapels (c. 1824) 249
Malibran, Maria (1808–36), soprano: SW's song on the death of 280
manic depression *see* bipolar affective disorder
Mannheim School 316
Map, Walter (c. 1140–c. 1209), Welsh writer and cleric: 'Mihi est propositum' set by SW 268
Mara, Gertrud Elisabeth (1749–1833), soprano 220, 256
Marconi, Mme, singer 147, 148
Marenzio, Luca (1553/4–99), Italian composer 128
Margate, Kent 108, 124–6
  vicar of in 1812 *see* Baylay, William
Marsh, John (1752–1828), amateur musician and diarist 135
Martin, Charlotte Louisa *see* Wesley, Charlotte Louisa
Martin y Soler, Vicente (1754–1806), Spanish composer: *Una cosa rara* (1786) 315

Marylebone Gardens 220
Méhul, Etienne-Nicolas (1763–1817), French composer: *Joseph* (1807) 208
Melville, Miss, singer 95
Mendelssohn, Felix (1809–47), German composer 213, 214, 272, 276
  contributes to Eliza's album (1836) 213
  meets SW at Christ Church, Newgate Street 228
Methodism and Methodists 1–4, 12–14, 21, 194–5
  Book Room 194, 199, 212
  City Road Chapel 22, 36, 194, 195
  Foundery, Moorfields 2–3, 7
  Protestant Methodist Connexion 199
  West Street Chapel 194
  attitudes to child-rearing and education 12–14
  attitudes to Freemasonry 38
  comments on family concerts 20–1
  role of music in worship 26
Methodist Hymn Book (1933) 250
Millgrove, Benjamin, of Bath 8
Milton, John (1608–74), English poet 121
  Comus 252
  Paradise Lost 148
Missa pro Angelis 113
modes, Greek 59
Moncrieff, William Thomas (1794–1857), dramatist: *Elijah raising the Widow's Son* (1815) 144
Monro and May, music publishers 309
Monthly Magazine 69, 104, 140, 278, 313, 316
  reviews of SW's Op. 6 voluntaries in 298–9
Moore, Joseph (1766–1851), organizer of Birmingham Festival 107, 119, 198
Moore, Thomas (1779–1852), Irish poet:
  translations of Anacreon set by SW 272, 279
Moralt, Johannn Wilhelm (1775–1847), viola player 60
Moravian Church 2, 200
Morelli, Giovanni (fl. 1787–1815), bass 60
Mori, Nicolas (1796/7–1839), violinist 213, 289
  contributes to Eliza's album (1836) 213
Morley, Thomas (1557/8–1602), composer 218
Mornington, Earl of (1735–81), amateur composer 17, 221
  music perf. at family concerts 24
Mortimer, Mrs, Wesley family friend 151
Moscheles, Ignaz (1794–1870), German pianist, composer 189, 216
Mozart, Wolfgang Amadeus (1756–91), Austrian composer 4, 22, 71, 224
  concerto form 287
  music of 15, 60, 70, 133, 136, 219–20, 226, 232, 268, 317
  works:
    accompaniments to Handel's *Messiah* 131
    concertos 286

Mozart, Wolfgang Amadeus, works (*cont.*):
  Masses 54, 242
    Mass in C Minor: 'Laudamus te' 257
  operas:
    La clemenza di Tito: 'Ah! Perdona' 61, 63, 120, 147
    Così fan tutte: 'Come scoglio' 257
    Don Giovanni 161, 315
    Die Entführung: 'Martern allen Arten' 257
    Le nozze di Figaro 120, 161, 184
    Die Zauberflöte 141
      March of the Priests arr. SW for barrel organ 164
      Overture arr. SW for barrel organ 164
  Requiem 141, 147, 189, 208, 256
  Sonata for Piano Duet in F, K 497: 316
  Sonata for Piano Duet in C, K 521: 316
  Sonata for Two Pianos, K 448/375a: 111, 318–19
  Symphony (unspecified) perf. in SW's 1802 concert series 63
  Variations on Fischer's Minuet, K 179/189a, arr. SW for barrel organ 164
music festivals 58, 95 *see also* Birmingham, Gloucester, Hereford, Ipswich, Norwich, Tamworth, Three Choirs Festival, Worcester
music profession 14, 31, 35
music publishing 31, 72–3, 93
music teaching 87, 90
Musical World 213, 215, 216, 265
  list of SW's works in (1837) 302, 305, 309

NMMR see New Musical Magazine, Review and Register
Napoleon I (1769–1821), Emperor of France 144
Napoleon III (1808–73), Emperor of France 309
Nares, James (1715–83), organist, composer 15
New English Hymnal 250
New Musical Fund 144, 226, 279
New Musical Magazine, Review and Register (NMMR) 92–3, 98–100
News of Literature and Fashion 172, 174
Newton, Robert (1780–1854), Methodist minister 200
Nichols, W. A. A., organ builder 198n
Nightingale, John Charles (1790–1833), organist 139
Noblemen and Gentlemen's Catch Club *see* Catch Club
Nolcken, Baron, Swedish ambassador 22
'Non nobis, Domine', canon formerly attributed to Byrd 299
Norfolk, Duchess of (Catherine Howard) (1718–84) 28
Norfolk and Norwich Hospital 149

Northesk, Earl *see* Carnegie, William
Norwich, Norfolk 95, 108, 143, 145–6, 149, 160, 166
Novello, Clara (1818–1908), soprano, daughter of Vincent Novello 259
Novello, Francis (b. 1779), bass, brother of Vincent Novello 54, 172
Novello, Joseph Alfred (1810–96) music publisher, son of Vincent Novello 54, 114, 212, 280, 293, 311
Novello, Mary Sabilla, née Hehl (1789–1854), wife of Vincent Novello 114–15
  salon of 116, 174
Novello, Mary Victoria, daughter of Vincent Novello *see* Clarke, Mary Cowden
Novello, Sidney (1816–20), son of Vincent Novello 161
Novello, Vincent (1781–1861), organist, composer, and music publisher 84, 108, 110, 141, 159, 172–3, 223, 239, 271, 277, 316
  letters from SW to quoted or cited 125, 128, 130, 134, 136–7, 138, 139, 140, 149, 153, 160, 161, 163, 164, 166, 167, 168, 169, 170, 173–4, 177, 181, 185, 242, 259, 270, 273, 303, 318
  early life and career 54
  relationship with SW (1811–25) 113–14
  as member of Pantheon opera company (1812) 121
  performances with SW 105–7, 110, 123, 133, 142, 302–3
  and Fitzwilliam collection (1824–5) 179–80, 186, 190
  quarrels with SW (1826) 186, 189–90
  reconciliation with SW (1830) 210
  arrangements:
    Bach's Prelude in E♭, BWV 552, for organ duet and orchestra 133, 134, 141, 145
    Bach's 'St Anne' Fugue, BWV 552, for organ duet 142, 145, 302
  publications:
    A Collection of Sacred Music (1811) 54, 112, 239, 240, 311
    The Fitzwilliam Music (1825–6) 180, 190
    The Psalmist 212, 215, 250
    Select Organ Pieces 212, 290, 311
    Short Melodies for the Organ 294, 311
Novello & Co 212

Oglethorpe, James Edward (1696–1785), colonist of Georgia 2, 22
O'Leary, Arthur (1729–1802), Irish Roman Catholic priest 28
Oliver, George, Charlotte's trustee 119, 196
opera *see* Italian opera, English opera
'Opera House', *see* King's Theatre, Haymarket
oratorio concerts *see* concerts
Ordo Recitandi Divini Officii 156

General Index

Organs (in London unless otherwise specified):
  at SW's 1809 Royal Institution lectures 85–6
  at SW's 1811 Surrey Institution lectures 110
  at SW's 1813 Argyll Rooms concert 135
  The Argory, Co. Armagh 163–4
  Christ Church, Blackfriars 121
  Christ Church, Newgate Street 214
  Foundling Hospital chapel 55
  King's College, Cambridge 183
  Peterhouse, Cambridge 183
  Portuguese Embassy Chapel 84, 239
  St Lawrence, Jewry 169
  St Mary the Great, Cambridge 183
  St Nicholas, Great Yarmouth 145
  St Paul's Cathedral *see separate entry*
  St Sepulchre-without-Newgate 169
  Savoy Chapel, Strand 169–70
  Tamworth (St Editha) 96–7
  Trinity College, Cambridge 183
  Surrey Chapel 294–5 (Fig. 3)
Ossian (pseudonym of James MacPherson (1736–96)): 'Alone on the sea-beat rock' (*The Sorrows of Winter*) set by SW 274
Owslebury, near Winchester 185
Oxford, Bishop of (1777) 19
Oxford 2, 6, 74
Oxford House (Mrs Barnes's school) 33, 35, 38, 44, 67, 68, 89–91

Pacchierotti, Gaspare (1740–1821), Italian castrato 220, 314
Page, John (*c.* 1760–1812): *Harmonia sacra* 244
Paine, Thomas (1737–1809), radical writer 266
Paisible, Louis-Henry (1748–82), French violinist, composer 286
Paisiello, Giovanni (1740–1816), Italian composer 220, 233
Pantheon *see* concert venues
Paoli, Pascal (1725–1807), Corsican patriot 22
Parke, William (1762–1847), oboist, writer: *Musical Memoirs* (1830) 104n, 129
Parker, Thomas (*fl. c.* 1764–87), organ builder 55
Parsons, Robert (*c.* 1530–70), composer 218
Paton, Mary Ann (1802–64), soprano 184, 189, 259
Paxton, Stephen (1735–87), composer 221
  theme by used by SW 299
Pearce, Charles Edward (1856–1928), organist, writer 215, 247, 297n
Peat, Sir Robert (1771/2–1837), of Brentford, friend of SW 172–3
Peile, Joseph Stageldoir (1787–1840), pianist 61, 63
Pergolesi (1710–36), Italian composer 220, 224, 232
  La serva padrona (1733) 220
  Stabat Mater (1749) 230, 231

Pettet, Alfred (bapt. 1788–1837), Norwich organist 145–6, 149, 166–7, 171
Original Sacred Music (*c.* 1825) 235
Pettit, James, Bank of England official 117
Philharmonic Society 132–3, 156, 159, 167, 285
  concerts 136, 146, 227, 267
  SW and 133, 146, 161, 226
Phillips, Henry (1801–76), bass 116, 184, 189, 259
Piccinni, Niccolò (1728–1800), Italian composer
  La buona figliuola (1760) 220
  La morte d'Abel 252
Pindar, Peter (pen name of John Wolcot (1738–1819)) writer: 'O Delia, every charm is thine' set by SW 110, 272
Pinto, George Frederick (1785–1806), violinist, composer 60, 71–2, 270, 301
Pius VI (1717–99), Pope 29–30
plainchant *see* Gregorian chant
plainsong *see* Gregorian chant
Pleyel, Ignace Joseph (1757–1831), composer, publisher, piano maker 70, 125, 133, 222
Pollen, James, of Guildford 22
Pomeroy, Hon. George (b. 1764), amateur musician 99
Pope, Alexander (1688–1744), poet, dramatist 182, 270
  quoted by SW 181
  The Dunciad 253
  'Here shall the morn her earliest tears bestow' (adapted from *Elegy to the Memory of an Unfortunate Lady*) set by SW 270
Portogallo, Marcos Antonio (1762–1810), Portuguese composer:
  Merope 62
  Semiramide 118
Portuguese Embassy Chapel 25, 26, 54, 160, 172, 216, 223, 224, 229, 234, 237, 239, 302
  'musical meeting' at (1808) 84
  Novello and SW at 112–14, 126, 145
  organ 84, 239
Pouchée, Edward Dixon, publisher 175
Preston, Thomas, music publisher 121, 305
Price, James (1752–83), experimental scientist 17, 19, 22
  legacy to SW 22, 33–5, 40, 67
Price, Mr, doctor, of Brighton 198
Prince of Wales *see* George IV
Prince Regent *see* George IV
Professional Concert 219
Pucitta, Vincenzo (1778–1861), Italian composer:
  La caccia di Enrico IV 136
'Pug', nickname of friend of SW 169
Purcell, Henry (1659–95), composer 173, 182, 210, 216, 217, 218, 245, 249, 274, 280
  music by perf. at family concerts 24
  Mad Bess ('From silent shades') 24, 221
  Te Deum in D 219

Pymar, Thomas (c. 1764–1854), organist of Beccles, Suffolk 146, 171

QMMR see Quarterly Musical Magazine and Review
Quarterly see Quarterly Musical Magazine and Review
Quarterly Musical Magazine and Review 160
  review of SW's Service in F in 180, 184–5, 227, 247, 299
    SW's reply to 181–2

Ramsgate, Kent 124–6
  vicar of (1812) see Harvey, Richard
Ranelagh pleasure gardens 220
Rauzzini, Venanzio (1746–1810), Italian castrato, composer 87, 220
Rees, Abraham: Cyclopaedia 82
Reinagle, Alexander (1756–1809), violinist 23
Reinagle, Hugh (1758/9–85), cellist 23, 287–8, 292
Repository of Arts 140
  review of SW's The Deserter's Meditations in 321–2
Reynolds, Sir Joshua (1723–92), painter 62
Ricci, Francesco Pasquale (1732–1817), Italian composer 221
Rich, John (?1692–1761), playwright, theatre manager 5, 193
Rich, Priscilla (c. 1713–83), wife of John Rich 5, 7, 193, 217
Ridge, Herts. see under Wesley, Samuel
Ridgeway, Mr, friend of SW 191
Rimbault, Stephen Francis (1773–1837), organist 161
Roberts, Richard (?1729–1823) High Master of St Paul's School 66, 67
Roberts, Thomas (1765/6–1832), Methodist minister 194
Robertson, Henry, Treasurer of Covent Garden theatre 171, 184
Robinson, Henry Crabb (1775–1865), diarist 201
Robson, Joseph, organ builder 197 see also Flight and Robson
Roche Court, Fareham, home of James Gardiner 185
Rode, Pierre (1774–1830), French composer 293
Rogers, Mr, early teacher of Charles Wesley jun. 8
Roman Catholicism see under Wesley, Samuel
Romberg, Andreas Jakob (1767–1821), German composer 133, 293
Rooke, Mr, early teacher of Charles Wesley jun. 5
Rossini, Gioacchino (1792–1868), Italian composer 226–7
Royal Academy of Music 163
Royal College of Music 54, 310

Royal Harmonic Institution 170, 175
Royal Institution of Great Britain 70, 76, 79, 85, 86, 87, 88, 92, 97
  SW's lectures at 110, 187–8, 198, 208, 209, 227
Russell, John (1711–1804), printer, mayor of Guildford 17, 22
Russell, John, RA (1745–1806), artist 17
  portrait of SW 17, 18 (Pl. 2)
Rudall, George 293
Russell, Mary Ann (1781–1854), widow of William Russell 175
Russell, William (1777–1813), organist, composer 57, 137–8, 145, 175
  committee for performance of Job (1814) 142
  Job (1814) 142, 175
  publication of (1825, 1826) 175
Russell Institution 198

Sacchini, Antonio (1730–86), Italian composer 220, 233
Sacred Harmonic Society 212, 248
Sadler, James (d. 1828), balloonist 145
Sainsbury & Co (publishers): A Dictionary of Musicians 98, 171–2
St Katherine's Dock 198
St Katherine's Hospital, Regent's Park 198
St Luke's Hospital 150, 152, 154
St Paul's Cathedral 19, 22, 104, 134, 185, 219
  SW's 'O Lord God of Hosts' sung at (1770s) 244
  abortive plans for performance of SW's Litany Responses at (1806) 70
  SW's Litany Responses and Te Deum and Jubilate sung at (1807) 84–5
  SW's Magnificat and Nunc Dimittis sung at (1823) 166
  SW's Service sung at (1824) 167–8, 247
  Mendelssohn plays at (1837) 214
St Paul's School 66, 67, 69, 74
Sale, John Bernard (1779–1828), bass 189
Salomon, Johann Peter (1745–1815), violinist, impresario 47, 97, 105, 222, 270–1, 291
  performances of Haydn's Creation (1800) 59–60, 96, 224
  advises SW on promotion of Bach (1808) 75–6
  benefit concerts (1812, 1813) 121, 135
  theme by used by SW as subject of fugue in piano sonata 317
Santley, Charles (1834–1922), baritone 260
Sardinian Embassy Chapel 25, 26, 54, 223, 229
Sarti, Giuseppe (1729–1802), Italian composer 63
Saust, Charles (b. 1773), flautist, composer 270–1
Savage, William (1720–89), composer 217
Savage, William (1770–1843), secretary to Royal Institution 88–9
Savoi, Signor, singer 20

Saxe-Coburg-Saalfeld, Leopold, Prince of 148
Scarlatti, Alessandro (1660–1725), Italian composer 23, 24, 192
Scarlatti, Domenico (1685–1757), Italian composer 8, 9, 15, 217, 314
 harpsichord sonatas 8, 9, 217, 314
Schobert, Johann (c. 1735–67), Austrian composer 15, 218
Schubert, Franz (1797–1828), Austrian composer 317
Schunke, Andreas and Gottfried, horn players 141
'Scots wha' hae with Wallace bled' arr. SW for barrel organ 163
separation, marital 102–3, 119–20
seraphine, reed organ 214, 311
Seward, William (1747–99), man of letters 224, 297–8
Shakespeare, William (1564–1616), playwright 75, 129
Shepherd, Antony (1721–1796), Dean of St George's Chapel, Windsor 22
Shepherd, Mary Freeman (1730–1815), confidante of SW 27–8, 30–1, 37, 40, 42–3, 64, 66
Sheppard, Dr Edward (1731–1813), of Bath 88
Sheridan, Elizabeth, née Linley (1754–1792), soprano 74
Sheridan, Richard Brinsley (1751–1816), playwright, MP 74, 75, 86
Sherriff, Deborah, SW's landlady in Bristol (1830) 207
Shield, William (1748–1829), viola player, composer 61, 63, 71, 146, 170
Shirley, James (1596–1666), dramatist, poet: 'The glories of our birth and state' set by SW 266
Siddons, Sarah (1755–1831), actress 220
Skarratt, Robert, music engraver 128
Smart, George (1776–1867), conductor, impresario 122, 128–9, 159, 161, 170, 188, 189, 226
 and Drury Lane oratorio concerts 129–31, 141, 144, 147–8
Smith, Charles (1786–1856), singer, organist 145
Smith, 'Father' (Bernhardt Schmidt), (c. 1630–1708), organ builder 183
Smith, George, of Faversham, Kent 90–2
Smith, John, Bristol organ builder 203, 204
Smith, John Christopher (1712–95), amanuensis and copyist of Handel 191–2, 217
 Gideon 191–2
Smith, John Stafford (1750–1836), composer, musical antiquarian 83
Smith, John Thomas (1776–1833): *Nollekens and his Times* (1828) 108
Smith, Revd Sydney (1771–1845), clergyman, wit 76
Smith, Theodore, (c. 1740–c. 1810) English or German composer 315–16
Smith, William, of Leeds 200
Smith, Miss, daughter of George Smith, pupil of SW at Mrs Barnes's school 90–2
Snetzler, John (1710–85), organ builder 168, 183
Society of Harmonists 70, 265
'The Soldier, tir'd of war's alarms' *see* Arne, Thomas Augustine
Soler, Vincente Martin y *see* Martin y Soler, Vicente
Somers Town 161
Southern, Henry (1799–1853), writer, editor of *London Magazine* 185
Southey, Robert (1774–1843): 'You are old, father William' set by SW 267
Spagnoletti, Paolo (1768–1834), violinist 110
Spanish Embassy Chapel 54
Spencer, Knight, Secretary of Surrey Institution 99–100, 109–10
Spohr, Louis (1784–1859), German composer 293
Stamitz, Johann (1715–57), composer 219
Stanley, John (1712–86), organist, composer 5, 217
Stephens, Catherine (1794–1882), soprano 125, 147, 148
Stephenson, Edward (1759–1833), Bach enthusiast 104
Sterne, Laurence (1713–68): 'Harsh and untuneful are the notes' (*Tristram Shandy*) set by SW 263
Stevens, Richard John Samuel (1757–1837), composer, teacher 55, 83, 85n, 170, 265, 271
 Recollections and diary cited or quoted 70, 75, 138, 152, 211, 312–13
Stevenson, George J. (1818–88), Methodist writer: *Memorials of the Wesley Family* (1876) 33, 101n
Stokes, Charles (1784–1839), pianist, organist 110, 318
Street, Joseph Edward, son of Joseph Payne Street 175
Street, Joseph Payne, friend of SW 51–2, 69, 105, 170, 175, 185, 234
Surrey Chapel 75, 97, 98, 114, 122, 149, 302
 organ specification 295 (Fig. 3)
Surrey Institution 97–8, 99, 101, 109–10
Sussex, Duke of (Augustus Frederick, Duke of Sussex) (1773–1843) 122, 129, 139, 272
Suter, Sarah (1793/4–1863), partner of SW 101–2, 114, 124, 134, 153–4, 155, 156, 162, 165, 182, 183, 192, 194, 198, 201, 216
 SW's letters to 107–8, 109
 quoted or cited 109, 143, 191, 192, 197, 200, 204, 205–6
Sutherland, Alexander (?1781–1861), doctor 150, 153

Swieten, Gottfried van (1733–1803), diplomat, amateur musician 71
Swift, Jonathan (1667–1745), writer, divine 182
Symonds, Miss, singer 198

Talbot, James (1726–90), Vicar Apostolic of the London District 28–30, 31
Tallis, Thomas (*c.* 1505–85), composer 182, 218
Tamworth, Staffs. 94–7, 99, 101, 104, 105, 118, 225, 288
  music festival at (1809) 94–6
Taylor, Edward (1784–1863), bass, of Norwich 143
Taylor, J., author, 148
Taylor, William (*c.* 1753–1825), manager of Covent Garden Theatre 120–1, 135–6
teaching, music *see* music teaching
temperament, musical *see* tuning and temperament
Thelyphthora, *see* Madan, Revd Martin
Thomson, James (1700–48), Scottish dramatist and poet 96, 261
  'Father of Light and Life' (*The Seasons*) set by SW 96, 267–8
Three Choirs Festival 95, 185, 256, 259 *see also* Gloucester, Hereford, Worcester
Thurlow, Edward (1731–1806), Lord Chancellor: 'Hurly burly, blood and thunder' set by SW 271
Tietjens, Therese (1831–77), soprano 260
The Times 61, 118, 131, 123, 136, 171
  review of rival oratorio concerts (1813) 131
  obituary of SW (1837) 29n, 35–6
  account of funeral of SW (1837) 216
Tinney, Charles, bass 147, 148
Tolly, Mr, of Birmingham 198
Tomkins, Thomas (1572–1656), composer 218
Tooke, John Horne (1736–1812), politician 268
Tooth, Eliza (1793–*post* 1851), friend of Wesley family 192–3, 207, 210–11
Tooth, Samuel, builder, friend of Wesley family 22
Tottenham Street Rooms (Hyde's Concert Rooms) *see* concert venues
Tower of London 69
Traetta, Tommaso (1727–79), Italian composer 220
Traquair, Earl and Countess of 27–8
tuning and temperament 55, 81–2, 86, 89
  equal temperament 81
  SW's lecture on 92, 109–10, 208
Tunstall, Suffolk 108–9, 110, 117, 137
Turle, James (1802–1882), organist of Westminster Abbey 216
Tuthill, Dr, doctor 153
Twiss, Richard (1714–1821), traveller, writer 22, 108–9
Tydemann, Zebedee, music teacher of Framlingham, Suffolk 107, 191

Tyson, Alan (1926–2000), English musicologist and collector of music 314

United Methodist Hymnal 250
D'Urfey, Thomas (*c.* 1623–1723): *Wit and Mirth, or, Pills to Purge Melancholy* (1699–1700): 'Tobacco's but an Indian weed' from set by SW 267, 276
'Ut queant laxis', plainsong hymn 113, 240

Valabrègue, Paul, husband of Angelica Catalani 120–1
Van Swieten, Gottfried *see* Swieten, Gottfried van
Vaughan, Elizabeth, soprano 78, 95, 105, 136, 280
Vaughan, Thomas (1782–1843), tenor 78, 95, 105, 107, 120, 136, 189, 278, 280
Vauxhall Gardens 136
Vazeille, Molly *see* Wesley, Molly
Vento, Mattia (1735–76), Italian composer 8, 217, 218, 219, 230
Victoria (1819–1901), Queen of England 177, 214, 248, 322
Vincent, J., alto 51–2
Viotti, Giovanni Battista (1755–1824), Italian violinist, composer 133
Vocal Concerts *see* concert series
Vocal Magazine (1781) 263, 274, 276

Wagner, Henry Michell (1792–1870), Vicar of Brighton 197–8
Wait, Daniel Guilford (1789–1850) friend of SW 179, 180, 182–4, 186, 203–5, 206, 207–8
Ward, John (1571–1638), composer 128
Wateringbury, Kent 64, 66
Waterloo, Battle of (1815) 144
  song by SW commemorating British victory at 279
Watford, Herts. 207
Webb, Edward (d. 1788) organist of St George's Chapel, Windsor 37
Webbe, Samuel, the Elder (1740–1816), composer, organist 26, 38, 44n, 54, 124, 242
  Masses 221
  influence on SW 223
  A Collection of Music as used in the Chapel of the King of Sardinia (*c.* 1785) 242
Webbe, Samuel, the Younger (1768–1843), composer, organist 23, 38
  visits Margate and Ramsgate with SW (1812) 124–6
  benefit (1813) 136
Weber, Carl Maria von (1786–1826), German composer 175, 188, 189, 227
  Der Freischütz 175, 184, 188, 227, 319
  Hunting Chorus 175

Lied der Hirtin 319
Oberon 184, 188, 189, 227
Weichsell, Elizabeth, *see* Billington, Elizabeth
Weichsell, Charles (*c.* 1766–*post* 1805) violinist, composer 20
  arrangement of Beethoven string quartet 141, 308
Weldon, John (1676–1736), composer 218
Wellington, Duke of (Arthur Wellesley (1769–1852), First Duke of Wellington), Field Marshal 144, 197
Wellings, Mr and Miss, of Brighton 197–8
Wells Cathedral 203
Welsh, Thomas (*c.* 1780–1848), composer and bass 170
Wesley, ?, infant daughter of SW and Sarah Suter (d. 1813) 134
Wesley, ?, infant son of SW and Sarah Suter, (d. 1816) 149
Wesley, Charles senior (1707–88), father of SW 1, 2, 3, 10, 19, 26, 30, 36–7, 98, 181, 192, 194, 195, 249, 273–4
  account of his sons' musical education 4–5, 7–9, 14–15, 217–19
  and family concerts 20–2
  alleged acquaintance with Handel 192–3
  and SW's conversion to Roman Catholicism 28–9
  attitudes to child-rearing and education 12–14
  declining health and death 36–7, 168
  relationship with SW 12–13, 32–3, 37, 168
  'And is he then set free?' (Ode on the Death of William Kingsbury) set by SW 275
  'Might I in thy sight appear' set by SW 249
  'Omnia vanitas' set by SW 168, 243
  'There are by fond Mama supplied' set by SW 263
  attitude to music profession 14, 20–1
  hymns set by Handel 192, 223, 273–4, 275, 281
Wesley, Charles junior (1757–1834), brother of SW 1, 11, 12, 14, 15, 25, 28, 37, 46, 49–50, 64, 88, 116–17, 126, 149–50, 170, 171, 177, 192, 195, 196, 199, 200–1, 224, 284, 288, 296
  SW's letters to quoted or cited 69–70, 72, 78, 83–4, 103, 116, 265
  early musical education 4–5, 7–9, 217–18
  and family concerts 20–4, 36, 268
  and organist's position at Windsor (1788) 37
  concert series with SW (1802) 60–3, 116, 284
  article on in *Public Characters of all Nations* (1824) 171
  invited to play at Leeds (1828) 199–200
  death 211
  will 212
  as keyboard player 83
  conservatism of 83, 217–18
  dependency on Sarah in later life 195
  relationship with SW 83, 212

Ode on the the Death of Boyce (1780) 23
Wesley, Charles III (1793–1859), son of SW and Charlotte 46, 49–50, 64, 109, 116–17, 152, 153, 201, 216, 270
  birth 46
  attends St Paul's School (1805) 66
  removed from St Paul's school (1806) 67
  educated by SW (1806) 69
  later relationship with SW 176–7
  setting by SW of 'Life is a jest' (translation of Greek verse) 270
Wesley, Charlotte Louisa, née Martin (1761–1845), wife of SW 32, 38, 40, 53, 60, 64–5, 66, 101–3, 107, 116, 117–18, 119–20, 127, 151, 153, 176–7, 194, 195, 196, 201, 216
  appearance 33
  character and family background 33, 44–5
  extravagance 45, 49, 68, 101
  mental illness 48–9, 51
  physical violence of towards SW 57
Wesley, Eliza (1819–95), daughter of SW and Sarah Suter 159, 211, 214–15, 252, 280, 292, 310, 311, 318
  bequeathes SW's manuscripts to British Museum 160, 188, 208
  organ music by SW for 310–11
  edition of SW's letters to Jacob (*Bach Letters*) 208
  autograph album (1836) 213
Wesley, Emma Frances (1806–65), daughter of SW and Charlotte 66, 67, 68, 101, 109, 119, 152
Wesley, John (1703–91), uncle of SW 1, 2, 3, 5, 6, 13, 21, 22, 27, 28, 29, 36, 37, 42, 43, 98, 181, 207, 217
  attitude to music 13
  attends family concerts (1781, 1784) 22
  reaction to SW's conversion to Roman Catholicism (1784) 29
  concerns about Charles jun. and Samuel (1788) 36–7
  writings and publications:
    The Christian's Pattern; or, a Treatise of the Imitation of Christ (1735) 39
    A Collection of Hymns for the Use of the People called Methodists (1780) 194
    An Extract of the Life of Monsieur de Renty 1741) 39
    The Life of Gregory Lopez (1735) 39
    On the Power of Music (1780) 13
Wesley, John (1825–*ante* 1876), son of SW and Sarah Suter 183, 202, 211
Wesley, John James (b. and d. 1768), son of Charles and Sarah Gwynne Wesley 7
Wesley, John William (1799–1860), son of SW and Charlotte 57, 64, 68, 109, 117, 127, 152, 153, 201, 216

General Index

Wesley, Matthias Erasmus (1821–1901), son of SW and Sarah Suter 162, 211, 212, 216
Wesley, Molly, formerly Vazeille (1710–81), wife of John Wesley 3
Wesley, Robert Glenn (1830–1915), son of SW and Sarah Suter 211, 247
Wesley, Rosalind (b. c. 1814), daughter of SW and Sarah Suter 153, 159, 211, 214
Wesley, Samuel (1662–1735), Vicar of Epworth, grandfather of SW 1, 252, 253
Wesley, Samuel (1691–1739), uncle of SW 54, 279

Wesley, Samuel (1766–1837)
life:
  birth (1766) 1, 7
  childhood and early musical education 7–10, 15–18
  plays a psalm at Bristol 9
  plays organ at Bath Abbey 9
  composes *Ruth* 9–10
  family visited by Boyce (1774) 10, 15
  visits with Martin Madan 14
  composes march for Guards regiment 16
  visits Russell family (1776) 17
  friendship with James Price (1776) 17, 19
  plays in concert at Hickford's Rooms (1777) 19–20
  family concerts (1779–87) 20–4
  early involvement with Roman Catholicism (1778) 25–7
  first Roman Catholic church music (1780) 26
  meets Charlotte (1782) 32–3
  converts to Roman Catholicism (1784) 26–7, 27–30
  composes *Missa de Spiritu Sancto* (1784) 29–30
  adolescent rebelliousness 30–1
  interest in Latin and Greek 31–2
  composes 'Qualem ministrum' (1785) 31–2
  proposes publication of 'Qualem ministrum' (1785) 31–2
  attains majority (1787) 33
  inheritance from Price 33
  alleged fall and head injury (1787) 35–6
  becomes a Freemason (1788) 38
  continuing relationship with Charlotte 40, 44–5
  opposition to marriage and marriage ceremony 40–1
  disagreements with Roman Catholic Church over doctrine (1792) 43–4
  sets up house with Charlotte at Ridge (1792) 44
  pregnancy of Charlotte (1793) 45–6
  marriage to Charlotte (1793) 45
  birth of son Charles (1793) 45–6
  deterioration of relationship with Charlotte (1794) 47–8
  birth of daughter Susanna (1797) 48
  composes *Ode to St Cecilia* (1794) 48
  separation from Charlotte (1795) 49–50
  moves to Finchley (1797) 53
  renews musical activities in London (1797) 53
  death of Susanna (1797) 53–4
  resumes composition (1798) 54
  applies for organist's position at Foundling Hospital (1798) 55–7
  moves to Hornsey Lane (1798) 57
  birth of son John William (1799) 57
  moves to Highgate (1799) 57
  performance of *Ode to St Cecilia* (1799) 57–8
  composes *Confitebor* (1799) 59
  renews acquaintance with Burney (1799) 59
  sends score of *Confitebor* to Burney (1799) 59
  plays organ concerto at performance of Haydn's *Creation* (1800) 59–60
  love affair with Anne Deane (c. 1799) 60
  separation from Charlotte (1801)
  concert series at Tottenham Street Rooms (1802) 60–3
  extended period of depression (c. 1802–5) 63
  reconciliation with Charlotte and move to Camden Town (1805) 66
  birth of daughter Emma Frances 66
  financial problems (1806) 67–9
  copies '48' (1806) 69
  reviews Callcott's *A Musical Grammar* (1807) 70
  discovers music of J. S. Bach (1808) 71
  renews friendship with Burney (1808) 72
  consults Burney on promoting and publishing Bach (1808) 72
  converts Burney to Bach cause (1808) 73–4
  introduces William Linley to Burney (1808) 74–5
  consults Burney on lecturing (1808) 76
  Hanover Square Rooms concert (1808) 76–7
  resumes involvement with Freemasonry (1808) 77–8
  visits Cambridge (1808) 78–9
  beginning of correspondence with Jacob (1808) 79
  promotes Bach with Jacob (1808) 79–84
  demonstration of Elliot organ with Jacob 81–2
  plans edition of Bach's '48' with Horn (1808–9) 82
  takes part in 'musical meeting' at Portuguese Embassy chapel (1808) 84–5
  Te Deum and Jubilate sung at St Paul's (1808) 84–5
  invited to lecture at Royal Institution (1808) 85
  consults Burney about lectures (1808–9) 85
  portrait painted by Bacon (1809) 86
  visits Bath (1809) 87–8
  lectures at Royal Institution (1809) 85–6, 88–9
  dismissed from Mrs Barnes's school (1809) 89–90

dispute with Smith over piano lessons (1809) 91–2
NMMR controversy (1809) 92–3, 98–100
publishes edition of Bach's organ trio sonatas with Horn (1809) 93–4
Hanover Square Rooms concert (1809) 94
directs music festival at Tamworth (1809) 94–7
gives concert in Birmingham (1809) 97
plays Bach violin sonatas to Burney (1809) 97, 105
lectures at Surrey Institution (1809) 97–8
gives recital with Jacob at Surrey Chapel (1809) 98
beginning of relationship with Sarah Suter (1809) 101
final separation from Charlotte (1810) 101–3
publishes first volume of edition of '48' with Horn (1810) 104
Hanover Square Rooms concert (1810) 105
performs *Goldberg Variations* with Novello to Burney (1810) 105–7
birth of son Samuel Sebastian (1810) 107
visits Birmingham (1810) 107
visits Jeaffreson in Tunstall (1811) 108
gives second course of lectures at Surrey Institution (1811) 110–11
Hanover Square Rooms concert (1811) 110–11
begins correspondence with Novello (1811) 112
directs Birmingham Festival (1811) 118
agrees formal Deed of Separation (1812) 119
Hanover Square Rooms concert (1812) 120–2
appointed Masonic Grand Organist (1812) 122
harmonizes Gregorian chant (1812) 123
visits Margate and Ramsgate (1812) 124–6
visits Burney with Butler (1812) 126
publishes edition of Bach's Six Little Preludes (?1812) 127
composes 'O sing unto mie roundelaie' for Madrigal Society prize (1812) 128–9
appointed organist at Covent Garden oratorio concerts (1813) 128–9
joins Philharmonic Society as associate (1813) 133
death of infant daughter (1813) 134
Argyll Rooms concert (1813) 135–6
plays at music festival in Ipswich (1813) 137
applies for organist's position at Foundling Hospital (1813) 137–9
takes part in Union of two Grand Lodges of England (1813) 139
invited to write reviews for *European Magazine* (1814) 140–1
member of committee on performance of Russell's *Job* (1814) 141
takes part in performance of *Job* at Foundling Hospital (1814) 142
benefit with Ashley at Covent Garden (1814) 142

visits Norwich (1814) 143, 145
plans edition of Credo of Bach's *B Minor Mass* (1815) 145–6
visits Great Yarmouth and Norwich (1815) 145
becomes full member and director of Philharmonic Society (1815) 146
shares benefit with Ashley (1816) 148
illness and death of infant son (1816) 149
collapse on road to Norwich (1816) 149
deteriorating health and breakdown (1816–17) 150–3
incarceration at Blacklands House (1817–18) 153–7
convalescence at Southend (1818) 157
resumes career (1818) 157–9
copies music for Philharmonic Society (1818) 159
birth of daughter Eliza (1819) 159
begs for work as copyist (1820) 162, 163
composes Latin Magnificat (1821) 162–3
granted honorary membership of Royal Academy of Music (1822) 163
arranges music for McGeough's barrel organ (1822) 163–4
composes Anglican Magnificat and Nunc Dimittis (1822) 164
applies for organist's post at St Lawrence, Jewry (1823) 166
Magnificat and Nunc Dimittis perf. at St Paul's (1823) 166
complete Service in F perf. at St Paul's (1824) 167–8
appointed to Camden Chapel (1824) 168
composes *Carmen Funebre* 168–9
plays organs of London churches with friends (1824) 169–70
arranges music by Handel for Royal Harmonic Institution (1824) 170
publishes Service in F (1824) 170–1
correspondence on Sainsbury's *Dictionary of Music* article (1824) 171–2
visits Peat in Brentford (1824) 172–3
Service in F reviewed in *Harmonicon* (1825) 173
reacts angrily to review of Service in *Harmonicon* (1825) 173–4
replies to *Harmonicon* review of Service (1825) 174
arranges accompaniments to Russell's *Job* for Mary Russell (1825) 175
acts as 'umpire' at Brixton (1825) 175–6, 177–8
arrested and imprisoned for debt (1825) 176–7
enquires about publication of Fitzwiliam music (1825) 179
Service in F reviewed in *QMMR* (1825) 180

Wesley, Samuel (1766–1837), life (*cont.*):
  reacts angrily to *QMMR* review of Service in F (1825) 180–1
  publication of reply to Harmonicon review (1825) 181–2
  visits Cambridge and transcribes music from Fitzwilliam collection (1825) 182–3
  plans publicatin of *Confitebor* (1825) 183
  performs *Confitebor* with Novello in Cambridge (1825) 183–4
  attempts publication of reply to *QMMR* review (1825) 184–5
  visits Gardiner at Roche Court (1825) 185–6
  granted permission to transcribe music from Fitzwilliam collection (1826) 186
  quarrel with Novello (1826) 186
  visits Cambridge (1826) 187
  lectures at Royal Institution (1826) 187–8
  plans edition of motets from Byrd's *Gradualia* (1826) 187
  Confitebor perf. in London (1826) 188–9
  discovers Handel hymns (1826) 191–2
  publishes Handel hymns (1826) 193–4
  renews relationship with Methodists (1826–7) 194
  attends Breakfast for the Children of the Methodist Preachers (1827) 195
  visits Brighton (1827) 197–8
  gives lectures on music in London (1828) 198
  gives organ recitals at St Peter's, Dale End, Birmingham (1828) 198
  composes and publishes *Original Hymn Tunes* (1828) 199
  gives organ recitals at Brunswick Chapel, Leeds (1828) 199–200
  gives organ recitals in Bristol (1829) 203–7
  gives concert at Watford (1829) 207
  lectures at Bristol Institution (1830) 207–9
  reconciliation with Novello (1830) 210
  illness (1830) 210–11
  offers services at Handel Commemoration (1834) 211
  plays at Sacred Harmonic Society concert (1834) 212
  composes hymns for Novello's *The Psalmist* (1834) 212
  writes *Reminiscences* (1836) 212
  writes article for *Musical World* (1836) 213
  writes out score of *Ode to St Cecilia* from memory (1837) 213–14
  plays to Mendelssohn (1837) 215
  final illness and death (1837) 216
  funeral (1837) 216
musical works *see* Index of Wesley's Works
publications:
  edition of '48' (with Horn) 107, 108, 137, 308
  edition of Bach organ trios (with Horn) 93–4
  edition of Bach's Six Little Preludes (?1812) 127
  edition of Handel hymns (1826, 1827) 193–4, 249–50
  Original Hymn Tunes (1828) 199
  Service in F (1824) 166, 170–1
writings:
  Vindex to Verax (1792) 42–3
  review of Callcott's *A Musical Grammar* (1807) 70
  satirical verse on 'J. P.' (1809) 99
  reviews of music for *European Magazine* (1814–16) 140–1, 150
  Reminiscences (1836) 9, 212–13
    cited 20, 47, 58, 59, 71, 93n, 114, 130, 189, 212–13, 222, 285
  'A Sketch of the State of Music in England' (*Musical World*, 1836) 213
addresses:
  Ridge (1792–7) 33, 44–50, 51, 53
  Church End, Finchley (1797–8) 53, 57
  Hornsey Lane, near Highgate (1798–9) 57
  Five Mile Stone, Highgate (1799–1803) 57, 60, 64
  Arlington Street, Camden Town (?1805–10) 66, 69, 210, 270
  Adam's Row, Hampstead Road (1810–12) 102, 107, 109, 121
  Tottenham Court (1812–13) 121, 124
  Gower Place, Euston Square (1813–17) 157
  Blacklands House, Chelsea (1817–18) 153, 154–7
  Euston Street, Euston Square (*c.* 1818–30) 66, 102, 161, 195
  Mornington Place (1830–2) 210
  King's Row, Pentonville (1832–7) 210n, 211
attitudes and relationships:
  attitude to music profession 31–2, 35
  attitude to Roman Catholicism 25–30 35, 36, 38, 39, 42, 42–3, 45, 54, 67, 124, 156, 184, 221, 229, 234
  relationship with Charles Wesley sen. (father) 12–13, 32–3, 37, 168
  relationship with Charles Wesley jun. (brother) 83–4, 212
  relationship with Charles Wesley III (son) 69, 176–7
  relationship with Charlotte 21–3, 40, 44–50 *passim*, 66, 101–3, 153
  relationship with Sarah Gwynne Wesley (mother) 164–5
  relationship with Sarah Wesley (sister) 195–6, 201–2
  relationship with Methodism and Methodists 35, 67, 194–5
concerts and recitals:
  Hickford's Rooms (20 May 1777) 19–20
  family concerts (1779–87) 21–4, 220–1

Covent Garden (22 Feb. 1799) (*Ode to St Cecilia*) 57–8
King's Theatre (21 Apr. 1800) (*Creation*) 59–60
Tottenham Street Rooms series (Feb.–May 1802) 60–3
Surrey Chapel (15 Mar. 1808) 75
Hanover Square Rooms (11 June 1808) 76–7
Hanover Square Rooms (3 June 1809) 94
King's Theatre (22 June 1809) 94
Green Man Inn, Blackheath (26 June 1809) 94
Tamworth (21, 22 Sept. 1809) 96–7
Birmingham (23 Sept. 1809) 97
Surrey Chapel (29 Nov. 1809) 98
Covent Garden (30 Jan. 1810) 104
Covent Garden (12 Mar. 1810) 104
Hanover Square Rooms (27 Apr. 1811) 110–11
Birmingham Festival (2–4 Oct. 1811) 118
Vocal Concerts (9 Mar. 1812) 120
Christ Church, Blackfriars (10 May 1812) 121
Hanover Square Rooms (16 May 1812 (Salomon's benefit) 121
Hanover Square Rooms (3 June 1812) 120–2
Ramsgate (3 Oct. 1812) 124–5
Covent Garden oratorio concerts (1813) 130–2
Hanover Square Rooms (26 Apr. 1813) (Salomon's benefit) 135
Argyll Rooms (4 May 1813) 135–6
Ipswich (6–8 July 1813) 137
Covent Garden oratorio concerts (1814) 141–2
Covent Garden (28 May 1814) 142
Foundling Hospital Chapel (15 June 1814) 142
Norwich (20 Oct. 1814) 143
Covent Garden oratorio concerts (1815) 144–5
Great Yarmouth (12 July 1815) 145
Norwich (27, 28 July 1815) 145
Covent Garden (13 May 1815) 146–8
Covent Garden (1 June 1816) 148
High Wycombe (25 Sept. 1816) 150
Covent Garden oratorio concerts (1817) 150
Covent Garden oratorio concerts (1819) 159
Covent Garden oratorio concerts (1825) 175
Argyll Rooms (4 May 1826) (*Confitebor*) 188–9
St Saviour's Southwark (1 Mar. 1827) 196
Christ Church, Newgate Street (27 Apr. 1827) 196
Beresford Chapel, Walworth (8 June 1827) 196
Somers Town Chapel (24 June 1827) 196–7
Birmingham, St Peter's, Dale End (23 May 1828) 198
Leeds, Brunswick Chapel (12 Sept. 1828) 199
Watford (Nov. 1829) 207
Bristol (Sept.–Oct. 1829) 203–7
Sacred Harmonic Society (7 Aug. 1834) 212
finances:
  income
    from teaching 312–13
    as organist at Covent Garden oratorio concerts (1813–16) 133–4, 142, 145, 148
    from reviews for *EM* (1814) 140
    from publication of Handel hymns (1826, 1827) 193–4
    from Bristol recitals (1829) 206–7
    from Bristol lectures (1830) 208
    annuity from Methodist Book Room (1834–7) 212
  expenditure
    maintenance to Charlotte 117–18, 176
    maintenance agreement with Charlotte 119–20
  problems and crises
    in May 1811: 116–18
    in Oct. 1812: 126–7
    following collapse on road to Norwich (Aug. 1816) 149–50
    following breakdown (1817–18) 157–9
    imprisonment for debt (May 1825) 176–7
    in Jul. 1826: 191
    in Nov. 1829: 207
freemasonry:
  membership of Preston's Lodge of Antiquity 38
  membership of Somerset House Lodge 77–8, 122, 211
  appointed Grand Organist (1812) 122
  takes part in Union of two Grand Lodges of England (1813) 139–40
health and illnesses:
  bipolar affective disorder (summer 1785) 31
  alleged fall and head injury (1787) 35–6
  depression (late 1780s) 38
  depression (1802–5) 63–4
  depression (1806–7) 68–9, 70
  breakdown (1816–17) 149–157
  depression (1818–23) 160–3
  breakdown (1830) 210–11
lectures:
  Royal Institution (1809) 85–6, 88–9
  Surrey Institution (1809) 97–8
  Surrey Institution (1811) 110–11
  Royal Institution (1826) 187–8
  London Institution (1828) 198
  Royal Institution (1828) 198
  Russell Institution (1828) 198
  Bristol Institution (1830) 207–9
music manuscripts:
  'Pasticcio Book, 1774–5' (BL, Add. MS 34998) 10, 244, 262, 273–4, 281, 288, 291, 294, 296
  'Harmony 1798' (RCM, MS 4020) 54, 234
  'Harmony 1800' (BL, Add. MS 71107) 234, 279

Wesley, Samuel (1766–1837), life (*cont.*):
  music teaching:
    at Oxford House, Marylebone (Mrs Barnes's school) 33, 35, 38, 44, 67, 68, 89–92
    'school' and 'private' lessons 90
Wesley, Samuel Sebastian (1810–76), son of SW and Sarah Suter 107, 108, 109, 116, 124, 143, 153, 154–5, 159, 165, 183–4, 185–6, 191, 194–5, 196, 197
  placed with Hawes at Chapel Royal (1817) 156, 157
  sings before George IV (1821) 163, 196
  accompanies SW on visit to Peat in Brentford 172–3
  accompanies SW to Bristol (1829) 204–6
  directs music at SW's funeral 216
  Overture in E 281
  Overture to *The Dilosk Gatherer* 281
  The European Psalmist (1872) 249
  A Few Words on Cathedral Music (1849) 244
Wesley, Sarah (1759–1828), sister of SW 1, 4, 25, 31, 36, 37, 40, 46, 47, 48, 64, 88, 126, 150–1, 152, 177, 193, 194, 195
  character 201–2
  death 200, 202
  failing health 195, 199–200
  letters and memoranda of cited or quoted 17, 39, 40, 47, 48, 60, 162, 165, 195
  relationship with SW 176–7, 195–6, 201–2
  SW's financial demands on 40, 46, 47, 48, 49–50, 60, 116, 149–50
  SW's letters to cited or quoted 42, 48, 63, 190, 191, 195 will 201, 202
Wesley, Sarah Gwynne (1726–1822), mother of SW 3, 4, 46, 48, 64, 88, 107, 164–5, 194
  failing health and death 164–5
  SW's financial demands on 116–17, 126–7
  SW's letters to cited or quoted 60, 69–70, 116
Wesley, Susanna (1669–1742), grandmother of SW 1, 12, 48
Wesley, Susanna (1795–7), daughter of SW and Charlotte 48, 49–50, 53–4, 279
  'Beneath, a sleeping infant lies' (epitaph on by SW) 54, 279
Wesley, Thomasine (1827–82), daughter of SW and Sarah Suter 211
Wesley Banner and Revival Record 33, 151

Wesleyan Methodist Magazine 192–3, 194, 199
West Street Chapel, *see* Methodism
Westminster Abbey 83, 128, 211, 216, 221
Westminster School 2, 6
Wilbye, John (1574–1638) composer 128
  'Adieu, sweet Amaryllis' 273
Williams, David, Bristol organist, early teacher of SW 9
Williams, George Ebenezer (1783–1819), organist 83
Williams, Hannah, Wesley family servant 48
Williams, Robert (b. 1794), organist 175–7
Willis's Rooms *see* concert venues
Wilson, Charles (b. 1796), pianist, pupil of SW 136, 143, 149, 290
Winchester 108, 185
Windsor, James (1776–1853), composer, organist of Bath 88
Windsor, St George's Chapel 37
Winter, Peter (1754–1825), German composer 144
  Elijah raising the Widow's son 144
  The Liberation of Germany 147
Wise, Matthew (*c.* 1647–87), composer 218
Wölfl, Joseph (1773–1812), Austrian pianist, composer 133
Woodbridge, Suffolk 108
Worcester, Three Choirs Festival meeting at (?1809) 256
Worgan, John (1724–90) organist, harpsichordist, composer 5, 6, 7, 8–9, 14, 17, 22, 56, 217, 251
  Manasseh 7
  Six Sonatas (1769) 218
  edition of harpsichord sonatas of Scarlatti 9
Wynn, Watkin Williams (1749–89), subscriber to family concerts 220

'X.Y.Z.', correspondent to *NMMR* 99

Young, Edward (1683–1765), poet 261
  'Thou happy wretch' (*Night Thoughts*) set by SW 262

Zinzendorf, Count Nikolaus von (1700–60), Moravian bishop 2